Handbook of Language and Social Psychology

Handbook of Language and Social Psychology

Edited by

HOWARD GILES
University of California at Santa Barbara, USA

and

W. PETER ROBINSON
University of Bristol, UK

JOHN WILEY & SONS
Chichester · New York · Brisbane · Toronto · Singapore

Copyright © 1990 by John Wiley & Sons Ltd.
Baffins Lane, Chichester
West Sussex PO19 1UD, England

Other Wiley Editorial Offices

John Wiley & Sons, Inc., 605 Third Avenue,
New York, NY 10158–0012, USA

Jacaranda Wiley Ltd, G.P.O. Box 859, Brisbane,
Queensland 4001, Australia

John Wiley & Sons (Canada) Ltd, 22 Worcester Road,
Rexdale, Ontario M9W 1L1, Canada

John Wiley & Sons (SEA) Pte Ltd, 37 Jalan Pemimpin 05–04,
Block B, Union Industrial Building, Singapore 2057

Library of Congress Cataloging-in-Publication Data:

Handbook of language and social psychology / edited by Howard Giles
   and Peter Robinson.
       p.   cm.
     Includes bibliographical references.
     ISBN 0 471 92481 4
     1. Psycholinguistics.   2. Sociolinguistics.   I. Giles, Howard,
   II. Robinson, W. P. (William Peter)
   P37.H33   1990
   308.4′4—dc20   89-24874
                                                          CIP

British Library Cataloguing in Publication Data:

Handbook of language and social psychology.
   1. Sociolinguistics
   I. Giles, Howard   II. Robinson, W. P. (William Peter)
   401′.9
   ISBN 0 471 92481 4

Typeset by Inforum Typesetting, Portsmouth
Printed and bound in Great Britain by Courier International Ltd, Colchester

Contents

Contributors

LYNDA A. ANDERSON
  School of Public Health, University of Michigan, Ann Arbor, USA

RICHARD Y. BOURHIS
  Department of Psychology, University of Quebec, Montreal, Canada

JAMES J. BRADAC
  Department of Communication Studies, University of California, Santa Barbara, USA

MICHAEL BURGOON
  Department of Communication and Department of Family and Community Medicine, University of Arizona, Tucson, USA

JOSEPH N. CAPPELLA
  Department of Communication Arts, University of Wisconsin–Madison, USA

RICHARD CLÉMENT
  School of Psychology, University of Ottawa, Canada

MICHAEL J. CODY
  Department of Communication Arts and Sciences, University of Southern California, Los Angeles, USA

JUSTINE COUPLAND
  Centre for Applied English Language Studies, University of Wales College of Cardiff, UK

NIKOLAS COUPLAND
  Centre for Applied English Language Studies, University of Wales College of Cardiff, UK

HOLLY K. CRAIG
  Communicative Disorders Clinic, University of Michigan, Ann Arbor, USA

BRENDA DANET
   *Departments of Communication and Sociology/Social Anthropology, Hebrew
   University of Jerusalem, Israel*

JOHN EDWARDS
   Department of Psychology, St Francis Xavier University, Antigonish, Canada

MARY ANNE FITZPATRICK
   Center for Communication Research, University of Wisconsin–Madison, USA

HOWARD S. FRIEDMAN
   Department of Psychology, University of California, Riverside, USA

ADRIAN FURNHAM
   Department of Psychology, University College, London, UK

ROBERT C. GARDNER
   Department of Psychology, University of Western Ontario, London, Canada

WILLIAM B. GUDYKUNST
   *Department of Speech Communication, California State University, Fullerton,
   USA*

BETH HASLETT
   Department of Communication, University of Delaware, Durham, USA

E. TORY HIGGINS
   Department of Psychology, New York University, USA

JACQUELINE HINCKLEY
   Communicative Disorders Clinic, University of Michigan, Ann Arbor, USA

THOMAS HOLTGRAVES
   Department of Psychological Science, Ball State University, Muncie, USA

CHERIS KRAMARAE
   Department of Speech Communication, University of Illinois, Urbana, USA

IVANA MARKOVA
   Department of Psychology, University of Stirling, UK

C. DOUGLAS McCANN
   Department of Psychology, York University, Toronto, Canada

MARGARET L. McLAUGHLIN
   *Department of Communication Arts and Sciences, University of Southern
   California, Los Angeles, USA*

SIK HUNG NG
   Department of Psychology, University of Otago, Dunedin, New Zealand

MARK T. PALMER
   Department of Communication Studies, Northwestern University, Evanston, USA

MILES L. PATTERSON
   Department of Psychology, University of Missouri-St Louis, USA

ITESH SACHDEV
   Department of Applied Linguistics, Birkbeck College, London, UK

WESLEY N. SHELLEN
   Department of Interpersonal Communication, University of Montana, Missoula, USA

RICHARD L. STREET, JR
   Department of Communication, Texas A & M University, College Station, USA

STELLA TING-TOOMEY
   Department of Speech Communication, California State University, Fullerton, USA

KAREN TRACY
   Department of Rhetoric and Communication, Temple University, Philadelphia, USA

JOAN S. TUCKER
   Department of Psychology, University of California, Riverside, USA

TEUN VAN DIJK
   Department of General Literary Studies, University of Amsterdam, The Netherlands

WILLIAM W. WILMOT
   Department of Interpersonal Communication, University of Montana, Missoula, USA

WARD M. WINTON
   Department of Psychology, College of St Thomas, St Paul, USA

J. MALLORY WOBER
   Independent Broadcasting Authority, London, UK

Prologue

W. PETER ROBINSON AND HOWARD GILES

One of us wrote what we believe to have been the first text on social psychology and language. This claim is neither a confession nor a boast of personal longevity. Its Gricean significance is to draw attention to the difference between 1972 and 1990. In that earlier book it took somewhat fewer than 200 pages to give reasonable coverage to the field. In 1990 we are aware of many omissions from this handbook; sufficient topics for a second volume would have been easy to specify. Within what is presented, one of our sad surgical editorial tasks was to cut down the reference lists of authors, giving economy priority over scholarliness.

The last 17 years have witnessed a very vigorous growth in the field. In 1972 it was possible to contemplate a review of gender and language that could be confined to two pages. For a 1979 revision, the books and articles on the intersect of gender and language were so numerous that the idea of writing a second edition was abandoned. Now, a few years later, the proliferation of knowledge has reached a stage where a handbook is timely. No single author could hope to do justice to the whole field; however, an array of specialists can capture the contemporary scene with verbal photographs of the state of the art.

What is this field that was omitted altogether from the original *Handbook of social psychology* (Lindzey, 1952), and appeared in the second edition (Lindzey and Aronson, 1968), but written by a polymath who would not call himself a social psychologist? There were several main directions from which encouragement for its development came.

Chomsky's (1957) *Syntactic structures* gave a strong impetus both to linguistics and to psychology. Psycholinguists invented themselves and tried to check whether or not transformational rules were indeed the operational rules for the production of real speech. Since Chomsky also made claims about the nature of language acquisition in children, developmental psychologists switched their studies from cognition

Handbook of Language and Social Psychology
Edited by H. Giles and W.P. Robinson. © 1990 John Wiley & Sons Ltd

to language and eventually to the relations between the two. Not surprisingly it quickly emerged that there was more to development than an innate Language Acquisition Device; there needed to be a Language Acquisition Support System (Bruner, 1981), mediated by the activities of other human beings. It also became evident that there was more to language than syntax and transformational rules. The tri-stratal system of phonology, lexico-grammar and semantics had to be related to the *use* of language, in pragmatics. It is as dangerous to study *langue* without *parole* as it is to study *parole* without *langue*. The study of *language* requires attention to the dialectic between the two. No list of functions of language contains 'emitting grammatically acceptable strings of units' as one of its number. Early lists all contained social functions (e.g. Ervin-Tripp, 1964; Halliday, 1969; Jakobson, 1960; Searle, 1975). These could be set into a social psychological framework (Robinson, 1972), and the relations between language and social behaviour could be examined from a social psychological perspective.

Sociological perspectives provided two other points of departure. Bernstein (1961) proposed the operation of two social class-related codes of language use and asserted that confinement to one of these was a major reason why lower working class children were not equipped to take advantage of the apparent equality of opportunity in education provided by the Western democracies. This was invoked by others as a 'deficit' position and eventually clashed with a second sociological perspective formulated by Labov (1966) through his studies of social stratification in Martha's Vineyard and New York City. Social psychologists have subsequently attempted to set down ideas which might serve to effect a reconciliation in the difference–deficit debate, but have had no noticeable success (Edwards, 1979; Robinson, 1978). Studies of similarities and differences between social classes led to comparable studies on ethnic groups, then gender and eventually to studies on other forms of social categories and groupings.

A fourth strand was initiated by a social psychologist. Lambert (1967) invented the Matched Guise Technique with which it was shown that the same person was evaluated differently if speaking in French rather than English. Inferences about personality from speech alone set a pattern for a wide variety of work on inferences from different components of language used within a language, e.g. accent. With Labov's (1966) work, this source provided a point of departure for studies of accent convergence and divergence (Giles, 1973) and these in turn gave birth to Speech Accommodation Theory (Giles, Taylor, and Bourhis, 1973).

Such a skeletal history of the social psychology of language, with its roots in psycholinguistics, sociolinguistics and social psychology itself is no more than a brief caricature and very much underestimates our debt to anthropology (e.g. Fishman, 1968, 1972; Gumperz and Hymes, 1972; Malinowski, 1923), to ethnographers of communication (Hymes, 1967) and to mass communication studies. Our concerns as social psychologists are not so much with how language works as a system or even with what the units and structures of the system are. We have to know these things, however, in order to cope with our problems. We have to describe and explain how language is used to communicate messages to other people. We have to find out what messages can be sent and which ones are sent by whom, where, when and how. We have to find out why they are being sent. The social psychological perspective requires that we answer such questions in respect of individuals as persons and as members of social groups. Both personal and social identity are significant to us, as is context of situation.

Our perspective can merge into the sociological and anthropological as we move towards the study of systems for human living. It moves towards sociolinguistics and ethnography of communication if we focus on the linguistic interests of sociologists and ethnographers.

However, now that the necessity has been accepted of including a social psychological perspective if we are to describe and explain any context of communication, we find ourselves somewhat overwhelmed by the infinite variety of such contexts and issues. One suspects that a social psychological perspective is relevant even to intrapersonal as well as interpersonal and intergroup communication. With the field still in the vigour of its youth, it is hardly surprising that some topics have received much more attention than others.

The chapters show this diversity of development across problems. In some areas the theoretical and empirical progress allows authors to write with clear confidence as we move forward within what appears to be well-founded explanatory frameworks. Another set of areas is at the stage of collecting together insightful observations and speculative ideas. A third set offers opportunities for conceptual nightmares. (For example, what are we to do with emotions? Our culture has given us and requires us to use a vast and unordered vocabulary based on a trait-centred view of human nature.) A fourth set chases the shifting chimera of deception; what we manage to discover becomes the basis for training people to control the 'leaks'. This variation in progress is itself both reassuring and challenging.

We hope we have added to the attraction of the book by having recognizably human authors write the chapters. Reviews can be excellent and dull: the computer search, the compilation and collation of the list of studies all reported with mechanical thoroughness. Whilst we encouraged each contributor to conduct a sufficient literature review to provide readers with helpful lists of references, we also invited authors to do more. We asked them to ride their hobby-horses and to offer their personal points of view. We asked them to say where they thought current difficulties and weaknesses lay and to speculate about ways forward. Fortunately authors have subscribed to these editorial requests to varying degrees, and the chapters cover the range from objective and interesting reviews on the one hand to healthy selling and preaching on the other.

Critics will not be slow to notice our omissions. What they cannot know is whether these arise because the editors were negligent or because consenting authors were delinquent. Contemplating the manuscript before us we have our regrets as well as our satisfactions and, as seems to be one of the ironic characteristics of *le comédie humaine*, both can arise from the same source.

We have become specialists. The reference lists are replete with social psychologists and their work, but the cross-referencing to other species of academic are fewer than would be desirable in the best of all possible worlds. Such pioneering thoughts as one mustered and expressed orally in the late 1960s were likely to be uttered in the presence of anthropologists, linguists, philosophers and sociologists. It was dangerous not to have read Malinowski (1923) or Sapir (see Mandelbaum,

1949). It was risky not to know the difference between a phone and a phoneme, even if you were then reminded that neither existed. We read Aristotle (1909) and Cicero (1942) as well as Grice (1975), and Wittgenstein (1951) as well as Austin (1962). The sociology books were sometimes very weighty, but Voloshinov (1973) was essential reading. In retrospect, some us were probably too overawed by the power of other disciplines, especially when some less than sympathetic professors expressed their disdain for the emergent social psychologists. (One suspects that Europeans are more often victims of their entrenched power hierarchies than North Americans, and it is not surprising that the greater growth has been in North America.) While we can be delighted that there is more than enough work now for us to have our specialist handbook, we must also look forward to a time when two other handbooks appear: a Handbook of Language in which the social psychological perspective is properly represented and a Handbook of Social Psychology in which the same is true for the representation of language.

Meanwhile we must be grateful for the energy, assertiveness and constructiveness of academics in North America. An old definition of a standard language is that it is a dialect with a national flag. We hope this handbook will be our disciplinary flag. That it is so heavily North American carries a cost as well as bringing benefits. Not surprisingly, most of the work has been done by North Americans with North Americans in North America. So the social psychology is set in particular cultural contexts. The particular values of these cultures underpin and limit the data and theory. Taking a God's-eye view across space and time, North America is an open society: individualistic rather than collective. It is achieved position rather than assigned status that counts. The society is assertive rather than compliant; it is competitive rather than cooperative. Personally negotiated change is expected; rights are mentioned more than obligations; freedom is valued more than duty. So, for example, a study of the use of language in marriage in Wisconsin will not transfer immediately to Kyoto or Ching Mei. Answers to questions about learning a second language in Canada may not readily transfer to Tashkent and the questions arising may be different in Arusha. We must be careful. Human beings may be all alike in some ways, but there are cultural, subcultural and individual differences which limit the nature of some of the generalizations we ought to make. This is not a matter for regret. It is certainly not a matter for complaint. Nor is it a warning. It is a reminder to be open-minded and careful in the application of models derived in one culture when attempting to export them to others. What will prove to be universal to the species will be determined by evidence yet to be collected and theories yet to be created. We have come a long way in a short time, but there is a very long way to go yet.

Having noted the rapid specialization and the legitimate colonization of part of our territory, and having indicated the potential cultural biases in most of the chapters, we can also identify several shifts of interest in the field that have occurred in recent years.

In terms of social groups and their ways of using language, we have noted already that the interest in the 1960s was predominantly in black English vernacular and socio-economic status differences. Contributions to the debate of 'differences versus deficits' were made by almost all the disciplines except social psychology. Although social psychologists have been interested in the marking of social identity by both speech and non-verbal indicators and this remains a focus of attention, concern with the developmental and intellectual implications of differential commands and/or use of particular language varieties has faded from the scene. Other social categories suffering from discrimination have attracted more and more interest. Gender still leads the field, but the elderly are gaining ground, as are those who are defined administratively or socially as physically, mentally or emotionally disabled.

If we look at work on the sociological orders of society, then education generally has faded. The use of language and its relevance to effective teaching and self-fulfilling prophecies have been studied with vigour and success (Brophy and Good, 1986), but the work is psychologically relatively atheoretical (Robinson, 1984), and currently educational concerns are more with efficiency than with justice.

Justice itself has been a growth area, and the law courts have provided a morally and socially important arena for social psychologists to work in. Alas, Gorgias is still defeating Socrates so far as verdicts are concerned; at least the fact that some of the likely reasons for this can be made explicit and 'explained' by social psychologists may help judges and juries to discount the influence of rhetorical devices.

In the medical world, doctor–patient communication has become a growth area, for reasons which are less clear. The medical profession seems to have moved its focus from cases of illness to people with problems. Certainly there has been a growth in the wish to communicate effectively with patients and this has fortunately been translated into a willingness to have social psychologists study current practice and its implications. Patient demand has also been strong.

The kinship order has appeared in the growth of work on marriage, perhaps mainly because we are concerned about the high incidence of marriage breakdowns. There has been less concern with the qualities of interaction between persons occupying familial roles other than those of husband and wife. Social relationships more generally have been a growth area in social psychology, as is witnessed by the massive volumes edited by Duck and Gilmour (1981a,b,c; also Duck, 1982). Quite properly, language has loomed large as a feature of developing, maintaining and dissolving relationships, as several chapters in this handbook demonstrate.

So many other major sections of society remain to be studied that it is not overly helpful to try to list them. We do not as yet have much information about communication in the military and religious orders. Commerce and industry are more concerned to 'solve' their communication problems than to study them. And what is being done in North America and Europe stands in need of replication elsewhere.

There have also been changes in the aspects of language and non-verbal codes studied over the years. The listing, classification and explanations of the modes and functioning of non-verbal signals have been very successful. The exploration of their integration with verbal communication is likewise a success story. Similarly phonology in its guise as accent has been investigated in a wide variety of situations and cultures and has been an integral component of Speech Accommodation Theory. Studies of grammar and lexis have faded somewhat with the loss of interest in education and its differential availability to different social groups. The semantic level of language remains dormant as a focus of social psychological investigation.

Pragmatically related studies have increased greatly. Discourse analysis has been and is a major development. In reminding us that words are deeds it is correct, but some of its protagonists may be in temporary danger of forgetting that there are deeds which are not words and that the meanings of wordings are often not as transparent as social psychologists would like them to be. On the other hand, however, if discourse analysts become too self-critical, they will not generate the work.

In the study of the relations between use of language and social behaviour, one major source of difficulty stems from the reflective agentive properties of human beings. Once valid rules of inference are discovered and publicized, people can learn to use and abuse those rules, thereby invalidating them. Just as agrochemists, insects and insecticides are in dynamic and potentially unstable equilibrium, so are liars and liar detectors, sincere people and Machiavellians who are efficient with their facework. Furthermore, the rules themselves can change. Just as gold can change its value, so can a post-vocalic /r/. Struggles in the social mobility game are reflected in changes in the social value of particular qualities and forms of speech. Hence, although we can offer general explanations of phenomena, their specific forms of realization may be highly localized in time and place.

A second related difficulty stems from the character of the communicative process and human nature. It is a commonplace in psychology that, within limits, we adapt to what is constant and react to what is new. To gain attention to their messages, the media have to upgrade their adjectives and adverts. Movies hyped themselves into colossal blockbusters. Superstars became megastars. What was 'skill' four years ago became 'ace' and then 'bril'. The contemporary accolade for 'the good' changes rapidly in certain groups. Hence in language use we have understandable and predictable shifts, except that we cannot predict which specific changes will gain a temporary hegemony. This is compounded by the synchronous changing fashions of non-verbal behaviour.

However, probably our greatest hazard lies with psychology itself: we have not achieved a consensual theory of human motivation. Why should this be selected as a crucial handicap? As we have already indicated, one of the advantages of a communicative approach to language is its encouragement of a functional/structural perspective. We can then ask which units and which structures are combined to perform which functions. But from where is our taxonomy of functions to come? Searle (1975) provided a bridge with Speech Act Theory, and his set of five functions may have been preferable to three (Bühler, 1934) or an infinite number (Wittgenstein, 1951). Whatever taxonomy eventually gains ascendance, we know that it will have to allow for more than one function being performed at a time. It will have to accept that combinations of both non-verbal and verbal units are the determinants of any function. We know that the taxonomy will be multilevel in that single remarks may be intended or received as both very general and very specific statements. As Labov and Fanshel (1977) show, 'You haven't put sugar in my tea?' can serve to remind the miscreant addressee that he or she is a worthless person incapable of showing any measure of human consideration.

Functions must at some point link with motivational theory. Why people do what they do in the way that they do are motivational questions. At present the motivational reasons cited are close to everyday explanations: to give a good impression, to be approved of, to show you like the other, to avoid threatening face, to be polite. These are perfectly good reasons for the selection of utterances, but are generally diagnosed *post hoc* and not pursued into deeper stories. We have always had too many theories of motivation (see, for example, Hall and Lindzey, 1957) and, until we can achieve a consensus in motivational theory, we shall not be able to take our explanations of language behaviour beyond the everyday and the proximal.

Nevertheless, as the 27 chapters show, we can achieve and have achieved great progress in but a flash of time, and doubtless the revised edition in 5 years time will be more than twice as large.

REFERENCES

Aristotle (1909). *The rhetoric of Aristotle* (transl. R. Claverhouse). Cambridge: Cambridge University Press.

Austin, J.L. (1962). *How to do things with words*. Oxford: Oxford University Press.

Bernstein, B. (1961). Social structure, language and learning. *Educational Research*, **3**, 163–176.

Brophy, J. and Good, T.L. (1986). Teacher behaviour and student achievement. In M.C. Wittrock (Ed.), *Handbook of research on teaching*, 3rd edn, pp. 328–375. New York: Macmillan.

Bruner, J.S. (1983). *Childs talk*. Oxford: Oxford University Press.

Bühler, K. (1934). *Sprachtheories: Die Darstellungsfunktion der Sprache*. Jena (GDR): Fischer.

Chomsky, N. (1957). *Syntactic structures*. The Hague: Mouton.

Cicero, M.T. (1942). *De oratore* (transl. E.W. Sutton). London: Heinemann.

Duck, S. and Gilmour, R. (Eds) (1981a). *Personal relationships*, Vol. 1, *Studying personal relationships*. London: Academic Press.

Duck, S. and Gilmour, R. (Eds) (1981b). *Personal relationships*, Vol. 2, *Developing personal relationships*. London: Academic Press.

Duck, S. and Gilmour, R. (Eds) (1981c). *Personal relationships*, Vol. 3, *Personal relationships in disorder*. London: Academic Press.

Duck, S. (Ed.) (1982). *Personal relationships*, Vol. 4, *Dissolving personal relationships*. London: Academic Press.

Edwards, J. (1979). *Language and disadvantage*. London: Arnold.

Ervin-Tripp, S.M. (1964). An analysis of the interaction of language, topic and listener. In J.J. Gumperz and D. Hymes (Eds), *The ethnography of communication. American Anthropologist*, **66** (2), 86–102.

Fishman, J.A. (1968). *Bilingualism in the barrio*. Final Report. Contract No. OEC–1–7–062817–0297 US Department of Health, Education and Welfare. Washington, DC.

Fishman, J.A. (1972). *The sociology of language*. Cambridge, MA: Newbury Press.

Giles, H. (1973). Accent mobility: A model and some data. *Anthropological Linguistics*, **15**, 87–105.

Giles, H., Taylor, D.M., and Bourhis, R.Y. (1973). Towards a theory of interpersonal accommodation through language: Some Canadian data. *Language in Society*, **2**, 177–192.

Grice, H.P. (1975). Logic and conversation. In P. Cole and J.L. Morgan (Eds), *Syntax and semantics*, Vol. 3, pp. 41–58. New York: Academic Press.

Gumperz, J.J. and Hymes, D. (Eds) (1972). *Directions in sociolinguistics*. New York: Holt.

Hall, C.S. and Lindzey, G. (1957). *Theories of personality*. New York: Wiley.

Halliday, M.A.K. (1969). Relevant models of language. *Educational Review*, **22**, 26–37.

Hymes, D. (1967). Models of the interaction of language and social setting. *Journal of Social Issues*, **27**, No. 2.

Jakobson, R. (1960). Linguistics and poetics. In T.A. Sebeok (Ed.), *Style in language*. New York: Wiley.

Labov, W. (1966). *The social stratification of speech in New York City*. Washington, DC: Center for Applied Linguistics.

Labov, W. and Fanshel, D. (1977). *Therapeutic discourse: Psychotherapy as conversation*. New York: Academic Press.

Lambert, W.E. (1967). A social psychology of bilingualism. *Journal of Social Issues*, 23, 91–109.

Lindzey, G. (Ed.) (1952). *Handbook of social psychology* (2 Vols). Cambridge, MA: Addison-Wesley.

Lindzey, G. and Aronson, E. (1968). *Handbook of social psychology*, 2nd edn. Cambridge, MA: Addison-Wesley.

Malinowski, B.K. (1923). The problem of meaning in primitive societies. Republished in 1949 in C.K. Ogden and I.A. Richards (Eds), *The meaning of meaning*, 10th edn, pp. 296–336. London: Routledge.

Mandelbaum, D. (Ed.) (1949). *Selected writings of Edward Sapir on language, culture and personality*. Berkeley, CA: University of California Press.

Robinson, W.P. (1972). *Language and social behaviour*. Harmondsworth (England): Penguin.

Robinson, W.P. (1978). *Language management*. Sydney: Allen and Unwin.

Robinson, W.P. (1984). Social psychology in classrooms. In G.W. Stephenson and V.H. Davis (Eds), *Progress in applied social psychology*, Vol. 2, pp. 93–128. Chichester (England): Wiley.

Searle, J.R. (1975). A classification of Illocutionary acts. *Language in Society*, 5, 1–23.

Voloshinov, V.N. (1973). *Marxism and the philosophy of language* (transl. L. Matejka and I.R. Titunik). New York: Seminar Press.

Wittgenstein, L. (1951). *Philosophical investigations*. Oxford: Blackwell.

Section 1

Social Psychology and Language: Perspectives

Introduction to Section 1

It was hope rather than sadism that motivated our requests to authors to tackle relations between language and such broad and fuzzy concepts as social cognition, emotion, social influence and personality. The potential hazards are different in the four fields. 'Social cognition' has grown dangerously fast into a highly desirable label of somewhat indeterminate reference. Studies of emotion and the ways we talk about it have shown up the conceptual confusion of the professionals and the varied assumptions of lay people. The diversity of personality theories extant and the doubting of the very notion of stable generalizable characteristics as useful predictors of behaviour have compounded difficulties of examining the intersect of emotion with speech. Social influence in its guise of attitude development and change was not yielding clear patterns of explicable results when approached by either traditional social psychologists or communication specialists. Here each author manages to bring constructive order out of diversity and uncertainty, and possible ways ahead are signposted with well-founded confidence.

If social cognition is defined as the processes and structures that determine and are determined by presumed knowledge about self and others, then McCann and Higgins can justify their separation of the field into effects of sender on communication and of communication on sender, followed by similar separations for receivers. They note that such binary splits have an analytic convenience, but run the risk of implying that communicative acts are static one-off units having detectable origins and impacts. Communication is dynamic, sequential and negotiable, as McCann and Higgins point out. They are able to show what an empirically productive vein ideas from social cognition have opened up for studies both of general processes and of individual differences. They remind us of the dangers of neglecting process at the expense of structure and of neglecting affect for knowledge.

Winton wishes we had more knowledge about affect in its emotional aspects. What seemed to be a quietly settled and informative field with the geometric models of face recognition became messy as a result of two confrontations. The pursuit of

---

Handbook of Language and Social Psychology
Edited by H. Giles and W.P. Robinson.   © 1990 John Wiley & Sons Ltd

appraisal and prototype models gave rise to questions about the status of words for emotions. Which are really emotions? What is the correspondence between everyday usages and a psychologically well-founded theory of emotion? The last provides the second stumbling block. We still seem to have to refer to James–Lange, Cannon–Bard and Schachter, whilst being unhappy about each of them. Recognizing these difficulties, Winton is still able to offer a range of substantive studies linking uses of emotional speech to determinants, consequences and accompaniments, and to offer suggestions for where we might go next.

Burgoon provides a welcome relief from what used to be rather inconsequential studies of attitude change, which perhaps inevitably relied on single independent-variable manipulations of not-very-crucial-to-life attitudes and hence generated but weak and evanescent effects. Reminding us of the presumed power of rhetoric down the ages, Burgoon develops Expectancy Theory as a framework for considering combinative and interactive effects. This theory of influence and the taxonomy of compliance-gaining strategies originally presented by Marwell and Schmitt serve both as integrative ideas and as bases for forward projections.

Wide as the fields of social cognition, emotion and social influence are, we would have to concede that personality is the most daunting of the titles in this section. As Furnham points out, over and above problems of definition and measurement, personality theorists have traditionally been relatively uninterested in language, and speech and language experts have had but little interest in personality. Whatever the difficulties of defining ethnicity or social class, social groups are easier comparative targets than variations along dimensions of personality, touched as these are by psychometric concerns that have become unpopular. Furnham helps to define a research agenda. He illustrates some of the potential for work in the area and demonstrates this cogently using the example of extraversion.

All four chapters remind us that we are pioneers.

1

Social Cognition and Communication

C. DOUGLAS McCANN AND E. TORY HIGGINS

Department of Psychology, York University, Canada and Department of Psychology, New York University, USA

One of the more curious observations that results from considering traditional research and theory in social psychology is the relative lack of attention paid to language and communication both as important processes in their own right and as critical mediators of such things as person perception and impression formation. Social psychologists are presumably concerned with explaining and understanding the nature of human social interaction, and it would seem that communication has an important role to play in such contexts. Until recently, however, communication issues received little attention in the social psychological literature. The current interest of social psychologists in information-processing models (i.e. social cognition) has led to renewed interest in communication issues and has the potential to serve as a bridge between traditional social psychology and the study of communication and language.

This is not to suggest that the traditional social psychological literature has completely ignored the role of communication. This early work, however, was guided by what now seems to be an overly restrictive perspective, loosely based upon the mathematical model of communication proposed by Shannon and Weaver (1949). Communication was conceptualized as a linear process of information transmission (see Higgins, 1981) between a communicator who had a single purpose (e.g. persuasion) and a passive recipient. In this context, social psychologists examined such things as the effects of source, message and recipient characteristics on persuasive impact (e.g. Hovland, Janis, and Kelley, 1953;

Handbook of Language and Social Psychology
Edited by H. Giles and W.P. Robinson. © 1990 John Wiley & Sons Ltd

McGuire, 1969). Although other aspects of communication were studied (e.g. Mehrabian and Reed, 1968), communication and language issues were not generally highlighted.

It seems that communication and language have now reappeared as important topics in their own right. While no single conceptual model has emerged to replace those concerned with information transmission, recent research derived from the current interest in social cognition has served to present a more elaborate view of the role of language and communication in interpersonal interaction. The findings of this recent work are in close agreement with what most of us know intuitively about the important role played by communication in our everyday interactions.

We know that the impressions we form of others are often based upon what those others say and how they say it (see Chapter 19, by Bradac). This seems to be especially important in our conversations with relatively unfamiliar others. For example, few of us can forget how intently we listened to the parents of our first date the first time we met with them. It was important for us to find out what they were like so that our subsequent interactions would go smoothly. It is also clear that we use our knowledge and/or preconceptions about certain types of people to guide our communicative interactions with them. Thus, for example, we use our knowledge about the typical interests of 5-year-olds to steer a conversation with a young niece toward topics that will engage her.

In addition to these examples that focus on the 'other' in communicative inter-actions, it is also clear that our interpersonal communication has 'self' relevance. Much of what we say and how we say it reflects our central beliefs and important characteristics. Thus, our communicative activity is affected by our idiosyncratic beliefs about the world in general and by beliefs we hold about ourselves. For example, we tend to direct conversation away from issues that embarrass us. Finally, under some circumstances, it seems that our verbalizations can, in turn, affect the very beliefs that direct our conversation. Sometimes the mechanisms underlying this effect are clear to us, such as when, through the process of trying to persuade someone else to adopt our position, we discern the inadequacy of the arguments that form the basis of a cherished belief (see Chapter 3, by Burgoon). In other cases, the process is much less accessible.

The objective of this chapter is to review the recent literature that has considered each of these issues. This research has emerged from the area of social cognition, which provides a bridge between the concerns of social psychologists and those of researchers working in the area of language and communication. The potential for such an integration has been enhanced by the fact that each field has recently undergone a shift toward a greater use of information-processing analysis in the examination of issues of interest. This means that researchers in the two fields can more easily communicate with one another through the use of common meth-odologies and theoretical models.

Focus of this Review

Social cognition represents one of the most rapidly developing areas in psychology. In this field of study, traditional social psychological issues are approached from the perspective of information-processing models originally developed in cognitive psychology (e.g. Markus and Zajonc, 1985). Although it has been defined in many ways (see Ostrom, 1984), most working in the area would agree that social cognition is a branch of social psychology that involves *the study of the processes and structures that determine and are determined by knowledge of self and others*.

Although social psychologists have always been interested in cognition (see Zajonc, 1980), the current information-processing orientation dates mainly from the late 1970s (Ostrom, 1984). Accordingly, in reviewing research at the interface between social cognition and communication, we focus mainly on work that has appeared in the last decade or so. However, we also include discussion of earlier work that anticipated current trends (e.g. Krauss, Vivekananthan, and Weinheimer, 1968; Zajonc, 1960).

In this review, we have decided to focus on research examining four *interrelated* issues (for other reviews see Clarke, 1985; Higgins, 1981; Kraut and Higgins, 1984; McCann and Higgins, 1984, 1988). First, we consider the impact of the self, including the communicator's self-concept, beliefs and personal goals, on the nature of interpersonal communication. Second, we examine the ways in which the communicator's verbalizations can affect the communicator him- or herself in terms of knowledge, evaluations and beliefs. Third, we consider the effects of the communicator's knowledge and preconceptions about the recipient on how the communicator formulates messages for specific listeners. Finally, we consider the ways in which what a communicator says can influence the impressions formed of him or her by the recipients. It should be clear to the reader that these issues are more formal restatements of the intuitively based observations on the role of language to which we referred above.

EFFECTS OF SELF (COMMUNICATOR) ON COMMUNICATION

The self as an object of inquiry has recently evidenced a remarkable resurgence of interest in social psychology. In large part this ascendancy is due to the powerful and innovative approaches taken by those working within the social-cognitive tradition (e.g. Kuiper and Derry, 1981; Markus, 1977; Rogers, 1981). The self is no longer conceptualized as being identical with self-esteem (e.g. Wylie, 1979). Instead, it is seen as a dynamic, multifaceted entity (e.g. Higgins, 1987; Markus and Nurius, 1986) that has an important directive influence on both intra- and interpersonal responses (for a review, see Markus and Wurf, 1987).

In this section, we examine some of the ways in which the self and related characteristics of the communicator such as constructs, beliefs and goals have an effect on the nature of the communicative and interpersonal behaviors produced by an individual. The work reviewed in this section represents some of the richest and most influential examples of social-cognitive analyses of interpersonal communication. We begin with an examination of work exploring the implications of personal constructs and identity.

A major line of investigation has been the continuing work on 'constructivist' models of interpersonal communication (e.g. Applegate and Delia, 1980; Delia and

O'Keefe, 1979; Delia, O'Keefe, and O'Keefe, 1982; O'Keefe and Delia, 1982, 1985; O'Keefe and Shepard, 1987). Although initially designed to explore the relation between impression formation and message production, more recent formulations have moved increasingly toward sophisticated analyses of interpersonal interaction. This approach focuses on the role played by personal construct systems (Crockett, 1965; Kelly, 1955) in the creation and communication of meaning and interpretation both for self and others.

In this approach, communication is viewed as an interpersonal event that focuses on meaning generation and exchange and that takes place in distinct contexts to serve specific purposes (e.g. O'Keefe and Delia, 1985). Primary consideration is given to the impact on message construction of the communicator's personal constructs (both idiosyncratic and shared) and other 'interpretive schemes' (O'Keefe and Delia, 1982). These are seen to influence the individual's interpretation of the communication situation and other participants, as well as the communicator's recognition of alternative courses of action and strategies. Inherent in this orientation is the notion that the communication intentions of the participants are a major focus of personal and interpersonal activity. Since the personal construct systems of the actors are critical to social construction processes, it is assumed that differences in construct development (i.e. differences in differentiation and abstractness) will influence variety in message production and the extent to which multiple goals are realized in the message.

Support for this line of reasoning has been found in research employing a variety of communication contexts and tasks, including persuasion, comforting and regulating others, and arguments. In this work, individual differences in degree of construct differentiation and abstractness have been found to be positively related to the tendency of communicators to produce messages that incorporate multiple dimensions of the interpersonal context (Applegate, 1982; Delia, Kline, and Burelson, 1979; O'Keefe and Shepard, 1987). For example, O'Keefe and Shepard (1987) examined the relationship between construct differentiation and the tendency to incorporate multiple objectives. They had subjects participate in an interaction that elicited argument and conflict, and suggested that in such situations several goals are relevant, including facework and interaction maintenance (see Chapter 10, by Tracy).

In dealing with such multiple goals, an individual may adopt one of three strategies: (a) *selection*, in which the individual emphasizes one goal and ignores the others; (b) *separation*, in which the individual deals with all the goals but in a sequential manner; (c) *integration*, in which the individual produces messages that simultaneously advance multiple aims. Consistent with expectations, the results indicated that it was the high-differentiation subjects who tended to pursue the last strategy most often. This finding complements earlier work in demonstrating the *interpersonal* consequences of construct differentiation. In addition, this model has been shown to have important implications for understanding the nature of individual differences in message production both within and across age groups (O'Keefe and Delia, 1982).

A second major model relating self and communicative activity has been the 'speech-accommodation' theory. Innovative work associated with this model has shown, for example, that self-identity needs, activated by contexts and other participants, dramatically influence the nature of the communications produced (e.g. Ball, Giles, and Hewstone, 1985; Bourhis, Giles, Leyens, and Tajfel, 1979; Giles, Bourhis, and Taylor, 1977; Giles and Hewstone, 1982; Street and Giles, 1982; Thakerar, Giles, and Cheshire, 1982).

This theory was originally developed to account for the way in which interactants converge or diverge in speech. It was suggested that speakers are motivated under certain circumstances to adjust their speech style in order to fulfil identity concerns (see also Eastman, 1985). Convergence was seen to express a desire for social integration, whereas divergence was thought to be employed to promote social distance (Street and Giles, 1982; see Ball *et al.*, 1985, for a more recent perspective). Speech accommodation, then, is a motivated linguistic strategy used to produce linguistic markers that can be used in identity-relevant situations (cf. Tajfel and Turner, 1979) to make salient either ingroup or outgroup identity. For example, if an important element of an individual's ingroup identity was threatened by the status or behavior of an interaction partner who was a member of an outgroup, the individual might intensify his or her production of linguistic features distinctive to the ingroup (Ryan, 1979).

The 'speech-accommodation' model, linking interpersonal processes and identity concerns with speech, has had an important impact on the field of social cognition and has served as a basis for many empirical investigations. Taken together, the 'constructivist' and 'speech-accommodation' models clearly reveal the important influence that relatively stable self features can have on the form and content of interpersonal communication. Next we review formulations that consider the impact on communication of what is unknown or, at most, hypothesized about the self (or others).

Berger and his associates have conceptualized communicative interactions in terms of a process of uncertainty reduction (e.g. Berger, 1979, 1986; Berger and Bradac, 1982; Berger and Calabrese, 1975; see also Hewes and Planalp, 1982). Here the focus is on how communication functions to reduce uncertainty and to assist us in our attempts to acquire knowledge and understanding of ourselves and others. The task that faces many interactants is one of acquiring sufficient knowledge about their interaction partners to be able to predict the actions of the latter (Athay and Darley, 1981). Berger and Bradac (1982), for example, describe the range of strategies available to communicators to reduce such uncertainty. These strategies presumably are especially important determinants of initial communicative activity. Communicators use a variety of linguistic cues to assist them in their attempt to gain knowledge about their interaction partners, including such things as fluency, intensity and grammatical proficiency. These cues allow for judgments of similarity, which can then be used as a basis for action. Variation in experimentally induced information-seeking has been shown to reflect itself in discernible behavioral differences in dyadic interaction (e.g. Kellerman and Berger, 1984).

Another example of this orientation is reflected in the 'hypothesis-testing' research carried out by Snyder and Swann (Snyder, 1984; Snyder and Swann, 1978; Swann, 1984; see Higgins and Bargh, 1987, for a review). This research documents the influence of a belief or hypothesis in channeling the nature of interpersonal interactions. For example, in their initial research, Snyder and Swann (1978) presented subjects with a 'getting-acquainted' task in which they were to select a set of questions to ask a target person in an upcoming interaction. Subjects were also given a hypothesis to test about their partner. For some subjects it was suggested that their interaction partner was extraverted and for some it was suggested that the other person was introverted. Subjects tended to select questions that would serve preferentially to elicit confirmatory evidence. In addition, in the course of the actual interactions, it was clear that the questions that were asked of the targets channeled the interactions so that the targets tended to display confirmatory behavioral evidence regardless of their own true dispositions.

Another communicator variable that has been addressed in the recent literature concerns the role of motivation and personal goals. The notion of communication as a set of motivated strategies has been acknowledged in many research studies and theoretical models (e.g. Canary, Cody, and Marston, 1987; Gilbert, Jones and Pelham, 1987; O'Keefe and Delia, 1982; O'Keefe and McCormack, 1987; Sypher and Applegate, 1984). We now describe two approaches to this issue that serve to illustrate this general orientation.

In the 'communication-game' model of interpersonal communication (e.g. Higgins, 1981; Higgins and McCann, 1984; Higgins, Fondacaro, and McCann, 1981; McCann and Hancock, 1983; McCann and Higgins, 1984, 1988), personal goals and motives are accorded a critical role in explanations of communicative behavior. Interpersonal communication is conceptualized as a rule-following exercise in which variations in rule-following behavior are mediated by personal goals (e.g. McCann and Hancock, 1983). For example, one rule of the communication game is that speakers should modify or tune their messages to suit the characteristics of their audience. McCann and Hancock (1983) examined the implications of individual differences in personal goal orientation for this process by having high and low self-monitors communicate about a stimulus person to a listener who they were told either liked or disliked the stimulus person. The results indicated that it was only the high self-monitors who modified their messages to suit the attitudinal characteristics of their audience. High self-monitors are particularly concerned with face goals (Snyder, 1979) and tend to use contextual cues (e.g. the recipient's attitude) to guide their ongoing behavior. Low self-monitors, on the other hand, are concerned with enacting behavior consistent with their own attitudes and beliefs (see Chapter 12, by Friedman and Tucker). Thus, differences in personal goal orientation were found to influence communicative activity through their impact on rule-following behavior. The traditional work on the topic of impression management and self-presentation is clearly related to this in terms of its focus on the effects of personal motivations on interpersonal strategies and behavior (e.g. Baumeister, 1982; DePaulo, Kenny, Hoover, Web, and Oliver, 1987; Goffman, 1959; Greenwald and Breckler, 1985; Jones and Pittman, 1982; Schlenker and Leary, 1985; Tedeschi and Norman, 1985).

A final example related specifically to the involvement of the self is the innovative work of Wicklund and Gollwitzer (1982; Gollwitzer and Wicklund, 1985) on symbolic self-completion theory. It has important implications for the understanding of some of the processes underlying verbal self-description. According to this theory, individuals are frequently committed to establishing and maintaining specific types of self-definitions or personal identities. Individuals sometimes find themselves in an 'incomplete state' in which, for example, they have not completely fulfilled the socially recognized requirements for identities they would like to claim. Under such conditions of incomplete self-identity, individuals are motivated to engage in compensatory symbolic self-completion activities – such as active self-description – which serve to bolster their claim. This theory is elaborate in its specification of the conditions under which this type of message would be produced. As of yet, however, it has seen only limited exposure in the communication literature.

As should be clear from the above review, research and theory linking self and self-relevant processes to communication are abundant and quite comprehensive. This research has highlighted the important effects that the communicator's self-concept, beliefs and motivations can have on the nature of interpersonal communication. This trend stands in contrast to much of the earlier work in this area, which tended to focus on the effects of communicator characteristics (e.g. credibility) on, for example, the tendency of message recipients to accept persuasive messages. Although not derived from any single theoretical formulation, this more recent work parallels developments in conceptualization of the self and its links to motivation and behavior. It seems likely that these interpersonal implications of the self and self-relevant processes will continue to stimulate research in the future.

COMMUNICATION EFFECTS ON THE COMMUNICATOR'S SOCIAL COGNITIONS

In this section, we review the social-cognitive effects of communication on the communicator. Although a focus of interest in early work (e.g. Bernstein, 1960; Whorf, 1956), this issue has received relatively less attention in the more recent literature. This relative lack of attention is most likely the result of two converging influences. First, classic models of communication (e.g. Shannon and Weaver, 1949) have conceptualized communication as a static and linear process, and this tends to highlight the impact of the message on the target or recipient. These classic models rarely consider the effects on the communicator except in terms of temporarily negotiated situated identities (for a review of traditional symbolic interactionist perspectives on this, see O'Keefe and Delia, 1985). Second, many recent social-cognitive models of social information processing have concentrated on the role played by 'theory-driven processes' (see Higgins and Stangor, 1986, for a review) which tend to relate to assimilation rather than accommodation (e.g. Ross, Lepper, and Hubbard, 1975). In this work the emphasis is on how the cognitive structures of the actor serve to influence the encoding and retrieval of social information (Fiske and Taylor, 1984). The effects of contextual or data-driven processes on information processing and social judgment have received less attention. This imbalance in focus, however, appears to be diminishing somewhat in the recent social-cognition literature. This shift in emphasis is also evident in recent work on social cognition and communication, which has followed the lead of some classic work in this area.

The early work by Zajonc (1960) and others (e.g. Brock and Fromkin, 1968; Cohen, 1961; Harvey, Harkins, and Kagehiro, 1976; Higgins, McCann, and

Fondacaro, 1982; Leventhal, 1962) on 'cognitive tuning' showed the effect of merely adopting a speaker (or listener) role on the manner in which the communicator represented social information. For example, Zajonc's work demonstrated that speakers tend to represent information in a relatively differentiated and polarized fashion compared to listeners, whose role allows them to represent information in a less differentiated and non-unified fashion.

Another classic and well-known literature examined the effects of counter-attitudinal advocacy on the communicator's beliefs (e.g. Bem, 1972; Festinger, 1957; Janis and King, 1954). More recently, Burgoon and Miller (1971, 1985; see also Chapter 3, by Burgoon) conceptualized the counter-attitudinal advocacy effect within the context of a broader 'expectancy' model that integrates the persuasive effect of communication both on passive (i.e. listeners) and active (i.e. speakers) participants. These authors suggest that linguistic and communicative activities take place within a larger set of norms or expectations and that matching or violating prescriptions can influence the persuasiveness of a message both for recipients and originators of messages. One of the linguistic variables about which we have expectations is the 'intensity' of the persuasive appeal. Burgoon and Miller argue that part of the counter-attitudinal advocacy effect on communicators is due to the intensity of the language produced in situations that violate personal norms. They experimentally manipulated intensity and found it played an important mediating role in terms of the amount of communicator attitude change that was produced (e.g. Burgoon and Miller, 1971).

Other work in this area has examined the identity implications of language shifts for bilingual speakers. One recent example is the work by Bond (1983), who had bilingual Chinese subjects in Hong Kong report on auto- and heterostereotypes regarding values (using a modified form of Rokeach's (1973) Values survey) either in their native Cantonese or in English. The language of response was shown significantly to affect reported values on several indices (see earlier work by Taylor, Dagot and Gardner, 1969). This line of investigation has intriguing social-cognitive implications (see also Hoffman, Lau, and Johnson, 1986).

Research conducted in the context of the 'communication-game' model (Higgins, 1981) has also considered this issue. In a development of earlier work on labeling effects on memory in experimental psychology (e.g. Carmichael, Hogan, and Walter, 1932; Thomas, DeCapito, Caronite, LaMonica, and Hoving, 1968), Higgins and his colleagues explored the implications of their assumption that the verbal encoding of stimulus information will, over time, serve as a basis for the reconstruction of that information (cf. Bartlett, 1932; Neisser, 1967). Thus contextual and personality factors that influence how information is encoded were hypothesized to influence the subsequent reconstruction of that information.

In the initial study in this program of research, Higgins and Rholes (1978) had subjects communicate about a stimulus person they had read about to a recipient who they believed either liked or disliked the stimulus person. It was predicted that subjects would modify their messages to suit the attitudes of their listener and that this message modification would lead over time to evaluative change in subjects' memory for, and attitudes about, the stimulus person. Both sets of predictions were confirmed. For example, subjects who communicated to someone they thought liked the stimulus person produced a more positive message and subsequently recalled and evaluated the stimulus person's behavior more positively than subjects who communicated to someone they thought disliked the stimulus person. Later research has replicated and extended these initial findings (e.g. Higgins *et al.*, 1982; Higgins and McCann, 1984; McCann and Hancock, 1983).

Although consistent in their implications, the results of the above lines of research only begin to address the range of effects that message production may have on the communicators themselves. Many other issues have yet to be considered. One of these bridges the concerns of both this and the previous section. Most of the work examining communicator effects has focused on the effects of communication either on general beliefs or on knowledge and evaluations of specific other persons. An important unexamined issue concerns the extent to which similar effects would be observed in terms of the communicator's beliefs about self (i.e. self-concept). For example, would communicating a positive message about self under theoretically relevant conditions lead to a more positive self-concept for individuals with low self-esteem or depression? In addition to its theoretical importance, such research has clear applied relevance.

EFFECTS OF OTHER (RECIPIENT) ON COMMUNICATION

Every interpersonal encounter necessarily involves at least two individuals. Communicators, therefore, can, and typically do, adopt the audience's standpoint in their communicative interaction. An interesting question, then, is what are the effects of an audience's characteristics on communication? This has been a classic and well-researched question in the communication literature.

It is assumed in most classic treatments of communicative competence that to be an effective and efficient communicator one should tune or modify one's messages to suit the characteristics of the listener (e.g. Mead, 1934; Piaget, 1926). This has been a critical feature of most analyses of communication (e.g Higgins and Rholes, 1978; Manis, Cornell, and Moore, 1974; Newtson and Czerlinsky, 1974) and is a prominent communication rule or norm according to the 'communication-game' model (for a review, see Higgins, 1981).

Several aspects of this tendency have been of interest. One line of research has concentrated on examining the developmental antecedents of this aspect of effective communication. Most traditional approaches have focused on the development of perspective-taking as a necessary basic skill (see Flavell, Botkin, Fry, Wright, and Jarvis, 1968; Glucksberg, Krauss, and Higgins, 1975; Higgins, 1977). Here it is assumed that in order to be able adequately to tailor a message to suit an audience one must be able to adopt their role or to see things from their perspective. The ability to take the perspective of the listener is then a precondition for effective message modification. This ability is assumed to be dependent upon mature cognitive development and increased differentiation of the personal construct system (e.g. O'Keefe and Delia, 1985).

In addition to this developmental literature, a great deal of research has been devoted to documenting and explaining the conditions under which message modification will occur. These efforts have examined message modification as a result of both chronic and temporary attributes of the listener. Perhaps one of the most powerful early demonstrations of this came from the work of Krauss *et al.* (1968), who compared the messages produced by communicators for themselves with those produced for others. Interesting here was the finding that message production for the general 'other' (i.e. a social message) was more effective for a specific 'other' than a message produced for the self, i.e. a non-social message (see Krauss, 1987, for a review). Most other research has compared the form and content of messages produced for different types of 'others'.

One focus in examining audience effects in communication has concerned easily categorizable, highly salient audience characteristics. For example, research has described the shifts in linguistic form and content that occur when adults address children (e.g. Gelman and Shatz, 1977; Sachs and Devin, 1976). Much of this interest has centered on the characteristics and use of the 'baby-talk' register (e.g. DePaulo and Bonvillian, 1978; Ferguson, 1977; Gleason and Weintraub, 1978; Snow, 1977; Snow and Ferguson, 1977). In a recent study extending this work, DePaulo and Coleman (1986) had subjects encode messages in a training context for each of the following: a 6-year-old child, a retarded adult, a peer who spoke English as a second language (i.e. a foreigner) and a peer who spoke English as a first language. Two conclusions derived from this study are of special interest. First, evidence was found suggesting the presence both of message modification in the face of salient social category cues (e.g. differences in encoding for similar peers versus foreigners) and of fine tuning to suit the individual needs of category members (i.e. differential modification for more or less sophisticated foreigners). Thus, even when using highly salient cues to tailor their messages, communicators are still sensitive to individual variation. The precise parameters of this latter effect are still unknown. Second, the results suggested that baby talk may be a prototype or basic register from which other specialized registers are derived. In addition to baby talk and 'foreign talk' (Ferguson, 1975, 1977; Freed, 1981), research has focused on the registers used in conversing with elderly adults (e.g. Caporael, Lukaszewski, and Culbertson, 1983; see Chapter 22, by Coupland and Coupland) and on the speech variations used by broadcasters for different audiences (e.g. Bell, 1982).

Although the effect of audience characteristics on the form and content of communication has been well documented, several additional issues need to be considered. For example, we know little about the nature of the underlying social-cognitive processes that contribute to successful message modification or about how such attempts are monitored by the communicator. Here, work on feedback (see Kraut and Lewis, 1984) and on editing standards (e.g. Hample and Dallinger, 1988) may be relevant. In addition, we need to know more about the conditions under which communicators *do not* successfully tailor their messages. Some innovative work along this line has recently been conducted by Goranson (1986) in his examination of 'communication overconfidence' and its cognitive and motivational bases.

COMMUNICATION EFFECTS ON THE RECIPIENT'S SOCIAL COGNITIONS

In many traditional approaches to the study of communication, message recipients were treated as relatively passive participants who served mainly as targets for the communicative activity of the speakers. Their task was simply to decode the message content directed at them. In some treatments, however, message recipients have been conceptualized as active participants who engaged in a variety of evaluative and information-seeking processes with respect to the speaker (see Berger and Bradac, 1982; McGuire, 1985). This perspective raises issues concerning the social-cognitive responses of recipients to speaker attributes and how these effect information transmission. From the listener's perspective, who the speakers are, what they say, how they say it and why they say it are all factors worthy of consideration (see Eagly and Chaiken, 1984; McGuire, 1969). A few important processes seem to be implicated in the evaluations of speakers by listeners.

According to Berger and Bradac (1982), the recipients' 'linguistic based judgments of a speaker's psychological makeup and affiliations' (p. 55) allow recipients to engage in the process of uncertainty reduction. Since effective interpersonal behavior is predicated upon being able to anticipate what the other will do, listeners use linguistic cues to reduce their uncertainty about the speaker. In addition, many of these speaker evaluations occur as a result of theory-driven expectations based upon salient social category attributes (e.g. McCann, Ostrom, Tyner, and Mitchell, 1985). Certain person types are expected to emit certain language forms and content. Disconfirmation of these expectations can have important consequences for evaluations of them (e.g. Burgoon and Miller, 1985). Expectancy disconfirmation may also negatively impact on the objectives of the speaker, as was shown by Burgoon and Stewart (1975) in their examination of language intensity and the persuasiveness of female communicators.

In addition to this interest in process, there are two general categories of research examining the effects of specific communicator cues. The first focuses on reactions to messages produced by members of distinct social groups (e.g. males, females) and the second focuses on the effects of specific aspects of language form (e.g. intensity).

A great deal of interest has centered on evaluations of the speech of females as compared to that generally produced by males. For example, women's speech is often judged to be less forceful because, in part, they tend to use a greater proportion of indirect speech acts (e.g. Lakoff, 1979; McCann and Higgins, 1984). Accordingly, women using this style are judged to be less hostile (see Kraut and Higgins, 1984). Whether or not this is a valued judgment is, of course, dependent on the context and goals of the communicator.

In addition to gender differences in language (see Chapter 17, by Kramarae) and their relation to social judgment and evaluation, research has also examined the impact of salient cues such as accent (e.g Ryan and Bulik, 1983) and old age (e.g. Sebastian and Ryan, 1985; Stewart and Ryan, 1982). This latter focus is especially noteworthy given the recent concern with stereotypes and treatment of the elderly. Disconfirmation of expectations here can sometimes lead to more positive evaluations, as when elderly communicators are perceived to use fast-paced speech

(Stewart and Ryan, 1982). Sebastian and Ryan (1985) suggest that two mechanisms may possibly mediate the evaluative reactions of recipients. In their consideration of the role of accent, these authors propose that speaker evaluations may be due to a 'negative affect mechanism' associated with the difficulties encountered in decoding unusual speech cues. In addition, listeners may use unusual speech cues to make inferences about the speaker's ethnicity and probable social status (i.e. low), which in turn may produce more general negative evaluations (see Chapter 14, by Sachdev and Bourhis, and Chapter 19, by Bradac).

Research has also focused on the evaluative implications of various speech factors, including multiple-goal representation (e.g. O'Keefe and McCormack, 1987), voice quality (e.g. Pittan and Gallois, 1987), the relative contribution of voice quality and content factors (e.g. O'Sullivan, Ekman, Friesen, and Scherer, 1985), similarity in speech rate between speaker and listener (Street, Brady, and Putman, 1983), dialect hostility (Hopper, 1986), the use of direct and indirect speech forms (Holtgraves, 1986) and intensity, loudness, pitch and immediacy (e.g. Ray, 1986; see Berger and Bradac, 1982, for a review; see also Chapter 6, by Street). This research is more descriptive than explanatory, and more process-oriented models need to be developed which consider factors such as the recipient's ability to decode speaker intent (e.g. Gaelick, Bodenhausen, and Wyer, 1985).

Finally, there are two other recent orientations that have important potential for research in this area. First, Mulac and colleagues (e.g. Mulac, Incontro, and James, 1985; Mulac, Lundell, and Bradac, 1986) have examined the relative contribution of theory- and data-driven processes in the evaluation of male/female speech differences. In this work they have examined the relative contribution of gender stereotypes and the 'gender-linked language effect' to the evaluation of male and female speakers. This focus on the role of theory and data is consistent with current trends in social cognition.

A second example of the rich potential inherent in integrating social cognition and communication research in the area of speaker evaluation is the work of Davis and her colleagues on 'responsiveness' (e.g. Davis and Holtgraves, 1984). Communicator responsiveness is conceptualized as being a function of four contingencies between communicative interactants: probability of response, response relevance, appropriateness of response latency and appropriateness of response elaboration. Variation in speaker responsiveness has been shown to be implicated in a host of reactions, including personal evaluations, competence judgments and assessments of motivation. Further work on this model will undoubtedly add to our knowledge of the social-cognitive and interpersonal processes involved in such situations.

CONCLUSIONS AND FUTURE DIRECTIONS

In this chapter, we have reviewed and considered research and theory representing an integration of work in the areas of social cognition and communication. This is an active and exciting field of study, which serves as an interface for researchers in psychology, sociology and communication. As is clear from our review, there is a wealth of innovative research and theory that has served, over the last decade or so, to provide new directions for, and conceptualizations of, the nature of interpersonal communication. Although significant advances have been made, some limitations of current work are evident. These in themselves should provide direction for new work. Some of these limitations or concerns have been pointed out in the context of our review. There are, however, some additional, more general, points that are worthy of mention.

First, it is clear that, when considering the nature either of the self or of other cognitive structures invoked in the above analyses, these conceptions are in many cases based on earlier structural models that neglect some recent developments in the field. For example, the self is now considered to be a dynamic, multifaceted entity that has cognitive, motivational and affective implications (e.g. Higgins, 1987; Markus and Nurius 1986; McCann and Higgins, 1988). In large measure, most of the research and theory examining the relations between self and communication has focused on issues related to the traditional formulation of self-concept (i.e. beliefs a person has about what he or she is actually like). Not only does this ignore the implications of other aspects of the self (i.e. standards for the self or future aspirations; see Higgins, 1987, for a review) that are 'motivationally rich', but the essential affective quality of the self is absent. Failure to consider these facets of the self may have contributed to the overly static conception of communication conveyed by most recent work.

In addition, most models concerned with 'constructivism' in communication have similarly ignored more recent conceptions. For example, the models focusing on personal constructs have adopted a traditional emphasis on *structure* at the expense of *process*. Thus, in an attempt to understand individual differences in communication, these models concern themselves with differences in the 'availability' of knowledge and fail to consider systematically differences in knowledge 'accessibility' which have been found in other areas to be critical mediators of information processing (see Higgins and Bargh, 1987, and McCann and Higgins, 1984, for reviews). This has also impacted on interest in the development of these personal constructs. Traditional work has focused on the development of such things as perspective-taking (but see O'Keefe and Delia, 1985) and has failed to consider systematically the implications of development in ability to represent multiple elements that could impact on the communicator's ability to deal with multiple and competing goals.

Most of the work reviewed above has also failed to capture the dynamic quality of communicative interactions. One example will suffice to illustrate what we mean. As we suggested above, communicators typically modify their messages to suit the characteristics of their audience. Demonstrations of this abound in the literature. What has not been considered in any detail is how communicators make inferences about the relative success or failure of their attempts, what adjustments they make for unsuccessful attempts and the extent to which these adjustments may vary according to the communicator's goals (e.g. persuasion, impression management, task, etc.), type of recipient or the nature of their relationship. Research into these issues would serve to illustrate more of the 'on-line' nature of motivated communication.

Finally, some mention must be made regarding the isomorphism inherent in the four research areas we have reviewed. The classification we presented is arbitrary in nature, but it is one that reflects the explicit directions taken in current research. This orientation is most likely a carry-over from classic models of communication that failed to highlight the dynamic nature of interpersonal communication. The problem confronting reseachers in their attempts to redress this limitation is that there is no single process model that has emerged to replace these classic formulations. We know intuitively, however, that each of the issues reviewed above is interrelated with the others. For example, self and other relevant processes are related. Speakers engage in message modification. This process is guided by their impressions or conceptions of the listener. Listeners are most likely aware of this process and probably adjust their evaluations of, and feedback to, the speaker accordingly. The speaker then uses this information to adjust further the form and content of his or her message. It is this quality of interpersonal communication that we believe will more quickly emerge as a result of integrating social cognition and communication, given the focus in each area on process.

ACKNOWLEDGMENTS

Preparation of this article was partially supported by a Social Sciences and Humanities Research Council of Canada Grant (410–87–0099) awarded to the first author and a National Institute of Mental Health Grant (MH39429) awarded to the second author. The authors thank Alexander Mackenzie, Howard Giles and Peter Robinson for their insightful comments on an earlier draft.

REFERENCES

Applegate, J.L. (1982). The impact of construct system development on communication and impression formation in persuasive contexts. *Communication Monographs*, **49**, 277–289.

Applegate, J.L. and Delia, J.G. (1980). Person-centered speech, psychological development, and the contexts of language use. In R. St Clair and H. Giles (Eds), *The social and psychological contexts of language use*, pp. 213–241. Hillsdale, NJ: Erlbaum.

Athay, M. and Darley, J.M. (1981). Toward an interaction-centered theory of personality. In N. Cantor and J.F. Kihlstrom (Eds), *Personality, cognition and social interaction*, pp. 281–308. Hillsdale, NJ: Erlbaum.

Ball, P., G'les, H. and Hewstone, M. (1985). Interpersonal accommodation and situational construals: An integrative formalisation. In H. Giles (Ed.), *Recent advances in language, communication and social psychology*, pp. 263–286. Hillsdale, NJ: Erlbaum.

Bartlett, F.C. (1932). *Remembering*. Cambridge: Cambridge University Press.

Baumeister, R.F. (1982). A self-presentational view of social phenomena. *Psychological Bulletin*, **91**, 3–26.

Bell, A. (1982). Radio: The style of news language. *Journal of Communication, 32*, 150–164.

Bem, D.J. (1972). An experimental analysis of self-persuasion. *Journal of Experimental Social Psychology*, **1**, 199–218.

Berger, C.R. (1979). Beyond initial interaction: Uncertainty, understanding and the development of interpersonal relationships. In H. Giles (Ed.), *Language and social psychology*, pp. 122–144. Oxford: Blackwell.

Berger, C.R. (1986). Social cognition and intergroup communication. In W.B. Gudykunst (Ed.), *Intergroup communication*, pp. 51–61. London: Arnold.

Berger, C.R. and Bradac, J.J. (1982). *Language and social knowledge: Uncertainty in interpersonal relations*. London: Arnold.

Berger, C.R. and Calabrese, R.J. (1975). Some explorations in initial interaction and beyond: Toward a developmental theory of interpersonal communication. *Human Communication Research*, **1**, 99–112.

Bernstein, B. (1960). Language and social class. *British Journal of Sociology*, **11**, 271–276.

Bond, M.H. (1983). How language variation affects intercultural differentiation of values by Hong Kong bilinguals. *Journal of Language and Social Psychology*, **2**, 57–66.

Bourhis, R.Y., Giles, H., Leyens, J.P., and Tajfel, H. (1979). Psycholinguistic distinctiveness: Language divergence in Belgium. In H. Giles and R. St Clair (Eds), *Language and social psychology*, pp. 158–185. Oxford: Blackwell.

Brock, T.C. and Fromkin, H.L. (1968). Cognitive tuning set and behavioral receptivity to discrepant information. *Journal of Personality*, **36**, 108–125.

Burgoon, M. and Miller, G.R. (1971). Prior attitudes and language intensity as predictors of message style and attitude change following counterattitudinal advocacy. *Journal of Personality and Social Psychology*, **20**, 240–253.

Burgoon, M. and Miller, G.R. (1985). An expectancy interpretation of language and persuasion. In H. Giles and R. St Clair (Eds), *Recent advances in language, communication, and social psychology*, pp. 199–229. Hillsdale, NJ: Erlbaum.

Burgoon, M. and Stewart, D. (1975). Empirical investigations of language intensity: I. The effects of sex of source and language intensity on attitude change. *Human Communication Research*, **1**, 244–248.

Canary, D.J., Cody, M.J., and Marston, P.J. (1987). Goal types, compliance-gaining and locus of control. *Journal of Language and Social Psychology*, **5**, 249–269.

Caporael, L.R., Lukaszewski, M.P., and Culbertson, G.H. (1983). Secondary baby talk: Judgments by institutionalized elderly and their caregivers. *Journal of Personality and Social Psychology*, **44**, 746–754.

Carmichael, L., Hogan, H.P., and Walter, A.A. (1932). An experimental study of the effect of language on the reproduction of visually perceived form. *Journal of Experimental Psychology*, **15**, 72–86.

Clark, H.H. (1985). Language and language users. In G. Lindzey and E. Aronson (Eds), *The handbook of social psychology*, Vol. 2, pp. 179–232. New York: Random House.

Cohen, A.R (1961). Cognitive tuning as a factor affecting impression formation. *Journal of Personality*, **29**, 234–245.

Crockett, W.H. (1965). Cognitive complexity and impression formation. In B.A. Mahler (Ed.), *Progress in experimental personality research*, Vol. 2, pp. 47–90. New York: Academic Press.

Davis, D. and Holtgraves, T. (1984). Perception of unresponsive others: attributions, attraction, understandability, and memory for their utterances. *Journal of Experimental Social Psychology*, **20**, 383–408.

Delia, J.G., Kline, S.L., and Burelson, B.R. (1979). The development of persuasive communication strategies in kindergarteners through twelfth-graders. *Communication Monographs*, **46**, 241–256.

Delia, J.G. and O'Keefe, B.J. (1979). Constructivism: The development of communication in children. In E. Wartella (Ed.), *Children communicating*, pp. 157–185. Beverly Hills: Sage.

Delia, J.G., O'Keefe, B.J., and O'Keefe, D.J. (1982). The constructivist approach to communication. In F.E.X. Dance (Ed.), *Comparative human communication theory*, pp. 147–191. New York: Harper & Row.

DePaulo, B.M. and Bonvillian, J.D. (1978). The effect on language development of the special characteristics of speech addressed to children. *Journal of Psycholinguistic Research*, **7**, 189–211.

DePaulo, B.M. and Coleman, L.M. (1986). Talking to children, foreigners and retarded adults. *Journal of Personality and Social Psychology*, **51**, 945–959.

DePaulo, B.M., Kenny, D.A., Hoover, C.W., Webb, W., and Oliver, P.V. (1987). Accuracy of person perception: Do people know what kinds of impressions they convey? *Journal of Personality and Social Psychology*, **52**, 303–315.

Eagly, A.H. and Chaiken, S. (1984). Cognitive theories of persuasion. In L. Berkowitz (Ed.), *Advances in experimental social psychology*, Vol. 17, pp. 45–63. New York: Academic Press.

Eastman, C. (1985). Establishing social identity through language use. *Journal of Language and Social Psychology*, **4**, 1–20.

Ferguson, C.A. (1975). Toward a characterization of English foreigner talk. *Anthropological Linguistics*, **17**, 1–14.

Ferguson, C.A. (1977). Baby talk as a simplified register. In C.A. Ferguson and C. Snow (Eds), *Talking to children: Language input and acquisition*, pp. 209–235. Cambridge: Cambridge University Press.

Festinger, L. (1957). *A theory of cognitive dissonance*. Stanford CA: Stanford University Press.

Fiske, S.T. and Taylor, S.E. (1984). *Social cognition*. Reading, MA: Addison-Wesley.

Flavell, J.H., Botkin, P.T., Fry, C.L., Wright, J.W., and Jarvis, P.E. (1968). *The development of role-taking and communication skills in children*. New York: Wiley.

Freed, B. (1981). Foreigner talk, baby talk, native talk. *International Journal of the Sociology of Language*, **28**, 19–40.

Gaelick, L., Bodenhausen, G.V., and Wyer, R.S. (1985). Emotional communication in close relationships. *Journal of Personality and Social Psychology*, **49**, 1256–1265.

Gelman, R. and Shatz, M. (1977). Appropriate speech adjustment: The operation of conversational constraints on talk to two year olds. In M. Lewis and L. Rosenblum (Eds), *Interaction, conversation and the development of language*, pp. 116–145. New York: Wiley.

Gilbert, D.T., Jones, E.E., and Pelham, B.W. (1987). Influence and inference: What the active perceiver overlooks. *Journal of Personality and Social Psychology*, **52**, 861–870.

Giles, H., Bourhis, R.Y., and Taylor, D.M. (1977). Towards a theory of language in ethnic group relations. In H. Giles (Ed.), *Language, ethnicity, and intergroup relations*, pp. 32–65. London: Academic Press.

Giles, H. and Hewstone, M. (1982). Cognitive structures, speech and social situations: Two integrative models. *Language Sciences*, **4**, 187–219.

Gleason, J.B. and Weintraub, S. (1978). Input language and the acquisition of communication competence. In K.E. Nelson (Ed.), *Children's language*, pp. 171–222. New York: Garden Press.

Glucksberg, S., Krauss, R.M., and Higgins, E.T. (1975). The development of referential communication skills. In F. Horowitz, E. Hetherington, S. Scarr-Salapatek, and G. Seigel (Eds), *Review of child development research*, Vol. 4, pp. 304–345. Chicago: University of Chicago Press.

Goffman, E. (1959). *The presentation of self in everyday life*. New York: Doubleday.

Gollwitzer, P.M. and Wicklund, R.A. (1985). Self-symbolizing and the neglect of other's perspectives. *Journal of Personality and Social Psychology*, **48**, 702–715.

Goranson, R.E. (1986). Bias in judgments of communication effectiveness. Paper presented at Meeting of the Canadian Psychological Association, Toronto, Canada.

Greenwald, A.G. and Breckler, S.J. (1985). To whom is the self presented? In B.R. Schlenker (Ed.), *The self in social life*, pp. 126–146. New York: McGraw-Hill.

Hample, D. and Dallinger, J.M. (1988). Individual differences in cognitive editing standards. *Human Communication Research*, **14**, 123–144.

Harvey, J.H., Harkins, S.G., and Kagehiro, D.K. (1976). Cognitive tuning and the attribution of causality. *Journal of Personality and Social Psychology*, **34**, 708–715.

Hewes, D.E. and Planalp, S. (1982). There is nothing as useful as a good theory . . . : The influence of social knowledge on interpersonal communication. In M.E. Roloff and C.R. Berger (Eds), *Social cognition and communication*, pp. 107–150. Beverly Hills: Sage.

Higgins, E.T. (1977). Communication development as related to channel, incentive and social class. *Genetic Psychology Monographs*, **96**, 75–141.

Higgins, E.T. (1981). The 'communication-game': Implications for social cognition and persuasion. In E.T. Higgins, C.P. Herman, and M.P. Zanna (Eds), *Social cognition: The Ontario symposium*, Vol. 1, pp. 343–392. Hillsdale, NJ: Erlbaum.

Higgins, E.T. (1987). Self-discrepancy: A theory relating self and affect. *Psychological Review*, **94**, 319–341.

Higgins, E.T. and Bargh, J.A. (1987). Social cognition and social perception. In M. Rosenzweig and L. Porter (Eds), *Annual review of psychology*, Vol. 38, pp. 469–495. New York: Annual Reviews.

Higgins, E.T., Fondacaro, R.A., and McCann, C.D. (1981). Rules and roles: The 'comunication-game' and speaker–listener processes. In W.P. Dickson (Ed.), *Children's oral communication skills*, pp. 289–312. New York: Academic Press.

Higgins, E.T. and McCann, C.D. (1984). Social encoding and subsequent attitudes, impressions and memory: Context-driven and motivational aspects of processing. *Journal of Personality and Social Psychology*, **47**, 26–39.

Higgins, E.T., McCann, C.D., and Fondacaro, R.A. (1982). The 'communication-game': Goal directed encoding and cognitive consequences. *Social Cognition*, **1**, 21–37.

Higgins, E.T. and Rholes, W.S. (1978). 'Saying is believing': Effects of message modification on memory and liking for the person described. *Journal of Experimental Social Psychology*, **14**, 363–378.

Higgins, E.T. and Stangor, C. (1986). Context-driven social judgment and memory: When behavior 'engulfs the field' in reconstructive memory. In D. Bar-Tal and A. Kruglanski (Eds), *Social psychology of knowledge*, pp. 42–75. Cambridge: Cambridge University Press.

Hoffman, C., Lau, I., and Johnson, D.R. (1986). The linguistic relativity of person cognition: An English–Chinese comparison. *Journal of Personality and Social Psychology*, **51**, 1097–1105.

Holtgraves, T. (1986). Language structure in social interaction: Perception of direct and indirect speech acts and interactants who use them. *Journal of Personality and Social Psychology*, **51**, 305–314.

Hopper, R. (1986). Speech evaluation of intergroup dialect differences: The shibboleth schema. In W.B. Gudykunst (Ed.), *Intergroup communication*, pp. 127–136. London: Arnold.

Hovland, C.I., Janis, I.L., and Kelley, H.H. (1953). *Communication and persuasion in psychological studies of opinion change*. New Haven: Yale University Press.

Janis, I.L. and King, B.T. (1954). The influence of role-playing on opinion change. *Journal of Abnormal and Social Psychology*, **49**, 211–218.

Jones, E.E. and Pittman, T.S. (1982). Toward a general theory of strategic self-presentation. In J. Suls (Ed.), *Psychological perspectives on the self*, Vol. 1, pp. 231–267. Hillsdale, NJ: Erlbaum.

Kellerman, K. and Berger, C.R. (1984). Affect and social information acquisition: Sit back, relax, and tell me about yourself. In R.N. Bostrom (Ed.), *Communication yearbook*, Vol. 8, pp. 412–455. Beverly Hills: Sage.

Kelly, G.A. (1955). *A theory of personality*. New York: Norton.

Krauss, R.M. (1987). The role of the listener: Addressee influences on message formulation. *Journal of Language and Social Psychology*, **6**, 81–9.

Krauss, R.M., Vivekananthan, P.S., and Weinheimer, S. (1968). Inner speech and external speech: Characteristics of communication effectiveness of socially and nonsocially encoded messages. *Journal of Personality and Social Psychology*, **9**, 292–300.

Kraut, R.E. and Higgins, E.T. (1984). Communication and social cognition. In R.S. Wyer and T.K. Srull (Eds), *Handbook of social cognition*, Vol. 3, pp. 67–128. Hillsdale, NJ: Erlbaum.

Kraut, R.E. and Lewis, S.H. (1984). Some functions of feedback in conversation. In J. Applegate and H.E. Sypher (Eds), *Understanding interpersonal communication: Social cognition and strategic processes in children and adults*, pp. 231–260. Beverly Hills: Sage.

Kuiper, N.A. and Derry, P. (1981). The self as a cognitive prototype: An application to person perception and depression. In N. Cantor and J.F. Kihlstrom (Eds), *Personality, cognition and social interaction*, pp. 215–232. Hillsdale, NJ: Erlbaum.

Lakoff, R. (1979). Stylistic strategies within a grammar of style. In J. Orasanu, M. Slater, and L. Adler (Eds), *Language, sex, and gender: Does La Difference make a difference? Annals of the New York Academy of Science*, **327**, 53–80.

Leventhal, H. (1962). The effects of sex and discrepancy on impression change. *Journal of Personality*, **30**, 1–15.

Manis, M., Cornell, S.D., and Moore, J.C. (1974). Transmission of attitude-relevant information through a communication chain. *Journal of Personality and Social Psychology*, **30**, 81–94.

Markus, H. (1977). Self-schemata and processing information about the self. *Journal of Personality and Social Psychology*, **35**, 63–78.

Markus, H. and Nurius, P. (1986). Possible selves. *American Psychologist*, **41**, 954–969.

Markus, H. and Wurf, E. (1987). The dynamic self-concept: A social psychological perspective. In M.R. Rosenzweig and L.W. Porter (Eds), *Annual review of psychology*, Vol. 38, pp. 299–337. New York: Annual Reviews.

Markus, H. and Zajonc, R.B. (1985). The cognitive perspective in social psychology. In G. Lindzey and E. Aronson (Eds), *The handbook of social psychology*, Vol. 1, pp. 137–230. New York: Random House.

McCann, C.D. and Hancock, R.D. (1983). Self-monitoring in communicative interaction: Social-cognitive consequences of goal-directed message modification. *Journal of Experimental Social Psychology*, **19**, 109–121.

McCann, C.D. and Higgins, E.T. (1984). Individual differences in communication: Social cognitive determinants and consequences. In H.E. Sypher and J.L. Applegate (Eds), *Understanding interpersonal communication: Social cognitive and strategic processes in children and adults*, pp. 172–210. Beverly Hills: Sage.

McCann, C.D. and Higgins, E.T. (1988). Motivation and affect in interpersonal relations: The role of personal orientations and discrepancies. In L. Donahew, H.E. Sypher, and E.T. Higgins (Eds), *Communication, social cognition and effect*, pp. 53–79. Hillsdale, NJ: Erlbaum.

McCann, C.D., Ostrom, T.M., Tyner, L.K., and Mitchell, M.L. (1985). Person perception in heterogeneous groups. *Journal of Personality and Social Psychology*, **49**, 1449–1459.

McGuire, W.J. (1969). The nature of attitudes and attitude change. In G. Lindzey and E. Aronson (Eds), *The handbook of social psychology*, Vol. 3, pp. 136–314. Reading, MA: Addison-Wesley.

McGuire, W.J. (1985). Attitudes and attitude change. In G. Lindzey and E. Aronson (Eds), *Handbook of social psychology*, Vol. 2, pp. 233–246. New York: Random House.

Mead, G.H. (1934). *Mind, self and society*. Chicago: University of Chicago Press.

Mehrabian, A. and Reed, H. (1968). Some determinants of communication accuracy. *Psychological Bulletin*, **70**, 365–381.

Mulac, A., Incontro, C.R., and James, M.R. (1985). Comparison of the gender-linked language effect and sex on role stereotypes. *Journal of Personality and Social Psychology*, **49**, 1098–1109.

Mulac, A., Lundell, T.L., and Bradac, J.J. (1986). Male–female language differences and attributional consequences in a public speaking situation: Toward an explanation of the gender-linked language effect. *Communication Monographs*, **53**, 115–129.

Neisser, U. (1967). *Cognitive psychology*. New York: Appleton-Century-Crofts.

Newtson, D. and Czerlinsky, T. (1974). Adjustment of attitude communications for contrasts by extreme audiences. *Journal of Personality and Social Psychology*, **30**, 829–837.

O'Keefe, B.J. and Delia, J.G. (1982). Impression formation and message production. In

M.E. Roloff and C.R. Berger (Eds), *Social cognition and communication*, pp. 33–72. Beverly Hills: Sage.

O'Keefe, B.J. and Delia, J.G. (1985). Psychological and Interactional dimensions of communicative development. In H. Giles and R.N. St Clair (Eds), *Recent advances in language, communication and social psychology*, pp. 41–85. Hillsdale, NJ: Erlbaum.

O'Keefe, B.J. and McCormack, S.A. (1987). Message design logic and message goal structure: Effects on perceptions of message quality in regulative communicative situations. *Human Communication Research*, **14**, 68–92.

O'Keefe, B.J. and Shepard, G. (1987). The pursuit of multiple objectives in face-to-face persuasive interactions: Effects of construct differentiation on message organization. *Communication Monographs*, **54**, 369–419.

Ostrom, T.M. (1984). The sovereignty of social cognition. In R.S. Wyer and T.K. Srull (Eds), *The handbook of social cognition*, Vol. 1, pp. 1–38. Hillsdale, NJ: Erlbaum.

O'Sullivan, M., Ekman, P., Friesen, W., and Scherer, K. (1985). What you say and how you say it: The contribution of speech content and voice quality to judgments of others. *Journal of Personality and Social Psychology*, **48**, 54–62.

Piaget, J. (1926). *The language and thought of the child*. New York: Harcourt-Brace.

Pittan, J. and Gallois, C. (1987). Predicting impressions of speakers from voice quality: Acoustic and perceptual measures. *Journal of Language and Social Psychology*, **5**, 233–247.

Ray, G.B. (1986). Vocally cued personality prototypes: An implicit theory approach. *Communication Monographs*, **53**, 266–276.

Rogers, T.B. (1981). A model of the self as an aspect of the human information processing system. In N. Cantor and J.F. Kihlstrom (Eds), *Personality, cognition and social interaction*, pp. 193–214. Hillsdale, NJ: Erlbaum.

Rokeach, M. (1973). *The nature of human values*. New York: Free Press.

Ross, L., Lepper, M.R., and Hubbard, R. (1975). Perseverance in self perception: Biased attributional processes in the debriefing paradigm. *Journal of Personality and Social Psychology*, **32**, 880–892.

Ryan, E.B. (1979). Why do low prestige language varieties persist? In H. Giles and R.N. St Clair (Eds), *Language and social psychology*, pp. 145–157. Baltimore: University Park Press.

Ryan, E.B. and Bulik, C.M. (1983). Evaluations of middle class and lower class speakers of standard American and German-oriented English. *Journal of Language and Social Psychology*, **1**, 51–61.

Sachs, J. and Devin, J. (1976). Young children's use of age-appropriate speech styles in social interaction and role-playing. *Journal of Child Language*, **3**, 81–98.

Schlenker, B.R. (1985). Identity and self-identification. In B.R. Schlenker (Ed.), *The self and social life*, pp. 65–100. New York: McGraw-Hill.

Sebastian, R.J. and Ryan, E.B. (1985). Speech cues and social evaluations: Markers of ethnicity, social class and age. In H. Giles and R.N. St Clair (Eds), *Recent advances in language, communication and social psychology*, pp. 112–143. Hillsdale, NJ: Erlbaum.

Shannon, C.E. and Weaver, W. (1949). *The mathematical theory of communication*. Urbana, IL: University of Illinois Press.

Snow, C.E. (1977). Mothers' speech research: From input to interaction. In C.E. Snow and C.A. Ferguson (Eds), *Talking to children*, pp. 31–49. Cambridge: Cambridge University Press.

Snow, C.E. and Ferguson, C.A. (Eds) (1977). *Talking to children*. Cambridge: Cambridge University Press.

Snyder, M. (1979). Self-monitoring processes. In L. Berkowitz (Ed.), *Advances in experimental social psychology*, Vol. 12, pp. 86–128. New York: Academic Press.

Snyder, M. (1984). When beliefs become reality. In L. Berkowitz (Ed.), *Advances in experimental social psychology*, Vol. 18, pp. 247–305. New York: Academic Press.

Snyder, M. and Swann, W.B. (1978). Hypothesis-testing processes in social interaction. *Journal of Personality and Social Psychology*, **36**, 1202–1213.

Stewart, M.A. and Ryan, E.B. (1982). Attitudes toward younger and older adult speakers: Effects of varying speech rates. *Journal of Language and Social Psychology*, **1**, 91–109.

Street, R.L., Brady, R.M., and Putman, W.B. (1983). The influence of speech rate stereotypes and rate similarity on listener's evaluations of speakers. *Journal of Language and Social Psychology*, **2**, 37–56.

Street, R.L. and Giles, H. (1982). Speech accommodation theory: A social cognitive approach to language and social behavior. In M.E. Roloff and C.R. Berger (Eds), *Social cognition and communication*, pp. 193–226. Beverly Hills: Sage.

Swann, W.B. (1984). Quest for accuracy in person perception: A matter of pragmatics. *Psychological Review*, **91**, 457–477.

Sypher, H.E. and Applegate, J.L. (1984). Organizing communication behavior: The role of schemas and constructs. In R.N. Bostrom (Ed.), *Communication yearbook*, Vol. 8, pp. 310–329. Beverly Hills: Sage.

Tajfel, H. and Turner, J.C. (1979). An integrative theory of group conflict. In W.C. Austin and S. Worchel (Eds), *The social psychology of intergroup relations*, pp. 7–24. Monterey, CA: Brooks-Cole.

Taylor, D.M., Dagot, E.D., and Gardner, R.C. (1969). The use of semantic differentials in cross-cultural research. *Philippine Journal of Psychology*, **2**, 43–51.

Tedeschi, J.T. and Norman, N. (1985). Social power, self-presentation, and the self. In B.R. Schlenker (Ed.), *The self in social life*, pp. 292–323. New York: McGraw-Hill.

Thakerar, J.N., Giles, H., and Cheshire, J. (1982). Psychological and linguistic parameters of speech accommodation theory. In C. Fraser and K.R. Scherer (Eds), *Advances in the social psychology of language*, pp. 205–255. Cambridge: Cambridge University Press.

Thomas, D.R., DeCapito, B., Caronite, A., LaMonica, G.L., and Hoving, K.L. (1968). Mediated generalization via stimulus labeling: A replication and extension. *Journal of Experimental Psychology*, **78**, 531–533.

Whorf, B. (1956). *Language, thought and society*. New York: Wiley and MIT.

Wicklund, R.A. and Gollwitzer, P.M. (1982). *Symbolic self-completion*. Hillsdale, NJ: Erlbaum.

Wylie, R. (1979). *The self-concept*, Vol. 2. Lincoln, NE: University of Nebraska Press.

Zajonc, R.B. (1960). The process of cognitive tuning and communication. *Journal of Abnormal and Social Psychology*, **61**, 159–167.

Zajonc, R.B. (1980). Cognition and social cogition: A historical perspective. In L. Festinger (Ed.), *Retrospections on social psychology*, pp. 180–204. New York: Oxford University Press.

2

Language and Emotion

WARD M. WINTON

Department of Psychology, College of St Thomas, USA

This chapter concerns language and emotion, a broad topic which encompasses several disparate areas of research. Some of the questions to be addressed include the following: How is the language of emotion represented in our minds? Do a few prominent categories such as anger and happiness play a special role in the cognitive representation of emotion? Under what circumstances does the expression of emotion foster intimacy between two people, and how do these differ from situations in which emotional disclosure might cause a person to be rejected by others? How does research on language and emotion relate to general theoretical issues, such as the notion that affective reactions are so fast as to require minimal cognitive activity?

In this chapter, the noun 'affect' will be treated as essentially synonymous with 'emotion' or 'feeling', and the adjective 'affective' as akin to 'emotional'. Where appropriate, we shall consider how future research might integrate the views of different investigators.

MODELS OF EMOTION

Geometric Models

Geometric models have influenced research on emotion throughout the century. Such an approach was first proposed by Wundt (1896). He proposed that affective reactions are underpinned by three dimensions: pleasantness/unpleasantness, excitement/depression, and strain/relaxation. Similar views were expressed later by

Handbook of Language and Social Psychology
Edited by H. Giles and W.P. Robinson. © 1990 John Wiley & Sons Ltd

various researchers. Perhaps the best-known example of a dimensional model is the 'semantic differential' discussed by Osgood, Suci, and Tannenbaum (1957). They presented extensive evidence that affective communication essentially concerns three dimensions: evaluation, activity, and potency. These terms are not quite the same as those used by Wundt, but it is noteworthy that there is any similarity at all, considering that Wundt did not have the benefit of such modern research techniques as factor analysis. Another well-known stance is that of Schlosberg, who investigated the dimensional structure of facial expressions. He first suggested two dimensions – pleasantness/unpleasantness and attention/rejection – and he noted that the facial expressions corresponding to happiness, surprise, fear, anger, disgust, and contempt can be described by a 'roughly circular' surface in two-dimensional space (Schlosberg, 1952). He later proposed a third dimension: sleep/tension or activation (Schlosberg, 1954).

In the 1960s and 1970s, several investigators presented empirical findings that had much in common with the work of Wundt (1896), Schlosberg (1952, 1954), and Osgood *et al.* (1957). These studies showed that the language and/or facial manifestations of emotion can be described in a two- or three-dimensional space. Additional dimensions sometimes emerged (for a review see Smith and Ellsworth, 1985). For example, Averill (1975) presented evidence that subjective feeling states reflect four dimensions: evaluation, activation (arousal), control, and depth of experience. The first two are robust and familiar, having emerged in virtually all studies of the dimensional structure of emotionally toned words and facial expressions, but the same cannot be said of the other two.

A frequently cited, and representative, set of studies was presented by Russell (1980). In one study, he asked participants to assess the similarity of pairs of affect words. Examples of such words include *happy, calm, sad, tired, annoyed, afraid*, and *astonished*. Altogether 28 words were used. Multidimensional scaling showed that these judgments can be described quite well by a two-dimensional solution, where the two dimensions are pleasantness/unpleasantness and arousal. Further, the terms can be arranged in a circle similar to that proposed by Schlosberg. In another study, Russell showed that this circumplex model accounts for 'a substantial proportion, but not all, of the variance in self-reported affective states' (p. 1174). He concluded that the cognitive structure of affect is 'conveniently summarized' by a circumplex model. A similar view was expressed by Plutchik (1980).

In the 1980s, research concerning the structure of the language of emotion departed from bidimensional and tridimensional approaches in at least two respects. First, some investigators strongly questioned whether such structures are adequate, presenting evidence that additional dimensions may emerge consistently if different methods are used. To a large extent, these additional dimensions reflect the role of cognitive appraisal in emotion. In addition, non-geometric models began to figure prominently in the literature. Instead of describing emotions in multidimensional space, some studies presented emotions from the standpoint of prototype theory.

Appraisal Models

Smith and Ellsworth (1985) argued that methodological factors are partly responsible for the frequent reports of bidimensional and tridimensional structures. For instance, the range of stimuli sampled may limit the dimensions that can be found. In addition, when making similarity judgments, subjects may not use consistent criteria to judge different stimulus pairs, and may be influenced only by the most salient cognitive dimensions. Further, Smith and Ellsworth noted that previous research was not strongly tied to specific theories of emotion.

To remedy these difficulties, Smith and Ellsworth (1985) asked subjects to recall past experiences associated with each of 15 emotions and to rate these emotions along eight dimensions. These dimensions were derived from appraisal theories, which emphasize that emotional experience is closely associated with the organism's appraisal of its environment (e.g. Lazarus, 1968). Principal components analysis and multidimensional scaling each yielded similar solutions consisting of six orthogonal dimensions: pleasantness, anticipated effort, certainty, attentional activity, self–other responsibility/control, and situational control. Related findings were presented in a subsequent study (Smith and Ellsworth, 1987).

Differences among emotions may be described in terms of these dimensions. For example, some of the qualities that characterize anger include unpleasant valence, appraisals of human agency, and a sense that someone other than oneself is responsible for the anger-inducing event. In contrast, sadness is distinguished from anger and other emotions by appraisals of situational control. 'Apparently, the belief that the unpleasant situation is controlled by impersonal circumstances . . . is crucial to sadness' (Smith and Ellsworth, 1985, p. 834).

The Smith–Ellsworth approach may be classified as representing both geometric and appraisal models. It is in the tradition of geometric models insofar as it depicts the cognitive structure of emotion in multidimensional terms. At the same time, it proposes dimensions that are expressly tied to the view that cognitive appraisal is critical to emotion.

Scherer (1984) discussed several features of the cognitive antecedents of emotion that are similar to those proposed by Smith and Ellsworth (1985, 1987), but he posited a specific sequence of events as well. Appraisal, in his view, proceeds as a series of stimulus evaluation checks. A novelty check is first, followed by asessments of intrinsic pleasantness, goal/need significance, coping potential, and norm/self compatibility, in that order. Several subchecks are involved, including judgments about power and control in the coping potential stage. Scherer used cluster analysis to show that emotion terms can be classified by a tree structure that is not inconsistent with his proposed sequence theory. In interpreting the results of the analysis, he observed that 'a criterion that closely resembles goal/need conduciveness/obstruc- tiveness determines the top-level branching, followed by a clear coping potential criterion including the subchecks for power and control' (p. 49).

To reconcile his approach with the circumplex models proposed by Russell (1980) and Plutchik (1980), Scherer (1984) contends that those models concern reactions to stimuli and situations rather than antecedents of emotional processes. He also shares the methodological concerns raised by Smith and Ellsworth (1985), arguing that the results supporting a circumplex model might be artifactually produced by the particular labels studied. He faults Russell's inclusion of the words *tired*, *drowsy*, *sleepy*, *tranquil*, and *calm* because many researchers and laypersons might not consider them emotion terms, and he notes that a preponderance of near-synonyms may bias the scaling.

Roseman (1984) proposed a model of relationships between several cognitive appraisal dimensions and resulting discrete emotions. The positive/negative dimension is tied to the conception of events as consistent or inconsistent with motivations; 'good' events are those consistent with a motive, and 'bad' events are not. Other dimensions include certainty, power or legitimacy, and causal agency. According to Roseman, various dimensional combinations create specific emotional reactions. For example, if a person is in a weak position and is certain of the occurrence of an event that is inconsistent with an appetitive motive, then sorrow will be felt. However, if a person in a weak position believes that such an event is merely possible rather than certain, then the resulting reaction will be fear, not sorrow.

Thus, Roseman (1984), Scherer (1984), and Smith and Ellsworth (1985, 1987) all contend that bidimensional and tridimensional models are not adequate to describe the structure of emotion, and that at least two or three additional dimensions must be taken into account. In addition, Scherer emphasizes a particular sequence of events in the appraisal process.

Prototype Models

A different approach has been taken by researchers influenced by the prototype perspective associated with Rosch (1978) and other cognitive psychologists. This viewpoint emphasizes the hierarchical relations among categories. Three levels of inclusiveness are typically defined: superordinate (exemplified by furniture), basic (chair or table), and subordinate (armchair or coffee table). Basic-level categories have special properties. They are more informative than those at the superordinate level and also more economical than subordinate categories. In addition to stressing hierarchical organization, prototype researchers note the 'fuzziness' of categories, contending that classes are separated by vague rather than sharp boundaries.

That the affective lexicon can be described hierarchically is illustrated by the work of Shaver, Schwartz, Kirson, and O'Connor (1987, Study 1). Their subjects were asked to sort 135 emotion terms into categories representing 'judgments about which emotions are similar to each other and which are different from each other'. Cluster analysis suggested five basic-level categories: *love, joy, anger, sadness,* and *fear.* A sixth possibility, *surprise,* also emerged, but it was less differentiated than the others. Within each of the five well-differentiated groupings presumed to represent the basic level, a number of smaller subclusters emerged, presumably corresponding to subordinate categories. *Love,* for instance, subsumes three subordinate clusters. One includes such terms as *adoration, affection,* and *fondness;* another includes *lust, passion,* and related terms; and the third is *longing.*

Shaver *et al.* (1987) subjected the participants' responses to multidimensional scaling, and the familiar tridimensional solution provided a good fit to the data. However, the authors observed that the geometric model did not reveal certain properties of the similarity judgments that emerged in the cluster analysis. For example, the multidimensional scaling results did not reveal that frustration is more closely related to anger than to fear or sadness. Yet this fact did emerge in cluster analysis, for a subordinate grouping within the anger cluster included frustration.

In a second study, subjects wrote accounts of emotional experiences. Content analysis produced a list of prototypical features for each of the five basic categories. These lists bolster the notion that a tridimensional structure is not adequate to describe emotion. Consider the characteristic 'judgment of illegitimacy or unfairness', which Shaver et al. (1987) found to be associated with anger. The usual tridimensional description of anger – high in activity, high in potency, and evaluatively negative, to use the terminology of the semantic differential – does not capture this feature. However, it can be accommodated within the appraisal models discussed above. As Smith and Ellsworth (1985) noted, the perceived fairness of an unpleasant experience is related to appraisals of responsibility and control; 'if someone else is responsible for a bad situation, it is seen as less fair than if you yourself are responsible' (p. 831).

That emotions may constitute 'fuzzy sets' with graded membership criteria is implied by the work of Fehr, Russell, and Ward (1982). Subjects in that study responded 'true' or 'false' to such statements as 'anger is an emotion', 'awe is an emotion', and 'joy is a sport', among others. Prototypical exemplars of the emotion concept (anger, joy) were identified more quickly and more accurately than less typical exemplars (awe, pride). That subjects were apparently unsure how to classify peripheral cases indicates that judgments about emotion category membership are not absolute and are instead a matter of degree. Further applications of prototype theory in the emotion domain were reported by Fehr and Russell (1984) and Russell and Bullock (1986).

Prototype researchers have interpreted their findings as complementing rather than contradicting geometric models. Shaver et al. (1987) stated that 'both hierarchical and dimensional representations' (p. 1081) can illumine the cognitive structure of emotion, and Russell and Bullock (1986) drew a similar conclusion. However, it should be noted that prototype models are generally more comprehensive than geometric structures, especially bidimensional ones. Well-established features of emotion, such as pleasantness and arousal, are revealed by the work of Shaver et al. (1987), but so is much more, including additional cognitive dimensions and distinctions between antecedents and reactions.

HAVE RESEARCHERS DEFINED EMOTION ADEQUATELY?

The views of Ortony, Clore, and Foss (1987) and Clore, Ortony, and Foss (1987) are, in some ways, at odds with several of the positions discussed above. They presented criteria for distinguishing emotions from non-emotional states. Their taxonomy is not a theory of emotion but is 'an approach to identifying those psychological states that need to be accounted for in theories of emotion' (Clore et al., 1987, p. 754). In their view, the affective lexicon can be understood in terms of four broad classes: affective conditions (the best examples of emotion terms), external conditions, cognitive conditions, and physical and bodily states.

Genuine emotions should be rated as such when presented in two different linguistic contexts: *feeling* and *being*. Thus *feeling angry* and *being angry* should both be judged as emotions. A different pattern should hold for words in the external conditions class; for example, *feeling abandoned* should be seen as more emotional than *being abandoned*, and Clore and colleagues (Clore *et al.*, 1987; Ortony *et al.*, 1987) would therefore argue that *abandoned* is not a clear example of an emotion term. Words in the cognitive conditions class should be seen as only marginally emotional, and physical and bodily states should not be seen as emotional (e.g. neither *feeling hungry* nor *being hungry* refer to emotions). Clore and colleagues presented subjects with words in both the *feeling* and *being* contexts, and asked participants to judge whether the phrase described an emotion. (Slightly different methods were used for nouns. They were rated in the context of *feeling* and without a context, but were not rated in the *being* context.) The results generally supported the proposed taxonomy, although some of the empirical classifications departed from the investigators' expectations.

Clore and colleagues (Clore *et al.*, 1987; Ortony *et al.*, 1987) questioned whether other researchers have studied terms that refer to true emotions. Their strongest criticisms were directed toward Plutchik (1980), who presented a circumplex model based on a study of 40 affect terms. They argued that 17 of these 40 words (e.g. *inquisitive*, *puzzled*, *receptive*) are questionable examples of emotions. A similar point was made about Russell's (1980) work, with 5 of his 28 stimulus words (e.g. *tired*, *drowsy*) classified as non-affective. Further, Ortony (1987) argued that guilt is not a good example of an emotion, noting the different connotations of *feeling guilty* and *being guilty*. This viewpoint raises questions about several of the studies discussed above. Shaver *et al.* (1987) and Scherer (1984) included *guilt* and related terms in their lists of emotion words, and Smith and Ellsworth (1985) and Roseman (1984) also considered guilt an emotion. (It should be noted that Clore and colleagues empirically classified *guilty* and *guiltless* as external conditions, but *guilt* emerged in the affective conditions class.)

The work of Clore and colleagues (Clore *et al.*, 1987; Ortony *et al.*, 1987) makes an important point. Care must be taken to ensure that studies of the affective lexicon really refer to genuine emotional states. However, it is not clear whether their views compel substantive changes in the approaches taken by all of the researchers mentioned above. If we were to repeat such studies as those of Shaver *et al.* (1987) or Scherer (1984) while changing the methods – that is, restricting the lists of emotion terms to those that Clore and colleagues would consider genuine emotions – the results might not differ dramatically from those originally reported. Of course, this is an empirical question, and future research might address this issue.

Other researchers (e.g. Mees, 1985; Shields, 1984) have undertaken to distinguish emotions from non-emotions, and their work is not inconsistent with the research just discussed (see Ortony *et al.*, 1987, p. 360). However, an important qualification was suggested by Shimanoff (1985c), who showed that some words have emotional connotations for one sex but not the other. For example, 74.1% of the women in her study considered *astonished* a reference to an emotion, but a similar judgment was made by only 47.1% of the men. *Bewildered* was considered emotive by 70.4% of the women and 33.3% of the men. These sex differences may help to explain why Clore, Ortony, and Foss, who are male, pre-experimentally classified *astonished* and *bewildered* as cognitive conditions and then found that they should be empirically classified as affective conditions. The empirical classification probably stems from the judgments of the female subjects, although we do not know this for certain because sex differences were not examined. Future research should consider the extent to which men and women agree on affective classifications. Indeed, the degree of agreement among other social groupings within and across cultures might also merit investigation.

One additional point should be made concerning the work of Clore and colleagues. They questioned the logic of the prototype researchers, arguing that conceptions of emotions as prototypes are not necessarily warranted by the data presented by those investigators. Clore and colleagues contend that classical definitions – which stress that concepts are definable in terms of necessary and sufficient features – may still be tenable, and they also suggest that a hybrid of prototype and classical theories may prove valuable.

EMOTION IN CONVERSATION

In much of the research just discussed, individual words were the primary focus of study. A different approach to the study of emotion and language can be taken by examining sentence structure and the flow of conversation. Several researchers have investigated the role of emotion in these contexts.

Shimanoff (1985a) conducted a study in which college students were asked to tape their conversations for one complete day. Twenty-six dyadic conversations of 5 minutes in length were chosen at random from the tapes, and the content was analyzed for affective references. References to unpleasant emotions occurred almost twice as often as references to pleasant emotions. Further, comments about unpleasant affect tended to refer to the speaker's behavior rather than the hearer's, and the reverse pattern emerged for references to positive affect.

Shimanoff (1985a) interpreted the results as reflecting rules concerning appropriate and inappropriate affective displays. An excessively positive, 'Pollyanna-ish' person may be seen as unrealistic and simplistic, but a constant complainer is devalued as well, so speakers need to strike a balance between positive and negative affect. Politeness and self-effacement also come into play, explaining the different references to speaker's and hearer's behavior.

A related study of married couples (Shimanoff, 1985b; see also Chapter 21, by Fitzpatrick) showed that certain kinds of emotional disclosures occur more frequently than others. 'Face-honoring' comments (pleasant emotions regarding the hearer) and 'face-compensating' ones (regrets for transgressions against the hearer) were preferred to 'face-threatening' remarks (e.g. hostile emotions concerning the hearer). A subsequent study (Shimanoff, 1987) showed that some forms of disclosure, such as those concerning personal vulnerabilities, enhance feelings of intimacy and cause the hearer to feel honored, and Shimanoff related these findings to the face-honoring and face-saving value of disclosures (see Chapter 10, by Tracy). Additional research concerning strategies that people use to promote 'positive face' has been reported recently by Cashion, Cody, and Erickson (1986), who studied humor, and Cupach, Metts, and Hazleton (1986), who investigated reactions to embarrassment.

Shimanoff (1985b) reported that husbands and wives did not differ in overall levels of emotional disclosure, consistent with an earlier finding (Shimanoff, 1983) that male and female college students do not differ in linguistic references to emotional states. However, the 1983 study also showed that men were more emotionally expressive in opposite-sex dyads than in same-sex dyads, perhaps because they consider women nurturing and supportive of affective disclosures, whereas females did not alter their emotional expressiveness as a function of audience sex.

In a study by Notarius and Johnson (1982), husbands and wives discussed a significant interpersonal issue for up to 30 minutes. The couples were asked to 'work toward a mutually satisfactory solution to a salient relationship issue' while being videotaped. In some ways, wives were more expressive than husbands. Wives' speech included more negative and less neutral behavior than did husbands' speech. Wives also reciprocated their husbands' behavior (positive and negative), while husbands did not reciprocate wives' speech. Insofar as these results suggest that women were more expressive than men, they differ from those reported by Shimanoff (1983, 1985b). Methodological factors might help to explain these differences. Perhaps men are self-conscious, and therefore unexpressive, when engaging in a videotaped discussion of a significant interpersonal issue, as they did in the Notarius–Johnson study. Shimanoff studied naturally occurring conversations that might be less emotionally loaded.

In addition to examining emotional behavior, Notarius and Johnson (1982) also measured physiological reactivity. Skin potential responses were continuously monitored throughout the conversation. Husbands displayed a greater tendency than wives to emit skin potential reactions to the partner's negative comments. The authors considered these findings to be consistent with a 'discharge' or hydraulic model of emotional expression, which assumes that people who are not overtly expressive must discharge their feelings through covert means. However, these results should be interpreted cautiously. Sex differences in physiological reactivity were only marginally significant ($p < .09$), and evidence for the discharge model is inconsistent (Winton, Putnam, and Krauss, 1984).

Gurtman (1987) showed his subjects a videotape of a student who said that she had not done well on an exam and then presented either depressive disclosures ('It's obvious by now that I am a failure . . . My prospects seem bleak.') or non-depressive comments ('I was thinking how I could improve myself . . . My prospects are still bright.'). Happy, sad, or flat affect was displayed as well. The effects of the depressive disclosures were fairly consistent across affect conditions. Such comments caused the viewer to reject and derogate the speaker.

It is interesting to compare these results with Shimanoff's (1987) finding that the disclosure of personal vulnerabilities can cause the hearer to feel honored. Of course the methods of the two studies are different, and a vulnerable comment in Shimanoff's sense is not the same as a depressive remark in Gurtman's study. Nonetheless, to the extent that some disclosures can fall into both categories, self-disclosure might cause the hearer to feel personally flattered *and* to reject the speaker as well. In fact, if a listener feels flattered by another's disclosure, it is conceivable that a listener's initial reaction might be to encourage additional revelations – but the listener might wind up rejecting the discloser anyway. Such a dual reaction would certainly not raise the intimacy level of the relationship between speaker and hearer and might have devastating consequences for the depressed, vulnerable individual, who realizes too late that he has bared his soul to the wrong person. Future research should investigate these possibilities, which seem to contradict the popular notion that emotional expressiveness is generally beneficial.

Hooley's (1986) work provides additional evidence that high levels of emotional expressiveness do not have uniformly salutary consequences. Spouses of depressed patients were classified as either high or low in the tendency to express emotion (EE), and interactions between these individuals and their depressed partners were observed. Compared with low-EE spouses, high-EE spouses were more likely to make critical remarks toward their depressed partner and were generally more negative toward them.

Discussions pertaining to unpleasant experiences may be generally characterized by a reluctance to acknowledge or deal with negative affect. This possibility is implied by Osgood and Hoosain (1983), who argued that negative stimuli produce 'avoidance of cognizing'. Findings consistent with this notion were presented by Collier, Kuiken, and Enzle (1982, Experiments 1 and 2). They showed that communications about negative affect were grammatically more complex than affectively positive communication. Along similar lines, Preston (1984) noted that pleasant concepts are easier to describe than unpleasant ones, and found that pleasant content was characterized by shorter words and less verbal output than negative content. However, while unpleasant affect may foster grammatical complexity, the reverse sequence does not necessarily hold true. Collier et al. (1982, Experiment 3) experimentally manipulated the grammatical complexity of written communications and asked subjects to judge the emotional experience of the writer of the material. Complexity attenuated the extremity of the reactions, lowering the degree of pleasantness perceived to be associated with positive material while also dampening the degree of negativity associated with unpleasant material.

Collier et al. (1982) defined grammatical complexity in terms of a number of specific linguistic features. To illustrate their work, consider the grammatically complex version of a description of an unpleasant event (reactions to the movie *The Exorcist*) that they used in Experiment 3:

Sure when I go to sleep at night, I'll see her head turn around like she's a yo-yo or something like that . . . What I really disliked in the movie was the way they presented the statue which represented Christ. For people who don't have a religion, it might not matter very much. But a religion for me is my search for a meaning in life. If I didn't have a religion, I'd be lost.

In contrast, here is the grammatically simple version of the same text:

Sure I go to sleep at night and I see her head turn around. She looks like a yo-yo or something . . . I really disliked the way they presented the statue of Christ. It might not matter to people without a religion, but a religion is my search for meaning. Without it, I am lost.

A related study by Kuiken (1981) showed that inconsistency between expressed and felt affect is associated with a non-immediate language style, which is indicated by such modes of expression as negation (saying 'I am not nervous' instead of 'I am calm') and reluctance to affirm assertions ('He is sort of shy' rather than 'He is shy'). Inconsistency between expressed and felt affect was operationally defined by asking subjects to describe a desirable aspect of a disliked trait or an undesirable aspect of a liked trait. For instance, if subjects first thought of a quality that they liked about themselves, and then tried to describe the *undesirable* aspects of that trait, they tended to use a non-immediate language style.

Related points were made by Schlenker and Leary (1985) in their discussion of social anxiety, a negative affective state that may be related to depression, but is conceptually distinct from it. They contend that high social anxiety fosters a self-protective style of self-presentation that includes minimal self-disclosure, cautious self-descriptions and a passive interaction style that avoids disagreement. Empirical findings consistent with this viewpoint were presented by Leary, Knight, and Johnson (1987).

It would be informative to integrate research on grammatical complexity and language style with the work on depression discussed above. To what extent does the form and style of language, distinct from content, play a role in the rejection of depressives noted by Gurtman (1987)? Perhaps the disclosure of negative or vulnerable feelings does not lead to rejection when the comments have been couched in a complex or non-immediate style that makes them easier to deal with, while the likelihood of rejection might be enhanced by raw, direct expression of depressive sentiments.

Future research on conversation should take into account Paulhus and Levitt's (1987) intriguing concept of 'automatic egotism'. Their subjects responded 'me' or 'not me' to trait adjectives presented on a microcomputer. Affect was manipulated by distractor words presented nearby. Some distractors were emotionally significant (e.g. *sex*, *blood*, *death*, *slut*) and others were not. The presence of the affect-laden words enhanced socially desirable responding; they increased and speeded up endorsements of positive traits and denials of negative traits.

Paulhus and Levitt (1987) offered an arousal interpretation. Affective stimuli are presumed to augment arousal and therefore increase dominant (socially desirable) responses. Some implications for conversation are as follows:

> Consider the speed at which social discussions and arguments can move. If the affect associated with a speaker's word choice or phrasing automatically inflates egotism, then the rest of the speaker's sentence may be processed under polarized evaluation. Moreover, the listener's response may be generated within a polarized evaluation system. Similar effects . . . might result from affective reactions to the speaker's appearance or a brief nonverbal behavior . . . (Paulhus and Levitt, 1987, p. 256)

Future research should examine the implications of this approach for self-presentation, self-disclosure, and other aspects of conversational dynamics while also noting predictions that can be made from other viewpoints. Consider the work of Isen and colleagues, who have shown in several studies that happiness fosters unusual, creative responses (e.g. Isen and Daubman, 1984; Isen, Johnson, Mertz, and Robinson, 1985). They rejected arousal interpretations on the grounds that the subjects' reactions could not be understood as dominant responses. For example, Isen *et al*. (1985) showed that happiness fostered statistically unusual responses in a word-association procedure. From this standpoint, if one assumes that affectively positive remarks elevate the mood of either the speaker or the listener, one would expect such remarks to shift a conversation in an unusual or creative direction but not an egotistical one. Yet another perspective is implied by Bower (1981), who has conducted a variety of studies showing that affective stimuli render emotion categories accessible. This approach suggests that happy comments should foster additional positive thoughts and remarks; whether such talk should also be construed as egotistical or unusual is open to question. Thus, the views of Paulhus and Levitt (1987), Bower (1981), and Isen and colleagues (Isen and Daubman, 1984; Isen *et al*., 1985) all have somewhat different implications for the study of conversation, and future research should examine these issues empirically.

INTERACTION OF VERBAL AND NON-VERBAL CHANNELS

Because non-verbal communication is discussed elsewhere in this handbook (see Section 2), it is beyond the scope of this chapter to discuss this topic at length. However, a few studies comparing verbal and non-verbal means of communication will be mentioned.

Krauss, Apple, Morency, Wenzel, and Winton (1981) asked participants to judge the affective content of certain interactions (a political debate in one study and interviews of college women in another). Some participants viewed 'full-channel' videotapes, which included both video and audio information. Others made judgments on the basis of single channels such as video only, content-filtered audio that preserves paralinguistic cues, and verbal only (written transcripts). Regression analyses showed that the full-channel judgments could be predicted quite well from the ratings based on transcripts. The judgments based on paralinguistic and video channels added little predictive power. On this basis, Krauss *et al*. (1981) questioned the contention that affect is primarily conveyed by non-verbal means, a notion that has frequently appeared in the non-verbal communication literature. A similar point was made by Ekman, Friesen, O'Sullivan, and Scherer (1980).

Wallbott and Scherer (1986) presented subjects with depictions of affective states portrayed by professional actors, and asked subjects to judge which of four emotions (joy, anger, sadness, and surprise) was displayed – i.e. to 'decode' the actors' emotional displays. The stimuli presented to the subjects involved four channel combinations: audiovisual, video only, audio only, or content-filtered speech. Decoding accuracy was generally higher for the two conditions involving video than for the other two conditions. However, the six actors differed from one another in their ability to use particular channels to display specific emotional states, and complex interactions emerged when decoding accuracy was examined as a function of all experimental variations (actor, type of emotion, communication channel, and type of dramatic scene; this last factor reflected whether the scene involved a child). Wallbott and Scherer noted that different non-verbal cues are used to depict various emotions and that 'differences between channels and between actors strongly affect decoding accuracy'.

In a study by Apple and Hecht (1982), speakers role-played discrete emotions such as sadness and anger while reading sentences whose content was either emotionally appropriate or neutral. Later, listeners tried to identify the emotions based only on paralinguistic information (content-filtered audio tapes). Multidimensional scaling of listeners' judgments showed that stimuli with neutral semantic content were seen as having higher 'energy levels' – akin to activation or arousal – than those with emotionally appropriate content, independent of the affective state that the speakers were trying to convey.

Apple and Hecht (1982) interpreted this finding as meaning that speakers put more effort into vocally encoding particular affects when neutral content was being read. This, in turn, suggests that verbal and vocal channels compensate for one another. When the verbal channel lacked emotional content, speakers put more effort into role-playing so as to compensate vocally for this deficiency, but they did not try so hard to communicate affect paralinguistically when the verbal content was emotionally appropriate. This compensation notion helps explain other aspects of their results. For example, semantically emotional material facilitated the identification of sadness, a low-energy affect that was probably obscured by the high energy level conveyed by speakers reading neutral material. Anger, a high-energy emotion, was more successfully conveyed with neutral material than with angry content.

Somewhat different results were presented by Plazewski and Allen (1985). In their study, children recited statements that were either positive or negative in verbal content, and they did so using five different tones of voice ranging from extremely unfriendly to extremely friendly. Adults later judged paralinguistic affect from audio recordings. Accuracy was greatest when verbal and paralinguistic cues were consistent. These results contradict the Apple–Hecht compensation notion.

The methods of these two studies were quite different. Plazewski and Allen's (1985) encoders were sixth graders, and emotional inconsistency was operationally defined in terms of positive and negative affect. Apple and Hecht (1982) studied college students and contrasted specific emotion categories with neutral content. These methodological factors might help to explain the differences between the two studies. Nonetheless, the different results illustrate an interesting question: are verbal and vocal channels compensatory or redundant? The question has a measure of general theoretical significance; consider Izard's (1971) claim that one emotion system can 'recruit' or activate another. Plazewski and Allen's findings support this idea, but those of Apple and Hecht do not. Future research should seek to identify circumstances under which compensation and redundancy each operate.

THEORIES OF EMOTION

Throughout the 1980s, a major question of interest to researchers has been the extent to which emotion is influenced by cognition. Disparate views are illustrated by the exchange between Lazarus (1982, 1984), who believes that appraisal and other cognitive processes are critical to affective experience, and Zajonc (1980, 1984), who holds that many emotional reactions are non-cognitive. Several of the researchers discussed in this chapter, especially Roseman (1984) and Smith and Ellsworth (1985), are aligned with the former stance.

Additional evidence consistent with the cognitive approach comes from studies showing that people generally agree on the relationships between specific emotional reactions and particular situations (Doré and Kirouac, 1986; Harrison, 1986). In other words, emotion elicitors are generally not idiosyncratic. These results are consistent with Schachter's (1964) assumption that people attach 'cognitive labels' to situations. The studies illustrate agreement concerning how a certain situation should be appraised or interpreted.

This is not to say that research on language and emotion uniformly supports Lazarus (1982, 1984), Schachter (1964), and other cognitive theorists. Bock (1986) showed that words are evaluated for their emotional content at an early stage of information processing. He considered this finding to support Zajonc's (1980, 1984) view that a stimulus often has an immediate emotional impact that does not depend on extensive reflection by the individual. Related results were presented by Bock and Klinger (1986). In addition, the above-mentioned views of Harrison (1986) and Doré and Kirouac (1986) are qualified by the work of Rychlak and Williams (1984), who reported that individuals differ in the affective connotations they attach to terms like *serious* and *thrifty*. (Note, however, that Rychlak and Slife (1984) disagreed with Zajonc in some ways.)

Lyman and Waters (1986) asked participants to describe the loci of sensations associated with different emotions. Fairly distinctive patterns of sensory loci, primarily concerning the stomach, face, head, heart, eyes, and hands, emerged for various affects. These results are consistent with the James–Lange theory (e.g. James, 1890), a formulation that is less cognitive than that of Schachter (1964) but not so automatic and non-cognitive as Zajonc's (1980, 1984) stance.

Lyman and Waters (1986) emphasized neo-Jamesian 'facial feedback' theories in their discussion, and argued that their findings were partly supportive of such notions. However, there is mixed evidence for facial feedback formulations. A number of studies have shown that facial movement can produce global hedonic effects, but at present there is minimal direct evidence for specific categorical effects (Winton, 1986). Some reviewers do not consider the findings in this area to be particularly strong or consistent (Manstead, 1988; Matsumoto, 1987); null results have been reported in several studies relating facial expressions to mood. Further, Zajonc (1985) argued that facial movement can alter affective state by changing cerebral blood flow, a process that differs from the sensory mechanisms emphasized in neo-Jamesian theories like that of Izard (1971).

EPILOGUE

Several possible avenues for future research have been identified in the present review. They include the following:

(1) Research on the structure of the affective lexicon should continue to examine

ways in which bidimensional and tridimensional models can be supplemented by additional dimensions or even replaced altogether by different models such as prototypes. Sex differences in judgments about emotion should also be considered more extensively in future research.

(2) The consequences of self-disclosure deserve further study. Some studies show that the disclosure of vulnerable feelings can foster intimacy and make the listener feel honored, while there is also evidence that depressive self-disclosure can lead to rejection. To the extent that vulnerable and depressive comments can overlap, the apparent contradiction has not been resolved. The complexity and style of language might be related to these issues. Perhaps the direct, forthright disclosure of depressive sentiments is likely to foster rejection, whereas a non-immediate style might not have the same result.

(3) Paulhus and Levitt (1987) presented evidence for affect-induced 'automatic egotism' and speculated about the implications of this notion for the flow of conversation. Somewhat different predictions concerning the impact of emotion on conversation can be derived from other perspectives, including those of Isen and Daubman (1984) and Bower (1981). Empirical research along these lines is needed.

(4) The relationships among different channels of communication need to be clarified. Apple and Hecht (1982) suggested that verbal and vocal channels are compensatory, while findings presented by Plazewski and Allen (1985) imply that these channels are redundant. Future research should try to identify circumstances under which each relationship holds.

(5) Broad theoretical issues, such as the extent to which cognition governs emotion, are relevant to a number of studies of language and affect. Future research might profitably adopt McGuire's (1983) 'contextualist' epistemology, which emphasizes that different theories can hold true under different circumstances. Investigators might try to establish precisely when and how appraisal processes influence emotion and distinguish these circumstances from those in which affect is immediate and non-cognitive.

An integrative approach to some or all of these five research areas would draw on different branches of social psychology. Some studies of the second topic in the above list are closely related to sociology and anthropology. Shimanoff's (1985b, 1987) work, for instance, focused on naturalistic conversations and yielded results that were interpreted in terms of Goffman's (1967) concept of 'face'. In contrast, the third topic in the list generally encompasses studies that are theoretically and methodologically rooted in experimental psychology. Paulhus and Levitt (1987), for example, relied on the notion that arousal enhances dominant responses, an idea that stems from Hullian learning theory (Hull, 1943). If the Paulhus–Levitt notion of automatic egotism is studied in naturalistic contexts like those investigated by Shimanoff, very different aspects of social psychology would be usefully integrated. Situational limitations on different principles might be identified – for example, when does the motive to 'save face' override egotism, and when does the reverse hold? As another example of potential synthesis, general theoretical issues (topic 5 above) may be elucidated by research on whether different communication channels 'recruit' one another (topic 4 above) as well as by studies indicating the importance of cognitive appraisal (topic 1).

Thus, research on language and emotion need not be fragmented. Such research can combine different areas of social psychology and illuminate basic theoretical questions. It is to be hoped that future studies will pursue the issues described above in an integrative manner.

REFERENCES

Apple, W. and Hecht, K. (1982). Speaking emotionally: The relation between verbal and vocal communication of affect. *Journal of Personality and Social Psychology,* **42**, 864–875.

Averill, J.R. (1975). A semantic atlas of emotional concepts. *JSAS Catalog of Selected Documents in Psychology*, **5**, 330 (Ms No. 1103).

Bock, M. (1986). The influence of emotional meaning on the recall of words processed for form or self-reference. *Psychological Research*, **48**, 107–112.

Bock, M. and Klinger, E. (1986). Interaction of emotion and cognition in word recall. *Psychological Research,* **48**, 99–106.

Bower, G.H. (1981). Mood and memory. *American Psychologist*, **36**, 129–148.

Cashion, J.L., Cody, M.J., and Erickson, K.V. (1986). 'You'll love this one . . . ': An exploration into joke-prefacing devices. *Journal of Language and Social Psychology*, **5**, 303–312.

Clore, G.L., Ortony, A., and Foss, M.A. (1987). The psychological foundations of the affective lexicon. *Journal of Personality and Social Psychology*, **53**, 751–766.

Collier, G., Kuiken, D., and Enzle, M.E. (1982). The role of grammatical qualification in the expression and perception of emotion. *Journal of Psycholinguistic Research*, **11**, 631–650.

Cupach, W.R., Metts, S., and Hazleton, V., Jr (1986). Coping with embarrassing predicaments: Remedial strategies and their perceived utility. *Journal of Language and Social Psychology*, **5**, 181–200.

Doré, F. and Kirouac, G. (1986). Reliability of accuracy and intensity judgments of eliciting situations of emotions. *Canadian Journal of Behavioural Science*, **18**, 92–103.

Ekman, P., Friesen, W.V., O'Sullivan, M., and Scherer, K. (1980). Relative importance of face, body, and speech in judgments of personality and affect. *Journal of Personality and Social Psychology*, **38**, 270–277.

Fehr, B. and Russell, J.A. (1984). Concept of emotion viewed from a prototype perspective. *Journal of Experimental Psychology: General*, **113**, 464–486.

Fehr, B., Russell, J.A., and Ward, L.M. (1982). Prototypicality of emotions: A reaction time study. *Bulletin of the Psychonomic Society*, **20**, 253–254.

Goffman, E. (1967). *Interaction ritual; essays on face-to-face behavior*. Chicago: Aldine.

Gurtman, M.B. (1987). Depressive affect and disclosures as factors in interpersonal rejection. *Cognitive Therapy and Research*, **11**, 87–100.

Harrison, R.H. (1986). The grouping of affect terms according to the situations that elicit them: A test of a cognitive theory of emotion. *Journal of Research in Personality*, **20**, 252–266.

Hooley, J.M. (1986). Expressed emotion and depression: Interactions between patients and high-versus low-expressed-emotion spouses. *Journal of Abnormal Psychology*, **95**, 237–46.

Hull, C.L. (1943). *Principles of behavior*. New York: Appleton-Century-Crofts.

Isen, A.M. and Daubman, K.A. (1984). The influence of affect on categorization. *Journal of Personality and Social Psychology*, **47**, 1206–1217.

Isen, A.M., Johnson, M.M.S., Mertz, E., and Robinson, G.F. (1985). The influence of positive affect on the unusualness of word associations. *Journal of Personality and Social Psychology*, **48**, 1413–1426.

Izard, C.E. (1971). *The face of emotion*. New York: Appleton-Century-Crofts.

James, W. (1890). *The principles of psychology*. Republished 1950. New York: Dover.

Krauss, R.M., Apple, W., Morency, N., Wenzel, C., and Winton, W. (1981). Verbal, vocal, and visible factors in judgments of another's affect. *Journal of Personality and Social Psychology*, **40**, 312–320.

Kuiken, D. (1981). Non-immediate language style and inconsistency between private and expressed evaluations. *Journal of Experimental Social Psychology*, **17**, 183–196.

Lazarus, R.S. (1968). Emotions and adaptation: Conceptual and empirical relations. In W.J. Arnold (Ed.), *Nebraska symposium on motivation, 1968*, pp. 175–266. Lincoln, NE: University of Nebraska Press.

Lazarus, R.S. (1982). Thoughts on the relations between emotion and cognition. *American Psychologist*, **37**, 1019–1024.

Lazarus, R.S. (1984). On the primacy of cognition. *American Psychologist*, **39**, 124–129.

Leary, M.R., Knight, P.D., and Johnson, K.A. (1987). Social anxiety and dyadic conversation: A verbal response analysis. *Journal of Social and Clinical Psychology*, **5**, 34–50.

Lyman, B. and Waters, J.C.E. (1986). The experiential loci and sensory qualities of various emotions. *Motivation and Emotion*, **10**, 25–37.

Manstead, A.S.R. (1988). The role of facial movement in emotion. In H.L. Wagner (Ed.), *Social psychophysiology: Theory and clinical applications*, pp. 105–129. London: Wiley.

Matsumoto, D. (1987). The role of facial response in the experience of emotion: More methodological problems and a meta-analysis. *Journal of Personality and Social Psychology*, **52**, 769–774.

McGuire, W.J. (1983). A contextualist theory of knowledge: Its implications for innovation and reform in psychological research. In L. Berkowitz (Ed.), *Advances in experimental social psychology*, Vol. 16, pp. 1–47. Orlando, FL: Academic Press.

Mees, U. (1985). What do we mean when we speak of feelings? On the psychological texture of words denoting emotions. *Sprache und Kognition*, **4**, 2–20.

Notarius, C.I. and Johnson, J.S. (1982). Emotional expression in husbands and wives. *Journal of Marriage and the Family*, **44**, 483–489.

Ortony, A. (1987). Is guilt an emotion? *Cognition and Emotion*, **1**, 283–298.

Ortony, A., Clore, G.L., and Foss, M.A. (1987). The referential structure of the affective lexicon. *Cognitive Science*, **11**, 341–364.

Osgood, C.E. and Hoosain, R. (1983). Pollyanna II: Two types of negativity. *Journal of Psychology*, **113**, 151–160.

Osgood, C.E., Suci, G.J., and Tannenbaum P. (1957). *The measurement of meaning*. Urbana, IL: University of Illinois Press.

Paulhus, D.L. and Levitt, K. (1987). Desirable responding triggered by affect: Automatic egotism? *Journal of Personality and Social Psychology*, **52**, 245–259.

Plazewski, J.G. and Allen, V.L. (1985). The effect of verbal content on children's encoding of paralinguistic affect. *Journal of Nonverbal Behavior*, **9**, 147–159.

Plutchik, R. (1980). A general psychoevolutionary theory of emotion. In R. Plutchik and H. Kellerman (Eds), *Emotion: Theory, research, and experience*, Vol. 1, *Theories of emotion*, pp. 3–33. New York: Academic Press.

Preston, J.M. (1984). Referential communication: Some factors influencing communication efficiency. *Canadian Journal of Behavioural Science*, **16**, 196–207.

Rosch, E. (1978). Principles of categorization. In E. Rosch and B.B. Lloyd (Eds), *Cognition and categorization*, pp. 27–48. Hillsdale, NJ: Erlbaum.

Roseman, I.J. (1984). Cognitive determinants of emotion: A structural theory. In P. Shaver (Ed.), *Review of personality and social psychology*, Vol. 5, pp. 11–36. Beverly Hills: Sage.

Russell, J.A. (1980). A circumplex model of affect. *Journal of Personality and Social Psychology*, **39**, 1161–1178.

Russell, J.A. and Bullock, M. (1986). Fuzzy concepts and the perception of emotion in facial expressions. *Social Cognition*, **4**, 309–341.

Rychlak, J.F. and Slife, B.D. (1984). Affection as a cognitive judgmental process: A theoretical assumption put to test through brain-lateralization methodology. *Journal of Mind and Behavior*, **5**, 131–150.

Rychlak, J.F. and Williams, R.N. (1984). Affective assessment and dialectical oppositionality in the cognitive processing of social descriptors. *Personality and Social Psychology Bulletin*, **10**, 620–629.

Schachter, S. (1964). The interaction of cognitive and physiological determinants of emotional state. In L. Berkowitz (Ed.), *Advances in experimental social psychology*, Vol. 1, pp. 49–80. New York: Academic Press.

Scherer, K.R. (1984). Emotion as a multicomponent process: A model and some cross-cultural data. In P. Shaver (Ed.), *Review of personality and social psychology*, Vol. 5, pp. 37–63. Beverly Hills: Sage.

Schlenker, B.R. and Leary, M.R. (1985). Social anxiety and communication about the self. *Journal of Language and Social Psychology*, **4**, 171–192.

Schlosberg, H. (1952). The description of facial expressions in terms of two dimensions. *Journal of Experimental Psychology*, **44**, 229–237.

Schlosberg, H. (1954). Three dimensions of emotion. *Psychological Review*, **61**, 81–88.

Shaver, P., Schwartz, J., Kirson, D., and O'Connor, C. (1987). Emotion knowledge: Further exploration of a prototype approach. *Journal of Personality and Social Psychology*, **52**, 1061–1086.

Shields, S.A. (1984). Distinguishing between emotion and nonemotion: Judgments about experience. *Motivation and Emotion*, **8**, 355–369.

Shimanoff, S.B. (1983). The role of gender in linguistic references to emotive states. *Communication Quarterly*, **30**, 174–179.

Shimanoff, S.B. (1985a). Expressing emotions in words: Verbal patterns of interaction. *Journal of Communication*, **35**, 16–31.

Shimanoff, S.B. (1985b). Rules governing the verbal expression of emotions between married couples. *Western Journal of Speech Communication*, **49**, 147–165.

Shimanoff, S.B. (1985c). Verbal references to emotions. *Psychological Documents*, **15**, 9–10 (Ms No. 2689).

Shimanoff, S.B. (1987). Types of emotional disclosures and request compliance between spouses. *Communication Monographs*, **54**, 85–100.

Smith, C.A. and Ellsworth, P.C. (1985). Patterns of cognitive appraisal in emotion. *Journal of Personality and Social Psychology*, **48**, 813–838.

Smith, C.A. and Ellsworth, P.C. (1987). Patterns of appraisal and emotion related to taking an exam. *Journal of Personality and Social Psychology*, **52**, 475–488.

Wallbott, H.G. and Scherer, K.R. (1986). Cues and channels in emotion recognition. *Journal of Personality and Social Psychology*, **51**, 690–699.

Winton, W.M. (1986). The role of facial response in self-reports of emotion: A critique of Laird. *Journal of Personality and Social Psychology*, **50**, 808–812.

Winton, W.M., Putnam, L.E., and Krauss, R.M. (1984). Facial and autonomic manifestations of the dimensional structure of emotion. *Journal of Experimental Social Psychology*, **20**, 195–216.

Wundt, W. (1896). *Outlines of psychology*. Republished 1902 (transl. C.H. Judd) Leipzig: Engelmann.

Zajonc, R.B. (1980). Feeling and thinking: Preferences need no inferences. *American Psychologist*, **35**, 151–175.

Zajonc, R.B. (1984). On the primacy of affect. *American Psychologist*, **39**, 117–123.

Zajonc, R.B. (1985). Emotion and facial efference: A theory reclaimed. *Science*, **228**, 15–21.

3

Language and Social Influence

MICHAEL BURGOON

Department of Communication and Department of Family and Community Medicine, University of Arizona, USA

Questions about the factual and value dimensions of persuasive communication have been pervasive in the writings of scholars from the ancient Greek and Roman theorists to present-day social psychologists of various schools of thought. In the *Gorgias* and the *Phaedrus*, Plato contrasts the ethical and unethical practices of persuasion. In the *Gorgias*, the interchanges between Socrates and Gorgias envision rhetoric as founded on evil persuasion. Plato's description of rhetoric in the *Phaedrus* embodies a just and noble persuasion. In the twentieth century, we still worry about hidden persuaders, gullible people, and unethical uses of language to persuade and move people to action. However, no one would deny the importance of understanding better how we use language to change the perceptions, affect, cognitions, and behaviors of those with whom we interact.

The importance of strategic language choices in constructing messages designed for social influence[1] is manifest to the community of scholars interested in language and social psychology today. Burgoon and Miller (1985) introduced their theoretical exposition on the relationship between language and persuasion with the following words:

> Our language affects our lives powerfully. Others make attributions about social and professional status, background and education, and even the intent of communication by evaluating our language choices. Those intrigued with social influence, whether classical scholars or media image-makers, have long pondered the influence of such language choices on the success or failure of persuasive attempts. The decision to appeal to people's logic or emotional side is manifest in the language used in persuasive

Handbook of Language and Social Psychology
Edited by H. Giles and W.P. Robinson. © 1990 John Wiley & Sons Ltd

messages: persuaders try to mollify, justify, terrify or crucify by altering the language in their appeals. (Burgoon and Miller, 1985, p. 199)

The importance of language is recognized by those concerned with social influence processes and evidenced by the voluminous amount of empirical research on language variables that impact the alteration of attitudes and/or behaviors. Yet there has been a lag in the development of explanatory theoretical models which incorporate functional statements about the relationship between language and social influence. This lack of theoretical development has had unfortunate consequences for those interested in communication and social psychology because: (a) research over the past decade on language choices, message strategies, and persuasion has been relatively moribund, (b) extant research has been dismissed by many as hopelessly confused and confounded, and (c) recent theoretical models have simply ignored the large body of classic studies that attest to the suasory power of language.

The variable-analytic tradition of social psychology prior to this decade contributed heavily to the present discontent with the quality of knowledge claims emanating from various research efforts. Without theoretical guidance, the prevailing research paradigm has been an inductive, exhaustive examination of a single language variable and its relationship to persuasion. Much of this research focused on language behavior designed to appeal to the emotions, or what classical scholars call *pathos*, as a vehicle to facilitate change in attitudinal positions or modify behavior. When main-effect findings demonstrated relationships between the selected variable and some measure of attitude/behavior change, additional variables such as source characteristics, power, and receiver variables were investigated.

In many studies, main-effect findings were not replicated or interaction effects overrode conclusions about the impact of the selected language variable. It was not uncommon for claims advanced about the impact of language choices on attitude change to be immediately challenged by null findings or, in many cases, research reporting the obverse. For example, some research attests to the superiority of strong fear appeals over weak fear-arousing messages in suasory attempts. Other findings suggest that strong fear appeals are ineffective and lead to boomerang effects where receivers believe or behave in a manner opposite to that desired by the advocate. The fear-appeal literature is but one area of social influence replete with confounded claims and conflicting conclusions. Bodies of research dealing with language intensity, obscenity, opinionatedness, and humor and warmth present similar, often uninterpretable, findings.

The problems identified with this research tradition are not limited to the language of emotional appeals. Research on logical appeals and message organization has followed the same mechanistic empiricism paradigm, resulting in equally confounded accumulations of evidence. While beyond the scope of this chapter, programs of research investigating the relationship between logical consistency, evidence, message structure, and message organization manifest a similar pattern. Disputed main-effect findings, confusing interactions, and lack of functional explanatory mechanisms have precluded informed conclusion-drawing about logic, language, and organization in the attitude-change process.

One approach to this conceptual muddle, taken by such researchers as Petty and

Cacioppo (1986) with their development of the Elaboration Likelihood Model, is simply to ignore this wealth of empirical data and relegate persuasive message variables to the status of unobserved intervening variables. The labeling of arguments as central or peripheral is often derived from inferring antecedents from consequents, or a teleological method of explanation. Thus, *if* specific outcomes occur (e.g. attitude change), then certain kinds of intrapsychic message processing had to have occurred. Such an explanatory mechanism is relatively unproductive for people interested in the social effects of language strategy choices. The more appropriate approach is to specify *a priori* how language variables affect the persuasive process.

The argument advanced in this chapter is that much could be gained by examining related, but distinct, lines of research in a different organizational format. An analytic framework can be constructed to explain the relationship between language and social influence by focusing first on micro-level language choices and extending empirically based findings to more macro-level tactics and strategies. Results of change attempts based on specific language choices such as fear-arousing messages, messages varying in language intensity, and variables important in emotional appeals provide a foundation for analyzing language choices beyond the sentence level. The macro-analytic studies of social influence involving persuasive themes, typologies of compliance-gaining strategies, and sequential message strategies that have received so much attention during the past decade can be seen as a complement to, and extension of, this earlier research.

The following discussion will review, critique, and synthesize previous research and draw generalizations about language behavior and its relationship to social influence. Expectancy Theory (Burgoon and Miller, 1985) serves as a useful theoretical umbrella under which these generalizations can be meaningfully subsumed and understood. An expectancy interpretation of the relationship between language and social influence allows explanation and interpretation of what have been heretofore seemingly contradictory findings. It also suggests fruitful lines of research for exploration which may assist in reviving systematic inquiry in areas of theoretical and practical import.

AN OVERVIEW OF EXPECTANCY THEORY

The logic undergirding the original formulation of Expectancy Theory, one of the few extant language-based theories of persuasion, is that, since language is a rule-governed symbolic system, people develop sociological norms and expectations for the contextual appropriateness of language choices in suasory attempts. In many communication transactions, language usage conforms to and confirms these norms, often enhancing the normative status of individuals who engage in specific kinds of language behavior. In other words, relatively rigid norms of appropriateness develop in a language community. When an advocate attempts to alter, maintain, or reinforce the attitude and/or behaviors of people and intentionally or accidentally violates social norms governing language usage, expectations of targets are violated, affecting receptivity to persuasive messages.

The basic premises of Expectancy Theory are difficult to articulate in a summary chapter within the space limitations imposed. However, Miller and Burgoon (1985) have devoted considerable effort to articulating each proposition embedded within this formulation and the reader is directed to their paper for increased understanding of the work that undergirds much of this chapter. Contingent on a host of moderator variables, violations of expectations may enhance or inhibit the persuasive efficacy of a message. A key variable in persuasive effectiveness is whether a source's language choices positively or negatively violate receivers' expectations. Language behavior viewed as culturally or socially inappropriate represents a *negative violation* of expectations and predictably inhibits a target's receptivity to the advocated position. If a change in attitudinal position and/or behavior is advocated, the consequences of a negative violation include: (a) lack of attitudinal change and/or modification of behaviors, or (b) actual movement of attitudes and modification of behaviors in the direction *opposite* to that desired by the advocate.

Predicting the impact of *positive violations* of expectations posed conceptual and operational problems for Expectancy Theory researchers. Work by McPeek and Edwards (1975) first suggested that positive violations of expectations increase persuasibility only when sources were initially evaluated negatively. Burgoon and Miller (1985) more formally advance the proposition that a positive violation of expectations occurs when an advocate is expected to deviate from normative language use in a negative manner and subsequently conforms to social norms governing language choices. This conceptualization is based on the notion that there is a band-width of appropriate normative language behavior. Positive violations of expectations occur only when one expects a source to communicate out of the boundary of appropriate language behavior and the source tailors his or her message to fall within the acceptable range of conduct. Conformity to norms results in receiver's overestimations of the positiveness of language behavior and, thus, promotes significant modifications of behavior and/or changes in attitudes.

Such a conceptualization of positive violations of expectations precludes the possibility that a person who routinely constructs persuasive messages in an expected, normative manner will ever positively violate expectations. Taken one step further, the original formulation of Expectancy Theory would have little, if any, explanatory power for attitude change obtained by moderately or highly valued sources. This conceptual restriction obviously unduly limits the theory's domain of discourse. The addition of a proposition is needed that allows for the occurrence of positive violations of expectations when a speaker who is expected to conform to normative language use behaves unexpectedly. For example, an 'average' speaker unexpectedly delivering an eloquent, moving oration is likely to benefit from the contrast between expected and obtained behaviors. Certainly, a wealth of social influence research attests to how a discrepancy between expected and enacted behavior is causally related to desired persuasive outcomes. Figure 3.1 provides a modified version of Expectancy Theory and summarizes predictions about the impact of positive and negative violations of expectations on attitude/behavior change.

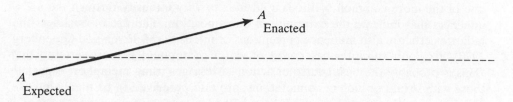

AREA OF POSITIVE VIOLATIONS OF LANGUAGE NORMS

BAND-WIDTH OF NORMATIVE, EXPECTED LANGUAGE BEHAVIORS

AREA OF NEGATIVE VIOLATIONS OF LANGUAGE NORMS

FIGURE 3.1 Summary of Expectancy Theory predictions about language behaviors and attitude/behavior change.

Case A. Positive violation of expectations by performing better than expected. Enacted behavior outside expected, normative band-width in positive direction. Attitude/behavior change predicted in direction advocated by source.

Case B. Positive violation of expectations by negatively evaluated source conforming more closely to norms of language behavior. Enacted behavior within the expected, normative band-width. Attitude change in direction advocated by source because of overly positive evaluation of source behavior.

Case C. Negative violation of expectations by performing of language behavior outside normative band-width in negative direction. No attitude/behavior change or actual changes in opposite direction advocated by the source predicted.

MICRO-LEVELS ANALYSES OF LANGUAGE BEHAVIORS

Most micro-level analyses of language behavior and its relationship to social influence began with an examination of linguistic properties of messages. Some attitude-change research involved manipulations within sentences of verb tense, adjectival and adverbial qualification, and type–token ratios to create varying experimental conditions (McEwen and Greenberg, 1970). Other research examined the impact of specific language choices on attitude change. For example, Bowers (1963, 1964) identified the variable of concern as language intensity or the degree to which a source indicates his or her deviation from neutrality. The statement 'That is a very good idea' is more intense than the statement 'That is a good idea'.

Though the perceived intensity of a message can be manipulated in several ways, one of the more common methods utilized is to vary intensity through the use of qualifiers that indicate the extremity of one's position. The use of qualifiers that indicate certainty also influence perceptions of intensity (McEwen and Greenberg, 1970). 'No doubt this is the best course of action' communicates more certainty than 'This is probably the best course of action'. Messages using metaphor, especially those with sexual or violent connotations, are also perceived to be highly intense. The statement 'Current economic policies in the United States are raping the poor' is an example of a highly intense metaphor. Unfortunately, though such research led to interesting, if not easily interpretable results, it was not guided by explanatory theoretical models.

These early research efforts experimentally manipulating micro-level variables such as adjectival and adverbial qualification provided the foundation for Expectancy Theory. Burgoon and Chase (1973) first suggested that, while much research had examined the impact of a communicator advancing an unexpected argument or an unexpected position, little evidence existed about the general expectations people have about the *linguistic* properties of messages. Working in the resistance to persuasion paradigm, Burgoon and Chase (1973) found that, when pretreatment inoculation messages differed structurally from attack messages, the amount of induced resistance to persuasion varied. The explanation offered was that pretreatment messages provided expectations about the linguistic form or appropriate style of subsequent persuasive attack messages. Burgoon and Stewart (1974) and Burgoon (1974) posited and found that, when a communicator positively violates linguistic expectations, attitude change toward the advocate's position significantly increases; conversely, when a source negatively violates expectations, a boomerang effect occurs such that targets change in directions contrary to those advanced by the persuader.

Findings based on an expectancy paradigm suggest that: (a) people have highly developed expectations about the appropriate lexical properties of persuasive messages, (b) individuals' expectations may not be driven by conscious thought processes, (c) violations of expectations can either enhance or inhibit desired changes, and (d) specific subgroups in the population have a very wide band-width of expected behavior while others have restricted linguistic freedom and often negatively violate normative expectations.

The foregoing within-sentence, linguistic-based research also allowed explanatory principles to be derived that pertain to the effects of language choice at the argument level. Research on such variables as fear appeals, opinionatedness, language intensity, and/or powerful or powerless speech has produced conflicting results. The next portion of this chapter will review several seemingly disparate lines of research conducted more than a decade ago, present empirical findings, and report the most parsimonious explanations advanced at the time for such results. It will be argued that, both in terms of conceptual origins and patterns of results, these lines of research have basic similarities that cannot be explained without reference to the previously articulated tenets of Expectancy Theory.

Fear Appeals

An age-old, yet widely used, persuasive tactic is to use fear-inducing language to sway an audience toward some predetermined end. Fear appeals are messages that attempt to convince persuadees that harm will befall them, or people important to them, if the advocate's claims are not adopted. 'Stop smoking or you will be dead within a year', 'This country faces economic ruin if my fiscal policies are not adopted', and 'If you don't buy enough life insurance, your family will suffer after you are gone' are appeals containing language designed to arouse people to action through fear.

Though a number of studies report conflicting results, two major theoretical positions support the notion that strong fear appeals are generally more effective than weak ones in suasory attempts (Baron and Byrne, 1977; Higbee, 1969). The general cognitive consistency paradigm (Festinger, 1957; Heider, 1946; Osgood and Tannenbaum, 1955) addresses issues related to an advocate's use of language to arouse fear and how such arousal affects persuasion. Variations on the consistency model suggest that fear appeals should utilize explicit, rather than mild, language to emphasize the harmful consequences of non-compliance. Strong language about the consequences of not following the advocate's prescriptions for behavior should increase stress and/or inconsistency in the target and motivate compliance in order to restore cognitive consistency. A reasonable person would obviously want to act in a manner that avoids harmful consequences and maintains a perception of rationality. A competing, perhaps more parsimonious, explanation for the relative superiority of strong fear appeals is a drive-reduction explanation (Baron and Byrne, 1977; Higbee, 1969). The drive-reduction model assumes that strong fear appeals lead to an increased state of arousal in the receiver. When presented with recommendations for how negative outcomes can be avoided (acceptance of the claim), the receiver is reassured and the arousal is reduced. This reduction in negative forms of arousal is reinforcing and enhances the probability that an advocate's claims and suggestions will be accepted, thus inducing attitude change (Baron and Byrne, 1977) and/or behavioral modification. Other studies (Leventhal and Niles, 1964; Niles, 1964; Singer, 1965) report a similar positive relationship between level of fear arousal and attitude change.

Early on, Janis and Feshbach (1953) stimulated controversy by suggesting that mild fear appeals were more effective than more intensely constructed fear-arousing messages, both in terms of immediate compliance and enduring resistance to subsequent persuasive attacks. Other research, soundly criticized for procedural imperfections (De Wolfe and Governale, 1964; Janis and Terwilliger, 1962), also reported a negative relationship between level of fear-arousing language and subsequent attitude change. To add to the theoretical confusion, yet others found no relationship between the intensity of fear appeals and attitude change (Beach, 1966; Powell, 1965).

Obviously, when such contradictory findings exist in the literature, it is reasonable to conclude that other variables are important determinants of the effects of fear-inducing language on attitude change. A flurry of research activity in the late 1960s and early 1970s found several factors that add to the effectiveness of strong fear appeals. For example, fear appeals that point out immediate and severe consequences of non-compliance are more effective than those which focus on more long-term or delayed effects. Strong fear appeals supported with evidence are more likely to be effective than those without evidence. Highly credible communicators can effectively use fear appeals when low-credibility communicators cannot. Finally, fear appeals linking non-compliance to harm befalling a receiver's loved one are likely to be more effective than appeals where threats are directed only at the target.

Language Intensity

It has become almost a cultural truism that effective speakers are people who choose language that passionately communicates their ideas. We have also come to believe that intense speakers are usually effective in gaining compliance and changing attitudes. However, research on the effectiveness of appeals varying in language intensity indicates that highly intense messages are generally *less* persuasive than messages using more moderate levels of intensity (Bowers, 1964; Bradac, Bowers, and Courtwright, 1979; Chase and Kelley, 1976; Miller and Burgoon, 1979). Some communicators seem to have more options in the levels of language intensity they can effectively use. Highly credible speakers, for example, can use strongly worded messages and retain or even increase their persuasive impact.

One key determinant of the level of intensity that should be used is what is considered *appropriate* by one's audience. Burgoon and associates have demonstrated in several studies that using unexpectedly or inappropriately intense language is highly detrimental to one's persuasive effectiveness (Burgoon and Chase, 1973; Burgoon, Jones, and Stewart, 1974; Burgoon and Stewart, 1974). For example, females in North America are expected to use less intense language than males. When they negatively violate normative expectations by being highly intense, they are ineffective in influence attempts. The same is true for sources of either sex who are perceived to be low in credibility.

Opinionated Language

Closely related to the use of intense language is the use of opinionated language. Opinionated statements actually convey two messages: the source's attitude toward the topic and his or her attitude toward those people who agree or disagree with the advocated position. The statement 'England is a beautiful country and anyone who thinks otherwise is an idiot' would be considered opinionated since it conveys the persuasive claim ('England is a beautiful country') and the source's attitude towards those who would disagree with the claim ('. . . is an idiot'). Because it derogates those who disagree, the statement about England is an opinionated *rejection* statement. An opinionated statement which praises those who agree ('Any bright person would agree that England is a beautiful country') is an opinionated *acceptance* statement.

Not surprisingly, opinionated language is perceived as more intense than non-opinionated language and is an effective strategy for highly credible sources but not for those with low credibility (Miller and Lobe, 1967). The strictures concerning the use of intense language also apply to the use of opinionated statements. Non-opinionated language is more effective than opinionated language when the audience is highly involved in the topic and when strong opinions about the issue are held by the audience. If the audience is neutral on the topic, opinionated *rejection* statements can be more effective than statements containing no opinionated language (Mehrley and McCroskey, 1970).

Obscenity

The use of obscene language should be viewed as a special form of language intensity. A limited amount of quality research exists on the relationship between obscenities and attitude change. Bostrom, Baseheart, and Rossiter (1973) and Mulac (1976) found that the use of obscenity reduced evaluations of certain dimensions of source credibility. Pawlovich (1969) found that the credibility of female, but not male, speakers was severely reduced when obscenity was used in persuasive messages. Because the findings are similar to those suggesting contrast effects for highly intense language, opinionated language and obscenity should be considered a subset of highly intense language options. This assumption allows some general conclusions to be drawn about the combined research efforts on language intensity, opinionated-ness, and obscenity:

(1) Receivers of suasory discourse have normative expectations about an appropriate level of fear-arousing appeals, opinionated language, and magnitude of language intensity, broadly defined to include lexical choices, opinionatedness, and obscenity.
(2) When an audience thinks the source is highly credible, various types of intense language can be used to support the claim. When communicators are advocating a position counter to beliefs or opinions important to receivers or are unsure of their credibility, or know it to be low, as a matter of strategy they should choose less intense language.
(3) Receivers have gender-specific normative expectations about the appropriateness of language choices in persuasive messages. Males have the freedom to use a number of forms of intense language without negatively violating expectations; females have less freedom of language choice and are more persuasive when they use language low in intensity and opinionatedness, and use fewer fear appeals and obscenities.

In summary, males and highly credible advocates have a relatively wide bandwidth of acceptable language behavior and can elect to use a variety of persuasive strategies without negatively violating cultural and sociological expectations. Low-credibility sources and females have restricted degrees of freedom when it comes to language options if they wish to function effectively as change agents. For the past decade, the research on the impact of these micro-level strategies has been moribund, in part due to the inability of scholars to make sense of the empirical data. With the publication of the first formalization of Expectancy Theory in 1985, there appears to be the possibility for parsimonious explanations for what appeared to be a hopelessly confused body of research. Questions about how expectations are developed and/or changed as social structure changes are intriguing but unanswered. The effectiveness of often-used strategies such as humor and symbolic displays of warmth is similarly interesting and might be assessed under the umbrella of Expectancy Theory.

MACRO-LEVEL ANALYSES OF LANGUAGE BEHAVIORS

Compliance-gaining Strategy Research

Background

Contiguous in time with social-psychological laboratory research efforts to explain micro-level language behaviors and their relationship to persuasion, Marwell and Schmitt (1967a,b) developed a language-choice model of compliance-gaining strategies that dramatically altered the research agenda for the social psychology of language and communication. The compliance-gaining typology of Marwell and Schmitt (1967b) represents a synthesis of the social control and power literature (Etzioni, 1961; French and Raven, 1960; Goffman, 1959). This control or power orientation almost completely ignored the message-choice research on emotional appeals and the prevailing logic of the time. Marwell and Schmitt's approach was largely geared toward identifying macro-scale characteristics of social power that allowed actors to exert control and gain compliance from targets. The resulting typology of 16 compliance-gaining strategies, which Marwell and Schmitt (1967a,b) viewed as a preliminary attempt, was sufficiently exhaustive to generalize across a variety of compliance-gaining situations. Table 3.1 presents the Marwell and Schmitt typology and an example of a persuasive appeal for each strategy.

Ten years after the initial research, communication researchers discovered the Marwell and Schmitt (1967a,b) typology and opened the floodgates for a wave of empirical investigations of compliance-gaining strategies. Miller, Boster, Roloff, and Seibold (1977) completed a classic study of compliance-gaining strategy selections in which they used the Marwell and Schmitt typology to: (a) identify the control strategies available to potential persuaders, (b) study the effects of situational differences on choice of specific control strategies, and (c) understand the relationship between individual differences of potential persuaders and their choice of control strategies.

While the research questions posed by Miller *et al.* (1977) are interesting and important, the authors commit an egregious error in judgment and/or in interpretation when they claim that the field has devoted so much energy to an examination of the effects of source characteristics that there has been a 'relative lack of concern for message choices made by the potential persuader' (p. 37). They further erroneously claim that 'little research has systematically examined the relationship of source characteristics to subsequent choices of particular compliance-gaining strategies' (p. 38). The publication of such a rationale is especially ironic since Miller contributed so much to the previously discussed work on the relationship between language variables and attitude change. Unfortunately, Miller and associates may have

TABLE 3.1 Marwell–Schmitt (1967a,b) Typology of Compliance-gaining Strategies

	Strategy	
(1)	Promise	If you will comply, I will reward you.
(2)	Threat	If you do not comply, I will punish you.
(3)	Expertise (positive)	If you comply, you will be rewarded because of 'the nature of things'.
(4)	Expertise (negative)	If you do not comply you will be punished because of 'the nature of things'.
(5)	Liking	Actor is friendly and helpful to get target in a 'good frame of mind' so that he will comply with the request.
(6)	Pregiving	Actor rewards target before requesting compliance.
(7)	Aversive stimulation	Actor continuously punishes target, making stimulation cessation contingent on compliance.
(8)	Debt	You owe me compliance because of past favors.
(9)	Moral appeal	You are immoral if you do not comply.
(10)	Self-feeling (positive)	You will feel better about yourself if you comply.
(11)	Self-feeling (negative)	You will feel worse about yourself if you do not comply.
(12)	Altercasting (positive)	A person with 'good' qualities would comply.
(13)	Altercasting (negative)	Only a person with 'bad' qualities would not comply.
(14)	Altruism	I need your compliance very badly, so do it for me.
(15)	Esteem (positive)	People you value will think better of you if you comply.
(16)	Esteem (negative)	People you value will think worse of you if you do not comply.

promoted the dismissal of a great deal of message/language-choice research (e.g. fear appeals, intensity, logical appeals, and message organization) with what appears to be an overzealous embracing of the Marwell and Schmitt (1967a,b) typology.

The Miller *et al.* (1977) article deserves the label of 'classic study' for several reasons. First, since publication of the article in 1977, compliance-gaining strategy selection research has dominated the interest of social influence scholars. Second, three of the four authors proceeded to attack the original effort which carried their names (Boster and Stiff, 1984; Hunter and Boster, 1987; Roloff and Barnicott, 1979; Seibold, Cantrill, and Meyers, 1985). Finally, the field had an intellectual reunion of sorts when, a decade later, Miller, Boster, Roloff, and Seibold (1987) produced a review and critique of research that followed the group's maiden effort. This critique is recommended to those desiring a more technical treatment on the controversies surrounding this body of compliance-gaining research.

The body of knowledge

A review of the burgeoning body of compliance-gaining research completed in the last decade is somewhat disappointing. Unfortunately, the accumulated efforts of many researchers have progressed little beyond attempts to answer the three questions posed by Miller *et al.* (1977). The basic research paradigm used in compliance-gaining investigations has remained relatively unchanged over the past decade and across several dozen studies. Research protocols typically specify or manipulate persuasive scenarios and then measure the *likelihood* of strategy usage in such situations. Thus, the focus of almost every research effort has been on *what* strategy is used *when*.

Considerable activity of a reductionistic nature followed the publication of the article by Miller *et al.* (1977) in an attempt to uncover the underlying structure of the Marwell and Schmitt (1967a,b) typology. Marwell and Schmitt identified five dimensions paralleling French and Raven's (1960) bases of social power. Miller *et al.* (1977) found eight dimensions based on situation-specific scenarios. Kaminski, McDermott, and Boster (1977) in an immediate follow-up found two dimensions: positive and negative strategies. Roloff and Barnicott (1978), in an oft-cited article, coined the terms prosocial and antisocial strategies to identify these two dimensions of the typology. Unfortunately, researchers who adopted Roloff and Barnicott's prosocial and antisocial labels ignored methodological errors and interpretative problems in their research, and the terms became normative descriptors of the underlying dimensions of compliance-gaining strategies. All of the attempts at specifying the multiple dimensions of the typology produced little, for the best evidence (Burgoon, Dillard, Koper, and Doran, 1984; Dillard and Burgoon, 1985; Hunter and Boster, 1987) suggests that the typology is probably unidimensional. Further, it appears to make little difference whether one summative score of all 16 scale items is the criterion measure or each individual item is used as a dependent variable.

Considerable controversy has surrounded the use of the typology as a precoded checklist. Schenck-Hamlin, Wiseman, and Georgacarakos (1982) fired the opening salvo in what turned out to be a continuing war of words about an inductively derived, subject-generated approach to compliance-gaining strategy development. These arguments were quickly met with counter-evidence provided by Boster, Stiff, and Reynolds (1985) that deductive or inductive approaches produced very similar typologies. Although these two articles capture the argument in a nutshell, the question of how valuable likelihood-of-use checklists are in indexing actual communicative behavior has remained an issue (Dillard and Burgoon, 1985). Recently,

Burleson *et al.* (1988) claimed that the entire ten years of research using such protocols has resulted in little more than a measure of the social desirability of the individual items, rendering it virtually worthless. They claim the checklist approach is insensitive to situational and/or individual differences and that people over-report using positive strategies and under-report using negative strategies.

Another line of research has attempted to systematize a portion of the message-selection research by specifying situational influences affecting compliance. Cody and McLaughlin (1980; and see also Chapter 11, by these authors) report a dimensional analysis of compliance-gaining *situations* that resulted in the following six-factor solution:

(1) Degree of intimacy between target and actor;
(2) Extent to which compliance personally benefits the actor;
(3) Consequences of the compliance-gaining attempt for the relationship between target and actor;
(4) Rights of the actor in the situation;
(5) Extent to which the target typically dominates the actor;
(6) Degree of resistance to the compliance-gaining attempt expected from the target.

Cody, Woelfel, and Jordan (1983) replicated these findings and this dimensional solution has become an operational template for research aimed at specifying or manipulating situational variables.

Related research has examined individual differences in strategy selection choices (Boster and Stiff, 1984; Clark, 1979; Roloff and Barnicott, 1978; Sillars, 1980) with meager results. Efforts have expanded the domain by examining the number, type, and likelihood of use of strategies across gender (Burgoon, Dillard, and Doran, 1983) and culture (Burgoon, Dillard, Doran, and Miller, 1982). Again, the reported results produce few important significant differences.

The social effects approach to compliance-gaining strategies

There are two problematic areas in this line of research: (a) the over-reliance on likelihood-of-use ratings as the dependent measure of concern, which results in a lack of concern for the social impact of various strategies, and (b) the lack of theoretical development that incorporates compliance-gaining strategy use with a more comprehensive explanation of attitude-change processes. Hunter and Boster (1987) published an empathy interpretation of strategy selection based upon data that had been collected almost ten years ago. They argue that the Marwell and Schmitt (1967a,b) typology represents a Guttman-type continuum ranging from messages that produce positive emotional reactions to those that promote negative emotional reactions. Further, they claim that each actor has an empathy or ethical threshold that determines which strategies are acceptable or unacceptable. Due in part to the lag-time in publication and accumulated evidence that the empathy model suffers under empirical scrutiny, Hunter and Boster (1987) have conceded that empathy is probably not the underlying dimension of compliance-gaining strategy use.

Indeed, Hunter and Boster (1987) concur with Burgoon *et al.* (1983) and Dillard and Burgoon (1985) that the most appropriate conceptualization of the typology is a continuum of instrumental verbal aggression. In a break with the prevailing research tradition, Burgoon *et al.* (1983), working from an Expectancy Theory perspective, ignored likelihood-of-use ratings and posited that, if the underlying continuum was viewed as instrumental verbal aggression, normative expectations about the appropriateness of use of message strategies would differ for males and females (see Table 3.2).

Support was found for an interaction hypothesis predicting that males are expected to use more verbally aggressive persuasive strategies than females and, when they deviate from such strategies, negatively violate expectations and are less persuasive. Moreover, the results supported the claim that females are expected to be less verbally aggressive than males and are penalized by being less persuasive when they deviate from such an expected strategy. Manipulation checks indicated that people have different expectations for strategy use by males and females and that neither psychological sex role nor biological sex alter these expectations.

This research expands the potential utility of the Marwell and Schmitt (1967a,b) typology by focusing beyond what people claim they would use or actually use in compliance-gaining attempts. Knowledge is provided of the *effects* of using certain persuasive strategies differing in verbal aggressiveness. Though much of the likelihood-of-use research reports that people avoid verbally aggressive strategies (antisocial/negative-language choices), this research suggests that, especially for males, such avoidance might be an unwise strategic choice and inhibit persuasive effectiveness.

Burgoon *et al.* (in press, a,b) have tested this expectancy-based approach to compliance-gaining in an applied field setting, namely physician–patient relationships. Results suggest that physicians generally eschew *both* the most verbally aggressive and unaggressive language options when dealing with patients. Physicians rely primarily on expertise strategies, which may not be the most effective in gaining patient compliance with suggested treatment regimens and lifestyle alterations. When physicians use verbally aggressive language, more compliance is gained with

TABLE 3.2   Ratings of Likelihood of use by Male and Female Sources of Different Persuasive Message Strategies

Likely use by male sources	No gender differences expected	Likely use by female sources
Threat	Negative altercasting	Promise
Aversive stimulation	Negative esteem	Pregiving
		Positive moral appeal
Negative expertise	Negative moral appeal	Altruism
Debt	Positive expertise	Liking
	Positive self-feeling	
	Positive altercasting	
	Positive esteem	
	Negative self-feeling	

specific kinds of patients. Interestingly, in no case does the use of more verbally aggressive language reduce patient satisfaction with the quality of health care. The expectancy interpretation suggests that because of the normative status conferred upon physicians, they are expected to be verbally aggressive. Thus, physicians might be more effective in their clinical practice if they were to select more aggressive language behaviors.

Needed research directions

Research is overdue which demonstrates the effects of various combinations of compliance-gaining strategies. Stochastic models of attempts to change attitudes or modify behaviors might reveal that, while nearly everyone would prefer to begin with prosocial/positive language choices, at different time-lags people may abandon unaggressive language and move to antisocial strategies like threat, guilt, or fear. Ignoring the previous micro-level research in emotional and logical appeals has resulted in repeated use of a set of less than exhaustive strategies. The major propositions outlined by Burgoon and Miller (1985) in their exposition of Expectancy Theory provide an overarching framework for analyzing micro- and macro-level language behaviors. Close parallels exist when the language used in social influence is conceptualized on a continuum; that is, emotional appeals are special cases of language intensity and compliance-gaining strategies are special cases of instrumental verbal aggression. Much can be gained by synthesizing under one theoretical umbrella yesterday's variables of concern with today's more global interests in tactical and strategic communication.

Sequential Message Strategies

The previously discussed research dealt with the manipulation of one variable (e.g. evidence, language intensity) or a combination of variables in a single persuasive message (e.g. verbally aggressive strategies: threat, debt, aversive stimulation). Yet many influence attempts are sequential in nature; that is, multiple persuasive attempts carried out over time may take on the form of a campaign. Two of these sequential compliance-gaining strategies have received significant attention in the literature.

Foot-in-the-door

The first of these techniques ('foot-in-the-door') is based on the premise that we are often forced to choose language that will gain compliance with minimal pressure (DeJong, 1979; Dillard, Hunter, and Burgoon, 1984; Foss and Dempsey, 1979; Seligman, Bush, and Kirsch, 1976; Snyder and Cunningham, 1975). Situational pressures or moral or ethical constraints may inhibit or prevent the use of overtly manipulative strategies to gain compliance. A foot-in-the-door technique initially requires the persuader to make a relatively small request, to which he or she is certain the target will agree. Some time later, the target is again approached, with a larger request – that which the source originally desired. A number of studies confirm that

people who comply with a small initial request are more likely to comply with a
second larger request than are those who are approached with only a single large
request (DeJong, 1979; Dillard *et al.*, 1984). Presumably, this effect is due to a
change in the way targets see themselves after complying with the first request. In
other words, this technique manipulates *expectations about self* to promote desired
changes. Freedman and Fraser (1966) explain the phenomenon in this way:

> Once he has agreed to a request, his attitude may change. He may become in his own
> eyes a person who does this sort of thing, who agrees to requests made by strangers, and
> who takes actions on things he believes in, who cooperates with good causes. (Freedman
> and Fraser, 1966, p. 201)

The procedure used in one of Freedman and Fraser's (1966) experiments illustrates the effect of the foot-in-the-door technique. The large request put to a group of
homeowners was that they install a large sign in their front yard that read 'DRIVE
CAREFULLY'. Only 17% of the homeowners who were not first approached with a
small request were willing to comply. In contrast, 50% to 76% of the homeowners
who had first been approached with a small request complied with the subsequent
request to put the sign in their front yard.

Perhaps the most crucial aspect of the foot-in-the-door technique is determining
the size of the initial request. Since failure initially to gain compliance eliminates any
chance of success in the sequential request strategy, the first request must be small
enough that the receiver complies. However, the initial request cannot be so small
that it is perceived as trivial. For foot-in-the-door to work, compliance with the first
request must be a significant-enough act that the receiver comes to see himself or
herself as the type of individual committed to similar types of action (Burgoon and
Bettinghaus, 1980). One interesting aspect of the foot-in-the-door technique is that
an astute persuader can actually turn another's prior success in securing a target's
compliance into his or her own advantage. An individual may be attempting to gain
compliance from someone who has recently acceded to a similar, yet smaller, request
from another persuader. A foot-in-the-door strategist would suggest that the target is
now more vulnerable to the appeals of the second advocate. Such findings have
implications for applied settings. For example, once a patient has complied with a
mediated message regarding appropriate health care, a physician might later seek
and successfully obtain a large behavioral or lifestyle change.

Door-in-the-face

The second sequential technique, 'door-in-the-face', takes a very different approach
to gaining compliance (Cann, Sherman and Elkes, 1975). The target is first approached with language clearly indicating a very large request which the persuader
assumes will be *refused*. Later the target is approached with a second, more
moderately worded, request. The action requested in the second message is the
response desired by the persuader. Although more than one explanation has been
advanced for the effectiveness of the door-in-the-face strategy (Cann *et al.*, 1975;
Snyder and Cunningham, 1975), the research seems to support an explanation based

on the norm of reciprocity. Cialdini *et al.* (1975) argue that people feel obligated to make concessions to those who have made concessions to them. If a persuader makes a smaller or less demanding request of a target after an initial request has been rejected, the target presumably feels some pressure likewise to concede to a second, more reasonable appeal. Another explanation could be advanced from Burgoon and Miller's (1985) Expectancy Theory. The first request may set a target's expectations about the likely message strategies an actor would use. When the second request is unambiguously smaller, a positive violation of expectations occurs, promoting the desired changes. Such an expectancy interpretation has not previously been applied to this body of literature.

Several conditions are necessary for the door-in-the-face technique to be successful. First, the initial request must be refused. Since the initial request asks even more from the target than is actually desired, the size of the initial or 'throw-away' request must be carefully considered. While the first request must be large, it must not be so large as to be considered absurd, nor must it lead the target to begin viewing himself or herself as the type of person who refuses all requests of this type. In other words, the very mechanism (self-attribution) that allows the foot-in-the-door technique to be effective must be prevented from occurring and becoming a motivational factor in the door-in-the-face strategy. The second request must be unambiguously smaller than the first so that the persuader will be seen as making a significant concession in the appeal, or positively violating established expectations. Since door-in-the-face depends on targets feeling they have an obligation to make some type of reciprocal concession or that the source is positively violating expectations, it is evident that successful use of door-in-the-face requires that the same person make both requests (Burgoon and Bettinghaus, 1980).

Needed research directions

Given the demonstrated persuasive efficacy of these sequential strategies, research attention should focus on examining variables, other than size of request, in a stochastic manner. The use of fear, intensity, or any of the other micro-level appeals might be assessed for a gradualism effect, for example with beginning messages using mild fear appeals and subsequent messages escalating the level of fear. Conversely, high-fear appeals might initially be used to attain significant attitudinal shifts, followed by milder fear appeals which serve as positive violations. The same sequential, time-ordered message manipulations could be used to gain more information about the processual nature of the relationship between language choices and social influence by creating different combinations of aggressive/unaggressive compliance-gaining strategies, including, but not limited to, those suggested by Marwell and Schmitt (1967a,b).

CONCLUSION

Miller and Burgoon (1978) discussed the apparent decline in interest in both general persuasion research and specific language-choice research. They discuss a number of possible reasons for this decline. First, they argue that in the field of communication there appears to be a fascination with 'in vogue' methodologies and little concern about whether the data generated by these techniques are isomorphic with theory, past research, or common sense. One need only to observe the current overuse and misuse of meta-analytic techniques to realize this argument is as valid today as it was ten years ago when factor-analytic techniques were prevalent.

Second, they argue that some scholars in the field believe it is more fruitful to engage in the difficult and important task of describing 'talk' or 'conversation' than it is to do relatively 'trivial' and 'easy' systematic research with the goal of explaining and predicting the relationship between language and social influence. These scholars seem to believe that, because of the complexity with which variables interact in naturally occurring situations, isolating message effects does not contribute to the knowledge base of suasory discourse.

To be sure, certain variables present problems to scholars interested in building theory in the area of message effects. As previously stated, the language-effects research is replete with examples of confounded and confusing findings. Part of this confusion is the result of less than careful use of methodologies to generate knowledge. Another antecedent condition leading to this present state of knowledge is that the utilization of variable-analytic techniques has been unguided by theoretical concerns. While description of naturally occurring communicative activity is a noble and heuristic endeavor, one must recognize that building data sets and building theory are not synonymous. While some variables central to message research are relatively easy to deal with, others are more difficult to explain. Inquiry about the persuasive impact of many variables has been prematurely abandoned. Clearly, systematic research in the area of language effects is essential to our understanding of social influence.

This chapter was actually an examination of choices. The first focus of concern, at the micro-level of analysis, indicates that lexical choices have a powerful impact on persuasive success. It can be argued that there is a tendency to ignore important work simply because it was conducted two decades ago and its popularity has declined. A revival of interest in pursuing lexical-choice research and integrating it with extant areas of inquiry and theoretical developments seems overdue. The second area of focus concerned clusters of tactical and strategic choices used in the service of gaining compliance. The final area reviewed was stochastic lag-sequential choices about what language strategies will be most efficacious in efforts to change attitudes and/or behaviors over time. The conceptual parallels among these choices are evident when one considers that most micro-level emotional appeals are special cases involving language intensity and more macro-strategies are special cases involving instrumental verbal aggression. It is obvious that language behaviors are the markers with which level of intensity and/or aggression are judged. Moreover, given the evidence that (a) expectations about the appropriateness of language choices are somewhat universal, and (b) violations of such expectations dramatically impact the success of persuasive attempts, it is manifest that theoretical integration of seemingly disparate areas of inquiry is possible. A language-based conceptualization like Expectancy Theory must be invoked that explains the relationship between language and social influence across contexts and across levels of analysis. The fact that influence behavior simply cannot be explained without reference to such a theory provides a case for continued, and in some cases renewed, research efforts.

NOTE

1 The terms social influence, persuasion, attitude change, and compliance-gaining have become almost synonymous in the research literature. For the purposes of this chapter, social influence is the umbrella term for which persuasion and compliance-gaining become subsets. Persuasion is usually inclusive of attempts to change perceptions, affect, and cognition. The compliance-gaining literature has been more concerned with message attempts designed to gain behavioral compliance with various strategic attempts.

REFERENCES

Baron, R. and Byrne, D. (1977). *Social psychology*. Boston: Allyn and Bacon.

Beach, R.I. (1966). The effect of a fear-arousing safety film on physiological, attitudinal and behavioural measures. *Traffic Safety Research Review*, 10, 53–57.

Boster, F.J. and Stiff, J.B. (1984). Compliance-gaining message selection behavior. *Human Communication Research*, 10, 539–556.

Boster, F.J., Stiff, J.B., and Reynolds, R.A. (1985). Do persons respond differently to inductively-derived and deductively-derived lists of compliance gaining message strategies? A reply to Wiseman and Schenk-Hamlin. *Western Journal of Speech Communication*, 49, 177–187.

Bostrom, R.N., Baseheart, J.R., and Rossiter, C.M. (1973). The effects of three types of profane language in persuasive messages. *Journal of Communication*, 23, 461–475.

Bowers, J.W. (1963). Language intensity, social introversion and attitude change. *Speech Monographs*, 30, 345–352.

Bowers, J.W. (1964). Some correlates of language intensity. *Quarterly Journal of Speech*, 50, 415–420.

Bradac, J.J., Bowers, J.W., and Courtwright, J.A. (1979). Three language variables in communication research: Intensity, immediacy, and diversity. *Human Communication Research*, 5, 257–269.

Burgoon, M. (1974). Empirical investigations of language intensity: III. The effects of source credibility and language intensity on attitude change and person perception. *Human Communication Research*, 1, 251–256.

Burgoon, M. and Bettinghaus, E.P. (1980). Persuasive message strategies. In M.E. Roloff and G.R. Miller (Eds), *Persuasion: New directions in theory and research*, pp. 141–169. Beverly Hills: Sage.

Burgoon, M., Birk, T., Parrott, R., Coker, R., Pfau, M., and Burgoon, J. (in press, a). Research in patient–physician communication: Perceptions and effects of the use of verbally aggressive communication strategies; Compliance-gaining strategy selection in physician–patient communication: Primary care physicians' perceptions. *Health Communication*.

Burgoon, M. and Chase, L.J. (1973). The effects of differential linguistic patterns in messages attempting to induce resistance to persuasion. *Speech Monographs*, 40, 1–7.

Burgoon, M., Dillard, J.P., and Doran, N. (1983). Friendly or unfriendly persuasion: The effects of violations of expectations by males and females. *Human Communication Research*, 10, 283–294.

Burgoon, M., Dillard, J.P., Doran, N., and Miller, M.D. (1982). Cultural and situational influences on the process of persuasive strategy selection. *International Journal of Intercultural Relations*, 6, 85–100.

Burgoon, M., Dillard, J.P., Koper, R., and Doran, N. (1984). The impact of communication context and persuader gender on persuasive message selection. *Women's Studies in Communication*, **7**, 1–12.

Burgoon, M., Jones, S.B., and Stewart, D. (1974). Toward a message-centered theory of persuasion: Three empirical investigations of language intensity. *Human Communication Research*, **1**, 240–256.

Burgoon, M. and Miller, G.R. (1985). An expectancy interpretation of language and persuasion. In H. Giles and R. St Clair (Eds), *Recent advances in language, communication, and social psychology*, pp. 199–229. London: Erlbaum.

Burgoon, M., Parrott, R., Coker, R., Birk, T., Pfau, M., and Burgoon, J. (in press, b). Research in patient–physician communication: Perceptions and effects of the use of verbally aggressive communication strategies; Compliance-gaining strategy selection in physician–patient communication: Patients' perceptions. *Health Communication*.

Burgoon, M. and Stewart, D. (1974). Empirical investigations of language intensity: I. The effects of sex of source, receiver, and language intensity on attitude change. *Human Communication Research*, **1**, 244–248.

Burleson, B.R., Wilson, S.R., Waltman, M.S., Goering, E.M., Ely, T.K., and Whaley, B.B. (1988). Item desirability effects in compliance-gaining research: Seven empirical studies showing why the checklist methodology produces garbage. *Human Communication Research*, **14**, 429–486.

Cann, A., Sherman, S.J., and Elkes, R. (1975). Effects of initial request size and timing of the second request on compliance: The foot in the door and the door in the face. *Journal of Personality and Social Psychology*, **32**, 774–782.

Chase, L.J. and Kelley, C.W. (1976). Language intensity and resistance to persuasion: A research note. *Human Communication Research*, **3**, 82–85.

Cialdini, R.B., Vincent, J.E., Lewis, S.K., Catalan, J., Wheeler, D., and Darby, B.L. (1975). Reciprocal concessions procedure for inducing compliance: The door-in-the-face technique. *Journal of Personality and Social Psychology*, **31**, 206–215.

Clark, R.A. (1979). The impact of self-interest and desired liking on selection of persuasive strategies. *Communication Monographs*, **46**, 257–273.

Cody, M.J. and McLaughlin, M.L. (1980). Perceptions of compliance-gaining situations: A dimensional analysis. *Communication Monographs*, **47**, 132–148.

Cody, M.J., Woelfel, M.L., and Jordan, W.J. (1983). Dimensions of compliance-gaining situations. *Human Communication Research*, **9**, 99–113.

DeJong, W. (1979). An examination of self-perception mediation of the foot-in-the-door effect. *Journal of Personality and Social Psychology*, **37**, 2221–2239.

De Wolfe, A.S. and Governale, C.N. (1964). Fear and attitude change. *Journal of Abnormal and Social Psychology*, **69**, 119–123.

Dillard, J.P. and Burgoon, M. (1985). Situational influences on the selection of compliance-gaining messages: Two tests of the predictive utility of the Cody–McLaughlin typology. *Communication Monographs*, **52**, 289–304.

Dillard, J.P., Hunter, J.E., and Burgoon, M. (1984). Sequential-request persuasive strategies: Meta-analysis of foot-in-the-door and door-in-the-face. *Human Communication Research*, **10**, 461–488.

Etzioni, A. (1961). *A comparative analysis of complex organizations*. New York: Free Press.

Festinger, L. (1957). *A theory of cognitive dissonance*. Stanford, CA: Stanford University Press.

Foss, R.D. and Dempsey, C.B. (1979). Blood donation and the foot-in-the-door technique: A limiting case. *Journal of Personality and Social Psychology*, **37**, 580–590.

Freedman, J.L. and Fraser, S. (1966). Compliance without pressure: The foot-in-the-door technique. *Journal of Personality and Social Psychology*, **4**, 195–202.

French, J.R.P. and Raven, B. (1960). The bases of social power. In D. Cartwright and A. Zander (Eds), *Group Dynamics*, 2nd edn, pp. 607–623. New York: Harper and Row.

Goffman, E. (1959). *The presentation of self in everyday life*. Garden City: Doubleday.

Heider, F. (1946). Attitudes and cognitive organization. *Journal of Psychology*, **21**, 107–112.

Higbee, K. (1969). Fifteen years of fear arousal: Research on threat appeals: 1953–1968. *Psychological Bulletin*, **72**, 426–444.

Hunter, J.E. and Boster, F.J. (1987). A model of compliance-gaining message selection. *Communication Monographs*, **54**, 63–84.

Janis, L.L. and Feshbach, S. (1953). Effects of fear-arousing communications. *Journal of Abnormal and Social Psychology*, **48**, 79–92.

Janis, L.L. and Terwilliger, R. (1962). An experimental study of psychological resistance to fear-arousing communication. *Journal of Abnormal and Social Psychology*, **65**, 403–410.

Kaminski, E., McDermott, S., and Boster, F. (1977). The use of compliance-gaining strategies as a function of machiavellianism and situation. Paper presented at the Annual Meeting of the Central States Speech Association, Southfield, MI.

Leventhal, H. and Niles, P. (1964). A field experiment on fear arousal with data on the validity of questionnaire measures. *Journal of Personality*, **32**, 459–479.

Marwell, G. and Schmitt, D.R. (1967a). Compliance-gaining behavior: A synthesis and model. *Sociological Quarterly*, **8**, 317–328.

Marwell, G. and Schmitt, D.R. (1967b). Dimensions of compliance-gaining behavior: An empirical analysis. *Sociometry*, **30**, 350–364.

McEwen, W.J. and Greenberg, B.S. (1970). Effects of communication assertion intensity. *Journal of Communication*, **20**, 340–350.

McPeek, R.W. and Edwards, J.D. (1975). Expectancy disconfirmation and attitude change. *Journal of Social Psychology*, **96**, 193–208.

Mehrley, S. and McCroskey, J. (1970). Opinionated statements and attitude intensity as predictors of attitude change and source credibility. *Speech Monographs*, **37**, 47–52.

Miller, G.R., Boster, F., Roloff, M., and Seibold, D. (1977). Compliance-gaining message strategies: A typology and some findings concerning effects of situational differences. *Communication Monographs*, **44**, 37–51.

Miller, G.R., Boster, F., Roloff, M., and Seibold, D. (1987). MBRS rekindled: Some thoughts on compliance gaining in interpersonal settings. In M.E. Roloff and G.R. Miller (Eds), *Interpersonal processes: New directions in communication research*, pp. 89–116. Newbury Park: Sage.

Miller, G.R. and Burgoon, M. (1978). Persuasion research: Review and commentary. In B.D. Ruben (Ed.), *Communication yearbook*, Vol. 2, pp. 29–47. New Brunswick, NJ: Transaction.

Miller, M.D. and Burgoon, M. (1979). The relationship between violations of expectations and the induction of resistance to persuasion. *Human Communication Research*, **5**, 301–313.

Miller, G.R. and Lobe, J. (1967). Opinionated language, open- and closed-mindedness and response to persuasive communications. *Journal of Communication*, **17**, 333–341.

Mulac, A. (1976). Effects of obscene language upon three dimensions of listener attitude. *Communication Monographs*, **43**, 300–307.

Niles, P. (1964). The relationship of susceptibility and anxiety to acceptance of fear-arousing communications. Unpublished Doctoral Dissertation, Yale University.

Osgood, C.E. and Tannenbaum, P.H. (1955). The principle of congruity in the prediction of attitude change. *Psychological Review*, **62**, 42–55.

Pawlovich, K.J. (1969). The effects of offensive language on initial impressions of unknown communication sources. Unpublished Master's Thesis, Michigan State University.

Petty, R.E. and Cacioppo, J.T. (1986). *Communication and persuasion: Central and peripheral routes to attitude change*. New York: Springer-Verlag.

Powell, F.A. (1965). The effects of anxiety-arousing messages when related to personal, familial, and interpersonal referents. *Speech Monographs*, **32**, 102–106.

Roloff, M.E. and Barnicott, E. (1978). The situational use of pro- and anti-social compliance-gaining strategies by high and low machiavellians. In B.D. Ruben (Ed.), *Communication yearbook*, Vol. 2, pp. 193–208. New Brunswick, NJ: Transaction.

Roloff, M.E. and Barnicott, E. (1979). The influence of dogmatism on the situational use of pro- and anti-social compliance-gaining strategies. *Southern Speech Communication Journal*, **45**, 37–54.

Schenck-Hamlin, W.J., Wiseman, R.L., and Georgacarakos, G.N. (1982). A model of properties of compliance-gaining strategies. *Communication Quarterly*, **30**, 92–100.

Seibold, D.R., Cantrill, J.G., and Meyers, R.A. (1985). Communication and interpersonal influence. In M.L. Knapp and G.R. Miller (Eds), *Handbook of interpersonal communication*, pp. 551–614. Beverly Hills: Sage.

Seligman, C., Bush, M., and Kirsch, K. (1976). Relationship between compliance in the foot-in-the-door paradigm and size of first request. *Journal of Personality and Social Psychology*, **33**, 517–520.

Sillars, A.L. (1980). The stranger and the spouse as target persons for compliance-gaining strategies: A subjective utility model. *Human Communication Research*, **6**, 265–279.

Singer, R.P. (1965). The effects of fear-arousing communication on attitude change and behaviour. Unpublished Doctoral Dissertation, University of Connecticut.

Snyder, M. and Cunningham, M.R. (1975). To comply or not comply: Testing the self-perception explanation of the foot-in-the-door phenomenon. *Journal of Personality and Social Psychology*, **31**, 64–67.

4

Language and Personality

ADRIAN FURNHAM

Department of Psychology, University College, UK

Men use thought only to justify their wrongdoing, and speech only to conceal their thoughts.

(Voltaire)

I shall christen this style the Mandarin, since it is beloved by the literary pundits. It is the style of all those writers whose tendency is to make their language convey more than they mean or more than they feel, it is the style of most artists and all humbugs.

(Cyril Connolly)

How are personality and individual difference features marked linguistically? How do personality dimensions mediate social evaluations of linguistic performances? Indeed are some individual differences shaped or moulded by language input?

Despite the volume of research, on the one hand by personality theorists on traits and individual differences and on the other hand by psycholinguists and sociolinguists on the structure, function and use of speech, there is comparatively little programmatic research on the relationship between personality and language. Although some personality theorists have used some linguistic features like 'slips of the tongue' or self-references to illustrate psychological processes associated with personality types, few personality theorists or researchers have been particularly interested in language. In contrast, psycholinguists have been interested in individual differences, though rarely does their work relate to well-established personality traits or derive directly from psychological theories (Burleson, 1985; Delia, 1983).

Scherer (1979) has argued that many sociological and psychological models of speech have 'disregarded, among other things, individual differences between speakers in terms of types or traits and psychological states such as emotions or

Handbook of Language and Social Psychology
Edited by H. Giles and W.P. Robinson.   © 1990 John Wiley & Sons Ltd

moods'. Similarly Delia (1983) has noted: 'There currently is little agreement about how or exactly what to study about individual differences in language. The analysis of individual differences in language does not yet have a status of a defined subject within either linguistics or the broader multi-disciplinary domain of language and language behaviour research' (p. 208). We know for a fact that traits and psychological states of this sort affect speech behaviour quite strongly and we also know that listeners use speech markers of traits and state to infer or attribute a wide variety of speaker characteristics. However, we know very little about the details of trait/state effects on speech and the nature of the inferences made on the bases of these. Whereas animal-communication researchers have long since realized that individual differences among animals and their emotional states have a strong impact on the nature of signalling and have started to study these effects systematically, students of speech and language have been remarkably reticent in this respect (Scherer, 1979). 'This is true even for psychology, the discipline that is presumably in charge of phenomena such as personality or emotion . . . While there were some early flurries of excitement in psychology in the 1930s and 1940s, the enthusiasm died very rapidly and, as systematic reviews of the literature for both personality and emotion show, we can find little more than some isolated, and often rather weak pieces of research in the field' (Scherer, 1979, pp. 233–234).

Perhaps it is worth speculating why there has been so little *rapprochement* between personality theorists and social psychologists of language. There may be a number of reasons for this. First, from the point of view of personality theorists, most aspects of speech and language have never seemed particularly important as factors relating to personality and individual differences. Biological factors, early and late learning experiences and even cognitive styles have been thought to be determinants of personality, but language has very rarely been considered central or important enough to merit study. Second, language has not been considered a particularly interesting or important dependent variable for personality researchers. Although personality and individual differences have been related to a large number of cognitive processes including learning, memory and perception, there has been far less interest in communication style, for example. A third problem may have occurred because of the level of analysis; that is, paralinguistic and other aspects of speech are frequently considered at a detailed (molecular) level of behavioural analysis, while personality researchers are interested primarily in broad, higher-level behavioural patterns considered at a molar level.

Equally psycholinguists, sociolinguists and social psychologists of language have been less interested in the *actual* personality determinants of speech than in the *inference* of personality from speech. There may be various reasons for the relative paucity of studies on personality and speech. For instance, social psychologists of language are faced with a perplexing array of personality theories and systems all purporting to be *the* theory and to have isolated *the* salient basic dimensions of personality. From the outside it is not always clear which approach is the most valid and veridical or indeed which or how personality traits or cognitive styles might be related to speech. Second, there is a persistent debate as to whether personality traits are stable across time and consistent over situations, or whether social behaviour (presumably including speech) is situationally determined (Furnham and Argyle,

1981). Third, whilst it may be recognized that certain individual differences at the extremes (of intelligence or adjustment) are marked linguistically, there are other more interesting and more powerful determinants of speech which warrant more careful analysis before turning to those variables (personality) that may account for comparatively little of the variance.

However, it should not be thought that there exists no literature on the relationship between personality and speech. It may be true to say that the research that exists does not represent a consistent programmatic effort on the part of a definable group in the academic community. On the contrary, though there has been excellent and sustained research on the part of a few individuals and groups, it could not be said that there is a robust body of knowledge or an accepted theoretical stance in this area. Nevertheless, this chapter will attempt to review the extant literature critically and to make some recommendations for future research.

DEFINITIONAL DISTINCTIONS

The relationship between personality and language/speech requires, if not definitions, then at least some delineation of the domain in which the relationship applies.

There is no clear unequivocal definition of personality; nor is there any agreement about the fundamental dimensions of personality or their determinants (Furnham, 1988). Textbooks on personality theory provide a bewildering array of theories about personality and highlight quite different traits and types. Although these may loosely be classified into various categories such as psychoanalytic or trait, many differences exist between theories within each category. However, it would be misleading to assume that there is no agreement or that there is not a reasonable amount of overlap between differential theoretical traditions. Eysenck (1981) makes a persuasive argument for his three-dimensional structure to represent a paradigm in the field. Furthermore, whereas most personality theories are concerned with traits, some are interested in cognitive styles, attributional styles and behaviour patterns. Although it is infrequently stated as such, it does appear to be the case that investigators of cognitive style tend to stress cognitive as opposed to genetic/ biological variables and to believe in the essential modifiability of styles, whereas trait-theorists appear to see traits as relatively invariant and immutable. Also, there is no agreement as to what the major cognitive styles are or indeed the relationship between those investigated. However, what emerges seems to be the following. First, some personality traits seem much more obviously related to language and speech than others. For instance, the impulsivity and sociability associated with *extraversion*, one of the most fundamental of all personality dimensions, would seem to indicate that it is related to a number of linguistic and paralinguistic cues (Scherer, 1979). Second, the anxiety and obsessionality associated with *neuroticism* would appear to indicate that it is closely related to language and speech. On the other hand, there are some well-established individual difference traits like locus of control or conservatism which do not appear to be closely related to language or speech variables.

Linguists since Saussure (1916) have distinguished between *language (langue)*, the underlying system of shared grammatical and other rules, and *speech* (*parole*), which is concerned with how people actually talk. Whilst some researchers may believe there are personality correlates of language, most research has been aimed at speech. Over the years a large number of separate speech and language variables have been isolated, which include: bi/multilingualism, diglossia, elaborate/restricted code use, vocabulary, grammar/sentence construction, accent, speed, volume, pitch, discourse and dysfluency. Again, whilst some of these may seem to relate to specific personality traits or cognitive styles (such as paralinguistic and dysfluency cues), others may not (like multilingualism and code use).

Various 'theories' have been proposed to account for variations in speech. These include emphasizing the social groups to which speakers belong (Gudykunst, 1986; see Chapter 15, by Gudykunst and Ting-Toomey) and the social situation in which people communicate (Argyle, Furnham, and Graham, 1981). One might just as easily develop a theory concerned with personality determinants of speech from which certain empirically tested hypotheses may be derived. Consider for instance Table 4.1 adapted from Furnham (1986a). If indeed a speech-related theory of introversion–extraversion were derived, then this sort of pattern might emerge and would easily lead to testable hypotheses. In fact, as reviewers have shown, hypotheses very like those suggested in Table 4.1 have been tested.

It is suggested that extraverts differ from introverts on a number of speech and language dimensions: *form*, which refers to how formal is the language used; *code*, which refers to vocabulary size and grammatical construction; *grammar*, which refers to the type of words that a person chooses to use; *vocabulary* or lexicon, which refers to how many, how correct and how unusual are the words used; *accent*, which refers to regional and class-related ways of pronouncing words and phrases; *speed*, which refers quite obviously to the speed at which people talk; and *paralanguage*, which refers to dysfluencies like 'ums', 'errs', etc. What is being suggested in Table 4.1 is that, compared to extraverts, introverts generally use more formal speech with more careful grammatical constructions, perhaps a bigger vocabulary, etc. This is mere speculation based on a knowlege of the characteristics of introverts and extraverts, but may provide a useful model for hypothesis setting.

Some work along these lines has been conducted. Thorne (1987) placed introverts and extraverts in mixed and matched dyads and analysed their conversations. She

TABLE 4.1 Possible Speech Variations According to Personality Traits

Speech and language	Trait	
	Introvert	Extravert
Form	High	Low
Code	Elaborated	Restricted
Grammar	More nouns, adjectives, prepositions	More verbs, adverbs, pronouns
Vocabulary	Correct	Loose
Accent	Received	Local
Speed	Slow	Fast
Paralanguage	Few dysfluencies	Many dysfluencies

Adapted from Furnham (1986a).

found introverts with introverts engaged in focused problem talk, whereas extraverts with extraverts showed a wider range of topics and more claims of common ground. Introverted and extraverted dyads differed across numerous measures of conversational content and style. Although this study looked more at interactional and less at speech variables, there is good reason to support differences in the latter between extraverts and introverts.

RELATIONSHIP BETWEEN PERSONALITY AND SPEECH

The relationship between any two variables or factors can take many forms; it may be correlational or causal, and, if it is causal, different directions of causality are possible. Thus any of the following relationships between personality and speech/language could occur:*

(1) $P \neq S$ *(no relationship between personality and speech)*. This possibility would assume that there is no systematic relationship between any major personality factor and any dimension of speech. This may only appear to be so because the relationship which actually does exist is too subtle to be measured, too unstable, or is frequently 'washed out' or moderated by other more powerful and salient variables. However, it may be that there simply is no relationship at all.

(2) $P \rightarrow S$ *(personality 'determines' speech)*. This position assumes that some (but not all) personality traits determine in some sense various features of speech. People who adopt this position may well argue that different traits relate to, influence and determine different features of speech, or that some traits relate to all major speech features or that most traits relate to one particular speech feature. The crucial axiom of this position is that it is personality traits that 'causally' determine speech, along with perhaps other related variables (non-verbal behaviour)

(3) $S \rightarrow P$ *(speech 'determines' personality)*. This more unusual position assumes that personality traits are in some sense a function of speech variables (but see Chapter 1, by McCann and Higgins). In a sense the Whorfian hypothesis that language (through culture) shapes thought could be seen as a manifestation of this position in that speech shapes ways of thinking and behaving which become set in behaviourally replicable traits. Precisely how this occurs or which aspects of personality are shaped by which features of speech and language is not clear, but what does appear to be at the core of this position is that personality traits and cognitive style are primarily a function of language and speech variables.

(4) $P \leftrightarrow S$ *(personality and speech are reciprocally determined)*. This somewhat more realistic cybernetic view suggests both that personality is a function of speech *and* vice versa; that is, there is bidirectional causality between personality and speech. Of course this position allows for one direction of causality to be primary

* For speech, read speech *and* language.

and the other secondary so long as each have influence on the other. There may also be differences within the position as to which aspects of personality and which of speech are singled out for reciprocal determinism.

(5) $P_1 \leftrightarrow S_2$; $P_2 \rightarrow S_2$; $S_3 \rightarrow P_3$; $P_4 \approx S_4$ *(mixed relationships)*. Some theorists may argue that, as both personality and speech are multifaceted, it is possible that all the above four relationships occur *simultaneously*; that is, some personality variables reciprocally determine some speech variables; some personality variables unidirectionally determine some speech variables and vice versa; and finally some personality traits are not determined by, nor determine, speech and some speech variables are not determined by, nor determine, personality.

(6) $P \times S$ *(personality and speech are moderated by other variables)*. This approach suggests that both personality and speech are determined by another variable or group of variables. This moderator-variable approach can take many forms (see Figure 4.1) varying in the complexity of pathways and number of variables. Given the complexity of both speech *and* personality, it is hard to see how most theorists would opt for this 'path-analysis' moderator-variable approach. In a sense, this approach encapsulates all the other models as well. Though this well might be true, there is certainly no agreement on which are the salient personality, speech *or* moderator variables that are important, *or* on the precise causal links. Thus, while agreeing that the relationship is complex, multifaceted and multicausal, there are few explicit models of this process.

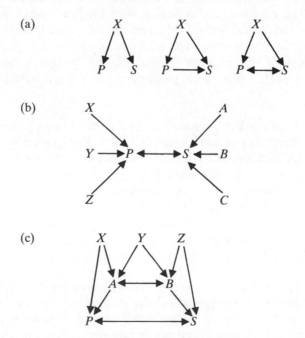

FIGURE 4.1   Different ways in which moderator variables (A, B, C, X, Y, Z) might determine personality (P) and speech (S).

A REVIEW OF REVIEWS

Despite the fragmented and relatively unprogrammatic literature in this field, a number of comprehensive and critical reviews have been published. A few of these will be considered in detail with particular emphasis on their conclusions.

Scherer (1979), one of the most important and active researchers in the field of personality markers in speech, executed an excellent review 10 years ago. This review has the advantage not only of being comprehensive but of examining research concerning non-English as well as English speakers. Furthermore it is critical but sympathetic to the problems of such research. The review is divided essentially into two parts: the first deals with studies concerned with the association between personality dispositions of speakers and objectively measured distal speech cues; and the second, studies concerned with the attributes of personality traits based on specific distal speech cues. In all, *four* aspects of speech are considered as they relate to personality:

(1) *Voice (frequency, intensity and quality)*. Higher fundamental frequency seems to be associated with competence and dominance in American and German speakers, as well as with discipline and dependability in American females and German males. The explanation for this phenomenon is given in terms of habitually elevated levels of arousal. There is some, albeit weak, indication that vocal intensity is associated with extraversion and emotional stability. Voice quality or timbre (resonant, metallic, strident versus muffled, mellow) seems to be determined by overall levels of muscle tension which are related to arousal dimensions of personality (i.e. extraversion) (Laver, 1975; Mallory and Miller, 1958).

(2) *Fluency*. There is some evidence, not all of which has been replicated, that pauses and speech rate are significantly related to extraversion (greater tempo, fewer pauses) and anxiety (the proportion of silences in highly anxious speakers is lower than in less anxious speakers). Similarly there is some research to suggest that speech discontinuities are related to anxiety, though the direction of causality is unclear (Siegman, 1978).

(3) *Morphology and syntax*. Despite the attractiveness of the commonsensical hypothesis that there is an association between linguistic style and personality, there are relatively few studies using a range of both variables. All sorts of formal characteristics (length of words, length and complexity of sentences, length of noun or verb phrases) have been considered to relate to cognitive-style variables but the results have been minimal. Further work relating the semantic function of self-reference to egocentricism has only met with limited success. Syntactical functions (abstract versus concrete nouns; verbs of action versus locomotion) have been related to personality dimensions such as need for achievement, authoritarianism and sociability, and some theoretically consistent but weak patterns of association have been found. Finally pragmatic functions (like evidence of silences, use of the proper pronoun) have been considered as they

relate to stable personality characteristics, but the results have yielded few significant results (Moerk, 1972).

(4) *Conversational behaviour*. Speech acts, turns and total verbal output have been related to a number of personality variables, but extraversion is the only trait which has consistently found to be associated with a greater amount of verbal output or longer total speaking time (Cope, 1969).

There appears to be more work on the inference of personality traits from speech style (see also Chapter 19, by Bradac). According to Scherer (1979) there have been four major techniques used to investigate this phenomenon:

(1) *Correlational*. Assessing relevant speech parameters and correlating them with personality attributions. This technique does not reveal which of the many cues available have been utilized by judges, or to what extent the cues measured correlate with other important cues that went unmeasured.

(2) *Masking*. Removing specific types of cues from speech samples so that specific features (high pitch, strong vocal effort) can be examined.

(3) *Manipulation*. Actors or performers systematically vary specific voice and speech parameters to provide better control.

(4) *Synthesis*. The development of synthetic speech samples conforming exactly to a desired pattern.

Scherer (1979) summarized the results of inference patterns of speech cues under the headings: *fundamental frequency*, high variability of which is seen as indicative of a dynamic, extraverted and outgoing personality – though results are somewhat inconsistent; *speech rate*, for which there is some evidence of a linear relationship with perceived competence, but of an inverted-U relationship with perceived benevolence; *other variables* such as length of utterances and participation rate for which no clear findings emerge.

Scherer (1979) concludes that there are two ways to assess the evidence for the existence of personality markers: check for studies in which accurate judgments of personality from speech style have been demonstrated and locate those studies demonstrating significant correlations between specific personality traits and specific speech cues. On both counts the reviewer is pessimistic, not only as regards the methodological quality of the existent work but also as regards the possibility of there being a clear link between personality and speech.

However, what Scherer (1979) is rightly most concerned with is the theoretical basis to this research:

> It is not sheer scientific curiosity which stimulates further inquiry into the origins, functions and mechanisms of personality marking. It has become painfully clear in the course of this review that most research done in this area has been carried out in the

spirit of dragnet fishing expeditions . . . In order to develop a theoretical framework and to generate hypotheses which could guide further research efforts, it seems necessary to speculate about the possible origins and mechanisms of personality marking in speech.

. . . Among the factors that could account for a lawful relationship between personality dispositions and speech are (i) biophysical or psychological factors, in which case the respective speech cues would be *concomitants* of these factors, and (ii) the functional efficiency of certain speech cues in producing certain interaction outcomes or attaining goals that serve important functions for the respective personality disposition, in which case it is the *effect* of the speech cues that explains the association. (Scherer, 1979, pp. 194–195)

Scherer (1979) is also interested in the nature (development structure) of the inference rules which people apply in attributing personality characteristics to speech variables. Further he argues:

Given the existence of strong stereotypical speech–personality inference rules, it is not impossible that the appropriate externalization will develop. This could happen either by speakers with the respective speech style developing the personality dispositions which are seen to correspond to it in the particular group or culture, or by speakers with the respective personality dispositions adapting the appropriate speech style. The former case we could call self-fulfilling prophesy, the latter self-presentation. (Scherer, 1979, p. 199)

A more recent review by Brown and Bradshaw (1985) extends Scherer's (1979) analysis. These authors attempt to summarize and classify the literature succinctly under these headings:

(1) *Accuracy*. Can judges identify personality type from voice?
(2) *Externalization*. What are the vocal concomitants of various personality types?
(3) *Attribution*. How will variations in specific vocal characteristics affect attributions of personality to the speaker?

Brown and Bradshaw (1985) argue that, whereas there are problems in the measurement of both speech and personality for the externalization issue (that is, how and which personality variables relate to which vocal features), these do not exist to the same extent for attribution studies. In their analysis, these authors put forward some highly debatable theories. For instance, they write:

In every review of accuracy research only one conclusive finding emerges: There is always astonishingly high inter-judge agreement despite the poor accuracy (in the sense of personality ratings agreeing with the standardized tests of the trait in question). . . . We propose . . . that the accuracy of personality judgments from voice has far more to do with the inadequacy of the personality measures used than the incompetency of judges to assess traits from vocal properties . . . Although personality identity seems to be a very stable thing, personality tests are notably unreliable with little agreement among alternate measures of the supposed same trait. (Brown and Bradshaw, 1985, pp. 153–154)

Psychometricians would have no truck with such a gross and inaccurate generalization. Though it may be true that some researchers have used personality measures of dubious validity and that the reliability of speech markers are usually higher, it is naive to blame the weak and equivocal findings exclusively on personality measurement. A glance at the manual of the Eysenck Personality Questionnaire (Eysenck and Eysenck, 1975) is sufficient proof of both the validity and reliability of the measure. Not all individual difference measures have been properly psycho-metrically assessed, and some show poor reliability. It behoves researchers in this field then to make judicious choices and not to blame personality measures for weak findings.

Brown and Bradshaw (1985), like Scherer (1979), report a number of one-off early externalization studies but seem most at home considering attribution studies. Indeed they report on a number of technologically sophisticated studies, using fast Fourier transforms and multifactorial statistics to show a map of what traits are attributed to which speech variable. These data are intriguing, but are not theory-driven. Perhaps it is time to attempt to develop a pan-cultural model of personality attribution from speech characteristics before seeking yet more sophisticated ways of experimentation. On the other hand methodological advancement in both person-ality *and* speech measurement provides much more powerful reasons to test extant theories, rather than develop new ones.

Reviews of the current literature are easier to group than to summarize. In general the research has been disappointingly atheoretical, unprogrammatic and, possibly as a result, highly equivocal. Finally, since it is social psychologists, rather than personality theorists, who have worked in this area, there has been much more research on the attribution of personality traits from specific speech patterns than on the actual personality correlates of speech.

THE LANGUAGE OF PERSONALITY DESCRIPTION

Hampson (1988) has argued that there are three overlapping but independent (in origin) perspectives on personality: the *explicit* psychological perspective of theor-ists; the implicit or *lay* perspective of ordinary people; and the *self*-perspective – our self-awareness of our own personality. The question remains as to whether the language for describing personality is different in these three domains. (See Chapter 2, by Winton, for a comparable concern about emotion.)

There is no doubt that the language of the explicit perspective of personality theorists is different from that of the average or typical lay person in describing their own or others' personalities. First, theoretical psychologists may use ordinary, everyday trait words like 'agreeableness' or 'culture' in a specific technical sense. Second, they may use trait words rarely used and only infrequently perfectly understood by the lay person, like 'psychoticism' or 'ego strength'. Third, to overcome the ambiguity of ordinary language and to encourage precision of descrip-tion, some personality theorists have actually invented personality terms like 'alexia', 'desurgency' and 'protension'.

More recently, based on the work of Rosch and Mervis (1975), there has been some interesting empirical work on the lexicography of lay personality language.

According to Rosch and Mervis, semantic categories are summary mental representations of similar objects. Many of these categories can be organized hierarchically, such that some categories (clothing, furniture) are more superordinate, inclusive or broad than others (shirt, chair). Members of a category at any level are referred to as instances, and instances are composed of attributes. Category membership is based on prototypicality. Instances may be more or less prototypical members of the category, depending on their proportions of shared attributes. It was demonstrated that for many categories of natural objects there is a preference of a basic level of categorization which falls between the superordinate and the subordinate levels. For example, when describing the object upon which you sit at your desk, you will probably call it a *chair* (basic level) rather than an item of furniture (superordinate level) or an office chair (subordinate level).

This model has been extended to traits by Hampson, John, and Goldberg (1986). In their approach, traits are viewed as categories for behaviours. Behaviours are characterized by attributes which include situational and motivational components as well as motor movements. Each trait category has an associated set of attributes, and behaviour is assigned to a category on the basis of its prototypicality with respect to these attributes. Traits are viewed as being hierarchically organized; broad, superordinate traits (extraverted) subsume narrow, subordinate traits describing the same aspect of personality (talkative).

Although it is intuitively reasonable to suppose that traits vary on a breadth dimension, establishing their relative breadth is thought to be an empirical question. Hampson *et al.* (1986) developed two converging measures of breadth based on subjects' judgments. Some of the broadest traits identified so far include active, competent, emotional, extraverted, irresponsible, sensitive and unpredictable; some of the narrowest traits are fault-finding, fidgety, jittery, miserly, overstudious, punctual, musical and wordy.

In addition, Hampson *et al.* (1986) have established that hierarchical class-inclusion relations are judged to exist between some traits differing in breadth. Using an asymmetry task to measure degree of class inclusion ('To be talkative is a way of being extraverted' is judged by most subjects as more meaningful than 'To be extraverted is a way of being talkative'), several hierarchies of traits describing the same aspect of personality at differing levels of breadth have been located. These hierarchies are composed of two levels (e.g. stable (broad)/calm (narrow)) or three levels (e.g. kind (broad)/generous (middle)/charitable (narrow)) and have been found for desirable and undesirable traits describing the five main areas of personality.

In this way researchers have done excellent and useful work on the language of personality. The same researchers (Hampson, Goldberg, and John, 1987) have recently looked at the category breadth and social desirability of 573 personality terms. For instance, traits considered desirable include affectionate, benevolent, cheerful and competent, while those thought undesirable include antagonistic, bad, bitter, cruel and dishonest.

This recent stress on the language of personality description is both interesting and useful. Indeed it has been argued that people's judgments about the personality of others (and no doubt themselves) are based more on the semantic and conceptual similarity between trait terms than the relationship between actual behaviours. Although this thesis (Shweder and D'Andrade, 1980) has been challenged (Romer and Revelle, 1984), there seems no doubt that actual language plays an important part in how we think about and describe personality. Indeed there is some evidence that different cultures taxonomize personality quite differently (Hampson, 1988). In other words a person's vocabulary may partly determine the way they think about their own and others' personality. In this sense there is some evidence of a neo-Whorfian hypothesis whereby lexicon determines thinking about personality.

Certainly attributional studies would be greatly enriched by a better understanding of many features (category breadth, social desirability, relatedness) of personality terms frequently attributed from speech.

PERSONALITY AND PREFERENCES FOR COMMUNICATION MEDIA

There is a fairly large empirical literature on differences in the communication process (for instance, the content and style of interactions) and outcome (the transmission of information, problem solving, persuasion and person perception) as a function of communication (Rutter, 1984; 1987; Short, Williams, and Christie 1976). For instance, Rutter, Stephenson, and Dewey (1981) found both the content and style of conversations differed as a function of the medium of communication. In their study they compared face-to-face interaction with audio-only communication and found fewer instances of simultaneous speech; a greater percentage of utterances ending as a question; a greater speech disturbance ratio (per 100 words); and fewer attention and acknowledgment signals. Clearly this has important implications for negotiating or counselling on the telephone.

Many people will acknowledge the advantages and disadvantages associated with various popular communication media. For instance, one may conceal one's age by using the telephone; it is probably easier but less effective to be assertive in a letter than face to face, etc. Given that different communicative media used frequently by ordinary people – telephone, telegram, letter, fax, face to face, television link-up – appear to lead to different communication styles, is it not plausible that personality differences may be reflected in the preferential choice of communication media? Just as there is a rich literature on person–job environment fit (Furnham and Schaeffer, 1984) which suggests that personality types are attracted to and satisfied by particular work environments, so might one not suspect that there is a personality–communication media fit such that people with certain personality dimensions are attracted to and would prefer, if given the choice, particular media?

Indeed Furnham (1982) has argued that, when people have specific messages, ideas or intentions to communicate to others, they usually choose to do so in social situations or through a specific media which will facilitate, rather than inhibit, the nature and intention of the message. For instance, people may prefer to use the telephone if they wish to disguise their age, or they may choose face-to-face interaction if they believe the other person is lying (see Chapter 12, by Friedman and Tucker). Thus the presumed effectiveness of messages is partly determined by an astute choice of the medium and/or context in which to deliver them. Certain social

situations of media, by virtue of their social rules and conventions, spatial arrangements, number of people present, quality or quantity of feedback, help to control
and regulate social interaction and hence communication. Some messages, particularly those concerned with assertiveness, which have subtle, emotional, persuasive or unpleasant features, may be far more effectively communicated through
media which prescribe or regulate certain types of behaviour relevant to the
communication.

Furnham (1986b) looked at the relationship between two personality variables –
assertiveness and fear of punishment – and preference for expressing messages
through different media. Subjects are required to indicate how much discomfort or
anxiety they experienced (or imagined experiencing) when delivering a series of
assertive messages through different media. Nearly all the subjects found the
communication of specific messages by letter the least difficult and face-to-face
interaction most difficult. However, although there were main effects for the
personality variables (the more assertive one is, the less difficulty one experiences
giving most messages through most media), there were no interactions suggesting
that, in this case, different personality types would choose different media through
which to communicate.

It is possible though that people may infer or attribute personality characteristics
to others, as a function of both their habitual or preferred choice of communication
medium *and* the way that medium reduces or accentuates verbal or non-verbal cues.
Thus, although the limited literature does not seem to support the assumption that
personality characteristics actually determine the preference for different everyday
means of communication, it may be that this is a fairly important feature in the
attribution of personality traits.

PSYCHOPATHOLOGY, LANGUAGE AND SPEECH

Even if one cannot be sure that personality in some way determines speech, can one
detect mental illness from language and speech? Do neurotics and/or psychotics have
characteristic speech or paralinguistic styles? Are everyday dysfluencies an indication of pathology like anxiety, or is it that state rather than trait-like aspects of
pathology can be detected by speech? Scherer (1979) has noted that most work in this
field has been done by psychologists mainly interested in diagnosis:

> It is regrettable that few researchers primarily interested in language have looked at the
> effects of psycho-pathological syndromes on speech. In many disciplines, the study of
> deviations, abnormalities and experimental destruction provides an important tool to
> discover the normal functions of the structures and processes under investigation. Since
> psychopathology often consists of mood and/or personality disorders, such researches
> would have thrown light on the role of 'personality and emotion in speaking behaviour'
> (Scherer, 1979, p. 234)

There is no doubt that both expert diagnostic and lay observations suggest that
certain 'mental illnesses' can be detected from speech. All psychiatric nomenclatures
have references to particular, specific and unusual speech patterns, voice qualities

and language usage. Indeed there are a number of psychologically recognized disturbances of verbal communication associated with the psychoses. These include:

Neologism: A newly made-up word having private meanings for the patient.
Echolalia: The repetition of words spoken by someone else.
Word salad: A jumble of apparently meaningless and unrelated words.

Lay people also recognize specific speech and linguistic features associated with mental states: depression is associated with slow, flat speech; anxiety is related to fast, dysfluent speech (Scherer, 1979). Not only trait but state features (i.e. drunkenness, anger) are frequently thought to manifest themselves in speech (Furnham, 1988).

Indeed there has been fairly extensive research on whether psychiatric disturbance can be detected from voice quality (Darby, 1985). Using both spectrographic analyses as well as more conventional content analysis of pitch, intensity and duration, there seems to be evidence that voice quality may be related to psychopathology but that vocal abnormalities are situation-specific and not stable over time or social contexts.

There is also a fairly extensive literature on the relationship between speech disturbances and anxiety. Speech disturbances include filled pause ('ums', 'ers') and 'non-ah' disturbances (omissions, repetitions, incompletions, stuttering). Whereas some studies have looked at trait anxiety, others have looked at experimentally induced state anxiety. The results from numerous studies (Cook, 1969; Scherer, 1979) seem to indicate that speech disturbance is affected by situational or transient anxiety, but the evidence on trait anxiety is far from unequivocal (Murray, 1971).

Temporal characteristics of speech have also been linked to trait and state psychopathology. These include speech rate, silences, number and length of utterances, and interruptions. As Rutter (1987) has noted, the main concern in this area has been anxiety, and the principal measures have been verbal productivity (time spent speaking and the number of words spoken) and speech rate. As with quality of voice, results have been rather equivocal, no doubt because studies have not been able to take into consideration other intervening and moderating variables. Although there is some evidence that anxiety raises verbal output and leads to more frequent and longer pauses, the self-presentational strategies and the perceived demands of listeners may be important moderator variables (Pope, Blass, Siegman, and Kaher, 1970).

The conclusion to draw from the literature in this field is twofold: first, that gross disturbance in speech or very unusual use of language is related to psychopathology and, second, that both state and trait anxiety may be detectable in certain speech features.

PERSONALITY TRAITS AND SPEECH VARIABLES

Various personality traits and, to a lesser extent, cognitive styles have been related to speech variables. For instance, Burleson (1985) recently investigated individual differences in the quality of the comforting strategies people produce; these ranged from the relatively insensitive and unresponsive to the highly empathic and sensitive. Three quite different 'recognized' traits will be considered in this section. A number of studies have considered extraversion, no doubt because it is a powerful and salient individual difference variable which relates to many forms of social behaviour. Two other individual difference variables, both correlated with extraversion, will also be considered, as they quite clearly relate to speech and are currently two of the most investigated of all individual difference concepts.

Extraversion

Although there is a comparative paucity of literature looking at the association between established personality traits and language/speech variables, a number of studies have looked at extraversion. This is no doubt partly due to the fact that the trait of extraversion seems fundamental to a number of personality typologies (Jung, Eysenck, etc.). Also it is comparatively easy to derive empirically testable and also common-sensical hypotheses from the prototypic descriptions of a typical extravert or introvert. Consider, for instance, the following description by Eysenck and Eysenck (1975):

> The typical extravert is sociable, likes parties, has many friends, needs to have people to talk to, and does not like reading or studying by himself. He craves excitement, takes chances, often sticks his neck out, acts on the spur of the moment, and is generally an impulsive individual. He is fond of practical jokes, always has a ready answer, and generally likes change; he is carefree, easy-going, optimistic, and likes to 'laugh and be merry'. He prefers to keep moving and doing things, tends to be aggressive and lose his temper quickly; altogether his feelings are not kept under tight control, and he is not always a reliable person.
>
> The typical introvert is a quiet, retiring sort of person, introspective, fond of books rather than people; he is reserved and distant except to intimate friends. He tends to plan ahead, 'looks before he leaps' and distrusts the impulse of the moment. He does not like excitement, takes matters of everyday life with proper seriousness, and likes a well-ordered mode of life. He keeps his feelings under close control, seldom behaves in an aggressive manner, and does not like losing his temper easily. He is reliable, somewhat pessimistic, and places great value on ethical standards. (Eysenck and Eysenck, 1975, p. 9)

It is quite simple given the above to derive hypotheses about extraversion such as:

(1) Extraverts will talk faster than introverts.
(2) Extraverts will have fewer unfilled pauses in their speech than introverts.
(3) Extraverts will have shorter response latencies than introverts.

As a consequence a number of research studies have been done on this topic, usually of a correlational nature. Essentially what they involve is measuring the extent of a person's introversion through questionnaires, then recording his or her (natural) speech in a specific social situation and correlating the two.

Studies using extraversion as the independent variable have been fairly numerous (Rutter, 1987). Siegman and Pope (1965), for example, found that extraversion was associated with shorter latencies, fewer brief filled pauses and fewer silent pauses, and Ramsay (1966, 1968) reported that silences between sound bursts were on average shorter for extraverts than introverts. American studies have indicated a positive association between verbal productivity and extraversion or related traits (Cope, 1969; Weinstein and Hanson, 1975), and British studies have reported the same (Campbell and Rushton, 1978; Carment, Miles, and Cervin, 1965; Patterson and Holmes, 1966; Rutter, Morley, and Graham, 1972). Extraversion has been shown to relate to measures of voice intensity and quality (Mallory and Miller, 1958). It has also been shown to relate to conversational behaviour, especially total verbal grammar output, fewer hesitations and longer pauses (Scherer, 1979).

Scherer (1979) has in fact noted that:

> . . . extraversion seems to be virtually the only personality trait which is likely to be definitely marked by special cues. However, while extraversion is one of the personality dispositions most important for social interaction and may be a prime candidate for marking, there are still possibilities for alternative explanations. Extraversion may easily stand out in terms of speech marking, since this trait has been studied much more frequently than any other personality trait. Consequently, further research using more personality traits and, it is hoped, more satisfactory assessment methods, may yet find that many more personality dispositions are marked in speech. (Scherer, 1979, p. 193)

Type A Behaviour

Since it was first isolated over 30 years ago as a behaviour pattern (but not as a personality trait or cognitive style) associated with coronary heart disease, there has been a plethora of studies on the Type A behaviour pattern.

Type A individuals are characterized as being highly competitive, frenetic, aggressive, achievement-oriented, ambitious, impatient and hard-driving (Price, 1983). Various research projects have also demonstrated that compared to Type B, Type A individuals are neurotic and anxious and extraverted (Friedman, Hall, and Harris, 1985). A central concern of all the research on this behaviour pattern is whether it is causally related to heart disease and attacks. The now extensive literature on this remains frustratingly equivocal. However, there is also an extensive extant literature on perceptual cognitive and attitudinal correlates of this behaviour pattern (Price, 1983).

There is some evidence that the speech style of Type A individuals is different from that of Type B. Type A individuals are thought to have a number of interesting speech behaviours: explosive conversational intonations, speech hurrying, accentuations in the ordinary rhythm of speech, as well as nascent vibrancy and aggressive timbre of voice. Essentially all observable speech and related motor characteristics have been said to be associated with, and to reflect, time-urgency (Price, 1983).

Indeed some of the diagnostic indicators of Type A behaviour relate quite clearly to speech patterns. These conclusions drawn from the empirical literature are taken from an original list published by Price (1983):

(1) The Type A individual interrupts with the answer when the interviewer, in

posing a question whose answer is already clear from context, hesitates, becomes laboriously tedious or repetitive, and then stammers.

(2) The Type A subject reports that, during conversation with others, he also thinks about other matters, rarely giving the other person his undivided attention.

(3) Type A subjects habitually substitute numerals for metaphors in speech.

(4) Type A subjects have an explosive, staccato, frequently unpleasant-sounding voice.

(5) Type A subjects exhibit irrationality and rage when asked about some past event in which they have become angered.

One may infer various other speech patterns from the characteristic irrational beliefs. These are set out below in Table 4.2. This has been adapted from Thurman (1984), whose primary concern was with helping people change their Type A behaviour.

There have been a number of other studies that have shown interesting and characteristic differences between Type A and B individuals. Scherwitz, Graham, Grandits, Buehler, and Billings (1989) examined self-involvement, defined as grammatical involvement of self in speech, through frequent use of the words 'I', 'me', 'my' and 'mine'. They argue that this definition assumes that egocentric, self-focused cognitive and emotional processes are reflected in speech. They tested the hypothesis that Type A individuals are more self-involved than Type B by counting all self-references spoken. By and large their results supported their hypothesis. This was in accordance with previous studies, which have shown that self-references are correlated with Type A behaviour, intensity of expressed anger and hostility, age, cigarette smoking and blood pressure reactivity. Clearly self-involvement is an important individual difference variable that is manifest in speech.

Studies that have concentrated on the non-verbal behaviour of Type A individuals have also tended to confirm such hypotheses. Hughes *et al.* (1983) demonstrated that, compared to Type B, Type A individuals tended to show greater activity, restlessness, exploratory behaviour and gestures, in everyday interaction. Hence these authors argued that the addition of non-verbal behaviours improves the discrimination of the Type A behaviour pattern obtained from the verbal behaviour alone. More recently Friedman *et al.* (1985) have identified two Type A and two Type B behaviour patterns. Type A individuals can either be healthy charismatics or hostile competitives, while Type B can be either relaxed, quiet persons or tense, overcontrolled inhibitors. Hence there are healthy and unhealthy Types A and B individuals, and this may be detected partly by their non-verbal expressive style. For instance, Friedman *et al.* (1985) found that unhealthy Type B individuals seemed nervous, inhibited and tense and, whereas their words sounded relatively most friendly, their tone of voice sounded relatively least friendly.

Certainly the *plethora* of studies on Type A behaviour relating a personality trait to health have shown the relevance of language and speech variables. Both the content and style of speech and accompanying non-verbal cues have consistently been shown to be related to the trait in a predictable manner (Price, 1983).

TABLE 4.2 Type A Irrational Beliefs and Rational Counter-challenges and Possible Speech Patterns Associated with Each

Type A irrational belief	Rational counter-challenge	Possible speech patterns
Quantity of output is more important than quality of output.	The quality of one's work is more related to success than the quantity of one's work.	Verbal speech
Faster is always better.	Many things need to be done slowly in order to be done well.	Very fast speech pattern
It is horrible when things are not done.	It is inconvenient when people or things are late, not the end of the world.	Constant references to deadlines
Winning or losing a competition is a reflection of one's worth as a person.	The outcome of a competition reflects relative performance, not relative human worth.	Competitive, comparative analogies used
One is only as good as one's accomplishments.	Worth as a human being is defined more by who one is than by what one does.	Constant references to accomplishments
Most events that slow one down are avoidable.	Situations that cause delay are an inescapable part of life.	
An endless string of accomplishments ensures that one will like oneself.	Numerous accomplishments are no guarantee that one will like oneself.	
Non-achievement-orientated activities are a waste of time.	Activities do not have to result in achievement to be worthwhile.	
One can have complete control over one's life if one just tries hard enough.	Total effort will not bring total control.	
Speeding up the pace of one's activities is the best way to keep or regain control.	Slowing down the pace of one's activities often helps regain a sense of control.	
Being perfectionistic is the best way to ensure high-quality achievements.	Setting challenging but reasonable goals helps promote high-quality achievements.	
Openly expressing anger and hostility makes other people pay for getting in my way.	When feeling angry and hostile, I'm the one who pays.	

Adapted from Thurman (1984).

Self-monitoring

There is a vast literature on personality and social psychology of self-presentation and impression management which is positively related to both extraversion and Type A behaviour (Furnham, 1989). There are both academic theories and 'lay theories' and observations about the way in which people change various aspects of their behaviour in order to create a particular impression. The 'telephone voice' – the modification of pitch, tone, accent and vocabulary – is a well-known attempt at impression management. Similarly the way in which people subtly and indirectly communicate approval or disapproval of one another by altering their speech so as to be more similar or different from one another can also be seen as a manifestation of self-management and impression formation (see Chapter 19, by Bradac).

Whilst there have been numerous attempts to relate self-variables like self-esteem, self-confidence and self-consciousness to aspects of speech, these self-variables have not been treated as traits. However, over the past 15 years, there has been an enormous interest in the 'trait' of *self-monitoring*, which is very clearly related to speech (Snyder, 1974, 1986). Whilst Snyder (1986) has argued that self-monitoring is a unique psychological construct, his critics have argued not only that the trait is multidimensional (Furnham and Capon, 1983; Lennox and Wolfe, 1984), but also that it is clearly correlated with both extraversion and neuroticism (Gabrenya and Arkin, 1980). Nevertheless there appear to be impressive reliability and validity data on the measure.

According to the theory, high self-monitors carefully regulate their expressive self-presentation to fit with what they perceive to be a desirable and appropriate behaviour pattern, and hence vary considerably as a function of situational constraints. Low self-monitors, on the other hand, do not or cannot regulate their self-presentation and are hence more stable in their expressive behaviours, which closely reflect their beliefs and feelings. These two characteristic interpersonal orientations differ in a number of the dynamics of social interaction. Pragmatic high self-monitors are highly flexible and adaptable, while principled low self-monitors tend to be more internally motivated and hence less adaptable. Thus the two types choose to inhabit and indeed create different social worlds and attribute different measures to friendship (Snyder, 1986).

Although neither Snyder (1986) nor other self-monitoring researchers have actually considered the relationship beween self-monitoring and language, one could make a number of predictions based on the original construct. For instance:

(1) High self-monitors would accommodate more to the language and speech styles of those they are with than low self-monitors.
(2) The language and speech of high self-monitors would be more varied than that of low self-monitors.
(3) High self-monitors would be more articulate and fluent than low self-monitors.
(4) Non-verbal and paralinguistic cues accompanying speech would be more appropriate, varied and synchronized in high self-monitors than they would in low self-monitors.
(5) High self-monitors would be better able to lie than low self-monitors.

Although both theoretically and empirically related to other personality variables like extraversion and neuroticism, it seems as if self-monitoring is a potentially very useful trait to relate to work on speech.

CONCLUSION

The extant literature on the relationship between personality/cognitive style and speech is unsatisfactory and frustrating for three basic reasons. First, there are no parsimonious, consistent, fruitful theories described specifically for, or derived from, the personality markers of speech. Where there is theoretical work, it appears to be derivative in the sense that theoretical hypotheses are derived from theories in the area of speech and personality. Furthermore the 'theories' that do exist are frequently at an inappropriate level – too molecular in that they deal specifically with the relationship between a restricted number of selected variables or too molar in the sense that by being overinclusive they are either unverifiable or unfruitful in the extent to which they generate testable hypotheses.

Second, the methodological problems in the area are considerable. It is not so much that research has been restricted to what Scherer (1979) called 'one-shot, single culture studies with small groups of college undergraduates in rigged "waiting-room" encounters' (p. 202). Rather the problem lies in the fact that there is a bewildering array of ways to measure *both* personality and speech, each of which has individual strengths and weaknesses and taps slightly different features of what the researchers are trying to measure. It is unfair either for social psychologists interested in language to blame personality measures, or for personality theorists to blame speech/language variables for the disappointing findings to date. Clearly the choice of measurement instrument or method needs to be both theoretically and empirically driven. Alas, scepticism about personality variables has frequently led social psychologists to be ignorant about the most useful criteria for choosing robust tests. Similarly general lack of interest in language may have handicapped personality theorists in their choice of variables.

Third, whilst few researchers would deny that anthropological (culture), sociological (class) and sociopsychological (appearance) variables affect a range of features (speech) as well as trait (personality) and state (emotional) individual differences, they rarely point out which of or how these factors interact. No personality theorist (it is hoped) would suggest that all variations in language and speech are determined by personality variables, and it would only be the most naive social psychologist who would argue that all the variance in language and speech may be accounted for by state or situational variables. The question remains, not *how much* of each variable (personality, situational) contributes to the resultant behaviour but *how* these variables interact. For this we still await a testable, parsimonious and robust theoretical model.

As numerous reviewers have pointed out, for research and theorizing to develop more fully in the area of personality/individual differences in speech and communication, a multidisciplinary approach needs to be undertaken using multiple variables (Delia, 1983; Fillmore, Kempler, and Wang, 1979).

REFERENCES

Argyle, M., Furnham, A., and Graham, J. (1981). *Social situations*. Cambridge: Cambridge University Press.

Brown, B. and Bradshaw, J. (1985). Towards a social psychology of voice variations. In H. Giles and R. St Clair (Eds), *Recent advances in language, communication and social psychology*. London: Erlbaum.

Burleson, R. (1985). The production of comforting messages: Social-cognitive foundations. *Journal of Language and Social Psychology*, **4**, 253–273.

Campbell, A. and Rushton, J. (1978). Bodily communication and personality. *British Journal of Social and Clinical Psychology*, **17**, 31–36.

Carment, D., Miles, C., and Cervin, V. (1965). Persuasiveness and persuasibility as related to intelligence and extraversion. *British Journal of Social and Clinical Psychology*, **4**, 1–7.

Cook, M. (1969). Anxiety, speech disturbances and speech rate. *British Journal of Social and Clinical Psychology*, **8**, 13–21.

Cope, C. (1969). Linguistic structure and personality development. *Journal of Counselling Psychology*, **16**, 1–19.

Darby, J. (Ed.) (1985). *Speech and language evaluation in neurology: Adult disorders*. New York: Grune and Stratton.

Delia, J. (1983). Social psychology, competency and individual differences in communication action. *Journal of Language and Social Psychology*, **2**, 207–218.

Eysenck, H. (1981). *A model for personality*. New York: Springer.

Eysenck, H. and Eysenck, S. (1975). *Eysenck Personality Questionnaire*. London: Hodder and Stoughton.

Fillmore, C., Kempler, D., and Wang, W. (1979). *Individual differences in language ability and language behavior*. New York: Academic Press.

Friedman, H., Hall, J., and Harris, M. (1985). Type A behaviour, non-verbal expressive style, and health. *Journal of Personality and Social Psychology*, **48**, 1299–1315.

Furnham, A. (1982). The message, the context and the medium. *Language and Communication*, **2**, 33–47.

Furnham, A. (1986a). Situational determinants of intergroup communication. In W. Gudykunst (Ed.), *Intergroup communication*. London: Edward Arnold.

Furnham, A. (1986b). Assertiveness through different media. *Journal of Language and Social Psychology*, **5**, 10–11.

Furnham, A. (1988). *Lay theories: Everyday understandings of problems in the social sciences*. Oxford: Pergamon.

Furnham, A. (1989). Personality correlates of self-monitoring. *Personality and Individual Differences*, **10**, 35–42.

Furnham, A. and Argyle, M. (Eds) (1981). *The psychology of social situations*. Oxford: Pergamon.

Furnham, A. and Capon, M. (1983). Social skills and self-monitoring processes. *Personality and Individual Differences*, **4**, 171–178.

Furnham, A. and Schaeffer, R. (1984). Person–environment fit, job satisfaction and mental health. *Journal of Occupational Psychology*, **57**, 295–307.

Gabrenya, W. and Arkin, R. (1980). Factor structure and factor correlates of the Self-Monitoring Scale. *Personality and Social Psychology Bulletin*, **6**, 13–22.

Gudykunst, W. (1986). *Intergroup communication*. London: Edward Arnold.

Hampson, S. (1988). *The construction of personality: An introduction*, 2nd edn. London: Routledge.

Hampson, S., Goldberg, L., and John, O. (1987). Category-breadth and social-desirability values for 573 personality terms. *European Journal of Personality*, **1**, 241–258.

Hampson, S., John, O., and Goldberg, L. (1986). Category breadth and hierarchical structure in personality: Studies of asymmetries in judgements of trait implications. *Journal of Personality and Social Psychology*, **26**, 140–154.

Hughes, J., Jacobs, D., Schuker, B., Chapman, D., Murray, D., and Johnson, C. (1983). Nonverbal behaviour of the type A individual. *Journal of Behavioural Medicine*, **6**, 279–289.

Laver, J. (1975). Individual features in voice quality. PhD Thesis, University of Edinburgh.

Lennox, R. and Wolfe, R. (1984). Revision of Self-Monitoring Scale. *Journal of Personality and Social Psychology*, **46**, 1349–1364.

Mallory, P. and Miller, V. (1958). A possible basis for the association of voice characteristics and personality traits. *Speech Monograph*, **25**, 255–260.

Moerk, E. (1972). Factors of style and personality. *Journal of Psycholinguistic Research*, **1**, 257–265.

Murray, D. (1971). Talk, silence, and anxiety. *Psychological Bulletin*, **75**, 244–260.

Patterson, M. and Holmes, D. (1966). Social interaction correlates of the MMPI extraversion–introversional scale. *American Psychologist*, **21**, 724–725.

Pope, B., Blass, J., Siegman, A., and Kaher, J. (1970). Anxiety and depression in speech. *Journal of Consulting and Clinical Psychology*, **35**, 128–133.

Price, V. (1983). *Type A behaviour pattern*. London: Academic Press.

Ramsay, R. (1966). Personality and speech. *Journal of Personality and Social Psychology*, **4**, 116–118.

Ramsay, R. (1968). Speech patterns and personality. *Language and Speech*, **11**, 54–63.

Romer, D. and Revelle, W. (1984). Personality traits: Fact or fiction. *Journal of Personality and Social Psychology*, **47**, 1028–1042.

Rosch, E. and Mervis, C. (1975). Family resemblances; Studies in the internal structure of categories. *Cognitive Psychology*, **7**, 573–605.

Rutter, D. (1984). *Looking and seeing: The role of visual communication in social interaction*. Chichester: Wiley.

Rutter, D. (1987). *Communicating by telephone*. Oxford: Pergamon.

Rutter, D., Morley, J., and Graham, J. (1972). Visual interaction in a group of introverts or extraverts. *European Journal of Social Psychology*, **2**, 371–384.

Rutter, D., Stephenson, G., and Dewey, M. (1981). Visual communication and the content and style of conversation. *British Journal of Psychology*, **20**, 41–52.

Saussure, F. de (1916). *Cours de linguistique générale*. Paris: Payot.

Scherer, K. (1979). Personality markers in speech. In K. Scherer and H. Giles (Eds), *Social markers in speech*. Cambridge: Cambridge University Press.

Scherwitz, L., Graham, L., Grandits, G., Buehler, J., and Billings, J. (1986). Self-involvements and coronary heart disease incidence in the multiple risk factor intervention trial. *Psychosomatic Medicine*, **48**, 187–199.

Short, J., Williams, E., and Christie, B. (1976). *The social psychology of telecommunications*. London: Wiley.

Shweder, R. and D'Andrade, R. (1980). The systematic distortion hypothesis. In R. Shweder (Ed.), *Fallible judgement in behavioral research*. San Francisco: Jossey-Bass.

Siegman, A. (1978). The tell-tale voice: Non-verbal messages of verbal communication. In A. Siegman and S. Feldstein (Eds), *Nonverbal behaviour and communication*. Hillsdale, NJ: Erlbaum.

Siegman, A. and Pope, B. (1965). Personality variables associated with productivity and verbal fluency in the initial interview. In B. Compton (Ed.), *Proceedings of the 73rd Annual Conference of the APA*. Washington: APA.

Snyder, M. (1974). The self-monitoring of expressive behaviour. *Journal of Personality and Social Psychology*, **30**, 526–537.

Snyder, M. (1986). *Public appearances, private realities: The psychology of self-monitoring.* New York: Freeman.

Thorne, A. (1987). The press of personality: A study of conversation between introverts and extraverts. *Journal of Personality and Social Psychology*, **53**, 718–726.

Thurman, C. (1984). Cognitive–behavioural interventions with Type A faculty. *Personnel and Guidance Journal*, **3**, 358–362.

Weinstein, M. and Hanson, R. (1975). Personality trait correlates of verbal interaction levels in an encounter group context. *Canadian Journal of Behavioural Science*, **7**, 192–200.

Section 2

Channels and Their Analysis

Introduction to Section 2

The study of non-verbal components of communicative behaviour is one of the success stories in social psychology and perhaps helps to show the likely direction in which other research fields may find it desirable to go. Whether we are studying actions or reactions, we no longer conceptualize the problems in terms of single variables operating on each other.

Patterson demonstrates the need for a comprehensive approach to non-verbal behaviour. We need a typology of functions and of cues. We need to be aware that even a single act will involve an array of cues, each of which may be operating multifunctionally. Fortunately, we now have enough observations from natural and experimental situations to permit us to work with this complexity.

Likewise, prosody and paralanguage can be securely set into a strong literature. Like Patterson, Street shows how the earlier analytic 'slicing' of the communicative stream of information has given way to attempts to resynthesize the slices into the whole. The qualities of the pattern become the basis for inference of meaning and significance.

The task of Cappella and Palmer is to go one step further and integrate the verbal and non-verbal, and this they do. They test models of ways of combining variables against criteria of meaningful patterning. They show that aggregation which incorporates temporal covariation is far superior to distributional covariation as a device for exposing patterns. Such achievements have of course required the development of multichannel recording equipment and of computer programs capable of the number crunching necessary for the appropriate calculations. Just 20 years ago the technology would not have allowed Cappella and Palmer to have tested their ideas.

At present it is the known number of variables and the range of values they can take that sets drastic limits to what is experimentally feasible. In the next 20 years it may be that the theoretical models too will have become very complicated. That is particularly likely with discourse analysis. Whether we focus on conversations or monologues, both the analysis and synthesis are daunting. For monologue we have

Handbook of Language and Social Psychology
Edited by H. Giles and W.P. Robinson.   © 1990 John Wiley & Sons Ltd

yet to improve upon the rules of Aristotle and Cicero. The semantics of conversational analysis remain at the stage of apt illustration. In his chapter van Dijk selects
particular themes, more to show the potential value of the approach than to reveal its
achievements. He establishes a theoretical framework on which work may proceed.
The representation of ethnic prejudice in natural talk and writing necessarily has
ecological validity in a way in which ticks on checklists of adjectives for particular
ethnic groups cannot. Van Dijk lays down the challenge that methods of investigation ultimately have to yield results which predict and explain what people actually
say and write. We shall not be short of hard work to do in the immediate or distant
future.

5

Functions of Non-Verbal Behavior in Social Interaction

MILES L. PATTERSON

Department of Psychology, University of Missouri-St Louis, USA

The primary purpose of this chapter is to provide a representative review of the role of non-verbal behavior in social interaction. The discussion will be organized around a classification of the social functions of non-verbal behavior. The paralinguistic and prosodic functions of speech will not be covered in this chapter because they are considered in detail in Chapter 6. To facilitate an understanding of the functional perspective, it is useful to consider the context in which this approach developed. Consequently, I will start with a brief overview of the empirical and theoretical work that preceded the functional model of non-verbal exchange.

EARLY TRENDS

Before 1960, there were relatively few studies on non-verbal behavior in interaction. Sommer's (1959, 1961, 1962, 1965) work on 'personal space' marked a turning point in the development of empirical research on non-verbal behavior. Around the same time, Exline and his colleagues (Exline, 1963; Exline, Gray, and Schuette, 1965; Exline and Winters, 1965) began studying patterns of gaze in interaction. The investigation of individual behaviors in isolation, or the 'channel' approach, was characteristic of much of the early research on non-verbal behavior. There were others, however, who emphasized the importance of studying multivariate constructs such as 'proxemics' (Hall, 1963, 1966), 'intimacy' (Argyle and Dean, 1965),

Handbook of Language and Social Psychology
Edited by H. Giles and W.P. Robinson. © 1990 John Wiley & Sons Ltd

and 'immediacy' (Mehrabian, 1969). Although these constructs differed somewhat from one another, they all emphasized *patterns* of behavior across different channels and not a single channel at a time.

The first important theoretical model was built upon the construct of interpersonal intimacy (Argyle and Dean, 1965). In their model, Argyle and Dean (1965) proposed that, in any interaction, interpersonal intimacy was behaviorally manifested in the distance, gaze, smiling, and verbal intimacy shared between the interactants. If the overall behavioral intimacy were too discrepant from an appropriate or comfortable level for the partners, it was predicted that adjustments in one or more of the component behaviors would help to compensate for the inappropriate intimacy. Thus, a too close approach by one person might lead to a decrease in gaze and smiling by the partner.

Although much of the early research supported equilibrium theory (see Cappella, 1981; Patterson, 1973), there was an important deficiency in the theory. Specifically, equilibrium theory could not explain instances in which people matched or reciprocated their partner's behavior. For example, sometimes a close approach or increased gaze leads to an increase, not a decrease, in the partner's level of non-verbal involvement. This particular shortcoming stimulated the development of several different explanations for both compensatory and reciprocal patterns (Andersen and Andersen, 1984; Burgoon, 1978; Cappella and Greene, 1982; Patterson, 1976).

These different theoretical approaches shared two important characteristics. First, they all assumed that there was a consistency between the affective reactions and the behavior of an individual. In general, compensatory behaviors were judged to be the product of negative affect and/or less favorable impressions of one's partner, whereas reciprocated behaviors were judged to be the product of positive affect and/or more favorable impressions of one's partner. Second, all of these models were reactive in nature; that is, a person's behavior at a given point in time was assumed to be the product of the partner's preceding behavior.

These two characteristics reflect, I think, distinct limitations in the explanatory power of these models. First, not all interactive behavior is consistent with the actor's underlying affect (e.g. Bond, 1972; Ickes, Patterson, Rajecki, and Tanford, 1982). For example, the independence of behavior and affect may be seen in a deceptive exchange, such as smiling and trying to be friendly to someone you dislike. Second, because these various models were reactive in nature, they ignored those instances in which an actor's behavior is guided by goals or motives that are, at least, partially independent of the partner's behavior. Furthermore, some interactive exchanges, such as greetings or farewells, involve mutually coordinated patterns of behavior. In such instances, the interactants are simultaneously responding to a common script (Abelson, 1981) and not just reacting to each other.

The functional model of non-verbal exchange (Patterson, 1982, 1983) was an attempt to resolve these limitations. In contrast to the affect-based models, this approach posited that an individual's naive perception of the function or purpose of the interaction was sometimes a more important determinant of the exchange than was affect.

A FUNCTIONAL MODEL

I will not attempt to discuss the model in detail, but such information may be found elsewhere (Patterson, 1982, 1983). Instead, a brief overview of the model will be presented here. The model proposes that different influences combine to determine the initiation and development of an interaction. The relationships among the various determinants are shown in Figure 5.1. First, the basic determinants are the genetic and environmental factors. Each person's genetic make-up reflects some characteristics that are representative of the species in general and others that are unique to the individual. The environment exerts some direct influence, but it also helps to shape the gene pool through the process of natural selection.

These basic determinants exert their influence on the remote antecedents of culture, gender, and personality. The remote antecedents, in turn, directly affect a person's habitual behavioral style (behavioral predispositions), arousal, and expectancies regarding the interaction (cognitive–affective reactions). Culture, gender, and personality also influence the choice of situations and relationships. The nature of the situation and the relationship between the interactants also affect the course of the pre-interaction mediators.

In general, to the extent that the pre-interaction mediators lead to similar preferences for non-verbal involvement and to complementary perceptions of the function of the interaction, the exchange between partners will tend to be smooth and stable. Instability in the interaction will lead to arousal and an assessment of the interaction. These changes will precipitate an adjustment in the level of involvement and/or a change in the perceived function of the interaction. If these adjustments and reassessments are successful, the interaction will stabilize. If not, the interaction will recycle through another adjustment phase until either stability is achieved or the interaction is terminated.

The specific patterns of non-verbal involvement and their role in the interaction are very much a product of the functions activated in a particular exchange. The remainder of this chapter will focus on a discussion of different functions of non-verbal behavior and the particular ways in which they are manifested in interaction.

FUNCTIONS OF NON-VERBAL BEHAVIOR

In analyzing the functions of non-verbal behavior, I will be looking across individual channels (e.g. distance, visual behavior, touch, facial expression) to identify the common purposes served by different patterns of non-verbal behavior. A basic assumption of this functional approach is that different patterns of behavior may serve the same function and, in turn, the same pattern of behavior (on different occasions) may serve different functions. A common 'metric' considered across various studies is the degree of involvement reflected in specific behavior patterns. Conceptually, like the constructs of intimacy (Argyle and Dean, 1965), immediacy (Mehrabian, 1969), and proxemics (Hall, 1968), involvement describes the cumulative behavioral 'closeness' between individuals in an interaction (Patterson, 1982). Operationally, the involvement construct includes behaviors not subsumed under

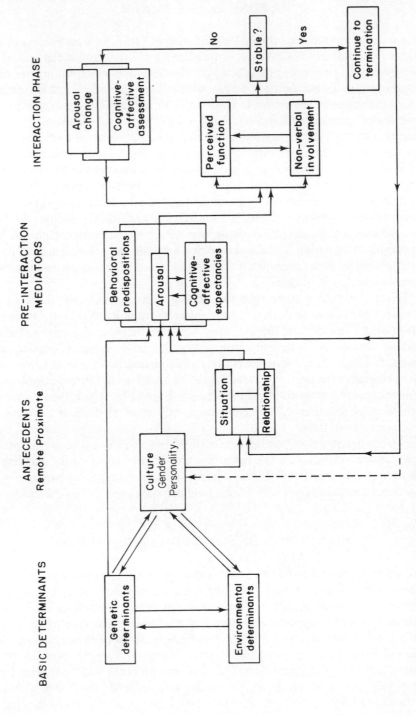

FIGURE 5.1   The functional model of non-verbal exchange.

the other constructs, e.g. facial expressiveness, postural openness, head nods, and paralinguistic cues. This focus on functions, looking across behaviors, should provide a better understanding of the complexity of interactive behavior than is possible with a serial treatment of each channel in isolation.

The description and analysis of non-verbal behavior in terms of its functions is not a new endeavor. A number of different classifications has been offered in the past (e.g. Argyle, 1972; Ekman and Friesen, 1969; Harrison, 1973). Across these classifications, three basic functions emerge: (a) providing information; (b) regulating interaction; and (c) expressing intimacy. From the perspective of the decoder or receiver, all of the encoder's behavior is potentially informative. Of course, at any given point in time, only a fraction of the encoder's behavior may be noticed and evaluated. The function of regulating interaction refers primarily to the role of non-verbal behaviors in facilitating the give-and-take in interactions. Expressing intimacy refers to the spontaneous expression of interpersonal affect (positive and negative) in a person's non-verbal behavior. For example, a closer approach, increased gaze, and smiling might reflect liking toward another person. Conversely, remaining distant, avoiding gaze, and not smiling might reflect disliking toward a different person.

In addition to the three functions identified by previous researchers, four additional categories are proposed, including: (a) social control; (b) presenting identities and images; (c) affect management; and (d) facilitating service and task goals (Patterson, 1982, 1987). Social control involves the deliberate use of non-verbal behavior to influence the interaction partner. For example, one might gaze and smile more at a person from whom a favor is requested. Next, the presentational function describes the purposeful use of non-verbal behavior to create an identity or image for observers. Like the social control behavior, presentational behavior is managed for a purpose but, in this case, the target is the group of observers, not the interaction partner. The next category is termed 'affect management' because adjustments in interactive behavior help to regulate or modify the experience of affect and its consequences. For example, strong negative reactions such as embarrassment, shame, or social anxiety may lead to increased avoidance of others and decreased gaze. The final category, the service–task function, describes the influence of service and task constraints on non-verbal behavior. For example, service relationships such as those between a physician and patient or a dentist and patient are professional exchanges that require a high level of involvement, typically tactile in nature.

The remainder of the chapter discusses the research representative of each of these functions. There is a considerable amount of empirical research on the first four functions, but relatively little on the last three. Consequently, the discussion of the last three functions is more speculative than that on the first four. In any case, the chapter should provide a useful overview of the important and diverse roles served by non-verbal behavior in social interactions.

Providing Information

It is obvious that an individual's non-verbal behavior has informational value to observers. Much of the research on non-verbal behavior relates, in some fashion, the behavior of the actors to the impressions of interaction partners or other observers. Because this is such an extensive area of research, only a few general highlights will be presented here. The informational utility of non-verbal behavior is discussed at length in books by Ekman and Friesen (1975), Kleinke (1986), and Mehrabian (1981) and in edited volumes by Siegman and Feldstein (1985, 1987).

First, facial expressions provide a great deal of information about an individual's emotional state. Research by Ekman indicates that posed expressions of happiness, anger, fear, disgust, sadness, and combined fear/surprise seem to be universally encoded and decoded (Ekman, 1972, 1973; Ekman *et al.*, 1987). When spontaneous expressions of emotion are used, the accuracy of identifying particular emotions decreases, but does remain above chance levels (Wagner, MacDonald, and Manstead, 1986). Vocal cues of speech, such as pitch, loudness, rate, and other qualities, also permit above-chance accuracy in identifying emotion (Frick, 1985). Decoding accuracy is generally higher for combined audiovisual or visual-only channels than it is for the audio channel alone, but this difference is affected by the type of emotion and by the individual expressive styles of encoders (Scherer, 1986; Wallbott and Scherer, 1986).

A few generalizations may be offered concerning the role of involvement behaviors such as distance, gaze, and touch. Usually, people are judged more favorably as they initiate higher levels of involvement (i.e. closer approaches, more gaze, and possibly touch) up to the point where such involvement is seen as inappropriate (see Andersen, 1985; Kleinke, 1986; Patterson and Edinger, 1987; Thayer, 1986, for reviews of some of this research). This upper limit, reflected in an individual's expectancies about the partner, will vary depending on factors such as culture, gender, personality, and the relationship between the interactants (see Figure 5.1).

In the instances described so far, the informational value of the behavior relates to the decoding process; that is, different behaviors by an actor can lead to different inferences being made about the meaning of the behaviors. Very little research relates the informational function to the encoding process, but some basic suggestions might be offered. Specifically, Hall (1966, 1968) has proposed that the selection of different distances in interaction facilitates the gathering of different kinds of sensory information. For example, in order to gain tactile and olfactory information about another person, one must stand very close. In contrast, visual input may be received at considerably greater distances. Hall has even proposed that cultural differences in preferred interaction distances are a product of different cultures emphasizing different kinds of sensory input. For example, Hall (1966) suggested that Latin Americans and Southern Mediterranean people interact more closely than do the English and Northern Europeans because the former groups emphasize tactile and olfactory information and the latter groups emphasize visual information.

There is another sense in which non-verbal behavior may serve an informational function for the actor or encoder. Specifically, the actor's own behavior may help to inform him or her about personal feelings or reactions. Facial feedback theory proposes that the feedback provided by facial muscle activity is critical in determining the experience of specific emotional states (Tomkins, 1982). In a similar fashion, self-perception theory (Bem, 1967, 1972) states that actors use their own behavior to make attributions about feelings or attitudes; that is, in cases where individuals might not easily know how they feel about a person, they look to their own behavior as an indicator of those feelings or judgments. For example, John might use the knowledge that he gazed and smiled a great deal at Mary to infer that he likes her.

In summary, from the observer's perspective, non-verbal behavior can provide important information about an actor, including the person's emotional reactions, interpersonal affect, and personality characteristics. The actor's own behavior may also be self-informative regarding personal affective and cognitive states.

Regulating Interaction

Interaction regulation refers to the role of non-verbal behavior in facilitating smooth, orderly interactions. First, the arrangement of individuals in an interaction (e.g. distance and orientation) sets some limits on what is possible in a conversational exchange (Ciolek and Kendon, 1980; Kendon, 1976, 1977). To understand the flow of interaction reflected in turn-taking, however, we have to look to other more dynamic behaviors. There is an extensive literature on turn-taking and a number of excellent reviews (Cappella, 1985; Duncan and Fiske, 1977; Feldstein and Welkowitz, 1987; Wiemann, 1985) may be consulted for details that are beyond the scope of this chapter.

Nevertheless, several general patterns may be identified. First, there are regularities that may be seen in the behaviors of speakers and listeners. Speaker movement, including hand and arm movements and postural adjustments, seems to be concentrated around the junctures of phonemic clauses, i.e. segments of speech from one to several syllables in length that seem to be spoken as a unit (Boomer, 1978; Boomer and Dittmann, 1962). The scope or range of movement may also be related to the size of the spoken segment; that is, smaller, briefer movements may be related to smaller speech segments, whereas larger postural shifts may mark changes in content or topic (Scheflen, 1964; Thomas and Bull, 1981). In general, speakers gaze less at listeners than listeners do at speakers, but listener-directed gaze may decrease even more when there are hesitations and non-fluent speech, and when judgmental evaluations are taking place (Allen and Guy, 1977; Kendon, 1967).

Listener movement, like speaker movement, seems to be related to the structure of speech. In particular, listeners are most likely to indicate agreement with speakers by verbal comments (e.g. 'mm-hmm') and head nods between phonemic clauses than at other points in speech (Dittmann and Llewellyn, 1967, 1968).

As the speaker and listener are about to switch roles, distinct patterns emerge in the behaviors of each person. Duncan (1972) identified several cues that signal a speaker's readiness to yield a turn, including the following:

(1) a change in pitch in the last word in a phonemic clause;
(2) a drawl or stretching out of the last word or syllable in a phomenic clause;
(3) cessation of gestures;
(4) sociocentric sequences such as 'you know';
(5) a decrease in pitch or loudness at the end of sociocentric sequences;
(6) the completion of a grammatical clause.

There is also some evidence that, as speakers are about to end their turn, they gaze more at the listener than they do at other points in their turn (Harrigan and Steffen, 1983; Kendon, 1967). Although the changing pattern of gaze can serve as a turn-yielding signal to the listener, it also provides the speaker with an opportunity to assess the listener's reaction to the completed comments.

As listeners make the transition to speakers in the turn-taking process, the following behaviors are likely to be initiated (Duncan and Niederehe, 1974):

(1) a shift of the head away from the speaker;
(2) an audible inhalation;
(3) the initiation of a gesture;
(4) overloudness in the first segments of speech.

More recently, other researchers have found additional support for increased gesturing (Harrigan, 1985) and head movements (Hadar, Steiner, Grant, and Rose, 1984) as speakers initiate a turn.

The patterns discussed here suggest that there are substantial regularities in the way speakers and listeners behave in the course of an interaction. It is clear that the behavioral patterns described here are correlated with speaker and listener roles and with the turn-taking process. It is quite another thing to claim that those behaviors alone are responsible for the regulation of interaction. Nevertheless, from the functional perspective, it is still useful to appreciate that some minimal level of involvement, represented in speaker and listener cues, is related to efficient give-and-take in interaction (Duncan and Fiske, 1977; Kendon, 1967).

Expressing Intimacy

A third function of non-verbal involvement is that of expressing intimacy. Since the time of Argyle and Dean's (1965) theory, the concept of intimacy has been central in the analysis of non-verbal behavior in social interactions. Intimacy may be described as a bipolar dimension that reflects the degree of union with or openness toward another person. Practically, intimacy is represented in an affective attachment toward a person. In general, it is assumed that the strength and valence of the intimacy felt towards a partner is spontaneously reflected in the actor's non-verbal behavior. Of course, this is qualified by the social norms operating in different settings.

Numerous studies show that, as the relationships between individuals becomes more intimate, the level of non-verbal involvement increases. Most of this research examines behavioral differences as a function of relationship intimacy in hetero-sexual pairs. Typically, in closer relationships, interpersonal distances become smaller (Aiello and Cooper, 1972; Heshka and Nelson, 1972; Willis, 1966); touch increases in frequency and/or intimacy (Greenbaum and Rosenfeld, 1980; Heslin and Boss, 1980; Jones and Yarbrough, 1985; Jourard, 1966; Rosenfeld, Kartus, and Ray, 1976); and mutual gaze increases (Goldstein, Kilroy, and Van de Voort, 1976; Rubin, 1970). An important moderating variable in the patterns described here is the sex composition of interacting pairs. In comparably intimate same-sex relationships, males typically initiate lower levels of involvement than do females (e.g. Foot, Chapman, and Smith, 1977; Greenbaum and Rosenfeld, 1980; Heshka and Nelson, 1972; Heslin and Boss, 1980).

The existing research indicates that intimacy is one important factor in interactive behavior, but when is the intimacy function most likely to be seen? The likelihood that non-verbal involvement will reflect the intimacy function is greater under the following three conditions (Patterson, 1983):

(1) when there is a strong and clear affective reaction to one's partner;
(2) when the particular form or level of non-verbal involvement is socially appropriate in that situation;
(3) when task constraints and goals of interpersonal influence are not salient in the interaction.

Of course, in many situations, a person's non-verbal behavior is not the spontaneous consequence of affect towards the partner. Instead, behavior is more deliberate and managed, guided by a motive of trying to influence the partner.

Social Control

The social control function involves the purposeful or goal-directed use of non-verbal behavior to influence an interaction partner. An individual may sometimes be aware of initiating a particular behavior pattern to influence another person (e.g. I'll have to be sure to smile and look impressed at his inane comments). More commonly, I suspect, there is some awareness of the motive (e.g. I want to be hired for this job; I want to make a sale to this customer), but little or no awareness of the specific behaviors initiated. In the latter case, the behavior patterns may simply be scripted routines (e.g. Abelson, 1981) activated by the goals of 'making a good impression' or 'making a sale'. Social control may be manifested in several different interpersonal processes including: (a) status and power; (b) persuasion and compliance; and (c) impression management. Deception is also a manifestation of social control, but deception will be thoroughly covered in Chapter 12, by Friedman and Tucker.

Status and power

Status and power are terms that are relevant to the vertical structure of social relationships (Schlenker, 1980). Status refers to one's position in a social hierarchy, whereas power refers to the consequence or benefit of having high status. Most of the research on status, power, and non-verbal behavior focuses either on the perceptions of power or status that are inferred from different patterns of non-verbal behavior or on the non-verbal correlates of differential status. The former approach involves a decoding methodology; the latter involves an encoding methodology.

From the decoding studies, it appears that those who initiate higher levels of involvement with a partner are judged as having higher status or greater power. For example, individuals who gaze relatively more at a partner are judged more dominant or potent than those who gaze less (Thayer, 1969; Zimmerman, 1977). In a study of posed facial expressions, lowered brows and non-smiling mouths resulted in higher rated dominance than did contrasting poses (Keating, Mazur, and Segall, 1977).

The encoding studies provide a somewhat more complicated picture of the behavioral consequences of having status. The results of different studies show that higher-status individuals typically initiate more touch, talk more, and take up more space than do lower-status individuals (Goffman, 1967; Henley, 1973; Leffler, Gillespie, and Conaty, 1982; Reynolds, 1984). Higher status does not, however, necessarily result in increased involvement toward a lower-status partner. Exline (1972; Exline, Ellyson, and Long, 1975) found that, compared to the lower-status person, the higher-status member of a pair gazed less. This effect was qualified by speaker–listener roles. The higher-status person gazed at the partner more while talking, whereas the lower-status person gazed more while listening. In another study, lower-ranked individuals were more expressive facially to higher-ranked individuals, whereas the higher-ranked individuals exhibited no difference in expressiveness as a function of partner rank (Hottenstein, 1978). In an interesting observational study, lower-status members of a state legislature touched a higher-status member more frequently than vice versa (Goldstein and Jeffords, 1981). In this circumstance, touch might be used by the lower-status person in making a request to the higher-status person.

Gender is a generic status characteristic that can also determine the non-verbal display of power. Henley (1973, 1977) has proposed that, in the United States, males are more likely to exercise non-verbal power than are females, particularly in terms of touch. Relative task expertise can overshadow gender effects. For example, when females were discussing a feminine task (e.g. sewing) in mixed-sex pairs, they showed more non-verbal power (more looking while talking and less looking while listening and more gestures) than did their male partners (Dovidio, Brown, Heltman, Ellyson, and Keating, 1988). This pattern was reversed in the discussion of a masculine task (changing oil) and a non-gender task (gardening).

The mixed results from the encoding studies suggest that higher status provides greater flexibility in the initiation of increased non-verbal involvement; that is, higher-status individuals can exert their power non-verbally either by increasing gaze, touch, and other forms of involvement or by disengaging from their lower-status partners. In contrast, lower-status individuals do not have the prerogative of power, and they typically have to attend to the higher-status person.

Persuasion and compliance

Although attempts to change attitudes typically focus on a verbal message, the accompanying non-verbal cues may be especially important in contributing to attitude change. Mehrabian and Williams (1969) found that, when subjects were instructed to be more persuasive, behaviors such as gaze, head nodding, gesturing, and facial expressiveness all increased. Very high levels of involvement, however, can be distracting and even arouse a person's defenses, resulting in less attitude change (Albert and Dabbs, 1970). Close approaches, touch, or increased gaze are usually more effective in persuasive attempts when they are initiated by people who are viewed positively by the recipients (Burgoon, 1978, 1983).

Compliance, unlike attitude change, does not imply any long-term change in cognitions but only agreement to a specific behavioral request. Simple requests for help (e.g. returning a dime left in a phone booth, donations to charity, taking a leaflet, signing a petition) are usually more successful if gaze, touch, or a close approach accompanies the request (Baron, 1978; Baron and Bell, 1976; Brockner, Pressman, Cabitt, and Moran, 1982; Bull and Gibson-Robinson, 1981; Kleinke, 1977; Kleinke and Singer, 1979; Patterson, Powell, and Lenihan, 1986; Valentine and Ehrlichman, 1979). Different interpretations for the effect of high involvement on compliance have been offered. Specifically, high involvement by a requester can produce one or more of the following reactions in the target person:

(1) increased attraction toward the requester;
(2) increased dominance of the requester (with the target person feeling intimidated);
(3) increased stress that may be terminated by compliance.

Impression management

The strategic use of non-verbal behavior to create favorable reactions in a partner is a common occurrence. In studies on employment interviews, applicants who initiate higher levels of involvement, in terms of increased gaze, smiling, and head movement, are typically evaluated more positively (Forbes and Jackson, 1980; Imada and Hakel, 1977; McGovern, 1977; Young and Beier, 1977).

In less-structured interactions, an individual's expectancies about a partner may affect behavioral strategies. Previous research on expectancies and social behavior suggests that the self-fulfilling prophecy (Merton, 1948; Rosenthal, 1966) or behavioral confirmation process (Snyder and Swann, 1978; Snyder, Tanke, and Berscheid, 1977) can affect the development of interaction; that is, the existence of a particular expectancy about a partner causes the actor to behave in a way that elicits the expected behavior from the partner. Thus, if you expected someone to be friendly, you would be relaxed and friendly which, in turn, would make it easier for your partner to behave that way. Consequently, the expectancy is fulfilled or confirmed. In this way, the actor may be seen as reciprocating the behaviors that are *anticipated* from the partner. In these cases, there is consistency between the actor's expectancy and later behavior.

Sometimes expectancies may produce a different behavioral strategy: one that may be described as compensation. For example, the anticipation of an unfriendly or cold interaction may lead an actor to behave in a more friendly way in order to compensate for the anticipated behavior of the partner (Bond, 1972; Coutts, Schneider, and Montgomery, 1980; Ickes *et al.*, 1982). In such instances, people may smile and gaze more at their partners, even though they are feeling quite negative about them.

Generally, smiling seems to be an important component in managed displays such as being polite (Bugental, 1986), covering negative affect (Ekman and Friesen,

1982), ingratiation (Lefebvre, 1975), and signaling interest in meeting another person (Walsh and Hewitt, 1985). Of course, there are smiles and then there are smiles. Ekman and Friesen (1982) note that 'felt' smiles can be distinguished from phony ones in terms of both the pattern of facial muscles activated and the onset and duration of the smiles.

Across these various circumstances, it is clear that non-verbal behavior can be managed for specific interpersonal goals. Furthermore, the behavior initiated can be inconsistent with the affect felt toward the partner. These two characteristics are also common to the presentational function, but there remains an important distinction between the social control and presentational functions.

Presenting Identities and Images

Although presentational patterns necessarily involve an interaction partner, the purpose of the behavior is *not* to influence the partner. Instead, presentational patterns are designed to create an identity or image for third-party observers (Patterson, 1987). In Goffman's (1959, 1963, 1967, 1972) dramaturgical approach, such behavior patterns are described as 'performances' that are enacted for a surrounding 'audience'. Goffman's treatment of presentational patterns does not distinguish between presentations directed toward a partner and those directed toward observers. Nevertheless, such a distinction seems useful in understanding the origin of different presentations.

Sometimes these purposeful patterns are self-presentational. For example, in the presence of his boss, a father may interact closely and intently with his young daughter in order to create the impression that he is a loving and devoted parent. Other presentations, however, are designed to show a relationship or pair identity. In social gatherings, couples may stand close, hold hands, or occasionally touch one another. Goffman (1972) described such patterns as 'tie-signs', whereas Scheflen (1974; Scheflen and Ashcraft, 1976) termed them 'withness' cues.

Dyadic presentations are usually, though not always, cooperative in some sense; that is, both partners will have some investment in supporting a particular relationship identity. For example, a husband and wife who are in the midst of an argument may still decide to portray an image of marital harmony in a social gathering with friends. Consequently, they might stand close, hold hands, and appear concerned about one another, even though they may not feel that way. In a different situation, one member of a pair may display exaggerated independence by staying physically aloof and ignoring the partner.

In summary, individual and dyadic presentation patterns can result in exaggerated levels of involvement with interaction partners; that is, increased or decreased levels of involvement with a partner may be initiated to establish or reinforce a specific identity or image for members of a surrounding audience.

Affect Management

Adjustments in interactional involvement can also serve to modify the experience of affect, especially, strong affect; that is, the initiation of strong affect can result in behavioral adjustments that serve to maximize positive affect and minimize negative affect. Affect management patterns are often spontaneous and temporally limited.

One set of negative affective reactions including embarrassment, shame, and social anxiety seems to be characterized by high levels of public self-consciousness (Buss, 1980). In turn, this negative self-focus often leads to the temporary avoidance of others. When embarrassment is precipitated in interactions, typical reactions include a decrease in gaze toward the partner and an increase in gestural activity, movement, and smiling (Edelmann and Hampson, 1979, 1981; Modigliani, 1971). Some of these reactions, particularly gaze avoidance and smiling seem to vary across cultures (Edelmann et al., 1987; Edelmann and Iwawaki, 1987). In addition, an individual's experiences of fear (Schachter, 1959) and grief are likely to lead to increased involvement with others, as a means of providing some comfort or support.

At the positive end of the emotional spectrum, touch seems to be particularly important. Unexpected success, intense happiness, or good fortune may lead to hugs, kisses, and the sharing of smiling and laughter. In athletic contests, important plays and scores often result in the initiation of touch among team members. Sometimes relatively intimate touch, such as hugs or slapping the buttocks, occurs among the most masculine sports heroes, often in front of thousands of spectators and even millions of viewers on TV. It should be noted that some of the touch exchanges in athletic contests are quite ritualized, especially those initiated across competing teams, e.g. the congratulatory handshake after the game (Heckel, Allen and Blackmon, 1986).

Facilitating Service and Task Goals

In some situations, the patterns of interactive behavior are determined, not by interpersonal affect or by attempted influence but, by the service or task constraints of the setting. For example, professional service exchanges such as those with physicians, dentists, and barbers (hair stylists) typically involve close distances, touch, and careful visual scrutiny; that is, the particular service, not a personal relationship, requires the high level of involvement by the practitioner. In such cases, the behavior of the professional and the client may follow a predictable, scripted routine.

Task goals may also constrain patterns of interactive behavior in a variety of settings. Work that is detailed, cognitively complex, or confidential is often completed in relative physical isolation; that is, arrangements will be selected that increase the separation between people and reduce the opportunity for visual and auditory intrusion. For example, students using libraries for serious studying seem more concerned about choosing seating locations that avoid distractions and the noise from other people than about choosing locations near desired reference material (Schaeffer and Patterson, 1977; Sommer, 1966, 1968). In contrast, in many work settings, such as those involving assembly lines, the task demands may force individuals into very close arrangements.

To the extent that the service and task constraints determine the course of an interaction, the resulting behavior patterns reflect little about the interactants or their personal relationships. It seems likely, however, that self-selection is a factor in individuals choosing those kinds of careers or jobs that are consistent with their personal preferences for involvement with others. Thus, extraverts, rather than introverts, are likely to choose those settings in which the interactions are characterized by close distances, high levels of gaze, and greater expressiveness.

In summary, behavior patterns characteristic of the service–task function tell us more about the norms surrounding various work and service settings than they do about individuals in those settings and their relationships with one another. In fact, a behavior–setting analysis (Barker, 1968; Wicker, 1979) would suggest that in many situations, once the particular roles are determined, individuals are interchangeable or substitutable. For example, exchanges between physicians and patients tend to be relatively constant in form even though different physicians and different patients are involved.

CONCLUSION

This chapter provides an overview of non-verbal behavior in interaction in terms of the various functions served by different patterns of non-verbal behavior. I will not attempt to summarize or review the material already discussed but, instead, I will focus on three issues regarding the functional perspective and classification. First, most interactive sequences (especially those longer than a few seconds) are likely to serve more than one function. Thus, a particular pattern may both provide information and serve to regulate the interaction. Alternatively, a similar pattern in a different interaction may reflect a mix of the intimacy and social control functions; that is, interpersonal affect may generally determine the actor's behavior, but the actor is also trying to influence his or her partner. So, in addition to the moderately involving behavior characteristic of good friends, the actor strategically tries to persuade his or her friend on a particular issue by standing even closer, gazing more, and initiating touch.

Second, the activation of different functions and the specific behavior patterns in the service of those functions are affected by a variety of background variables including: (a) culture; (b) gender and personality of the interactants; (c) setting characteristics; and (d) the relationship between the interactants (see Figure 5.1). Because non-verbal behaviors are typically ambiguous and may have a number of different meanings (Schneider, Hastorf, and Ellsworth, 1979), different people in different cultures and settings may vary considerably in the expression and interpretation of different functions. In effect, the meaning of a particular pattern of behavior is very much a product of its social context. Consequently, a given behavior pattern may serve a variety of different functions.

Finally, it is important to appreciate that a comprehensive understanding of interaction requires a study of the relationship between non-verbal and verbal components (see Chapter 7, by Cappella and Palmer). It is clear that verbal behavior and non-verbal behavior can serve similar functions (Spitzberg and Cupach, 1984), but the manner in which the verbal and non-verbal elements are combined is undoubtedly very complex. Some attempts have already been made at classifying and analyzing verbal behavior. For example, Wiener and Mehrabian's (1968) analysis of verbal behavior along an immediacy dimension parallels the non-verbal immediacy (Mehrabian, 1969) dimension. In addition, Stiles' (1978) taxonomy of verbal response modes provides a means of classifying the intent of verbal behavior (e.g. advisement, interpretation, confirmation, question, disclosure, etc.) that is clearly functional in nature. Although the particular form of such a synthesis is difficult to anticipate, a functional approach may provide a means for understanding the interplay of verbal and non-verbal behavior.

REFERENCES

Abelson, R.P. (1981). Psychological status of the script concept. *American Psychologist*, **36**, 715–729.

Aiello, J.R. and Cooper, R.E. (1972). Use of personal space as a function of social affect. *Proceedings of the 80th Annual Convention of the American Psychological Association*, **7**, 207–208.

Albert, S. and Dabbs, J.M. (1970). Physical distance and persuasion. *Journal of Personality and Social Psychology*, **15**, 265–270.

Allen, D.E. and Guy, R.F. (1977). Ocular breaks and verbal output. *Sociometry*, **40**, 90–96.

Andersen, P.A. (1985). Nonverbal immediacy in interpersonal communication. In A.W. Siegman and S. Feldstein (Eds), *Multichannel integrations of nonverbal behavior*, pp. 1–36. Hillsdale, NJ: Erlbaum.

Andersen, P.A. and Andersen, J.F. (1984). The exchange of nonverbal intimacy: A critical review of dyadic models. *Journal of Nonverbal Behavior*, **8**, 327–349.

Argyle, M. (1972). Non-verbal communication in human social interaction. In R.A. Hinde (Ed.), *Non-verbal communication*, pp. 243–260. Cambridge: Cambridge University Press.

Argyle, M. and Dean, J. (1965). Eye-contact, distance and affiliation. *Sociometry*, **28**, 289–304.

Barker, R.G. (1968). *Ecological psychology: Concepts and methods for studying the environment of human behavior*. Stanford, CA: Stanford University Press.

Baron, R.A. (1978). Invasions of personal space and helping: Mediating effects of invader's apparent need. *Journal of Experimental Social Psychology*, **14**, 304–312.

Baron, R.A. and Bell, P.A. (1976). Physical distance and helping: Some unexpected benefits of 'crowding in' on others. *Journal of Applied Social Psychology*, **6**, 95–104.

Bem, D.J. (1967). Self perception: An alternative interpretation of cognitive dissonance phenomena. *Psychological Review*, **74**, 183–200.

Bem, D.J. (1972). Self perception theory. In L. Berkowitz (Ed.), *Advances in experimental psychology*, Vol. 6, pp. 1–62. New York: Academic Press.

Bond, M.H. (1972). Effect of an impression set on subsequent behavior. *Journal of Personality and Social Psychology*, **24**, 302–305.

Boomer, D.S. (1978). The phonemic clause: Speech unit in human communication. In A.W. Siegman and S. Feldstein (Eds), *Nonverbal behavior and comunication*, pp. 245–262. Hillsdale, NJ: Erlbaum.

Boomer, D.S. and Dittmann, A.T. (1962). Hesitation pauses and juncture pauses in speech. *Language and Speech*, **5**, 215–220.

Brockner, J., Pressman, B., Cabitt, J., and Moran, P. (1982). Nonverbal immediacy, sex and compliance: A field study. *Journal of Nonverbal Behavior*, **6**, 253–258.

Bugental, D.B. (1986). Unmasking the 'polite smile': Situational and personal determinants of managed affect in adult–child interaction. *Personality and Social Psychology Bulletin*, **12**, 7–16.

Bull, R. and Gibson-Robinson, E. (1981). The influences of eye-gaze, style and dress, and locality on the amounts of money donated to a charity. *Human Relations*, **34**, 895–905.

Burgoon, J.K. (1978). A communication model of personal space violations: Explication and an initial test. *Human Communication Research*, **4**, 129–142.

Burgoon, J.K. (1983). Nonverbal violations of expectations. In J.M. Wiemann and R.P. Harrison (Eds), *Nonverbal interaction*, pp. 77–111. Beverly Hills, CA: Sage.

Buss, A.H. (1980). *Self-consciousness and social anxiety*. San Francisco, CA: Freeman.

Cappella, J.N. (1981). Mutual influence in expressive behavior: Adult–adult and infant–adult dyadic interaction. *Psychological Bulletin*, **89**, 101–132.

Cappella, J.N. (1985). Controlling the floor in conversation. In A.W. Siegman and S. Feldstein (Eds), *Multichannel integrations of nonverbal behavior*, pp. 69–103. Hillsdale, NJ: Erlbaum.

Cappella, J.N. and Greene, J.O. (1982). A discrepancy–arousal explanation of mutual influence in expressive behavior for adult and infant–adult interaction. *Communication Monographs*, **49**, 89–114.

Ciolek, T.M. and Kendon, A. (1980). Environment and the spatial arrangement of conversational encounters. *Sociological Inquiry*, **50**, 3–4.

Coutts, L.M., Schneider, F., and Montgomery, S. (1980). An investigation of the arousal model of interpersonal intimacy. *Journal of Experimental Social Psychology*, **16**, 545–561.

Dittmann, A.T. and Llewellyn, L.G. (1967). The phonemic clause as a unit of speech decoding. *Journal of Personality and Social Psychology*, **6**, 341–349.

Dittmann, A.T. and Llewellyn, L.G. (1968). Relationship between vocalization and head nods as listener responses. *Journal of Personality and Social Psychology*, **9**, 79–84.

Dovidio, J.F., Brown, C.E., Heltman, K., Ellyson, S.L., and Keating, C.F. (1988). Power displays between women and men in discussions of gender-linked traits: A multichannel study. *Journal of Personality and Social Psychology*, **55**, 580–587.

Duncan, S., Jr (1972). Some signals and rules for taking speaking turns in conversations. *Journal of Personality and Social Psychology*, **23**, 283–292.

Duncan, S., Jr and Fiske, D.W. (1977). *Face-to-face interaction: Research, methods, and theory*. Hillsdale, NJ: Erlbaum.

Duncan, S., Jr and Niederehe, G. (1974). On signaling that it's your turn to speak. *Journal of Experimental Social Psychology*, **10**, 234–247.

Edelmann, R.J., Asendorpf, J., Contarello, A., Georgas, J., Villanueva, C., and Zammuner, V. (1987). Self-reported verbal and non-verbal strategies for coping with embarrassment in five European cultures. *Social Science Information*, **26**, 869–883.

Edelmann, R.J. and Hampson, S.E. (1979). Changes in nonverbal behavior during embarrassment. *British Journal of Social and Clinical Psychology*, **18**, 385–390.

Edelmann, R.J. and Hampson, S.E. (1981). Embarrassment in dyadic interaction. *Social Behavior and Personality*, **9**, 171–177.

Edelmann, R.J. and Iwawaki, S. (1987). Self-reported expression and consequences of embarrassment in the United Kingdom and Japan. *Psychologia*, **30**, 205–216.

Ekman, P. (1972). Universals and cultural differences in facial expressions of emotion. In J.K. Cole (Ed.), *Nebraska symposium on motivation, 1971*, Vol. 19, pp. 163–206. Lincoln, NE: University of Nebraska Press.

Ekman, P. (1973). Cross-cultural studies of facial expressions. In P. Ekman (Ed.), *Darwin and facial expression*, pp. 169–229. New York: Academic Press.

Ekman, P. and Friesen, W.V. (1969). The repertoire of nonverbal behavior: Categories, origins, usage and codings. *Semiotica*, **1**, 49–97.

Ekman, P. and Friesen, W.V. (1975). *Unmasking the face*. Englewood Cliffs, NJ: Prentice-Hall.

Ekman, P. and Friesen, W.V. (1982). Felt, false, and miserable smiles. *Journal of Nonverbal Behavior*, **6**, 238–252.

Ekman, P., Friesen, W.V., O'Sullivan, M., Chan, A., Diacoyanni-Tarlatzis, I., Heider, K., Krause, R., LeCompte, W.A., Pitcairn, T., Ricci-Bitti, P.E., Scherer, K., Tomita, M., and Tzavaras, A. (1987). Universals and cultural differences in the judgments of facial expressions of emotion. *Journal of Personality and Social Psychology*, **53**, 712–717.

Exline, R.V. (1963). Explorations in the process of person perception: Visual interaction in relation to competition, sex and need for affiliation. *Journal of Personality*, **31**, 1–20.

Exline, R.V. (1972). Visual interaction: The glances of power and preference. In J.K. Cole (Ed.), *Nebraska symposium on motivation, 1971*, Vol. 19, pp. 163–206. Lincoln, NE: University of Nebraska Press.

Exline, R.V., Ellyson, S.L., and Long, B. (1975). Visual behavior as an aspect of power role relationships. In P. Pliner, L. Krames, and T. Alloway (Eds), *Advances in the study of communication and affect*, Vol. 2, pp. 21–51. New York: Plenum.

Exline, R.V., Gray, D., and Schwette, D. (1965). Visual behavior in a dyad as affected by interview content and sex of respondent. *Journal of Personality and Social Psychology*, 1, 201–209.

Exline, R.V. and Winters, L.C. (1965). Affective relations and mutual glances in dyads. In S. Tomkins and C. Izard (Eds), *Affect, cognition, and personality*, pp. 316–350. New York: Springer.

Feldstein, S. and Welkowitz, J. (1987). A chronography of conversation: In defense of an objective approach. In A.W. Siegman and S. Feldstein (Eds), *Nonverbal behavior and communication*, pp. 435–500. Hillsdale, NJ: Erlbaum.

Foot, H.C., Chapman, A.J., and Smith, J.R. (1977). Friendship and social responsiveness in boys and girls. *Journal of Personality and Social Psychology*, 35, 401–411.

Forbes, R.J. and Jackson, P.R. (1980). Nonverbal behaviour and the outcome of selection interviews. *Journal of Occupational Psychology*, 53, 65–72.

Frick, R.W. (1985). Communicating emotion: The role of prosodic features. *Psychological Bulletin*, 97, 412–429.

Goffman, E. (1959). *Presentation of self in everyday life*. Garden City, NY: Anchor.

Goffman, E. (1963). *Behavior in public places*. New York: Free Press.

Goffman, E. (1967). *Interaction ritual*. Garden City, NY: Anchor.

Goffman, E. (1972). *Relations in public*. New York: Harper Colophon.

Goldstein, A.G. and Jeffords, J. (1981). Status and touching behavior. *Bulletin of the Psychonomic Society*, 17, 79–81.

Goldstein, M., Kilroy, M., and Van de Voort, D. (1976). Gaze as a function of conversation and degree of love. *Journal of Psychology*, 92, 227–234.

Greenbaum, P.E. and Rosenfeld, H.M. (1980). Varieties of touching in greetings: Sequential structure and sex-related differences. *Journal of Nonverbal Behavior*, 5, 13–25.

Hadar, U., Steiner, T.J., Grant, E.C., and Rose, F.C. (1984). The timing of shifts of head postures during conversation. *Human Movement Science*, 3, 237–245.

Hall, E.T. (1963). A system for the notation of proxemic behavior. *American Anthropologist*, 65, 1003–1026.

Hall, E.T. (1966). *The hidden dimension*. New York: Doubleday.

Hall, E.T. (1968). Proxemics. *Current Anthropology*, 9, 83–108.

Harrigan, J. (1985). Listeners' body movements and speaking turns. *Communication Research*, 12, 233–250.

Harrigan, J.A. and Steffen, J.J. (1983). Gaze as a turn-exchange signal in group conversations. *British Journal of Social Psychology*, 22, 167–168.

Harrison, R.P. (1973). Nonverbal communication. In I.S. Pool, W. Schramm, N. Maccoby, F. Fry, E. Parker, and J.L. Fern (Eds), *Handbook of communication*, pp. 93–115. Chicago: Rand McNally.

Heckel, R.V., Allen, S.S., and Blackmon, D.C. (1986). Tactile communication of winners in flag football. *Perceptual and Motor Skills*, 63, 553–554.

Henley, N.M. (1973). Status and sex: Some touching observations. *Bulletin of the Psychonomic Society*, 2, 91–93.

Henley, N.M. (1977). *Body politics: Power, sex, and nonverbal communication*. Englewood Cliffs, NJ: Prentice-Hall.

Heshka, S. and Nelson, Y. (1972). Interpersonal speaking distance as a function of age, sex, and relationship. *Sociometry*, 35, 491–498.

Heslin, R. and Boss, D. (1980). Nonverbal intimacy in airport arrival and departure. *Personality and Social Psychology Bulletin*, 6, 248–252.

Hottenstein, M.P. (1978). An exploration of the relationship between age, social status, and facial gesturing. *Dissertation Abstracts International*, 38, 5648B–5649B.

Ickes, W., Patterson, M.L., Rajecki, D.W., and Tanford, S. (1982). Behavioral and cognitive consequences of reciprocal versus compensatory responses to pre-interaction expectancies. *Social Cognition*, **1**, 160–190.

Imada, A.S. and Hakel, M.D. (1977). Influence of nonverbal communication and rater proximity on impressions and decisions in simulated employment interviews. *Journal of Applied Psychology*, **62**, 295–300.

Jones, S.E. and Yarbrough, A.E. (1985). A naturalistic study of the meanings of touch. *Communication Monographs*, **52**, 19–56.

Jourard, S.M. (1966). An exploratory study of body-accessibility. *British Journal of Social and Clinical Psychology*, **5**, 221–231.

Keating, C.F., Mazur, A., and Segall, M.H. (1977). Facial gestures which influence the perception of status. *Sociometry*, **40**, 374–378.

Kendon, A. (1967). Some functions of gaze-direction in social interaction. *Acta Psychologica*, **26**, 22–63.

Kendon, A. (1976). The F-formation system: The spatial organization of social encounters. *Man–Environment Systems*, **6**, 291–296.

Kendon, A. (1967). Spatial organization in social encounters: The F-formation system. In A. Kendon (Ed.), *Studies in the behavior of social interaction*. Lisse: Peter de Ridder Press, Holland.

Kleinke, C.L. (1977). Compliance to requests made by gazing and touching experimenters in field settings. *Journal of Experimental Social Psychology*, **13**, 218–223.

Kleinke, C.L. (1986). *Meeting and understanding people*. New York: Freeman.

Kleinke, C.L. and Singer, D.A. (1979). Influence of gaze on compliance with demanding and conciliatory requests in a field setting. *Personality and Social Psychology Bulletin*, **5**, 386–390.

Lefebvre, L.M. (1975). Encoding and decoding of ingratiation in modes of smiling and gaze. *British Journal of Social and Clinical Psychology*, **14**, 33–42.

Leffler, A., Gillespie, D.L., and Conaty, J.C. (1982). The effects of status differentiation on nonverbal behavior. *Social Psychology Quarterly*, **45**, 153–161.

McGovern, T.V. (1977). The making of a job interviewee: The effect of nonverbal behavior on an interviewer's evaluations during a selection interview. *Dissertation Abstracts International*, **37**, 4740B–4741B.

Mehrabian, A. (1969). Some referents and measures of nonverbal behavior. *Behavior Research Methods and Instrumentation*, **1**, 203–207.

Mehrabian, A. (1981). *Silent messages: Implicit communication of emotions and attitudes*. Belmont, CA: Wadsworth.

Mehrabian, A. and Williams, M. (1969). Nonverbal concomitants of perceived and intended persuasiveness. *Journal of Personality and Social Psychology*, **13**, 37–58.

Merton, R.K. (1948). The self-fulfilling prophecy. *Antioch Review*, **8**, 193–210.

Modigliani, A. (1971). Embarrassment, facework, and eye contact: Testing a theory of embarrassment. *Journal of Personality and Social Psychology*, **17**, 15–24.

Patterson, M.L. (1973). Compensation in nonverbal immediacy behaviors: A review. *Sociometry*, **36**, 237–252.

Patterson, M.L. (1976). An arousal model of interpersonal intimacy. *Psychological Review*, **83**, 235–245.

Patterson, M.L. (1982). A sequential functional model of nonverbal exchange. *Psychological Review*, **89**, 231–249.

Patterson, M.L. (1983). *Nonverbal behavior: A functional perspective*. New York: Springer-Verlag.

Patterson, M.L. (1987). Presentational and affect management functions of nonverbal involvement. *Journal of Nonverbal Behavior*, **11**, 110–122.

Patterson, M.L. and Edinger, J.A. (1987). A functional analysis of space in social interaction. In A.W. Siegman and S. Feldstein (Eds), *Nonverbal behavior and communication*, pp. 523–562. Hillsdale, NJ: Erlbaum.

Patterson, M.L., Powell, J.L., and Lenihan, M.G. (1986). Touch, compliance, and interpersonal affect. *Journal of Nonverbal Behavior*, **10**, 41–50.

Reynolds, P.D. (1984). Leaders never quit: Talking, silence, and influence in interpersonal groups. *Small Group Behavior*, **15**, 404–413.

Rosenfeld, L.B., Kartus, S., and Ray, C. (1976). Body accessibility revisited. *Journal of Communication*, **26**, 27–30.

Rosenthal, R. (1966). *Experimenter effects in behavioral research*. New York: Appleton-Century-Crofts.

Rubin, Z. (1970). Measurement of romantic love. *Journal of Personality and Social Psychology*, **16**, 265–273.

Schachter, S. (1959). *The psychology of affiliation*. Stanford, CA: Stanford University Press.

Schaeffer, G.R. and Patterson, M.L. (1977). Studying preferences, behavior, and design influences in a university library. In P. Suedfeld, J.A. Russell, L.M. Ward, F. Szigeti, and G. Davis (Eds), *The behavioral basis of design*, Book 2, pp. 301–305. Stroudsberg, PA: Dowden, Hutchison, and Ross.

Scheflen, A.E. (1964). The significance of posture in communication systems. *Psychiatry*, **27**, 316–331.

Scheflen, A.E. (1974). *How behavior means*. Garden City, NY: Anchor.

Scheflen, A.E. and Ashcraft, N. (1976). *Human territories: How we behave in space–time*. Englewood Cliffs, NJ: Prentice-Hall.

Scherer, K.R. (1986). Vocal affect expression: A review and a model for future research. *Psychological Bulletin*, **99**, 143–165.

Schlenker, B.R. (1980). *Impression management*. Monterey, CA: Brooks/Cole.

Schneider, D.J., Hastorf, A.H., and Ellsworth, P.C. (1979). *Person perception*, 2nd edn. Reading, MA: Addison-Wesley.

Siegman, A.W. and Feldstein, S. (Eds) (1985). *Multichannel integrations of nonverbal behavior*. Hillsdale, NJ: Erlbaum.

Siegman, A.W. and Feldstein, S. (Eds) (1987). *Nonverbal behavior and communication*, Hillsdale, NJ: Erlbaum.

Snyder, M. and Swann, W. (1978). Behavioral confirmation in social interaction: From social perception to social reality. *Journal of Experimental Social Psychology*, **14**, 148–162.

Snyder, M., Tanke, E.D., and Berscheid, E. (1977). Social perception and interpersonal behavior: On the self-fulfilling nature of social stereotypes. *Journal of Personality and Social Psychology*, **35**, 656–666.

Sommer, R. (1959). Studies in personal space. *Sociometry*, **22**, 247–260.

Sommer, R. (1961). Leadership and group geography. *Sociometry*, **24**, 99–110.

Sommer, R. (1962). The distance for comfortable conversation: A further study. *Sociometry*, **25**, 111–116.

Sommer, R. (1965). Further studies of small group ecology. *Sociometry*, **28**, 337–348.

Sommer, R. (1966). The ecology of privacy. *Library Quarterly*, **36**, 234–248.

Sommer, R. (1968). Reading areas in college libraries. *Library Quarterly*, **38**, 249–260.

Spitzberg, B.H. and Cupach, W.R. (1984). *Interpersonal communication competence*. Beverly Hills, CA: Sage.

Stiles, W.B. (1978). Verbal response modes and dimensions of interpersonal roles: A method of discourse analysis. *Journal of Personality and Social Psychology*, **36**, 693–703.

Thayer, S. (1969). The effect of interpersonal looking duration of dominance judgments. *Journal of Social Psychology*, **79**, 285–286.

Thayer, S. (1986). History and strategies of research on social touch. *Journal of Nonverbal Behavior*, **10**, 12–28.

Thomas, A.P. and Bull, P. (1981). The role of pre-speech posture change in dyadic interaction. *British Journal of Social Psychology*, **20**, 105–111.

Tomkins, S.S. (1982). *Affect, imagery, and consciousness,* Vol. 3. New York: Springer.

Valentine, M.E. and Ehrlichman, H. (1979). Interpersonal gaze and helping behavior. *Journal of Social Psychology*, **107**, 193–198.

Wagner, H.L., MacDonald, C.J., and Manstead, A.S.R. (1986). Communication of individual emotions by spontaneous facial expressions. *Journal of Personality and Social psychology*, **50**, 737–743.

Wallbott, H.G. and Scherer, K.R. (1986). Cues and channels in emotion recognition. *Journal of Personality and Social Psychology*, **51**, 690–699.

Walsh, D.G. and Hewitt, J. (1985). Giving men the come-on: Effect of eye contact and smiling in a bar environment. *Perceptual and Motor Skills*, **61**, 873–874.

Wicker, A.W. (1979). *An introduction to ecological psychology*. Monterey, CA: Brooks/Cole.

Wiemann, J.M. (1985). Interpersonal control and regulation in conversation. In R.L. Street and J.N. Cappella (Eds), *Sequence and pattern in communication behavior*, pp. 85–102. London: Arnold.

Wiener, M. and Mehrabian, A. (1968). *Language within language. Immediacy: A channel in verbal communication*. New York: Appleton-Century-Crofts.

Willis, F.N. (1966). Initial speaking distance as a function of the speakers' relationship. *Psychonomic Science*, **5**, 221–222.

Young, D.M. and Beier, E.G. (1977). The role of applicant nonverbal communication in the employment interview. *Journal of Employment Counseling*, **14**, 154–165.

Zimmerman, L.E.S. (1977). First impressions as influenced by eye contact, sex, and demographic background. *Dissertation Abstracts International*, **37**, 6414B–6415B.

6

The Communicative Functions of Paralanguage and Prosody

RICHARD L. STREET, JR

Department of Speech Communication, Texas A & M University, USA

The maxim is resounded repeatedly: 'It's not what you said; it's how you said it!' The acoustical elements of communication perform important functions in social inter-action in that they facilitate listeners' efforts to interpret the semantic content of utterances and are relied upon to ascertain a speaker's personal characteristics and intentions. Non-verbal speech – variously labeled prosody, paralanguage, extra-linguistic speech, and vocalics – has enjoyed a rich tradition of empirical inquiry within psychology, linguistics, and communication sciences. Historically, studies of non-verbal speech usually stem from one of four paradigms. First, speech scientists have been interested in the *physiology of sound production* as they explicate interrelationships between, for example, muscle systems, the vocal tract, facial and dental characteristics, the pharynx, and respiratory volume (see Abercrombie, 1967; Laver and Trudgill, 1979). Second, researchers in the area of 'language attitudes' and 'message effects' have examined the *attributional correlates* of various speech styles or vocal characteristics. For example, these scholars might solicit listeners' evalua-tions of speakers exhibiting differences in accent, speech rate, vocal pitch, etc. (Giles and Powesland, 1975; Scherer, 1979b; Street and Hopper, 1982).

Third, some investigators have studied the extent to which an individual's *personal characteristics* (e.g. personality, emotional state, sex, age, etc.) are represented in vocal behavior (Scherer, 1986; Scherer and Giles, 1979; Siegman, 1978). For example, extraverts typically pause less than introverts (Scherer, 1979a; Siegman and Pope, 1965); young adults generally speak faster than children and elderly adults

---

Handbook of Language and Social Psychology
Edited by H. Giles and W.P. Robinson.   © 1990 John Wiley & Sons Ltd

(Sabin, Clemmer, O'Connell, and Kowal, 1979). Finally, scholars with linguistic orientations have long been interested in the manner in which prosody and paralanguage influence the *meaning* listeners assign to utterances (e.g. the rise or fall of pitch cues listeners to interpret an utterance as a question or a statement) (Crystal, 1969; Martin, 1981; Trager and Smith, 1951).

The references above provide in-depth reviews of non-verbal speech research and will not be duplicated here. Rather, the purpose of this chapter is to take a somewhat different approach by examining non-verbal speech behaviors from a 'communicative function' perspective. Although the research traditions listed above have implications for communication processes, each typically focuses upon the behavior of the *individual*, speaking alone or to an immediate or removed (as in a tape-recording) other.

In this chapter, I examine non-verbal speech as an *interactive* phenomenon which significantly impinges upon interpersonal communication processes and outcomes. The chapter unfolds as follows. First, I describe the various speech behaviors normally treated as prosodic and paralinguistic. This is followed by a discussion of the processes by which non-verbal speech is produced by communicators. This section specifically focuses both on how non-verbal speech is encoded with little or no cognitive awareness and on how these processes are facilitated by an *interlocutor's* speech style and the speaker's expectancies for the interaction. Finally, I conclude with an examination of communicative functions which are in part accomplished by interactants' non-verbal speech exchange.

PROSODY AND PARALANGUAGE DEFINED

Non-verbal speech refers to the acoustical properties of communication. Types of non-verbal speech are defined in accordance with their phonetic definition and function. While this approach is somewhat simplistic, I will follow Martin's (1981) lead and describe two general categories of non-verbal speech: prosody and paralanguage.

Prosody represents *discretely coded* non-verbal speech behaviors. Based on Martin's (1981) classification, the following are examples of prosodic cues. *Stress* refers to vocal prominence typically accomplished by loudness and/or pitch. *Center* is a form of stress that marks the peak of vocal prominence or primary stress. For example, in the sentence, 'He went *home yesterday*?', the words 'home' and 'yesterday' are stressed with center on the last word. Whereas stress and center create the rhythmic nature of an utterance, *juncture* breaks up the rhythm with a pause, lengthening of syllables, or a change in pitch or articulation rate. Finally, *pitch direction* (rise, fall, and maintenance of pitch) and *pitch height* and *range* are perceptually represented as tone and inflection of the voice (Lieberman, 1967; Martin, 1981).

Paralanguage, on the other hand, constitutes *continuously coded* behaviors and includes *vocal intensity* (loudness), *fundamental frequency* (pitch), *silence* within an utterance (pause) and between speaker switches (response latency), *speech duration* (length of a monologue, or amount of time a conversant holds the floor), and *speech rate* (number of words or syllables uttered within a particular time frame) (Scherer, 1979a; Siegman, 1978).

Accent has both prosodic and paralinguistic features. Within a speech community, a characteristic accent is derived from a specific set of phonemic rules governing the intonation of vowels and consonants (Laver and Trudgill, 1979). These phonemic systems vary across speech communities. On the other hand, speakers may have varying 'degrees' of accentedness as they accentuate or attenuate intonational markers of accent (Giles and Powesland, 1975). For example, there are at least eight degrees of Mexican-accented English in the United States (Brennan, Ryan, and Dawson, 1975).

PRODUCING NON-VERBAL SPEECH

Only recently have researchers begun unraveling the intricacies of factors regulating the production of paralanguage and prosody. On the one hand, non-verbal speech is a product of the speaker's physiology, emotion, and arousal. For example, the experience of arousal often constricts the vocal cords, thereby creating an increase in vocal pitch (Scherer, 1986). On the other hand, many aspects of non-verbal speech style are 'managed' and serve the speaker's communicative intent. For example, a speaker may increase speech rate and loudness in order to emphasize a particular point or to be perceived as dynamic (Giles and Street, 1985). While this section of the paper overviews these processes, detailed attention is reserved for the manner in which the communicator's goals and partner's behavior contribute to the production of non-verbal speech.

Non-Verbal Speech as a Physiological Response

There are certain aspects of a speaker's voice over which he or she may have little or no control. First, the physical characteristics of the vocal and respiratory apparatus (e.g. vocal tract length, facial and dental features, mass of the vocal cords, respiratory volume, etc.) determine some qualities of the speaker's voice, particularly pitch, loudness, and tone (Abercrombie, 1967). These rather invariant features of the voice have been labeled 'extralinguistic' because they are, to some degree, beyond volitional control. For example, males and large people usually have louder, lower-pitched voices than do females and small persons as a result of having a larger respiratory volume and an extended vocal tract (Laver and Trudgill, 1979). Elderly individuals often experience changes in voice quality, vocal pitch, and vocal intensity due to such factors as ossification of the vocal cords, diminished respiratory capacity, and reduced coordination within the central nervous system (Helfrich, 1979).

Second, transient emotional and affective states (e.g. anxiety, anger, excitement, fatigue) can impact significantly upon a speaker's non-verbal speech characteristics in two respects. On the one hand, the experience of arousal and emotions affects the pliability of the vocal cords and alters breathing patterns. For example, when sexually aroused, men and women lose fine control of their voice characterizations (Laver and Trudgill, 1979). When experiencing 'hot' anger, an increase in both the level and variability of a speaker's vocal pitch and intensity usually occurs (Scherer, 1986).

On the other hand, the experience of arousal, particularly as it relates to anxiety, affects speech style to the extent that it influences the ability to encode and articulate utterances. Moderate or mild levels of anxiety tend to facilitate or 'energize' communication production processes by enhancing the ability to make semantic and syntactic choices, to be non-verbally expressive, and to monitor a partner's responses (Siegman, 1978; Street and Cappella, 1985). Relative to individuals experiencing very high or very low arousal, moderately aroused speakers typically speak faster, with briefer response latencies, fewer disfluencies, longer speech durations, and greater vocabulary diversity (Kasl and Mahl, 1965; Murray, 1971; Siegman and Pope, 1965, 1966). The speech of low and highly anxious persons may be somewhat similar to each other but for different reasons. Among the former, the verbal and vocal production mechanisms become inefficient and inadequately activated, as in boredom or fatigue; among the latter, anxiety disrupts production processes by interfering with the motor and cognitive operations regulating articulation and lexical selections (Laver and Trudgill, 1979; Siegman, 1978).

Non-Verbal Speech as a Communicative Act

Although some aspects of non-verbal speech are either impossible or difficult to control, many features of paralanguage and prosody are deliberately 'managed', or strategically manipulated, to serve communicative purposes and functions. While scholars are certainly knowledgeable about various ways in which non-verbal speech is related to communicative goals and outcomes (to be discussed later), relatively little is known about the encoding of non-verbal speech for these purposes. Recently, researchers have been delving into this issue, particularly with regard to communicative behavior production in general. As Berger (1980) has pointed out, 'competent' verbal and non-verbal responses often unfold with little conscious attention to the acts themselves, that is, to the specific syntactic and semantic choices, gestural coordination with speech acts, accents, speech rate, etc. A problematic question remains unanswered: how are communicators able to manipulate non-verbal speech levels within milliseconds and toward various ends with little or no awareness and without involving complex cognitive operations? Drawing from recent work in cognitive psychology, several theorists have undertaken initial steps toward accounting for cognitive and behavioral processes underlying the production of communicative behavior (see Brown, Warner, and Williams, 1985; Greene, 1984a; Natale, 1975; Scherer, 1986). These writers generally postulate the existence of an integrated hierarchy of cognitive operations linking communicative goals and strategies (of which the communicator may be aware) to motor responses of speech and movement (of which the communicator is usually unaware).

While it is not the intention of this chapter to put forth a model of non-verbal speech production, some discussion of issues related to these processes is warranted in a review of paralanguage and prosody, especially given the communicative significance of these behaviors. The phenomena of interest here are the *adaptation* and *habituation* of non-verbal speech style. There is a substantial amount of evidence indicating that, during the course of an interaction, communicators tend to adapt their non-verbal speech in relation to an interlocutor's performances of these behaviors. These adaptations may reflect moves toward similarity (convergence) or toward differences (divergence or complementarity) and have been observed for speech rate, accent, pauses, speech duration, and loudness levels (Cappella and Planalp, 1981; Feldstein and Welkowitz, 1978; Giles and Powesland, 1975; Street, 1984).

Although communicators readily modify speech in relation to a partner's behavior, and although they often display somewhat different communicative styles from one encounter to the next, there are rarely *dramatic* variations in their speech behavior either within or across interactions. In other words, speakers display some degree of consistency in their non-verbal speech styles (Cappella, 1983; Giles and Street, 1985). Speech consistency and adaptation are not necessarily contradictory phenomena. A conversant's speech style may remain relatively stable, not varying significantly during the course of an interaction, or across different interactions with the same partner or with different partners. However, what variations are produced relative to the normal or baseline speech style may be toward or away from a partner's speech performance. Most of the research examining speech consistency and adaptation has focused on paralinguistic behaviors. Statistically significant trends for consistency and adaptation have been observed for speech rate, the duration of speaking turns, response latencies, and pauses within speaking turns (Cappella and Planalp, 1981; Jaffe and Feldstein, 1970; Street, 1984; Street and Buller, 1988; Street and Murphy, 1987).

Adaptations in non-verbal speech

Why do communicators adapt their communicative style in general and speech in particular in relation to that of partners? First, there is strong evidence indicating that speech adaptation is related to a communicator's interaction goals. Communicators typically converge speech if they wish to win approval from or socially assimilate with one another or if they seek to enhance accuracy and coherence when communicating with one another (Giles, Mulac, Bradac, and Johnson, 1987). For example, speech convergence has been observed among interactants instructed to create a favorable impression (Putman and Street, 1984), who are interpersonally oriented (Street and Murphy, 1987), who have a high need for approval (Natale, 1975), who report that they were trying to improve the accuracy of communicating information to interlocutors (Bourhis, Roth, and MacQueen, 1989), and who have placed a premium on communicative intelligibility (Natale, 1975). Divergence of speech has been observed among interactants wishing to dissociate from their partners (Bourhis and Giles, 1977; Bourhis, Giles, Leyens, and Tajfel, 1979), who are intentionally creating ambiguity in a communicative exchange by periodically switching linguistic styles (e.g. from more to less to more formal speech) during the course of the interaction (Scotton, 1985), and who are reacting adversely to the communicative response of another (Cappella and Greene, 1982).

Second, it appears that speech adaptation follows a developmental progression and is contingent upon specific cognitive and social abilities. The proclivity to adapt communicative response (including vocal behavior) appears early in life, prompting some to say it is an innate, genetically predisposed 'response set' in the human species (Hoffmann, 1977; Meltzhoff, 1985). For example, in some instances, infants adapt their vocalic (duration of vocalizing, vocal pitch) and kinesic (gaze and gestural durations) behavior toward that of caregivers (Beebe, Jaffe, Feldstein, Mays, and Alson, 1985; Stern, Jaffe, Beebe, and Bennett, 1975); in other instances, infants adjust these responses to compensate those of adults (see Cappella, 1981, for review). Vocal and behavioral reciprocity and compensation appear to be means by which infants integrate themselves in a social environment, share affective experiences, and regulate arousal and stimulation levels (Beebe *et al.*, 1985; Cappella, 1981; Meltzhoff, 1985).

While the *propensity* to adapt vocal behavior exists at the onset of life, the *ability* to do so only emerges and becomes more stable as children acquire linguistic, cognitive, and pragmatic skills. For example, during the first year of life, the establishment of particular patterns of infant–caregiver response sequences is accomplished in large part by the caregiver; that is, the mother responds to the child's behavior in a reciprocal or compensatory fashion. However, in the second year of life, children become more active communicators and display more initiative and consistency in matching or compensating the adult's communicative behaviors (Beebe *et al.*, 1985; Bruner, 1981; Stern *et al.*, 1975). Among verbal children, the ability to adapt response latency, speech duration, and speech rate in relation to corresponding behaviors of partners has been related to age, normal (as opposed to delayed) development, and social responsiveness (Feldstein, Konstantareas, Oxman, and Webster, 1985; Street, 1983; Street and Cappella, in press; Welkowitz, Cariffe, and Feldstein, 1976).

In sum, adaptation appears early but the skills with which children coordinate vocal responses with those of interlocutors emerge with linguistic, cognitive, and social maturation. Among adults, vocal responses and adaptations are goal-oriented, fine-tuned, and often produced spontaneously and non-consciously (Cappella and Planalp, 1981). The question now arises: in addition to an elaborated verbal repertoire, the knowledge of conversational rules, and a motivational impetus, what cognitive mechanisms facilitate matching and compensation such that they occur automatically and within fractions of seconds? Natale (1975), extrapolating from the work of Lane and Tranel (1971), proposed that speech adaptation (particularly convergence) is an automatic response due to the existence of a 'public feedback loop', the function of which is to incorporate ambient speech stimuli (e.g. a partner's loudness and rate) into the speaker's vocalic repertoire, thereby circumventing the need for conscious deliberations.

In support of this contention, Natale (1975) reviews evidence indicating that speakers are often 'unaware' of their speech convergence (see also Cappella and Planalp, 1981; Street, 1982; Webb, 1972). The automaticity of convergence can also explain anecdotal evidence suggesting that communicators have difficulty 'faking' an unfamiliar accent (e.g. a British speaker trying to talk like a Texan); yet, after becoming immersed within a speech community for a period of time, speakers often 'discover', either through self-awareness or from reports of others, that their speech now contains phonological variants of the speech community. According to Natale, the function of the public feedback loop is to promote communicative efficiency during interaction; that is, it enables the conversants to achieve an optimal speech 'format' for the interaction. In a more general sense, one could infer that a mechanism predisposing behavioral convergence is also functionally significant for humans to the extent that it promotes the experience of interpersonal rapport and assimilation into a social system (Bavelas, Black, Chovil, Lemery, and Mullett, 1988). Unfortunately, Natale's model only addresses the issue of convergence. It does not elaborate on how the proclivity to converge is 'overridden' by a communicator's goal to maintain or diverge speech and subsequently how this response is accomplished.

Consistency in non-verbal speech

The automatic nature of a mechanism generating speech adaptation should not be taken to imply that it is beyond the communicator's control. Non-verbal speech also reveals consistency within an interaction and sensitivity to situational and role constraints which may characterize the interaction. For example, interviewees often display longer talk durations, slower speech rates, and fewer interruptions than do interviewers (Matarazzo, Wiens, Matarazzo, and Saslow, 1968; Street, 1984), a phenomenon that Giles (1977) has described as the maintenance of optimal 'sociolinguistic distance' given differences in the participants' role or power relationship. In fact, in such communicative encounters, changes in the speech of one partner often lead to corresponding changes in the speech of the other such that the 'pattern' of speech differentiation is maintained (Matarazzo and Wiens, 1972; Street, 1984; Street and Buller, 1988).

Representations of various situation-specific communicative strategies appear to be stored in the communicator's reserve of experiential knowledge (Giles and Street, 1985). When encountering a situation requiring a specific non-verbal speech style, the proclivity to adapt communicative behavior toward or away from a partner's speech levels is likely overridden in favor of a particular response style. For example, upon encountering a slow-talking, posturally relaxed, regionally accented interviewer, an employment interviewee may nonetheless speak with a moderately fast speech rate, with an erect posture, and with a more standard accent because of his or her concerns for deference and impression management (Street, 1986). With experience and practice, these response styles may become scripted or habituated (Berger and Roloff, 1980) such that they can be invoked and unfold automatically with little cognitive effort after the communicator recognizes their appropriateness for a particular context. For example, Greene (1984b; Greene, O'Hair, Cody, and Yen, 1985) has demonstrated that, when giving an organizing scheme and just a short time to prepare to speak on a topic, speakers produce more fluent speech and pause less than when talking on an unfamiliar topic with no prior preparation.

The fact that communicators tend to display consistency in their non-verbal speech behaviors is probably the result of their efforts to 'economize' communicative behavior production processes. Drawing from the work of Langer (1978), Berger and Roloff (1980) have argued that, if some forms of communicative behavior such as non-verbal speech can be accomplished with little or no conscious deliberation, the communicator can then direct attentional resources to such issues as developing a conversational topic, monitoring a partner's behavior, and coordinating interaction goals. Thus, communicators may seek to routinize many features of their communicative styles so that they can be deployed smoothly and with little effort. Because individuals are limited in their ability to store and process information, they are further motivated to develop self-presentation styles which are cross-situationally appropriate. For example, Snyder (1979) has argued that, although concerned about situation-appropriate behaviors, high self-monitors are not chameleon-like. Rather, one aspect of the high self-monitor's skill is the ability to develop communicative routines which are cross-situationally suitable yet can be tailored to situational nuances. Indeed, greater consistency has been observed in the speech of interpersonally oriented individuals (Street and Murphy, 1987) and high self-monitoring interactants (Dabbs, Evans, Hopper, and Purvis, 1980) than in the speech of their counterparts.

Summary

Non-verbal speech represents one component of communicative style. Consistency among these behaviors typically reflects the extent to which a particular self-presentation is appropriate for a specific communicative event. The routinization or 'scripting' of these responses enables the communicator to direct cognitive resources to other aspects of interaction such as topic development and monitoring the partner's communication. Consistency in speech performance, however, does not preclude conversants from adapting speech to different partners depending on their goals, the situation, and their partners' communicative styles. Modifications in non-verbal speech can occur automatically because the speech production system allows for efficient, effortless adjustments relative to an interlocutor's speech either by incorporating a partner's speech features into the communicator's own paralinguistic and prosodic responses or by compensating a partner's speech levels. Demonstrating the versatility of speech production processes, several investigations have indicated that speech convergence, consistency, and the maintenance of role-appropriate speech differences are not an either–or phenomenon. Rather, within the same interaction, communicators have maintained role-appropriate differences for some speech behaviors (e.g. speech duration, interruptions, speech rate), converged other speech behaviors to achieve similarity for the intensity and timing of conversational responses (e.g. response latency, loudness), and compensated other behaviors (e.g. duration of speaking turns) in order to coordinate floor-holding exchanges (Cappella and Planalp, 1981; Jaffe and Feldstein, 1970; Matarazzo and Wiens, 1972; Street, 1986).

COMMUNICATIVE FUNCTIONS AND NON-VERBAL SPEECH

Overview

Historically, researchers have assumed a 'channel' approach to the study of communicative behavior; that is, they have sliced the communicative 'stream' horizontally into various behavioral channels such as language, non-verbal behavior, vocalic behavior, and, more specifically, into subcategories of these channels such as self-disclosure, gaze, interpersonal distance, speech acts, and speech rate (see, e.g., Feldstein and Welkowitz, 1978; Harper, Wiens, and Matarazzo, 1978). Given the complexity of communicative processes, the channel approach is appealing because researchers can define and thus focus upon a particular communicative form. The study of a single communicative behavior (e.g. speech rate) or class of behaviors (e.g. non-verbal speech) has enabled researchers to identify and describe characteristics of the behaviors under scrutiny. However, communicators typically do not behave within one channel to the exclusion of others. In oral communication, every linguistic message is 'packaged' with accompanying vocalic behavior. In face-to-face interaction, non-verbal behaviors are also ubiquitous. The validity of a 'channel' approach is suspect, given the fact that a particular behavior within one channel can have dramatically different meanings depending on co-occurring behaviors in other channels. Gaze at a partner can signal anger when accompanied by negative facial affect and loud speech, or it can signal intimacy if accompanied by positive facial affect and soft speech. A fast speech rate can reflect anger, anxiety, elation, or impression management, depending on the presence of other behaviors (Giles and Street, 1985; Scherer, 1986).

The limitations of the channel approach have given rise to 'functional' models of communicative behavior. Rather than dividing the communicative stream horizontally into the various channels, advocates of communicative function models opt for slicing interaction behaviors 'vertically' by examining the collection of responses which accomplish particular functions (Burgoon, Buller, Hale, and de Turck, 1984; Cappella and Street, 1985; Patterson, 1983). Communicative functions of interest have included coherence in discourse (Tracy, 1985); intimacy, social control, and dominance (Burgoon and Hale, 1988; Edinger and Patterson, 1983); impression management (Giles and Street, 1985); task (Patterson, 1983; Poole, 1985); and feedback/reinforcement (Patterson, 1983).

One objective of this chapter is to examine non-verbal speech from a functional perspective; that is, to describe how these speech behaviors in conjunction with other communicative responses promote coherent conversational exchanges, foster intimacy and affiliation, and reflect patterns of communicative control and dominance. Paralinguistic behaviors are also instrumental to the management and formulation of interpersonal impressions. However, the research on this topic is reviewed by Bradac in Chapter 19 and will not be duplicated here.

Non-Verbal Speech and Coherence

In a variety of ways, non-verbal speech contributes to the coherence, understanding, and coordination of communicative exchanges. Prosody and paralanguage function somewhat differently to this end and thus are discussed separately.

Prosody

Prosodic speech features perform a metacommunicative function by providing interpretive cues for linguistic behaviors (Martin, 1981) and speaker switches (Duncan and Fiske, 1977). These responses function to determine which language features are stressed, what is to be taken literally, whether an utterance is completed or in process, what is 'new' information in the utterance relative to what information has already been given, and whether the utterance should be interpreted as sarcasm, humor, or deception. This is accomplished in a variety of ways.

Stress. Vocal stress, via the manipulation of pitch and loudness, draws the listener's attention to particular word(s) within the utterance. The stressed word or word phrase highlights the salience of the semantic function of that particular word(s). For example,

'This is *John's* car'

emphasizes the significance of the car belonging to John, whereas

'*This* is John's car'

draws attention to the car itself. Of course, stress – in conjunction with language – does not *determine* meaning; rather, it serves as an interpretive guide for the interface between language and context. In the first sentence, stress on 'John's' could mean that the speaker is surprised that John would have this kind of car or that the speaker inferred the car belonged to someone else. As Oliva (1982) has pointed out, non-verbal speech is indexical to the extent that it draws attention to a change, emphasis, deformation, or some characteristic (e.g. what is new versus old information in the utterance) of language. Using the collectivity of verbal behaviors, non-verbal responses, and context, the listener seeks to 'fill in' meaning and intention in the speaker's utterance (Cicourel, 1973; Grice, 1975; Hopper, 1981).

Juncture. Juncture represents breaks and boundaries in the linguistic stream and may be achieved by silence, lengthening of boundary segments of utterances, and changes in pitch, rate, and loudness. According to Martin (1981), the role of juncture is to break the communication flow into manageable units for the listener (e.g. into utterances or utterance groups) and secondarily to clarify potential syntactic ambiguities such as

'It's starting to rain now/ let's go inside'
'It's starting to rain/ now let's go inside'

and semantic ambiguities such as

'You want beer/ and wine?'
'You want beer and wine?'

Intonation. Rises and falls in intonation clarify the function of utterances (e.g. questions versus statements), whether the utterance is completed or in progress

(Martin, 1981), and when a speaker is relinquishing the floor (Duncan and Fiske, 1977). For example,

'I should write Jim a letter'

is a question,

'I should write Jim a letter'

suggests a statement, and

'I should write Jim a letter'

indicates an incomplete or continuing utterance.

Vocal exaggeration. Exaggerated vocal stress and disruptions of speech rhythm are often employed to alert the listener not to interpret an utterance literally but as humor, sarcasm, teasing, etc. Of course, vocal exaggeration need not be present for a non-literal translation. For example, a speaker at a formal dinner may presume listeners share interpretations of a phenomenon (e.g. very casual dress) and perceive as sarcastic the comment, 'That's elegant attire', even in the absence of vocal exaggeration. However, in the absence of the obvious, vocal exaggeration alerts the listener to a reframing of the literal content of an utterance:

'Now / that's / a beautiful / tie!'

Paralanguage

Paralinguistic behaviors are also influential in the creation of coherent communicative exchanges. As reviewed earlier, there is a preponderance of evidence revealing that, during the course of interaction, communicators tend to converge toward one another's speech and non-verbal behaviors (Feldstein and Welkowitz, 1978; Street, 1986). Although disagreement exists regarding the motivational impetus underlying communicative convergence (for discussions of these issues, see Cappella and Greene, 1982; Giles *et al.*, 1987; Natale, 1975; Patterson, 1983), there is evidence indicating that speech matching facilitates the ease with which speakers coordinate communicative exchanges and achieve understanding. For example, Giles and Smith (1979) reported that a Canadian speaker who slowed his normal rate of speech such that it approximated the speech rate typical of the English audience to which he was speaking was perceived by the audience as a more effective communicator than when he maintained his relatively fast speech rate. Natale (1975) reviews evidence suggesting that interactants' convergence of vocal intensity represents their joint efforts toward intelligible speech. Natale posits that, by achieving 'congruence' (i.e. similarity) among speech behaviors regulating the timing, tempo, and intensity of social interactions (e.g. speech rate, pauses, response latencies, loudness), conversants are mutually creating an optimal vocal 'format' for the interaction.

As mentioned in the section on non-verbal speech production, speech convergence can occur with little or no communicative awareness, assuming there are no normative constraints preventing convergence. One could surmise, then, that speech convergence promotes effective communication, not only to the extent that the interactants have achieved an acceptable paralinguistic mode for the interaction, but also because it emerges effortlessly so that attentional resources can be directed to other communicative objectives such as topic development and monitoring a partner's reactions. Thus, unexpected or unacceptable differences between interactants' speech rates, response latencies, loudness, etc. should be conspicuous, communicatively awkward, and brought to consciousness. In partial support of this view, Street (1982; Street and Brady, 1982) has reported that listeners tend not to notice when a speaker's speech rate and response latency are similar to their own or when a conversant converges these behaviors. However, divergence is noticed (and denigrated) by listeners as is the maintenance of speech differences (i.e. no adaptation) when the speaker's speech style is *significantly* or *inappropriately* different from that of an interlocutor (see also Giles *et al.*, 1987).

When roles of interactants are asymmetrical, speech complementarity (and not convergence) will appropriately emerge among some speech behaviors to reflect social differences. Complementarity among these speech behaviors may also promote coherence among communicative exchanges. If the participants have expectations for complementary patterns of interaction (e.g. interviewee–interviewer; manager–employee), maintaining differences along appropriate communicative dimensions reinforces the interactants' shared perceptions of the situation and of their respective social roles. The exchange will then be 'stable' as each interactant's goals and behaviors are compatible (Patterson, 1983). The mutual commitment to a complementary pattern of communicative exchange may explain the evidence reviewed earlier indicating that, although producing speech at different levels, interactants may reciprocate changes in one another's speech (e.g. increasing turn and pause durations in response to similar adjustments by a partner) such that the pattern of communicative differences is maintained (Matarazzo and Wiens, 1972; Street, 1984; Street and Buller, 1988).

Non-Verbal Speech and Communicative Control

There are numerous verbal and non-verbal markers of status, power, and control in social interactions. Two dramatically different communicative (and speech) patterns may emerge, depending on whether conversants are trying to *acquire* control of the encounter or to *maintain* a particular pattern of dominance–submissiveness.

Acquiring control

Some non-verbal speech behaviors are particularly powerful in that they regulate floor-holding patterns or the intensity of interaction. When having no prior expectations regarding each other's respective status, communicators who interrupt partners more frequently, talk for longer durations, and speak louder and faster than do their interlocutors tend to emerge or be perceived as powerful, dominant, and influential (Rogers and Jones, 1975; Scherer, 1979a; Stang, 1973). When two individuals are each vying for communicative control, both may exhibit these speech behaviors and create a pattern of 'competitive reciprocity' as each attempts to 'out-talk' the other (Giles, 1977; Street and Cappella, 1985). Not surprisingly, such an exchange is unstable and typically of short duration as one party eventually concedes the floor to the other or withdraws from the interaction.

These speech behaviors function in a powerful and controlling fashion for several reasons. First, an interruption disrupts the speech flow, thereby taking away an interlocutor's opportunity to complete the utterance (Wiemann, 1985). Second, loud and (to some extent) higher-pitched speech is 'acoustically' powerful to the extent that it stimulates arousal more than does soft and low-pitched speech, and thus likely draws substantial attention toward the speaker (Bradac and Street, 1986).

Third, a fast rate of speech may enhance the speaker's power in several respects. At least in Western cultures, moderate and relatively fast speech stereotypically evokes ratings of competence-related attributes such as intelligence, status, edu-catedness, dynamism, and confidence (Street, Brady, and Putman, 1983; Thakerar and Giles, 1981). Another factor is that speech rate reflects the tempo with which linguistic inputs are presented to listeners; the faster the tempo, the faster the listener must process utterances. This may create greater cognitive load upon the listener as more attentional resources are directed toward understanding the utterances rather than toward developing counter-arguments, carefully formulating a response, daydreaming, etc. (see e.g., Miller, Maruyama, Beaber, and Valone, 1976). Collec-tively, these factors can account for findings which show that speakers with relatively fast speech rates are usually perceived as more competent, persuasive, interesting, and confident than are slower-paced speakers (Brown, 1980; Mehrabian and Williams, 1969; Street and Brady, 1982).

Finally, duration of talk is related to the acquisition of power and influence to the extent that the listener's attention is directed toward the speaker holding the floor. Not only do long floor-holdings preclude others from speaking, but they also force listeners to consider the content of the speaker's utterances. In group interaction, several studies have reported that talk time alone (regardless of the quality of the speaker's contribution) was directly related to the speaker's perceived influence, dominance, and leadership emergence (Cappella, 1985; Stang, 1973).

Patterns of dominance and submissiveness

In relationships characterized by an asymmetrical distribution of power and/or status, the interactants' relative non-verbal speech performances (as well as other non-verbal behaviors) can reflect and reinforce the power relationship. On their own, these behaviors may not signal powerfulness or powerlessness; however, collectively, they complement one another to index a dominance–submissive rela-tionship such as that characteristic of teacher–student, manager–employee, doctor–patient, domineering spouse–submissive spouse interactions, to name a few. The pattern of communicative dissimilarities may reflect differences in interactants' goals, roles, and/or licenses to use various status markers.

In their interactions with higher-status or more socially powerful persons, lower-power conversants are often engaged in impression management, whereas their interlocutors are not (e.g. employment interviewee–interviewer; employee–manager). Thus, communicators with less status often speak faster, with less pausing, and with more vocal variety (i.e. variations in pitch, loudness, tempo) than do their partners (Giles and Street, 1985; Siegman, 1978; Street, 1984, 1986; Thakerar and Giles, 1982). Second, high-status persons often presume the right to exercise dominance by speaking for longer periods (Hershey and Werner, 1975; Street and Buller, 1988), interrupting more (West, 1984; Wiemann, 1985), and speaking louder (Scherer, 1979a) than their lower-status partners. Even in interactions in which the controlling participant speaks less than his or her interlocutor (e.g. appraisal and employment interviews), the former often controls the interaction by regulating topic development and the allocation of speaking turns (Street, 1986).

Finally, high-status communicators often are allowed to violate normative expectations for communicative behavior. In fact, violating expected behaviors can result in more status and influence because rule violations may accentuate their positions of power (Bradac and Street, 1986). Thus, among vocal behaviors, a dominant communicator may speak softer or louder, slower or faster, and/or with a more standard or non-standard accent than interlocutors. Scotton (1985) has observed a similar phenomenon in the markers of language formality (e.g. terms of address, accent, and use of slang as in 'What the heck, Sir?') and labels such moves 'style-shifting'. According to Scotton, such shifts change the nature of the communicative code characterizing the interaction. Style-shifting enhances the speaker's power because it (a) creates uncertainty in the listener regarding appropriate communicative forms and (b) reinforces the speaker's license and power to produce changes in communicative style. Of course, one could infer that, if an interlocutor wished to challenge the speaker's status, influence, or power, shifts in style and non-normative behavior would be an easy target for such a challenge.

In sum, in stable relationships characterized by an unequal distribution of power, the behavior of the powerful conversant does not by itself reflect or reinforce communication control. Rather, it is the profile of the communicative acts of the high-power individual *vis-à-vis* the rather powerless behavior of the lower-status party which indexes relative dominance. Thus, the dominance–submissive pattern is created *mutually* by the interactants and is reflected in a complementary pattern of communicative exchange (Cappella and Street, 1985; Giles *et al.*, 1987; Patterson, 1983).

Non-Verbal Speech and Affiliation

Although research is limited, several non-verbal speech behaviors are salient cues to expressions of affiliation and intimacy. When discussing highly personal, intimate, or anxiety-provoking topics, conversants often produce relatively slower and quieter speech, with more pauses and (sometimes) more disfluencies (Siegman, 1979; Siegman and Reynolds, 1982). Siegman (1979) attributes these phenomena to the problematic aspects of encoding language on personal topics. Not only are communicators cautious about discussing intimate and personal matters, they also may experience difficulty in producing appropriate or adequate descriptions of their emotion and feelings (Bowers, Metts and Duncanson, 1985). In addition, there are likely cultural expectations for personal topics to be discussed slowly and quietly. Such a vocal code perhaps cues the 'privacy' or seriousness of the utterance.

More generally, interactants who reciprocate one another's communicative responses, particularly non-verbal speech, are not only expressing the intensity of an affiliative response but also creating a mutually preferred format for expressing interpersonal involvement (Cappella, 1983; Cappella and Greene, 1982). The intensity of affiliation is reflected in behavioral *levels* through the interactant's speech rate, vocal animation, gaze, touch, distance, loudness, intimacy of self-disclosure, etc. (Burgoon and Hale, 1988; Mehrabian, 1972). The mutuality of the interactants' preferences for non-verbal expressiveness is indexed by *patterns* of reciprocal exchange (Cappella, 1983; Patterson, 1983). Several studies have reported that interactants reciprocating their interlocutor's speech rates, accents, and response latencies are perceived by partners and observers as more socially attractive, warm, and communicatively competent than are conversants not reciprocating partners' speech (Giles and Smith, 1979; Putman and Street, 1984; Street, 1982, 1984; Street *et al.*, 1983; Welkowitz and Kuc, 1973). This research complements related findings among other affiliative behaviors indicating that similarity between interactants' postures and body positions is related to perceptions of rapport and interpersonal involvement (Bavelas *et al.*, 1988; LaFrance, 1982). In sum, the social attraction and affiliation between two conversants may be better indexed by their relative similarity among non-verbal behaviors, including speech, than by the levels of these behaviors *per se* (Cappella and Palmer, 1988).

FUTURE DIRECTIONS

In this paper, I have attempted to examine the nature and function of non-verbal speech in social interaction. While researchers have extensively studied the physiology and perceptual correlates of, and speaker characteristics reflected in, speech behaviors, two topics remain seriously understudied. First, the processes by which non-verbal speech unfolds automatically as well as the social consequences of stability and variability in speech style warrant explication. These issues are not only of theoretical interest but also of practical concern because they impinge upon broader questions related to communicative skill development and disorders of communication (cf. Crown, Feldstein, Jasnow, Beebe, and Jaffe, 1985).

For example, within the context of communicative competence, one could argue that, as communicators become more competent, their communicative styles will reveal greater consistency. Communicators develop self-presentation styles as they discover a set of responses which facilitate the accomplishment of personal goals (Schlenker, 1980). Furthermore, for the sake of efficiency, given limited cognitive and behavioral resources, competent communicators probably are motivated to formulate only a few styles which would be appropriate for various communicative situations (cf. Snyder, 1979). On the other hand, as communicators become more competent, they may exhibit greater adaptation in their communicative responses. For example, experiences with different interlocutors, contexts, and speech communities may allow communicators to develop a sufficiently diversified communicative repertoire so that responses can be efficiently and appropriately modified, given the characteristics of a partner or the situation (Giles and Street, 1985).

This issue also has implications for how communicators are perceived by others. A particular communicative style (e.g. relatively fast speech with vocal animation) may consistently evoke positive impressions for the employment interviewee (e.g. dynamic, confident, intelligent), but elicit negative reactions for the conversationalist (e.g. too formal, overbearing, out of tempo). Likewise, adaptive responses may generate positive impressions of an interactant if the adaptation promotes smooth and rhythmic conversational exchanges or if it makes the speaker appear accommodating and as 'fitting in'. Yet, modifying one's communicative style may generate unfavorable attributions if the speaker appears ingratiating or insincere (Giles, 1977).

Second, by not examining multiple levels of naturally occurring communicative behaviors, social speech researchers may be limiting the ecological validity of their findings. For example, in experiments manipulating a communicator's vocal levels and controlling (or excluding) other behaviors, non-verbal speech has been shown to have a tremendous impact on social evaluations (Brown, 1980; Hayes and Meltzer, 1972). However, in conjunction with other behaviors, the impact of a particular speech variable, while perhaps significant, is often attenuated as perceivers evaluate the *total* communicative response in relation to the particular communicative functions of import in the interaction (Street, Mulac, and Wiemann, 1988). From a functional perspective, then, non-verbal speech influences outcomes of social interaction because of its importance in the classes of behaviors regulating the accomplishment of interaction functions such as affiliation, control, the formation of interpersonal impressions, and coherence within communicative exchanges.

REFERENCES

Abercrombie, D. (1967). *Element of general phonetics*. Edinburgh: University of Edinburgh Press.

Bavelas, J.B., Black, A., Chovil, N., Lemery, C., and Mullett, J. (1988). Form and function in motor mimicry. *Human Communication Research*, **14**, 275–300.

Beebe, B., Jaffe, J., Feldstein, S., Mays, K., and Alson, D. (1985). Interpersonal timing: The application of an adult dialogue model to mother–infant vocal and kinesic behavior. In T.M. Field and N.A. Fox (Eds), *Social perception in infants*, pp. 217–247. Norwood, NJ: Ablex.

Berger, C.R. (1980). Self-consciousness and the study of interpersonal interaction. In H. Giles, W.P. Robinson, and P. Smith (Eds), *Language: Social psychological perspectives*, pp. 49–53. Oxford: Pergamon.

Berger, C.R. and Roloff, M.E. (1980). Social cognition, self-awareness, and interpersonal communication. In B. Dervin and M.J. Voigt (Eds), *Progress in communication sciences*, Vol. 2, pp. 1–49. Norwood, NJ: Ablex.

Bourhis, R.Y. and Giles, H. (1977). The language of intergroup distinctiveness. In H. Giles (Ed.), *Language, ethnicity, and intergroup relations*, pp. 119–135. London: Academic Press.

Bourhis, R.Y., Giles, H., Leyens, J.-P., and Tajfel, H. (1979). Psychological distinctiveness: Language divergence in Belgium. In H. Giles and R. St Clair (Eds), *Language and social psychology*, pp. 158–185. Oxford: Blackwell.

Bourhis, R.Y., Roth, S., and MacQueen, G. (1989). Communication in the hospital setting: A survey of everyday and medical language use among patients, nurses, and doctors. *Social Science and Medicine*.

Bowers, J.W., Metts, H.M., and Duncanson, W.T. (1985). Emotion and interpersonal communication. In M.L. Knapp and G.R. Miller (Eds), *Handbook of interpersonal communication*, pp. 500–550. Beverly Hills, CA: Sage.

Bradac, J. and Street, R.L., Jr (1986). Powerful and powerless styles of talk. Paper presented to the Annual Meeting of the Speech Communication Association, Boston.

Brennan, E.M., Ryan, E.B., and Dawson, W.E. (1975). Scaling of apparent accentedness by magnitude estimation and sensory modality matching. *Journal of Psycholinguistic Research*, **4**, 27–36.

Brown, B.L. (1980). Effects of speech rate on personality attributions and competency evaluations. In H. Giles, W.P. Robinson, and P. Smith (Eds), *Language: Social psychological perspectives*, pp. 293–300. Oxford: Pergamon.

Brown, B.L., Warner, C.T., and Williams, R.N. (1985). Vocal paralanguage without unconscious processes. In A.W. Siegman and S. Feldstein (Eds), *Multichannel integrations of nonverbal behavior*, pp. 149–193. Hillsdale, NJ: Erlbaum.

Bruner, J. (1981). The social context of language acquisition. *Language and Communication*, **1**, 155–178.

Burgoon, J.K., Buller, D., Hale, J., and de Turck, M.A. (1984). Relational messages associated with nonverbal behaviors. *Human Communication Research*, **10**, 351–378.

Burgoon, J.K. and Hale, J. (1988). Nonverbal expectancy violations: Mode elaboration and application to immediacy behaviors. *Communication Monographs*, **55**, 58–79.

Cappella, J.N. (1981). Mutual influence in expressive behavior: Adult–adult and infant–adult dyadic interaction. *Psychological Bulletin*, **89**, 101–132.

Cappella, J.N. (1983). Approaching and avoiding others: Involvement in dyadic interactions. In J.M. Wiemann and R.P. Harrison (Eds), *Nonverbal interaction*, pp. 113–148. Beverly Hills, CA: Sage.

Cappella, J.N. (1985). Controlling the floor in conversation. In A.W. Siegman and S. Feldstein (Eds), *Multichannel integrations of nonverbal behavior*, pp. 69–103. Hillsdale, NJ: Erlbaum.

Cappella, J.N. and Greene, J.O. (1982). A discrepancy–arousal explanation of mutual influence in expressive behavior for adult–adult and infant–adult interaction. *Communication Monographs*, **49**, 80–114.

Cappella, J.N. and Palmer, M. (1988). Attitude similarity and attraction: The mediating effects of kinesic and vocal behavior. Paper presented to the Annual Meeting of the International Communication Association, New Orleans.

Cappella, J.N. and Planalp, S. (1981). Talk and silence sequences in informal conversation III: Interspeaker influence. *Human Communication Research*, **7**, 117–132.

Cappella, J.N. and Street, R.L., Jr (1985). A functional approach to the structure of communicative behavior. In R.L. Street, Jr and J.N. Cappella (Eds), *Sequence and pattern in communicative behavior*, pp. 1–29. London: Arnold.

Cicourel, A.V. (1973). *Cognitive sociology*. London: Macmillan.

Crown, C.L., Feldstein, S., Jasnow, M., Beebe, B., and Jaffe, J. (1985). A strategy for investigating autism as a prelinguistic disorder of social development. *Australian Journal of Human Communication Disorders*, **13**, 61–76.

Crystal, D. (1969). *Prosodic systems and intonation in English*. Cambridge: Cambridge University Press.

Dabbs, J.M, Jr, Evans, M.S., Hopper, C.H., and Purvis, J.A. (1980). Self-monitors in conversation: What do they monitor? *Journal of Personality and Social Psychology*, **39**, 278–284.

Duncan, S. and Fiske, D.W. (1977). *Face-to-face interaction*. Hillsdale, NJ: Erlbaum.

Edinger, J.A. and Patterson, M.L. (1983). Nonverbal involvement and social control. *Psychological Bulletin*, **93**, 30–56.

Feldstein, S., Konstantareas, M., Oxman, J., and Webster, C.D. (1985). The chronography of interaction with autistic speakers. *Journal of Communicative Disorders*, **15**, 451–460.

Feldstein, S. and Welkowitz, J. (1978). A chronography of conversation: In defense of an objective approach. In A.W. Siegman and S. Feldstein (Eds), *Nonverbal behavior and communication*, pp. 435–499. Hillsdale, NJ: Erlbaum.

Giles, H. (1977). Social psychology and applied linguistics: Toward an integrative approach. *ITL: A Review of Applied Linguistics*, **35**, 27–42.

Giles, H., Mulac, A., Bradac, J., and Johnson, P. (1987). Speech accommodation theory: The first decade and beyond. *Communication Yearbook*, **10**, 13–48.

Giles, H. and Powesland, P.F. (1975). *Speech style and social evaluation*. London: Academic Press.

Giles, H. and Smith, P.M. (1979). Accommodation theory: Optimal levels of convergence. In H. Giles and R. St Clair (Eds), *Language and social psychology*, pp. 45–65. Oxford: Blackwell.

Giles, H. and Street, R.L., Jr (1985). Communicator characteristics and behavior. In M.L. Knapp and G.R. Miller (Eds), *Handbook of interpersonal communication*, pp. 205–261. Beverly Hills, CA: Sage.

Greene, J.O. (1984a). A cognitive approach to human communication: An action assembly theory. *Communication Monographs*, **51**, 289–306.

Greene, J.O. (1984b). Speech preparation processes and fluency. *Human Communication Research*, **11**, 61–84.

Greene, J.O., O'Hair, H.D., Cody, M.J., and Yen, C. (1985). Planning and control of behavior during deception. *Human Communication Research*, **11**, 335–364.

Grice, H.P. (1975). Logic and conversation. In P. Cole and J.L. Morgan (Eds), *Syntax and semantics: Speech acts*, pp. 41–58. New York: Academic Press.

Harper, R.G., Wiens, A.N., and Matarazzo, J.D. (Eds) (1978). *Nonverbal communication: The state of the art*. New York: Wiley.

Hayes, D.P. and Meltzer, L. (1972). Interpersonal judgments based upon talkativeness I: Fact or artifact? *Sociometry*, **35**, 538–561.

Helfrich, H. (1979). Age markers in speech. In K.R. Scherer and H. Giles (Eds), *Social markers in speech*, pp. 63–108. Cambridge: Cambridge University Press.

Hershey, S. and Werner, E. (1975). Dominance in marital decision-making in women's liberation and non-women's liberation families. *Family Processes*, **14**, 223–233.

Hoffmann, M.L. (1977). Empathy, its development, and prosocial implications. In C. Keasey (Ed.), *Nebraska symposium on motivation, 1977*, pp. 169–217. Lincoln, NE: University of Nebraska.

Hopper, R. (1981). The taken-for-granted. *Human Communication Research*, **7**, 195–211.

Jaffe, J. and Feldstein, S. (1970). *Rhythms of dialogue*. New York: Academic Press.

Kasl, W.V. and Mahl, G.F. (1965). The relationships of disturbances and hesitation in spontaneous speech to anxiety. *Journal of Personality and Social Psychology*, **1**, 425–433.

LaFrance, M. (1982). Posture mirroring and rapport. In M. Davis (Ed.), *Interaction rhythms*, pp. 279–297. New York: Human Sciences.

Lane, H.L. and Tranel, B. (1971). The Lombard reflex and role of hearing in speech. *Journal of Speech and Hearing Research*, **14**, 677–709.

Langer, E.J. (1978). Rethinking the role of thought in social interaction. In J. Harvey, W.J. Ickes, and R.F. Kidd (Eds), *New directions in attribution research*, Vol. 2, pp. 35–58. Hillsdale, NJ: Erlbaum.

Laver, J. and Trudgill, P. (1979). Phonetic and linguistic markers in speech. In K.R. Scherer and H. Giles (Eds), *Social markers in speech*, pp. 1–32. Cambridge: Cambridge University Press.

Lieberman, P. (1967). *Intonation, perception, and language*. Cambridge, MA: MIT Press.

Martin, H. (1981). The prosodic components of speech melody. *Quarterly Journal of Speech*, **67**, 81–92.

Matarazzo, J.D. and Wiens, A.N. (1972). *The interview: Research on its anatomy and structure*. Chicago: Aldine.

Matarazzo, J.D., Wiens, A.N., Matarazzo, R.G., and Saslow, G. (1968). Speech and silence behavior in clinical psychotherapy and its laboratory correlates. In M.J. Schlien, H. Hunt, J.D. Matarazzo, and C. Savage (Eds), *Research in psychotherapy*, Vol. 3, pp. 347–394. Washington, DC: American Psychological Association.

Mehrabian, A. (1972). *Nonverbal communication*. Chicago: Aldine.

Mehrabian, A. and Williams, M. (1969). Nonverbal concomitants of perceived and intended persuasiveness. *Journal of Personality and Social Psychology*, **13**, 37–58.

Meltzhoff, A.N. (1985). The roots of social and cognitive development: Models of man's original nature. In T.M. Field and N.A. Fox (Eds), *Social perception in infants*, pp. 1–30. Norwood, NJ: Ablex.

Miller, N., Maruyama, G., Beaber, R.J., and Valone, K. (1976). Speed of speech and persuasion. *Journal of Personality and Social Psychology*, **34**, 615–624.

Murray, D.C. (1971). Talk, silence, and anxiety. *Psychological Bulletin*, **75**, 224–260.

Natale, M. (1975). Convergence of mean vocal intensity in dyadic communication as a function of social desirability. *Journal of Personality and Social Psychology*, **32**, 790–804.

Oliva, J. (1982). The structure and semiotic function of paralanguage. In M. Davis (Ed.), *Interaction rhythms*, pp. 195–206. New York: Human Sciences Press.

Patterson, M.L. (1983). *Nonverbal behavior: A functional perspective*. New York: Springer-Verlag.

Poole, M.S. (1985). Tasks and interaction sequences: A theory of coherence in group decision-making interaction. In R.L. Street, Jr and J.N. Cappella (Eds), *Sequence and pattern in communicative behavior*, pp. 206–224. London: Arnold.

Putman, W. and Street, R.L., Jr (1984). The conception and perception of noncontent speech performance: Implications for speech accommodation theory. *International Journal of the Sociology of Language*, **46**, 97–114.

Rogers, W.T. and Jones, S.E. (1975). Effects of dominance tendencies on floor-holding and interruption behavior in dyadic interaction. *Human Communication Research*, **1**, 113–122.

Sabin, E.J., Clemmer, E.J., O'Connell, D.C., and Kowal, S. (1979). A pausological approach to speech development. In A.W. Siegman and S. Feldstein (Eds), *Of speech and time*, pp. 35–55. Hillsdale, NJ: Erlbaum.

Scherer, K.R. (1979a). Personality markers in speech. In K.R. Scherer and H. Giles (Eds), *Social markers in speech*, pp. 147–209. Cambridge: Cambridge University Press.

Scherer, K.R. (1979b). Voice and speech correlates of perceived social influence in simulated juries. In H. Giles and R. St Clair (Eds), *Language and social psychology*, pp. 88–120. Oxford: Blackwell.

Scherer, K.R. (1986). Vocal affect expression: A review and model for future research. *Psychological Bulletin*, **99**, 143–165.

Scherer, K.R. and Giles, H. (Eds) (1979). *Social markers in speech*. Cambridge: Cambridge University Press.

Schlenker, B.R. (1980). *Impression management: The self-concept, social identity, and interpersonal relations*. Monterey, CA: Brooks/Cole.

Scotton, C.M. (1985).'What the heck, Sir?': Style shifting and lexical coloring as features of powerful language. In R.L. Street, Jr and J.N. Cappella (Eds), *Sequence and pattern in communicative behavior*, pp. 103–119. London: Arnold.

Siegman, A.W. (1978). The tell-tale voice: Nonverbal messages of verbal communication. In A.W. Siegman and S. Feldstein (Eds), *Nonverbal behavior and communication*, pp. 183–244. Hillsdale, NJ: Erlbaum.

Siegman, A.W. (1979). The voice of attraction. In A.W. Siegman and S. Feldstein (Eds), *Of speech and time*, pp. 89–114. Hillsdale, NJ: Erlbaum.

Siegman, A.W. and Pope, B. (1965). Efects of question specificity and anxiety producing messages on verbal fluency in the initial interview. *Journal of Personality and Social Psychology*, **4**, 188–192.

Siegman, A.W. and Pope, B. (1966). The effects of interviewer-ambiguity and topical focus on interviewee vocabulary diversity. *Language and Speech*, **9**, 242–249.

Siegman, A.W. and Reynolds, M. (1982). Interviewee–interviewer nonverbal communications: An interactional approach. In M. Davis (Ed), *Interaction rhythms*, pp. 249–276. New York: Human Sciences.

Snyder, M. (1979). Self-monitoring processes: In L. Berkowitz (Ed.), *Advances in experimental social psychology*, Vol. 12, pp. 85–128. New York: Academic Press.

Stang, D.J. (1973). Effect of interaction rate on ratings of leadership and liking. *Journal of Personality and Social Psychology*, **27**, 405–408.

Stern, D., Jaffe, J., Beebe, B., and Bennett, S. (1975). Vocalizing in unison and alternation. *Transactions of the New York Academy of Sciences*, **263**, 89–101.

Street, R.L., Jr (1982). Evaluation of noncontent speech accommodation. *Language and Communication*, **2**, 13–31.

Street, R.L., Jr (1983). Noncontent speech convergence and divergence in adult–child interactions. *Communication Yearbook*, **7**, 369–395.

Street, R.L., Jr (1984). Speech convergence and speech evaluation in fact-finding interviews. *Human Communication Research*, **11**, 139–169.

Street, R.L., Jr (1986). Interaction processes and outcomes in interviews. *Communication Yearbook*, **9**, 215–250.

Street, R.L., Jr, and Brady, R.M. (1982). Speech rate acceptance ranges as a function of evaluative domain, listener speech rate, and interaction context. *Communication Monographs*, **49**, 290–308.

Street, R.L., Jr, Brady, R.M., and Putman, W. (1983). The influence of speech rate stereotypes and rate similarity on listeners' evaluations of speakers. *Journal of Language and Social Psychology*, **2**, 37–56.

Street, R.L., Jr, and Buller, D. (1988). Patients' characteristics affecting physician–patient nonverbal communication. *Human Communication Research*, **15**, 60–90.

Street, R.L., Jr, and Cappella, J.N. (1985). Sequence and pattern in communicative behavior: A review and commentary. In R.L. Street, Jr and J.N. Cappella (Eds), *Sequence and pattern in communicative behavior*, pp. 243–276. London: Arnold.

Street, R.L., Jr, and Cappella, J.N. (in press). Social and linguistic factors influencing adaptation in children's speech. *Journal of Psycholinguistic Research*.

Street, R.L., Jr, and Hopper, R. (1982). A model of speech style evaluation. In E.B. Ryan and H. Giles (Eds), *Attitudes toward language variation: Social and applied contexts*, pp. 175–188. London: Arnold.

Street, R.L., Jr, Mulac, A., and Wiemann, J.M. (1988). Speech evaluation differences as a function of perspective (participant versus observer) and presentational medium. *Human Communication Research*, **14**, 333–363.

Street, R.L., Jr, and Murphy, T. (1987). Interpersonal orientation and speech behavior. *Communication Monographs*, **54**, 42–62.

Thakerar, J.N. and Giles, H. (1981). They are–so they speak: Noncontent speech stereotypes. *Language and Communication*, **1**, 251–256.

Thakerar, J.N. and Giles, H. (1982). Psychological and linguistic parameters of speech accommodation theory. In C. Fraser and K.R. Scherer (Eds), *Advances in the social psychology of language*, pp. 205–255. Cambridge: Cambridge University Press.

Tracy, K. (1985). Conversational coherence: A cognitively grounded rules approach. In R.L. Street, Jr and J.N. Cappella (Eds), *Sequence and pattern in communicative behavior*, pp. 30–49. London: Arnold.

Trager, G.L. and Smith, H.L., Jr (1951). *An outline of English structure*. Norman, OK: Battenburg.

Webb, J.T. (1972). Interview synchrony: An investigation of two speech rate measures. In A.W. Siegman and B. Pope (Eds), *Studies in dyadic communication*, pp. 115–133. New York: Pergamon.

Welkowitz, J., Cariffe, G., and Feldstein, S. (1976). Conversational congruence as a criterion for socialization in children. *Child Development*, **47**, 269–272.

Welkowitz, J. and Kuc, M. (1973). Interrelationships among warmth, genuineness, empathy, and temporal speech patterns in interpersonal interactions. *Journal of Consulting and Clinical Psychology*, **41**, 472–473.

West, C. (1984). *Routine complications: Trouble with the talk between doctors and patients*. Bloomington, IN: University of Indiana Press.

Wiemann, J.M. (1985). Interpersonal control and regulation in conversation. In R.L. Street, Jr and J.N. Cappella (Eds), *Sequence and pattern in communicative behavior*, pp. 85–102. London: Arnold.

7

The Structure and Organization of Verbal and Non-Verbal Behavior: Data for Models of Production

JOSEPH N. CAPPELLA AND MARK T. PALMER

Department of Communication Arts, University of Wisconsin-Madison and Department of Communication Studies, Northwestern University, USA

The purpose of this chapter is to present some issues concerning the structure and organization of verbal and non-verbal behavior at the individual level. Our concern is not only with the generation of such behavior, that is, how it is organized in its manifest production, but also with how it is perceived, that is, how individuals see and hear its organization. This distinction is often called the encoding–decoding distinction. But fundamentally the distinction is one between two quite different locations for meaning, namely in the sender's intention and motivation on the encoding side, and in the receiver's perception and reaction on the decoding side. In short, the interrelation of verbal and non-verbal behaviors is the search for common meanings, in intention or motivation and in perception or reaction, that tie these behaviors together.

In all matters concerning this organization the primary concern is with the empirical organization and structure of non-verbal and verbal behavior and not necessarily with the underlying mechanisms which contribute to the organization and structure. This orientation toward the empirical is not a slap at cognitive models of production or reception. Quite the contrary! We will be suggesting (albeit in a limited way) certain theoretical and explanatory aspects of production and reception. Rather, the orientation toward the empirical is taken up because cognitive

Handbook of Language and Social Psychology
Edited by H. Giles and W.P. Robinson.   © 1990 John Wiley & Sons Ltd

models of reception and production must be models of some phenomenon and, we fear, the phenomenon of verbal and non-verbal organization is incompletely specified.

In short, the task is to describe a portion of the available evidence on verbal and non-verbal structure, to present bits and pieces of new evidence, to outline some methods for acquiring better evidence, and lastly to describe some of the theoretical approaches which would explain production and comprehension at the individual level.

IMPORTANCE

It is fair to ask why the question of the organization of verbal and non-verbal behavior is so important that we should direct our attention to it. The alternatives are in some sense simpler. One could focus upon each type of behavior separately. One could produce behavioral indices based on criteria of face validity for their combination. Neither of these approaches is acceptable for the same reasons that they would not be acceptable approaches to item grouping in personality-test construction. No self-respecting researcher would group items together only on the basis of their face validity and no competent researcher would treat multiple, parallel test items as distinct. Why should verbal and non-verbal behaviors emitted by individuals be treated any differently from self-report test items?

Next let us consider some of the motivations for studying empirically and theoretically the meaning patterns of verbal and non-verbal behaviors.

Theories of Production

If we are to understand how people produce verbal and non-verbal behavior, then our theories of production must be both precise and valid. But if the data upon which these theories are posited are very limited in scope, general rather than specific, temporally imprecise rather than precise, then the theories themselves may be incomplete or, worse, inaccurate in significant ways. For example, the timing of head nods or other body movements relative to vocal stress is very important information for theories of speech or motor primacy in speech production (Butterworth and Hadar, 1986; McNeill, 1985). The absence of such information allows no disconfirmable theoretical claims on which mechanism of production is causally prior or, more interestingly, whether both behavioral outcomes are generated from the same underlying representation.

Theories of Reception

The temporal variation in aural and visual stimulation created during an ordinary interaction is very high. Individual participants could not reasonably be processing even a fraction of the information present in this stimulation. The interesting cognitive question is how this information-dense stimulation is mapped into perceptions about the other and the other's meanings. Certainly the two extreme positions are incorrect: 'all stimulation but one channel is ignored' cannot be correct, given all of the research on the mitigating effects of inconsistent verbal and non-verbal messages (Burgoon, 1985a); 'all stimulation is processed' cannot be correct, given the usually accepted limits of the human information-processing system (Kahneman, 1973). Thus, the interesting theoretical questions will be ones of what heuristics people regularly use to reduce the complexity that they must handle and how effective these heuristics are. For example, deception research comes to mind here since people's perception of what is deceptive is often different from what is actually associated with deception (Zuckerman, De Paulo, and Rosenthal, 1981).

Measurement Issues

One of the most frustrating and taxing problems facing interaction researchers is the costly problem of measuring and coding numerous verbal and non-verbal behaviors. The necessity for this multiplicity is created by concerns for ecological validity and by concerns that actions (or their absence) in one modality will be compensated in another modality. In such a case, measurement of only one modality will fail to show variation that occurred in a complementary modality. Thus, for example, researchers in self-disclosure reciprocity have found persons reciprocating high levels of self-disclosure even though their liking for these high self-disclosers does not follow (Chaiken and Derlega, 1974; Cozby, 1972). Studies employing multiple behaviors may show that persons compensate in other modalities while reciprocating verbally by staying on topic (Rubin, 1975).

The effect of a resurgent interest in multiple behaviors is an ocean of data with little concomitant reduction in dimensionality. The equivalent effect in personality or attitude research would be data analyses with dozens or perhaps hundreds of individual items. The solution in the self-report domain is to carry out various sorts of data reduction of the individual items into clusters. The equivalent solution in the behavioral domain is to ascertain if behavioral clustering exists either among the behaviors that are produced by persons in interaction or in the mapping between behaviors and the perceptions that they produce. The former strategy seeks to find empirical covariation as the basis for clustering and the latter seeks to find functional equivalence as the basis for clustering of behaviors.

If two different behaviors give rise to the same perception, then one could treat them as functionally equivalent (that is, as having the same meaning); if at the same time they regularly exhibit high temporal covariation, then not only are they functionally equivalent but they are in fact redundant. We should not expect such simplicities in the complex world of social interaction, but these extreme cases set the stage for understanding why it is necessary to study empirical covariations among behaviors, both verbal and non-verbal. When redundancies or functional equivalences are discovered, then aggregate scales can be constructed and data-handling and coding problems can be reduced.

In sum, the study of the organization of the verbal and non-verbal domains has implications for the study of production models and reception models, and has the potential for advancing measurement and coding in social interaction research.

METHODOLOGICAL APPROACHES

Although there are as many ways of studying the organization of verbal and non-verbal behaviors as there are researchers, a few quantitative procedures stand out as having been widely used or as having unexploited potential. Three distinctions differentiate types of studies by methodology: multiple versus single behavior studies, production versus reception studies, and distributional versus temporal studies.

Single behavior studies usually focus on a single verbal or non-verbal behavior and its relation to some other behavior. Perhaps the most common example of this type of inquiry is the qualitative or quantitative examination of the relationship between a behavior such as iconic gesture and some aspect of the spoken word (McNeill and Levy, 1982). Multiple behavior studies typically examine a variety of behaviors and their interrelation. The distinction is basically one between a bivariate and multivariate analysis.

Production studies are concerned with the covariation among behaviors as they are manifested by an individual actor in some social context. Organization or structure is manifested in the ability to predict from one behavior (or behavioral set) to another. Reception studies, on the other hand, are concerned with how people respond (especially in terms of conscious cognitive judgments) to behaviors manifested by another person. Responses may include judgments of affiliation, involvement, dominance, and so on. By focusing on reactions to behaviors, one gets a sense of how behaviors function in producing judgments and attitudes and in the process one gains some understanding of the similarity and dissimilarity in meaning that various behaviors have (where 'meaning' here is defined in terms of its effect on judgment).

Distributional studies are concerned with covariation across behaviors in the aggregate. By using mean or total durations of various behaviors one can get a sense of which behaviors co-occur in the aggregate. However, in order to understand when covariation is truly simultaneous, rather than simply occurring in the same interaction, one needs to have temporal data.

Each of the above distinctions carries different types of information about the organization of verbal and non-verbal behavior. The three two-valued distinctions above produce eight types of studies of organization (e.g. production–temporal–single). Examples of each type exist, although single variable, distributional studies predominate. In our view, studies of both production and reception are necessary and equally important in understanding the organization and structure of verbal and non-verbal behavior. However, because one can always go from temporal to distributional and from multiple to single behavior analyses, temporal, multiple behavioral studies are to be preferred in terms of the information they are capable of providing.

Thus, the types of studies of the organization of non-verbal and verbal behavior include:

Production–Single–Distributional
Production–Single–Temporal
Production–Multiple–Distributional

Production–Multiple–Temporal
Reception–Single–Distributional
Reception–Single–Temporal
Reception–Multiple–Distributional
Reception–Multiple–Temporal

In the remainder of this chapter, we will review some of the empirical literature and some of the substantive theory relevant to the first four classes of studies. Length restrictions necessitate that reception studies be discussed elsewhere (see Cappella and Palmer, 1988a).

SOME CAVEATS

Certainly the reader might object at the outset that attempting to ascertain organizational patterns among behaviors, while complex in itself, is made even more complex by the fact that the patterns would be expected to vary by situation, personality type, social role, and other factors known to influence the production and reception of verbal and non-verbal behaviors (Burgoon, 1985b; Giles and Street, 1985). Further, problems of generalization will be compounded by variations in the size of time units and observation units across studies, variation in types of measures such as averages, raw durations, rates, frequencies, short and long events, etc., and by the sheer ingenuity of researchers in inventing new variables to describe the same stimulus sequence (e.g. mutual gaze, face-directed gaze, gaze while speaking, gaze–dominance ratio, and so on).

All of these problems are real but represent no greater complexity than exists in any other study of social behavior and, indeed, in any attempt to build a personality or state assessment instrument. Additionally, it is not unreasonable to seek generalizations both within and across those complicating factors creating variation. Generalizations across personality types may be difficult to achieve but they would provide powerful guides for both methodology and theory.

PRODUCTION APPROACHES

The goal of production studies is to establish patterns of empirical covariation among behaviors spontaneously manifested or experimentally induced in competent speakers and actors. The goals are to provide empirical grist for the cognitive theories of production and to assess empirical redundancy for the purposes of scale building and data reduction.

Distributional–Single Studies

In the class of studies labeled 'distributional–single', the most common type of research assesses the covariation between a particular motivational or personality state and some observable, behavioral manifestation of that state. For example,

Siegman (1979, 1987) has shown that cognitive load in the form of uncertainty about the situation or the other person leads to increases in pausing in speech. Links between behavioral domains, however, are indirect at best. For example, if one combines Siegman's results with research by Nielsen (1962) showing greater gaze aversion with more difficult tasks, then one might be led to infer that gaze aversion and pausing in speech covary. Although not an unreasonable inference, the inference is nonetheless indirect. It may be the case that these two indicators do not covary at all but rather are merely different manifestations of the same underlying causal force preferentially employed by one individual as opposed to another. In such a case, the inference of covariation between behaviors would be incorrect.

The reason for such inferences is that the multiple behaviors are not studied in the same design and, much more importantly, actual patterns of temporal covariation are not observed. If one does study gaze aversion and pausing within the same design (say as a function of induced interpersonal hostility) but only obtains means values, then the means could covary significantly in the aggregate without covarying at all temporally. Such are the weaknesses of distributional rather than temporal data, whether gathered singly or in multiples.

Despite these inferential weaknesses, studies in this category can be useful and are certainly much more numerous than their counterparts in the 'temporal' category. Several summaries of literature which seek to group individual behaviors on the basis of their being common consequents of similar underlying forces have appeared elsewhere (Cappella and Street, 1984; Coker and Burgoon, 1987; Edinger and Patterson, 1983; and see Chapter 6, by Patterson) and will not be repeated here. We will consider several studies in which covariation between various speech features and kinesic behaviors is studied.

Cappella (1985b) studied various vocal and kinesic responses to two types of interview questions under conditions evaluated as high and low in social anxiety. An independent sample of judges rated two groups of interview questions: the second group was judged to be more difficult, more complex, more thought-provoking, and more anxiety-producing than the first group. All interviewees were asked the less-taxing questions first, followed by the more-taxing questions. The expectation was that the more difficult questions would promote more complex verbal responses. Indeed, the responses to the more difficult questions took longer and (after adjustment for length differences) produced more pausing, more gaze aversion, more body-focused gestures, and more object-focused gestures. Thus, the more verbally complex responses may be associated with compensatory reactions in terms of vocal hesitancy (pauses), reduced informational input (gaze aversion), and motor spillover (body-focused gestures).

These findings are consistent with other research on the relationship between complex, ambiguous, and difficult verbal materials, on the one hand, and pausing (Goldman-Eisler, 1968; Greene, 1984b; Siegman, 1979), gaze aversion (Exline and Winters, 1965; Kendon, 1967), and body-focused gestures (Butterworth and Beattie, 1978; Jurich and Jurich, 1974) on the other. Despite this consistency, the distributional covariation found in these studies cannot be interpreted as strong evidence for production processes and the mechanisms underlying behavioral production. Temporal covariation is necessary for such inferences.

Distributional–Multiple Studies

As researchers use increasingly sophisticated video, audio, and computer technologies to gather more complete and detailed verbal and non-verbal behaviors within social interactional contexts, they inevitably will turn to reducing the complexity of these data through various forms of aggregate clustering of mean and average behaviours.

The argument for doing so is a rather straightforward extension of similar techniques used in test construction. Social and behavioral scientists regularly employ the tenets of classical test theory to develop internally consistent scales from individual items. The basic purpose is to produce a more reliable measure of an underlying state or trait of a person from several independent, and presumably parallel, measures of the state or trait. The composite measure, if psychometrically acceptable, will usually have greater internal consistency (and hence reliability) than will the separate items; additionally, the researcher achieves some efficiency by having to analyze a much smaller set of variables. The reduction is achieved precisely because there is redundancy among the items tapping into the underlying construct. Capitalizing on this redundancy is advantageous both theoretically and statistically.

An analogous argument can be made for multiple behaviors generated in research on multiple verbal and non-verbal behaviors. To the extent that the behaviors are redundant, it makes neither conceptual nor practical sense to treat them as distinct. Rather, their multiplicity should be reduced in the same way and for the same reasons that redundant test items should be reduced: to increase reliability and statistical efficiency. In short, clustering behaviors can have the same effects as clustering test items.

Some very important cautions must be noted, however, in this proposal. First, aggregate covariation (for example, in mean durations of behaviors) does not necessarily imply temporal covariation for exactly the reasons noted earlier. Second, the patterns of covariation observed may change as the units across which aggregation occurs either increase or decrease. For example, we would not be surprised to find that covariational patterns across conversations as time units would differ from those observed with turns or phrases as time units. Third, the patterns of covariation observed may change as the social conditions under which the patterns take place change. For example, it would be unsurprising to find that behavioral covariation for socially secure persons differed from that for socially insecure persons, if only because certain behaviors may have restricted ranges. Fourth, the patterns of covariation may vary as a function of the type of behavioral data gathered. For example, correlations among rate variables would not necessarily be the same as patterns among durational or frequency measures.

Finally, and most important, the theoretical purpose of the index must be taken into account when methods for its construction are chosen. The key point here is this: when an index of behaviors is being constructed because the research is aimed at studying behavioral production, then empirical covariation among behaviors is a sufficient criterion for index construction. However, when the index is being constructed for some other purpose, say the response of partners to hostility, then the index building must be based on the effectiveness of a particular behavioral grouping in determining partner response, and not necessarily on the covariation among sender behaviors. Partners may be responding to different 'packages' of social stimulation by senders than the 'packages' determined by the production forces driving the sender's actions. In short, the nature of the index construction must be determined by the purposes to which it will be put. This section focuses upon production, and thus simple covariation among behaviors is an acceptable basis for index construction. When reception is the goal, then covariation between behaviors and outcome judgments must be the basis for clustering.

These caveats may be summarized in one admonition at these early stages of index construction: each study must construct its own indices based upon the particular purposes, social conditions, measures, and time units pertinent to the application. Time will tell whether any regular patterns of behavioral covariation will emerge.

Early studies

Mehrabian (1970) hypothesized a three-dimensional structure describing the organization of non-verbal interaction behaviors. The three dimensions were labeled:

    I. Evaluation
   II. Social Control
  III. Responsiveness

Mehrabian suggested that those cues which describe non-verbal immediacy (i.e. increased touching, forward lean, direct orientation, greater eye contact, and decreased distance) also represented an evaluation dimension (Mehrabian, 1969) and that cues representing 'relaxation' (i.e. increased body lean and limb asymmetry) were most closely associated with social control.

Mehrabian and Ksionsky (1972, 1974; Mehrabian, 1971), noting the lack of empirical work directly relating dimensions to multiple sets of behaviors, attempted to test that relationship in a series of laboratory studies. In one typical study (Mehrabian and Ksionsky, 1972) subjects interacted with same-sex confederates displaying slightly positive affect (smiling once, looking at the subject 30% of the time), initiating topics about one-third of the time, and making short responses. Some 26 behavioral categories were selected, all of which related to the hypothesized dimensions of Evaluation, Social Control (also called Power), and Responsiveness. Table 7.1 shows the results of the oblique factor analyses of these behaviors.

Table 7.1 reveals that there are more than the three dimensions hypothesized by Mehrabian and Ksionsky (1972). Mehrabian (1972) described the first three dimensions as equivalent to the three hypothesized dimensions: Affiliation was interpreted as the Evaluative dimension, Relaxation as the Power or Social Control dimension, and Responsiveness was interpreted to be as predicted. Also, an Ingratiation factor was found to be part of Affiliation in a different study (Mehrabian, 1971) and, according to Mehrabian and Ksionsky (1972), 'Further analysis of this measure has shown that a distinction between affiliative and ingratiating behavior is helpful when situational factors force mutual dependence between participants, such as situations in which one person is less confident of his abilities or is in a more subservient role'

TABLE 7.1 Behavioral Groupings

Behavioral Factor	Behaviors
I. Affiliative Behavior	Total number of statements per minute Number of declarative statements per minute Percent duration of eye contact with confederate Percent duration of subject's speech Percent duration of confederate's speech Positive verbal content Head nods per minute Pleasantness of facial expression
II. Responsiveness to the Confederate or Salience of Confederate for Subject	Total (positive plus negative) vocal expressions Speech rate Speech volume
III. Relaxation	Rocking movements per minute (negative loading) Leg and foot movements per minute (negative loading) Body lean
IV. Ingratiation	Pleasantness of vocal expressions Negative verbal content (negative loading) Verbal reinforcers given per minute Number of questions per minute Self-manipulations per minute
V. Behavioral Index of Distress	Percent duration of walking Object manipulations per minute Arm-position asymmetry
VI. Intimate Position	Shoulder orientation away from confederate Distance from confederate (negative loading) Head turns per minute (looking around)

From Mehrabian, A. and Ksionsky, S. (1972).

(p. 431). Apparently, interaction with a slightly positive stranger was such a condition.

Factor V, Distress, appears to describe behaviors reflecting heightened activity and arousal. The last factor, Intimate Position, is something of an anomaly since it was expected that closer personal distances and direct orientation should signal liking (Mehrabian, 1969) and Affiliation; and as shown in Table 7.2, the Intimate Position factor did not correlate with any other factor.

Table 7.2 also reveals a small to moderate negative correlation between Affiliative Behavior and Relaxation, and this is equivalent to a negative correlation between affective evaluation of partners and degree of social control exhibited. In other words, in the waiting situation with a slightly positive stranger, the degree of expressed positive affect is inversely related to the degree of expressed control. Mehrabian and Ksionsky (1974) interpreted the relationship between Affiliative

TABLE 7.2   Intercorrelation Among Behavioral Factors

Behavioral Factor	II	III	IV	V	VI	VII
I. Affiliative Behavior	.26*	−.26*	.39*	.12	−.18*	.41*
II. Responsiveness		.02	−.10	−.03	−.12	.08
III. Relaxation			−.29*	−.17*	.19*	−.17*
IV. Ingratiation				.29*	−.26*	.13
V. Distress					−.33*	.03
VI. Intimate Position						−.05

From Mehrabian, A. and Ksionsky, S. (1972).
* $p < .05$.

Behavior and Relaxation (Power or Status dimension) in the following way. Increased Tension (i.e. decreased Relaxation) accompanied by increased positive affect (i.e. Affiliative Behavior) indicates 'respect' due to a power difference between partners. Increased Tension with decreased positive affect indicates 'vigilance', which is required in uncertain situations. Thus, the moderate negative correlation between Affiliative Behavior and Relaxation in the factor analytical data is interpreted as an indication of 'respect'. There is no test of this explanation in the study and so the conclusion remains speculative. Furthermore, oblique factor solutions invite greater intercorrelations between factors than do orthogonal solutions and the interpretation of these intercorrelations cannot be made without careful consideration of convergent findings. However, it is important to note the possibility of an interrelationship between factors contributing to an interpersonal state. In other words, there is some indication that multiple sets of behaviors may combine to produce a single interpersonal function.

Mehrabian and Ksionsky's (1972, 1974) work is particularly interesting in that it represents the first comprehensive attempt to factor-analyze a set of previously studied interaction behaviors of proven relational importance. The factors that resulted in the analyses were named for the clusters of behaviors on the basis of how these behaviors had been shown to be used in the past individually or in smaller sets. These researchers chose to code variables which they knew had some relational effects. They then factored these behaviors and found that they clustered in more or less the same way as they had expected. These clusters or factors were then named for the chief function of the behavioral set as they had been used in previous research. However, there was never a comparison, in the same study, of the behavioral set and independent judgments or perceptions of their use. In other words, these studies were encoding studies alone and the function of the behaviors in the particular 'waiting with a stranger' situation was assumed on the basis of previous research alone. The only corroborating evidence that a function was indeed operating through a set of behaviors came with the positive correlation of Affiliation Behavior (i.e. total number of statements per minute; number of declarative statements per minute; percent duration of eye contact, subject's speech, and of

confederate's speech; positive verbal content; head nods per minute; and pleasantness of facial expression) with positive evaluations of the confederate (Mehrabian
and Ksionsky 1972, 1974).

Later studies

A cursory glance at the published correlation matrices among non-verbal and verbal
behaviors is not encouraging. Matrices published by Cegala, Savage, Brunner, and
Conrad (1982), Duncan and Fiske (1977), and some developed from our own studies
(Cappella and Greene, 1984; Cappella and Palmer, 1988b) do not exhibit much
similarity. Factor analysis of correlations among eight behaviors from Cappella and
Greene's study yielded four clear groupings: affiliation (gaze plus directness of
posture and orientation), gesture (body-focused minus object-focused), speech
(vocalization minus pauses minus latency), and smiles and laughter. These groupings
made both conceptual and statistical sense, but a later study by Cappella and Palmer
(1988b) using similar coding rules but a different social context yielded a substantially different correlational pattern; in turn these correlations were quite different
from those of Mehrabian. These data are presented in Table 7.3.

One of the reasons for this failure to produce interesting and consistent findings
may be the aggregate nature of the data. Correlations are generated from the mean
or total durations of an individual's behavior. Of course, a correlation of this sort says
little about simultaneous occurrence but only describes co-occurrence across a much
larger interval of time (i.e. a conversation). Additionally, mean levels are known to
vary considerably as a function of individual differences, situational differences, and
the like. The consequence is that correlations of these mean or total values can be
radically altered as a function of variations in persons and situations, the types of

TABLE 7.3   Correlations Among Kinesic and Vocal Behaviors

	Talk	Sim. Spch	Spch rate	Po.1	Po.2	Gaze	BFG	OFG	Sm./ La.
Floor	.75	.00	−.13	−.06	−.10	−.31	−.07	.22	−.10
Talk		.55	.53	−.30	.00	.02	−.05	.36	.00
Sim. spch			.81	−.27	.17	.21	.07	.37	.20
Spch rate				−.44	.16	.44	−.01	.25	.16
Po.1					−.02	−.28	.02	.05	−.15
Po.2						.14	.06	.17	−.12
Gaze							−.16	.14	.19
BFG								−.01	.04
OFG									−.06

Floor = duration of holding the floor; Talk = duration of vocalization; Sim. spch = duration of
simultaneous speech; Spch rate = rate of speaking; Po.1 = forward posture and shoulder orientation;
Po.2 = away posture and orientation; Gaze = face-directed eye gaze; BFG = body-focused gestures;
OFG = object-focused gestures; Sm./La. = duration of smiles and laughter.
$r > .221$ or $< -.221$, $p < .05$; $.185 < r < .220$, $.05 < p < .10$.
From Cappella and Palmer (1988b).

summary measures employed, and so on, distorting the correlations that would be obtained under more constant conditions.

Manipulating sender states

A somewhat different approach to understanding how behaviors emitted by individuals covary is to manipulate the individual's motivational state and observe the pattern of covariation in verbal and non-verbal concomitants. Coker and Burgoon (1987) conducted a complex study, part of which was aimed at encoding differences under conditions of high and low involvement. One of the conceptual components of involvement was assumed to be immediacy. Subjects engaged in two 10-minute interactions in which they were ostensibly practicing interviewing skills. After the first interaction, one of the persons was recruited to behave as a confederate and told greatly to increase or greatly to decrease their involvement. No guidance was given to the confederates as to how to change their actions to show more or less involvement; the decisions were based on the subjects' naive views of how to accomplish this end. The interactions were videotaped and rated[1] by judges on 59 non-verbal behaviors at 2-minute intervals. The rating scales were grouped via factor analysis to reduce the complexity of the analysis. Twenty-two groupings resulted. Compared with those in the low-involvement condition, confederates in the high-involvement condition displayed: (a) more immediacy (direct body and facial orientation, gaze, positive reinforcers, gestures, closer distance), (b) more facial animation and vocal expressiveness, (c) fewer silences, latencies, and more coordinated body movements, (d) more vocal warmth and interest, and (e) less anxiety (more composure, vocal relaxation, vocal attentiveness, and fewer self-adaptors).

Coker and Burgoon (1987) also compared the involvement levels of the confederates between the baseline and changed periods. Results indicated that as involvement was increased by the confederates so did: (a) immediacy, (b) expressiveness, (c) body and speech coordination, and (d) vocal warmth and interest, while ratings of anxiety decreased and there were fewer silences.

Summary

The pattern of inconsistent results revealed across studies above should not be taken to suggest that the search for behavioral indices is hopeless. Rather it suggests that attempts to find behavioral groupings on the basis of aggregate, encoding-based data are best carried out within the confines of the purposes of particular research applications. The gain in reliability and efficiency alone may be worth the effort.

Individual–Temporal Studies

Probably the most common approach to assessing the covariation among verbal and non-verbal behaviors is the experimental or quasi-experimental study assessing the relationship between some kinesic feature and some feature of the speech stream, either content or non-content. When the coordination observed between behaviors is temporally precise, the study should be categorized with the 'temporal' rather than distributional data. Temporal precision allows theorists to use results in actual process models of verbal and non-verbal production.

Perhaps the best known program of research in this tradition is that of Beattie (1978, 1979; Butterworth and Beattie, 1978). Henderson, Goldman-Eisler, and Skarbek (1966) were the first to report evidence for cycles of fluency and hesitancy in spontaneous monologues. Although the methods employed to specify cycles were roundly criticized by Power (1983, 1984), less subjective methods employed by Beattie (1979, 1980) indicated that cycles existed for unplanned, relatively lengthy monologues. These periods are presumably ones during which the speaker is under greater (hesitant periods) and lesser (fluent periods) cognitive load as revealed by the pause to phonation ratio during the period. Of special interest are the other kinesic behaviors during these periods. Beattie (1978) found that fluent phases tended to be associated with greater gaze toward the listener. These same periods are also associated with a greater number of illustrative gestures (Butterworth and Beattie, 1978).

Greene and Cappella (1986) hypothesized that, in the absence of the opportunity to plan a pending monologue, subjects would exhibit decreases in speech fluency just after identified idea boundaries. Interrupted time-series regression procedures were employed to verify this hypothesis; the experiment was successful. A follow-up study in which subjects were given the opportunity to plan before a monologue showed that decreases in fluency were not so pronounced as when no planning was permitted. This research not only corroborates that of Butterworth (1975) by using a more precise statistical methodology but parallels the findings of Chafe (1980) and of Gee and Grosjean (1983, 1984).

The importance of the above research is found in the relationship between the production of non-verbal behavior and the 'state' of the verbal stream. Obviously the two streams are interdependent. Finding variation in the verbal stream that is both theoretically and empirically predictive of non-verbal concomitants is not so obvious. Periods of fluency and hesitancy are one such variant in the verbal stream and, in light of the research by Greene and Cappella (1986), these periods are determined by the introduction of new idea boundaries. The search for other variations in the verbal stream has had a limited scope.

A theoretically exciting line of study that has received some empirical attention is the relationship between structural and semantic features of the verbal stream and various vocal and kinesic behaviors. Kendon (1970) was one of the earliest researchers to give attention to the speech–gesture relationship in particular. His detailed observations led to the claim that the hierarchical structure of language was paralleled by body movements of larger and smaller magnitude. Thus, major topical shifts, not unlike those of paragraph shifts in discourse, would be accompanied by large postural shifts, for example orientational changes by seated conversationalists. To the best of our knowledge these potentially interesting observations have not been carefully replicated. On theoretical grounds a close association between kinesic shifts and verbal shifts would have significant implications for the forces leading to production of both verbal and motor behaviors.

Hadar (in press) calls these kinesic accompaniments to speech changes the 'speech productive' functions of body movements. The work of Dittmann (1972; Dittmann and Llewellyn, 1969), Hadar, Steiner, Grant, and Clifford Rose (1984), Ragsdale and Silvia (1982), and others has led to significant insights into the speech–movement relationship. In short, the type of relationship depends upon the type of movement that is being considered. Condon and Ogston (1969) initially claimed that body movements occurred primarily during restarted speech, after speech hesitancies. But research by Butterworth and Beattie (1978), Hadar *et al.* (1984), and Ragsdale and Silvia (1982) showed that body movements tended to occur prior to word choices for illustrative movements although head movements tended to be simultaneous with or occur just after the onset of speech. The precise temporal covariation between speech and certain types of movements at least suggests that they may be generated from the same set of underlying forces.

McNeill (1985, 1986; McNeill and Levy, 1982) has taken this proposal one step further, arguing that 'gestures and speech have parallel semantic and pragmatic function' (McNeill, 1985, p. 355). He tries to demonstrate through example and from controlled research that the meanings of certain gestures are equivalent to the meanings of the verbs that they accompany. Although the examples are poignant, the research studies are not controlled well enough to inspire confidence. Were McNeill's proposition to be found valid, certain aspects of gestural behavior would be redundant with the semantic information carried verbally and would be a window to the semantic encoding process. Before such leaps can be undertaken, a great deal more evidence is necessary (Butterworth and Hadar, 1986; Feyereisen, 1987). This is one area of non-verbal behavior where the interesting theory has outrun the data.

Temporal–Multiple Studies

A third type of study takes advantage of time-series techniques to assess the contemporaneous and lagged covariation between various behaviors. The advantage of this statistical technique is that it can be used to determine the degree of correlation in naturally occurring behavior streams among behavior sets which occur simultaneously or at a slightly later time. The method provides data far superior to that provided by the distributional studies and which supplements the single be-havior, usually experimental, studies described in previous sections.

Some preliminary studies conducted in our laboratory are described in this section. In an exploratory analysis, we focused on three 30-minute conversations from a corpus of 49 which had been coded in 0.3-second units for face-directed gaze; object- and body-focused gestures; smiles and laughter; and pauses, vocalizations, and switching pauses. Six data files (one for each person in each conversation), consisting of 6000 observations for each of the above variables as 1–0 (on–off) scores, were analyzed for patterns of temporal covariation within a person's behavior. The major results were unsurprising (in retrospect). Positive and consistent intercorrela-tions among floor-holding, vocalization, object-focused gestures, and gaze aversion were found across the six persons studied. No other behaviors showed consistent temporal covariation. The results are not surprising in that they show that, when persons have the floor for speaking, they tend to avert gaze more, use illustrative gestures, and talk more than pause. More informative is the result that gaze while holding the floor correlated negatively with vocalization and positively with within-pauses, suggesting that gaze while speaking tends to occur at pauses while speaking rather than at vocalizations – a finding also noted by Duncan and Fiske (1977).

The above results were consistent across the six people who were studied and were based on relatively precise timing (0.3-second units). Non-significant results for body-focused gestures, and for smiles and laughter, indicate that these behaviors may not be tied to the same production forces as the speech-related behaviors of gaze and gesture.

In a more comprehensive follow-up to the above study, the same set of behaviors was studied in a group of four socially anxious and four socially secure persons who interacted with other members of their group once each. This yielded 12 dyadic interactions. Although these data were coded in 0.3-second time units, two aggregate time units (one shorter and one longer) were tried. The patterns of intercorrelations among behaviors for each person in each interaction were compared. Little difference among individuals was observed in the correlational patterns even when they came from different groups of high and low social anxiety. As before, gaze aversion, floor-holding, object-focused gestures, and vocalization were systematically intercorrelated. Indices for these four behaviors were constructed and their internal consistency was calculated to be .75 for the smaller time units and .86 for the larger time units averaged across persons. In short, results from three different samples of people using three different time units produced similar findings. Although the substantive findings are not surprising, the grouping of gaze aversion, vocalization, holding the floor, and gesturing may indicate a behavioral 'package' that should be studied as a unit, while body gestures and smiles can be treated as distinct from this package.

THEORETICAL APPROACHES TO BEHAVIORAL PRODUCTION

Little theoretical attention has been given to accounting for patterns of covariation among verbal and non-verbal behaviors. Part of the reason for this is that the empirical data necessary for theoretical advancement are limited and part of the reason is that theorists themselves have been concerned either with general theories of production or with much narrower theories pertinent to a limited subset of behaviors. In this section, only a cursory review of theoretical work will be offered.

Cappella (1985b) was interested in the relationship between social anxiety and turn-taking. In trying to account for the possibility that high socially anxious persons might employ different turn-taking rules than low socially anxious persons, he was led to an explanation of the observed covariation among floor-holding, vocalization, pausing, gaze aversion, and gesture. The work of Humphreys and Revelle (1984) shows that the usual inverted-U relationship between stimulation and performance can be explained by appealing to the effects of arousal and task type on short-term memory capacity. Since pausing, gaze aversion, and body-focused gesturing are all known to increase under conditions of greater arousal or greater cognitive load (see Cappella, 1985a, for summary), then any factor that significantly increases cognitive load or somatic activity and arousal should also lead to increased pausing, gaze aversion, and body-focused gestures (decreased object-focused gestures). Speaking versus listening, hesitant versus fluent speaking, introduction of new and unrehearsed ideas, increased self-cognitions, and greater social anxiety are several factors producing greater cognitive load and/or arousal, and should be associated with behavioral changes indicative of the load. This proposition is well supported by the literature as the previous review has shown.

Much recent attention has focused on the speech–gesture relationship and how to account for the close interdependence. McNeill's (1985) work has been the most stimulating and controversial. He has argued that gesture and speech share a computational stage in their generation by which is meant that they arise together and develop in parallel. By gestures, McNeill means illustrators (in the sense of Ekman and Friesen, 1969, 1975) and not emblems or adaptors. McNeill's position is based on five arguments about speech and gesture:

(1) Gestures, as he has defined them, only occur during speech and not during listening.
(2) Classes of gestures parallel the semantic and pragmatic functions of speech. For example, iconic gestures are parallel to and occur with concrete referential meanings.
(3) Gestures are synchronized in time with speech output.
(4) Gestures and speech are affected similarly in aphasia with, for example, patients with Broca's aphasia having little problem with referring terms or with iconic gestures but having considerable difficulty with grammatical structure and with gestural 'beats' (structuring gestures).
(5) Gestures develop parallel to speech in children with more concrete verbal symbols developing at the same time as iconic gestures.

McNeill's (1985) thesis is both appealing and exciting for its implications about a common cognitive mechanism responsible for the production of two, obviously related, but distinct forms of behavioral output. His position has certainly not met with uniform acclaim. Feyereisen (1987) has criticized sections of the evidence that McNeill marshalls as being incomplete or erroneous (but see McNeill, 1987). Butterworth and Hadar (1986) criticize the evidence on timing (among other things) but especially take McNeill to task for failing to specify a realistic production mechanism that will satisfy cognitive, linguistic, and motoric constraints.

On this question, Levelt, Richardson, and La Heij (1985) have conducted some revealing experiments on deictic expressions. They argue that three theoretical stances are possible concerning the relationship between speech and gestures (in particular deictic gestures):

(1) The two systems are independent of one another and, once formulated, must be separately run off, regardless of interference in the vocal or motor channel.
(2) The two systems are quite dependent upon one another such that there are adaptive reactions of each system to the other during the phases of planning and execution.

(3) The two systems are interdependent during planning but independent in the execution phase – the *ballistic* view.

Some ingenious research by Levelt *et al.* (1985) indicates that the third position is supported. Their experiment involved subjects pointing and speaking as lights on a board came on. The pointing gesture could be interfered with by including a weight timed to be interposed at precise instances of gesturing. The authors found that, when the weight interfered with pointing early in the sequence (before the onset of speech), there was also interference with the onset of speech. When the weight interfered with pointing slightly later in the gesture (but also before the onset of speech), there was no interference with the onset of speech. Thus, it appears that the ballistic view is correct in the sense that interfering with execution in one domain does not have an effect on execution in the other domain. McNeill's (1985) position that speech and gesture have a common source is supported by these data, but their execution is presumed to occur through different systems. Obviously the theoretical claims being advanced are currently well beyond the necessary process data to support them.

Finally, Greene (1984a, in press) takes a much broader view of production than is found in any of the models discussed above. His action assembly theory attempts to specify both the cognitive structures and the processes necessary to account for all forms of behavioral production. The structures are specified by a set of 'procedural records', which are the repositories of experience linking actions to outcomes. These records exist at a variety of levels of abstraction from sensorimotor to high-level plans. The production of action is dependent upon the *retrieval* of procedural records from memory and their *assembly* into an organized sequence.

These two aspects of production, activation–retrieval and assembly, are the cognitive processes necessary for production. Greene (1984a, in press) assumes that the activation–retrieval process can occur in parallel so that any number of activating conditions can push associated procedural records above threshold, simultaneously leading to parallel retrieval. The assembly process organizes the procedural records into a coherent pattern of action to be executed. Unlike the activation process, assembly is assumed to occur serially so that the more records to be assembled, or the more complex or unfamiliar the assembly, and so on, then the greater the cognitive load and the greater the delay in responding, the more likely the attempts at reducing extraneous stimulation, and so on.

Greene has tested his theory in a variety of contexts with some success (Greene, 1984b; Greene and Cappella, 1986; Greene, O'Hair, Cody, and Yen, 1985). The strength and weakness of the theory is found in its generality. The theory could be applied to a wide variety of production questions because it has not been constructed for particular applications in speech production (Dell, 1986), motor coordination (MacKay, 1982), or other areas. At the same time the theory is too general in that the content of the procedural records is specified in only broad terms, the activation process is a function of unspecified pertinent factors, and, perhaps most important, the nature of the assembly process is unclear. Despite these limitations (or strengths if one believes in generality above all), the theory has significant potential as an overarching paradigm for production processes into which less general, and more specific models, might be folded.

SUMMARY AND CONCLUSIONS

The purpose of this paper was to make an argument and present some data. The argument is that the clustering of verbal and non-verbal behaviors ought to be seriously studied, especially with methods and technologies which will allow for information on the temporal covariation among behaviors or between behaviors and outcome judgments. The tradition of aggregating or summing across measures is common in a variety of areas in social psychology and communication. The reasons are simply ones of achieving efficiency and greater reliability. So it is with the variety of verbal and non-verbal behaviors. While studying them separately may be a requirement of certain research applications, it is certainly not a requirement of all research applications.

We have also tried to argue that distributional covariation is not as informative as temporal covariation. Results based on distributional covariation appear to be less consistent than the little data available on temporal covariation. Also, process theories of production are much less informed by aggregate covariation than by temporal covariation; process theories require process data.

NOTE

1 There is a substantial difference between rating and coding behavior. Coding is usually more precise but also more burdensome in energy and effort. For example, coding pauses in speech involves timing every audible pause at every moment of interaction. Rating is less precise but also more efficient. For example, rating pauses involves giving an overall assessment of the frequency of pauses (from 'none at all' to 'almost constant') in a 30-second segment of interaction.

ACKNOWLEDGMENT

We wish to thank Bonny Donzella for her work on preparing for analysis the data for the study described on p. 155.

REFERENCES

Beattie, G. (1978). Floor-apportionment and gaze in conversational dyads. *British Journal of Social and Clinical Psychology*, **17**, 7–15.

Beattie, G.W. (1979). Planning units in spontaneous speech: Some evidence from hesitation in speech and speaker gaze direction in conversation. *Linguistics*, **17**, 61–78.

Beattie, G.W. (1980). The role of language production processes in the organization of behavior in face-to-face interaction. In B. Butterworth (Ed.), *Language production, Vol. 1: Speech and talk*, pp. 69–107. London: Academic Press.

Burgoon, J.K. (1985a). The relationship of verbal and nonverbal codes. In B. Dervin and M.J. Voight (Eds.), *Progress in communication sciences*, Vol. VI, pp. 263–298. Norwood, NJ: Ablex.

Burgoon, J.K. (1985b). Nonverbal signals. In M.L. Knapp and G.R. Miller (Eds), *Handbook of interpersonal communication*, pp. 344–392. Newbury Park, CA: Sage.

Butterworth, B. (1975). Hesitation and semantic planning in speech. *Journal of Psycholinguistic Research*, **4**, 75–87.

Butterworth, B. and Beattie, G.W. (1978). Gesture and silence as indicators of planning in speech. In R.N. Campbell and P.T. Smith (Eds), *Recent advances in the psychology of language: Formal and experimental procedures*. New York: Plenum.

Butterworth, B. and Hadar, U. (1986). Gesture, speech, and computational stages: A reply to McNeill. Unpublished manuscript, Department of Psychology, University College London, London.

Cappella, J.N. (1985a). Production principles for turn-taking rules in social interaction: Socially anxious vs socially secure persons. *Journal of Language and Social Psychology*, **4**, 193–212.

Cappella, J.N. (1985b). Production principles for turn-taking rules in social interaction: Socially anxious vs. socially secure persons. *Journal of Language and Social Psychology*, **4**, 193–212.

Cappella, J.N. and Greene, J.O. (1984). The effects of distance and individual differences in arousability on nonverbal involvement: A test of discrepancy–arousal theory. *Journal of Nonverbal Behavior*, **8**, 259–286.

Cappella, J.N. and Palmer, M.O. (1988a). The structure and organization of verbal and nonverbal behavior: Data for models of reception. Unpublished paper, Department of Communication Arts, University of Wisconsin-Madison.

Cappella, J.N. and Palmer, M.O. (1988b). Attitude similarity and attraction: The mediating effects of kinesic and vocal behaviors. Unpublished paper presented at the International Communication Association meetings, New Orleans, LA.

Cappella, J.N. and Street, R.L., Jr (1985). A functional approach to the structure of communicative behavior. In R.L. Street, Jr and J.N. Cappella (Eds), *Sequence and pattern in communicative behavior*, pp. 1–29. London: Edward Arnold.

Cegala, D.J., Savage, G.T., Brunner, C.C., and Conrad, A.B. (1982). An elaboration of the meaning of interaction involvement: Toward the development of a theoretical concept. *Communication Monographs*, **49**, 229–248.

Chafe, W.L. (1980). The development of consciousness in the production of a narrative. In W.L. Chafe (Ed.), *The pear stories: Cognitive, cultural, and linguistic aspects of narrative production*, pp. 9–50. Norwood, NJ: Ablex.

Chaiken, A.L. and Derlega, V.J. (1974). Variables affecting the appropriateness of self disclosure. *Journal of Consulting and Clinical Psychology*, **42**, 588–593.

Coker, D.A. and Burgoon, J.K. (1987). The nature of conversational involvement and nonverbal encoding patterns. *Human Communication Research*, **13**, 463–494.

Condon, W.S. and Ogston, W.D. (1969). A segmentation of behavior. *Journal of Psychiatric Research*, **5**, 221–235.

Cozby, P.C. (1972). Self-disclosure, reciprocity and linking. *Sociometry*, **35**, 151–160.

Dell, G.S. (1986). A spreading activation theory of retrieval in sentence production. *Psychological Review*, **93**, 283–321.

Dittmann, A.T. (1972). The body movement–speech rhythm relationship as a cue to speech encoding. In A.W. Siegman and S. Feldstein (Eds), *Studies in dyadic communication*, pp. 135–152. New York: Pergamon.

Dittmann, A.T. and Llewellyn, L.G. (1969). Body movement and speech rhythm in social conversation. *Journal of Personality and Social Psychology*, **11**, 98–106.

Duncan, S. and Fiske, D.W. (1977). *Face to face interaction*. Hillsdale, NJ: Erlbaum.

Edinger, J.A. and Patterson, M.L. (1983). Nonverbal involvement and social control. *Psychological Bulletin*, **93**, 30–56.

Ekman, P. and Friesen, W.V. (1969). The repertoire of nonverbal behavior: Categories, origins, coding and usage. *Semiotica*, **1**, 49–98.

Ekman, P. and Friesen, W.V. (1975). *Unmasking the face*. Englewood Cliffs, NJ: Prentice-Hall.

Exline, R.V. and Winters, L.C. (1965). Affective relations and mutual glances in dyads. In S. Tomkins and C. Izard (Eds), *Affect, cognition, and personality*. New York: Springer.

Feyereisen, P. (1987). Gestures and speech, interactions and separations: A reply to McNeill (1985). *Psychological Review*, **94**, 493–498.

Gee, J.P. and Grosjean, F. (1983). Performance structures: A psycholinguistic and linguistic appraisal. *Cognitive Psychology*, **8**, 59–85.

Gee, J.P. and Grosjean, F. (1984). Empirical evidence for narrative structure. *Cognitive Science*, **8**, 59–85.

Giles, H. and Street, R.L. (1985). Communicator characteristics and behavior. In M.L. Knapp and G.R. Miller (Eds), *Handbook of interpersonal communication*, pp. 205–262. Newbury Park, CA: Sage.

Goldman-Eisler, F. (1968). *Psycholinguistics: Experiments in spontaneous speech*. New York: Academic Press.

Greene, J.O. (1984a). A cognitive approach to human communication: An action assembly theory. *Communication Monographs*, **51**, 289–306.

Greene, J.O. (1984b). Speech preparation processes and verbal fluency. *Human Communication Research*, **11**, 61–84.

Greene, J.O. (in press). The stability of nonverbal behavior: An action-production approach to problems of cross-situational consistency and discriminativeness. *Journal of Language and Social Psychology*.

Greene, J.O. and Cappella, J.N. (1986). Cognition and talk: The relationship of semantic units to temporal patterns of fluency in spontaneous speech. *Language and Speech*, **29**, 141–157.

Greene, J.O., O'Hair, H.D., Cody, M.J., and Yen, C. (1985). Planning and control of behavior during deception. *Human Communication Research*, **11**, 335–364.

Hadar, U. (in press). Two types of gesture and their role in speech production. *Journal of Language and Social Psychology*.

Hadar, U., Steiner, T.J., Grant, E.C., and Clifford Rose, F. (1986). The timing of shifts of head posture during conversation. *Human Movement Science*, **3**, 237–245.

Henderson, A., Goldman-Eisler, F., and Skarbek, A. (1966). Sequential, temporal patterns in spontaneous speech. *Language and Speech*, **9**, 68–71.

Humphreys, M.S. and Revelle, W. (1984). Personality, motivation, and performance: A theory of the relationship between individual differences and information processing. *Psychological Review*, **91**, 153–184.

Jurich, A.P. and Jurich, A.P. (1974). Correlations among nonverbal expressions of anxiety. *Psychological Reports*, **34**, 199–204.

Kahneman, D. (1973). *Attention and effort*. Englewood Cliffs, NJ: Prentice-Hall.

Kendon, A. (1967). Some functions of gaze direction in social interaction. *Acta Psychologica*, **26**, 22–63.

Kendon, A. (1970). Movement coordination in social interaction: Some examples described. *Acta Psychologica*, **32**, 100–125.

Levelt, W.J.M., Richardson, G., and La Heij, W. (1985). Pointing and voicing in deictic expressions. *Journal of Memory and Language*, **24**, 133–164.

MacKay, D.G. (1982). The problems of flexibility, fluency and speed-accuracy trade-off in skilled behavior. *Psychological Review*, **89**, 483–506.

Maxwell, G.M., Cook, M.W., and Burr, R. (1985). The encoding and decoding of liking from behavioral cues in both auditory and visual channels. *Journal of Nonverbal Behavior*, **9**, 239–263.

McNeill, D. (1985). So you think gestures are nonverbal? *Psychological Review*, **92**, 350–371.

McNeill, D. (1986). Iconic gestures of children and adults. *Semiotica*, **1**, 107–128.

McNeill, D. (1987). So you *do* think gestures are nonverbal! Reply to Feyereisen (1987). *Psychological Review*, **94**, 499–504.

McNeill, D. and Levy, E. (1982). Conceptual representations in language activity and gesture. In R.J. Jarvella and W. Klein (Eds), *Speech, place, and action*, pp. 271–295. New York: Wiley.

Mehrabian, A. (1969). Some referents and measures of nonverbal behavior. *Behavior Research Methods and Instrumentation*, **1**, 203–207.

Mehrabian, A. (1970). A semantic space for nonverbal behavior. *Journal of Consulting and Clinical Psychology*, **35**, 248–257.

Mehrabian, A. (1971). Verbal and nonverbal interaction of strangers in a waiting situation. *Journal of Experimental Research in Personality*, **5**, 127–138.

Mehrabian, A. (1972). *Nonverbal communication*. Chicago: Aldine-Atherton.

Mehrabian, A. and Ksionsky, S. (1972). Categories of social behavior. *Comparative Group Studies*, **3**, 425–436.

Mehrabian, A. and Ksionsky, S. (1974). Some determinants of social interaction. In S. Weitz (Ed.), *Nonverbal communication*, 1st edn, pp. 312–329. New York: Oxford University Press.

Nielsen, G. (1962). Studies in self confrontation. Cited in Beattie, G.W., The role of language production processes in the organization of behavior in face-to-face interaction. In B. Butterworth (Ed.), *Language production*, Vol. 1. London: Academic Press.

Power, M.J. (1983). Are there cognitive rhythms in speech? *Language and Speech*, **26**, 253–261.

Power, M.J. (1984). 'Are there cognitive rhythms in speech?': A reply to Beattie. *Language and Speech*, **27**, 197–200.

Ragsdale, J.D. and Silvia, C.F. (1982). Distribution of kinesic hesitation phenomena in spontaneous speech. *Language and Speech*, **25**, 185–190.

Rubin, Z. (1975). Disclosing oneself to a stranger: Reciprocity and its limits. *Journal of Experimental Social Psychology*, **11**, 233–260.

Siegman, A.W. (1979). Cognition and hesitation in speech. In A.W. Siegman and S. Feldstein (Eds), *Of speech and time*, pp. 151–178. Hillsdale, NJ: Erlbaum.

Siegman, A.W. (1987). The telltale voice: Nonverbal messages of verbal communication. In A.W. Siegman and S. Feldstein (Eds), *Nonverbal behavior and communication*, 2nd edn, pp. 351–434. Hillsdale, NJ: Erlbaum.

Zuckerman, M., De Paulo, B., and Rosenthal, R. (1981). Verbal and nonverbal communication of deception. In L. Berkowitz (Ed.), *Advances in experimental social psychology*, Vol. 14, pp. 1–59. New York: Academic Press.

8

Social Cognition and Discourse

TEUN A. VAN DIJK

Department of General Literary Studies, University of Amsterdam, The Netherlands

The social psychology of discourse is a new field of study that partly overlaps with the social psychology of language, dealt with in the other chapters of this handbook. This means that this single chapter deals with topics that have received less attention in the social psychology of language, such as specific structures and strategies of discourse (excluding grammatical or other properties of sentences) and those issues in social psychology that can most fruitfully be studied from a discourse analytical perspective.

Despite having its roots in some 2000 years of rhetoric, discourse analysis as an independent cross-discipline in the humanities and the social sciences has emerged only since the mid-1960s. Developing at the same time as, and sometimes in close relation to, other new disciplines, such as semiotics, pragmatics and sociolinguistics, its primary parent-disciplines were ethnography, linguistics, microsociology and poetics. In the 1970s, cognitive psychology and Artificial Intelligence joined the disciplines in which increasing interest in discourse constituted one of the major new developments of the last decade (for details, see van Dijk, 1985b).

The extension to the social psychology of discourse only took place in the 1980s (for recent discussions, see, e.g., Potter and Wetherell, 1987; Robinson, 1985). There are virtually no books in social psychology that feature concepts such as 'discourse' or 'text' in their subject index, and there are very few journal articles in the field that explicitly deal with discourse structures. This means that this chapter will not be able to review a large body of social psychological research that explicitly deals with discourse structures, although I take the liberty to reinterpret several

Handbook of Language and Social Psychology
Edited by H. Giles and W.P. Robinson. © 1990 John Wiley & Sons Ltd

studies in a discourse analytical framework. To compensate for a solid research tradition, part of this chapter will therefore be theoretical and programmatic, in order to chart and stimulate future directions and work in this new field.

Despite this lack of explicit interest in discourse, social psychology has many subdomains that allow or require a discourse analytical approach. After all, there are few fundamental sociopsychological notions that do not have obvious links with language use in communicative contexts, that is, with different forms of text or talk. Social perception, impression management, attitude change and persuasion, attribution, categorization, intergroup relations, stereotypes, social representations (SRs) and interaction are only some of the labels for the major areas of current social psychology in which discourse plays an important, but as yet rather disguised, role. True, language and especially communication have played a prominent part in the history of social psychology (see especially Brown, 1965), as is abundantly made clear in the other chapters of this handbook, but the essentially discursive nature of language use has been mostly reduced to a more or less intuitive study of 'messages', and at present social psychology mainly focuses on properties of 'speech'. In other words, after linguistics and its sister-disciplines of psycho- and sociolinguistics, discourse analysis has something to offer to most social psychologists. The reverse is equally true: social psychological insights are of primary importance for the development of discourse analysis.

While a 'definition' of the notion of discourse cannot of course be given (the whole discipline, or at least a whole theory, provides such a definition), I understand 'discourse' in this chapter both as a specific form of language use, and as a specific form of social interaction, interpreted as a complete communicative event in a social situation. What distinguishes discourse analysis from sentence grammars is that discourse analysis in practice focuses specifically on phenomena beyond the sentence. Obviously, uttered words or sentences are integral parts of discourse. Since, empirically speaking, the 'meaning' of discourse is a cognitive structure, it makes sense to include in the concept of discourse not only 'observable' verbal or nonverbal features, or social interaction and speech acts, but also the cognitive representations and strategies involved during the production or comprehension of discourse. I here ignore multiple problems related to the precise delimitation of discourse with respect to others (forms of) interaction, with respect to non-verbal communication, or with respect to other cognitive structures and strategies. The notion of 'text', sometimes used as the purely verbal aspect of discourse, sometimes as the abstract linguistic form underlying discourse as a form of language use, is here used mostly in its everyday sense of 'written discourse'.

SOCIAL COGNITION AND INTERACTION

To restrict the discussion about the potentially vast field of the social psychology of discourse, I focus on a number of basic concepts that in my opinion may be fruitful in establishing a solid theoretical framework. First, I pay special attention to the interplay between discourse and social cognition (Fiske and Taylor, 1984; Wyer and Srull, 1985; see Chapter 1, by McCann and Higgins). Social cognition is here discussed mainly in terms of shared SRs of group members (Farr and Moscovici, 1984); that is, I shall neglect the more individual domains of social psychology. Social cognition research dovetails with schema–theoretic orientations in cognitive and Artificial Intelligence research into text processing and the role of knowledge scripts (Schank and Abelson, 1977; van Dijk and Kintsch, 1983). Thus, I hope to show that SRs such as stereotypes or ethnic prejudices, just like socially shared knowledge, are essentially reproduced in society through discourse (see also Kraut and Higgins, 1984; Roloff and Berger, 1982; Rommetveit, 1984). This notion of 'reproduction' will play a prominent role in the framework presented in this chapter.

Second, the discursive reproduction of social cognitions also requires a proper social (sociological) dimension, which, however, has often been neglected in social psychology (Forgas, 1983). The basic notions here are those of interaction and social situation (Argyle, Furnham, and Graham, 1981; Forgas, 1979). Processes of social perception, communication, attribution, attraction, impression management and intergroup contact, among many others, are also to be defined in such a conceptual framework.

My main thesis will be that these socially situated cognitive representations and processes at the same time have an important discourse dimension. Social representations are largely acquired, used and changed, through text and talk. Therefore, discourse analysis may be used as a powerful instrument to reveal the underlying contents, structures and strategies of SRs.

My major criticism of both traditional work in social psychology and the more recent approaches is that on the one hand they are not cognitive enough, neglecting to specify mental representations and strategies, and on the other hand they are not social enough, neglecting social context and functions. Thus, whereas I share the recognition of the fundamental role of discourse in social psychology with the authors of the only book on the subject (Potter and Wetherell, 1987), I differ from these authors in my approach to cognitive SRs or attitudes, which they tend to 'explain away' by reducing them essentially to properties of social discourse. In my opinion, no sound theoretical or explanatory framework can be set up for any phenomenon dealt with in social psychology without an explicit account of socially shared cognitive representations. Whereas discourse is of course of primary importance in the expression, communication and reproduction of SRs (which is also the main thesis of this paper), this does not mean that discourse or its strategies are identical with such representations.

Thus, for this chapter, I define the role of discourse in social psychology essentially in terms of the interplay between social cognition and situated interaction in processes of societal reproduction. Thus, cognitively monitored interactions are linked to other important social dimensions, such as those of group dominance and social structure. This link is necessary in an adequate explanation of the functions of group prejudices and ideologies, as well as of their discursive reproduction in society. Obviously, the study of these relationships overlaps with research in both micro- and macrosociology, which have both neglected the important cognitive dimensions of social interaction (however, see Cicourel, 1973).

STRUCTURES OF SOCIAL REPRESENTATIONS

I must be brief about the first step of the theoretical framework, that is, about the structures of SRs. Actually, very little is known about the precise organization of such representations, despite some interesting early attempts to model them after the structure of knowledge in terms of scripts (Abelson, 1976).

Recall that social cognition is here defined as a socially shared system of SRs, a system which, however, also includes a set of strategies for their effective manipulation in social interpretation, interaction and discourse. Located in 'semantic' (or, rather, social) memory, SRs may be conceptualized as hierarchical networks, organized by a limited set of relevant node-categories. Social representations of groups, for instance, may feature nodes such as Appearance, Origin, Socio-economic goals, Cultural dimensions and Personality. These categories organize the propositional contents of SRs, which not only embody shared social knowledge, but also evaluative information, such as general opinions about other people as group members. The traditional social psychological notion of 'attitude' thus is here redefined in terms of these generalized SRs. The social dimension of SRs not only resides in the fact that these cognitions are about social groups, classes, structures or social issues. SRs are also social because they are acquired, changed and used in social situations; that is, they are cognitions that are shared by all or most members of a group (Brown and Turner, 1981; Moscovici, 1982). This implies that they are abstracted from purely personal knowledge and experiences, from personal or context-bound opinions, as well as from unique situations, and have undergone a process of generalization, adaptation and normalization. Finally, it should be noted that the notion of 'social representation' has been developed mainly by Serge Moscovici and his associates (see, e.g., Moscovici, 1984, and other papers in the edited volume by Farr and Moscovici, 1984), in order, for example, to conceptualize common-sense notions of complex sociocultural or scientific phenomena (such as 'psychoanalysis'). My use of the notion is somewhat different, and includes any socially shared cognitive representation about social phenomena, including social groups, social relationships, or social issues or problems (e.g. nuclear energy, disarmament).

Besides these general, group-based SRs, I introduce the important notion of '(situation) models' (Johnson-Laird, 1983; van Dijk, 1987c; van Dijk and Kintsch, 1983). These mental models have recently played a vital role in psycholinguistics and the psychology of text processing. Whereas socially shared SRs are located in social memory, models are cognitive representations of personal experiences and interpretations, including personal knowledge and opinions, and are located in episodic memory. Models represent the interpretations individuals make of other persons, of specific events and actions, and essentially are the cognitive counterpart of situations. When people witness a scene or an action, or read or hear about such events, they construct a unique model of that situation or update an old model. Models, thus, are also the referential basis of text understanding. They are organized by a fixed schema, featuring such well-known categories as Setting (Time, Location), Circumstances, Participants and Event/Action, each possibly accompanied by an evaluative modifier (Argyle et al., 1981; Brown and Fraser, 1979). Not surprisingly, these categories also show up in the semantics of sentences and discourse, simply because such expressions routinely describe situations. We see that cognitive model theory provides the essential missing link between cognitive structures, situational structures and discourse structures.

Models are crucial for the theoretical framework of this chapter. They form the interface between generalized SRs, on the one hand, and the individual uses of these SRs in social perception, interaction and discourse, on the other hand. The interpretation of social scenes, but also the planning of discourse or interaction, is based on models. Personal models explain individual variation in the application of general knowledge and attitudes. People may have personal opinions that may be at variance with the general opinions of their group, for example because of their own personal experiences. On the other hand, models are also the basis of general knowledge and other SRs. Through processes of generalization and decontextualization (sets of) models may be transformed into scripts or attitudes. For my discussion, it is especially relevant to note that models play a central role, at the interpersonal communicative level, in the group-based reproduction of SRs through discourse. For social psychology in general, the introduction of the notion of models solves many classical problems of the interface between individual and social dimensions of cognition and interaction, such as those of the famous 'attitude–behavior' link (Cushman and McPhee, 1981).

A special type of situation model is the episodic representation which speech participants make of the current communicative situation. This 'context model' features knowledge and opinions about (the actual) self, the other speech participant, about goals of interaction and about important social dimensions of the current situation (e.g. 'classroom instruction', 'talk with boss' or 'consulting the doctor'). Hence, context models monitor talk, guide strategies of impression formation and generally translate general social norms and rules into specific constraints of discourse. Again, we see how social cognitions may be linked to discourse structures through models.

HISTORICAL BACKGROUND

We have earlier observed that social psychology does not pay much attention to the important discursive nature of the phenomena it studies. A closer look at the history of social psychology in our century does not seem to change this picture of the benevolent neglect of discourse. In the three books published in 1980 that look back at the making of the discipline, the notion of discourse hardly comes up as a relevant concept (Evans, 1980; Festinger, 1980; Gilmour and Duck, 1980). In Jones and Gerard's well-known book of the 1960s, the concepts of discourse, text and message do not appear in the index, and language is treated only as a factor of socialization (Jones and Gerard, 1967). Communication, however, receives more attention in that book, mostly in relation to persuasion, attitude change and processes of social comparison. Since a detailed analysis of the history of discourse in social psychology cannot be given here, I briefly summarize some of the highlights of that history that are of interest for a discourse approach.

The early work by Bartlett (1932) may be recognized as a milestone, not only for schema theory and the psychology of text processing, but also for the social psychology of discourse. His method of serial reproduction, applied to stories and rumors, is the first important contribution to the theory of discursively based reproduction of social cognitions. Bartlett shows that recall of discourse is not purely personal, but that its contents and forms may also depend on sociocultural constraints, viz. as to whether to provide a brief summary of an event or a long and detailed report. Allport and Postman's (1947) later book on the reproduction of rumors in society, finding similar processes of 'sharpening' and 'levelling' in such discourses, remains an important later application of the framework developed by Bartlett (see also Shibutani, 1966).

The founding fathers (as in all academic disciplines, women were hardly allowed to play such a role) of social psychology have little explicit to say about discourse, even when it does play an implicit role in their work. Heider (1958) recognizes the relevance of stories in the analysis of social action and attribution, but in the rest of his book he focuses more generally on the structures of action (ideas which are, however, relevant for a theory of pragmatics or a semantics of narrative). Festinger's early work on social communication and influence also deals with the analysis and explanation of rumors. He concludes that rumors may be reproduced in such a way that they contribute to the future actions of individuals as well as to the reduction of their cognitive dissonance (Festinger, 1950, 1957). For the perspective of our discussion, it is important to note that Festinger also found that persuasive discourse is especially effective when its opinions are assumed to be generally supported by others. Apparently, group sharing is a fundamental condition of the acquisition and reproduction of social cognitions. It was further found that face-to-face conversations in this case may be more effective than monologue or text (Festinger, Schachter, and Back, 1950; Lewin, 1947). Indeed, it appears that informal talk with age, status or gender peers may have an important function in the acquisition of knowledge and opinions (Katz and Lazarsfeld, 1955). In these various studies, we find some of the roots for a modern theory of consensus formation and social reproduction through discourse. Important for us is the early recognition of the social dimensions in the cognitive structures, acquisition and reproduction of SRs. Unfortunately, the analysis of the role of discourse in this process has generally remained intuitive in this early work.

PREJUDICE AND DISCOURSE: AN EXAMPLE FROM CURRENT RESEARCH

In order to make the general framework sketched above more concrete, and to develop further the ideas formulated in early social psychology on the relations between discourse, communication and social cognitions, I summarize some research findings from my own work on the reproduction of racism in discourse and communication. This research analyzes how ethnic prejudice is represented and manipulated in cognition, and expressed in discourse and communication, by white group members of Western multi-ethnic societies. Data for this research were gathered from different sources, viz. informal conversation, information interviews conducted in Amsterdam and San Diego (van Dijk, 1984, 1987a), news reports in the press (van Dijk, 1988a) and school textbooks (van Dijk, 1987b).

The Structures and Strategies of Prejudice

Ethnic prejudice, while superficially defined in terms of 'negative attitudes' of group members about other groups (see also Allport, 1954), is primarily analyzed in terms of organized SRs, shared by many or most members of dominant groups, about dominated groups. These specific SRs feature contents, structures and strategies that optimally organize concrete models and actions in such a way that (for instance ethnic or racial) dominance may be effectively reproduced.

The categories of prejudiced attitude schemata include Origin, Appearance, Socio-economic goals, Socio-cultural norms and values, and Personality; that is, in experiences with minority group members or 'ethnic events' in society, majority group members establish, or draw upon, general knowledge or opinions about where the outgroup members come from, what they look like, why they are 'here', what cultural norms and values they have (e.g. what language they speak, what habits they have) and what kind of personality 'those people' have (e.g. are they aggressive, criminal, etc.?). Social position, and hence group membership of social members, may further influence specific variations, contents or strategic uses of such prejudices. Thus, blue-collar workers, also in their everyday stories, may emphasize the belief that immigrants or minorities 'take away our houses and jobs', because it is this belief that is most relevant to the protection of their own interests and the interpretation of their social frustrations (Miles, 1982; Miles and Phizacklea, 1979; Wellman, 1977). People with more education and better jobs may focus on stereotypes or prejudices about 'deficient' culture, education or language knowledge, a form of prejudice often labeled 'modern' or 'symbolic' racism (Dovidio and Gaertner, 1986).

Depending on the representation of the context, these general, prejudiced attitude schemata influence the concrete models of the ethnic situation that dominant group members build and express in talk or interaction. For instance, in such models, causes of their own negative experiences or social problems may be attributed to minority groups or their members (and not, for instance, to the economy or urban decay); that is, there are 'biased' transformations of the causality relations or agency roles in the model. Also, dominant group members, especially those of lower socio-economic position, may reverse the victim role in such models. They will tend to say that they themselves rather than the minority groups are being discriminated against. Such biased attributions are related both to the familiar 'fundamental attribution error' (Pettigrew, 1979; Stephan, 1977), and to the illusory correlations established between the observed presence of minorities and the experience of their own poverty (Hamilton, Dugan, and Trolier, 1985). Biased models not only instantiate prejudice schemata (e.g. as prototypes, see Cantor and Mischel, 1977, 1979), but also are strategically devised in such a way that they seem to conform such general SRs (Snyder, 1981a,b). Thus, models, and their expression in text and talk, show how group members interpret and represent ethnic events as a function of both social context and general group schemata.

Discourse and Prejudice

Structures and processes of prejudiced SRs also appear in talk and text (for details, see Potter and Wetherell, 1987; van Dijk, 1984, 1987a; van Dijk and Wodak, 1988; Windisch, 1978). The social functions of such prejudiced communications are to share and normalize social knowledge and opinions with other ingroup members, to exhibit and confirm ingroup membership and allegiance or to exchange practical information that shows 'how to deal with them'. At the same time, such talk must contextually obey the usual rules of conversation and interaction, and respect general social norms and goals, including those that prohibit discrimination (Billig, 1988). These general norms are also translated into the context model for the current conversation: a good impression must be made on the hearer or interviewer, or, rather, a bad one must be avoided (Arkin, 1981). This means that prejudiced people cannot simply express negative opinions about 'foreigners', because in that case they might be seen as racists. Thus, they resort to strategic tactics in which negative 'other-presentation' is combined with tactics of impression management, such as positive self-presentation or face-keeping. Hence, discourse about minorities is full of disclaimers, such as denials ('I am not a racist, but . . .'), apparent concessions ('There are good ones among them, but . . .') and other moves (see also Hewitt and Stokes, 1975).

These analyses show that specific properties of everyday discourse and interaction are systematically related to the structures of situation models, context models and general SRs. At the same time, they show how specific SRs are reproduced in the ingroup. These links become manifest not only in the semantic moves of disclaiming, but also in story structure, argumentation and dominant topics of talk. Similarly, conversational phenomena, such as hesitations, false starts and correction, may be related to the cognitive strategies of production, as monitored by the context models of a conversation (viz. by the goal of positive impression formation). Structures of stories about minorities sometimes rather closely reflect the organization of underlying models of the ethnic situation (van Dijk, 1985b). Thus, the normally obligatory Resolution category of the story schema may be left out because storytellers see ethnic situations as essentially problematic and unresolved. Also, as we saw earlier, dominant group members may represent themselves as 'victims' in both stories and models. Conversational topics, on the other hand, rather seem to reflect the contents of the general prejudices about ethnic difference, group threat and intergroup competition, and of the general feelings of ingroup superiority.

Other Research on Prejudice, Stereotypes and Discourse

Although most other research on intergroup relations, stereotypes and prejudices has not been particularly interested in discourse and communication, results from some of this other work may well be interpreted in our framework. A few examples may illustrate this assumption (see e.g. Brewer and Kramer, 1985, for a review).

Bodenhausen and Wyer (1985) studied the effects of ethnic stereotypes on decision-making and information-processing strategies. Among other things, they found that, when (white?) subjects read imaginary case files of personnel managers who had to make a decision about a job-related transgression by people with an Anglo or an Arab name, the recall protocols of the subjects tended to focus on stereotype-confirming information about the target persons. Although this study, like the other research we discussed, nicely shows that SRs condition social information processing, it unfortunately does not offer a detailed theoretical framework that explains the link between the structures and contents of the case files, the interpretation strategies of the readers, their models of the situation (and hence of the target persons), the general ethnic representations and the resulting recall processes and protocols. Better reproduction of stereotypical information may and must be explained in terms of the detailed interaction between these structures and strategies, for instance the role of ethnic SRs in the formation of model structures during text comprehension as well as text production. Thus, people will tend to rely on general SR information as soon as more detailed (possibly relevant) information of concrete models is no longer accessible. Once dominant group members have acquired prejudiced SRs, cognitive processes will generally favor the relatively easy application and hence the confirmation of such SRs during later reproduction or other tasks, instead of the search for possibly disconfirming information in situation models.

The important finding in the study by Bodenhausen and Wyer (1985), as well as in several other studies of the last decade, is that prejudices and stereotypes influence information processing, including reading, understanding and memorizing discourse, such as case files, stories or conversations (Hamilton, 1981). One of the cognitive strategies involved in this process is that information that is construed as an instantiation of, or that is consistent with, or inferable from, a 'biased' group schema may get specific focus and be better organized in 'ethnic' situation models. This is also because situation models are easier to build from prefabricated (instantiated) copies from stereotypes than from scratch, that is, on the basis of new, external information. On future occasions, information from such well-organized models will in turn be more easily recalled and applied in communication and interaction, thus further confirming both the cognitive and the social relevance and prominence of the stereotypical or prejudiced SRs (Duncan, 1976; Rothbart, Fulero, Jensen, Howard, and Birrell, 1978). In fact, in an early paper, Cooper and Jahoda (1947) show that information that aims at combating anti-semitism but that is inconsistent with prevalent stereotypes may not only be ignored or made irrelevant by the reader, but even be strategically misunderstood in the first place. Similarly, stereotypical schemata are used in hypothesis testing about other people, although social norms may also influence actual decisions made by subjects about stereotypical information they receive (Lord, Ross, and Lepper, 1979). It is assumed that less extensive knowledge about outgroups will probably lead to more polarized structures (Us versus Them) in model representations (Linville and Jones, 1980), a phenomenon which also finds confirmation in the contrastive rhetoric of the interviews I analyzed ('WE have to work hard, while THEY can throw parties every week').

While these tendencies found in the experimental literature agree with the basic principles of social information processing, there are some interesting complications; for example, the prominence of information during processing may be defined not only in terms of its relevance or agreement with existing belief schemata, but also by its deviance from such schemata. As is generally the case in story-telling, people also tend to recall interesting exceptions, that is, events that are remarkable (Hastie and Kumar, 1979) or people who play a 'solo' role in a group (Taylor, 1982; Taylor, Fiske, Etcoff, and Ruderman, 1978). While this is undoubtedly correct, it is also clear that deviance presupposes the application of knowledge about routine events or 'normal' people (Black, Galambos, and Read, 1984). We may conclude that mental models and their retrieval are also shaped by strategies of distinction: the more unique the event, the more unique its model, and the less such a model will tend to be confused with others. It is likely that processing such specific information takes more time, and this longer or 'deeper' processing will also result in more elaborated models (see also Brewer, Dull, and Lui, 1981). Remarkable episodes that are not sustained by general schemata are essentially model-based, however, and we may assume that such information will be easily forgotten after longer delays. Similarly, as soon as information is very complex, people will tend to rely on ready-made schemata, rather than on the many details of the actual situation (Rothbart, Evans, and Fulero, 1979). In other words, a more sophisticated theory of the interplay between SRs, models and discourse may explain several earlier results that have sometimes been seen as conflicting (van Dijk, 1985a).

We suggested that, unlike traditional prejudices about minorities (or women for that matter), current prejudices, especially among liberals, may seem more subtle, indirect, modern and 'symbolic' (Barker, 1981; Dovidio and Gaertner, 1986; Essed, 1987). They may focus on bussing, positive action or other forms of 'advantaging' the outgroup. Also, as I found in the interviews I conducted, many of the classical prejudices are not expressed. Sophisticated discourse analysis, as well as analyses of non-verbal or other less controllable features of talk and interaction, such as intonation or pitch, may therefore become necessary to establish underlying SRs (Crosby, Bromley, and Saxe, 1983; Weitz, 1972; Word, Zanna, and Cooper, 1974). Whites may have internalized the norm of non-discrimination (Billig, 1988), but not yet a set of unprejudiced feelings (see Kelman, 1961). Or rather, they may not yet have developed an anti-racist SR that enables them to recognize, represent or talk about (discriminatory) situations as such, or to view them from the perspective of minority group members.

Concluding this section, we find that although most other work on stereotypes and prejudice does not establish a link with discourse, their implications for a theory of the formation and reproduction of SRs are important. The results predict, for instance, that both prejudiced speakers and listeners of talk about minorities will tend to focus on those semantic topics or even microstructural details that are consistent with their SRs. Similarly, since such group attitudes emphasize differences between groups and similarities within groups, prejudiced language users will especially focus on those properties and actions of outgroups that will confirm their difference if not their 'deviance'. These and many other properties of prejudiced talk are largely to be explained in terms of the very specific models such people use or build during communication. Specification of these model structures and of the strategies applied in their expression in communication is, however, lacking in most work on ethnic stereotypes.

Another basic problem of this research, especially of the research done in the

USA, is that the cognitive processes studied are often isolated from their essential social functions in the reproduction of racism and the maintenance of white group power (van Dijk, 1988b). Indeed, prejudice and stereotypes are not universals of the social mind, or inherent properties of complex information processes. They are specifically developed, learned and reproduced in specific sociohistorical contexts, and among specific (dominant) groups. In other words, these social cognitions and processes always need to be related to actual group relationships, as is especially shown in much European research on intergroup relations (Tajfel, 1981; Turner and Giles, 1981). How exactly a social condition like group membership interfaces with detailed SRs and strategies is still largely unknown.

OTHER DOMAINS: PERSUASION, IMPRESSION FORMATION, ATTRIBUTION

Persuasion

A similar account may be given of the role of discourse and social cognitions in both classical and current research in other domains of social psychology, such as persuasion, impression formation and attribution. For example, classical research on persuasion and attitude change by Hovland and his associates (e.g. Hovland, Lumsdaine, and Sheffield, 1949) did give some attention to discourse characteristics, such as the nature and the order of arguments and their effects on persuasion (for review, see e.g., Eagly and Himmelfarb, 1978; Himmelfarb and Eagly, 1974; McGuire, 1969; Petty and Cacioppo, 1981; see Chapter 3, by Burgoon). The same is true for the study of the effect of fear appeals in propaganda (Janis and Feshbach, 1953), repetition or rhetorical questions (Cacioppo and Petty, 1979) in persuasive discourse and their relations with general credibility of the speakers. While some of this work is relevant in a modern theory of the reproduction of SRs, its major shortcomings, at least from our present discourse analytical point of view, are its neglect of a systematic theory of persuasive discourse that goes beyond the somewhat haphazardly chosen discourse properties just mentioned, as well as the lack of a detailed cognitive processing theory that would relate such discourse structures with model structures, and these again with 'attitudes'. In much of this research, personal opinions of models have usually been confused with the more general, socially shared opinions of SRs, which are much more difficult to change, both by definition and also because their change mostly requires extensive social interaction and communication (Jaspars and Fraser, 1984). Attitude-change theory has hardly paid attention to the detailed representation of attitudes themselves, so it is not surprising that much of this early research yields conflicting evidence about the role of specific discourse structures in such attitudes.

Recent persuasion and attitude-change research correctly emphasizes the lack of a direct link between persuasive discourse and opinion change (see Eagly and Chaiken, 1984, for a recent review). Within the perspective of a renewed emphasis on cognitive 'mediation' or cognitive 'responses' (a notion, however, that still betrays traces of behaviorism), it is argued that 'intervening thoughts', such as pro or con arguments, are esssential in opinion change (Petty, Ostrom, and Brock, 1981). While this is undoubtedly true, we find that the problem of description and explanation is not solved by a rather vague reference to 'thoughts' or cognitive arguments. We need to know what exactly these thoughts are, how and where they are represented, what cognitive strategies operate on them and how resulting opinions are formed and represented. The problem also remains of how relevant thoughts are engendered by persuasive discourse in the first place. For instance, repetition in (or of) discourse may affect text processing and model formation in different ways. It may provide the reader with more time to search for relevant models or SRs, to build more extensive models (including more or more detailed opinions) or to instantiate relevant opinions from SRs in models; at the same time, repetition may signal importance or relevance, which will affect the hierarchical structuring of models: macrostructural or topical information, high in the model, is often signalled by repeated information in discourse. These various processes will need to be made explicit if we want to explain whether and why repeated persuasive discourse has more, or less, effect on opinion formation in models (Cacioppo and Petty, 1979). The processes involved are too complex to be simply captured by the application of recall of argumentation schemata alone (Schmidt and Sherman, 1984): while these schemata are by definition of a general nature, and therefore shared and easily available, the contents of each argumentation are unique, or at least largely variable.

Impression Management

Some impression-management research, which has a more social orientation than most persuasion research (Tedeschi, 1981), also deals with the discursive ante- cedents of model transformations, such as the presence of positive self-description, or the performance of 'kind' verbal acts, such as greetings or self-disclosure (Schneider, 1981). As is also shown in some of the persuasion literature, moderation, reticence, avoidance or withdrawal in attitude expression may be conducive to positive evaluations, on the intuitive ground that aggression or radical positions may lead to more negative evaluations by the recipient (Arkin, 1981; Hass, 1981). This phenomenon is also encountered in interviews about minorities: people often express moderate views, for example by using strategic moves of mitigation, or else avoid delicate issues, for instance by withdrawing or changing the topic. A negative evaluation of the speaker does not always lead to less persuasion, however. This also depends on social characteristics of the speaker: people who are more credible or powerful, for example because of knowledge or status, may be more aggressive in defending their points of view than less impressive speakers (Burgoon and Miller, 1985).

   The important conclusion of this and similar findings is that discourse structures alone do not fully predict what will happen cognitively, as is well-known in the psychology of text processing (van Dijk and Kintsch, 1983). Structures, contents and availability of context models, of the current speaker, as well as of the recipient, and SRs about the group the speaker belongs to, will almost always strongly determine the actual processing of what the speaker says. There is practically no research that consistently demonstrates opinion-formation or impression-formation effects of specific language or discourse structures independent of topic or issue, or independent of the communicative context and independent of speakers and recipients (Berger and Bradac, 1982; Petty and Cacioppo, 1985; see Chapter 19, by Bradac).

Attribution

Although little attribution research is explicitly interested in the structures of discourse and their relations with the process of attribution, many experiments are based on 'information' about action and actors that is presented to experimental subjects in the form of discourse, for example stories (Hewstone, 1983a). Recall that stories, which are essentially about interesting human action, express prominent situation models in episodic memory (of course with many transformations, due to constraints of the context model, for example pragmatic or conversational relevance). Hence, attribution processes are basically strategies of 'making sense', that is, strategies of coherent model building. Relations of cause and reason are fundamental in the establishment of coherence (van Dijk, 1977). More generally, therefore, attribution might best be analyzed as a special case of understanding, viz. of human action as well as of (action) discourse, especially of causes, reasons or motivations of human action (see also Kelley, 1983). Understanding and explanation of action in terms of attributes of the actor or on the basis of context characteristics, which form the core phenomena studied by attribution theory, thus are only one of the many strategies of (action) understanding (see the contribution in the edited volume by Jaspars, Fincham, and Hewstone, 1983, for details).

Because the very notion of action presupposes actor control, and since models feature prominent actor categories, there will be a general tendency to explain actions in terms of actor characteristics rather than in terms of context (Jones and Nisbett, 1972). In speech acts such as defenses, excuses, accusations or justifications of action, this focus may be diverted to the usually less prominent context, for instance in explaining (and therefore excusing) our own negative actions or failures. This 'self-serving' aspect of attribution bias not only holds for individuals, but more generally also for group members, when they explain negative actions or failures of other ingroup members in a situation of intergroup conflict. On the other hand, negative actions of outgroup members tend to be explained in terms of their group characteristics and therefore blamed on them rather than explained or excused in terms of contextual conditions (Pettigrew, 1979; Stephan, 1977). Attribution as a form of excuse is also part of strategies of positive self-presentation, as we also saw in the analysis of conversation about minorities (see also Tedeschi and Reiss, 1981). Note, however, that these differences in the explanation of actions by/of in- and outgroup members are not simply cognitive 'errors'. On the contrary, they are (of course mostly unconscious) highly effective strategies, which ultimately have crucial social functions in the reproduction of group dominance (or resistance against such dominance).

Discourse analysis may be expected to show more explicitly the differences and the functions of the perspectives involved in the understanding, description or explanation of action (Farr and Anderson, 1983). It may show how people actually go about explaining their own actions or those of others (Antaki, 1981). Explanations of actions are not isolated cognitive activities, but part of the more complex process of understanding, that is, model building. These models in turn are often expressed in (personal) stories or accounts, which also have their proper interaction constraints. Therefore, these accounts may be taken as important data for the analysis of the attribution or explanation process, but should also be seen as an autonomous social practice (Harré and Secord, 1972). Social actors use attributions strategically, depending on relevance and context, and may apply effective procedures to express or understand explanations in line with their actual goals or interests. This implies that common-sense explanations of action, as well as the understanding of action discourse, are based on complex SRs, shared by social actors or language users as group members, and featuring vast sets of knowledge, attitudes, sociocultural norms and values, and ideologies, as well as the rules and strategies to handle this information (Hewstone, 1983b; Moscovici and Hewstone, 1983).

Unfortunately, we know very little of the detailed structures and strategies of language use and discourse that may express or influence attributional processes (Hewstone, 1983a). Work in critical linguistics shows how the syntactic structures of sentences, for instance in newspaper headlines, may reflect the ideologically based attribution of agency (Fowler, Hodge, Kress, and Trew, 1979; van Dijk, 1988c; see also Pryor and Kriss, 1977). The same is true for the use of action verbs, which may signal different attributions depending on whether they describe accomplishments, actions, opinions or emotions (McArthur, 1972). For instance, action descriptions referring to 'anger' of the actor will typically favor situational attributions, whereas descriptions of accomplishments will tend to focus on attributes of the persons themselves. Similarly, a whole range of stylistic phenomena, such as pronunciation, lexical choice and grammatical style, provides indicators about speakers/actors, or rather about group(s) they belong to, which will not only determine opinion formation but also guide the attribution process, for instance in interethnic communication (Giles and Hewstone, 1982; Giles and Powesland, 1975; Giles, Scherer, and Taylor, 1979). Lind and O'Barr (1979), among others, showed that the attribution of power in the courtroom may be influenced by the use of specific stylistic features, such as the presence or absence of hesitation markers or hedging. Here we touch upon one of the crucial tasks of social cognition research, viz. to establish a link between a social relation, namely power, on the one hand, and its representation in social cognition, and communication through discourse, on the other hand. In most of the research just mentioned, however, it is precisely the cognitive interface between social relationships and discourse style that is discussed in rather vague terms, if at all (van Dijk, 1988b).

Ideology

There are many concepts and areas of research of a sociocognitive nature that are neglected in mainstream social psychology but which have a vital role in the explanation of the processes of social cognition and its societal reproduction through discourse. One of these concepts is ideology, which is usually left to sociology and political science (but see Billig, 1982). However, from the early days of attitude research and the analysis of belief consistency, it has often been observed that social beliefs and attitudes seem to have some kind of consistency. Although social cognitions are not consistent in the proper logical sense, I nevertheless assume that they show various forms of coherence or *psycho*logical consistency. Attitudes about different social issues may feature the same basic opinions, similar explanations and, especially, the instantiation of the same general norms or values. Despite variations and contradictions, people have the intuitive ability to recognize such coherence and label it accordingly (for instance as 'conservative').

Against this background, I propose that an ideology is the group-based, shared framework that underlies this coherence. Ideology provides the basic building blocks, the selection principles of relevant norms and values, as well as the structural organization of SRs. In line with the analysis of ideologies in the social sciences, I also assume that ideologies are in part self-serving, and developed and applied in such a way that group members' social cognitions and practices are geared towards the maintenance of overall group interests (Centre for Contemporary Cultural Studies, 1978; Kinloch, 1981). Thus, ideologies of dominant groups monitor the development of SRs, the formation of models, and the production of action and discourse of group members in such a way that the group will maintain power and reproduce its hegemony with respect to dominated groups, as has been most obvious in classism, sexism and racism. Such dominance may also be exercised by the control of the means of ideological production, such as the media or education, and therefore indirectly by the control of public discourse that expresses those models that instantiate attitudes that are consistent with the dominant ideology. Ideological frameworks explain why attitudes are not formed or changed in an arbitrary way. Basic strategies of social information processing are not simply defined in terms of universals of cognition. Similarly, the formation of norms and values, and their application in opinion formation, must also be monitored by an underlying, ideological framework. Discourse plays a central role in the formation and change of ideologies. Through discourse, ideologies may be made partly explicit, and thus conveyed and normalized or legitimated. One of the major common tasks of social psychology and discourse analysis in the next decade is to analyze in detail these structures, processes and social practices of the ideological framework.

CONCLUSIONS

This survey of some of the literature in social psychology shows that discourse appears to be relevant in many ways in the study of social cognition, viz. as experimental materials, data and subject responses, as well as a direct object of study. We have also seen, however, that social psychologists have largely ignored this role of discourse, although some (and more recently many) of them have been interested in the role of language and communication. Discourse structures, for example of persuasive messages, of impression-formation strategies or of explanatory accounts of attribution, are seldom made explicit, nor are their relations with structures of social cognition analyzed in detail.

Despite this marginal role of an explicit theory of discourse in social psychology, we also found that existing research may partially be reinterpreted in such a way that insights may be obtained about the systematic relationships between the structures and strategies of discourse and those of social cognition. From my own work on the discursive expression and communication of ethnic prejudice in society, I have concluded that socially shared cognitions also systematically appear in text and talk, and that such discourse forms a necessary link in the group reproduction of ethnic beliefs. Other research on stereotypes shows how SRs induce 'biased' information processing about minority group members generally, and ingroup-favoring discourse use or recall about outgroups in particular. I have stressed, though, that the actual contents and strategies involved are not simply universals of the cognitive dynamics of group perception and interaction, as may be the case for processes of categorization or polarization. Rather, group power and interests, dominance and other social relations are involved for which SRs and their strategies play a very specific function. It is therefore imperative to specify how a social relation like power may be mapped into the structures and strategies of SRs, for instance by means of fundamental ideological frameworks of the interpretation of social reality.

The role of discourse, in the form of 'messages' or 'communication', is more prominent in both classical and recent attitude-change and persuasion research. Besides properties of communicators, message characteristics have often been taken as independent variables in experimental work on the antecedents of attitude change. In my critical evaluation of this research, I first reformulated the notions of attitude and attitude change in terms of a more explicit framework of social cognitions, representations and strategies. It was emphasized that the notion of 'attitude change', implied by all persuasion research, should be analyzed in terms of transformations of evaluative beliefs (opinions) in situation models, and that attitudes are complex schemata consisting of generalized opinions, inferred from models. Future work in this area thus should pay closer attention to the precise contents and structures of SRs, their relations with models, and the relations of models with persuasive discourse structures as well as social dimensions of persuasive interactions and situations. Similar remarks hold for impression management and attribution theory, and the presentation, interpretation and understanding of human action. Beyond a more explicit application of cognitive model theory in the analysis of explanations, justifications or excuses as forms of action understanding, I emphasized the need to analyze everyday explanatory discourse, for instance stories or argumentation, both as a source of information about underlying attribution processes, as well as the actual, socially situated practice of action explanations.

This chapter is limited to a brief discussion of some work in only a few major domains of social psychology. It is obvious, however, that there is virtually no domain in this discipline that does not involve discourse in some way, either as part of the domain or object of research, as is the case in persuasion, or as experimental materials, response formats (e.g. recall protocols) or other data (see also Ericsson and Simon, 1984). All fields of social psychology deal with how people make sense of the social world and each other, not only by thinking about each other, looking at each other or interacting, but also and primarily by talking to and about each other. In addition to the general sociocognitive processes discussed above, research should also focus on specific communicative events or discourse genres, such as cognition–interaction pairs in the courtroom, the classroom or the newsroom. In such situated interactions, various sociocognitive processes take place at the same time. In such discourse, persuasion, attribution, self-presentation or stereotyping may be integrated. Sophisticated analysis of the many properties of text and talk may yield insight both into the detailed structures of underlying situation or context models, SRs or ideologies, and into the social functions of such discourse and interaction.

ACKNOWLEDGMENT

I am particularly indebted to Miles Hewstone for his extensive comments and suggestions about the (much longer) first draft of this chapter, and to Mick Billig, whose important comments need to be taken into account in future versions of my theoretical framework.

REFERENCES

Abelson, R.P. (1976). Script processing in attitude formation and decision making. In J.S. Carroll and J.W. Payne (Eds), *Cognition and social behavior*, pp. 33–46. Hillsdale, NJ: Erlbaum.

Allport, G.W. (1954). *The nature of prejudice*. New York: Doubleday/Anchor.

Allport, G.W. and Postman, L. (1947). *The psychology of rumor*. New York: Holt.

Antaki, C. (Ed.) (1981). *The psychology of ordinary explanations*. London: Academic Press.

Argyle, M., Furnham, A., and Graham, J.A. (1981). *Social situations*. Cambridge: Cambridge University Press.

Arkin, R.M. (1981). Self-presentation styles. In J.T. Tedeschi (Ed.), *Impression management: Theory and social psychological research*, pp. 311–333. New York: Academic Press.

Barker, M. (1981). *The new racism*. London: Junction.

Bartlett, F.C. (1932). *Remembering*. London: Cambridge University Press.

Berger, C.R. and Bradac, J.R. (1982). *Language and social knowledge*. London: Arnold.

Billig, M. (1982). *Ideology and social psychology*. Oxford: Blackwell.

Billig, M. (1988). The notion of 'prejudice': Some rhetorical and ideological aspects. In T.A. van Dijk and R. Wodak (Eds), *Discourse, racism and social psychology*, pp. 91–110. *Text*, **8**, No. 1/2.

Black, J.B., Galambos, J.A., and Read, S.J. (1984). Comprehending stories and social situations. In R.S. Wyer, Jr, and T.K. Srull (Eds), *Handbook of social cognition*, Vol. 1, pp. 119–160. Hillsdale, NJ: Erlbaum.

Bodenhausen, G.V. and Wyer, R.S. Jr (1985). Effects of stereotypes on decision making and information-processing strategies. *Journal of Personality and Social Psychology*, **48**, 267–282.

Brewer, M.B., Dull, V., and Lui, L. (1981). Perceptions of the elderly: Stereotypes as prototypes. *Journal of Personality and Social Psychology*, **41**, 656–670.

Brewer, M.B. and Kramer, R.M. (1985). The psychology of intergroup attitudes and behavior. *Annual Review of Psychology*, **36**, 219–243.

Brown, P. and Fraser, C. (1979). Speech as a marker of situation. In K.R. Scherer and H. Giles (Eds), *Social markers in speech*, pp. 33–62. Cambridge: Cambridge University Press.

Brown, R. (1965). *Social psychology*. New York: Free Press.

Brown, R.J. and Turner, J.C. (1981). Interpersonal and intergroup behaviour. In J.C. Turner and H. Giles (Eds), *Intergroup behavior*, pp. 33–65. Oxford: Blackwell.

Burgoon, M. and Miller, G.R. (1985). An expectancy interpretation of language and persuasion. In N. Giles and R. St Clair (Eds), *Recent advances in language communication and social psychology*. London: Erlbaum.

Cacioppo, J.T. and Petty, R.E. (1979). Effects of message repetition and position on cognitive responses, recall and persuasion. *Journal of Personality and Social Psychology*, **37**, 97–109.

Cantor, N. and Mischel, W. (1977). Traits as prototypes: Effects on recognition memory. *Journal of Personality and Social Psychology*, **35**, 38–48.

Cantor, N. and Mischel, W. (1979). Prototypes in person perception. In L. Berkowitz (Ed.), *Advances in experimental social psychology*, Vol. 12, pp. 3–52. New York: Academic Press.

Centre for Contemporary Cultural Studies (1978). *On ideology*. London: Hutchinson.

Cicourel, A.V. (1973). *Cognitive sociology*. Harmondsworth (England): Penguin.

Cooper, E. and Jahoda, M. (1947). The evasion of propaganda: How prejudiced people respond to anti-prejudice propaganda. *Journal of Psychology*, **23**, 15–25.

Crosby, F., Bromley, S., and Saxe, L. (1980). Recent unobtrusive studies of black and white discrimination and prejudice: A literature review. *Psychological Bulletin*, **87**, 546–563.

Cushman, D.P. and McPhee, R.D. (Eds) (1981). *Message–attitude–behavior relationship*. New York: Academic Press.

Dovidio, J.F. and Gaertner, S.L. (Eds) (1986). *Prejudice, discrimination and racism*. New York: Academic Press.

Duncan, B.L. (1976). Differential social perception and attribution of intergroup violence: Testing the lower limits of stereotyping blacks. *Journal of Personality and Social Psychology*, **34**, 590–598.

Eagly, A.H. and Chaiken, S. (1984). Cognitive theories of persuasion. *Advances in Experimental Social Psychology*, **46**, 735–754.

Eagly, A.H. and Himmelfarb, S. (1978). Attitudes and opinions. *Annual Review of Psychology*, **29**, 517–554.

Ericsson, K.A. and Simon, H.A. (1984). *Verbal reports as data*. Cambridge, MA: MIT Press.

Essed, P.J.M. (1987). Academic racism: Common sense in the social sciences. Centrum voor Etnische Studies, Universiteit van Amsterdam: *CRES Publications*, No. 5.

Evans, R.I. (1980). *The making of social psychology: Discussions with creative contributors*. New York: Gardner Press.

Farr, R.M. and Anderson, T. (1983). Beyond actor–observer differences in perspective: Extensions and applications. In M. Hewstone (Ed.), *Attribution theory: Social and functional extensions*, pp. 45–64. Oxford: Blackwell.

Farr, R.M. and Moscovici, S. (Eds) (1984). *Social representations*. Cambridge: Cambridge University Press.

Festinger, L. (1950). Informal social communication. *Psychological Review*, **57**, 271–282.

Festinger, L. (1957). *A theory of cognitive dissonance*. Stanford: Stanford University Press.

Festinger, L. (Ed.) (1980). *Retrospections on social psychology*. New York: Oxford University Press.

Festinger, L., Schachter, S., and Back, K. (1950). *Social pressures in informal groups*. New York: Harper.

Fiske, S.T. and Taylor, S.E. (1984). *Social cognition*. Reading, MA: Addison-Wesley.

Forgas, J.P. (1979). *Social episodes*. London: Academic Press.

Forgas, J.P. (1983). What is social about social cognition? *British Journal of Social Psychology*, **22**, 129–144.

Forgas, J.P. (Ed) (1981). *Social cognition: Perspectives on everyday understanding*. London: Academic Press.

Fowler, R., Hodge, B., Kress, G., and Trew, T. (1979). *Language and control*. London: Routledge and Kegan Paul.

Giles, H. and Hewstone, M. (1982). Cognitive structures, speech, and social situations: Two integrative models. *Language Sciences*, **4**, 187–219.

Giles, H. and Powesland, P.F. (1975). *Speech style and social evaluation*. London: Academic Press.

Giles, H., Scherer, K.R., and Taylor, D.M. (1979). Speech markers in social interaction. In H. Giles and K.R. Scherer (Eds), *Social markers in speech*, pp. 343–381. Cambridge: Cambridge University Press.

Gilmour, R. and Duck, S. (Eds) (1980). *The development of social psychology*. London: Academic Press.

Hamilton, D.L. (Ed.) (1981). *Cognitive processes in stereotyping and intergroup behavior*. Hillsdale, NJ: Erlbaum.

Hamilton, D.L., Dugan, P.M., and Trolier, T.K. (1985). The formation of stereotypic beliefs: Further evidence for distinctiveness-based illusory correlations. *Journal of Personality and Social Psychology*, **48**, 5–17.

Harré, R. and Secord, P.F. (1972). *The explanation of social behavior*. Oxford: Blackwell.

Hass, R.G. (1981). Presentational strategies and the social expression of attitudes: Impression management within limits. In J.T. Tedeschi (Ed.), *Impression management: Theory and social psychological research*, pp. 127–146. New York: Academic Press.

Hastie, R. and Kumar, P.A. (1979). Person memory: Personality traits as organizing principles in memory for behaviors. *Journal of Personality and Social Psychology*, **37**, 25–38.

Heider, F. (1958). *The psychology of interpersonal relations*. New York: Wiley.

Hewitt, J.P. and Stokes, R. (1975). Disclaimers. *American Sociological Review*, **40**, 1–11.

Hewstone, M. (1983a). The role of language in attribution processes. In J. Jaspars, F.D. Fincham, and M. Hewstone (Eds), *Attribution theory and research: Conceptual, developmental and social dimensions*, pp. 241–260. London: Academic Press.

Hewstone, M. (Ed.) (1983b). *Attribution theory: Social and functional extensions*. Oxford: Blackwell.

Himmelfarb, S. and Eagly, A.H. (Eds) (1974). *Readings in attitude change*. New York: Wiley.

Hovland, C.I., Lumsdaine, A.A., and Sheffield, F.D. (1949). *Experiments on mass communication*. Princeton, NJ: Princeton University Press.

Janis, I.L. and Feshbach, S. (1953). Effects of fear-arousing communications. *Journal of Abnormal and Social Psychology*, **48**, 78–92.

Jaspars, J., Fincham, F.D., and Hewstone, M. (Eds) (1983). *Attribution theory and research: Conceptual, developmental and social dimensions*. London: Academic Press.

Jaspars, J. and Fraser, C. (1984). Attitudes and social representations. In R.M. Farr and S. Moscovici (Eds), *Social representations*, pp. 101–124. Cambridge: Cambridge University Press.

Johnson-Laird, P.N. (1983). *Mental models*. Cambridge: Cambridge University Press.

Jones, E.E. and Gerard, H.B. (1967). *Foundations of social psychology*. New York Wiley.

Jones, E.E. and Nisbett, R.E. (1972). The actor and the observer: Divergent perceptions of the causes of behavior. In E.E. Jones *et al.* (Eds), *Attribution: Perceiving the causes of behavior*, Morristown, N.J: General Learning Press.

Katz, E. and Lazarsfeld, P.F. (1955). *Personal influence*. New York: Free Press.

Kelley, H.H. (1983). Perceived causal structures. In J. Jaspars, F.D. Fincham, and M. Hewstone (Eds), *Attribution theory and research: Conceptual developmental and social dimensions*, pp. 343–369. London: Academic Press.

Kelman, H.C. (1961). Processes of opinion change. *Public Opinion Quarterly*, **25**, 57–78.

Kinloch, G.C. (1981). *Ideology and contemporary sociological theory*. Englewood Cliffs. NJ: Prentice-Hall.

Kraut, R.E. and Higgins, E.T. (1984). Communication and social cognition. In R.S. Wyer and T.K. Srull (Eds), *Handbook of social cognition*, Vol. 3, pp. 87–128. Hillsdale, NJ: Erlbaum.

Lewin, K. (1947). Group decision and social change. In T.M. Newcomb and E.L. Hartley (Eds), *Readings in social psychology*, pp. 330–344. New York: Holt.

Lind, E.A. and O'Barr, W.M. (1979). The social significance of speech in the courtroom. In H. Giles and R. St Clair (Eds), *Language and social psychology*, pp. 66–87. Oxford: Blackwell.

Linville, P.W. and Jones, E.E. (1980). Polarized appraisals of out-group members. *Journal of Personality and Social Psychology*, **38**, 689–703.

Lord, C., Ross, L., and Lepper, M.E. (1979). Biased assimilation and attitude polarization: The effects of prior theories on subsequently considered evidence. *Journal of Personality and Social Psychology*, **37**, 2098–2109.

McArthur, L.Z. (1972). The how and what of why: Some determinants and consequences of causal attributions. *Journal of Personality and Social Psychology*, **22**, 171–193.

McGuire, W.J. (1969). The nature of attitude and attitude change. In G. Lindzey and E. Aronson (Eds), *Handbook of social psychology*, 2nd edn, Vol. 3, *The individual in a social context*. Reading, MA: Addison-Wesley.

Miles, R. (1982). *Racism and migrant labour*. London: Routledge and Kegan Paul.

Miles, R. and Phizacklea, A. (Eds) (1979). *Racism and political action in Britain*. London: Routledge and Kegan Paul.

Moscovici, S. (1982). The coming era of representations. In J.-P. Leyens (Eds), *Cognitive analysis of social behavior*, pp. 115–150. The Hague: Nijhoff.

Moscovici, S. (1984). The phenomenon of social representations. In R.M. Farr and S. Moscovici (Eds), *Social representations*, pp. 3–70. Cambridge: Cambridge University Press.

Moscovici, S. and Hewstone, M. (1983). Social representations and social explanations: From the 'naive' to the 'amateur' scientist. In M. Hewstone (Ed.), *Attribution theory: Social and functional extensions*, pp. 99–125. Oxford: Blackwell.

Pettigrew, T.F. (1979). The ultimate attribution error: Extending Allport's cognitive analysis of prejudice. *Personality and Social Psychology Bulletin*, **5**, 461–476.

Petty, R.E. and Cacioppo, J.T. (1981). *Attitudes and persuasion: Classic and contemporary approaches*. Dubuque, IA: Brown.

Petty, R.E. and Cacioppo, J.T. (1985). The elaboration likelihood model of persuasion. In L. Berkowitz (Ed.), *Advances in experimental social psychology*. New York: Academic Press.

Petty, R.E., Ostrom, T.M., and Brock, T.C. (Eds) (1981). *Cognitive responses in persuasion*. Hillsdale, NJ: Erlbaum.

Potter, J. and Wetherell, M. (1987). *Discourse and social psychology: Beyond attitudes and behaviour*. Newbury Park, CA: Sage.

Pryor, J.B. and Kriss, M. (1977). The cognitive dynamics of salience in the attribution process. *Journal of Personality and Social Psychology*, **35**, 49–55.

Robinson, W.P. (1985). Social psychology and discourse. In T.A. van Dijk (Ed.), *Handbook of discourse analysis*, Vol. 1, pp. 107–144. London: Academic Press.

Roloff, M.E. and Berger, C.R. (Eds) (1982). *Social cognition and communication*. Beverly Hills, CA: Sage.

Rommetveit, R. (1984). The role of language in the creation and transmission of social representations. In R.M. Farr and S. Moscovici (Eds), *Social representations*, pp. 331–360. Cambridge: Cambridge University Press.

Rothbart, M., Evans, M., and Fulero, S. (1979). Recall for confirming events: Memory processes and the maintenance of social stereotypes. *Journal of Experimental Social Psychology*, **15**, 343–355.

Rothbart, M., Fulero, S., Jensen, C., Howard, J., and Birrell, P. (1978). From individual to group impressions: Availability heuristics in stereotype formation. *Journal of Experimental Social Psychology*, **14**, 237–255.

Schank, R.C. and Abelson, R.P. (1977). *Scripts, goals, plans and understanding*. Hillsdale, NJ: Erlbaum.

Schmidt, D.F. and Sherman, R.C. (1984). Memory for persuasive messages: A test of a schema-copy-plus-tag model. *Journal of Personality and Social Psychology*, **47**, 17–25.

Schneider, D.J. (1981). Tactical self-presentations: Toward a broader conception. In J.T. Tedeshi (Ed.), *Impression management. Theory and social psychological research*, pp. 23–40. New York: Academic Press.

Shibutani, T. (1966). *Improvised news: A sociological study of rumor*. Indianapolis, IN: Bobbs-Merrill.

Snyder, M. (1981a). On the self-perpetuating nature of social stereotypes. In D.L. Hamilton (Ed.), *Cognitive processes in stereotyping and intergroup behavior*, pp. 183–212. Hillsdale, NJ: Erlbaum.

Snyder, M. (1981b). Seek and ye shall find: Testing hypotheses about other people. In E.T. Higgins, C.P. Herman, and M.P. Zanna (Eds), *Social cognition: The Ontario symposium*, Vol. 1, pp. 277–304. Hillsdale, NJ: Erlbaum.

Stephan, W.G. (1977). Stereotyping: The role of ingroup–outgroup differences in causal attribution for behavior. *Journal of Social Psychology*, **101**, 255–266.

Tajfel, H. (1981). *Human groups and social categories*. Cambridge: Cambridge University Press.

Taylor, S.E. (1982). The availability bias in social perception and interaction. In D. Kahneman, P. Slovic, and A. Tversky (Eds), *Judgment under uncertainty: Heuristics and biases*, pp. 190–200. New York: Cambridge University Press.

Taylor, S.E., Fiske, S.T., Etcoff, N.L., and Ruderman, A.J. (1978). Categorical and contextual bases of person memory and stereotyping. *Journal of Personality and Social Psychology*, **36**, 778–793.

Tedeschi, J.T. (Ed.) (1981). *Impression management: Theory and social psychological research*. New York: Academic Press.

Tedeschi, J.T. and Reiss, M. (1981). Verbal strategies in impression management. In C. Antaki (Ed.), *The psychology of ordinary explanations of social behaviour*, pp. 271–309. London: Academic Press.

Turner, J.C. and Giles, H. (Eds) (1981). *Intergroup behaviour*. Oxford: Blackwell.

van Dijk, T.A. (1977). *Text and context*. London: Longman.

van Dijk, T.A. (1984). *Prejudice and discourse: An analysis of ethnic prejudice in cognition and conversation*. Amsterdam: Benjamins.

van Dijk, T.A. (1985a). Cognitive situation models in discourse production: The expression of ethnic situations in prejudiced discourse. In J.P. Forgas (Ed.), *Language and social situations*. New York: Springer.

van Dijk, T.A. (Ed.) (1985b). *Handbook of discourse analysis* (4 Vols). London: Academic Press.

van Dijk, T.A. (1987a). *Communicating racism*. Newbury Park, CA: Sage.

van Dijk, T.A. (1987b) *Schoolvoorbeelden van racisme* [*Textbook examples of racism*]. Amsterdam: Socialistische Uitgeverij Amsterdam.

van Dijk, T.A. (1987c). Episodic models in discourse processing. In R. Horowitz and S.J. Samuels (Eds), *Comprehending oral and written language*. New York: Academic Press.

van Dijk, T.A. (1988a). *News analysis*. Hillsdale, NJ: Erlbaum.

van Dijk, T.A. (1988b). Social cognition, social power and social discourse. *Text*, **8**, 129–157.

van Dijk, T.A. (1988c). How 'They' hit the headlines: Ethnic minorities in the press. In G. Smitherman-Donaldson and T.A. van Dijk (Eds), *Discourse and discrimination*, pp. 221–262. Detroit, MI: Wayne State University Press.

van Dijk, T.A. and Kintsch, W. (1983). *Strategies of discourse comprehension*. New York: Academic Press.

van Dijk, T.A. and Wodak, R. (Eds) (1988). *Discourse, racism and social psychology*. *Text*, **8**, No. 1/2.

Weitz, S. (1972). Attitude, voice and behavior: A repressed affect model of interracial interaction. *Journal of Personality and Social Psychology*, **24**, 14–21.

Wellman, D.T. (1977). *Portraits of white racism*. Cambridge: Cambridge University Press.

Windisch, U. (1978). *Xénophobie? Logique de la pensée populaire*. Lausanne: l'Age d'Homme.

Word, C.O., Zanna, M.P., and Cooper, J. (1974). The nonverbal mediation of self-fulfilling prophecies in interracial interaction. *Journal of Experimental Social Psychology*, **10**, 109–120.

Wyer, R.S. Jr, and Srull, T.K. (Eds) (1985). *Handbook of social cognition* (3 vols). Hillsdale, NJ: Erlbaum.

Section 3

Language and Interpersonal Facework

Introduction to Section 3

Having focused in the last section on the dynamics of different facets of our communicative repertoire, we turn now to how language is intricately involved in various ubiquitous social activities, namely self-disclosure, facework, accounting, deception, and control.

Holtgraves begins by examining the multidimensional nature of self-disclosures (e.g. their directness, level of intimacy) and shows how the very same disclosive act has differing interpretive potential, depending on the timing and social location of its divulgence. Moreover, the negotiative character of the phenomena is examined by considering how self-disclosures are introduced into conversation, managed, and responded to as well as how the disclosure can preconstruct the discursive climate in which the act is seemingly elicited. Holtgraves' emphasis, then, is on the *process* of self-disclosure and its pragmatic meaning for identity construction and relational development, and this is integrated in a compelling manner with social skills and self-presentational perspectives.

Tracy attends to the latter topic by critically examining different approaches to facework and the ways in which we can use language to present a particular image of ourselves as well as to ensure that interlocutors are treated as they would wish (positive and negative face, respectively). Whilst comparing and contrasting developments in politeness theory and research with the stances of Goffman and more contemporary self-presentation theorists, Tracy underscores the difficulty of achieving intended conversational outcomes, given the often *multiple* and sometimes *competing* face desires we possess at one and the same time. The complexity and potential of this important area of interpersonal communication, and the role of politeness within it, is articulated well in terms of Tracy's tenets or blueprint for a new theory of facework discourse.

Apart from trying to impose our identities on others, sometimes we feel the need, or are required, to account for our supposedly questionable actions, feelings, and

Handbook of Language and Social Psychology
Edited by H. Giles and W.P. Robinson.   © 1990 John Wiley & Sons Ltd

thoughts. Hence, Cody and McLaughlin provide a thorough review of this burgeoning area of defending our faces and reducing interactional costs. They examine the typologies available for describing different accounting types (e.g. excuses, justifications), identify some of the attributional dimensions underlying recipients' acceptance of them, and discuss the relative merits for their effectiveness in organizational and legal settings. The discoursal nature of (even multiple) accounting is also examined, not only in terms of the relationship between the natures of reproach and subsequent repair, but also in the ways people account for the same action in different contexts. Cody and McLaughlin, whilst invoking construals of moral action, provide a social cognitive framework for studying accounts by a reliance on causal schemata and scripts, and point out that the knowledge required to present accounts (verbally and non-verbally) is also that needed by others in understanding and interpreting them.

Accounting – as well as many other forms of facework and self-disclosure – sometimes involves speakers in acts of deception. Even if it does not, recipients are often wary, rightly or wrongly, that they might be the victims of deception. However, as Friedman and Tucker point out, we are not particularly adept at detecting deception, even though there is a social consensus about which verbal and non-verbal cues constitute its occurrence. These are not particularly reliable, given that such sociolinguistic recipes are also associated with other psychological states (e.g. arousal), although certain preconditions for deceiving do indeed lend themselves to specifiable leakages. The literature is reviewed by recourse to a new model which examines the individual and situational factors which mediate the deceiver's language behaviours, and the cognitive and motivational factors of the decoder which influence detection. This framework again underscores the *process* of deception as well as the skills required for performance on the one hand and sensitivity on the other.

All of the processes studied above involve, to varying degrees, different forms of asymmetrical power. The final chapter in this section by Ng examines the manner in which language not only determines others' actions but moulds their goals, wants, and understandings. By invoking a new framework for studying the language of control, Ng analyses the social and linguistic principles which, essentially and implicitly, underlie the management of self-disclosures, facework, accounting, and deception. If these language behaviours are decoded as intended, then their purveyors have created or maintained considerable interpersonal power. Hence, by the infrequent use of so-called 'powerless' verbal and discoursal devices, and the ability to dictate and/or endorse topic shifts, an individual will be perceived as interactionally and socially 'in control'. However, language is used for other control purposes and Ng's discussion of these lays well the ground for the next section on communication between social groups. Ng shows that language can act as an independent variable, determining our social reality by masking and misleading our understanding of political events according to certain sociolinguistic principles. The use of language to facilitate control by concealing it from both target and agent can be even more pernicious when it is 'routinized' in language by trivializing subordinate groups and rendering them invisible, as illustrated by means of the generic masculine and its sociopsychological consequences.

This section, then, will demonstrate the tactical and negotiative character of language in contextualized, mainly interpersonal, use.

9

The Language of Self-Disclosure

THOMAS HOLTGRAVES

Department of Psychological Science, Ball State University, USA

Self-disclosure has been a topic of continuous research for over 30 years. Social, personality, and clinical psychologists, as well as communication scholars, have all contributed to this research, reflecting the interdisciplinary interest in this topic. It is somewhat surprising, then, that there has been little explicit attention paid to the language of self-disclosure, or *how* individuals self-disclose. Much past research has examined self-disclosure as a behavior independently of how it is linguistically realized within conversations. Thus, despite the plethora of studies of self-disclosure, relatively little is known about what self-disclosure is and how it occurs and is managed within conversations. The major purpose of this chaper is to describe some of the properties of self-disclosure as a contextually grounded verbal activity, and more importantly, to argue what can be gained by doing so.

How people self-disclose is meant here to refer simply to the various ways in which disclosures can occur. Informal observation suggests a considerable amount of variability in terms of the form of disclosures, how disclosures are brought about, the reactions of recipients of disclosures, and so on. How people disclose is somewhat similar to what others have referred to as self-disclosure style (e.g. Berg, 1987; Chelune, 1975). Self-disclosure style, however, usually refers only to the non-verbal aspects of self-disclosure. In contrast, the primary focus in this chapter will be on the language of self-disclosure.

Handbook of Language and Social Psychology
Edited by H. Giles and W.P. Robinson. © 1990 John Wiley & Sons Ltd

To organize this chapter, I will first describe some features of self-disclosure within a turn (i.e. what disclosure is and some of its important dimensions), and self-disclosure within a conversation (i.e. how disclosures are brought about and managed within a conversation). These features of self-disclosure will then be discussed in terms of the facework involved in self-disclosure episodes. Finally, two strands of current research, impressions of disclosers and individual differences in disclosure, will be considered within this framework.

SELF-DISCLOSURE WITHIN A TURN

Self-disclosure generally is defined as information about oneself that is verbally communicated to another (e.g. Cozby, 1973). It usually is assumed also that the act of disclosing is voluntary (non-coercive) and intentional (Pearce and Sharp, 1973), and that the information disclosed is unavailable to others (Worthy, Gary, and Kahn, 1969). Linguistically, there appear to be few syntactic constraints on the form that self-disclosures can take, though there must be either an implicit or an explicit reference to the self (Berger and Bradac, 1982).

Obviously, many utterances that are non-equivalent on certain dimensions can be regarded as self-disclosures with these definitions. As a result, it has been argued (though not always followed) that self-disclosure should be viewed as a multidimensional concept (Chelune, 1979; Cozby, 1973). It is important to note that self-disclosure can be viewed as multidimensional at different levels of analysis. For example, a single disclosure (i.e. within-turn disclosure) can vary on important dimensions, as can an individual's self-disclosing behavior within a particular interaction, or an individual's self-disclosing in general. Many treatments of self-disclosure as multidimensional refer to an individual's disclosing behavior within an interaction. For example, Chelune, Skiffington, and Williams (1981) present evidence for the existence of five parameters of an individual's self-disclosure within an interaction. In this section, however, three selected dimensions of within-turn disclosure will be considered.

Direct and Indirect Disclosures

Within an interactional perspective (e.g. Watzlawick, Beavin, and Jackson, 1967), virtually any verbalization is self-disclosing from the hearer's perspective (see also Berger and Bradac, 1982). In this regard, Sousa-Poza and Rohrberg (1976) argue that disclosures can be classified as either direct or indirect. Although it is difficult to make a crystalline distinction between the two, direct self-disclosures can be regarded as utterances that express explicitly a speaker's self-view (e.g. 'I feel proud'). In contrast, indirect disclosures do not explicitly express the speaker's self-view, although such a view could be *inferred* by the hearer. For example, 'I got an A on my exam' could be, in many situations, regarded as an indirect disclosure of pride.

It could be argued that indirect disclosures are akin to 'expressions given off' rather than 'expressions given' (Goffman, 1959), and thus are not self-disclosures to the extent that the information is conveyed unintentionally (see Coupland,

Coupland, Giles, and Wiemann, 1988a). However, many speech acts can be performed indirectly (Searle, 1975) or 'off the record' (Brown and Levinson, 1987) for various reasons (see Chapter 10, by Tracy), and it is likely that indirectness plays some role in self-disclosure. Further, such differences may be important in the operation of face management processes, as will be discussed below.

Disclosure Intimacy

The dimension of self-disclosure that has received a great deal of attention is the intimacy or depth of a disclosure. However, intimacy and self-disclosure often have been equated, and there have been few attempts to define intimacy. Often, intimacy is manipulated on the basis of pilot subjects' perceptions of the intimacy of various topics (e.g. Won-Doornink, 1985). At times, the intimacy of the actual communications is rated, though often the communication is a monologue (Berg and Archer, 1982) or essay written by the subject (Brewer and Mittelman, 1980). These measures of intimacy gloss over important differences. While topics no doubt can be ordered in terms of the extent to which they are not routinely discussed (and hence presumably intimate), it would seem that intimacy does not necessarily reside solely in the topic, but rather in *how* the topic is brought up and talked about. There are several important considerations in this regard.

First, the perceived intimacy of a disclosure no doubt will vary as a function of various features of the *context* of the disclosure (Archer, 1979). For example, the same disclosure will probably be perceived as more intimate if it occurs between strangers rather than intimates, or during a business conversation rather than an informal conversation. One might also expect perceived intimacy to vary as a function of the placement of a disclosure within a conversation. A disclosure that occurs near the beginning of a conversation should, at times, be perceived as more intimate than the same disclosure occurring later in the conversation.

Second, *how* a topic is discussed can affect the intimacy of a disclosure. As Morton (1978) suggests, people can both trivialize intimate topics (and hence make them less intimate) and personalize non-intimate topics (and hence make them more intimate). The verbal mechanisms by which this occurs have been largely unexplored. However, Morton (1978) and others (e.g. Berg and Archer, 1982) have made a distinction between descriptive and evaluative disclosures. A descriptive disclosure refers to the revealing of facts about oneself, while an evaluative disclosure refers to the disclosure of some internal state such as an emotion, opinion, and so on. These two dimensions are somewhat independent. Thus, one can disclose a past event with or without a correspondingly intimate evaluation of the event. In this way, what is generally regarded as an intimate topic can be discussed in more or less intimate ways, depending on the degree of evaluative intimacy. It should be noted that evaluative intimacy is somewhat similar to language intensity, or degree of affective departure from what is being communicated (Bowers, 1963). However, with few exceptions (e.g. Bradac, Hosman, and Tardy, 1978), language intensity has not been examined in self-disclosure research.

Level of Speaker Identification

The topic of many disclosures concerns an individual's past actions. For any particular action that might be disclosed, however, there is variability in terms of the level of the speaker's identification with the action, or the extent to which the action is described in a way that is self-defining. For example, in response to the question 'What did you do last night?', an individual who spent the night watching TV could say 'I went home and turned on the TV', or 'I went home and vegetated in front of the TV'. Both responses describe the same past action. The second response, however, does so in a way that is more self-defining.

An important perspective in this regard is Vallacher and Wegner's (1987) theory of action identification. According to their theory, actions are open to many different interpretations and can be described at many different levels. Levels of action identification are assumed to be hierarchically organized, with lower levels conveying the details of an action (e.g. turning on the TV), while higher levels are more abstract and comprehensive (e.g. vegetating in front of the TV). As will be discussed in more detail below, levels of action identification have clear interpersonal implications. For example, a spouse accused of flirting may describe his or her actions at a very low level (e.g. 'We were talking') so as to avoid the self-defining implications of a higher-level description (e.g. 'We were getting to know one another').

Self-disclosure should be viewed as a multidimensional concept, not only in terms of one's overall disclosing behaviour (Chelune et al., 1981), but also in terms of the variability within a single disclosure. As will be seen below, the three within-turn disclosure dimensions discussed in this section have important implications for various inter- and intrapersonal processes.

SELF-DISCLOSURE WITHIN CONVERSATIONS

Disclosures do not occur in isolation (with the exception of many laboratory experiments), but rather within the context of some type of verbal interaction. How does this occur? How does one go about making a disclosure within a conversation? How do recipients react to another's self-disclosure? These are important questions in terms of understanding what self-disclosure is, and the role played by self-disclosure in various social pyschological processes.

Important as these questions may be, they rarely have been systematically addressed. An important exception to this trend, however, has been the recent research of the Couplands and their associates (Coupland, et al., 1988a; Coupland, Coupland, Giles, and Henwood, 1988b). On the basis of detailed examinations of 'getting acquainted' conversations between elderly and younger female interactants, they have proposed a framework for conceptualizing many important features of the *process*, or conversational dynamics, of painful self-disclosure (see also Chapter 22, by Coupland and Coupland). Although their framework was developed on the basis of this rather specific type of self-disclosure, much of their model seems applicable to self-disclosure in general, particularly so as their framework coincides well with other sociolinguistic theorizing. Of particular interest here is their treatment of what

precedes (the precontext) and what follows (recipient next-moves) a self-disclosure.
The following is a very brief description and comment on these two components of
their model as articulated by Coupland *et al.* (1988a) (all examples are mine).

Precontext

The precontext of a disclosure refers to the conversation remarks that precede, and
hence help bring about, a self-disclosure. Three broad types are identified and
ordered on two dimensions: the extent to which an individual is obligated to disclose,
and the response options he or she has in disclosing. A precontext that creates
something of an obligation to disclose is an elicitation of the disclosure by the future
disclosure recipient (recipient-determined disclosure). In other words, many disclosures are preceded by some type of elicitation by the recipient. Direct elicitations
create the strongest obligation to disclose. These are usually questions (e.g. 'How did
you do on the exam?') and hence greatly constrain a speaker's options in responding.
Disclosures may also be elicited in a less forceful manner with indirect elicitations, or
moves which invite a disclosure, but do not require one (e.g. 'Did you get your exam
results?').

A second type of precontext is one in which the disclosure is not elicited, but rather
is textually determined. In this case, the development of the conversation makes a
disclosure relevant. As a result, the obligation to disclose is less, and the options in
responding are greater, than when a disclosure is elicited. Two subtypes of textually
determined disclosures are noted. The first is the case where a response to another's
question requires a disclosure in order for the response to be truthful and interpretable. For example, in order to answer an 'innocent' question (e.g. 'Are you still going
to school?'), a speaker may need to elaborate on a simple yes or no answer in order to
produce a cooperative response (e.g. 'No, I'm afraid I couldn't keep my grades up').
The second subtype is a disclosure by the other interactant which can be regarded as
making one's own disclosure textually appropriate. This is an example of the well-
documented reciprocity effect that will be discussed in more detail below.

Finally, disclosures for which obligations and constraints are minimal fall within
the discloser-determined category. An important subtype of this category is an 'out
of the blue' disclosure, in other words, a disclosure for which there is *no* precontext.
Also included within the discloser-determined category are cases whereby an
individual enacts moves to create a context for his or her disclosure.

This model of disclosure precontexts raises a number of important issues. First, as
Coupland *et al.* (1988a,b) note, the precontext has important implications for what
self-disclosure *is*. Their data suggest that not all disclosures are completely voluntary
(a criterion for self-disclosure according to many definitions). Rather, many disclosures are elicited by an interactant, or made relevant by the tone and direction of
the conversation. Furthermore, even when a disclosure is not elicited, a speaker may
manufacture a context so that the disclosure does not appear to be voluntary.

Second, the precontext serves as a backdrop for the interpretation of a
disclosure. As a result, the interpersonal implications of a disclosure will depend,
in part, on the remarks that precede the disclosure. It will be argued below, for
example, that a speaker who makes an 'out of the blue' disclosure will be

perceived differently from a speaker who makes the exact same disclosure in response to another's elicitation.

Finally, when individuals want to disclose on a particular topic, they may strategically work to bring about the topic. An examination of the entire precontext can elucidate the strategies individuals may use to do this. For example, even though a disclosure may have been directly elicited, an examination of the moves *preceding* the elicitation may reveal the extent to which the discloser is responsible for getting the other to elicit the disclosure.

Recipient Next-Moves

Rarely do self-disclosures terminate a conversation. Rather, talk usually continues in some manner. Coupland *et al.* (1988a,b) provide a taxonomy of recipient next-moves (i.e. the receiver's response to the disclosure), which are ordered on a continuum regarding the extent to which the move either encourages or discourages further disclosure. Moves that are most encouraging are those that explicitly work to maintain the topic of the disclosure (e.g. requesting the speaker to clarify and/or elaborate on the disclosure). Still encouraging, but somewhat less so, are focused evaluative responses (i.e. positive evaluations of the disclosure). Both of these moves are reinforcing of the disclosure and would seem to encourage its continuation through several more turns. Moves that are clearly discouraging are those that switch or shift the topic away from that of the disclosure or, somewhat less discouragingly, refocus the disclosure (e.g. by making light of the disclosure, or by commenting on an irrelevant aspect of the disclosure). Finally, other moves are described that fall in the middle of this continuum. An important type here is a reciprocated self-disclosure, that is, when the recipient responds to a disclosure with his or her own self-disclosure. As the model makes clear, and as will be discussed in more detail below, this move neither encourages nor discourages further disclosure.

As with the precontext, a consideration of recipient next-moves illustrates the dynamics involved in the process of self-disclosure. For example, the amount of detail provided in a disclosure is, in large part, dependent on the receiver's response(s) to the disclosure. If the next-move is encouraging, then more detail and elaboration is likely to be provided, other things being equal. Thus, what traditionally has been viewed as the amount or breadth of a disclosure is, in part, an emergent phenomenon. Note that this stands in contrast to the frequent conceptualization of disclosiveness as a personality trait.

This perspective also dovetails nicely with sociological conceptions of self-disclosure. For example, at least in close relationships, the recipient's next-move is part of the process by which interactants negotiate the meaning and implications of a disclosure (Backman, 1983). In this view, it is misleading to consider self-disclosure as an individual phenomenon. Rather, the emphasis is on the joint contributions of the interactants through the give and take of a conversation. In the end, both what is disclosed, and its significance, are to be viewed as a collective, emergent phenomenon.

Self-disclosures occur within the larger context of some type of verbal interaction. Furthermore, within an interaction there are different ways in which self-disclosures are brought about and responded to. In the remainder of this chapter, some of the implications of this variability in the process of self-disclosure will be discussed.

SELF-DISCLOSURE AND FACE MANAGEMENT

Motivation for self-disclosure traditionally has been viewed in terms of relationship development (Altman and Taylor, 1973), and as a means of achieving psychological well-being (Jourard, 1971; Stiles, 1987). Similar to other verbal activities, however, self-disclosure can serve many different and sometimes simultaneous functions (Cappella and Street, 1985; see Chapter 5, by Patterson, and Chapter 7, by Cappella and Palmer). For example, individuals may disclose as a means of regulating intimacy, in order to elicit feedback from others, as a means of self-clarification, and so on. This has been recognized by Archer (Archer, 1987; Archer and Earle, 1983) and Derlega and Grzelak (1979) in their attempts to catalog the functions of self-disclosure, and by Miller and Read (1987), who view self-disclosure as a strategy for the achievement of a goal or set of goals (see also Dindia, 1985).

Alternatively, self-disclosure can also be viewed as self-presentation. In fact, some theorists (e.g. Schlenker, 1984) regard self-disclosure and self-presentation as synonymous, and suggest it is useless to distinguish between the two. The view taken here is that self-disclosure can and does serve multiple and often simultaneous functions. However, at another level, self-presentational concerns will *always* be operative during a disclosure episode, regardless of what higher-level functions may also be served. Self-disclosure is sensitive business and creates, in Goffman's (1967) terms, a face-threatening situation (see Chapter 10, by Tracy). The language of self-disclosure should reflect, to varying degrees, this feature.

It is necessary to elaborate briefly on the face-threatening nature of self-disclosure. According to Brown and Levinson (1987), all individuals have two basic face wants: positive face, or the desire to be well regarded, and negative face, or the desire not to be imposed upon. In disclosing negative information, a speaker is threatening his or her own positive face, and the recipient is placed in the role of helping to manage the speaker's spoiled identity, an imposition that can be regarded as threatening the recipient's negative face. Importantly, the disclosure of positive information may also activate face concerns. To disclose positive information can be damaging to the speaker's identity insofar as doing so implicates negative traits of brashness and egotism (Holtgraves and Srull, 1989; Jones and Pittman, 1982). In addition, to the extent that a positive disclosure is construed by the recipient as one-upmanship, the recipient may feel his or her identity (i.e. positive face) has been threatened (Gergen and Wishnov, 1965).

Given the interactionally sensitive nature of self-disclosure, disclosure episodes should be rich in face management strategies. Surprisingly, with the exception of the work of the Couplands and their associates (Coupland et al., 1988a; Coupland, Grainger, and Coupland, 1988), there have been few attempts to document the manner in which the language of disclosure episodes is sensitive to these self-presentational concerns. Nevertheless, our earlier discussion of the dimensions and context of self-disclosures provides a framework within which several observations can be made.

Disclosure Precontext

One important consideration for a potential discloser is the placement of the disclosure sequence within the conversation. By working a disclosure into a conversation in a smooth and natural way, the face-threatening implications of disclosing should be lessened. For example, a disclosure without a precontext (i.e. an 'out of the blue' disclosure) will be quite abrupt and noticeable, and will be somewhat difficult to manage interactionally. This of course is true of any utterance that violates conversational norms regarding topic changes (Tracy and Moran, 1983) or responsiveness (Davis and Holtgraves, 1984). However because of the potentially threatening nature of disclosures, the effect is increased.

The ability to integrate self-disclosures into a conversation should be a valuable skill. How might a speaker do this? One possibility would be to ask the other interactant to disclose, thereby creating a type of conversation in which the speaker's own disclosures would be appropriate (see discussion of reciprocity below). Another possibility would be to introduce a general topic which would provide a textual grounding for a later disclosure, and/or increase the probability of the other eliciting a disclosure. A more direct strategy would be to use a presequence, similar to the manner in which presequences are used (eventually) to make a request (Levinson, 1983). Thus, a speaker might say 'Did you hear about x?' or 'Did I tell you about x?' as a move prompting the other to then inquire about x.

Disclosure Dimensions

In addition to the context of a disclosure, face concerns should at times be related to the form of disclosures. Thus, a discloser may in some way attempt to mitigate the extent to which the disclosed information places him or her in a bad light. For example, a speaker may disclose embarrassing information in a cheerful manner as a means of managing face (Coupland et al., 1988a). Face concerns also may be related to some of the previously mentioned dimensions of self-disclosure.

First, as noted in the discussion of Vallacher and Wegner's (1987) theory of action identification, individuals can describe their actions at varying levels of abstraction. Furthermore, higher-level descriptions are more self-defining than lower-level descriptions. Vallacher, Wegner, and Frederich (1987) provide evidence for a link between levels of action identification and self-presentation goals. Their research demonstrates that individuals who believe they have performed poorly at a task will describe their actions at a lower level (to avoid self-definition) than will those who believe they have performed well. Their research also demonstrates that more specific self-presentation goals will affect action identification. For example, individuals who have succeeded at a task and are interacting with a person who values modesty will tend to use lower levels of identification in describing their successful performance. In this way, they avoid the inferences of bragging that would result from using a higher-level identification.

Second, the locus of causality for the actions being disclosed may be varied in subtle ways, and these implicit attributions may serve self-presentation functions. Thus, a speaker may minimize the face-threatening nature of a self-disclosure by making an implicit external attribution (e.g. 'He gave me a D in the course'). While there is a voluminous literature on self-serving attributions in general (e.g. Ross and Sicoly, 1979) there have been no attempts to examine implicit attributions in self-disclosure and their role in self-presentation concerns.

Third, indirect disclosure may be used as a face management technique. As Brown and Levinson (1987) and others (e.g. Tannen, 1981) have argued, indirectness appears to be a common strategy for minimizing the face threat inherent in verbal activities such as making requests, criticizing, disagreeing, and so on. The relevance of indirectness for self-disclosure can be seen most clearly in the use of indirect replies (Holtgraves, 1986). Imagine, for example, an interactant who is faced with an elicitation for negative information (e.g. 'What did you get on your history exam?'). Rather than replying directly (e.g. 'I did terribly on that exam'), a speaker can use an indirect reply (e.g. 'I thought that was a very difficult exam'). An indirect reply only implies that the information is negative, and so lessens the threat to the speaker's face.

Recipient Moves

An important assumption of facework is that interactants *collectively* manage each other's face (Goffman, 1967). Thus, face concerns should be salient for the *recipient* of a disclosure. As noted above, a recipient can help bring about a disclosure by using various types of elicitations, and evidence suggests that face considerations will play an important role in this process (Holtgraves, 1986). Most obvious here is the face-threatening nature of *direct* elicitations. To directly request a negative self-disclosure creates a face-threatening situation for both speaker and hearer. As a result, indirect elicitations, because they are less demanding and provide an out for the recipient, will be a less threatening way to invite a disclosure.

A disclosure carries with it an implicit demand for a response and, as Coupland *et al.* (1988a) suggest, this presents something of an interactional problem for the recipient (see also Jefferson, 1984). Consider, for example, the recipient of a negative disclosure who now must balance concerns for the discloser's face, with the conversational requirements of topical relevance. To maintain the topic may be risky as further talk may be embarrassing for the discloser. On the other hand, topic shifts or making light of the disclosure may also be threatening. One strategy in this regard is to be attentive to the discloser while initiating a topic change. For example, in Jefferson's (1984) corpus, moves away from trouble talk (negative self-disclosures) are almost always other-attentive in some way.

It has been argued here that the act of self-disclosing activates face concerns, and that there are various ways in which the process of self-disclosure can either increase or decrease the salience of face threat. If this is the case, then how individuals disclose should have predictable effects on perceptions of disclosers, and individual differences in disclosiveness may be due to differences in conversational skills. These possibilities are considered in the next two sections.

PERCEPTIONS OF DISCLOSERS

Most researchers have examined perceptions of disclosers on a general evaluative dimension such as liking, or related judgments such as mental stability. In terms of the act of disclosing, the research suggests greater liking for a discloser than a non-discloser (e.g. Johnson and Dabbs, 1976). However, when the intimacy of the disclosure is manipulated, a curvilinear effect (moderately intimate disclosers are evaluated more favorably than high- or low-intimate disclosers) is sometimes reported (e.g. Cozby, 1972; though see Rubin, 1975).

Probably more important than the act of disclosing is the contextual appropriateness of a self-disclosure (Chaiken and Derlega, 1974a). There are several studies illustrating the effects of disclosure context on liking, though few studies have examined explicitly the role of conversation context. Instead, much of this research has been concerned with characteristics of the recipient – for example, a discloser is liked more when disclosing to a friend rather than to a stranger, and when disclosing to a person of equal age rather than to one younger or older (Chaiken and Derlega, 1974b) – and with characteristics of the discloser such as gender – for example, disclosing females are evaluated more highly than disclosing males, at least on most topics (Kleinke and Kahn, 1980; see Chapter 17, by Kramarae).

A direct test of the effects of the conversation precontext on perceptions of a discloser was undertaken by Holtgraves and Srull (1989). In this study, a speaker made a number of positive self-statements that either were contextually grounded in an appropriate manner (in response to a question, or when the other interactant was also making positive self-statements) or were not so grounded. In general, it was found that the same disclosures resulted in decreased liking for the speaker, and perceptions of greater speaker egotism, when the remarks were not contextually grounded. In addition to this study, there are two lines of self-disclosure research that indirectly illustrate the role of a disclosure precontext on perceptions of a discloser.

First, there have been several demonstrations of a timing effect on perceptions of a discloser. In general, a person who discloses later in a conversation is evaluated more favorably than one who makes the same disclosure early in a conversation (Archer and Burleson, 1980; Jones and Gordon, 1972; Miell, Duck, and LaGaipa, 1979; Wortman, Adesman, Herman, and Greenberg, 1976). A popular interpretation of this effect is in terms of personalism (Jones and Archer, 1976). According to this view, a person who discloses early will be viewed as an indiscriminate discloser. When the disclosure occurs later in the conversation, however, the recipient should feel more singled out for the disclosure, and hence like the discloser more.

The timing effect also can be interpreted in terms of the precontext of a disclosure. Thus, an early disclosure should be regarded as less appropriate than a later disclosure because the latter is more likely to be contextually grounded in some way. It is somewhat difficult to interpret the timing studies in this way because naturalistic conversations typically are not examined. Berg (1987) however, makes something of a similar suggestion in arguing that the timing effect, and personalism effects in general, can be interpreted in terms of responsiveness; that is , the recipient of a late-occurring disclosure will be more likely to believe the discloser is being responsive to his or her remarks than will the recipient of a disclosure occurring early in the conversation.

2) The research on disclosure reciprocity can also be interpreted as evidence for the importance of the conversation precontext in mediating impressions of a discloser. Numerous studies have demonstrated that interactants match or reciprocate their partner's self-disclosures (e.g. Ehrlich and Graeven, 1971; Miller and Kenny, 1986). A common explanation for the reciprocity effect is the operation of a norm of reciprocity (Derlega, Harris, and Chaiken, 1973; see also Chapter 11, by Cody and McLaughlin). If this is the case, then violations of this norm (i.e. it is appropriate to reciprocate a disclosure) should affect perceptions of the speaker. Chaiken and Derlega (1974c) provide some evidence for this. Subjects in this experiment evaluated a target speaker who made either an intimate or a non-intimate disclosure following either an intimate or a non-intimate disclosure from a first speaker. Liking for the second speaker was a function of the match between the level of her disclosure and that of the first speaker. For example, when the second speaker made an intimate disclosure, she was evaluated more favorably if her disclosure followed an intimate disclosure from the first speaker, than when it followed a non-intimate disclosure.

The results of the studies by Chaiken and Derlega (1974c) and Holtgraves and Srull (1989) suggest that a normatively proper context for one's disclosure is a prior disclosure (of equal intimacy and/or valence) by the other speaker. Note, however, that this runs counter to what one would expect on the basis of the operation of certain conversation norms or rules. A disclosure recipient who reciprocates with a disclosure will often be changing the topic of the conversation, thereby not being responsive (Davis, 1982) or accommodative (Giles, Mulac, Bradac, and Johnson, 1987) to the first speaker. Now, it is of course possible to reciprocate a disclosure on the same topic, though in some ways this may not be as responsive as other moves. Two studies conducted by Berg and Archer provide some support for this observation. In one study, a speaker who responded to another's disclosure with concern (and was thus more responsive) was evaluated more favorably than a speaker who reciprocated with an equally intimate disclosure (Berg and Archer, 1980). In a second study, speakers who matched the intimacy of a prior speaker were evaluated more favorably than those who did not, but *only* when the disclosure was on the same topic (Berg and Archer, 1983). These studies indicate that a reciprocal disclosure is not always the preferred move following a disclosure, and conversely, another's disclosure is not always the most appropriate context for one's own disclosure.

It should be noted here that laboratory demonstrations of disclosure reciprocity illustrate one of the drawbacks of studying disclosure in non-natural interactions. In most of these experiments, the responses of the subjects were constrained by the experimental procedure. Typically, after subjects received a disclosure from another (usually an experimental confederate), they were allowed to choose to respond (or at least indicate their willingness to respond) from a set of topics provided by the experimenter. Berg (1987) argues that, with this procedure, a disclosure of equal intimacy may be the only way to be responsive to the other speaker. In contrast, there is a wide range of responses, in addition to disclosure reciprocity, for individuals involved in an *actual conversation* (see above section on recipient next-moves). Thus, immediate disclosure reciprocity may be, in part, an artifact of the experimental setting.

Although it appears that perceptions of a discloser will vary as a function of how the disclosure is brought about, this will not always be the case. In particular, there are individual differences in perceptions of disclosers as a function of the precontext. For example, individuals who are concerned with their self-presentation, such as those high in public self-consciousness (Carver and Humphries, 1981), should be relatively more sensitive to the contextual appropriateness of disclosures. In the Holtgraves and Srull (1989) study, it was predicted and found that individuals high in public self-consciousness were more affected by the context manipulation than those low in public self-consciousness. Conceptually similar results have been reported by Chelune (1977). He found that subjects high in disclosure flexibility (i.e. individuals who use different levels of disclosure in different situations) rated a person who disclosed intimately to a stranger more negatively than did subjects low in disclosure flexibility. This study, then, also illustrates individual variability in sensitivity to the contextual appropriateness of self-disclosures.

A major source of information in forming impressions of others is what they tell us, or what they self-disclose. The impressions that are ultimately formed, however, will depend not only on the content of a disclosure, but also the manner in which the disclosure is brought about within a conversation. Thus, an interaction-based evaluation of a speaker will depend both on what is disclosed, and how it is disclosed.

INDIVIDUAL DIFFERENCES IN SELF-DISCLOSURE

Much early research viewed self-disclosure as a personality trait (see also Chapter 4, by Furnham). This research has been criticized for inconsistent findings, and for ignoring situational factors that affect self-disclosure (Altman and Taylor, 1973; Archer, 1979). To the extent that there are individual differences in self-disclosure, these differences may be due, in part, to some of the aforementioned aspects of the process of disclosure.

First, the ability to carry on a conversation is a skill involving knowledge of the relevant rules, monitoring of the situation and the conversation as it develops, and so on (Spitzberg and Cupach, 1984). The ability to self-disclose successfully can also be regarded as a skill (Altman and Taylor, 1973; Solono, Batten, and Parish, 1982). In fact, given the face-threatening nature of self-disclosure, greater skill than usual would seem to be required; that is, a speaker must be able to work the disclosure into the conversation in a smooth and natural way, to disclose in such a way that his or her partner is not embarrassed and is able to respond, and so on. To the extent that there are individual differences in the frequency of self-disclosure, these differences may be due, in part, to differences in disclosure competence, and how an individual discloses would obviously be an important component of this skill. Thus, one might expect that high self-monitors, who appear to be socially skilled (Furnham and Capon, 1983; Snyder, 1987), would be quite adept at self-disclosure (see also Chapter 1, by McCann and Higgins). Research conducted by Shaffer, Smith, and

Tomarelli (1982) indicates that high self-monitors do reciprocate disclosures more than low self-monitors (though see Ludwig, Franco, and Malloy, 1986).

Second, because self-disclosures occur within conversations, differences in self-disclosure should be due, in part, to the person with whom the individual is interacting. Miller, Berg, and Archer (1983) have recently developed an Opener Scale, designed to assess individuals' ability to get others to 'open up' and disclose to them. The scale, which contains items such as 'I'm sympathetic to people's problems', and 'I can keep people talking about themselves', has been found to predict individual differences in the receipt of self-disclosures from others.

While it is clear that some individuals will be disclosed to more than others, it is less clear *why* they are chosen to be the recipient of self-disclosures. The Opener Scale is essentially a measure of the extent to which respondents report their ability to get others to talk, enjoy listening to others, and so on. Left unexplored are the strategies by which openers elicit self-disclosures. Some work in this direction has been done by Purvis, Dabbs, and Hopper (1984). Their research suggests that high openers (compared to low openers) maintain more eye contact and are rated as more involved with their conversation partners. Their focus is on non-verbal behavior, though it seems reasonable that verbal behaviors would constitute part of a high opener's repertoire. Several possibilities can be outlined.

First, the extent to which an interactant is verbally responsive should affect the likelihood of another's disclosure. Being verbally responsive (i.e. addressing the topic of the preceding remark) indicates interest in the other's remarks (Davis, 1982), and thus should increase the probability of disclosures. Second, the use of elicitations would obviously increase, indeed obligate, disclosures from an interactant. Importantly, though, elicitations would have to be used with great caution. Directly asking someone about intimate information would probably decrease the likelihood of the interaction progressing very far. There are, as noted above, strategic means by which information can be indirectly elicited, and it may be through these sorts of strategies that high openers are able to elicit disclosures.

In addition to individual differences in the tendency to elicit disclosures from others, there may also be differences in the extent to which some people get others to elicit disclosures from them. This was implicit in the above discussion of strategies for making disclosures contextually appropriate. Another possibility, however, is that people's expectations about the disclosiveness of a class of others (e.g. the elderly) may result in a type of behavioral confirmation (Snyder, 1987). Such a possibility has been suggested by Coupland *et al.* (1988a). They argue that younger people may expect the elderly to talk about their troubles, and this may result in the elderly's conversational partners tending to elicit disclosures from them (see Chapter 22, by Coupland and Coupland).

CONCLUSION

In the past, self-disclosure has been generally studied as a unitary behavior independent of how it actually occurs in conversations. In this chapter I have attempted to describe some of the important features of self-disclosure as a conversational activity, and the possible role these features might play in various inter- and intrapersonal processes.

While some topics for future research have been suggested, I have avoided the difficult task of suggesting various research strategies. Thus, a few comments on strategy are appropriate here. First, there is the obvious need for more descriptive analyses of self-disclosure as it occurs within conversations. Such efforts not only will result in an increased understanding of what self-disclosure is and how it occurs, but also can serve as a source of hypotheses that can then be tested within different frameworks. In this vein, one approach would be to examine conversations for the distribution of various moves as a function of theoretically meaningful variables. For example, a common finding in the literature is that females are more disclosing than males. However, this difference may be due, in part, to an *expectation* that females are more disclosive, and thus their partners tend to elicit disclosures from them. This possibility could be tested by comparing the frequency and type of elicitations of interactants paired with male versus female partners (see also Chapter 17, by Kramarae). Another framework would be to use a typical impression-formation paradigm to examine, for example, the effects of various forms of disclosures, and/or conversational contexts for disclosure, on impressions of a speaker (see Chapter 19, by Bradac).

Self-disclosure is a behavior with implications for many phenomena such as impression management, impression formation, relationship development, identity formation and change, and so on. However, as this chapter has hopefully made clear for the case of impression management and impression formation, understanding the role of self-disclosure in these phenomena will require a consideration of the language and process of self-disclosure.

REFERENCES

Altman, I. and Taylor, D.A. (1973). *Social penetration: The development of interpersonal relationships*. New York: Holt, Rinehart, and Winston.

Archer, R.L. (1979). Role of personality and the social situation. In G.J. Chelune and associates (Eds), *Self-disclosure*, pp. 28–58. San Francisco: Jossey-Bass.

Archer, R.L. (1987). Commentary. In V. Derlega and J.H. Berg (Eds), *Self-disclosure*, pp. 329–342. New York: Plenum Press.

Archer, R.L. and Burleson, J.A. (1980). The effects of timing of self-disclosure on attraction and reciprocity. *Journal of Personality and Social Psychology*, **38**, 120–130.

Archer, R.L. and Earle, W.B. (1983). The interpersonal orientations of disclosure. In P.B. Paulus (Ed.), *Basic group processes*, pp. 289–314. New York: Springer-Verlag.

Backman, C. (1983). Toward an interdisciplinary social psychology. In L. Berkowitz (Ed.), *Advances in experimental social psychology*, Vol. 16, pp. 219–261. New York: Academic Press.

Berg, J.H. (1987). Responsiveness and self-disclosure. In V. Derlega and J.H. Berg (Eds), *Self-disclosure*, pp. 101–130. New York: Plenum Press.

Berg, J.H. and Archer, R.L. (1980). Disclosure or concern: A second look at liking for the norm breaker. *Journal of Personality*, **48**, 245–257.

Berg, J.H. and Archer, R.L. (1982). Responses to self-disclosure and interaction goals. *Journal of Experimental Social Psychology*, **18**, 501–512.

Berg, J.H. and Archer, R.L. (1983). The discloser–liking relationship: Effects of self-perception, order of disclosure, and topical similarity. *Human Communication Research*, **10**, 269–282.

Berger, C.R. and Bradac, J.J. (1982). *Language and social knowledge*. London: Arnold.

Bowers, J.W. (1963). Language intensity, social introversion, and attitude change. *Speech Monographs*, **30**, 345–352.

Bradac, J.J., Hosman, L.A., and Tardy, C.H. (1978). Reciprocal disclosure and language intensity: Attributional consequences. *Communication Monographs*, **45**, 1–17

Brewer, M.B. and Mittelman, J. (1980). Effects of normative control of self-disclosure on reciprocity. *Journal of Personality*, **48**, 89–102.

Brown, P. and Levinson, S. (1987). *Politeness: Some universals in language use*. Cambridge: Cambridge University Press.

Cappella, J.N. and Street, R.L., Jr (1985). Introduction: A functional approach to the structure of communicative behavior. In R.L. Street and J.N. Cappella (Eds), *Sequence and pattern in communicative behavior*, pp. 1–29. London: Arnold.

Carver, C.S. and Humphries, C. (1981). Havana daydreaming: A study of self-consciousness and the negative reference group among Cuban-Americans. *Journal of Personality and Social Psychology*, **40**, 545–552.

Chaiken, A.L. and Derlega, V.J. (1974a). *Self-disclosure*. Morristown, NJ: General Learning Press.

Chaiken, A.L. and Derlega, V.J. (1974b). Variables affecting the appropriateness of self-disclosure. *Journal of Consulting and Clinical Psychology*, **42**, 588–593.

Chaiken, A.L. and Derlega, V.J. (1974c). Liking for the norm-breaker in self-disclosure. *Journal of Personality*, **42**, 117–129.

Chelune, G.J. (1975). Self-disclosure: An elaboration of its basic dimensions. *Psychological Reports*, **36**, 79–85.

Chelune, G.J. (1977). Disclosure flexibility and social-situational perceptions. *Journal of Consulting and Clinical Psychology*, **45**, 1139–1143.

Chelune, G.J. (1979). Measuring openness in interpersonal communication. In G.J. Chelune, (Ed.), *Self-disclosure*, pp. 1–21. San Francisco: Jossey-Bass.

Chelune, G.J., Skiffington, S., and Williams, C. (1981). Multidimensional analysis of observer's perceptions of self-disclosing behavior. *Journal of Personality and Social Psychology*, **41**, 599–606.

Coupland, J., Coupland, N., Giles, H., and Wiemann, J. (1988a). My life in your hands: Processes of self-disclosure in intergenerational talk. In N. Coupland (Ed.), *Styles of discourse*, pp. 201–253. London: Croom Helm.

Coupland, N., Coupland, J., Giles, H., and Henwood, K. (1988b). Elderly self-disclosure: Interactional and intergroup issues. *Language and Communication*, **8**, 109–133.

Coupland, N., Grainger, K., and Coupland, J. (1988). Politeness in context: Intergenerational issues. *Language and Society*, **17**, 253–262.

Cozby, P.C. (1972). Self-disclosure, reciprocity, and liking. *Sociometry*, **35**, 151–160.

Cozby, P.C. (1973). Self-disclosure: A literature review. *Psychological Bulletin*, **79**, 73–91.

Davis, D. (1982). Determinants of responsiveness in dyadic interaction. In W. Ickes and E. Knowles (Eds.), *Personality, roles, and social behavior*, pp. 85–140. New York: Springer-Verlag.

Davis, D. and Holtgraves, T. (1984). Perceptions of unresponsive others: Attributions, attraction, understandability, and memory of their utterances. *Journal of Experimental Social Psychology*, **20**, 383–408.

Derlega, V. and Grzelak, J. (1979). Appropriateness of self-disclosure. In G.J. Chelune (Ed.), *Self-disclosure*, pp. 151–176, San Francisco: Jossey-Bass.

Derlega, V., Harris, M.S., and Chaiken, A.L. (1973). Self-disclosure reciprocity, liking, and the deviant. *Journal of Experimental Social Psychology*, **9**, 277–284.

Dindia, K. (1985). A functional approach to self-disclosure. In R.L. Street and J.N. Cappella (Eds), *Sequence and pattern in communicative behavior*, pp. 142–160. London: Arnold.

Ehrlich, H.J. and Graeven, D.B. (1971). Reciprocal self-disclosure in a dyad. *Journal of Experimental Social Psychology*, **7**, 389–400.

Furnham, A. and Capon, M. (1983). Social skills and self-monitoring processes. *Personality and Individual Differences*, **4**, 171–178.

Gergen, J.J. and Wishnov, B. (1965). Others' self-evaluations and interaction anticipation as determinants of self-presentation. *Journal of Personality and Social Psychology*, **2**, 348–358.

Giles, H., Mulac, A., Bradac, J.J., and Johnson, P. (1987). Speech accommodation theory: The first decade and beyond. In M. McLaughlin (Ed.), *Communication yearbook*, No. 10, pp. 13–48. Beverly Hills, CA: Sage.

Goffman, E. (1959). *The presentation of self in everyday life*. Garden City, NY: Doubleday.

Goffman, E. (1967). *Interaction ritual*. New York: Pantheon.

Holtgraves, T. (1986). Language structure in social interaction: Perceptions of direct and indirect speech acts and interactants who use them. *Journal of Personality and Social Psychology*, **51**, 305–314.

Holtgraves, T. and Srull, T. (1989). The effects of positive self-descriptions on impressions: General principles and individual differences. *Personality and Social Psychology Bulletin*, **15**, 452–462.

Jefferson, G. (1984). On stepwise transition from talk about trouble to inappropriately next-positioned matters. In J.M. Atkinson and J. Heritage (Eds), *Structures of social action*, pp. 191–222. Cambridge: Cambridge University Press.

Johnson, C.F and Dabbs, J.M., Jr (1976). Self-disclosure in dyads as a function of distance and the subject–experimenter relationship. *Sociometry*, **39**, 257–263.

Jones, E.E. and Archer, R.L. (1976). Are there special effects of personalistic self-disclosure? *Journal of Experimental Social Psychology*, **12**, 180–193.

Jones, E.E. and Gordon, E.M. (1972). Timing of self-disclosure and its effects on personal attraction. *Journal of Personality and Social Psychology*, **24**, 358–365.

Jones, E.E. and Pittman, T. (1982). Toward a general theory of self-presentation. In J. Suls (Ed.), *Psychological perspectives on the self*, Vol 1, pp. 231–262. Hillsdale, NJ: Erlbaum.

Jourard, S. (1971). *Self-disclosure: An experimental analysis of the transparent self*. New York: Wiley-Interscience.

Kleinke, C.L. and Kahn, M.L. (1980). Perceptions of self-disclosers: Effects of sex and physical attractiveness. *Journal of Personality*, **48**, 190–205.

Levinson, S. (1983). *Pragmatics*. Cambridge: Cambridge University Press.

Ludwig, D., Franco, J.N., and Malloy, T.E. (1986). Effects of reciprocity and self-monitoring on self-disclosure with a new acquaintance. *Journal of Personality and Social Psychology*, **50**, 1077–1082.

Miell, D., Duck, S., and LaGaipa, J. (1979). Interactive effects of sex and timing in self-disclosure. *British Journal of Social and Clinical Psychology*, **18**, 355–362.

Miller, L.C., Berg, J.H., and Archer, R.L. (1983). Openers: Individuals who elicit self-disclosure. *Journal of Personality and Social Psychology*, **44**, 1234–1244.

Miller, L.C. and Kenny, D.A (1986). Reciprocity of self-disclosure at the individual and dyadic levels: A social relations analysis. *Journal of Personality and Social Psychology*, **50**, 713–719.

Miller, L.C. and Read, S.J. (1987). Why am I telling you this? Self-disclosure in a goal based model of personality. In V. Derlega and J.H. Berg (Eds), *Self-disclosure*, pp. 35–58. New York: Plenum Press.

Morton, T.L. (1978). Intimacy and reciprocity of exchange: A comparison of spouses and strangers. *Journal of Personality and Social Psychology*, **36**, 72–81.

Pearce, W.B and Sharp, S.M. (1973). Self-disclosing communication. *Journal of Communication*, **23**, 409–425.

Purvis, J.A, Dabbs, J.M., Jr, and Hopper, C.H. (1984). The Opener: Skilled use of facial expressions and speech pattern. *Personality and Social Psychology Bulletin*, **10**, 61–66.

Ross, M. and Sicoly, F. (1979). Egocentric biases in availability and attribution. *Journal of Personality and Social Psychology*, **37**, 322–336.

Rubin, Z. (1975). Disclosing oneself to a stranger: Reciprocity and its limits. *Journal of Experimental Social Psychology*, **11**, 233–260.

Schlenker, B.R. (1984). Identities, identifications, and relationships. In V.J. Derlega (Ed.), *Communication, intimacy, and close relationships*, pp. 71–104. Orlando: Academic Press.

Searle, J. (1975). Indirect speech acts. In P. Cole and J. Morgan (Eds), *Syntax and semantics*, Vol. 3; *Speech acts*, pp. 59–82. New York: Academic Press.

Shaffer, D.R., Smith, J.E., and Tomarelli, M. (1982). Self-monitoring as a determinant of self-disclosure reciprocity during the acquaintance process. *Journal of Personality and Social Psychology*, **43**, 163–175.

Snyder, M. (1987). *Public appearances, private realities*. New York: Freeman.

Solono, C.H., Batten, P.G., and Parish, E.A. (1982). Loneliness and patterns of self-disclosure. *Journal of Personality and Social Psychology*, **43**, 524–531.

Sousa-Poza, J. and Rohrberg, R. (1976). Communicational and interactional aspects of self-disclosure: A preliminary report on theory and method. *Semiotica*, **16**, 329–345.

Spitzberg, B.H. and Cupach, W.R. (1984). *Interpersonal communication competence*. Beverly Hills, CA: Sage.

Stiles, W.B. (1987). 'I have to talk to somebody': A fever model of self-disclosure. In V. Derlega and J.H. Berg (Eds), *Self-disclosure*, pp. 257–282. New York: Plenum Press.

Tannen, D. (1981). Indirectness in discourse: Ethnicity as conversation style. *Discourse Processes*, **4**, 221–238.

Tracy, K. and Moran, III, J.P. (1983). Conversation relevance in multiple goal settings. In R.T. Craig and K. Tracy (Eds), *Conversational coherence*, pp. 116–135. Beverly Hills, CA: Sage.

Vallacher, R. and Wegner, D.M. (1987). What do people think they're doing? Action identification and human behavior. *Psychological Review*, **94**, 3–15.

Vallacher, R., Wegner, D., and Frederick, J. (1987). The presentation of self through action identification. *Social Cognition*, **5**, 301–322.

Watzlawick, P., Beavin, J., and Jackson, D. (1967). *Pragmatics of human communication*. New York: Norton.

Won-Doornink, M.J. (1985). Self-disclosure and reciprocity in conversation: A cross-national study. *Social Psychology Quarterly*, **48**, 97–107.

Worthy, M., Gary, A.L., and Kahn, G.M. (1969). Self-disclosure as an exchange process. *Journal of Personality and Social Psychology*, **13**, 59–63.

Wortman, C., Adesman, P., Herman, E., and Greenberg, R. (1976). Self-disclosure: An attributional perspective. *Journal of Personality and Social Psychology*, **33**, 184–191.

10

The Many Faces of Facework

KAREN TRACY

Department of Rhetoric and Communication, Temple University, USA

'What could he do? If he let a comment like that go by, he would have *lost face*.' 'I was trying to give her an opportunity to *save face* and exit gracefully – it's not my fault it didn't work.' In everyday life, as these comments exemplify, people explain their own and others' behavior through appeals to 'face'. Face is also an important theoretical construct in social science research; work in psychology, linguistics, communication, anthropology, and sociology, to name but the most obvious disciplines, makes use of this concept.

While appeals to face are pervasive, examination of situated explanations raises the possibility that what one researcher means by face may not be the same thing meant by another. Face, for instance, is used to explain why people apologize when they make a request, why they notice people's haircuts or acquisition of a new pair of glasses, why they threaten others and call them names, why they joke when they spill a glass of milk, and why they change topics of conversation. If face is the explanation of such diverse communicative behaviors, not just a term used in very different ways, then the obvious question is: what is it?

The concept of face is Chinese in origin, having been used as early as the fourth century BC (Ho, 1975; Hu, 1944). The Chinese distinguish between two aspects of face. The first, *mien-tzu*, refers to social prestige, 'a reputation achieved through getting on in life, through success and ostentation' (Hu, 1944, p. 45), something that can 'be borrowed, struggled for, added to, padded' (p. 61). The second, *lien*, refers to a person's basic moral worth, his or her good character. Whereas *mien* is increased by having wealth or power, as long as people do not engage in unacceptable social behavior, all persons are entitled to *lien*. For the Chinese, then, face references people's concerns about personal reputation.

Handbook of Language and Social Psychology
Edited by H. Giles and W.P. Robinson.   © 1990 John Wiley & Sons Ltd

Current uses of the concept of face are more diverse than the traditional Chinese ones but are recognizable as extensions. In English-speaking countries, face has become a staple of people's everyday explanations of each other. While pervasive cross-culturally, not until the 1950s did 'face' and 'facework' become concerns of social scientists. In a seminal essay, entitled 'On face-work', Erving Goffman (1955) staked out this conceptual territory as one deserving careful systematic study. And although two distinct approaches can be seen, just about all current research traces its immediate intellectual roots to Goffman.

Before reviewing these approaches, let me offer beginning characterizations of 'face' and 'facework'. Face is a social phenomenon; it comes into being when one person comes into the presence of another; it is created through the communicative moves of interactants. Whereas face references the socially situated identities people claim or attribute to others, facework references the communicative strategies that are the enactment, support, or challenge of those situated identities. Both face and facework concern the relationship between communicative practices and situated identities; each concept requires the other but they differ regarding what is foregrounded.

For the most part, current approaches to the study of face reflect two camps: (a) the sociolinguistically based politeness theory; and (b) sociopsychologically based research. From a communication viewpoint, each approach is limited. Politeness theory uses simplistic, unelaborated notions about identity; sociopsychological approaches give inadequate attention to the discourse behaviors used to realize identity concerns.

The purpose of this chapter is twofold: to review and critique the two approaches, showing how the limitations of each could be offset by the strengths of the other; and to offer the beginnings of a communicative theory of facework, one that takes account of the full range of identity concerns people have in interaction and that attends to the ways these concerns are expressed in people's discourse practices.

THE POLITENESS-THEORY APPROACH TO FACE

Politeness theory, the name given to Brown and Levinson's (1978) comprehensive theory of how face wants, facework strategies, and situational influences come together, provides multiple examples of facework expression in three languages. Drawing upon Goffman (1955), Brown and Levinson define face as the public image every person wants to claim. Face claims, they argue, are of two kinds: positive and negative. Positive face concerns the desire to be appreciated and approved of by selected others. Negative face concerns a person's want to be unimpeded and free from imposition. These two classes of identity concerns motivate people and account for most instances of communication that do not adhere to Grice's (1975) model of communication as a maximally efficient information exchange. And except for a restricted set of circumstances, people can be expected to maintain each other's face.

Politeness theory begins its analysis with the linguistic unit of a speech act (Searle, 1969), where a 'speech act' refers to the function or action performed by a particular utterance. So, for instance, in uttering the words 'Close the door', a speaker performs a command and, in saying 'I hate rainy weather', a complaint. Many speech acts, Brown and Levinson argue, are face-threatening. A request, for instance, threatens a recipient's desire not to be imposed upon (negative face), while making an apology threatens a speaker's sense of his or her goodness and appropriateness (positive face).

The face-threat of acts (not given and inherent in the act) is influenced by three situational factors: the social distance between speaker and hearer, the relative power of the speaker compared to the hearer, and the intrinsic degree of imposition of an act. Thus, a request to borrow money would be more face-threatening if it were made of a superior rather than a peer, a stranger rather than a friend, and if the request were for a large sum of money rather than a small one. Putting the three factors together yields each speech act's expected amount of face-threat, which, in turn, influences which of five 'superstrategies' participants will use. Each super-strategy is associated with a characteristic amount of concern for the other's face, or 'politeness'. In determining how polite to be, communicators are expected to be 'rational humans', that is, to be as polite as needed but no more than necessary.

The least polite strategy is to perform an act 'baldly' with no attention to the hearer's face wants ('Lend me $500'). Next in politeness is to perform the action with positive politeness, a strategy that orients to the partner's needs to be appreciated and approved of ('Hey, old friend, you're a person I can really count on. Lend me $500, won't you?'). The third strategy is to perform the face-threatening act with negative politeness, a strategy that recognizes the individual's desire to be respected and not imposed upon ('Excuse me, I hate to ask this of you, and I wouldn't normally put you on the spot if I weren't in such dire straits, but could you lend me $500 for just a few days? I'd be forever in your debt.'). The fourth strategy is to go off record and hint, thereby making it possible for the partner not to recognize the act that is being performed ('You won't believe my problems; I have a phone bill that has to be paid by Monday or my telephone gets turned off.'). The fifth, and most polite, strategy is not to perform the face-threatening act.

Of note is the fact that the concept of 'politeness' is used in three related but conceptually distinct ways, only one of which bears a resemblance to the everyday meaning. The first type, negative politeness, refers to the communicative strategies interactants use to express recognition of others' needs for freedom from restraint. Negative politeness, unfortunately labeled because it suggests non-politeness, is, in fact, the most similar to what people in everyday life mean by 'being polite'. Doing things like offering an apology ('I hate to ask this of you, but . . .'), being pessimistic in requests for aid ('I don't suppose there is any chance you could help me out?'), being indirect, softening requests ('I wonder if you could help me out?'), minimizing imposition, recognizing that one is incurring a debt to the other, and using linguistic forms that create psychological distance for the speaker or hearer from an act (e.g. 'It's necessary for you to do the following things' versus 'I want you to do the following things') illustrate some of the discourse strategies used to evidence restraint and a desire not to impose on another.

Positive politeness, the second meaning of politeness, refers to language strategies that attend to people's needs to be appreciated and approved of; positive politeness strategies are communicative ways of building solidarity, showing that the other is

liked and seen as desirable. The kinds of communicative strategies Brown and
Levinson (1978) see as attending to this face want include things like noticing changes
in another ('You've got a new haircut'), showing sympathy to problems of the other
('How awful that it rained for your picnic'), giving gifts, selecting safe topics, seeking
agreement and avoiding disagreement, joking, offering or making promises to the
other, and taking for granted or asserting common ground.

Politeness
w/o a
preface

    Positive and negative politeness refer to specifiable language strategies. The last
kind of politeness – politeness without a preface – refers to a global level of concern
for the other's face and is hierarchically related to the other two. The more concern a
speaker gives to the other's face, the more polite is the action. The global level of
politeness used by a speaker is expected to be directly related to an act's degree of
face-threat (see Figure 10.1).

    Brown and Levinson's (1978) politeness theory is an elegant and impressive model
that brings together identity concerns, situational influences, and discourse strategies. In the decade since their original monograph was published, many researchers
have tested part of their theory or used their distinctions in new research arenas. For
instance, politeness theory has been used to ground studies of criticism and appraisal
in work situations (Fairhurst, Green, and Snavely, 1984; Tracy and Eisenberg,
1989), conversational interaction between pilots and crew members in airplane
crashes (Linde, 1988), talk between doctors and patients (Aronsson and Sätterlund-
Larsson, 1987), and exchanges among secretaries and office personnel (Shimanoff,
1977). Much politeness-generated research is reviewed in a recent book by Brown
and Levinson (1987). In the book, the original politeness-theory monograph is
retained and a 50-page introduction is added. The introduction not only reviews
research stimulated by politeness theory, but addresses basic criticisms that have
been made of the theory.

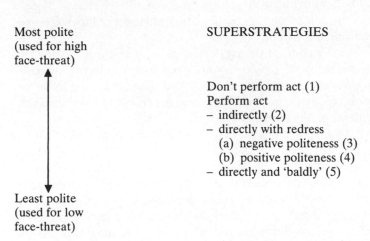

Most polite   SUPERSTRATEGIES
(used for high
face-threat)

                       Don't perform act (1)
                       Perform act
                       – indirectly (2)
                       – directly with redress
                          (a) negative politeness (3)
                          (b) positive politeness (4)
                       – directly and 'baldly' (5)

Least polite
(used for low
face-threat)

FIGURE 10.1   Relationship of expected amount of face-threat of speech act to superstrategy
used. Each superstrategy is associated with a characteristic amount of concern for the other's
face.

The new volume poses a fundamental dilemma for readers. On the one hand, it reveals the authors as sensitive to the many criticisms and problems noted in politeness theory. For instance, in the introduction, Brown and Levinson (1987) suggests that:

(1) basing their theory on speech acts had problems;
(2) the politeness ranking of their strategies will not always hold;
(3) there are probably more factors that affect the perceived face-threat of an act than power, distance, and rank;
(4) politeness as conceived in the theory may be culturally biased;
(5) positive and negative politeness may be different in kind, rather than higher and lower amounts of global politeness.

Since a number of criticisms seem to undermine their basic position, it is not obvious how the criticisms would be integrated into politeness theory. The decision not to revise the body of the monograph sends to readers an implicit message that the authors stand behind their initial claims. In a review essay, Coupland, Grainger, and Coupland (1988b) also highlight the difficulty of ascertaining Brown and Levinson's current claims.

In addition to Brown and Levinson's (1987) self-critique, critiques of politeness theory have been provided by Baxter (1984), Coupland *et al.* (1988b), Craig, Tracy, and Spisak (1986), Hymes (1982), Leech (1980, 1983), Lim (1988), and Penman (in press). While the thrust of each critique is different, most point to problems in equating identity concerns with the concept of positive/negative face.

Politeness theory provides us with a rich, linguistically elaborated sense of how two very general identity concerns are displayed; it does not, however, give an adequate picture of the complexity of identity issues that motivate communicative behavior. Such a picture comes more into focus when we look at how the study of face has been approached in several sociopsychological research areas.

SOCIOPSYCHOLOGICAL APPROACHES TO THE STUDY OF FACE

Three distinct areas of inquiry can be identified under the sociopsychological umbrella:

(1) inquiry directly related to Goffman's (1955) distinctions;
(2) self-presentation studies;
(3) bargaining and conflict research.

Each of these areas is different from the others in important ways but each offers an elaborated notion of how actors' own identity concerns guide communicative action, and how these concerns can produce actions that, at least on occasion, threaten others.

The Goffman Approach

Perhaps the most cited definition of face is the one given by Goffman in his early essay: face is 'the positive social value a person effectively claims for himself by the line others assume he has taken during a particular contact' (Goffman, 1955, p. 213). In subsequent work, Goffman (1959, 1961, 1971) developed a theory to explain the routine ways people present themselves in everyday life, support or challenge others' claims, and deal with challenges to identity claims. According to Goffman (1955, 1959), strategies used in orienting to face are of two main types: corrective practices and preventative ones.

1) Corrective practices are what people do *after* there has been an attack or threat to one party's face. For instance, if one person criticizes or finds fault with another ('This paper is a mess.'), the criticized person's response ('But, at least it's on time.') is likely to be one of several types of corrective practices. Research on 'accounts', verbal devices to make perceived failure or inappropriate behavior reasonable, is perhaps the most direct extension of this concern (e.g. Cody and McLaughlin, 1985; McLaughlin, 1984; Scott and Lyman, 1968; Semen and Manstead, 1983; Snyder, 1985; Tedeschi and Reiss, 1981). In a related vein are studies of the communicative events, variously called social confrontation (Newell and Stutman, 1988) or finding fault (Morris, 1988), that trigger the need for corrective practices.

2) In contrast to corrective practices are preventative ones: actions people take to avoid and prevent threats to self's or other's face. Preventative practices may be either defensive or protective. Defensive practices involve actions taken to avoid threats to self's face. The common practice of prefacing a comment with a disclaimer ('I'm not an expert, but . . .') (Hewitt and Stokes, 1975) is an example of this. Protective preventative practices, on the other hand, are geared to preventing or minimizing threats to the other's face. This is illustrated when people are studiously inattentive to small lapses of behavior from an interactional partner. Current work that examines how people handle embarrassing events (Cupach, Metts, and Hazelton, 1986; Edelman, 1985; Knapp, Stafford, and Daly, 1986) or deal with social anxiety (Daly and McCrosky, 1984; Leary and Schlenker, 1981; Schlenker and Leary, 1985) is a development of the focus on preventative practices.

Extensions of Goffman's (1955) work have emphasized aspects of identity management that are situationally triggered – for example, accounting for failure, dealing with embarrassment. The way people claim to be particular kinds of people (e.g. honest, strong, humorous, thoughtful) has been given little attention. In contrast, self-presentational research has focused primarily on these 'personality' aspects of identity.

Self-Presentation Theories

Strategic self-presentation concerns the way communicators shape their actions to create in others a specific desired response (Jones and Pittman, 1982; Schneider, 1981). While the words 'face' and 'facework' are rarely used in this tradition, the notion of self-presentation shares significant features with face. Like the notion of face, self-presentation assumes people have certain identities that are important and that they wish to be seen as possessing in social interaction. This tradition also highlights the necessity of the other's response in having claims supported. A third similarity between discussions of facework and self-presentation concerns what identity is claimed. According to self-presentation theorists, people often wish to claim that they are pleasant and likable (Jones and Pittman, 1982; Tetlock and Manstead, 1985; Tedeschi, in press). This is quite similar to the social identity claims to be appropriate, tactful, and poised seen in explicit studies of facework (Edelman, 1985; Gross and Stone, 1964; Modigliani, 1971) and to the wants for positive and negative face discussed in politeness theory (Brown and Levinson, 1978). Yet while recognizing the similarities, there are important differences.

First, while self-presentation occurs in social situations, it is conceived of and studied as a one-way phenomenon. Self-presentation largely ignores the fact that social situations involve at least two people. Not only is each person presenting self; each person is orienting to the other and presenting how he or she sees the other. Facework, then, includes self-presentation but also involves other-presentation; stated another way, it involves altercasting.

A second difference between self-presentation and the notion of face is the assumption by self-presentation theorists that there is a private or true self that manifests itself in some social interactions and a non-true, strategic self that is manifest in other situations (Baumeister, 1982; Rhodewatt, 1986; Tedeschi, 1986). A central concern within this tradition, then, becomes sorting out when people are presenting their private selves and when they are presenting their public selves.

The notion of face sidesteps the perplexing, and largely unanswerable, question of whether there is a true self that exists apart from interaction. In social interaction, people are, or try to be, particular kinds of people. Face references the identities claimed and attributed in specific social situations. Whether people 'really are that way' is relevant only if their communicative actions call into question the identity they seem to desire (e.g. confident communicative moves accompanied by nervous ones imply a nervous person trying to act confident).

Third and finally, self-presentation theorists highlight a range of identity claims that are virtually ignored in facework studies. For instance, in addition to the desire to be seen as pleasant and likable, self-presentation studies recognize that in specific situations people may want to be seen as intimidating, competent, needy, or dependent (Jones and Pittman, 1982). While the first two differences between self-presentation and facework highlight advantages of the facework construct, this third difference – the greater range of identity claims – is one that face theorists would do well to take more seriously and one that challenges Brown and Levinson (1978, 1987).

Bargaining and Conflict

Another line of research in which the idea of face is prominent is the study of negotiation and conflict. Face within this line of work is the image of strength a person wants to project in conflict (Brown, 1977; Deutsch, 1973; Folger and Poole, 1984; Pruitt and Smith, 1981; Tjosvold, 1983). Other identity claims, such as being seen as trustworthy, fair, and reasonable, while acknowledged as important, are not treated as face issues. This equating of face with an image of strength and firmness in a situation leads to a very different discussion of facework than seen thus far. Of note is the fact that the term 'facework' is never used; instead conflict researchers talk about 'saving face', 'restoring face', 'losing face', or 'maintaining face'. Similar to the self-presentational work, the face that is at stake is the speaker's; little attention is given to moves of interactants to respond to the face needs of the other. Face concerns, then, would be the equivalent of Goffman's (1959) corrective practices as well as more other-attacking strategies (name calling, threats).

Studies of face in conflicts between intimates (Harris, Gergen and Lannamann, 1986; Infante and Wigley, 1986) draw upon a related notion of facework as involving aggression toward the other. Insults, teasing, and profanity attacks on the other's character or competence are face-saving moves. A basic assumption is that one common way an individual saves face is by attacking an other. Thus, where the self-presentation work considers the strategies used to create largely positive impressions of self, the conflict tradition focuses on strategies that simultaneously minimize, or avoid, negative impressions of self by challenging and attacking the other.

Summary

Thus far we have considered how two research traditions, the linguistically based politeness theory and a cluster of sociopsychological lines of research, have used the concept of face. Each tradition can be seen as orienting to face as the identity claims people make in social interaction; the traditions differ with regard to:

(1) whether they give attention to self or the other's face needs;
(2) whether they consider only face support, or support and attack strategies;
(3) what people's face wants are assumed to be, and the degree to which the different facets of identity are elaborated;
(4) how much, if any, attention is given to the discourse practices that constitute facework.

A COMMUNICATIVE PERSPECTIVE ON FACEWORK

In an earlier article in which my colleagues and I (Craig *et al.*, 1986) critiqued politeness theory, we offered tenets for a theory of facework. These tenets essentially extended and modified politeness theory. Drawing upon our analysis of a large number of requests, we recommended that a theory of facework would need to have a more realistic notion of social interaction, recognizing the ever-present competitive aspect of interaction as well as the way selection of facework strategies in situated social roles (e.g. teacher–student) seems to be based on rights and obligations rather than on an abstract computation of distance, intimacy, and rank. In addition, we highlighted the importance of distinguishing between speakers' and hearers' face as well as positive and negative face. Finally, we argued for the importance of distinguishing between social judgments ('Basil is polite') and the language strategies that often – but not always – lead to such judgments.

The tenets to be offered in this chapter, while also influenced by politeness theory, take account of the broad range of ways facework has been thought about and studied.

Tenet 1: Facework refers to the identity implications of messages.

Communication has many functions (see Cappella and Street, 1985, for review) but an ever-present one is to put forth the kind of person one is and to suggest how one sees the other. One way to conceive of facework is as a more elaborated and discourse-grounded notion of the commonplace claim that all messages have a relational level (Watzlawick, Beavin, and Jackson, 1967). In particular, facework refers to the ways particular communicative moves speak to the identity claims of self and other in specific social situations. And while face concerns are not necessarily focal, they are always immanent.

A number of typologies offer descriptions of major facework moves. Shimanoff (1985, 1987), in the context of emotional disclosure between spouses, divides facework into four main types:

(1) face-honoring (disclosure of pleasant emotion);
(2) face-compensating (apologies);
(3) face-neutral (emotions about third parties);
(4) face-threatening (negative emotion toward other).

Her scheme provides elaboration of the face functions with regard to the other but ignores self-focused functions. In contrast, Katriel's (1986) scheme based on Hymes' (1982) earlier work attends to self-focused face strategies but retains a goodwill assumption also found operating in politeness theory; there is little recognition of other-directed 'bad' intentions. Katriel identifies four main strategies which cross two dimensions: strategies can be distinguished regarding whether they are hearer-focused or speaker-focused, and whether they are autonomy-focused (negative politeness) or emphasize solidarity (positive politeness).

The most comprehensive system is Penman's (in press). Drawing upon an analysis of courtroom discourse, she identifies and illustrates 16 major kinds of facework strategies. Penman's system distinguishes among strategies on the basis of whether they are oriented to self or other, whether they involve positive or negative face, and whether, and with what intensity, they attack or support.

Although only a start, these facework typologies give us a sense of the variety of message strategies that may relate to particular identity functions. More attempts to make these links, including going beyond Brown and Levinson's (1978, 1987) conception of identity, are needed.

Tenet 2: The face wants (i.e. identity claims) to which people orient are dependent on situation, personality, and culture.

Face involves those aspects of self that interactants present and wish to have ratified. Rhodewatt (1986), using the concept 'phenomenal self', argues that, because knowledge about the self is vast, at any moment of time, situational and motivational cues will render certain facets salient. Thus, for instance, in work situations, it seems likely that people would most value being seen in positive ways related to compe-tence. A professor, for example, might be concerned to be seen in the following ways: caring about students, keeping up with the field, fair, dependable, doing interesting research, etc. In all likelihood she would also want to be seen as a generally likable person. But this concern about being seen as likable would probably be more general than that she has with her spouse and close friends. This professor may also count being a good parent as an important part of who she is. In the work situation, however, she may not only minimize orientation to that face want but feel put off by people who attempt to appreciate her as a good parent.

If, as I have argued, face wants are highly situationally influenced, then it is important to be more specific than saying that people want to be appreciated and approved of by selected others. The face wants individuals pursue are different in different contexts. Thus, communicators need to decide which aspect of another's identity it is appropriate to orient to. Orienting to a contextually inappropriate face need of the other may be (or may be seen as) a sophisticated strategy to attack the other or enhance a claim of self. Coupland *et al.* (1988b) provide an example of this in a conversation between a nurse and geriatric patient.

In addition to situations influencing which face wants will be relevant, individuals bring their own particular concerns and weighing of concerns. These differences in face wants captured in traditional social psychology as individual differences (e.g. self-monitoring, reticence), lead people to use different facework strategies and the same ones with different frequencies (see Giles and Street, 1985, for review). Some people typically give more attention to taking account of others' face wants and reconciling them with their own (O'Keefe, 1988; O'Keefe and Shepherd, 1987).

Of particular interest, however, is the way differences among people's face wants can be related to cultural factors. Katriel (1986), in an ethnographic study of *dugri* speech in Israeli Sabra culture, challenges Brown and Levinson's (1978, 1987) assumption that all ways of talk are grounded in rules of considerateness. *Dugri* talk, speaking straight to the point, is an ideal of Israeli culture. In contrast to British people or Americans, for instance, Israelis give more weight to the identity claim of being forthright than the claim of being considerate. This leads to a communicative style which, in Israeli culture, is perceived as honest and forthright, but, in other cultures, is seen as inconsiderate and rude.

Other studies (Kochman, 1981; Tracy and Eisenberg, 1989; Tracy and McLaurin, 1988) suggest that American blacks and whites may also attach different values to being considerate. Blacks, Kochman argues, give more weight to the rights of speakers to be expressive of their feelings; whites, to the protection of others' sensibilities.

A host of studies give evidence of systematic ethnic/national (Carrell and

Konneker, 1981; Gumperz, 1982a,b; House and Kasper, 1981; Scollon and Scollon, 1981; Tannen, 1981, 1984) and gender (Baxter, 1984; Kemper,1984; Maltz and Borker, 1982; Shimanoff, 1977) differences, specifically in the valuing and use of politeness and, more broadly, in the importance attached to a set of face wants.

In sum, while concern over face may be universal, the particular aspects of face that are valued and pursued are highly influenced by culture, personality, and situation. A theory of facework, then, must be sensitive to individual and context-specific variation.

Tenet 3: Social situations involve tensions between different aspects of face.

Craig *et al.* (1986) argued that all social situations involve tensions between coopera-tion and competition, between self's and other's face. In an analysis of favor-asking requests, these authors showed that, even in situations where it is in the best interest of speakers to be cooperative, they will say things that are threatening and antagonis-tic. For instance, in asking a room-mate for help, a person said, 'Pat, how do you manage to do so well in that stupid class?' (Craig *et al.*, 1986, p. 461). As the authors argue, commenting that an activity in which another does well is 'stupid' can hardly be seen as being focused on the other's face needs. Rather, it is likely to be a threat to the other's face that arises, perhaps inadvertently, when speakers are focused on protecting their own face to ward off implications that they are 'dumb and stupid' at important things.

As the favor-asking situation illustrates, there are many everyday situations in which supporting another's face may raise threats to one's own. While there are times when interactants support their partner's face wants (e.g. 'I see you as a likable person who deserves to be treated respectfully') through orienting to their own face needs (displaying self as a polite, respectful person), there are numerous times when supporting self means challenging the other. Morris (1985) provides an interesting analysis of how this tension between the parties' face needs gets played out in an exchange between a teacher and student over the quality of an assignment. Both student and teacher implicitly claim to be competent performers of their specified role. To support their own face claims, each ends up attacking the other. The teacher suggests the student did a sloppy and careless job; the student implies the teacher gave inadequate, confused instructions.

The tension between self and other's face wants is particularly vivid in interview sessions. The general goal of an interviewer is to direct talk to specific topics. At the same time, interviewees have agendas regarding what they want to discuss (Hobbs and Agar, 1985). To the degree that interviewer and interviewee want to talk about different things, their face wants will conflict. Scollon and Scollon (1981) go so far as to argue that interactants' claims to negative face are inherently in tension. The more one person avoids imposing and impinging on another, the more that person is circumscribing his or her actions. While Scollon and Scollon's claim may be overstated – distance could create freedom for both parties – for most kinds of interaction, it seems accurate. To the extent that there are shared understandings of who should have greater freedom of action, it will not be an interactional problem; nonetheless self and other's desires for autonomy are fundamentally in tension.

Not only can one person's face wants come into tension with another's, the same person may want conflicting things. A professor may want his students not to impose upon him or make frequent demands on his time. At the same time, that professor may want to be a good teacher, one who is responsive to student needs and seeks to cultivate their talents. In this example, the professor's positive and negative face wants are in conflict.

A number of researchers (Bochner, 1982; Rawlins, 1983; Tannen, 1984) have argued that people have conflicting wants. They want to be connected, interdependent, intimate with others; at the same time, they want to be independent and autonomous. Too much connection threatens a person's sense of independence; too much autonomy threatens intimacy with another. This means, then, that in most situations discourse should evidence traces of an individual's orientations to both of these face wants; Aronsson and Sätterlund-Larsson (1987) illuminate this process in talk between doctors and patients.

In addition, other identity claims, what Brown and Levinson (1978, 1987) might think of as aspects of positive face, can come into conflict with each other. For instance, in negotiation situations, participants often want to appear both strong and trustworthy (Pruitt and Smith, 1981). The interactional difficulty is that many of the moves that signal a person has one quality, signal the absence of the other. For instance, making a concession may signal a person is bargaining in good faith but it may also be perceived as a sign of weakness; no concessions will signal an image of firmness but may also signal one cannot be trusted.

A common conflict in everyday life is that between a person's desire to be honest and his or her wish to be considerate. In a series of experiments, Bavelas and her colleagues (Bavelas, 1983, 1985; Bavelas, Black, Chovil, and Mullet, 1988; Bavelas and Chovil, 1986) show how participants deal with this conflict through a facework strategy called 'equivocating'. Equivocations allow communicators to sidestep what appears initially to be a choice between being honest and being considerate. For example, a person who does not like a gift, but who is asked if he or she does, may equivocate by responding, 'I appreciate your thoughtfulness'.

In sum, both within the self and between people, various aspects of face come into tension with each other. Sometimes communicators can resolve these tensions as is seen in the use of equivocation. Often, however, supporting one aspect of face will lead to an attack on another.

Tenet 4: The level of face-threat in a situation is first and foremost determined by the types of acts people perform.

Politeness theory is principally geared to explaining what situational factors make communicative acts more or less face-threatening. Yet, the first choice every communicator has concerns the act to be performed. In bargaining situations, Rubin and Lewicki (1973) have demonstrated how promises are more effective than threats. Researchers studying regulative situations – situations where one person is concerned with controlling another's behavior (O'Keefe and McCormack, 1987; Seibold, Cantrill, and Meyers, 1985) – have given considerable attention to this fact. For instance, if a person is angry with another, he or she can say, 'I'm feeling angry with you right now.' (expressive statement), 'You've been a real jerk recently.' (complaint), or 'If you're not more pleasant with my friends, I won't bring you.' (threat). It is likely that the kind of act performed will have as much if not more impact than the discourse variation seen within one act type. A satisfactory theory of facework needs to consider initial act selection.

Tenet 5: All interaction is potentially face-threatening.

Whenever people interact with each other, they make claims to be certain kinds of persons. These claims may not be personalized, psychological ones, but may be quite general (e.g. 'see me as someone who knows how to act appropriately in a supermarket'; 'recognize that I am a person in this situation'); however, they are nonetheless important. And, when people care about how they are perceived – which I would argue is most of the time – there is at least potential for face-threat.

Laver (1981) shows that, in addition to the well-documented relationship between forms of address and social rank (Brown and Gilman 1960), the kind of 'small talk' that occurs between people is also systematically related to relative rank. Small talk can be divided into three categories:

(1) factors common to both parties (e.g. the weather);
(2) self-oriented statements ('Walking up those stairs is a killer.');
(3) other-oriented statements ('How is your family doing?').

People similar or higher in status than their partner, Laver (1981) argues, could use any of the three categories; interactants lower in status, however, could not initiate other-oriented statements without risking a potential affront.

Thus, even the most routine situations of greeting and small talk involve potential face-threat. And while mismanagement of these routine situations is not frequent, when it does happen, as for instance when a person is not acknowledged in a social situation, one or both parties is likely to experience strong negative emotions such as embarrassment, humiliation, or anger. Goffman makes the argument that 'there is no occasion of talk so trivial as not to require each participant to show serious concern with the way in which he handles himself and the others present' (1955, p. 226).

CONCLUSIONS

Facework has many faces. It can be respectful and deferential; it can be friendly; it can be forthright; it can be hostile. Facework may be oriented to enhancement of the self and/or other; it may be oriented to self-defense and other-attack. Because people's self and other identity concerns are often complicated, many of the faces of facework may be visible in the same interaction. However, because language is multifunctional, serving other purposes besides facework; because meaning is culturally situated and contextually cued; and because desired identities may be in competition, the job of claiming and inferring identities is a highly complex one.

Future study of facework needs to take account of this complexity. Not only must future study consider the complexity of identity, something social psychological study has typically done, it must also consider the complexity of discourse expression. The need for social psychology, generally, to be more grounded in discourse has been cogently argued for by a number of theorists (Potter and Wetherell, 1987; Robinson, 1985). Potter and Wetherell (1987) go so far as to argue that 'any sociopsychological image of the self, in fact the very possibility of self-concept, is inextricably dependent on the linguistic practices used in everyday life to make sense of our own and other's actions' (p. 95).

The communicative perspective described in this chapter is a first start at compensating for the limitations of past approaches. While requiring considerable development, the perspective offers a beginning redefinition of the key issues requiring study. In particular, it moves researchers to study discourse *and* situated identity, seeing discourse as the only way to get at situated identity, and seeing elaborated notions of identity as critical to any interesting study of discourse.

In conclusion, let me suggest two directions for future research. The first would be to rethink established lines of research taking seriously the ever-present concern about face. For instance, one might study self-disclosure (see Chelune, 1979, for a review) in terms of the facework implications of expressing negative information and identify the language strategies used to pave the way for such expression.

Another direction, one that has just begun to receive attention, concerns how people manage multiple, and perhaps competing, face wants. In a recent conference, the focus of which was 'Multiple goals in discourse', scholars reported studies about a variety of identity tensions (e.g. see Coyle, Seibert, and Applegate, 1988; Hample and Dallinger, 1988; Rawlins, 1988; Spisak, 1988) including, for example, how conversational interaction between the elderly and the young reflected competing identity needs (Coupland, Coupland, Giles, and Henwood, 1988a), and how a nurse practitioner's discourse in gynecological exams reflected her concern to be medically task-focused and recognize the patient personally (Ragan, in press). Research that attempts to understand the multilayered relationships between discourse expression and competing face wants seem an especially promising area for future study.

REFERENCES

Aronsson, K. and Sätterlund-Larsson, U. (1987). Politeness strategies and doctor–patient communication: On the social choreography of collaborative thinking. *Journal of Language and Social Psychology*, **6**, 1–28.

Baumeister, R.F. (1982). A self-presentational view of social phenomena. *Psychological Bulletin*, **91**, 3–26.

Bavelas, J.B. (1983). Situations that lead to disqualification. *Human Communication Research*, **9**, 130–145.

Bavelas, J.B. (1985). A situational theory of disqualification: Using language to 'leave the field'. In J. Forgas (Ed.), *Language and social situations*, pp. 189–211. New York: Springer.

Bavelas, J.B., Black, A., Chovil, N., and Mullet, J. (1988). Equivocation as a solution to conflicting interpersonal goals. Paper presented at the 9th Annual Conference on Discourse Analysis, Temple University, Philadelphia.

Bavelas, J.B. and Chovil, N. (1986). How people disqualify: Experimental studies of spontaneous written disqualification. *Communication Monographs*, **53**, 70–74.

Baxter, L.A. (1984). An investigation of compliance-gaining as politeness. *Human Communication Research*, **10**, 427–456.

Bochner, A.P. (1982). On the efficacy of openness in close relationships. In M. Burgoon (Ed.), *Communication yearbook, 5*, pp. 109–124. New Brunswick, NJ: Transaction.

Brown, B.R. (1977). Face-saving and face-restoration in negotiations. In D. Druckman (Ed.), *Negotiations: Social-psychological perspectives*, pp. 275–300. Beverly Hills, CA: Sage.

Brown, P. and Levinson, S. (1978). Universals in language usage: Politeness phenomena. In E.N. Goody (Ed.), *Questions and politeness: Strategies in social interaction*, pp. 56–310. Cambridge: Cambridge University Press.

Brown, P. and Levinson, S. (1987). *Universals in language usage: Politeness phenomena*. Cambridge: Cambridge University Press.

Brown, R. and Gilman, A. (1960). The pronouns of power and solidarity. In T.A. Sebeok (Ed.), *Style in language*, pp. 253–276. Cambridge, MA: MIT Press.

Cappella, J.N. and Street, R.L. (1985). Introduction: A functional approach to the structure of communicative behaviour. In R.L. Street and J.N. Cappella (Eds), *Sequence and pattern in communicative behaviour*, pp. 1–29. London: Arnold.

Carrell, P.L. and Konneker, B.H. (1981). Politeness: Comparing native and non-native judgments. *Language Learning*, **31**, 17–30.

Chelune, G.M. (Ed.) (1979). *Self-disclosure: Origins, patterns, and implications of openness in interpersonal relationships*. San Francisco: Jossey-Bass.

Cody, M.J. and McLaughlin, M.L. (1985). Models for the sequential construction of accounting episodes: Situational and interactional constraints on message selection and evaluation. In R.L. Street and J.N. Cappella (Eds), *Sequence and pattern in communicative behaviour*, pp. 50–69. London: Arnold.

Coupland, N., Coupland, J., Giles, H., and Henwood, K. (1988a). My life in your hands: Strategic and discoursal processes in the management of elderly self-disclosure in intergenerational talk. Paper presented at the 9th Annual Conference on Discourse Analysis, Temple University, Philadelphia.

Coupland, N., Grainger, K., and Coupland, J. (1988b). Politeness in context: Intergenerational issues. *Language in Society*, **17**, 253–262.

Coyle, K., Seibert, J.H., and Applegate, J.L. (1988). The interaction of cognitive differentiation with gender and power on integration of face goals into persuasive messages. Paper presented at the 9th Annual Conference on Discourse Analysis, Temple University, Philadelphia.

Craig, R.T., Tracy, K., and Spisak, F. (1986). The discourse of requests: Assessment of a politeness approach. *Human Communication Research*, **12**, 437–468.

Cupach, W.R., Metts, S., and Hazelton, V. Jr (1986). Coping with embarrassing predicaments: Remedial strategies and their perceived utility. *Journal of Language and Social Psychology*, **5**, 181–200.

Daly, J. and McCrosky, J.C. (1984). *Avoiding communication: Shyness, reticence, and communication apprehension*. Beverly Hills, CA: Sage.

Deutsch, M. (1973). *The resolution of conflict*. New Haven, CT: Yale University Press.

Edelman, R.J. (1985). Social embarrassment: An analysis of the process. *Journal of Social and Personal Relationships*, **2**, 195–213.

Fairhurst, G.T., Green, S.G., and Snavely, B.K. (1984). Face support in controlling poor performance. *Human Communication Research*, **11**, 272–295.

Folger, J.P. and Poole, M.S. (1984). *Working through conflict*. Gleview, IL: Scott, Foresman.

Giles, H. and Street, R.L. (1985). Communicator characteristics and behavior. In M.L. Knapp and G.R. Miller (Eds), *Handbook of interpersonal communication*, pp. 205–261. Beverly Hills, CA: Sage.

Goffman, E. (1955). On face-work: An analysis of ritual elements in social interaction. *Psychiatry*, **18**, 213–231.

Goffman, E. (1959). *The presentation of self in everyday life*. Garden City, NY: Doubleday.

Goffman, E. (1961). *Encounters*. Indianapolis, IN: Bobbs–Merrill.

Goffman, E. (1971). *Relations in public*. New York: Basic.

Grice, H.P. (1975). Logic and conversation. In P. Cole and J. Morgan (Eds), *Syntax and semantics*, Vol. 3, *Speech acts*, pp. 41–58. New York: Academic Press.

Gross, E. and Stone, G.P. (1964). Embarrassment and the analysis of role requirements. *American Journal of Sociology*, **70**, 1–15.

Gumperz, J.J. (Ed.) (1982a). *Language and social identity*. Cambridge: Cambridge University Press.

Gumperz, J.J. (1982b). *Discourse strategies*. Cambridge: Cambridge University Press.

Hample, D. and Dallinger, J.M. (1988). The use of multiple goals in the cognitive editing of arguments. Paper presented at the 9th Annual Conference on Discourse Analysis, Temple University, Philadelphia.

Harris, L.M., Gergen, K.J., and Lannamann, J.W. (1986). Aggression rituals. *Communication Monographs*, **53**, 252–265.

Hewitt, J.P. and Stokes, R. (1975). Disclaimers. *American Sociological Review*, **40**, 1–11.

Ho, D.Y. (1975). On the concept of face. *American Journal of Sociology*, **81**, 867–884.

Hobbs, J.R. and Agar, M.H. (1985). The coherence of incoherent discourse. *Journal of Language and Social Psychology*, **4**, 213–232.

House, J. and Kasper, G. (1981). Politeness markers in English and German. In F. Coulmas (Ed.), *Conversational routine*, pp. 157–185. The Hague: Mouton.

Hu, D.H. (1944). The Chinese concepts of 'face'. *American Anthropologist*, **46**, 45–64.

Hymes, D. (1982). *Ethnolinguistic study of discourse in the classroom*. Final report to the National Institute of Education, University of Pennsylvania.

Infante, D.A. and Wigley, C.J. (1986). Verbal aggression: An interpersonal model and measure. *Communciation Monographs*, **53**, 61–69.

Jones, E.E. and Pittman, T.S. (1982). Toward a general theory of strategic self-presentation. In J. Suls (Ed.), *Psychological perspectives on the self*, pp. 231–262. Hillsdale, NJ: Erlbaum.

Katriel, T. (1986). *Talking straight: Durgri speech in Israeli Sabra culture*. London: Cambridge University Press.

Kemper, S. (1984). When to speak like a lady. *Sex Roles*, **10**, 435–443.

Knapp, M.L., Stafford, L., and Daly, L. (1986). Regrettable messages: Things people wish they hadn't said. *Journal of Communication*, **36**(4), 40–58.

Kochman, T. (1981). *Black and white styles in conflict*. Chicago: University of Chicago Press.

Laver, J. (1981). Linguistic routines and politeness in greeting and parting. In F. Coulmas (Ed.), *Conversational routine*, pp. 289–304. The Hague: Mouton.

Leary, M.R. and Schlenker, B.R. (1981). The social psychology of shyness: A self-presentation model. In J.T. Tedeschi (Ed.), *Impression management theory and social psychological research*, pp. 335–358. New York: Academic Press.

Leech, G.N. (1980). *Explorations in semantics and pragmatics*. Amsterdam: Benjamins.

Leech, G.N. (1983). *Principles of pragmatics*. London: Longman.

Lim, T.-S. (1988). Toward a new model of politeness. Paper presented at the Annual Meeting of the Speech Communication Association, New Orleans.

Linde, C. (1988). The quantitative study of communicative success: Politeness and accidents in aviation discourse. *Language in Society*, **17**, 375–399.

Maltz, D.N. and Borker, R.A. (1982). A cultural approach to male–female miscommunication. In J.J. Gumperz (Ed.), *Language and social identity*, pp. 195–216. Cambridge: Cambridge University Press.

McLaughlin, M.L. (1984). *Conversation: How talk is organized*. Beverly Hills, CA: Sage.

Modigliani, A. (1971). Embarrassment, facework and eye contact: Testing a theory of embarrassment. *Journal of Personality and Social Psychology*, **17**, 89–111.

Morris, G.H. (1985). The remedial episode as a negotiation of rules. In R.L. Street and J.N. Cappella (Eds), *Sequence and pattern in communicative behaviour*, pp. 70–84. London: Arnold.

Morris, G.H. (1988). Finding fault. *Journal of Language and Social Psychology*, **8**, 1–25.

Newell, S.E. and Stutman, R.K. (1988). The social confrontation episode. *Communication Monographs*, **55**, 266–285.

O'Keefe, B.J. (1988). The logic of message design: Individual differences in reasoning about communication. *Communication Monographs*, **55**, 80–103.

O'Keefe, B.J. and McCormack, S.A. (1987). Message design logic and message goal structure: Effects on perceptions of message quality in regulative communication situations. *Human Communication Research*, **14**, 68–92.

O'Keefe, B.J. and Shepherd, G.J. (1987). The pursuit of multiple objectives in face-to-face persuasive interactions: Effects of construct differentiation on message organization. *Communication Monographs*, **54**, 396–419.

Penman, R. (in press). Facework and politeness. Multiple goals in courtroom discourse. *Journal of Language and Social Psychology*.

Potter, J. and Wetherell, M. (1987). *Discourse and social psychology*. Newbury Park, CA: Sage.

Pruitt, D.G. and Smith, D.L. (1981). Impression management in bargaining: Images of firmness and trustworthiness. In J.T. Tedeschi (Ed.), *Impression management theory and social psychological research*, pp. 247–267. New York: Academic Press.

Ragan, S. (in press). Verbal play and multiple goals in the gynaecologic exam interaction. *Journal of Language and Social Psychology*.

Rawlins, W.K. (1983). Negotiating close friendship: The dialectic of conjunctive freedoms. *Human Communication Research*, **9**, 255–266.

Rawlins, W. K. (1988). Double agency and the discourse of friendship. Paper presented at the 9th Annual Conference on Discourse Analysis, Temple University, Philadelphia.

Rhodewalt, F.T. (1986). Self-presentation and the phenomenal self: On the stability and malleability of self-conceptions. In R.F. Baumeister (Ed.), *Public self and private self*, pp. 117–42. New York: Springer Verlag.

Robinson, W.P. (1985). Social psychology and discourse. In T.A. Van Dijk (Ed.), *Handbook of discourse analysis*, Vol. 1, *Disciplines of discourse*, pp. 107–144. London: Academic Press.

Rubin, J.Z. and Lewicki, R.J. (1973). A three-factor experimental analysis of promises and threats. *Journal of Applied Social Psychology*, **3**, 240–257.

Schlenker, B.R. and Leary, M.R. (1985). Social anxiety and communication about the self. *Journal of Language and Social Psychology*, **4**, 171–192.

Schneider, D.J. (1981). Tactical self-presentations: Toward a broader conception. In J.T. Tedeschi (Ed.), *Impression management theory and social psychological research*, pp. 23–40. New York: Academic Press.

Scollon, R. and Scollon, S.B.K. (1981). *Narrative, literacy and face in interethnic communication*. Norwood, NJ: Ablex.

Scott, M.B. and Lyman, S. (1968). Accounts. *American Sociological Review*, **33**, 46–62.

Searle, J. (1969). *Speech acts*. Cambridge: Cambridge University Press.

Seibold, D.R., Cantrill, J.G., and Meyers, R.A. (1985). Communication and interpersonal influence. In M.L. Knapp and G.R. Miller (Eds), *Handbook of interpersonal communication*, pp. 551–611. Newbury Park, CA: Sage.

Semen, G.R. and Manstead, A.S.R. (1983). *The accountability of conduct: A social psychological analysis*. New York: Academic Press.

Shimanoff, S.B. (1977). Investigating politeness. In E.O. Keenan and T.L. Bennet (Eds), *Discourse across time and space*, pp. 213–241. Los Angeles: University of Southern California Press.

Shimanoff, S.B. (1985). Rules for governing the verbal expression of emotions between married couples. *Western Journal of Speech Communication*, **49**, 147–165.

Shimanoff, S.B. (1987). Types of emotional disclosures and request compliance between spouses. *Communication Monographs*, **54**, 85–100.

Snyder, C.R. (1985). The excuse: An amazing grace. In B.R. Schlenker (Ed.), *The self and social life*, pp. 235–260. New York: McGraw-Hill.

Spisak, F. (1988). Multiple goals in dental hygienist–patient interaction. Paper presented at the 9th Annual Conference on Discourse Analysis, the Temple University, Philadelphia.

Tannen, D. (1981). Indirectness in discourse: Ethnicity in conversational style. *Discourse Processes*, **4**, 221–228.

Tannen, D. (1984). *Conversational style: Analyzing talk among friends*. Norwood, NJ: Ablex.

Tedeschi, J.T. (1986). Private and public experiences and the self. In R.F. Baumeister (Ed.), *Public self and private self*, pp. 1–20. New York: Springer-Verlag.

Tedeschi, J.T. (in press). Self-presentation and social influence: An interactionist perspective. In M.J. Cody and M.J. McLaughlin (Eds), *Psychology of tactical communication*. Clevedon (England): Multilingual Matters.

Tedeschi, J.T. and Reiss, M. (1981a). Identities, the phenomenal self, and laboratory research. In J.T. Tedeschi (Ed.), *Impression management theory and social psychological research*, pp. 3–22. New York: Academic Press.

Tedeschi, J.T. and Reiss, M. (1981). Identities, the phenomenal self, and laboratory research. In J.T. Tedeschi (Ed.), *Impression management theory and social psychological research*, pp. 3–22. New York: Academic Press.

Tetlock, P.E. and Manstead, A.S.R. (1985). Impression management vs. intra-psychic explanations: A useful dichotomy? *Psychological Review*, **92**, 59–77.

Tjosvold, D. (1983). Social face in conflict: A critique. *Internal Journal of Group Tensions*, **13**, 49–64.

Tracy, K. and Eisenberg, E.M. (1989). Multiple goals: Unpacking a commonplace. Paper presented to the Annual Meeting of the International Communication Association, San Francisco.

Tracy, K. and McLaurin, P. (1988). Race and gender differences in the face goals of recipients of criticism. Unpublished manuscript, Temple University.

Watzlawick, P., Beavin, J., and Jackson, D.D. (1967). *Pragmatics of human communication*. New York: Norton.

11

Interpersonal Accounting

MICHAEL J. CODY AND MARGARET L. McLAUGHLIN

Department of Communication Arts and Sciences, University of Southern California, USA

Anyone who ever made *excuses* to a professor for a late term paper, *apologized* to a spouse or romantic partner for failing to remember an anniversary, *justified* speeding in order to arrive at the airport on time, or *denied* that he or she cheated on a diet has used *accounts* in order to explain actions and, with any luck, avoid negative evaluations and/or penalties. An 'account', according to sociologists Marvin Scott and Stanford Lyman (1968), is 'a linguistic device employed whenever an action is subjected to valuative inquiry' (p. 171). By 'valuative inquiry', they meant that one person (whom we may call the 'reproacher') asks for an 'explanation' from another (the 'accounter') concerning either (a) an inappropriate or unexpected behaviour (Room-mate: 'Why did you wear *that* dress to a job interview?'), or (b) the *failure* on the accounter's part to engage in an appropriate or expected behaviour (Room-mate: 'Why didn't you lock the front door last night before you went to bed?'). Today, we use the term *failure event* (Cody and McLaughlin, 1985; Schönbach, 1980) to denote the specific (alleged) behaviour or 'offence' that resulted in an account's being requested, offered, and evaluated. Along similar lines, impression-management theorists have defined a 'social predicament' as 'any event that casts undesired aspersions on the lineage, character, conduct, skills, or motives of an actor' (Schlenker, 1980, p. 125; also see Tedeschi and Reiss, 1981, and Chapter 10, by Tracy).

Most accounts given daily probably deal with trivial matters. However, many accounts are important, for a number of reasons. First, the study of accounts tells us a

Handbook of Language and Social Psychology
Edited by H. Giles and W.P. Robinson. © 1990 John Wiley & Sons Ltd

good deal about how laypersons explain their world and use knowledge of causal relationships to make sense of it and interpret explanations. Second, improperly handled failure events can escalate to conflict (Schönbach, 1985, 1986; Schönbach and Kleibaumhuter, 1989), and we have found that (alleged) undischarged obligations and the accusations arising from them are a primary source of interpersonal conflict (Canary, Cunningham, and Cody, 1988). Third, there are any number of failure events involving traffic police, judges, and bureaucrats in which offering successful accounts pays, monetarily or otherwise. Further, accounts also have a direct bearing on the psychology of the accounter: they are fundamentally important in maintaining or sustaining a positive self-image, and avoiding a negative view of self. Snyder and Higgins (1989) argue that social actors use excuses to deny responsibility for negative acts, and use justifications to make negative acts appear less negative (if not positive); thus, actors foster a positive image of self and defend against a negative image.

The idea that verbal devices can be used to 'neutralize' negative evaluation is an old one (Scott and Lyman, 1968; Sykes and Matza, 1957: see the reviews by Semin and Manstead, 1983; Snyder, Higgins, and Stucky, 1983). However, only recently have scholars *systematically* focused research efforts of how accounts are offered and evaluated. We propose to introduce the reader to the study of interpersonal accounting by overviewing five topics:

(1) type of accounts;
(2) the canonical form of the account sequence;
(3) affective reciprocity in reproach–account sequences;
(4) effectiveness of accounts;
(5) future research: causal schemata.

We emphasize here the view of accounts as serving social, interpersonal, and interactional functions in that they are offered to others largely out of 'remedial' concerns so that reproachers or other audience members will not think unfavourably of the accounter (sections 1 through 4). The most recent research evaluates explanations in terms of a cognitive framework of causal schemata (section 5).

In our review, we emphasize studies on 'communicated' explanations; that is, communication episodes in which an accounter offers an apology, excuse, justification or denial to a parent or other family member, lover, friend, traffic officer, parole officer, judge, jury, etc. We will not be able to include literature on general explanations of either a public or private nature, such as explanations for success or failure of sports teams (Lau, 1984; Lau and Russell, 1980), poverty and affluence (Furnham, 1982, 1983), relational break-ups (Harvey, Weber, Galvin, Hustzi, and Garnick, 1986; Harvey, Weber, Yarkin, and Stewart, 1982; Weber, Harvey, and Stanley, in press), corporate success and failure (Bettman and Weitz, 1983), or for the functioning of combat veterans (see Harvey, Turnquist, and Agostinelli, 1988) (also see Antaki, 1981, 1988; Furnham, 1988).

TYPES OF ACCOUNTS

In their now-classic treatment of accounts, Scott and Lyman (1968) presented an exhaustive description of the two most commonly occurring types of accounts: *excuses* and *justifications*. An *excuse* was said to involve the offender's admitting that the act in question occurred, and that it was in fact harmful, but denying that he or she was fully responsible for it. Scott and Lyman suggested that since the world is imperfect and accidents occur beyond the control of social actors, one excuse, the *appeal to accidents*, would occur as standard fare, and, they speculated, should be deemed acceptable by reproachers and other audience members. However, little credibility can be assigned to a social actor who uses the same 'accident' as his or her excuse repeatedly over time. A worker may be late and report, truthfully, 'I had a flat tyre.' If such an excuse is given once, the supervisor may be inclined to accept it, and not hold the worker responsible. However, if the worker is late once a week and uses the same excuse each time, its credibility will quickly decay.

Besides the appeal to accident, Scott and Lyman (1968) included *appeal to biological drives*, *appeal to defeasibility*, and *scapegoating*. An *appeal to biological drives* generally deals with an appeal to *fatalism*: men are men; women are women; boys will be boys, etc. In the movie *Urban Cowboy*, an ex-convict is caught sleeping with another woman and announces, 'You can't expect a cowboy to love just one woman', meaning that a cowboy should not be blamed *personally* for his act – there are behaviours dictated by fate that cannot be controlled. Similar claims are made by alcoholics who excuse their behaviour because of ethnic origin. The *appeal to defeasibility* is basically an argument in which the accounter claims that he or she did not have full knowledge about an action and its consequences, and therefore should not be held responsible, or fully responsible, for what occurred. For instance, a teenager teases a sister about her boyfriend and the sister begins to cry. When asked why he behaved so cruelly, the teenager confesses that he didn't know that his sister and her friend had argued and separated (and that, since he didn't know, he should not be blamed and considered 'cruel'). Cases of *scapegoating* are fairly common: 'I am sorry, officer, this is my mom's car' (with a broken tail-light); 'But my secretary told me this was the correct form', etc.

When using a *justification*, the accounter accepts responsibility for the offence, but denies that it was harmful, or claims that there were positive consequences associated with the action that outweighed any negative consequences. Six common forms of justifications include *denial of injury*, *denial of the victim*, *appeal to loyalty*, *self-fulfillment*, *condemnation of condemners*, and the *sad tale* (Scott and Lyman, 1968). When using the form *denial of injury*, the accounter admits that an action occurred and that he or she was responsible for it, but that since no harm came from it, no penalty should be assessed; for instance, 'Yes, we (teenagers) took the car and stayed out last night but nothing happened. Everybody's okay.' In the *denial of the victim*, the accounter accepts responsibility for what occurred, but argues that the person who was hurt isn't worthy of the reproacher's concern: 'Who cares? She would have ripped me of if she could have.' When using an *appeal to loyalty*, the accounter asserts that loyalty to a group or friend is more important than any rules or laws that may have been violated.

A drug user may appeal to the principle of *self-fulfillment* when justifying the use of LSD as expanding the mind and consciousness. *Condemnation of the condemner* involves the claim that, because others break the same rules, the accounter should not be *personally* reprimanded – everybody, the argument goes, 'fudges' tax forms, drives a 'little' over the speed limit, etc. In the *sad tale,* the accounter claims (or rearranges the facts so that it appears) that a dismal past can be used to explain current behaviours. For example, a husband who is unfaithful to his wife may attempt to claim that, because he was a victim of divorce and an alcoholic, abusive mother, he has never fully learned to respect women, and that he has an insatiable need for love.

Some noteworthy papers appeared during the 1970s (Ditton, 1977; Shields, 1979; see reviews by Semin and Manstead, 1983; Snyder *et al.*, 1983). Most notably (in our view), Blumstein *et al.* (1974) assessed factors associated with the honouring of accounts (see section on 'Effectiveness of accounts' later in this chapter) and Coleman (1976) provided a typology of accounts offered by people protesting against traffic citations. However, work on accounts was expanded in the 1980s, as several proposals for extending the basic Scott–Lyman typology were offered. For example, Tedeschi and Reiss (1981) added to the list of specific examples of excuses and justifications (i.e. types of excuses included 'lack of intention (accounter asserts effects were not planned)', 'lack of volition (accounter asserts lack of bodily control)', and 'denial of agency'), and expanded the list of account types to include *meta-accounts, disclaimers, apologies*, and *blame*, in addition to *excuses* and *justifications*.

However, research by Schönbach (1980, 1985, 1986) in particular was instrumental in initiating several fundamental extensions. In his 1980 paper, Schonbach presented the notion of the account sequence (failure event, reproach, account, evaluation), and added two categories to the taxonomy of account forms. Not only can accounters use excuses or justifications, but they also may offer either a *concession* or a *refusal.* In a *concession*, the offender neither denies responsibility nor attempts to justify untoward conduct, but simply confesses or admits to the failure in question. Concessions are often accompanied by apologies, expressions of remorse, offers to make restitution, and so on (Darby and Schlenker, 1982; Schlenker and Darby, 1981). The *refusal* category includes such lines of defence as denial that the act in question was in fact committed, and refusal to grant the other party the right of reproach.

It should be clear to the reader that the types of accounts provided in the literature serve specific functions. By definition, an excuse attempts to exonerate the accounter of being held personally responsible for an offence, while a justification serves the function of making the action seem less negative (or even positive). The use of a concession communicates that the accounter agrees with the reproacher's assessment of responsibility and consequences, and, if appropriate forms of apologies are used, that the accounter will not engage in the act again and/or will make restitution. In the use of a refusal or denial, however, the accounter asserts (or proves) his or her innocence of the accusation, or refuses to grant the reproacher the right to ask about a questionable behaviour ('I am the father in this family and you can't question how I do the family budget.').

Beyond these functions served by accounts, however, the reader is cautioned against assuming that *one* type of account is uniformly more *credible* than another. Research on the credibility and effectiveness of accounts indicates that apologies and excuses (or a hybrid 'excuse–apology') are generally more effective than justifications and denials or refusals in reducing punishments or deflecting blame in interpersonal settings, when coping with embarrassment, when explaining actions to traffic officers, and even when explaining actions for white-collar crime (Rothman and Gandossy, 1982) (see below). However, it is often the case that *excuses* are the single most popular type of account generated and communicated, and excuses vary widely in terms of credibility. First, one type of excuse, 'denial of intent', is perceived to be more mitigating and effective than other types of excuses (see below; Cody and McLaughlin, 1988; Holtgraves, 1989). Second, attribution theorists investigating the use and perception of explanations (both excuses and justifications, but excluding apologies and denials; Folkes, 1982; Weiner, Amirkhan, Folkes, and Verette, 1987) indicate that explanations are preferred and more effective if they cite reasons that are unintentional, uncontrollable, unstable, and external, rather than intentional, controllable, stable, and internal (see below).

Some stark differences in the apparent credibility of accounts are evidenced by the results of Cody and McLaughlin (1988), comparing reactions to basic forms of oral messages offered in traffic court, and by the results of Hale (1987) – the only study which found that justifications were rated as more effective than excuses. Cody and McLaughlin assessed 375 cases of oral arguments made in traffic courts in the Greater Los Angeles area. Many merely involved *guilty pleas* ($n = 74$), and virtually all people making such an appeal were penalized. Most accounters used some type of an *excuse* in order to claim that they were not responsible ($n = 134$), and 75% of all accounters were penalized. Since a *justification* in this context means that the accounter is arguing that violating the law is *not* a negative act (or could even be viewed as a *positive* act), very few people opted to use justifications as a persuasive argument in traffic court ($n = 45$), and 91% of such accounters were penalized. Three types of *denials/refusals* were obtained: *challenge* to the authority of the police officer ('The officer ticketed the wrong person.') (91% were penalized), *denial of definition of the 'offence'* ('Well, the officer claims the light was red when I crossed through it, but I swear it was still yellow.') (81% were penalized), and *logical proofs* ('With these charts, diagrams, and photos, your Honour, I plan to prove that my '67 VW bug could not have accelerated to 47 mph in the residential streets indicated on this ticket . . .') (25% were penalized).

A judge in traffic court must decide whether an accounter is guilty as charged or whether there is 'reasonable doubt' of guilt. *Logical proofs* are the best way of raising doubts about a case. Second, in effectiveness are excuses; however, some excuses are more effective than others. Four subcategories of accounts were observed: 'lack of knowledge' ('I didn't know it was illegal') 'mitigating circumstances' ('I couldn't see the signs because the construction site obstructed the view'), 'appeal to illness/impairment' ('I was getting sick to my stomach . . .'), and 'denial of intention to break the law' ('I did not mean to screech my tyres when I accelerated. I really did not mean to do that.'). Of these, the 'denial of intention' excuses were more effective (only 30% were penalized), and the other excuses were considered 'lame' (70% to

80% were penalized). Thus, proofs and excusing oneself from responsibility on the grounds that one did not *intend* to commit the error were vastly more credible in traffic court than all other claims.

On the other hand, Hale (1987) assessed the credibility of accounts students might give to explain why a term paper was not turned in on time, and assessed both low- and high-quality concessions, apologies, excuses, and justifications. Hale found that excuses were rated no more credible than concessions and apologies. The high-quality justifications (students claimed the time they had devoted to job interviews precluded finishing the paper on time) were rated highest in credibility. Most studies on accounts assess 'one-shot' offences (running a red light, being late for work), and apologies and excuses are usually effective. Hale's project dealt with students who failed to complete an assignment over *weeks*, and one way to interpret her results is to conclude that excuses for chronic failure over time are regarded suspiciously. Good excuses are ones that offer reasons for the failure event that are external to the person, uncontrollable, unintentional, and unstable (Weiner *et al.*, 1987). Hale's 'quality' excuse involved the argument that the student was so burdened with homework that he or she could not complete the paper on time. This 'quality' excuse is actually poor, for three reasons. First, the student claims that he or she could not control his or her environment over *weeks*, and the alleged inability to control activities over time seems suspicious. Second, the 'quality' excuse harbours an insult, since the student claims that he or she decided to complete homework assignments in other, presumably more important, courses, while letting the work in this one course slide. Third, the excuse is simply a poor impression–management tactic (Schlenker, 1980) because the explanation makes the accounter appear weak, impotent, power-less. A 'better' excuse, involving uncontrollable, external, unintentional, and un-stable reasons, would involve arguing that a power shortage in the dorm caused the paper to be erased, a room-mate accidentally bent the diskette, or an illness in the family or on the student's part precluded completing the assignment.

The latter observation highlights a dilemma in research on accounts. Researchers themselves often construct a few samples of each of several types of accounts, and then require respondents to rate only these few samples in terms of credibility. An alternative would be to identify relevant samples of each possible argument that could be offered or to focus on a fine-grained analysis of what actors actually say. It is possible that at least some of the social actors observed in court, interacting with bureaucrats, explaining failures to parents, and so forth are more clever or creative than we give them credit for.

CANONICAL FORM OF THE ACCOUNT SEQUENCE

The results of research on accounts in the 1980s lead us to two conclusions: (a) accounts as they develop in interaction have a *canonical form*, which guides the way that they unfold; and (b) the relationships among the adjacent steps or 'slots' in the canonical form of the sequence (for example, reproach and account, or, account and evaluation) are to a certain extent governed by a principle of *affective reciprocity* with respect to level of mitigation. Let us consider each conclusion in turn.

That there is a basic structure to the repair of failure events has been noted by several scholars, under a variety of labels, including the *corrective interchange* (Goffman, 1967), the *remedial cycle* (Goffman, 1971), and the *remedial episode* (Morris, 1985). Our studies have led us to conclude that account sequences often unfold according to the following schedule: a failure event of some sort gives rise to a *reproach*, or request for repair, which is followed by an *account*, which is followed by an *evaluation* of the adequacy of the account in effecting repair (cf. Remler, 1978). If repair is effected, matters are restored (more or less) to their condition prior to the failure event.

We do not use the phrase 'canonical form' to imply that these steps will always be present. There is evidence that accounts are often given in the absence of an explicit reproach (Buttny, 1987; Dindia and Steele, 1987). Dindia and Steele found that 13% of patients' accounts to medical personnel were unsolicited, and 31% followed *implicit* reproaches. Similarly, accounts are not always followed prior to explicit evaluation (doctors or nurses frequently say little in response to a patient's excuse for not taking medicine as instructed; see also Chapter 25, by Hinkley, Craig, and Anderson). Dindia and Steele found that some accounts were followed by requests for clarification, or token responses.

Further, we do not suggest that the steps described above will always or even usually be immediately adjacent in conversation, for the sequence is subject to expansion by presequences, insertion sequences, and post sequences (Jackson and Jacobs, 1980; Jacobs and Jackson, 1979), and to the recycling of steps (e.g. the restatement of the reproach, the offering of additional accounts, etc.). What we do argue is that the reproach–account–evaluation sequence is canonical in the sense that (a) the explicit presence in interaction of the immediately prior step in the sequence sets up an expectation that the next step should ultimately appear; that is, it is sequentially implicative for the next action and would make its failure to materialize at some point remarkable; and (b) the sequence guides retrieval, comprehension, and behavioural output in the same way as do canonical story forms (McCartney and Nelson, 1981; McClure, Mason, and Barnitz, 1979) and persuasion scripts (Bisanz and Rule, 1989) for their respective forms of discourse.

AFFECTIVE RECIPROCITY IN REPROACH–ACCOUNT SEQUENCES

A second construct we have invoked in describing relationships among the acts in an account sequence is the level of mitigation/aggravation (Labov and Fanshel, 1977). We have argued that types of reproaches, accounts, and evaluations can be arrayed along a continuum, such that at one end are actions which ordinarily would serve to exacerbate the relational tension created by the failure event, and at the other are actions which would ordinarily serve to reduce it. In our early papers (McLaughlin, Cody, and O'Hair, 1983a; McLaughlin, Cody, and Rosenstein, 1983b), we tended to regard the location of accounts and other acts in the account sequence as relatively fixed with respect to the aggravation–mitigation continuum; that is, we regarded concessions and excuses as comparatively mitigating, and justifications and refusals as comparatively aggravating. We also argued for a general principle of reciprocity of affect in account sequences, such that mitigating reproaches lead to mitigating accounts (apologies or excuses), which would result in the offended parties responding in kind by accepting or *honouring* the accounts.

Support for our claims stems, first, from studies which confirm that a single mitigating versus aggravating continuum adequately accounts for how types of account messages are perceived, and, second, from research which demonstrates that types of reproaches (how accounts are requested) significantly influence the accounts that follow, and that types of accounts communicated to reproachers significantly influence the extent to which accounts are honoured (i.e. mitigating accounts result in more honouring).

A recent set of studies by Holtgraves (1989) found support for the mitigation–aggravation (or a 'justification–excuse–concession') dimension. Holtgraves had students sort 15 accounts (for instance, excuse – denial of intention, excuse – denial of volition, etc.) on the basis of similarity and found that a single dimension was adequate to account for the dissimilarity/similarity ratings (involving five categories or clusters of messages): *concession, excuse – denial of intention, excuse – denial of volition, justification – blame others*, and *justification – minimize harm* (the challenge/refusal category was not included). Next, Holtgraves gave students scenarios (for instance, a person is one and a half hours late to pick up his close friend for a concert, and it is too late to go), and had them rate the adequacy of seven types of accounts and hybrids of accounts: *full-blown apology* (involving an apology plus self-castigation plus restitution), *apology only* (a 'perfunctory' statement of being sorry), *regret, regret plus excuse, excuse, regret plus justification*, and *justification* ('It's not that big a deal; it wasn't going to be a good concert anyway.'). The students rated the accounts on the basis of *hearer satisfaction* (how satisfying it would be to the receiver to hear the type of account), *difficulty* (how difficult it would be for the accounter to communicate the particular type of account; apologies, for example, are satisfying to hear but often difficult to give), *helpfulness* (the extent to which the account would be helpful in solving the problem), and *likelihood of use* by the accounter in the context.

Holtgraves (1989) found that justifications were perceived as the least satisfying, followed by regret plus justification, excuse, regret, apology, regret plus excuse, and full-blown apology. Perceived helpfulness ratings indicated that justifications were rated lowest, followed by regret plus justification, excuse, regret, regret plus excuse, apology, and full-blown apology. Ratings of perceived difficulty paralleled the results of satisfaction and helpfulness, and the two forms of justifications were rated significantly *less* likely to be used than the other five accounts. Holtgraves concluded that apologies and excuses were more mitigating than justifications; however a perfunctory apology ('I am sorry') was rated as less satisfying than regret plus an excuse. Sometimes simply saying one is sorry is not sufficient.

Reciprocity effects, as noted earlier, occur when a blunt or less polite form of questioning (the reproach) results in a less polite account being offered, or, when polite and mitigating reproaches lead to mitigating accounts. We have used the term 'interactional constraint' to denote the situation in which speaker A's turn operates to constrain speaker B's freedom to use the full range of message responses he or she would normally have available. Our earlier studies (see Cody and McLaughlin, 1985) provide more support for the reciprocity effect for *aggravating actions*; for example, a projected refusal ('Don't try to deny it!') would be likely to lead to a justification or a refusal ('You have no right to accuse me!'), which might then lead to a reinstatement of the reproach and a protracted conflict sequence.

Some studies on the account sequence have examined how reproaches are phrased (as hostile, angry, derogatory), or have studied specific forms of reproaches. Our first study (McLaughlin *et al.*, 1983a) was based on retrospective reports of students; *reproaches* were coded into one of six categories:

(1) *Implicit reproach or silence.* 'I drove across a dead-end median so I wouldn't have to drive around and was waiting for traffic to pass so I could get on the street. A patrolman pulled me over so I got out. *He asked for my licence and that was all he said.*'
(2) *Behavioural cues.* 'The attendant kept shaking his head while he looked under the hood of my car. *His negative and disgusted reactions made me flubber and stumble with why I did not attend to my car regularly.*'
(3) *Projected concessions.* 'My grandparents and my younger brother came to campus from Greenwood to bring me items from home, and when they arrived on campus, I wasn't home. When I got back, my grandmother said, *"Well, it sure was nice of you to have us come down so you could be gallivanting all over the country."* '
(4) *Projected excuse.* 'My husband said, "Where the hell have you been? *Did you forget to wind your watch again?*" '
(5) *Projected justification.* 'She [my girlfriend] said, *"I suppose you're going to try and tell me it was just a joke."*'
(6) *Projected refusal.* 'The theatre owner . . . began degrading me for what he felt were inaccurate doorman reports . . . *"Now, why haven't you been filling these out with the truth?"* he said. *"You can't lie to me."*'

With respect to categories like *projected excuses*, *projected justifications*, etc., we argued that some forms of projected reproaches are more mitigating (projected excuses), while some are more aggravating (projected refusals), and that a particular form of reproach will elicit a matching level of account. Accounts in the McLaughlin *et al.* (1983a) study were coded into mutually exclusive types: *silence*, *concession*, *excuse*, *justification*, and *refusal*. The results provided modest support for the reciprocity principle: mitigating accounts generally were preceded by mitigating reproaches; aggravating accounts usually followed on the heels of aggravating reproaches.

In a study of what drivers say to traffic patrolmen, we found that patrolmen use only three basic types of reproaches:

(1) *projected excuse* ('Don't you know the speed limit here?');
(2) *projected justification* ('Is there some emergency?');
(3) *simple statement* of the putative offence ('I clocked you going 78 mph back there.').

Officers using the projected justification were likely to elicit a justification

('Well . . . , I am late for work.'), and officers who simply stated the nature of the offence (or who were rated as hostile and unfriendly) elicited *refusals* or complaints ('No, no. That's not right!'). However, projected excuses were not significantly related to the offering of excuses: rather, they were followed by any number of accounts (see Cody and McLaughlin, 1985).

In a third study (McLaughlin *et al.*, 1983b), participants met their partners for the first time as pairs of conversationalists engaged in a self-disclosure task, and were given a list of topics (Berger, 1973) which they could or could not use as needed in a 30-minute 'getting-acquainted' conversation. Conversations were transcribed and the transcripts searched for examples of account sequences. 'Offences' that emerged in conversations among strangers included:

(1) *taste/attitude/belief* offences, such as having doubts about religion or not liking science;
(2) *personal identity* offences, such as being a heavy drinker, a procrastinator, etc.;
(3) *work/school* offences, such as working for a female boss, working for minimum wage, or not having a major;
(4) *interaction* offences (here-and-now interaction problems, such as asking stupid questions, not listening, interrupting, yawning, etc.).

There were four types of reproaches:

(1) *surprise/disgust* ('You're a *male* secretary!?');
(2) *moral/intellectual superiority* ('I have enough problems of my own without getting all involved in some little fictional problem.');
(3) *direct request* for account ('Why would you want to live there?');
(4) *direct rebuke* ('You're prejudiced!').

We expected that a direct rebuke or assertion of moral/intellectual superiority would be more aggravating (likely to lead to a defensive account) than a direct request for an account.

Following reproaches were one of five forms of accounts, plus a 'silence/doesn't account' category for accounters who simply remained silent or switched topics. The five forms of accounts included *concession*, *excuse*, *refusal*, and *justification*. Four ways of evaluating accounts included:

(1) *honouring* ('That sounds good to me.');
(2) *retreating* (partial honouring, or making excuses for the other's behaviour, such as 'Yeah, I'm really tired, too.');
(3) *reject/take issue/restate reproach*;
(4) *dropping the issue/switching topics*.

We anticipated that more mitigating account forms would be met with honouring or retreating, while aggravating accounts would be more likely to be met with rejection or reiteration of the reproach.

Generally, predictions of congruent levels of mitigation/aggravation between steps in the account sequence were supported. Aggravating account forms like refusals were elicited by aggravating reproach forms (direct rebuke, moral/intellec-tual superiority), and were often followed by restatements of the reproach. Excuses were likely to be honoured, and concessions were often followed by a retreat by the reproacher. However, mitigating reproaches were not more likely to lead to mitigating accounts. As a general rule, politeness (see Chapter 10, by Tracy) in mitigating accounts led to honouring (primarily, excuses were honoured), but attempts were made quietly to ignore interactional mistakes (yawning, interrupting), and actors believed they did not need to account for matters of taste and preference. Nonetheless, some support was obtained for reciprocity in both reproach–account and account–evaluation segments of the sequence.

Schönbach and Kleibaumhuter (1989) asked respondents to imagine a scenario in which a child (who was in their care) sneaked into the kitchen, drank from a bottle of cleaning fluid, and had to be taken to hospital. Parents' reproaches were varied:

(1) *neutral question* (asking for an explanation);
(2) *derogation of self-esteem* ('How could that have happened to you? Apparently, you were occupied too much with yourself!?');
(3) *derogation of sense of control* ('Why haven't you been able to prevent this? We wouldn't have thought that you would lose sight so easily!').

Schönbach and Kleibaumhuter found that the neutral question elicited more conces-sionary statements than either of the derogating reproaches, with the derogation of the actor's sense of control producing the fewest concessionary statements. Each type of question produced the same number of excuses, but both the derogation con-ditions produced more justifications and refusals than the neutral condition.

It is tempting to conclude that the mitigation–aggravation continuum and re-ciprocity principle are generally valid outcomes of accounts given in *interpersonal settings*. However, in more formal contexts, reproachers may need to exert control over the interaction for legal or other responsibilities. The reproacher who is a judge or parole officer may assign little weight to a mere apology or to a single excuse, but *expect* to hear a number of components in an 'ideal' account (see next section). Also, a reproacher who is a medical doctor or nurse will respond very differently to the patient who failed to take medicine as directed. For example, Dindia and Steele (1987) assessed account sequences in health-care settings (involving hypertensive patients), and they found that: aggravating accounts were associated with aggravat-ing evaluations; aggravating evaluations (e.g. restating the reproach) led to ag-gravating second accounts; and mitigating evaluations (honouring or retreating) tended to be followed by mitigating second accounts (thus supporting notions of affective reciprocity for the last part of the sequence – the account–evaluation relationship). However, they found no relationship between the clinicians' *reproach* type and the clients' subsequent accounts, and no tendency for mitigating accounts to be followed by honouring or by the clinicians retreating from the original reproach. Clearly, however, one wouldn't expect research findings based on interpersonal settings like a friend's failing to be prompt for a concert to generalize to health-care settings in which patients are being monitored for a life-threatening illness. If a patient has not taken necessary precautions since the last appointment, it is unlikely that the patient will match the level of aggravation in the clinician's reproach (if the clinician initiates the account sequence in an aggravating reproach), and, if the patient does communicate an aggravating account, it is part of the clinician's role and responsibility to counter-argue or use aggravating evaluations.

EFFECTIVENESS OF ACCOUNTS

Interpersonal Settings

The distribution of types of accounts and the evaluation of accounts differ substantially between interpersonal settings and more formal ones, such as legal and organizational conflicts. As a general rule, in interpersonal settings, apologies and excuses should be more mitigating and polite, and are more likely to result in honouring than are justifications and refusals. Also, as noted above, Holtgraves (in press) found that a full-blown apology, an excuse plus regret, and an apology were rated higher in likelihood of solving the problem than other accounts. There are a number of studies that have found that apologies or statements of regret are important determinants of honouring. Mehrabian (1967) found that an apology can reduce a person's negative feelings if the person has been left waiting for an appointment. Another important study, although not dealing with *effectiveness per se*, found that even young children know that, if an offence has occurred (bumping into a person in a cafeteria line), an apology should be given, and that, as the severity (of this type of offence) increases (the victim falls down), increased penitence or restitution should be offered (Darby and Schlenker, 1982; Schlenker and Darby, 1981). Further, Blumstein *et al.* (1974) constructed a number of scenarios in which different offences had occurred (missing an important meeting, failing to bring home a birthday cake, and so forth), and manipulated types of accounts offered. Their results indicated that people were more likely to honour an account and forgive the offender if the accounter was repentant, seemed unlikely to repeat the offence, was not totally responsible for the offence, had high moral worth, had higher relative status, and committed a less severe offence.

One area in which apologies are both common and effective is the area of embarrassment. Cupach, Metts, and Hazleton (1986) examined coping with two types of embarrassing situations (loss of poise – an actor spilled gravy on himself or herself at dinner with friends – and an improper identity – an actor forgot his or her chequebook after the sales clerk had rung up the groceries). In the first study, apologies were rated more appropriate in both types of situations, whereas excuses and justifications were rated higher in appropriateness in the improper-identity situation than in the event concerning loss of poise. Further, since the improper-identity situation was probably more aggravating (the situation entailed greater possible negative implications for the other actor(s) and for the continuation of the episode, compared to the loss of poise event, in which the actor's friends were likely to sympathize with him or her), all strategies were rated as *less* satisfying in the improper-identity situation than in the event concerning loss of poise. Justifications were rated least preferred and more inappropriate than other tactics, even more so than avoidance.

In the second study, only three (of 86) respondents wrote that they would use justifications; most indicated they would use apologies, escape, humour, remediation (directly solve the problem causing the embarrassment), or a mere description (recount why they had not taken their chequebook with them). The preferred sequence of tactics during the loss of poise event involved escape, followed by an apology and then by humour, and the preferred sequence for improper identity was apology followed by description and remediation. Other studies on embarrassment also indicate that apologies, restitution, and remediational work (to solve the problem) are common, while excuses and justifications are less common (see Cupach et al., 1986; Petronio, 1984; Semin and Manstead, 1983).

Weiner et al. (1987) conducted four studies on excuses (they did not distinguish between apologies, excuses, and justifications), and found that excuses varied substantially in terms of mitigation and quality. In their first study, students were asked to recall and describe events in which they failed to do something expected of them, to write the reason given (true or false), and to indicate the evaluation of and consequences of the communicated reason. True reasons communicated for failure events included transportation problems, work or school commitments, other (personal) commitments, physical ailments, negligence, preference ('I just didn't want to do it'), and miscellaneous (10% of the reasons). Most of the *withheld* reasons, however, dealt with preference (53%) and negligence (28%) – accounters did not want to admit that they simply preferred not to fulfil social obligations, or (obviously) that they were negligent.

According to Weiner and his colleagues (Weiner, 1985; Weiner and Handel, 1985; Weiner et al., 1987), excuses vary in terms of four underlying dimensions:

(1) *intention* ('I was in a hurry to get home because it was dark and it was a high crime area.', compared to 'I didn't mean to spin my wheels and burn rubber when I accelerated.';

(2) *controllability* ('I ran out of gas' is certainly more controllable than 'The Dodgers game let out early because of the rain, and I unexpectedly got stuck in traffic.');

(3) *stability* ('The traffic was bad, as usual, at LAX'*, compared to 'A truck jack-knifed on the 405 [freeway] . . .');

(4) *locus of control* (internal ('I don't want to go') versus external ('My car was hit in my driveway by a hit-and-run driver and I can't go because I have to wait for the insurance adjuster.')).

Accounters know implicitly that good excuses are ones in which the reasons given include external, unstable, uncontrollable, and unintentional causes. Weiner et al. (1987) found that virtually all communicated reasons involved *unstable causes* and that withheld reasons were internal, controllable, and intentional ('I did not want to go') or internal, controllable, and unintentional ('I forgot'). Twelve per cent of all explanations were viewed suspiciously by receivers, mostly ones that were external, controllable, and unintentional (even though half of the explanations that were not

* Los Angeles International Airport.

believed were in fact truthful). Account episodes involving withheld reasons were associated with negative consequences for the relationship, increased responsibility attributed to the accounter, and increased expressed anger on the part of the receiver.

In a second study, Weiner *et al*. (1987) had students rate explanations, and the results indicated that failure events attributed to *preference* and *negligence* were related to angry reactions and to high ratings of internality, controllability, and intentionality. Of the four remaining reasons (*commitment, illness, work/study*, and *transportation*), the *commitment* reason (actually, the higher-involvement form of justification noted above) was rated higher in controllability, internality, and intentionality than other explanations (as one would expect with justifications, compared to excuses).

In the last two studies, Weiner *et al*. (1987) had confederates arrive late for experiments and offer (or fail to offer) explanations to the research partners they kept waiting. The confederates offered a good excuse (external, uncontrollable, unintentional), a bad excuse (internal, controllable, intentional), or no explanation at all (in study four, a fourth group was allowed to use any excuse they preferred – they gave 'good' excuses). Results indicated that those giving excuses were reacted to more positively. They were rated as more congenial and were perceived as having a more likable personality. Similarly accounters who offered good excuses or any excuse they liked were rated as more considerate, friendly, interesting, optimistic, rational, sensitive, and responsible than accounters who used either bad excuses or no excuses. Good excuses were found to evoke less anger, irritation, and dislike than bad excuses or no excuses.

There are two aspects of the work of Weiner and his colleagues that should be emphasized (besides the fact that explanations vary in terms of a set of important underlying factors). First, although they did not study apologies *per se*, excuses that were more mitigating in their study (involving external, uncontrollable, and unintentional reasons) were also found to be the more mitigating forms of excuses in other studies. In Holtgraves' (in press) multidimensional scaling project, the cluster of excuses labelled 'excuse–denial of intention' was perceived as more receiver-oriented and mitigating than other categories ('excuse–denial of volition', and all forms of justifications). Similarly, logical proofs and 'excuse–denial of intention' were observed to be the only two subcategories of accounts given in traffic court that were judged as credible.

A second aspect to be emphasized deals with the motivations actors have for communicating (or fabricating) accounts. Excuses, by definition, are intended to exonerate the giver, and are often viewed primarily in terms of the creation and maintenance of desired impressions (for instance, see Jones and Pittman, 1982; Schlenker, 1980; Tedeschi and Reiss, 1981; see Chapter 10, by Tracy). However, the studies reported in Weiner *et al*. (1987; also Folkes, 1982; Weiner and Handel, 1985) clearly indicates that accounters take into consideration emotions dealing with feelings of possible rejection, disappointment, anger, and so forth. Folkes (1982), for example, found that female college studies were significantly more likely to withhold true reasons for rejecting offers of dates in order to give 'better' reasons. Rejecters were likely to give reasons that were impersonal, uncontrollable, and unstable ('I have to study for finals') as their *public* reasons (64%), while private reasons included impersonal, uncontrollable, and unstable ones (30%), personal, uncontrollable, and stable ones (26%) (the requester was too old), or personal, controllable, and stable (14%) (the requester held incompatible religious views). In fact, 90% of the rejection messages given publicly cited impersonal causes, while only 53% of the private reasons were impersonal. Forty per cent of the true reasons were personal–stable, but only 9% of the causes communicated publicly were of a personal and stable nature. Rejecters clearly desired to avoid communicating negative information (the 'MUM' effect – people's reluctance to communicate negative information), and they desired to avoid anger, negative feelings, or being responsible for making the requester feel rejected.

Few studies have much to say about actors' attempts to *justify* alleged offensive behaviour. Two studies dealing with interpersonal relations which also support the mitigation-honouring relationship were conducted by McLaughlin and her colleagues. The McLaughlin *et al.* (1983a) project on failure events recalled by students indicated that guilt, severity of offence, (rated) importance of being exonerated of blame, and relational indices (intimacy or dominance in the reproacher–accounter relationship) were significantly related to use of accounts. Accounters who felt guilty were more likely to use a concession, while those who expressed little feeling of guilt either were silent or refused to account. More severe offences were associated with more frequent use of mitigating tactics (apologies). Respondents who indicated that being exonerated was an important goal used concessions, while those who rated the goal of securing honouring low were more likely to remain silent or to use justifications. The results also indicated that refusals were more likely to be offered to reproachers who were dominant (parents, professors, police, bosses), whereas justifications were more frequently offered to intimates; the later are more likely (one supposes) to take into consideration the accounter's personal motivations and reasons for engaging in behaviours that might otherwise be characterized as questionable. This project did not deal with honouring *per se*, but clearly demonstrated that accounters who desired honouring used concessions (apologies) and avoided aggravating tactics (justifications and 'silence').

McLaughlin *et al.* 1983b) found that four types of 'offences' were discussed during dyadic conversations among strangers: offences of *personal identity*, *taste/attitude/belief*, *work/school*, and of *interaction*. Accounters were significantly more likely to offer a verbal account for *taste/attitude/belief* offences, but were more likely to remain silent by ignoring the offence or the reproach for offences of *personal identity*, *work/school*, and *interaction* – probably for different reasons. For instance, interaction offences may be so trivial and beyond one's control (yawning) that accounters do not believe an account is warranted, or their occurrence may embarrass the accounter and silence is used as a form of escape. On the other hand, in cases where the reproach is for a *personal identity* ('You are a *male* secretary!?') or *work/school* ('You work for minimum wage?') offence, the alleged 'offence' clearly centres on the accounter's sense of self-worth and definition. In such events, the accounter probably believes that the reproacher has little right to request an account and that he or she is not obligated to offer one. McLaughlin *et al.* (1983b) also found that accounters offered either excuses or refusals for 'offences' involving personal identity and taste/

attitude/beliefs ('You don't like football?'). In this study, excuses resulted in *honouring*, while concessions and justifications resulted in the reproacher's *retreating* (partial honouring), and refusals, justifications, and silence tactics were associated with *reject/take issue/restate reproach*. Thus, while types of offences had a clear impact on the distribution of accounts offered, mitigating accounts resulted in either honouring or partial honouring, and aggravating accounts resulted in aggravating evaluations. The results of projects such as these indicate that social actors provide different types of responses when reproached for qualitatively different types of 'offences', self-concept, matters of taste, etc. It is probably the case that considerably different types of explanations and types of accounts are offered for different types of offences and attributions based on a need to be self-defensive, the deniability of the act in question (i.e. proof of its occurrence), relational implications, and so forth. While the adage 'There is no accounting for taste' may be partially true, we still have no fully developed model or theory of the use or effectiveness of accounts.

Organizational Settings

The few empirical studies on accounts offered in manager–worker dyads (Bies, 1987, in press; Bies and Moag, 1986; Bies and Shapiro, 1987, 1988; Bies, Shapiro, and Cummings, 1988; Mitchell, Green and Wood, 1981; Wood and Mitchell, 1981) suggest that certain additional constraints, such as workers' prior history and fairness in the organization, operate when reproachers evaluate accounts in organizational settings. Wood and Mitchell (1981), for example, conducted two studies on apologies and excuses nurses might offer for errors, such as failing to give medicine. They found that providing an excuse (for example, that a colleague went home sick halfway through the shift, leaving the nurse burdened) resulted in less *personal* responsibility for the error being assigned to the nurse, less agreement that the nurse needed supervision, and fewer punitive responses (compared to the case when an excuse was not provided). In the first study, which used a repeated-measures design, supervisors rated nurses who failed to apologize as more likely to receive punitive disciplinary actions and requiring closer supervision than nurses who did apologize. However, the second study was a between-subjects design and there was no strong support for mitigating effects of apologies – apparently, acts of apology were salient only when compared to accounts in which they were absent. Wood and Mitchell proposed that apologies, as impression-management tactics, should be studied in the larger context of the manager's past experiences with the worker, and the worker's previous work history.

　　Research by Bies and his colleagues focuses on the use of accounts as a means of reducing manager–worker conflict. In several projects, Bies (1987, in press) argues that accounts are fundamentally important to the maintenance of fairness in organizations (specifically, *interactional fairness*), and, further, argues that accounts (or explanations) function to reduce the likelihood of superior–subordinate conflict. Bies (in press) contends that, when managers communicate unfavourable information to workers (for instance, that the manager has decided not to increase the budget for the subordinate's work unit), three variables influence the extent to which workers experience anger and/or desire to retaliate:

(1) the manager's *apparent responsibility* for the decision;
(2) the manager's *motives* for making such a decision;
(3) the *undesirability* of the decision.

Three categories of accounts parallel these factors: *causal, ideological,* and *referential* (Bies, in press). In the first type of explanation, a *causal* account, the manager claims an external cause is to blame for the unfavourable decision, in the hope that he or she will not be held personally responsible for it. For example, the manager may explain that a freeze must be implemented because of a decline in the economy. The second, an *ideological* account, is an explanation in which a manager appeals to beliefs concerning values and goals that organizational members presumably share. He or she may impose a budget freeze and claim that the freeze was ordered to maintain 'competitive superiority' over rivals. Such explanations articulate the manager's motives (shared goals, integrative interests versus mutually exhaustive, distributive interests). In the third category of explanation, a *referential* account, the manager attempts to minimize negative feelings on the part of the workers by offering some positive comparison or referential standard to evaluate the negative information. For example, he may state: 'Your budget will be cut by 5%. But you are better off than the Speech Department. They were cut 20%, and Anthropology was cut 10%. Including such components in the communicated explanation can help to reduce the perceived undesirability of the decision. Bies (in press) further argues that three factors influence the effectiveness of accounts:

(1) the *timing* of the account;
(2) the perceived *adequacy* of the account;
(3) the perceived *sincerity* of the communicator.

In a series of studies, Bies and his colleagues (Bies and Shapiro, 1987; Bies *et al.*, 1988) confirmed that the adequacy of a causal account and perceived sincerity are in fact significant factors in honouring and avoiding conflict. Bies and Shapiro (Study I) found that respondents exposed to scenarios describing a manager as *unintentionally* appearing to take credit for workers' ideas rated the manager as behaving more fairly, and gave him or her higher ratings of approval, than did respondents who had not read the description denying intention. In Study II, respondents read scenarios in which a manager reduced the budget of a work unit. Half read a scenario that offered no causal account; the others read that the reduction in budget was attributed to declining orders because of sagging economic conditions (causes that are uncontrollable and external). Respondents who rated communicated explanations as more 'adequate' were more likely to regard the treatment as fair, and gave the manager higher approval ratings. In a third study, Bies and Shapiro surveyed advanced MBA students on their reactions to employment rejections. The *adequacy* of justifications for not being hired was significantly related to fairness and approval ratings, and affective reactions.

Using survey data, Bies *et al.* (1988) assessed how managers provided explanations to workers when refusing the subordinates' requests, and how subordinates reacted to the explanations. Subordinates made requests of a diverse nature (i.e. requests for equipment; for changes in departmental policy, organizational procedures, and product design; and requests for changes in job or task assignment). Seven categories of refusing the requests were identified: no reason given, political environment, upper management's (probable) refusal, subordinate's own behaviour or lack of preparation/planning, formal company policy, budget constraints, and company norms. The three rated highest in *adequacy* involved company norms, budget constraints, and formal company policy – three external, impersonal, and uncontrollable reasons. Besides the 'no reason given' category, the 'upper management' and 'political environment' claims were rated extremely low in adequacy, presumably because they are difficult to verify, simply reflect the manager's opinion, may seem irrelevant to the requests workers are making, and do not invoke causes beyond the control of the social actors (i.e. budgets, norms, and policies cannot be changed or controlled, but managers should be able to influence upper managers and the political environment). Bies *et al.* (1988) found that the adequacy of the account and the manager's perceived sincerity were significantly related to outcomes: subordinates expressed less anger, were less likely to disapprove of the manager, were less likely to bypass the manager by complaining to others in higher-status positions, and rated injustice lower (than in the case of inadequate claims or insincere messages).

Similar to the research of Blumstein *et al.* (1974), Bies's work indicates that the accounter's sincerity, truthfulness, moral worth, and/or credibility is strongly related to honouring in organizational settings. Further, adequacy of explanations is critically important, and the examples used by Bies and Shapiro (1987) (as well as the results of Bies *et al.*, 1988) suggest an implicit use of Weiner's (see, for example, Weiner *et al.*, 1987) dimensions of external, uncontrollable, and impersonal causes – and provide support for the claim that these dimensions are related to mitigation and honouring.

Legal Settings (see also Chapter 26, by Danet)

A survey of 156 drivers was briefly reported by Cody and McLaughlin (1985), and the results indicated that apologies and admissions of guilt (often subsumed into the same category of 'concessions' in earlier studies) provoked different outcomes when communicated to traffic officers. Apologies, or, more precisely, apologies plus excuses (since no traffic 'offender' *merely* offered a perfunctory apology), excuses and, in descending order, justifications resulted in more honouring than refusals and admissions of guilt (which resulted in almost 100% ticketing). Traffic officers must make a decision to ticket a person on the basis of severity of the offence, amount of evidence, and credibility of mitigating circumstances. Hence, the driver who apologizes as well as offering an excuse (presumably one specifying causes that are not internal, but which are unstable, uncontrollable, and unintentional) is more likely to communicate a desired image in the eyes of the officer – that is, that the driver did not mean to do it, is sorry that it occurred, would not have engaged in the behaviour if he or she could have avoided it, and will not engage in the behaviour in the future. Excuses ranked second in terms of credibility, followed by justifications. However, different subcategories of excuses (denial of intention) and justifications (medical emergencies, the 'worse things could have happened' was not more successful than logical proofs) carried more weight than other arguments.

Once in traffic court, however, offering apologies or just looking apologetic carried little weight (Cody and McLaughlin, 1988). Cody and McLaughlin found that only logical proofs (logic; letters of complaints filed at the county office; work orders from the city's office of public works; witnesses not known to, or affiliated with, the driver) were credible, with excuses following a distant second. Both of the projects on traffic violations would have provided more information about credibility of arguments if they had coded each account in terms of Weiner's (see, for example, Weiner *et al.*, 1987) underlying dimensions. In all of their studies, they have found that excuses are far more common than all other forms of accounts, and they have presented results for the undifferentiated global category of 'excuses', although excuses vary widely on a number of criteria. In fact, they referred to both excuses and justifications as 'utility' categories that are large indeed and often unrelated to specific reproach forms (Cody and McLaughlin, 1985). Both should be studied in terms of either subcategories of *types* (denial of intent, denial of volition, denial of injury, etc.) or clusters of types based on underlying factors (the unstable, uncontrollable, impersonal, extent dimensions).

McLaughlin, Cody, and French (1989) were interested in the differential effect that conventional accounting forms have on attributions made about the accounter's *moral character*. They proposed that availability of an acceptable account for a given course of action is often a crucial determinant of an actor's decision to choose a morally dispreferred or unlawful path, as opposed to following the straight and narrow. They argued that, in order to construct such accounts, actors need to have a knowledge base consisting of: (a) abstract moral principles; (b) situational determinants of the evaluation of conduct; (c) conventional accounting schemata; and (d) constraints which affect the way an account can be fashioned in interaction, including possible goals it might activate in the recipient (see McLaughlin *et al.*, 1989). McLaughlin and her colleagues further assumed that account recipients also function as account constructors, and that the knowledge required to construct accounts is also the knowledge required to comprehend and interpret them.

McLaughlin *et al.* (1989) developed a number of hypotheses about the conventional accounting forms and the attributions to which they might give rise. For example, they expected that dispositional attributions of the causes of the traffic offence would be greatest when the defendant used excuses and justifications, inasmuch as such arguments focus attention on character traits, motives, and values which might be used to explain questionable conduct. It was not anticipated that excuses and justifications would differ with respect to relieving the defendant of blame, inasmuch as Schultz and Wright (1985) have reported that, for harmful outcomes, persons are held responsible for their actions equally whether the actions are intentional or merely result from negligence. Thus, the excuse 'I was worried, and distracted, and I didn't realize how fast I was driving' should do no more to help the defendant avoid blame than 'I was in a hurry to get there before they closed'.

McLaughlin *et al.* (1989) selected 20 of the defendant accounts collected by Cody and McLaughlin (1988), choosing two accounts from each of the account categories (excluding concessions, and admissions of guilt) for two of the most common offences (speeding and running a red light). A total of 176 respondents (college students) rated the severity of the offence prior to reading each account, wrote open-ended essays on the topic 'your impression of the defendant', and evaluated each of the accounts on rating scales measuring the likelihood that the defendant was penalized, the extent to which the defendant was personally responsible for the failure event, etc. Although specific findings varied across offence types, it was clear that impressions of a defendant's moral responsibility for a traffic offence varied as a function of the type of account given. Often, the respondents' assessment of moral responsibility seemed to coincide with the court's. For example, Cody and McLaughlin found that 91% of the defendants using challenges and justifications received penalties from the court. McLaughlin *et al.* (1989) found that justification was rated as highest in likelihood of receiving a penalty in the 'speeding' data, and challenge received a similar assessment in the 'red-light' data.

Justification produced the highest attribution of the offence to the defendant's personal traits across both offence types. Justification produced the strongest attributions of intentional wrongdoing in the speeding data, while challenge fared similarly in the evaluations of accounts for running a red light. For the cases involving speeding, excuse produced the greatest attribution of the offence to 'circumstances' (that is, the environment caused the behaviour), and both excuse and justification were highly (and about equally) likely to result in the defendant being blamed for the offence. The latter findings did not hold for the 'red-light' data, however. It is likely that speeding, regardless of account given, produces more dispositional causal attributions than running a red light; it is easy to know when one is exceeding the speed limit, but it is often difficult to anticipate when a light will turn red and stop on time even if driving at a speed at or below the posted limit (Weiner's controllability factor; see, for example Weiner *et al.*, 1987).

A number of projects have investigated causal explanations or accounts for crimes more serious than traffic violations (Carroll and Payne, 1977; Felson and Ribner, 1981; Henderson and Hewstone, 1984; Riordan, Marlin, and Kellogg, 1983; Rothman and Gandossy, 1982). Carroll and Payne (1977) studied the impact of alleged causes of criminal actions (internal, stable, and intentional versus external, unstable, and unintentional) on perceptions of responsibility, severity of offence, sentencing, and the like. They did not assess the criminals' *communicated* account (apology, etc.). Carroll and Payne obtained support for predictions of attribution theory: crime caused by *internal* reasons led to more negative affect (higher ratings of severity, responsibility, punishments, and prison terms); *stable* long-term causes resulted in longer prison terms and higher ratings of responsibility; *internal–stable* causes led to higher ratings of criminality and responsibility than did external or unstable causes; and *internal–intentional* causes led to higher ratings of responsibility than did external or unintentional causes. Intentionality was the strongest predictor of judgments of responsibility for the crime. Students also assigned longer prison terms when both severity of offence and risk of recidivism were high, but experts assigned longer prison terms only when severity of the offence was high.

Felson and Ribner (1981) interviewed male prisoners who were convicted of serious crimes (felonious assault, manslaughter, etc.), and associated their communicated explanations for the crime with characteristics of the incident. While any number of studies on accounts in interpersonal settings indicated that most accounts that were communicated were excuses, Felson and Ribner found that over 50% of the accounts involved justifications. Seventeen per cent of explanations were *denials of wrongdoing*, 14% were mere *admissions of guilt*, 11.5% were *legal excuses* (appeals to accidents), 7% *other excuses*, 25.5% *legal justifications* (self-defence), and 25% were *other justifications*. Their results indicated that the types of accounts offered were occasionally self-defensive or 'strategic', and that only one type of account was related to length of sentence. The authors found that:

(1) legal excuses were more likely to be offered when the victim died, and when fewer physical blows were used when hitting the victim;
(2) excuses were more likely to be offered when the victim was female, whereas self-defence justifications were more likely to be offered if the victim was male;
(3) offenders denied engaging in the crime, refused to admit guilt, and used fewer legal excuses when the victim survived.

To assess the effect of type of account on sentencing, all communicated explanations were dichotomized into *denial of guilt* and *no denial of guilt*. Felson and Ribner found that denial interacted with type of charge in affecting sentencing. For murder and for first-degree assault cases, denial of guilt was associated with harsher minimum sentences (an additional 5.56 years for murder, 4.35 years for first-degree assault, compared to cases in which the criminal did not attempt to deny guilt) and harsher maximum sentences (13.40 and 8.64 years, respectively). Type of account communicated did not have an effect on sentencing for manslaughter and second-degree assault. For certain types of violent crime, then, denying guilt was perceived as quite aggravating.

Having been convicted of a serious crime, offenders used more arguments involving justifications than excuses. Since justifications can serve the function of defending the self-concept by casting a negative act in a more positive light, offenders appealed to self-defence and (negative) reciprocity. Further, the details or realities of a case strongly influenced the type of explanation communicated: males can rarely claim they committed violence against a female in self-defence, and it is implausible that a criminal 'accidentally' hit a victim *repeatedly*. It is also to the advantage of the criminal to claim low personal causation (excuse) if the victim dies.

Riordan *et al.* (1983) assessed students' reactions to hypothesized scenarios in which a US senator was described as soliciting prostitution or accepting bribes. Justification for the action ('I accepted the bribe because at the time I was doing my own investigation of bribery in Washington, DC') had predictable effects on minimizing the perceived wrongness of the act, and an excuse (the lobbyist was described as having gotten the senator drunk before the senator was given the money) was successful in exonerating the accused of personal responsibility. Also, there was some evidence that the senator's character was perceived *less* negatively when he offered an excuse than when he offered a justification. Offences were also judged more severely if the offences were related to work, as opposed to unrelated to work.

Riordan *et al.* (1983) found that type of communicated account had little impact on punishments. However, they only assessed excuses and justifications. Also, the Riordan *et al.* (1983) and Felson and Ribner (1981) studies neither assessed accounts in terms of underlying factors (i.e. external–uncontrollable–unintentional–unstable versus internal–controllable–intentional–stable), nor examined hybrids, multiple arguments (i.e. excuse plus apology), or conjunctive explanations (see below).

Henderson and Hewstone (1984) interviewed 44 violent offenders on 226 incidents of violence and found that external explanations were popular, as well as justifications (which accounted for 69% of the explanations). Justifications were particularly likely to be used if the victim was perceived as responsible for the crime, or when the criminal claimed that the situation was responsible for the occurrence of the act. Other findings indicated that:

(1) when third parties were present, attributions that the situation caused the crime increased and there were lower attributions assigned to victims, and less personal responsibility;
(2) excuses were more likely to be offered when the victim died (it is, as noted above, harder to justify (publicly) death);
(3) there were some effects due to relational qualities.

When the target was familiar or intimate, more victim-attribution causes were cited, while more situation-attribution causes were cited when the victim was a stranger or an authority figure. Finally, when the offender was himself hurt in the criminal act, more excuses were used and fewer justifications (compared to when the offender was not hurt). Since equity theory indicates that observers use being 'hurt in the action' in their calculations of fairness and possibly when sentencing, it is strategically in the best interest of an injured criminal to rely on a less aggravating tactic (excuse versus justification).

Relying on data collected by the Yale Law School/Law Enforcement Assistance Administration programme on the sentencing of white-collar offenders, Rothman and Gandossy (1982) focused on cases of bank embezzlement, credit and lending institution fraud, and securities violations. According to Rothman and Gandossy, judges who were interviewed in this project indicated that certain components of communicated explanations were important in the sentencing decision. The first two were 'universally recognized as important constituents of an effective explanation' (Rothman and Gandossy, 1982, p. 458): acknowledgement of moral and legal guilt, and assumption of personal responsibility. Two other ingredients included: (a) remorse ('statements which express contrition for the act itself, or which apologize to the victims of the crime, are thought superior to those that simply reveal sorrow for personal misfortunes stemming from the defendant's conviction' (p. 458)); and (b) justification for the defendant's behaviour; that is, defendants who provide 'good reasons' that led to their engaging in the crime are more favourably viewed than criminals who offer no explanation.

Rothman and Gandossy (1982) found that women's accounts more fully conformed to the judicial priorities, or ideal form of account. Women acknowledged personal responsibility more than men, more frequently provided justifications than men (i.e. living in marginal financial circumstances, need to feed and clothe children, and so forth), and women were more likely to apologize/express remorse for the conduct *per se* (rather than express regret for the personal consequences of having been caught). Accounts, according to Rothman and Gandossy, affected the evaluation of the defendant made by the probation officer, and these evaluations were found to affect significantly the severity of the sanction the defendant actually received. It pays to provide a characterization of self and offence that confirms to the judge's ideals of relevant components.

FUTURE RESEARCH

Given the work to date on effectiveness of accounts, we envision that future work will first provide additional information concerning the role of accounts in specific types of settings (family, friends, bureaucrats, organizations, legal, and medical), and that this research will assess how reproach–account–evaluation sequences are fashioned, given various types of 'offences'. However, little effort has been given to grounding the accounting process in a larger context, for example, in moral judgment and a theory of understanding. A logical place to begin that enterprise is in the theory of knowledge structures (Abelson and Lalljee, 1988; Leddo and Abelson, 1988; Read, 1987; Schank and Abelson, 1977; see also Chapter 1, by McCann and Higgins, and Chapter 21, by Fitzpatrick). Leddo and Abelson (1988) have argued against the notion that specialized structures and processes are required to account for the way people explain events: 'Explanation may . . . be conceived as a special case of the general process of understanding. The same knowledge structures used in understanding ought to be implicated in explanation' (p. 103).

To be sure, the process of explaining oneself to others involves a great deal more than simply coming to understand an event; conversational constraints, relational history, the prospect of evaluation, and other factors shape the process by which accounts unfold in interaction. But we believe, by and large, causal schemata, such as explanation prototypes (Abelson and Lalljee, 1988), play a far more important role in the process of interpersonal accounting than has been acknowledged heretofore. As Abelson and Lalljee argue, explanation prototypes, '*organized around ways that important but not totally controllable outcomes can occur*' (p. 185), are widely shared in Western culture, and are available as resources (places to go to find explanations) for parties to failed events. (For example, for the event 'stuck in traffic', the explanation-prototype set might contain RUSH-HOUR, HOLIDAY, ACCIDENT, CON-STRUCTION WORK, etc.). Most contemporary research on accounting has failed to factor in the causal schemata available to the account recipient (that is, what causal factors he or she would regard as plausible) and also the accounter's own view of the kind of causal scenario of the failure event that the offended party might construct.

One sort of failure event as we have described it in this chapter calls for the offending party to provide what attribution theorists have referred to as *contrastive explanation*: 'the individual must account for departure of an event from what might normally be expected' (Leddo and Abelson, 1986, p. 106). If the failed performance of a critical event is compared against the expected or prototypical performance of the event or one similar to it, an explanation for the failure may be constructed from the stereotyped sequence of actions (the script) associated with successful performance. An explanation for the failure event could be located in *goal failure* (goal absence, goal conflict, goal reversal, goal satisfaction, goal dissolution; Abelson and Lalljee, 1989), or, less likely, in *planning failure* (plan arrangement failure, plan consummation failure; Leddo and Abelson, 1986, p. 122), *execution failure*, or *interference*. Thus, in accounting for his failure to retrieve his wife's dress from the cleaners, an offending spouse could construct (and predict that his wife might construct) an explanation from goal failure (he only had time to go to the market or the cleaners, and they needed groceries more), a planning failure (he neglected to take the claim check), an execution failure (the dress wasn't ready), or interference (someone took his wife's cleaning order by mistake). As Read (1987) notes, also associated with scripts are *preconditions* that must be satisfied before scripts can be performed, and *initiating conditions* which give rise to the goal; an account could also be constructed from claims that preconditions were not met (he went to the cleaners on Tuesday when the claim check was for a Thursday pick-up) or that an original initiating condition no longer held (he thought she no longer needed the dress right away).

Leddo and Abelson (1986, p. 119) report that in terms of the sequence of actions in a script (preparation, entry, precondition, instrumental precondition, instrumental activation, instrumental actualization, doing, postcondition and exit), respondents are much more likely to attribute failure to the 'entry' and 'doing' steps than other steps. All other things being equal, the husband's failure to retrieve the dress is more likely to be attributed to the cleaner's being closed (an entry failure) or to the order's not being ready (a doing failure) than to, say, postcondition (the dress fell in a puddle) or instrumental precondition (the line was too long) failures. (We propose this as a model of accounting behaviour, in the abstract, and leave aside for the moment such issues as whether or not a particular explanation is true, whether it can be sustained, what the offender's 'account history' is *vis-à-vis* the reproacher (the cleaners can't be 'closed every' time), and so forth.)

Before closing, it is important to note that an adequate account of knowledge structures for explaining conduct must include among the knowledge components abstract moral principles and propositions about the situated evaluation of conduct. We have dealt at length elsewhere with Backman's (1985) notion of the account in the process of decision-making (McLaughlin *et al.*, 1989). Backman argues that most persons, when faced with a choice of action, the preferred one of which is prohibited by convention or morally disfavoured, will 'attempt to negotiate a definition of the situation . . . to blunt the effects of anticipated censure from self and others, either by reducing the strength of the rules operating in the situation or by providing a basis for accounts or explanations of the rule violation that excuse, justify or disguise the nature of the act' (Backman, 1985, p. 268). As Shaver (1985) notes in his study of the attribution of blame, different event descriptions lead to different attributions; disagreements about causation are often disagreements about the definition of the event taking place. If no plausible account or suitable 'situation definition' can be constructed, a person contemplating a morally dispreferred course may decide to abandon it.

Reducing 'the strength of rules' operating on the evaluation of conduct requires that an accounter have a knowledge of what Backman (1985) has called 'deep moral structure', in which concepts like 'fairness', 'need', 'justice', 'merit', and 'responsibility' are prominent. With respect to such concepts, however, Kurtines (1986) has demonstrated that the application of moral principles like *justice*, *benevolence*, and *pragmatism* is situationally determined, and that individuals vary in their preference for moral rule schemes. Similar conclusions were reached by Haan (1986).

There is extensive literature on moral judgments and responsibility attribution in social psychology (see, for example, Darley and Zanna, 1982; Finchem, 1985; Hamilton, 1978; Hamilton, Blumenfeld, and Kushler, 1988; Schultz and Wright, 1985). Schultz and Wright (1985), for instance, have demonstrated that the valence of an outcome (harmful versus beneficial) affects the way responsibility is assigned, such that (a) more responsibility is assigned for negligent harm than for negligent benefit, and (b) with respect to rewards and punishments, intentional and negligent harm are punished equally, and negligent and accidental benefits are equally rewarded. Hamilton *et al.* (1988) found that, even in children, there was a trend to be more sensitive to the presence of 'excusing conditions' (conditions which increase the probability of negative outcomes, or which make the actor's contribution to positive outcomes more remarkable) when the actions were harmful 'bad deeds' rather than good.

Finally, early research in accounting processes seems to have implicitly assumed that one type of account, an excuse or a justification, would be offered. However, for serious offences (white-collar crime), effective accounting requires more than a single tactic. The study of multiple excuses or justifications, as in the offering of conjunctive explanations (Abelson, Leddo, and Gross, 1987; Leddo, Abelson, and Gross, 1984; Read, 1987), is certainly in order.

REFERENCES

Abelson, R.P. and Lalljee, M. (1988). Knowledge structures and causal explanation. In D. Hilton (Ed.), *Contemporary science and natural explanation: Commonsense conceptions of causality*, pp. 175–203. London: Harvester Press.

Abelson, R.P., Leddo, J., and Gross, P.H. (1977). The strength of conjunctive explanations. *Personality and Social Psychology Bulletin*, **13**, 141–155.

Antaki, C. (1981). *The psychology of ordinary explanations of social behaviour*. London: Academic Press.

Antaki, C. (1988). *Analysing everyday explanation: A casebook of methods*. London: Sage.

Backman, C.W. (1985). Identity, self presentation, and the resolution of moral dilemmas: Towards a social psychological theory of moral behavior. In B.R. Schlenker (Ed.), *The self and social life*, pp. 261–289. New York: McGraw-Hill.

Berger, C.R. (1973). The acquaintance process revisited: Explorations in initial interaction. Paper presented at the Annual Meeting of the Speech Communication Association, December 1973, New York.

Bettman, J.R. and Weitz, B.A. (1983). Attributions in the board room: Causal reasoning in corporate annual reports. *Administrative Science Quarterly*, **28**, 165–183.

Bies, R.J. (1987). The predicament of injustice: The management of moral outrage. In L.L. Cummings and B.M. Staw (Eds), *Research in organizational behavior*, Vol. 9, pp. 289–319. Greenwich, CT: JAI Press.

Bies, R.J. (in press). Managing conflict before it happens: The role of accounts. In M.A. Rahim (Ed.), *Managing conflict: An interdisciplinary approach*. New York: Praeger.

Bies, R.J. and Moag, J.S. (1986). Interactional justice: Communication criteria of fairness. In R.J. Lewicki, B.H. Shepperd, and M.H. Bazerman (Eds), *Research on negotiation in organizations*, pp. 43–55. Greenwich, CT: JAI Press.

Bies, R.J. and Shapiro, D.L. (1987). Interactional fairness judgments: The influence of causal accounts. *Social Justice Research*, **1**, 199–218.

Bies, R.J. and Shapiro, D.L. (1988). Voice and justification: The influence on procedural fairness judgements. *Academy of Management Journal*, **31**, 676–685.

Bies, R.J., Shapiro, D.L., and Cummings, L.L. (1988). Causal accounts and managing organizational conflict: Is it enough to say it's not my fault? *Communication Research*, **15**, 381–399.

Bisanz, G.L. and Rule, B.G. (1989). Children's and adults' comprehension of narratives about persuasion. In M.J. Cody and M.L. McLaughlin (Eds), *The psychology of tactical communication*, pp. 48–69. Clevedon (England): Multilingual Matters.

Blumstein, P.W., Carssow, K.G., Hall, J., Hawkins, B., Hoffman, R., Ishem, E., Maurer, C., Spens, D., Taylor, J., and Zimmerman, D.L. (1974). The honoring of accounts. *American Sociological Review*, **39**, 551–566.

Buttny, R. (1987). Sequence and practical reasoning in accounts episodes. Unpublished paper. Department of Speech Communication, Ithaca College, Ithaca, New York.

Canary, D.J., Cunningham, E.M., and Cody, M.J. (1988). Goal types, gender, and locus of control in managing interpersonal conflict. *Communication Research*, **15**, 426–446.

Carroll, J.S. and Payne, J.W. (1977). Judgments about crime and the criminal: A model and a method for investigating parole decisions. In B.D. Sales (Ed.), *Perspectives in law and psychology*, pp. 191–239. New York: Plenum Press.

Cody, M.J. and McLaughlin, M.L. (1985). Models for the sequential construction of accounting episodes: Situational and interactional constraints on message selection and evaluation. In R.L. Street and J.N. Cappella (Eds), *Sequence and pattern in communicative behaviour*, pp. 50–69. London: Arnold.

Cody, M.J. and McLaughlin, M.L. (1988). Accounts on trial: Oral arguments in traffic court. In C. Antaki (Ed.), *Analysing everyday explanation: A casebook of methods*, pp. 113–126. London: Sage.

Coleman, R.V. (1976). Court control and grievance accounts: Dynamics of traffic court interactions. *Urban Life*, **5**, 165–187.

Cupach, W.R., Metts, S., and Hazleton, V. (1986). Coping with embarrassing predicaments: Remedial strategies and their perceived utility. *Journal of Language and Social Psychology*, **5**, 181–200.

Darby, B.W. and Schlenker, B.R. (1982). Children's reactions to apologies. *Journal of Personality and Social Psychology*, **43**, 742–753.

Darley, J.M. and Zanna, M.P. (1982). Making moral judgments. *American Scientist*, **70**, 515–521.

Dindia, K. and Steele, D.J. (1987). Account sequences in medical encounters. Paper presented at the Annual Meeting of the International Communication Association, May 1987, Boston, MA.

Ditton, J. (1977). Alibis and aliases: Some notes on the 'motives' of fiddling bread salesmen. *Sociology*, **11**, 233–256.

Felson, R.B. and Ribner, S.A. (1981). An attributional approach to accounts and sanctions for criminal violence. *Social Psychology Quarterly*, **44**, 137–142.

Finchem, F.D. (1985). Outcome valence and situational constraints in the responsibility attributions of children and adults. *Social Cognition*, **3**, 218–233.

Folkes, V. (1982). Communicating the reasons for social rejection. *Journal of Experimental Social Psychology*, **18**, 235–252.

Furnham, A. (1982). Why are the poor always with us? Explanation for poverty in Britain. *British Journal of Social Psychology*, **21**, 311–322.

Furnham, A. (1983). Attributions for affluence. *Personality and Individual Differences*, **4**, 31–40.

Furnham, A. (1988). *Lay theories: Everyday understanding of problems in the social sciences.* Oxford: Pergamon.

Goffman, E. (1967). *Interaction ritual.* Garden City, NY: Doubleday Anchor.

Goffman, E. (1971). *Relations in public.* New York: Basic.

Haan, N. (1986). Systematic variability in the quality of moral action, as defined in two formulations. *Journal of Personality and Social Psychology*, **50**, 1271–1284.

Hale, C.L. (1987). A comparison of accounts: When is a failure not a failure? *Journal of Language and Social Psychology*, **6**, 117–132.

Hamilton, V.L. (1978). Who is responsible? Toward a social psychology of responsibility attribution. *Social Psychology*, **41**, 316–328.

Hamilton, V.L., Blumenfeld, P.C., and Kushler, R.H. (1988). A question of standards: Attributions of blame and credit for classroom acts. *Journal of Personality and Social Psychology*, **54**, 34–48.

Harvey, J.H., Turnquist, D.C., and Agostinelli, G. (1988). Identifying attributions in oral and written explanations. In C. Antaki (Ed.), *Analysing everyday explanation: A casebook of methods*, pp. 32–42. London: Sage.

Harvey, J.H., Weber, A.L., Galvin, K.S., Hustzi, H., and Garnick, N. (1986). Attribution and the termination of close relationships: A special focus on the account. In R. Gilmour and S. Duck (Eds), *The emerging field of personal relationships*, pp. 189–201. Hillsdale, NJ: Erlbaum.

Harvey, J.H., Weber, A.L., Yarkin, K.L., and Stewart, B. (1982). An attributional approach to relationship breakdown and dissolution. In S. Duck (Ed.), *Dissolving personal relationships*, pp. 107–126. London: Academic Press.

Henderson, M. and Hewstone, M. (1984). Prison inmates' explanations for interpersonal violence: Accounts and attributions. *Journal of Consulting and Clinical Psychology*, **52**, 789–794.

Holtgraves, T. (1989). The form and function of remedial moves: Reported use, psychological reality, and perceived effectiveness. *Journal of Language and Social Psychology*, **8**, 1–16.

Jackson, S. and Jacobs, S. (1980). Structure of conversational argument: Pragmatic cases for the enthymeme. *Quarterly Journal of Speech*, **66**, 251–265.

Jacobs, S. and Jackson, S. (1979). Collaborative aspects of argument production. Paper presented at the Meeting of the Speech Communication Association, November 1979, San Antonio, Texas.

Jones, E.E. and Pittman, T.S. (1982). Toward a general theory of strategic self-presentation. In J. Suls (Ed.), *Psychological perspectives on the self*, pp. 231–262. Hillsdale, NJ: Erlbaum.

Kurtines, W.M. (1986). Moral behavior as rule governed behavior: Person and situation effects on moral decision making. *Journal of Personality and Social Psychology*, **50**, 784–791.

Labov, W. and Fanshel, D. (1977). *Therapeutic discourse: Psychotherapy as conversation.* New York: Academic Press.

Lau, R.R. (1984). Dynamics of the attribution process. *Journal of Personality and Social Psychology*, **46**, 1017–1028.

Lau, R.R. and Russell, D. (1980). Attributions in the sports pages. *Journal of Personality and Social Psychology*, **39**, 29–38.

Leddo, J. and Abelson, R.P. (1986). The nature of explanation. In J.A. Galambos, R.P. Abelson, and J.B. Black (Eds), *Knowledge structures*, pp. 103–22. Hillsdale, NJ: Erlbaum.

Leddo, J., Abelson, R.P., and Gross, P.H. (1984). Conjunctive explanations: When two reasons are better than one. *Journal of Personality and Social Psychology*, **47**, 933–943.

McCartney, K.A. and Nelson, K. (1981). Children's use of scripts in story recall. *Discourse Processes*, **4**, 59–70.

McClure, C., Mason, J., and Barnitz, J. (1979). An exploratory study of story structure and age effects on children's ability to sequence stories. *Discourse Processes*, **2**, 213–249.

McLaughlin, M.L., Cody, M.J., and French, K. (1989). Account-giving and the attribution of responsibility: Impressions of traffic offenders. In M.J. Cody and M.L. McLaughlin (Eds), *The psychology of tactical communication*, pp. 244–267. Clevedon (England): Multilingual Matters.

McLaughlin, M.L., Cody, M.J., and O'Hair, H.D. (1983a). The management of failure events: Some contextual determinants of accounting behavior. *Human Communication Research*, **9**, 209–224.

McLaughlin, M.L., Cody, M.J., and Rosenstein, N.E. (1983b). Account sequences in conversations between strangers. *Communication Monographs*, **50**, 102–105.

Mehrabian, A. (1967). Substitute for apology: Manipulation of cognitions to reduce negative attitude toward self. *Psychological Reports*, **20**, 687–692.

Mitchell, T.R., Green, S.G., and Wood, R. (1981). An attributional model of leadership and the poor performing subordinate. In L.L. Cummings and B.M. Staw (Eds), *Research in organizational behaviour*, Vol. 3, pp. 151–198. Greenwich, CN: Aijai Press.

Morris, G.H. (1985). The remedial episode as a negotiation of rules. In R.L. Street and J.N. Cappella (Eds), *Sequence and pattern in communicative behaviour*, pp. 70–84. London: Arnold.

Petronio, S. (1984). Communication strategies to reduce embarrassment: Differences between men and women. *Western Journal of Speech Communication*, **48**, 28–38.

Read, S.J. (1987). Constructing causal scenarios: A knowledge structure approach to causal reasoning. *Journal of Personality and Social Psychology*, **52**, 288–302.

Remler, J.E. (1978). Some repairs on the notion of repairs in the interest of relevance. *Proceedings of the Chicago Linguistic Society*, **14**, 391–402.

Riordan, C.A., Marlin, N.A., and Kellogg, R.T. (1983). The effectiveness of accounts following transgressions. *Social Psychology Quarterly*, **46**, 213–219.

Rothman, M.L. and Gandossy, R.P. (1982). Sad tales: The accounts of white-collar defendants and the decision to sanction. *Pacific Sociological Review*, **25**, 449–473.

Schank, R.C. and Abelson, R.P. (1977). *Scripts, plans, goals, and understanding*. Hillsdale, NJ: Erlbaum.

Schlenker, B.R. (1980). *Impression management*. New York: Brooks/Cole.

Schlenker, B.R. and Darby, B.W. (1981). The use of apologies in social predicaments. *Social Psychology Quarterly*, **44**, 271–278.

Schönbach, P. (1980). A category system for account phases. *European Journal of Social Psychology*, **10**, 195–200.

Schönbach, P. (1985). A taxonomy for account phases: Revised, explained and applied. Unpublished manuscript, Fakultat fur Psychologie, Ruhr-Universitat, Bochum, West Germany.

Schönbach, P. (1986). A theory of conflict escalation in account episodes. Unpublished manuscript, Fakultat fur Psychologie, Ruhr-Universitat, Bochum, West Germany.

Schönbach, P. and Kleibaumhuter, P. (1989). Severity of reproach and defensiveness of accounts. In M.J. Cody and M.L. McLaughlin (Eds), *The psychology of tactical communication*, pp. 229–243. Clevedon (England): Multilingual Matters.

Schultz, T.R. and Wright, K. (1985). Concepts of negligence and intention in the assignment of moral responsibility. *Canadian Journal of Behavioural Science*, **17**, 97–108.

Scott, M.B. and Lyman, S.M. (1968). Accounts. *American Sociological Review*, **33**, 46–62.

Semin, G.R. and Manstead, A.S.R. (1983). *The accountability of conduct: A social psychological analysis*. London: Academic Press.

Shaver, K.G. (1985). *The attribution of blame: Causality, responsibility, and blameworthiness*. New York: Springer-Verlag.

Shields, N.M. (1979). Accounts and other interpersonal strategies in a credibility detracting context. *Pacific Sociological Review*, **22**, 180–200.

Snyder, C.R. and Higgins, R.L. (1989). Reality negotiation and excuse-making: President Reagan's March 4, 1987 Iran Arms Speech and other literature. In M.J. Cody and M.L. McLaughlin (Eds), *The psychology of tactical communication*, pp. 207–228. Clevedon (England): Multilingual Matters.

Snyder, C.R., Higgins, R.L., and Stucky, R.J. (1983). *Excuses: Masquerades in search of grace*. New York: Wiley/Interscience.

Sykes, G.M. and Matza, D. (1957). Techniques of neutralization. *American Sociological Review*, **22**, 644–670.

Tedeschi, J. and Riess, M. (1981). Verbal strategies in impression management. In Antaki, C. (Ed.), *The psychology of ordinary explanations of social behaviour*, pp. 156–187. New York: Academic Press.

Weber, A.L., Harvey, H.L., and Stanley, M.A. (in press). The nature and motivations of accounts for failed relationships. In R. Burnett, P. McGhee, and D. Clark (Eds), *Accounting for relationships*. London: Methuen.

Weiner, B. (1985). An attributional theory of achievement motivation and emotion. *Psychological Review*, **92**, 548–573.

Weiner, B., Amirkhan, J., Folkes, V.S. and Verette, J. (1987). An attributional analysis of excuse giving: Studies of a naive theory of emotion. *Journal of Personality and Social Psychology*, **52**, 316–324.

Weiner, B. and Handel, S.J. (1985). A cognition–emotion–action sequence: Anticipated emotional consequences of causal attributions and reported communication strategy. *Developmental Psychology*, **21**, 102–107.

Wood, R.E. and Mitchell, T.R. (1981). Manager behaviour in a social context: The impact of impression management on attributions and disciplinary actions. *Organizational Behaviour and Human Performance*, **28**, 356–378.

12

Language and Deception

HOWARD S. FRIEDMAN AND JOAN S. TUCKER
Department of Psychology, University of California, USA

Rarely a day goes by when people do not engage in some sort of deceptive interaction. Indeed, deception seems to be a staple in our communication repertoire, relied upon to carry us through many different types of social encounters. Deception may facilitate pragmatic communication, protect the feelings of others, or serve a larger social purpose. For example, when answering the question, 'Hi, how are you?', people do not respond with the truth, the whole truth, and nothing but the truth. Similarly, most people learn that it is not always socially appropriate to say what is on their minds. And adults do not cry every time they feel sad or grin every time they feel happy. They hide their true thoughts and feelings and thus deceive others. Goffman called this 'face work' (Goffman, 1963; see Chapter 9, by Holtgraves, and Chapter 10, by Tracy). But these omissions and embellishments, while most certainly a form of deception, are usually more innocuous than sinister. Many deceptions and so-called 'white lies' are required by society's rules of social etiquette. On the other hand, many types of deception are not socially acceptable and may lead to harmful consequences for the deceived, the deceiver, or both. In the extreme, deception may be a part of manipulation, cheating, or fraud. In short, deception should not be narrowly conceptualized. It appears in many different situations, and for many different reasons.

In many social interactions, there is relatively little motivation to deceive successfully or for the perceiver to detect the deception. It does not matter much if the store clerk really does not want us to have a good day. As the stakes for deception go up, however, both the deceiver and detector will be more motivated to outwit the other. The deceiver must be able not only to give a convincing speech, but to present it in a style that the detector finds convincing and sincere. The detector, on the other hand, must not merely take the speaker's words at face value, but must attend to the subtleties of the speech and the non-verbal behavioral cues which accompany it, attempting to interpret accurately those which are indicative of deception. Thus both *verbal* (word) cues of veracity or plausibility, and *non-verbal* cues of deception or emotion are key elements of deceptive interchanges (see Chapter 7, by Cappella and Palmer).

Deception and detection are abilities which stem from the possession of certain basic communication skills. Skills in expressing or 'encoding' certain verbal and non-verbal behaviors while controlling others, as well as skills in perceiving or 'decoding' the verbal and non-verbal behaviors of others, seem to underlie deception and detection success. Some of this encoding and decoding ability is natural and spontaneous, but some is practiced and controlled. People differ markedly in their general communicative skills, and thus in their deception and detection abilities. Although deception is common in everyday social interaction, some unskilled individuals look deceptive when truth-telling and deceptive when deceiving. Other, more skilled, people look truthful when deceiving, and they look truthful when truth-telling. Note that this analysis differs from the assumption that people look honest when truth-telling and deceptive when deceiving. Analogously, some detectors are accurate, but some see deception when there is none, or miss real deception. In other words, deception skills are part of more general social skills. This skill approach provides a scientific and useful framework for understanding the outcomes of many social encounters (Friedman, 1979).

ACCURACY LEVELS

Given the amount of practice people presumably have in detecting deception, is it the case that people are generally accurate detectors? Many people certainly think that they can tell when they are being lied to. This question has interested deception researchers for many years. At first glance, it seems as if skilled detectors should be able to detect deception. But skilled deceivers are trying to mislead them! On the other hand, it is not so easy to be a successful deceiver if you are being watched by skilled detectors. So it is not surprising that detection accuracy in research typically falls in the modest range of 45% to 60%, with 50% accuracy being expected by chance (Kraut, 1980; see also Ekman, 1985). Most people can detect deception, but only at slightly above-chance levels. Or, from the other perspective, people can deceive, but only sometimes. As we will see, deceivers do not always give off cues of their deception, and detectors may make errors in judging which cues provide valid information.

Interesting questions that thus arise concern those individual factors that make successful deception more or less likely and those cues that are valid or invalid indicators of deception. Furthermore, how does the situation influence the behavior of the deceiver and the judgments made by the detector?

PERCEIVED AND ACTUAL CUES TO DECEPTION

There is often a discrepancy between the verbal and non-verbal cues which are *perceived* to be indicative of deception and the cues which are *actually* indicative of deception. When entering into social interactions, individuals bring with them naive theories about which cues are associated with deception. When asked which behaviors they believe to be clues to deception, people cite increased speech hesitations, high pitch, speech errors, speech latency, postural shifts, decreased speech rate, averted gaze, and increased smiling (see DePaulo, Stone, and Lassiter, 1985b; Zuckerman, Koestner, and Driver, 1981b).

However, research has found that these verbal and non-verbal cues are often not shown by deceivers during deceptive interactions. As we will see, informative behavioral cues displayed by deceivers are usually a function of the particular demands of the attempted deception. For example, if the deception causes the deceiver to become aroused, then signs of arousal such as raised pitch, pupil dilation, and increased use of adaptors (such as self-touching) may be more apparent in deceivers than truth-tellers. The challenge of generating a deceptive message may be reflected in message discrepancies, increased planning time, irrelevant information, speech hesitations, and decreased response length. Negative emotions felt by deceivers may be manifested in less immediate and more negative statements, as well as negative non-verbal cues (DePaulo *et al.*, 1985b; deTurck and Miller, 1985). Assuming that detectors are actually using the cues which they perceive (report) to be associated with the deception, the only clearly valid behaviors to which they are accurately attending are the paralinguistic cues of speech hesitations, raised pitch, and speech errors (see Chapter 6, by Street). But the validity of even these cues depends on certain assumptions.

Cues which seem to be indicative of deception in one study are found not to be so in another, and cues which seem to be utilized by one group of detectors are seemingly not attended to by others (sometimes rightly and sometimes wrongly). To resolve these matters, a more general approach must be taken. What follows is a comprehensive model of deception we have developed, which may help in understanding why these inconsistencies exist in the deception literature. It is based in part on the insightful work of Bella DePaulo, Robert Rosenthal, and Miron Zuckerman.

A MODEL OF DECEPTION

The deceptive communication process may be conceptualized in a model comprising three components (see Figure 12.1). On the left-hand side of the model is the component consisting of the deceiver and what may be termed 'input factors'. These input factors are situational and individual differences that influence the deceiver, affecting the deceiver's behavior. On the right-hand side of the model is the component consisting of the detector and 'detection factors'. Mediating the two sides of the model are the deceiver's behavioral cues: the expressive display engaged in during the deception.

Many studies deal simply with the center part of the model – what verbal and

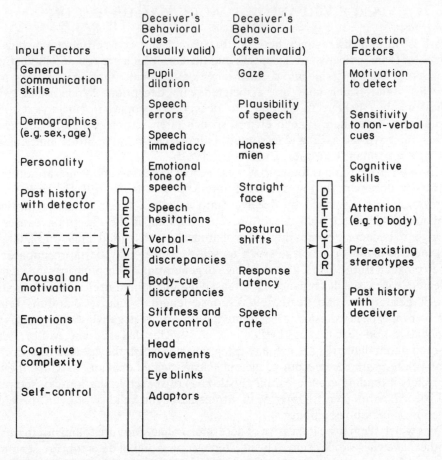

FIGURE 12.1   A model of deception.

non-verbal behaviors are associated with actual deception and which are perceived to be associated with deception. Fewer studies include input factors in the model, such as the deceiver's skill, motivation, and emotional state. Fewer still study influences on the detector, such as detection skill, attention, motivation, and cognitive decoding processes. Yet it is these factors which may qualify or moderate the relationships between behavioral cues and actual or perceived deception. It is also these factors which must be accounted for if one is to model accurately the subjects' typical social experiences (Funder, 1987).

Input Factors

Zuckerman, DePaulo, and Rosenthal (1981a) and others have described four basic input factors which influence the deceiver's behavior during a deceptive interaction. These factors are: the level of the deceiver's arousal; the cognitive complexity involved in generating the deceptive message; the emotions felt by the deceiver; and the self-control and self-monitoring of the deceiver. Note also that these four factors may have a differential impact, depending on the deceiver's personality, general communication skills, demographic characteristics, and past history with the detector.

Level of arousal seems to influence behavioral displays in various situations such as those involving deception, persuasion, or public performance. Linked to arousal is motivation; a highly motivated communicator will tend to have increased arousal. Deception research itself differs dramatically from study to study in terms of the level of arousal or motivation induced in the subjects. At the lowest level, studies eliciting relatively little arousal or motivation will ask subjects to tell an innocuous lie (about their occupation, for example) with little or no consequence for being caught (Geizer, Rarick, and Soldow, 1977). At the other end of the continuum are situations which seem to elicit a great deal of arousal or motivation, such as those in which subjects are 'set up' to engage in socially unacceptable behavior such as cheating and then are led to lie about their behavior in order to cover up their deed (e.g. Siegman and Reynolds, 1983). It would not be surprising that the behaviors engaged in by subjects across these two, and other, situations might differ as a function of arousal and motivation. It is important to note, however, that cues of arousal during deception might also be aroused in a *non-deceptive* situation involving performance anxiety.

From the work on non-verbal leakage which originated with Ekman and Friesen (1969), it is known that individuals are generally more successful in controlling certain aspects of their presentation than others. For example, the verbal content of a message and facial expressions are relatively easy to control, whereas paralanguage and body cues often 'leak' information indicative of deception (Ekman and Friesen, 1974; see also DePaulo and Rosenthal, 1979). The ability to control these various channels without appearing unnatural, however, may depend on the deceiver's level of arousal and motivation.

The unmotivated deceiver will not be careful in planning a lie since it does not really matter whether he or she is caught. Likewise, the deceiver is not apt to try to control his or her behavioral cues. On the other hand, relatively little information indicative of deception would be expected to 'leak' through the deceiver's non-verbal behaviors since the deceiver is not aroused. In other words, the deceiver will appear natural. As a result, the detector might find more behaviors indicative of deception in the verbal content of the deception than in non-verbal behaviors. When the deceiver is highly motivated to deceive, greater care will be taken in formulating the lie and controlling behavior, but the greater arousal in this situation may be evident in the deceiver's non-verbal behaviors: there may be 'leakage' of cues associated with deception, or the deceiver will try to overcontrol the body movements, resulting in a stiff appearance. In this case, the detector may be more successful if attending to the non-verbal behaviors of the deceiver.

Support for this analysis comes from DePaulo and her colleagues, who have found that deception is detected more from verbal cues when motivation is low and from non-verbal cues when motivation is high (see DePaulo, Lanier, and Davis, 1983; DePaulo, Stone, and Lassiter, 1985a; DePaulo et al., 1985b). Verbal cues such as irrelevant information and speech errors are associated with deception under low levels of motivation, but are not associated with deception when deceivers are highly motivated. Under high levels of motivation, deceivers tend to overcontrol their non-verbal behaviors and may appear stiff and unnatural to the detector. Specifically, highly motivated deceivers engage in less blinking, head movements, and postural shifts when deceiving. The arousal stemming from this high level of motivation is evident in the greater pupil dilation and higher voice frequency found in motivated liars (Zuckerman, *et al.*, 1981a).

The second input factor affecting the deceiver's behavior involves cognitive complexity. It is frequently more difficult cognitively to make up a lie than it is simply to tell the truth. Cognitive complexity in deceptive communication also differs markedly across studies. Little cognitive complexity is involved when subjects are provided with the deceptive messages to be presented (Hocking and Leathers, 1980), with a script to fall back on if necessary, or if the lie is simply a short answer like 'No, I didn't.' In most studies, however, the deceivers are required to generate their own deceptive responses, which may include rather involved, elaborate deceptions (e.g. Manstead, Wagner, and McDonald, 1984; Riggio and Friedman, 1983; Stiff and Miller, 1986). Furthermore, since it is more cognitively taxing to generate a lie spontaneously than to plan it, spontaneous lies should be easier to detect (Littlepage and Pineault, 1985).

Cognitive complexity should affect behavior by increasing the incidence of misstatements, increasing hesitation in speech, reducing speech fluency, decreasing gaze, increasing latency of response, and similarly affecting correlates of thinking. However, there is as yet rather weak support for this line of analysis (Zuckerman *et al.*, 1981a), with increased speech hesitations being one clear indicator of deception.

A third factor affecting how people behave when attempting to deceive involves the emotion the deceiver experiences during the deception. Two feelings, guilt and fear, are most readily associated with the act of deception (e.g. Ekman, 1980; Knapp, Hart, and Dennis, 1974; Kraut, 1980). Guilt may stem from an individual's upbringing which has taught him or her that lying is a wrongful and immoral act. Fear may stem from prior experiences which have taught the individual that punishment will follow if the lie is detected. The third affect, termed 'duping delight' (Ekman, 1980), is the feeling of elation which comes from successfully deceiving another.

These cues of emotion may then show up in facial expressions, voice tones, and body movements (see Chapter 2, by Winton). The expression of these emotions will usually be inappropriate to the given context and so indicate deception. For example, a mediocre salesperson might smile inappropriately at the closing of a sale, thus sending doubts through the buyer. Because they are indirect clues to deception, cues arising from leakage of emotion are sometimes distinguished from the 'cues of deception' that actually directly indicate deception. However, various cues of deception may be more apt to occur when one is experiencing an emotion while deceiving (Ekman, Friesen, and O'Sullivan, 1988). It should also be noted that proper communication of emotion is important to the general establishment of honesty. For example, a speaker who expresses true condolences at a funeral or congratulations at a wedding may be (erroneously) seen as deceptive if the speaker is introverted and unexpressive and does not seem to be feeling the expected feelings.

A fourth input factor involves the deceiver's success in attempting to control his or her behavior. There are large individual differences in self-control, self-monitoring, and acting abilities. A successful deceiver will control his or her behavior in such a way as to mask the clues to deception. If the individual uses too little control, then nervous behaviors, arousal, or inappropriate emotion will be displayed and the deceiver will probably be detected. If the individual's behavior is too controlled, however, he or she will probably be detected due to appearing too stiff, asynchronous, and unnatural.

Other factors such as personality and demographic characteristics (see Figure 12.1) will have an impact on the deception process, but only indirectly. For example, an individual with a rebellious nature, viewed with a skeptical eye in general, may be more likely to be suspected of deception than a straight-laced conservative. Likewise, adolescents with long hair or shaven heads may be suspected more than the elderly, males more than females, or politicians more than librarians. These suspicions are generally unfounded overgeneralizations, of course, since individuals with particular personality or demographic traits are not inherently more truthful or deceptive across the board. These characteristics do, however, affect the deceiver's overall appearance, perhaps leading to particular judgments of deceptiveness.

Detection Factors

Just as various factors affect the behaviors shown by a deceiver, so too various other factors affect the success of the perceiver or detector in correctly detecting deception. One important factor involves attention. As stated previously, certain verbal and non-verbal behaviors are more easily controlled than others, and so detectors aware of this will focus on 'leakier' channels when trying to detect deception (Ekman, 1985; Ekman and Friesen, 1969). It is relatively easy for detectors to learn to watch the deceiver's hands and feet, and to listen carefully to the voice.

A second detection factor involves the sensitivity of the detector to non-verbal cues. Some people are better able to read non-verbal cues and so might be better detectors of deception. For example, women are better decoders of non-verbal cues than are men (Hall, 1984). However, there is also evidence that women may not always apply this skill in order that they may not come to 'know too much' (Rosenthal and DePaulo, 1979). The spouse who suspects infidelity may choose, consciously or unconsciously, not to look too closely for deception cues.

A third factor influencing detection concerns the cognitive processing mechanisms employed by the detector. On the molecular level of behavioral cues, the detector cannot usually combine these cues in a simple fashion to form a general impression. Rather, the observer must use some more complex weighting and combination process. This process has not yet been identified, although it is clear that some subtleties (perhaps cue inconsistency) can be detected (DePaulo and Rosenthal, 1979; Riggio and Friedman, 1986). On a more molar level, the detector may choose to rely on cognitive strategies such as second-guessing in order to determine the truthfulness of a message (Hewes, Graham, Doelger, and Pavitt, 1985).

The detector's pre-existing stereotypes and past history with the deceiver will also influence the detector's judgments. For example, the detector may believe that certain 'types' or groups of people are generally untrustworthy and should be suspected of deception. Past history with the deceiver may lead the detector to assume that the deceiver is especially dishonest or perhaps especially honest. Or, the detector may notice some idiosyncratic behavior that has in the past been associated with the deceiver's lying. These stereotypes or predispositions on the part of the detector are biases that the detector brings to the general situation; they may or may not override the more immediate, situation-specific influences. Unfortunately, there is relatively little research in these areas.

A SKILLS APPROACH TO UNDERSTANDING THE DECEPTION PROCESS

As stated in the opening of this chaper, the abilities to deceive and to detect deception are abilities which presumably develop through practice in our everyday social interactions. The ability to deceive involves being able to successfully portray and control the verbal and non-verbal components of the deceptive message. But there is more.

Deception ability also involves the skill of being able to 'read' other people and interpret the *feedback* that they are providing. For example, a perceiver who is doubting the truthfulness of the message and a perceiver who is being successfully deceived will provide the deceiver with different sorts of feedback. The skilled deceiver should be able to modify his or her behavior depending on the feedback received. Deception is an ongoing process.

In terms of developing skill at deceiving versus detecting deception, the deceiver is at an advantage. Rarely does the detector receive immediate feedback regarding the accuracy of the detection (DePaulo, *et al.*, 1985b). If feedback is available, it is delayed and often only suggestive. As a result, the detector may not be able to form associations between certain behavioral cues and accurate detection (DePaulo and Pfeifer, 1986). Further, while the ability to deceive may be viewed as a necessary skill for social success (some have even viewed it as biologically adaptive), it is less clear that the ability to detect deception is always useful. In many cases, more problems are created than solved when we are able to determine that an individual is deceptive. In other cases, we may actively avoid making this judgment, preferring not to know the other individual's devious intentions. These pressures presumably help keep overall detection accuracy near chance levels.

Our general approach to studying the deception process, which views deceiving and detecting as abilities stemming from the possession of certain basic communication skills, makes intuitive sense. One might wonder why litle research has considered the influence of communication skills on the deception process. The answer is that viewing expressive communication from a skill perspective is a relatively new approach in the area of social interaction. Only in the last decade or so have relevant measures of expressive abilities been developed, allowing deception researchers more easily and validly to explore the links between communication skills, verbal and non-verbal behavioral cues, and actual and perceived deception ability.

The remainder of this chaper will be devoted to discussing the research relating skill measures to various facets of the deception process. At this early stage of investigation, trying to synthesize such a new and virtually untapped area may not only be futile, but actually do more harm than good. Very few studies have approached the deception process from a skill perspective and there is little conceptual or methodological consistency among the studies which have been done. Consequently, the results from these studies are inconclusive and can only be put into perspective as more work – both replications and extensions of what has been done thus far – is conducted. It is therefore our intent in this section to illustrate how these skill measures can be useful in conceptualizing and studying the deception process.

Skills and Deception

The Self-Monitoring Scale (SMS; Snyder, 1974, 1987) measures an individual's ability to observe others, and then regulate and control his or her own behavior in social interactions (see Chapter 1, by McCann and Higgins). High self-monitors are thought to be able to adapt to any social situation by modifying their behavior in order to fit into an appropriate role. Factor analysis of the SMS has revealed that the skill of self-monitoring actually comprises three different and more basic qualities: extraversion, other-directedness, and acting ability (Briggs, Cheek, and Buss, 1980; Riggio and Friedman, 1982; see also Chapter 4, by Furnham).

High self-monitors are expected to be successful deceivers due to their ability to regulate their own behavior – that is, because of their good performance ability and good self-control. If successful deception involves the ability to avoid and control the cues associated with deception, then high self-monitors should be less detectable than their low self-monitoring counterparts. High self-monitors, or at least those individuals scoring highly on the dimension of other-directedness, should be good detectors of deception as well. While other-directedness is generally the self-monitor's ability to assess the social situation in order appropriately to modify his or her behavior, in a deception situation it may serve as a skill which allows the self-monitor to attend to certain deception cues which would largely pass unnoticed by the average detector.

While various studies have found high self-monitors to be more successful deceivers and detectors than low self-monitors, Zuckerman et al. (1981a) concluded in their review of the literature that these advantages were not statistically reliable. The multidimensionality of the SMS may account for these inconsistencies. The acting and extraversion dimensions of the SMS are more theoretically related to deception ability than other-directedness, while the last skill is more related to detection success.

Since the Zuckerman et al. (1981a) review, several studies have begun investigating the relationship between the three SMS dimensions and deception ability. Individuals scoring highly on the SMS dimensions of extraversion and acting have been found to engage in significantly different levels of nervous behaviors when deceptive than when truthful (Riggio and Friedman, 1983) and are more successful deceivers when involved in unfeigned lies (Siegman and Reynolds, 1983). It has been proposed that extraverted individuals, as measured by the SMS, are more successful deceivers due to their overall honest demeanor (Riggio, Tucker, and Throckmorton, 1987). But the role of other-directedness in detection ability has not been studied. Although future research on self-monitoring ability should continue paying special attention to the relationship between deception and the separate SMS dimensions, situational factors should be considered as well. Situational variables (such as the opportunity to rehearse the lie (Miller, deTurck, and Kalbfleisch, 1983) or whether the lie is feigned or genuine (Siegman and Reynolds, 1983)) may be interacting with self-monitoring ability to affect deception success.

The Affective Communication Test (ACT; Friedman, Prince, Riggio, and DiMatteo, 1980), a measure of spontaneous non-verbal expressive ability, reflects a communication skill that might be indirectly relevant to deceptive situations. Non-verbal expressiveness can be thought of as dramatic flair. Individuals scoring highly on the ACT are generally enthusiastic and bubbly, but seem to lack control over their emotions. While having the ability to express their emotions accurately and with ease, they tend (unlike high self-monitors) not to be concerned with displaying socially appropriate behavior (Friedman et al., 1980). As a result, expressive individuals, scoring highly on the ACT, may not be successful deceivers due to the lack of control they have over their emotions. In fact, any affect experienced by the expressive individual during deception (for example, the previously mentioned 'duping delight') should be readily apparent to the detector. Consistent with this analysis, there is no evidence to suggest that these charismatic, expressive individuals, as measured by the ACT, are successful deceivers (Riggio and Friedman, 1983; Riggio et al., 1987). However, it may be the case that these highly expressive individuals have a generally honest demeanor which makes them appear truthful despite some intended deceptions.

The Social Skills Inventory (SSI; Riggio, 1986) measures six basic communication skills. Specifically, this instrument measures skills in sending, receiving, and controlling communication in the verbal (social) and non-verbal (emotional) domains. Individuals who are highly socially skilled should possess proportionate levels of skill in each of these six areas. The skills of particular relevance to deception ability are those involving control over communication. Emotional control should be a necessary component of deception since it involves the ability to manage and regulate one's non-verbal behavior. Social control, or role-playing ability, would allow the deceiver to present himself or herself in a manner which would be perceived as trustworthy by others. Analogously, individuals scoring highly on the scales of emotional and social sensitivity have the potential to be good detectors of deception. These individuals would have the ability to 'read' the verbal and non-verbal communication of others.

As expected, individuals skilled in the areas of social control have been found to be successful deceivers (Riggio, et al., 1987). The success of these individuals seems to be due to their appearing truthful regardless of whether they are lying or truth-telling. It is presently unclear what characteristics account for the honest demeanor of socially controlled individuals; it could be due (as hypothesized) to their superior ability appropriately to manage and regulate their behavioral display or it could be due to more indirect factors. The single study relating the emotional control subscale of the SSI to deception ability found no relationship between these two skills (Riggio et al., 1987). This study, however, did not use an emotionally arousing deception task and, as a result, did not require the deceivers to control their emotions in order to lie successfully.

The Profile of Non-verbal Sensitivity (PONS; Rosenthal, Hall, DiMatteo, Rogers, and Archer, 1979) measures the degree to which individuals are sensitive to non-verbal communication in various channels and combinations of channels: face, body, and figure; with and without voice tone. Unlike the previous three measures, the PONS is not a paper-and-pencil measure, but actually requires subjects to view scenes involving non-verbal behavior and identify correctly the content of the scene. Thus the subject must be able to interpret the non-verbal communication in order to be successful in this task.

Sensitivity to non-verbal communication and deception detection are two abilities which are theoretically related (cf. DiMatteo, Friedman, and Taranta, 1979). Particular communication channels (Ekman and Friesen, 1969, 1974) and particular behavioral cues (Zuckerman et al., 1981a) will provide more accurate information about deceptiveness than others. Those individuals sensitive to the more informative channels and cues will detect deception with greater accuracy. For example, individuals specifically instructed to pay attention to an informative channel, like tone of voice, are better able to distinguish truth from deception than individuals not given this information (DePaulo, Lassiter, and Stone, 1982). While very little research has investigated the relationship between the PONS and detection accuracy (e.g. Littlepage, McKinnie, and Pineault, 1983), the success which has been obtained in training individuals to be more sensitive to the deceptions and to the non-verbal communications of others (Rosenthal et al., 1979; Zuckerman, Koestner, and Alton, 1984) should encourage more research in this area.

CONCLUSIONS

In sum, it is useful to think of deception as part of a constantly negotiated social reality. Deception involves an actor who has various feelings, motivations, expressions, and styles that affect the behavioral cues that he or she gives off to a perceiver. The perceiver, in turn, uses various perceptual and cognitive processes to draw inferences about the actor and responds to the actor based on these inferences. As the perceiver's responses feed back to the actor, the cycle of communication and reality negotiation continues.

The time has come in the study of deception to move away from the commonly accepted 'lie-detector model' in which it is assumed that a red 'lie' light or a green 'truth' light will go on if we can only find a polygraph that is sensitive enough to 'read' our suspect. This approach ignores the interaction of actors and perceivers and sees deception as a static, simple behavior. However, communication is never a one-way street, and deceptive communication is no exception. It is an active, reactive, and interactive process. Future research, if it is to be representative of actual interactions, needs to account for the effects of communicative give-and-take between deceivers and detectors.

It is sometimes tempting for researchers to try to sidestep the thornier issues by concentrating only on observers' interpretations or 'attributions'. In other words, they may try to determine which cues result in which perceptions about veracity. For example, are shifty eyes seen as deceptive? As we have seen, this approach is only valuable if it is seen as addressing only one part of one issue. The issues of validity must be central – which cues validly indicate deception for which people under which circumstances.

However, a search for validity does not mean a search for a gold standard that is the single true indicator of deception. Although lawyers, judges, and sundry prosecutors may look for such an indicator, we have seen that such a search is hopeless from the start (see also Chapter 26, by Danet).

Just as successful communication through language depends upon a vast set of implicit assumptions, successful and unsuccessful deception depend on a host of variables surrounding any given social encounter. On the other hand, just as language is limited by certain biological and structural constraints, so, too, deception and its detection is defined by certain limits. Although it is true that there are no universal signs of deception and no universally successful deceivers, it is also true that the limits imposed by personality, motivation, and emotion make certain cues by certain people in certain situations more likely to be valid indicators of deception. A skillful, well-trained observer is more likely to detect deception than is an amateur; and, as charlatans of all kinds have proved, some people can deceive most of the people most of the time.

REFERENCES

Briggs, S.R., Cheek, J.M., and Buss, A.H. (1980). An analysis of the Self-Monitoring Scale. *Journal of Personality and Social Psychology*, **38**, 679–686.

DePaulo, B.M., Lanier, K., and Davis,T. (1983). Detecting the deceit of the motivated liar. *Journal of Personality and Social Psychology*, **45**, 1096–1103.

DePaulo, B.M., Lassiter, G.D., and Stone, J.I. (1982). Attentional determinants of success at detecting deception and truth. *Personality and Social Psychology Bulletin*, **8**, 273–279.

DePaulo, B.M. and Pfeifer, R.L. (1986). On-the-job experience and skill at detecting deception. *Journal of Applied Social Psychology*, **16**, 249–267.

DePaulo, B.M. and Rosenthal, R. (1979). Ambivalence, discrepancy, and deception in nonverbal communication. In R. Rosenthal (Ed.), *Skill in nonverbal communication*. Cambridge, MA: Oelgeschlager, Gunn and Hain.

DePaulo, B.M., Stone, J.I., and Lassiter, G.D. (1985a). Telling ingratiating lies: Effects of target sex and target attractiveness on verbal and nonverbal deceptive success. *Journal of Personality and Social Psychology*, **48**, 1191–1203.

DePaulo, B.M., Stone, J.I., and Lassiter, G.D. (1985b). Deceiving and detecting deceit. In B. R. Schlenker (Ed.), *The self and social life*, pp. 323–370. New York: McGraw-Hill.

de Turck, M.A. and Miller, G.R. (1985). Deception and arousal. *Human Communication Research*, **12**, 181–201.

DiMatteo, M.R., Friedman, H.S., and Taranta, A. (1979). Sensitivity to bodily nonverbal communication as a factor in physician–patient rapport. *Journal of Nonverbal Behavior*, **4**, 18–26.

Ekman, P. (1980). Mistakes when deceiving. Paper presented at the conference on the Clever Hans Phenomenon, New York Academy of Sciences, New York.

Ekman, P. (1985). *Telling lies*. New York: Norton.

Ekman, P. and Friesen, W. V. (1969). Nonverbal leakage and clues to deception. *Psychiatry*, **32**, 88–106.

Ekman, P. and Friesen, W.V. (1974). Detecting deception from the body or face. *Journal of Personality and Social Psychology*, **29**, 288–298.

Ekman, P., Friesen, W.V., and O'Sullivan, M. (1988). Smiles when lying. *Journal of Personality and Social Psychology*, **54**, 414–420.

Friedman, H.S. (1979). The concept of skill in nonverbal communication: Implications for understanding social interaction. In R. Rosenthal (Ed.), *Skill in nonverbal communication*. Cambridge, MA: Oelgeschlager, Gunn and Hain.

Friedman, H.S., Prince, L.M., Riggio, R.E., and DiMatteo, M.R. (1980). Understanding and assessing nonverbal expressiveness: The Affective Communication Test. *Journal of Personality and Social Psychology*, **39**, 333–351.

Funder, D.C. (1987). Errors and mistakes: Evaluating the accuracy of social judgment. *Psychological Bulletin*, **101**, 75–90.

Geizer, R.S., Rarick, D.L., and Soldow, G.F. (1977). Deception and judgment accuracy: A study in person perception. *Personality and Social Psychology Bulletin*, **3**, 446–449.

Goffman, E. (1963). *Behavior in public places: Notes on the social organization of gatherings*. New York: Free Press.

Hall, J.A. (1984). *Nonverbal sex differences*. Baltimore, MD: Johns Hopkins University Press.

Hewes, D.E., Graham, M.L., Doelger, J., and Pavitt, C. (1985). 'Second guessing': Message interpretation in social networks. *Human Communication Research*, **11**, 299–334.

Hocking, J.E. and Leathers, D.G. (1980). Nonverbal indicators of deception: A new theoretical perspective. *Communication Monographs*, **47**, 119–131.

Knapp, M.L., Hart, R.P., and Dennis, H.S. (1974). An exploration of deception as a communication construct. *Human Communication Research*, **1**, 15–29.

Kraut, R.E. (1980). Humans as lie-detectors: Some second thoughts. *Journal of Communication*, **30**, 209–216.

Littlepage, G.E., McKinnie, R., and Pineault, M.A. (1983). Relationship between nonverbal sensitivities and detection of deception. *Perceptual and Motor Skills*, **57**, 651–657.

Littlepage, G.E. and Pineault, M.A. (1985). Detection of deception of planned and spontaneous communications. *Journal of Social Psychology*, **125**, 195–201.

Manstead, A.S.R., Wagner, H.L., and MacDonald, C.J. (1984). Face, body, and speech as channels of communication in the detection of deception. *Basic and Applied Social Psychology*, **5**, 317–332.

Miller, G.R., deTurck, M.A, and Kalbfleisch, P.J. (1983). Self-monitoring, rehearsal, and deceptive communication. *Human Communication Research*, **10**, 97–117.

Riggio, R.E. (1986). Assessment of basic social skills. *Journal of Personality and Social Psychology*, **51**, 649–660.

Riggio, R.E. and Friedman, H.S. (1982). The interrelationships of self-monitoring factors, personality traits, and nonverbal social skills. *Journal of Nonverbal Behaviors*, **7**, 33–45.

Riggio, R.E. and Friedman, H.S. (1983). Individual differences and cues to deception. *Journal of Personality and Social Psychology*, **45**, 899–915.

Riggio, R.E. and Friedman, H.S. (1986). Impression formation: The role of expressive behavior. *Journal of Personality and Social Psychology*, **50**, 421–427.

Riggio, R.E., Tucker, J., and Throckmorton, B. (1987). Social skills and deception ability. *Personality and Social Psychology Bulletin*, **13**, 568–577.

Rosenthal, R. and DePaulo, B.M. (1979). Sex differences in accommodation in nonverbal communication. In R. Rosenthal (Ed.), *Skill in nonverbal communication*. Cambridge, MA: Oelgeschlager, Gunn and Hain.

Rosenthal, R., Hall, J.A., DiMatteo, M.R., Rogers, P.L., and Archer, D. (1979). *Sensitivity to nonverbal communication: The PONS Test*. Baltimore, MD: Johns Hopkins University Press.

Siegman, A.W. and Reynolds, M.A. (1983). Self-monitoring and speech in feigned and unfeigned lying. *Journal of Personality and Social Psychology*, **45**, 1325–1333.

Snyder, M. (1974). The self-monitoring of expressive behavior. *Journal of Personality and Social Psychology*, **30**, 526–537.

Snyder, M. (1987). *Public appearances/private realities*. New York: Freeman.

Stiff, J.B. and Miller, G.R. (1986). 'Come to think of it . . .' Interrogative probes, deceptive communication, and deception detection. *Human Communication Research*, **12**, 339–357.

Zuckerman, M., DePaulo, B.M., and Rosenthal, R. (1981a). Verbal and nonverbal communication of deception. *Advances in Experimental Social Psychology*, **14**, 1–59.

Zuckerman, M., Koestner, R., and Alton, A.O. (1984). Learning to detect deception. *Journal of Personality and Social Psychology*, **46**, 519–528.

Zuckerman, M., Koestner, R., and Driver, R. (1981b). Beliefs about cues associated with deception. *Journal of Nonverbal Behavior*, **6**, 105–114.

13

Language and Control

SIK HUNG NG

Department of Psychology, University of Otago, New Zealand

Society is impossible without control, which is communicated through language. Language, like society and control, is dynamic. It not only communicates control passively like a slave-messenger, but also contributes to control in various active ways. Owing to its malleable nature, language is a versatile cultural resource for control:

> Active control through language has become in our times the most devastating form of control, for it works at the source. Language is the extended arm, developed through millennia of evolution, by which our race has managed nature and built cooperative societies. It is material as well as instrument, a vicarious world in which anything can be arranged through verbal plans, then transferred to reality. (Bolinger, 1980, pp. 187–188)

Linguistic controls are seemingly endless in number (e.g. Cook-Gumperz, 1973) and their overview must by necessity be circumscribed in one way or another. For example, Wiemann (1985) has concentrated on conversation, Berger (1985) on interpersonal communication conduct from a social cognitive perspective, Miller (1987) on persuasion, and Giles and Wiemann (1987) have focused on the multiple relationships between language and society.

The present review aims at complementing the reviews above and furthering a heuristic framework that will sensitize us to the pervasiveness of linguistic control. The framework proposes three linguistic control functions, of which the most

---

Handbook of Language and Social Psychology
Edited by H. Giles and W.P. Robinson.   © 1990 John Wiley & Sons Ltd

obvious is the production of attitudinal and/or behavioural changes by persuasive speech, termed here *powerful speech* (see Chapter 3, by Burgoon).

Two other, less obvious, functions can be discerned from the two- and three-dimensional views of power. These views have already been summarized by Ng (1980), and a brief résumé will suffice for the present purpose. Bachrach and Baratz (1962) proposed the two-dimensional view to overcome the limitation of the then-prevalent view, which located power exclusively in the ability of winning a decision favourable to self. They extended the conception of power to include non-decision-making power.

> Of course power is exercised when *A* participates in the making of decisions that affect *B*. But power is also exercised when *A* devotes his energies to creating or reinforcing social and political values and institutional practices that limit the scope of the political process to public consideration of only those issues which are comparatively innocuous to *A*. (Bachrach and Baratz, 1962, p. 948)

Non-decision-making power, like decision-making power, associates power with, and only with, manifest conflict of interests, leaving out yet another power dimension:

> *A* may exercise power over *B* by getting him to do what he does not want to do, but he also exercises power over him by influencing, shaping or determining his very wants. Indeed, is it not the supreme exercise of power to get another or others to have the desire you want them to have? (Lukes, 1974, p. 23)

Non-decision-making power is often used in political (Orwell, 1954) and therapeutic (Greenley, 1973; Rubenstein and Lasswell, 1966) settings, and no less in families. It is reflected in, and facilitated by, certain linguistic forms, the main functions of which are to produce and manipulate information for *misleading* people and *masking* control (see Chapter 12, by Friedman and Tucker). I will call these interrelated functions the linguistic *depoliticization of control*. The third dimension of power is embodied in the desires that people have internalized. In pursuing these desires, people participate in their own control. The linguistic counterpart of the third power dimension is that language (or part of it) is biased against some people (e.g. women), and its mere *routine* use will disadvantage them. This control function will be called the *routinization of control*.

In the pages ahead, I will examine powerful speech and how language facilitates the depoliticization and routinization of control. My discussion will be drawn from the partly overlapping disciplines of social psychology, sociolinguistics, and linguistics. Wherever possible, I will articulate principles of behaviour and point out directions for research.

POWERFUL SPEECH

A powerful speech produces on the audience an intended effect such as attitude change and compliance. I will first examine relatively short, monologue speech, and then longer, interactive speech.

Short Monologue Speech

A powerful short speech, in one or more short sentences, can save lives. Imagine you are an innocent victim of a street-gang brawl, badly wounded as a result. You pick yourself up and look around for help. Not far from you gathers a crowd of bystanders, frightened, petrified, but otherwise physically fit to call an ambulance. Your life depends on such prompt intervention. However, from your knowledge of bystander apathy (Latané and Darley, 1970), you realize that the odds are against you. The bystanders are cognitively confused, and inhibited by diffusion of responsibility (see below). Unless you can trigger one or more of the bystanders to intervene, you will bleed to death before their eyes. Fortunately, your voice is relatively unharmed, and you can still muster a few words before you finally collapse. What would you say to save your life?

'Help! Help!' would not be effective. Neither would 'Help me, please!' A more powerful speech is, 'You, Sir! Call the police. I need an ambulance. Go!' As you say this, you should look this man in the eye, leaving him in no doubt of his specific responsibility. To another bystander, you may say, 'You, Madam – the lady with the red scarf! Get some hankies. My chest is bleeding.' The chances are that your words will transform apathy into active intervention. Lest you think that this is a purely abstract exercise, consider the anecdotal evidence. Richard Cialdini, a social psychologist, actually saved his life after an automobile collision by delivering precisely this sort of powerful speech (Cialdini, 1984, pp. 138–139).

The above scenario illustrates three principles of a powerful short speech. Sociologists William I. Thomas and Florian Znaniecki (1927) have advanced the insight that, when a person subjectively defines a situation as real, then the situation is real in its consequences. An implication of this insight is that bystanders do not necessarily define or perceive the victim's situation in the same way as the victim does. A powerful speech directed from victim to bystanders causes the latter to redefine the situation from the viewpoint of the victim: 'This person is not kidding or dangerous but is in need of urgent medical help.'

The second principle of a powerful speech is targeting. This is important in a crowd situation because each bystander tends to shift the responsibility of helping the victim to fellow bystanders. The resulting diffusion of responsibility discourages any particular bystander from giving the first helping hand (Latané and Darley, 1970). A powerful speech breaks down the diffusion, and targets particular bystanders. Targeting can be thought of as an attempt to individuate, single out, or particularize a person from the crowd (Zimbardo, 1969), and then to refocus this person's sense of pride or identity (see Reicher, 1982) on being able and willing to help the victim. The person no longer hides behind 'Why me?' but defines his or her identity at that moment as one who should be helping.

The third principle, drawn from persuasive communication research (Hovland, Janis, and Kelley, 1953; Jaspars, 1978), is simply that the request for help should be action-specific.

We shall label the three principles *definition of situation*, *targeting*, and *pinpointing action*, respectively. They are basic principles of a powerful speech relevant to emergency situations. Possibly, their relevance is generalizable to other nonemergency situations in which the sole means of influence is also a relatively short speech. It is hard to imagine how a speech that violates one or more of the principles could be effective in these other situations. There are, of course, various additional principles. For example, a request followed by a reason (e.g. '. . . because I am in a rush') is more effective than one without a reason. In situations where the request involves a small favour, even an empty reason is better than none (Langer, Blank, and Chanowitz, 1978). Apparently, the word 'because' can trigger the relevant 'favour-giving script' leading to compliance. Cialdini (1984) likens this to the automatic, fixed-action patterns observed in various infrahuman species. For example, by imitating the 'cheep-cheep' sound of a baby turkey, predators would invariably trigger a warm (but suicidal) embrace from the mother turkey. Cialdini (1984) cites several other speech techniques (e.g. larger-then-smaller-request, foot-in-the-door) to show how these could trigger human responses resembling fixed-action patterns. He labels the underlying general principle *primitive consent for an automatic age*, and warns of its increasing occurrence in a fast-paced, information-laden environment saturated with clever one-liners, 30-second commercials, political plugs, and sales and fundraising techniques.

Another principle, different from, but complementary to, the primitive-consent principle, stresses *cognitive* responses. It is based on attitude-change and persuasion research (see reviews by McGuire, 1985; Petty, Ostrom, and Brock, 1981). Actually, more than one cognitive principle is involved, but only the general underlying idea will be highlighted.

A message, once attended to and received, activates various thoughts in the recipient, some of which support and others which oppose the advocated stance. These thoughts will largely determine the message's persuasiveness (see Chapter 3, by Burgoon). How they do it is the subject of several cognitive theories of attitude change, including information-integration theory (Anderson, 1981), social judgment theory (see Eiser and Stroebe, 1972), balance theory (Heider, 1946), internalization-process theory (Kelman, 1961), and a good part of Ajzen and Fishbein's (1980) theory of reasoned action. A promising attempt at accounting for the diverse, and often contradictory, findings within a single theoretical framework is Petty and Cacioppo's (1985) elaboration-likelihood model. The model posits a central route to persuasion through the thoughtful (though sometimes biased) elaboration of the merit of the message. This mindful route, based on argument processing, is joined by a relatively mindless route based on processing of peripheral cues in the context (e.g. source's physical attractiveness). Both routes can lead to attitude change, but the change resulting from the central route is more enduring, more resistant to counter-persuasion, and a better predictor of behaviour than change resulting from the peripheral route.

The salience of one route over the other depends on ability (e.g. distortion, prior knowledge) and motivational (e.g. personal involvement, forewarning) variables. When these variables favour the central route, elaboration likelihood (argument processing) is high, and attitude change is affected by persuasive argument variables more than peripheral cue variables. Conversely, when elaboration likelihood is low, attitude may be changed by affective cues, or the recipient may attempt to form a reasonable opinion by making an inference about the likely correctness or desirability of a particular attitude through evaluation of cues such as message discrepancy, the recipient's own behaviour, and the characteristics of the source. One implication is that 'strong' arguments are persuasive only when elaboration likelihood is high. When elaboration likelihood is low, arguments serve as a peripheral cue for mindless processing; for example, an increase in the mere number of arguments, regardless of quality, will increase attitude change.

The elaboration-likelihood model, though comprehensive, has not been able to specify qualities that make arguments persuasive. It simply *defines* a strong message as one that generates thoughts favourable to the advocated stance, and a weak message as one that generates unfavourable thoughts. Clearly, a more adequate specification is necessary before the model can sharpen our understanding of the cognitive basis of a powerful message. Some of the plausible qualities of a powerful message are novelty, validity, and relevance (Burnstein, 1982; Vinokur and Burnstein, 1978), assuming, of course, that elaboration likelihood is high. Interestingly, Turner (1987) and Wetherell (1987) have argued that any one set of messages will be received as more persuasive if it comes from an ingroup rather than an outgroup source, and that a persuasive message is simply one which is seen as prototypical of the ingroup norm. This ingroup norm is often (Mackie, 1986), but not always (Ng and Wilson, 1989), extremitized, and may hold the key to intergroup communication and persuasion. Perhaps Petty and Cacioppo would counterargue that Turner and Wetherell's explanation only holds when elaboration likelihood is lowered by salient group membership cues.

Longer, Interactive Speech

Thus far, we have examined five principles relevant to short monologue speeches and messages. We now move on to longer, more interactive speeches to review the linguistic and paralinguistic features of power. Traditionally, this has been the domain of sociolinguists skilful in identifying speech forms in naturalistic settings. Lakoff (1973) observes in her sample that women's speech differs stylistically from men's (see Chapter 17, by Kramarae). The female style is characterized by the frequent use of *intensifiers* (so, very, really), *hedges* (sort of, kind of, you know, I guess, I think), *polite forms* ('Won't you please sit down?'), *rising intonation* (i.e. using rising intonation in declarative statements), and *tag questions* ('I had my glasses off. He was out at third, wasn't he?'). The effect of the frequent use of these features is that impressions of uncertainty, passivity, and ineffectiveness are created. For this reason, the female speech style has been dubbed as 'powerless'. But as Lind and O'Barr (1979) and O'Barr and Atkins (1980) have shown, use of the 'powerless' style is not confined to females but seems to correspond generally with speakers of a low social position *vis-à-vis* other interlocutors. To label female speech 'powerless' is misleading and other authors, choosing to evaluate female speech along a different dimension, have labelled it 'supportive' (Holmes, 1984).

Powerful speech features, by contrast, are relatively less well understood. One view is that the *less* frequent use of powerless features constitutes power. For example, in a simulated courtroom experiment, Lind and O'Barr (1979) showed that the infrequent use of powerless features by a witness, as compared to the more frequent use of the same features, elicited more favourable ratings on competence, social attractiveness, trustworthiness, social dynamism, and convincingness. Similar ratings were obtained by Erickson, Lind, Johnson, and O'Barr (1978), who also found a positive relation between a witness's infrequent use of powerless features and listeners' acceptance of the witness's advocated position.

Another, more promising, approach to powerful speech is to identify positive features the *more* frequent use of which would lead to high influence. This approach is exemplified by research on conversational groups. Unlike other research that relies on impression-formation techniques for measuring perceived powerfulness and casts the respondents in a listener or passive observer role (see review by Bradac and Street, 1986), conversational group research attempts to find out how the development of a social influence hierarchy among group members may be related to members' speech acts during conversation (e.g. Brooke and Ng, 1966). A consistent finding is that influence correlates positively with participation rates (Stein, 1975; Stein and Heller, 1979), especially with the number of successful turns (Brooke and Ng, 1986; Scherer, 1979).

Turn-taking may appear orderly on the surface, but there is much politics underneath. Turn allocation consists of either the current speaker selecting the next speaker, or the interlocutors selecting themselves (Sacks, Schegloff, and Jefferson, 1974; Zimmerman and West, 1975). In the former, the selected person has the right and obligation to speak. If some other, unselected, persons speak, they are seen as speaking out of turn or interrupting. When a turn is allocated by self-selection, the first starter gains the right of reply. In both cases, especially self-selection, success at turn-taking involves the skilful use of interruption markers, appositionals, increased amplitude, slowing tempo, and lengthened vowels applied competitively at transition-relevant places (Levinson, 1983).

Participation rates and turns are important parts of the organization of the talk exchange (who speaks, when, and for how long). Powerful speakers do not thrive on talk organization alone, though. Owsley and Scotton (1984) propose two additional arenas of power, namely, control of conversation content and evaluation of that content. Of these two, only the former has been studied at any great depth.

Control of conversation content can be thought of as topic management. As the conversation progresses, what is being talked about changes. Brooke (1988) found that group members who were perceived as changing the topic the most were also rated the most influential by fellow group members. The relationship between topic change and influence can be further specified by distinguishing topic nomination from its subsequent endorsement or rejection. The latter is particularly relevant to influence. For example, Fishman (1977) found that, although women made the greater conversational effort, it was men who exercised control by taking up or not taking up the topics suggested by women. Similarly, a minority of five men in a group discussion involving 32 other women controlled the discussion by insisting on topics that were important to them (Spender, 1980).

DEPOLITICIZATION OF CONTROL

A certain antagonism between those who control and those who are controlled is inherent in a control relationship. How to achieve control with only minimal antagonism is a practical problem for power-holders large and small. One solution is to depoliticize control, that is, to mislead people and to mask control.

Misleading People

To mislead people is to set them on a mental tract that leads further and further away from the forbidden truth. The potential of words to mislead is based partly on the high degree of voluntary controllability of verbal communication. However, although people can tell lies with words, their non-verbal gestures, being less consciously controllable, may give the lies away (Ekman and Friesen, 1969; see Chapter 12, by Friedman and Tucker). If humans had to rely solely on non-verbal communication, there would be less scope for deception.

More importantly, the potential of words to mislead is due to their evocative ability. Edelman (1977) argues that, as language is a symbol that condenses and rearranges feelings, memories, perceptions, beliefs, and explanations, it can be used to evoke a particular structuring of beliefs and emotions. For example, eyewitnesses' memory of the speed of cars involved in an accident can be distorted if it is evoked by single loaded words such as 'bump' and 'collide', instead of by more neutral words like 'contact' (Loftus and Palmer, 1974). The evocative potential of loaded words can be harnessed to set off a train of thoughts and associated emotions away from the real issue. This principle of evocation can be illustrated by linguistic categorization, to which Edelman (1977) attaches special importance. For example, in the context of mental institutions, the categorization of patients' basic personal freedoms and civil rights as 'privileges' evokes from staff responses that are different from those evoked by the category 'rights'. This is reminiscent of the effect of categorization on the accentuation of intercategory differences (Tajfel, 1981). Another example is the use of the categories 'unborn child' versus 'fetus' by anti- and pro-abortionists, respectively. A third example is provided by the description of couples without children as 'childless' versus 'childfree'.

A category can also be chosen to evoke a mythical reference group in support of oneself (e.g. President Nixon's 'silent majority'). The reference group may be idealized as a superordinate group and put up as a front to conceal the real conflict of interests. Consider the following example: *Ask not what your country can do for you; ask what you can do for your country*. The you–country categorization is clearly intended to mislead 'you' into believing that 'your' private selfish interests are at odds with the good of the country, when the real issue may in fact involve an élite trying to commit the country to war. Augmenting the chosen category are figures of speech such as metaphors (e.g. 'balance' between personal and communal interests), and vague syntactic structures such as non-transactives (Edelman, 1977).

Potter and Reicher (1987), working from the vantage point of discourse analysis, have examined the production and organization of categories in accounts of a 'riot'.

Although they are not concerned with the depoliticization effects of categories, their analysis clearly shows two opposing accounts and demonstrates the relevance of linguistic categories to the social psychology of intergroup relations. Social psychologists working in the minimal group tradition (e.g. Tajfel, 1982) have taken linguistic categories for granted, and left unexplored the fundamental facts that social categorization operates through speech and that much of intergroup conflict is about bad- and good-naming. There is potential here for an integrated study of the production and effects of linguistic categories, as well as the contributory roles of metaphors and syntax.

Masking Control

Fowler, Hodge, Kress, and Trew (1979) describe several linguistic devices that are relevant to masking. In command speech acts (e.g. rules and regulations), the writer or speaker seeks to direct the specific behaviour of his or her readers or listeners. When the speech is stated in the imperative form, both the source of command and the directness of the command are plain: *I*, the writer/speaker, *command you*, the addressees, *always to carry membership cards and show them on request*. To mask control, the source can be obfuscated by deleting *I*, and the directness of the command can be tempered by transforming second person *you* to third person *members*: *Members must always carry membership cards and show them on request*. The masking process can progress further by adopting the passive declarative form: *Membership cards must always be carried and shown on request*. In this way, the commander/commanded relationship that is expressed in the imperative form is replaced by a giver of information/recipient of information relationship, and thematic prominence shifts from persons to objects (membership cards).

In addition to the passivization principle above (agent deletion, replacement of second by third persons, and use of passive declaratives), another principle of masking is syntactic nominalization. In nominalization, a process clause is reduced to a noun. Consider the following example of nominalization: *Being absent for more than three consecutive sessions without explanation to the membership secretary means automatic expulsion*. Here *expulsion* is the reduced form of *someone expels you*, and serves to suppress the unpleasant detail of naming the expeller.

A third principle is pluralization, which works on both the source and the addressee. In the former, it aggrandizes and obscures the source (e.g. the Authorities); in the latter, it confirms the source's refusal to treat the individual addressee as an individual person.

A final principle to be considered here is reversal, which appears frequently in newspaper reporting, particularly in the editing of headlines. As its name implies, reversal casts victims (e.g. black Africans shot dead by the police) in the role of villains, implying that they are responsible for their own suffering. This is illustrated by the first of two newspaper headlines:

RIOTING BLACKS SHOT DEAD BY POLICE AS ANC LEADERS MEET

POLICE SHOOT 11 DEAD IN SALISBURY RIOT

In the first headline, 'blacks' are assigned to the beginning of a sentence normally reserved for the agent, whereas the 'police', who instigated the shooting, are concealed syntactically at the middle of the sentence. The reversal is bolstered by describing the blacks as rioting.

Reversals can be combined with agent deletion to conceal the instigator more completely than in the case above. For example, the instigator (Labour Department) does not even appear in the first headline below:

IMMIGRANTS' JOB APPLICATIONS FAILED TO MEET CRITERIA

LABOUR DEPARTMENT BARRED IMMIGRANT WORKERS FROM SUBSIDIZED JOBS

ROUTINIZATION OF CONTROL

Machiavelli advised the Prince to exercise control by fear instead of by love, for fear is a chain harder to break than love. The advice contradicts the much earlier teaching of Lao-Tzu, who ordered leadership on the following scale: leaders are good when no one seems to know they exist, not so good when people adore them, and bad when people fear them. The contradiction is not merely between pragmaticism and morality, but, more importantly, between an individualistic (Machiavelli) and a systemic (Lao-Tzu) view of power and control. The systemic view highlights the tendency of control relationships to embed in ways of life that have become a natural part of ourselves (see Ng, 1980). In this way, control is routinized. We shall now examine how language facilitates the routinization of control, using research on sexist language as our main reference (see also Chapter 17, by Kramarae).

Words that Conceal Females

It is customary in English to use feminine generics (she, her) to refer to physical objects (e.g. cars, ships, planes) that imply male control. Masculine generics (he, his, men) on the other hand, are the grammatically proper words for referring to sex-indefinite human referents. It is the routine use of masculine generics that serves to conceal women and girls.

Masculine generics were installed as legal usage by a British Act of Parliament in 1850, and much earlier, in 1746, as a grammatical rule by John Kirby. They are still frequently used, MacKay (1980), for example, has estimated that a person may come in contact with the generic 'he' over 10 million times during his or her lifetime.

Generic words are also masculine-specific words. In the course of language learning, it is the masculine-specific meaning that is learnt first, and only later the generic meaning. The masculine-specific meaning tends to stick. By means of the proactive inhibition procedure, Ng (in press) has demonstrated that 'man' and 'his' are coded in memory processes as part of the masculine but not the feminine category.

For the reasons above, masculine generics can hardly function in a truly inclusive way. Instead, they are androcentrically biased in their decoding. For example, individuals interpret the generics to be male-specific (MacKay and Fulkerson, 1979), associate them more frequently with male than female pictures (Harrison, 1975; Martyna, 1980; Schneider and Hacker, 1973), evaluate them as being biased against women (Briere and Lanktree, 1983) as well as being sexist (Murdock and Forsyth, 1985), and form a predominantly masculine impression when 'he' and 'man' are used in combination (Cole, Hill, and Dayley, 1983). Androcentric biases are also evident in the encoding of generics; that is, speakers and authors use generics mainly to refer to males (Ng, 1988). Third, there is also evidence suggesting that generic words instantaneously evoke visual images that are predominantly masculine (Wilson and Ng, 1988).

Owing to their pervasive androcentric biases, masculine generics conceal the existence of women and girls insofar as language affects our thoughts and perception. At the very least, they diminish the frequency of use of 'she', 'her', and 'woman' in our daily discourse, and, consequently, suppress the salience of the female category. The psychological cost to females is nothing less than being a non-person in one's own language (Moulton, Robinson, and Elias, 1978). The ascent of masculine generics, which eventuated in the assimilation of the generics into natural speech and important documents (e.g. law books, the Bible, Koran, Orthodox Jewish prayer books, Confucian classics), provides a rich source of historical evidence for the linguistic routinization of male dominance over females. Within the feminist movement, rejection of the generics has been a critical step towards greater visibility and a more positive social identity for females as a social category (Coates, 1986; William and Giles, 1978).

Words that Degrade Females

Once-neutral words have become degraded in meaning when applied later to females. 'Tart', for example, originally meant a small piece of pastry. It was first applied to younger women as a term of endearment, next to women who were sexually desirable, then to women who were careless in their morals, and most recently has been used in reference to women who are prostitutes (Schulz, 1975). The same process of degradation has occurred in initially positive words – for example, 'virago'. Some negative words, such as 'shrew', originally meant for males, have been transferred to females (Miller and Swift, 1977).

The linguistic devaluation of women goes further. Schulz (1975) has noted that titles for female (e.g. lady, governess, mistress) are devalued relative to their male counterparts (lord, governor, master). Similarly, words that are parallel in meaning (e.g. spinster versus bachelor) cast females in a less favourable light. There are 220 words in English for a sexually promiscuous female and only 20 for a sexually promiscuous male, even though there are fewer words describing females than males (Stanley, 1973, cited in Spender, 1980). Expressions acquire sexual connotations and have a narrower frame of reference when applied to women than to men (e.g. 'She is a professional' versus 'He is a professional'). Other similar examples abound in standard reference works such as *Roget's thesaurus* (see Bolinger, 1980).

Several authors have argued that the linguistic derogation of females is due to females' subordinate social position relative to males, including the lack of control by females over the making of language (Nielsen, 1977; Spender, 1980). In this respect, females as a social category are not unique in getting more than their fair share of unfavourable terms. Generally, non-élite groups in society who do not make their own language – servants, racial minorities, children, and the elderly – meet with the same fate. In other words, disparaging language in general, and sexist language more particularly, 'reflects' the context (Giles and Wiemann, 1987, p. 352). One may argue further that, given the existence of a sexist language, its usage will help maintain the subordination of females; that is, sexist language 'determines' the context (Giles and Wiemann, 1987, p. 363; see also McConnell-Ginet, 1978; Thorne and Henley, 1975). One may then argue still further that, if and when sexist language is used *routinely* as a matter of course, the subordination of females becomes routinized in daily discourse and does not require the extra effort of manipulation normally associated with depoliticization.

CONCLUSION

Much of politics is talk, talk, talk. Talk and, by extension, language afford valuable data on control. The recent string of relevant reviews recognizes the importance of the relations between language and control (Berger, 1985; Bradac and Street, 1986; Giles and Wiemann, 1987; Miller, 1987; Wiemann, 1985). In this chapter, we have examined five principles underlying short, monologue speech, and have noted a conceptual development in the direction of social cognition. We have also identified two methodological and conceptual developments in interactive speech research. The first is a change from studying passive observers to studying actual interlocutors in ongoing conversations. The second is a shift in focus from powerless to powerful speech. Associated with these developments has been an increase of research activities on talk organization and topic change. Research on powerful speech, both monological and interactive, has been and will continue to be a confluence of research for social psychologists and sociolinguists.

In addition to powerful speech, which occurs mostly in face-to-face situations and is easily detectable, there are other linguistic means of control that are less directive but nonetheless powerful. If we are to comprehend more fully how language affects our lives, we need to examine also these other subtle functions of language. Using the heuristic framework of the two- and three-dimensional views of power (Ng, 1980), we have proposed that language has both depoliticization and routinization functions.

Depoliticization comprises an array of linguistic devices for masking control and for misleading people. The masking devices of passivization, nominalization, pluralization, and reversal are endemic in rules, regulations, and news reporting. They are most fully unmasked by linguists in the tradition of George Orwell and M.A.K. Halliday (Edelman, 1977; Fowler *et al.*, 1979). The potential of language to mislead is due largely to the evocative ability of loaded words, especially those that form linguistic categories. The study of linguistic categories – how they are produced, organized, used, and with what effects – offers a promising lead in anchoring the social psychology of intergroup relations in the concrete, ongoing reality mediated by language and language use (Potter and Reicher, 1987; see also Potter and Wetherell, 1987; van Dijk, 1987).

Depoliticization involves a lot of effort in concocting phrases and speeches to mask control and to mislead people. By contrast, routinization of control is driven by the biases already coded in language and by the routine use of the (biased) language in daily discourse. One source of bias is masculine generics, which affect females uniquely. Available evidence shows that the generics are androcentric, suggesting that their routine use conceals or otherwise reduces the salience of females as a social category. Biases are also shown in degrading words the use of which burdens the degraded recipients with ridicule, shame, and defensiveness. In these ways, routinized linguistic sexism conceals the female category when referring to humans generally, and yet constitutes the same category particularly as a topic of derogatory discourse. Females born into such a language environment have three enemies, namely, the material conditions which give rise to the linguistic biases, people (including themselves) who use the language, and the language itself. Linguistic routinization of control is not confined to females or to the English language. Its study can be extended to other non-élite groups who are unable to control the language *about* themselves, such as the elderly (e.g. Coupland, Coupland, Giles, Henwood, and Wiemann, 1988), and to other languages (e.g. Blakar, 1975). There are other possibilities, especially linguistic changes *by* non-élite groups. For example, non-élite groups can break up routinization by effecting changes in vocabulary (e.g. jazz, yurky, Ms, s/he) or in phonology (e.g. final /–t/ glottalization, which is spreading among received-pronunciation speakers in New Zealand (D. Bayard, personal communication) as in Britain).

The three linguistic control functions – persuasion via powerful speech; depoliticization; and routinization – offer a way of viewing the pervasiveness of language power. In common with an old tradition in social psychology concerned with the hierarchy of power and social influence (see Kipnis, 1984; Ng, 1980; Raven, 1988), the functions convey a sense of increasing subtlety in which linguistic control operates. They sensitize us to the protean nature of power. Yet they are not meant to be exhaustive. One omission, for example, is the possibility raised by Orwell (1954) that language not only expresses an intended world-view but also functions 'to make all other modes of thought impossible' (p. 241).

REFERENCES

Ajzen, I. and Fishbein, M. (1980). *Understanding attitudes and predicting social behavior*. Englewood Cliffs, NJ: Prentice-Hall.

Anderson, N. (1981). Integration theory applied to cognitive responses and attitudes. In R.E. Petty, T.M. Ostrom, and T.C. Brock (Eds), *Cognitive responses in persuasion*, pp. 361–397. Hillsdale, NJ: Erlbaum.

Bachrach, P. and Baratz, M.S. (1962). Two faces of power. *American Political Science Review*, **56**, 947–952.

Berger, C.R. (1985). Social power and interpersonal communication. In M.L. Knapp and G.R. Miller (Eds), *Handbook of interpersonal communication*, pp. 439–499. Beverly Hills: Sage.

Blakar, R.M. (1975). How sex roles are represented, reflected and conserved in the Norwegian language. *Acta Sociologica*, **14**, 515–534.

Bolinger, D. (1980). *Language – The loaded weapon*. London: Longman.

Bradac, J.J. and Street, R. (1986). Powerful and powerless styles re-visited: A theoretical analysis. Paper presented at the Meeting of the Speech Communication Association, Chicago.

Briere, J. and Lanktree, C. (1983). Sex-role related effects of the sex bias in language. *Sex Roles*, **9**, 625–633.

Brooke, M.E. (1988). Topic change and social influence: A pilot study. Unpublished report, Department of Psychology University of Otago, New Zealand.

Brooke, M.E. and Ng, S.H. (1986). Language and social influence in small conversational groups. *Journal of Language and Social Psychology*, **5**, 201–210.

Burnstein, E. (1982). Persuasion as argument processing. In J.H. Davis and G. Stocker-Kreichgauer (Eds), *Group decision-making*. New York: Academic Press.

Cialdini, R.B. (1984). *Influence: How and why people agree to things*. New York: Morrow.

Coates, J. (1986). *Women, men and language*. London: Longman.

Cole, C.M., Hill, F.A., and Dayley, L.J. (1983). Do masculine pronouns used generically lead to thoughts of men? *Sex Roles*, **9**, 737–749.

Cook-Gumperz, J. (1973). *Social control and socialization: A study of class differences in the language of maternal control*. London: Routledge and Kegan Paul.

Coupland, N., Coupland, J., Giles, H., Henwood, K., and Wiemann, J. (1988). Elderly self-disclosure: Interactional and intergroup processes. *Language and Communication*, **8**, 109–133.

Edelman, M. (1977). *Political language: Words that succeed and policies that fail*. New York: Academic Press.

Eiser, J.R. and Stroebe, W. (1972). *Categorization and social judgement*. London: Academic Press.

Ekman, P. and Friesen, W.V. (1969). Nonverbal leakage and clues to deception. *Psychiatry*, **32**, 88–106.

Erickson, B., Lind, A.E., Johnson, B.C., and O'Barr, W.M. (1978). Speech style and impression formation in a court setting: The effects of 'powerful' and 'powerless' speech. *Journal of Experimental Social Psychology*, **14**, 266–279.

Fishman, P.M. (1977). Interactional shitwork. *Heresies*, **2**, 99–101.

Fowler, R., Hodge, B., Kress, G., and Trew, T. (1979). *Language and control*. London: Routledge and Kegan Paul.

Giles, H. and Wiemann, J.M. (1987). Language, social comparison, and power. In C.R. Berger and S.H. Chaffee (Eds), *Handbook of communication science*, pp. 350–384. Newbury Park: Sage.

Greenley, J.R. (1973). Types of authority and two problems of psychiatric wards. *Psychiatric Quarterly*, **47**, 191–202.

Harrison, L. (1975). Cro-Magnon woman – in eclipse. *Science Teacher*, **42**, 8–11.

Heider, F. (1946). Attitudes and cognitive organization. *Journal of Psychology*, **21**, 107–112.

Holmes, J. (1984). Hedging your bets and sitting on the fence: Some evidence for hedges as support structures. *Te Reo*, **27**, 47–62.

Hovland, C.I., Janis, I.L., and Kelley, H.H. (1953). *Communication and persuasion*. New Haven, CT: Yale University Press.

Jaspars, J.M.F. (1978). Determinants of attitudes and attitude change. In H. Tajfel and C. Fraser (Eds), *Introducing social psychology*, pp. 277–301. Harmondsworth (England): Penguin.

Kelman, H.C. (1961). Processes of opinion change. *Public Opinion Quarterly*, **25**, 57–78.

Kipnis, D. (1984). The use of power in organizations and in interpersonal settings. In S. Oskamp (Ed.), *Applied social psychology annual*, Vol. 5, *Applications in organizational settings*, pp. 179–210. Beverley Hills: Sage.

Lakoff, R. (1973). Language and woman's place. *Language in Society*, **2**, 45–80.

Langer, E.J., Blank, A., and Chanowitz, B. (1978). The mindlessness of ostensible thoughtful action: The role of 'placebic' information in interpersonal interaction. *Journal of Personality and Social Psychology*, **36**, 635–642.

Latané, B. and Darley, J.M. (1970). *The unresponsive bystander: Why doesn't he help?* New York: Appleton-Century-Crofts.

Levinson, S.C. (1983). *Pragmatics*. Cambridge: Cambridge University Press.

Lind, E.A. and O'Barr, W.M. (1979). The social significance of speech in the courtroom. In H. Giles and R. St Clair (Eds), *Language and social psychology*, pp. 66–87. Baltimore: University Park Press.

Loftus, F. and Palmer, J. (1974). Reconstruction of automobile destruction. *Journal of Verbal Learning and Verbal Behavior*, **13**, 585–589.

Lukes, S. (1974). *Power: A radical view*. London: Macmillan.

MacKay, D.G. (1980). Language, thought and social attitudes. In H. Giles, P. Robinson, and P.M. Smith (Eds), *Language: Social psychological perspectives*, pp. 89–96. Oxford: Pergamon.

MacKay, D.G. and Fulkerson, D.C. (1979). On the comprehension and producton of pronouns. *Journal of Verbal Learning and Verbal Behaviour*, **18**, 661–673.

Mackie, D. (1986). Social identification effects in group polarization. *Journal of Personality and Social Psychology*, **50**, 720–728.

Martyna, W. (1980). The psychology of the generic masculine. In S. McConnell-Ginet, R. Borker, and N. Fulman (Eds), *Women and language in literature and society*, pp. 69–78. New York: Praeger.

McConnell-Ginet, S. (1978). Intonation in a man's world. *Signs: Journal of Women in Culture and Society*, **3**, 541–559.

McGuire, W. (1985). The nature of attitudes and attitude change. In G. Lindzey and E. Aronson (Eds), *Handbook of social psychology*, 3rd edn, Vol. 2. Reading, MA: Addison-Wesley.

Miller, C. and Swift, K. (1977). *Words and women: New language in new times*. New York: Anchor.

Miller, G.R. (1987). Persuasion. In C.R. Berger and S.H. Chaffee (Eds), *Handbook of communication science*, pp. 446–483. Newbury Park: Sage.

Moulton, J., Robinson, G.M., and Elias, C. (1978). Sex bias in language use: Neutral pronouns that aren't. *American Psychologist*, **33**, 1032–1036.

Murdock, N.L. and Forsyth, D.R. (1985). Is gender-biased language sexist? A perceptual approach. *Psychology of Women Quarterly*, **9**, 39–49.

Ng, S.H. (1980). *The social psychology of power*. London: Academic Press.

Ng, S.H. (1988). *Masculine generics and sexism in language*. A Final Report prepared for the Social Sciences Research Fund Committee, Wellington.

Ng, S.H. (in press). The androcentric coding of *man* and *his* in memory. *Journal of Experimental Social Psychology*.

Ng, S.H. and Wilson, S. (1989). Self-categorization and belief polarization among Christian believers and atheists. *British Journal of Social Psychology*, **28**, 47–56.

O'Barr, W. and Atkins, S. (1980). 'Women's language' or 'powerless language'? In S. McConnell-Ginet, R. Borker, and N. Fulman (Eds), *Women and language in literature and society*, pp. 93–110. New York: Praeger.

Orwell, G. (1954). *Nineteen eighty-four*. Harmondsworth (England): Penguin.

Owsley, H.H. and Scotton, C.M. (1984). The conversational expression of power by television interviewers. *Journal of Social Psychology*, **123**, 261–271.

Petty, R.E. and Cacioppo, J.T. (1985). The elaboration likelihood model of persuasion. In L. Berkowitz (Ed.), *Advances in experimental social psychology*, Vol. 19, pp. 123–205. New York: Academic Press.

Petty, R.E., Ostrom, T.M., and Brock, T.C. (1981). *Cognitive responses in persuasion*. Hillsdale, NJ: Erlbaum.

Potter, J. and Reicher, S. (1987). Discourses of community and conflict: The organization of social categories in accounts of a 'riot'. *British Journal of Social Psychology*, **26**, 25–40.

Potter, J. and Wetherell, M. (1987). *Discourse and social psychology: Beyond attitudes and behaviour*. London: Sage.

Raven, B.H. (1988). French and Raven thirty years later: Power-interaction and interpersonal influence. Paper presented at the XXIV international Congress of Psychology, Sydney.

Reicher, S. (1982). The determination of collective behaviour. In H. Tajfel (Ed.), *Social identity and intergroup relations*, pp. 41–83. Cambridge: Cambridge University Press.

Rubenstein, R. and Lasswell, H.D. (1966). *The sharing of power in a psychiatric hospital*. New Haven, CT: Yale University Press.

Sacks, H., Schegloff, E.A., and Jefferson, G. (1974). A simplest systematics for the organization of turn-taking for conversation. *Language*, **50**, 696–735.

Scherer, K. (1979). Voice and speech correlates of perceived social influence in simulated juries. In H. Giles and R. St Clair (Eds), *Language and social psychology*, pp. 88–120. Baltimore: University Park Press.

Schneider, J.W. and Hacker, S.L. (1973). Sex role imagery and use of the generic 'man' in introductory texts: A case in the sociology of sociology. *American Sociologist*, **8**, 12–18.

Schuiz, M. (1975). The semantic derogation of women. In B. Thorne and N. Henley (Eds), *Language and sex: Difference and dominance*, pp. 64–75. Rowley, MA: Newbury House.

Spender, D. (1980). *Man made language*, 2nd edn. London: Routledge and Kegan Paul.

Stanley, J. (1973). Paradigmatic woman: The prostitute. Paper presented to the South Atlantic Modern Language Association. (Cited in Spender, 1980.)

Stein, T.R. (1975). Identifying emergent leaders from verbal and nonverbal communications. *Journal of Personality and Social Psychology*, **32**, 125–135.

Stein, T.R. and Heller, T. (1979). An empirical analysis of the correlates between leadership status and participation rates reported in the literature. *Journal of Personality and Social Psychology*, **37**, 1993–2002.

Tajfel, H. (1981). *Human groups and social categories: Studies in social psychology*. Cambridge: Cambridge University Press.

Tajfel, H. (1982). *Social identity and intergroup relations*. Cambridge: Cambridge University Press.

Thomas, W.I. and Znaniecki, F. (1927). *The Polish peasants in Europe and America*, 2nd edn. New York: Knopf.

Thorne, B. and Henley, N. (1975). Difference and dominance: An overview of language, gender and society. In B. Thorne and N. Henley (Eds), *Language and sex: Difference and dominance*, pp. 5–42. Rowley, MA: Newbury House.

Turner, J.C. (1987). The analysis of social influence. In J.C. Turner (Ed.), *Rediscovering the social group: A self-categorization theory*, pp. 68–88. Oxford: Blackwell.

van Dijk, T.A. (1987). *Communicating racism*. Newbury Park, CA: Sage.

Winokur, A. and Burnstein, E. (1978). Novel argumentation and social perceptions of simulated jurors. *Journal of Personality and Social Psychology*, **8**, 335–346.

Wetherell, M. (1987). Social identity and group polarization. In J.C. Turner (Ed.), *Rediscovering the social group: A self-categorization theory*, pp. 142–170. Oxford: Blackwell.

Wiemann, J.M. (1985). Interpersonal control and regulation in conversation. In R.L. Street and J.N. Cappella (Eds), *Sequence and pattern in communicative behaviour*, pp. 85–102. London: Arnold.

William, J. and Giles, H. (1978). The changing status of women in society: An Intergroup perspective. In H. Tajfel (Ed.), *Differentiation between social groups: Studies in the social psychology of intergroup relations*, pp. 431–446. London: Academic Press.

Wilson, E. and Ng, S.H. (1988). Sex bias in visual images evoked by generics: A New Zealand study. *Sex Roles*, **18**, 159–168.

Zimbardo, P.G. (1969). The human choice: Individuation, reason and order versus deindividuation, impulse and chaos. In W.J. Arnold and D. Levine (Eds), *Nebraska symposium on motivation*, Vol. 17. Lincoln, NE: University of Nebraska Press.

Zimmerman, D. and West, C. (1975). Sex roles, interruptions and silences in conversation. In B. Thorne and N. Henley (Eds), *Language and sex: Difference and dominance*, pp. 105–129. Rowley, MA: Newbury House.

Section 4

Language and Social Categories

Introduction to Section 4

Although *group* analogues of self-disclosure, facework (and self-presentation), accounting, and deception were not examined in the previous chapters, clearly they should be agendarized for future explorations and the astute reader will detect their, sometimes hidden, voices in this section. In the following chapters, we explore the manner in which language also can play crucial roles serving individuals' different *group* (as well as their own self-) identities and interests.

Most nations in the world comprise different cultural groups, each, more often than not, speaking its own distinct language. Hence, for effective communication to occur in multilingual settings, ethnic groups should have the ability and desire to code-switch between their respective language varieties. In their chapter, Sachdev and Bourhis examine the antecedents of code-switching by means of a wide variety of normative (e.g. situational rules), motivational (e.g. desire to emphasize ethnic solidarity), and sociostructural (e.g. institutional support for certain languages over others) factors. Attention is focused ultimately on the (under-studied) sociostructural factors and particularly by recourse to the authors' own independent work on the effects of group status, numbers, and power on intergroup perceptions and behaviours. Although different disciplinary traditions have afforded primacy to one or other set of these social forces, the present, more integrative, framework argues well for the necessity to take into account their actual *interaction*. This is well illustrated by overviewing studies which investigate the complex evaluative *consequences* of various kinds of code-switching, differentially sequenced under distinct sociocultural conditions.

Gudykunst and Ting-Toomey continue the focus on cultural groups by introducing some of the complex relationships between language and ethnicity which can exist across the world. It is argued that even dyadic conversations between members of different ethnic groups can be defined by the participants in 'interpersonal' or 'intergroup' terms – and hence different processes may determine the emergent events. A number of theoretical frameworks have been formulated in the social

Handbook of Language and Social Psychology
Edited by H. Giles and W.P. Robinson.   © 1990 John Wiley & Sons Ltd

psychology of ethnolinguistic communication, each of which relies upon different mediating processes and relates to different cognitive and behavioural outcomes. Having outlined these, Gudykunst and Ting-Toomey attempt to integrate them by means of a useful framework which posits different links between ethnic categorization, trait attribution and intergroup similarity judgments, uncertainty reduction, and communication breakdown.

We cannot of course consider interethnic relations without invoking notions of socio-economic status – given the prevailing isomorphism between them in many societies. Haslett, having first discussed the problems involved in defining and measuring 'class' (and later its meaning in terms of social identity), examines the ways in which language has been found to be a fairly reliable index of an individual's socio-economic status. She continues by overviewing the nature, functions, and origins of the so-called 'codes': language forms and communicative strategies which supposedly distinguish children and adults, and mother–child interactive patterns, of different social class categories. In addition to the indexical roles of language, Haslett also attends to the important ways in which language can act to *define* and *redefine* hierarchical status via the media as well as in interpersonal interaction.

In the next chapter, Kramarae argues forcibly for the need to take into account ethnicity and race, socio-economic status, *and gender together* if we are to account effectively for various social discriminations at the interactional, societal, and institutional levels. She reviews research in many traditions which has looked at the relationships between language and gender with attention to, for example, the ways in which sex group membership (as well as masculinity, femininity, and androgyny) is supposedly marked by various language forms and culturally determines grossly different communicative practices. But, in addition, she attends to the manner in which language maintains the gender hierarchy by its power to 'victimize' women in their *relationships* (friendly, loving, professional) with men. This analysis is, at least from the perspective of our own disciplinary base, unique and compelling in its attempts to reflect, disentangle, and confront the frustrations, anger, and abuse many women experience in many between-gender communications.

We belong of course to an array of social categories, some of which can be associated with social stigma, as the above implies. We shall conclude this section with a more 'clinical' contribution regarding our membership in mentally handi-capped or non-handicapped collectivities. Markova argues that the social consequences of possessing a handicapped identity may be more to blame for the communication problems that arise than the physiological potency of the actual disabilities themselves. She pinpoints the roles of social categorization, in-ference, and segregation, which can led to inadequate feedback and ultimately learned helplessness. Moreover, and while the handicapped have problems with referential communication and the frequency and multiplicity of them, she overviews studies grounding their lack of competence more in discoursal terms (e.g. coherent narrative) than along lexical or grammatical lines. This chapter brings us back full circle to the previous section as Markova articulates the kinds of communicative strategies (e.g. 'gap-filling') which the handicapped utilize in an attempt to manage the spoiled identities of which they are apparently so acutely aware. Indeed, and somewhat paradoxically, it is the invocation of such compensations which can contribute so forcibly to their perceived conversational incompetence.

This section, then, will show that we are uncovering the complex and subtle ways in which language, sometimes through the unwitting routines of everyday interaction, reflects, creates, and sustains our multiple group identities and power.

14

Bilinguality and Multilinguality

ITESH SACHDEV AND RICHARD BOURHIS

Department of Applied Linguistics, Birkbeck College, UK and Department of Psychology, University of Quebec, Canada

Bilinguality/multilinguality may be considered to be a psychological state of the individual who has access to two or more linguistic codes as means of communication (Hamers and Blanc, 1982). Bilingual and multilingual communication, where two or more languages (and dialects) are used, generally involve members of different ethnolinguistic groups. Regardless of the actual content of communication, innumerable events and studies around the world have shown that the actual languages themselves are clearly not 'neutral' media of communication. Which language(s) is(are) used when, why and by whom are important questions, given the crucial role that language plays as 'the recorder of paternity, the expressor of patrimony and the carrier of phenomenology' (Fishman, 1977). This chapter provides a review of research on bilingual and multilingual communication based on the framework proposed by Bourhis (1979, 1985).

In accordance with the theme of this handbook, a *social psychological* approach is employed to integrate micro-individual aspects with the macro-collective levels of bilingual and multilingual communication (Giles, Bourhis, and Taylor, 1977). This review is necessarily selective and the rich contributions from other conceptual and empirical orientations including sociolinguistics, the ethnography of speaking, interactional linguistics, linguistic anthropology, sociology of language, etc. are only briefly alluded to. The major recommendation of this review is to place the analyses of bilingual and multilingual communication in the oft-neglected sociostructural contexts within which such communications occur.

One of the most common phenomena in multilingual communication is code-

Handbook of Language and Social Psychology
Edited by H. Giles and W.P. Robinson. © 1990 John Wiley & Sons Ltd

switching, defined generally as 'the alternate use of two or more languages in the same utterance or conversation' (Grosjean, 1982). This general definition of code-switching is deliberately adopted for the present purposes, as a large variety of terms such as situational switching, metaphorical switching, code-mixing, style-shifting, etc. have been proposed for the different forms of code alternation in the literature and have generated considerable debate about their appropriateness (Brietborde, 1983; Gal, 1983; Saville-Troike, 1982; Scotton, 1983a).

Following Bourhis (1979, 1985), the determinants of code-switching are subsumed under three major sets of factors:

(1) *Normative factors*, including the situational taxonomies of speech norms defined by traditional sociolinguists (e.g. Gumperz, 1982), and the recent contributions of interactional sociolinguists concerning rules and maxims guiding code-switching (e.g. Scotton, 1983b);
(2) *Motivational factors*, including 'speech accommodation' (e.g. Giles and Powesland, 1975) and social categorization effects (Tajfel and Turner, 1979);
(3) *Sociostructural factors*, including the relative vitalities of language groups in terms of group numbers, group power and group status (e.g. Giles *et al.*, 1977; Sachdev and Bourhis, 1984).

In this conceptualization, the encoding and decoding of language choices in bilingual and multilingual communication depend crucially upon the interaction of normative motivational and sociostructural factors. The focus of this chapter is on language and dialect choice in bilingual and multilingual communication rather than on choice of accents, registers, etc.

NORMATIVE FACTORS

It has long been recognized by sociolinguists that the linguistic medium in which bilingual and multilingual communication take place is as important as the verbal content of the communication in understanding language behaviour (Fishman, 1972; Gumperz and Hymes, 1972). Traditional theoretical and empirical efforts by socio-linguists developed taxonomies of situational norms of code-switching according to topic of communication, the social setting in which it occurs, the purpose of the communication and the characteristics of the interlocutors (e.g. Hymes, 1972; Trudgill, 1974; see Giles and Powesland, 1975, for a review).

Early research in Israel (Herman, 1961), Tanzania (Beardsley and Eastman, 1971) and Japan (Ervin-Tripp, 1968) showed that bilinguals reverted to their native dialect or language when discussing emotional issues or when talking about topics relevant to the cultural contexts in which they lived. Similarly, in the Philippines and Paraguay, the use of the impersonal languages of English and Spanish (respectively) was normative amongst courting couples, who once wedded, would switch to Tagalog and Guarani (respectively) (Rubin, 1962; Sechrest, Flores, and Arellano, 1968). In all these cultural contexts and in numerous others, the local vernacular is restricted to the role of informal communication in private settings, while the more prestigious cosmopolitan language is considered the voice of intellect and of public formal communication. Similar situational determinants of language choice have been observed in Morocco (Bentahila, 1983), Hong Kong (Gibbons, 1986), Kenya (Scotton, 1983b), India (Pandit, 1979), Singapore (Platt, 1980) and many other settings across the world (Bourhis, 1979; Hamers and Blanc, 1989).

A variety of multilingual settings mentioned above may be termed diglossic (Ferguson, 1959; Fishman, 1967) or polyglossic (Platt, 1977) in the sense that certain codes are specifically reserved for high-status formal functions while others serve as modes of communication in informal situations. Extensive discussions of the relationships between diglossia, code-switching and bilingualism may be found in the publications by Fasold (1984), Hamers and Blanc (1989) and Scotton (1986) and are not considered here.

Dissatisfaction with traditional analyses of language switching arose from their conceptualization of interlocutors primarily as 'situational automatons'. The need to understand code-switching in non-automaton terms led some researchers to postulate 'cooperative' rules guiding discourse such as the Principles of Charity (Davidson, 1974) and Humanity (Grandy, 1973; Grice, 1975). Interactional sociolinguists have subsequently focused on identifying discourse strategies relevant in multilingual communication on the basis of the operation of a 'cooperativeness' maxim (e.g. Gumperz, 1982). Scotton (1980, 1983b) argued that these cooperative discourse principles assume that code choices are primarily concerned with communication efficiency and, moreover, serve to maintain the status quo. There is considerable evidence that language switches are not always designed to increase communication efficiency (Brown and Levinson, 1980) and code choices often aim to challenge the status quo (e.g. 'speech divergence' below).

Scotton (1983b) argued that language choices are determined by the negotiation of rights and obligations between interlocutors. *Unmarked* codes are chosen when interlocutors identify with their positions in well-defined role relationships, and *marked* codes are chosen to reject predefined roles. Scotton (1983b) systematized the 'negotiation of identities' approach in terms of six metamaxims determining code choices:

(1) the 'unmarked choice' maxim, where code choices affirm established roles;
(2) the 'deference' maxim, where choices show deference to interlocutors 'from whom you desire something';
(3) the 'virtuosity' maxim, where, due to a lack of linguistic ability, the marked code is chosen but does not imply rejection of defined roles;
(4) the 'exploratory choice' maxim, where code choice is made with a view to unmarking that choice in a weakly defined role relationship;
(5) the 'multiple-identities maxim', where more than one exploratory choice is made to express multiple identities;
(6) 'flouting the maxim' maxim, where code choices are made to disidentify with established rights and obligations.

Unlike traditional sociolinguists, Scotton's (1983b) approach is interactional and may be seen as complementing the social psychological approaches discussed below.

However, on a more cautious note, it should be appreciated that the social psychological status of her maxims is unclear and there is some potential for circularity in attributing code choices to the operation of maxims. This stems from the practice of defining original maxims using examples of code choices and then reciting those particular examples as 'independent' empirical evidence of the existence and operation of those maxims. Approaches attributing code-switching to the operation of multiple and competing situational norms are also likely to receive similar criticism.

Although code-switching in multilingual contexts may be attributed to social norms, rules and maxims, switching also occurs in the absence of, or in spite of the existence of, norms (Bourhis, 1979; Giles and Hewstone, 1982). In addition, even within normatively constrained settings there may be a wide latitude of acceptable language behaviours, and language use may be negotiated creatively to dynamically define and redefine social norms (Gal, 1983; Scotton, 1983b; cf. Brown and Fraser, 1979).

In Scotton's (1983b) theory, norms do not determine language choices, but language switches take place within a normative framework so that norms determine the relative markedness of linguistic codes. Scotton suggests that interlocutors are free to assert their individual motivations as all code choices are open to them, with interlocutors weighing up the relative costs and rewards in seeking their goals. Clearly, the motivational bases of language switching need to be examined more closely, and it is in this realm that social psychological approaches have made their greatest contribution.

MOTIVATIONAL FACTORS

Using a social psychological approach, Giles and his colleagues (e.g. Giles, Taylor, and Bourhis, 1973) developed a model of code-switching, now known as speech-accommodation theory (SAT; Giles, Mulac, Bradac, and Johnson, 1987b). Although SAT arose partly as a reaction to the normative bias in traditional socio-linguistics, it sought to account for code-switching in terms of interlocutors' motives, attitudes, perceptions and group loyalties. The value of SAT lies in its ability to explain and predict code-switching in terms of social psychological processes operating at both the interpersonal level (e.g. similarity-attraction; Byrne, 1969) and the intergroup level, where social categorization processes are of primary importance (Giles, 1978; Tajfel, 1982). The most recent developments also suggest extensions to 'couple' accommodation and relational identities (see Giles et al., 1987b).

The major focus of code-switching within SAT has been on speech convergence, speech divergence and speech maintenance, although other strategies have also been investigated. Briefly, in multilingual settings, speech convergence refers to interlocutors becoming more alike in the languages they use; speech divergence refers to interlocutors accentuating linguistic differences between themselves and others. It is noteworthy that these phenomena have been found to occur *simultaneously* on a variety of linguistic levels (paralinguistic, content, style, accent, etc), and that speakers are not always aware that they are modifying their codes. Levels of awareness about speech divergence appear to be higher than for speech convergence (e.g. Bourhis, 1983; Street, 1982). Recent research has also suggested that individuals may accommodate their speech not to the actual language used by their interlocutors but to the stereotypes they hold about the interlocutors' characteristics (e.g. Beebe, 1981).

Let us briefly examine the social psychological processes involved in speech convergence and speech divergence. It should be noted that, as a social psychological theory, SAT focuses on the effects of individuals' *perceptions* of their interlocutors' code-switching on their evaluative and communicative responses.

Central to SAT is the notion that interlocutors code-switch in order to satisfy a variety of motivations. The theory proposes that speech convergence reflects interlocutors' needs for social integration and social approval. Using research on similarity-attraction (e.g. Byrne, 1969) as a starting point, it was argued that, when interlocutors became more similar in the codes they used, there would be greater liking between them. Empirical support for this in a bilingual code-switching context was provided in a study by Giles *et al.* (1973). They found that anglophone Quebecers (AQs) perceived francophone Quebecers (FQs) more favourably and showed greater reciprocity in convergence to FQs (by using French) when FQs had converged to English than when they had maintained French. The results of this study and a plethora of others suggest that mutual language convergence facilitates interpersonal and intergroup interaction where linguistic dissimilarities may otherwise be a barrier to communication (Bourhis, 1979; Giles *et al.*, 1987b). In addition, research has shown that linguistic convergence is likely to increase interlocutors' intelligibility (Triandis, 1960), predictability (Berger and Bradac, 1982) and interpersonal involvement (LaFrance, 1979).

Speech-accommodation theory also considers convergence as part of a 'social exchange' (Homans, 1961) during which the interlocutors attempt to minimize costs and maximize rewards for code-switching. A recent study by van den Berg (1986) in a variety of naturalistic settings in Taiwan may be illustrative. Data from a variety of business transactions showed that salespeople in markets and departmental stores converged more than clients. From a social exchange perspective, convergence to clients' languages in such business transactions maximizes potential monetary gains from sales. Interestingly, in banks, where clients may have more to gain than clerks, it was the clients who tended to converge more than the clerks. Though alternative explanations for these data in terms of situational norms are possible, a social exchange analysis may be more revealing. Overall, in bilingual and multilingual encounters, interlocutors are more likely to converge when rewards (e.g. material rewards, social approval, etc.) outweigh the potential costs (e.g. linguistic effort, group-identity loss, etc.) of converging.

From an attributional perspective (e.g. Heider, 1958), the motives and intentions of interlocutors for code-switching are crucial in understanding bilingual and multilingual communication. Much social psychological research has shown that people evaluate others' behaviour on the basis of perceived effort, ability and the extent to which the behaviour is considered to be influenced by external pressures (Kelley, 1973). For instance, Simard, Taylor, and Giles (1976) found that FQ listeners evaluated AQs' convergence to French more favourably when it was attributed to the speakers' genuine and 'internal' desires to communicate than when it was attributed to situational demands forcing the speakers to converge. Conversely, AQs' maintenance of English was eveluted more negatively when attributions were made to speakers' lack of effort rather than to situational pressures. Thus, SAT proposes that evaluative and behavioural reactions to code-switching in multilingual communication may depend significantly on the attributions of interlocutors for code-switching.

Using Tajfel and Turner's (1979) social identity theory, SAT analyses phenomena of language maintenance and divergence mainly in terms of interlocutors' desires for differentiation from interlocutors. Laboratory research in 'minimal group' relations (e.g. Tajfel, 1978) repeatedly suggested that arbitrarily categorized group members chose to sacrifice absolute material gain for the sake of accentuating differentials between their own group and salient outgroups. Social categorization *pe se* appeared to be sufficient to induce intergroup discrimination in these studies. According to Tajfel and Turner (1979), this 'minimal group discrimination' allowed subjects to fulfil their motivations for *positive social (group) identities*. In multilingual contexts, language provides an important cue for social categorizations and is often considered to be the most important and valued dimension of group identity (Bourhis, 1984b; Giles, 1977). According to SAT, language maintenance and language divergence primarily reflect motivations to maintain or assert positive ethnolinguistic identities.

Perhaps the most dramatic multilingual demonstration of divergence was obtained in a language-laboratory study by Bourhis, Giles, Leyens, and Tajfel (1979) in Belgium. At this epoch in Belgium, English was generally considered to be the emotionally 'neutral' compromise for communication between the Flemish and francophone Walloon inhabitants. In the initial speaker turns of Bourhis *et al*'s (1979) study, trilingual Flemish subjects responded in English to emotionally neutral questions posed in English by an outgroup francophone Walloon (the confederate). However, in later speaker turns, in response to ethnically threatening questions and statements posed in English, about a third of the Flemish respondents spontaneously switched to Flemish rather than continuing their replies in English, i.e. they diverged. Analyses of the content of replies showed that all Flemish respondents responded negatively to the outgroup Walloon speaker's threats and disagreed with his views. In the final phase of the study, the francophone Walloon speaker emphasized his threats and ethnic identity by diverging to French from English. Under these circumstances, *all* Flemish subjects diverged from their francophone interlocutor by switching into Flemish and vehemently disagreeing with his statements. Evidence consistent with the Belgian findings has also been obtained in a variety of bilingual and multilingual settings including Wales and Quebec (e.g. Bourhis, 1984a; Bourhis and Giles, 1977; Bourhis, Giles, and Lambert, 1975; Giles and Johnson, 1986; Taylor and Royer, 1980).

SOCIOSTRUCTURAL FACTORS

Bilingual and multilingual communication primarily takes place between members of contrasting ethnolinguistic groups. As differences in the sociostructural factors of group numbers, power and status characterize such intergroup situations, bilingual and multilingual communication cannot be assumed to occur in a sociostructural vacuum. One of the most significant developments assessing the significance of sociostructural factors in the social psychology of language has been Giles *et al.*'s (1977) introduction of the construct of *ethnolinguistic vitality*. In an attempt to place social psychological processes mediating such communication in their appropriate sociostructural contexts, Giles *et al.* (1977) proposed a taxonomy of factors which were hypothesized to affect groups' ethnolinguistic vitalities, i.e. their ability to behave and survive as distinctive and active collective entities in intergroup settings.

According to Giles *et al.* (1977), group status, demographic strength, institutional support and control factors combine to make up the vitality of ethnolinguistic groups. Demographic variables relate to the sheer number of ethnolinguistic group members and their distribution throughout urban, regional and national territories. Demographic variables also include groups' rates of immigration, emigration and endogamy, as well as their birth rates. Institutional support and control factors refer to the extent to which a language group is formally and informally represented in, and controls, various educational, political, religious, economic, cultural and mass media institutions. Status variables pertain to language groups' sociohistorical prestige, social and economic status, as well as the status of the languages used by speakers locally and internationally. Groups' strengths and weaknesses on each of these dimensions may be assessed to provide a rough classification of ethnolinguistic groups as having low, medium or high vitality.

Since its introduction, the construct of ethnolinguistic vitality has been theoretically incorporated into a variety of models in second-language acquisition (e.g. Giles and Byrne, 1982; Giles and Johnson, 1987), language attitudes (e.g. Ryan, Giles and Sebastian, 1982), ethnic identification (e.g. Giles and Johnson, 1981) and relations between sexes (e.g. Kramarae, 1981), as well as in cross-cultural communication (e.g. Bourhis, 1979). The original formulations of Giles *et al.* (1977) focused largely on an 'objective' analysis of ethnolinguistic vitality gathered from available sociological and demographic information. The Subjective Vitality Questionnaire (SVQ; Bourhis, Giles, and Rosenthal, 1981) was developed to take into account individuals' representations of vitality which mediate ethnolinguistic behaviour (Johnson, Giles, and Bourhis, 1983; Moscovici, 1981; cf. Husband and Saifullah Khan, 1982).

Empirical work on subjective vitality in multilingual contexts has explored a variety of issues. For instance, in assessing the relationship between perceived and objective vitality, Giles, Rosenthal, and Young (1985) obtained impressive factor analytic support from SVQ responses for the social psychological reality of ethnolinguistic vitality along the dimensions of demography, status and institutional support and control. Other empirical studies have shown systematic effects of sociopolitical change on perceptions of vitality (e.g. Pierson, Giles, and Young, 1987; Young, Giles, and Pierson, 1986). Research assessing language attitudes in multilingual communication has shown that speakers who perceive their own group vitality to be high have more positive attitudes about the use of their own group language in a wider range of public and private settings than do speakers who perceive their group vitality to be low (Bourhis and Sachdev, 1984; Sachdev,

Bourhis, Phang, and D'Eye, 1987). Empirical findings in these and other areas including language acquisition (e.g. Giles, Garrett, and Coupland, 1987a; Giles and Johnson, 1987; Labrie and Clément, 1986) show that information about group vitality is important to understand better a variety of issues concerning bilingualism and multilingualism. However, the relationship between vitality and bilingual and multilingual code-switching has received little empirical attention.

INTEGRATIVE RESEARCH

There have been several theoretical attempts to integrate the influence of normative, motivational and sociostructural factors in code-switching (e.g. Bourhis, 1979, 1985; Giles et al., 1987a; Giles and Hewstone, 1982; Scotton, 1983b). However, empirical work has generally focused on the importance of a single factor or a limited set of factors operating at any one time. Traditional sociolinguistics emphasized the importance of social norms and rules and neglected the influence of social psycho-logical and sociostructural factors in communication. Recent approaches classified under the rubric of 'interactional sociolinguistics', emphasizing the negotiated aspects of code-switching between contrastive ethnolinguistic group speakers, have also received similar criticism. For instance, Singh, Lele, and Martohardjono (1988) are critical of current interactional sociolinguistic research for taking a dominant centric approach which fails to acknowledge that bilingual and multilingual com-munication usually occur between speakers who are members of groups of unequal power and status within majority/minority settings (e.g. Gumperz, 1982; Scotton, 1983b; see Chapter 15, by Gudykunst and Ting-Toomey). In the social psychology of language, the focus of a majority of studies in the speech-accommodation framework has been on communication situations where normative influences were ambiguous or non-existent, and the study of the role of sociostructural factors was restricted largely to that of description (e.g. Bourhis, 1984a; Giles et al., 1973).

Systematic empirical exploration of the interactive influence of normative, motivational and sociostructural factors in bilingual and multilingual code-switching is still in its infancy. Recent studies conducted in Montreal and Quebec City, whose resident anglophone and francophone populations differ greatly in terms of their relative vitalities, are worth discussing.

Historically, in Montreal, anglophones have long dominated the francophone majority (60% of the population) in economic, political and educational spheres in spite of being a numerical minority (20% of the population) (Bourhis 1984b). Indeed, some of the earliest studies in the social psychology of language showed that, in Montreal, both anglophones and francophones rated English speakers more favourably than French speakers on status and solidarity traits (e.g. Lambert, 1967). In the late 1970s, francophone vitality received a considerable boost when language legislation known as Bill 101 was adopted to promulgate French as the only official language of the province of Quebec (d'Anglejan, 1984). Threats and changes to the high ethnolinguistic vitality of the English-speaking minority effected by this legisla-tion have been associated with increased salience of anglophone categorization and anglophone identity (Bourhis, 1984b; Coleman, 1984). Bilingual Montreal, with its large anglophone minority, has remained at the centre of intense ethnolinguistic group conflict.

Quebec City is largely monolingual, with francophones comprising over 90% of the population. The differential in favour of francophone vitality over anglophone vitality is considerably greater in Quebec City than in Montreal, with francophones being overwhelmingly represented in all spheres of economic, political, educational and social endeavours. Relations between anglophones and francophones have also been less conflictive and more harmonious in Quebec City than in Montreal.

It was in the above two contexts that Genesee and Bourhis (1982, 1988) conducted their studies of the evaluative significance of code-switching (see Chapter 19, by Bradac). They argued that an ideal integrative approach to bilingual and multilingual communication involves a sequential analysis of language switching (Bourhis, 1985). Employing the segmented dialogue technique (Bourhis *et al.*, 1975), English and French Canadians were asked to evaluate code selection by anglophone and francophone actors heard in a simulated client–clerk interaction in a downtown retail shop. Four different patterns of code choice, consisting of three or four speaker turns, were played to listeners in each study and subjects were asked to form impressions after each speaker turn.

Results obtained in both Montreal and Quebec City revealed systematic patterns in listeners' evaluations of language switches, which depended on a complex and dynamic interplay between normative, social psychological and sociostructural factors. The most significant finding of these studies was that the bases of evaluation interactively *changed* over the course of the conversation.

Results of both studies showed that, in the initial speaker turns, normative constraints best accounted for listeners' evaluations of the code choices made by clerks. For instance, francophone and anglophone listeners in Montreal and Quebec City downgraded the clerk for failing to converge to the language of the client, thus violating the language norm favouring use of the client's language. Importantly, in accordance with a *normative* analysis, clerks in the Montreal study were not upgraded (rewarded evaluatively) for upholding the norm of switching to the clients' language.

Results of both studies also showed that listeners' evaluations of clerks' later code choices were influenced to a greater degree by interpersonal accommodation processes. Indeed, when both interlocutors maintained their respective ingroup languages at the onset of the bilingual encounter, subsequent language choices of the client were negatively evaluated. In contrast, when speakers showed their goodwill and respect through mutual convergence early in the conversation, subsequent language choices seemed emptied of their divisive ideological content and had little impact on listeners' evaluations.

Though there were a variety of similarities in results obtained in Montreal and Quebec City such as those reported above, there were some important differences. First, English maintenance by an anglophone clerk with a francophone client in the initial speaker turns, though violating the situational norm, was positively evaluated by anglophone listeners in Montreal but not in Quebec City. Second, in Quebec City, evaluations of clerk's switches to client's language were actually *upgraded* by anglophone and francophone subjects in both early and late phases of the conversation. Thus, unlike results from the Montreal study, speech-accommodation considerations appeared to be important throughout the conversation in Quebec City.

The above differences between the results obtained in the Quebec City study and the Montreal study highlight the importance of the sociostructural context in affecting evaluative reactions to code-switching in bilingual encounters. For instance, the ingroup-favouring evaluations of anglophone listeners in Montreal may be attributed to the high, but threatened, vitality traditionally enjoyed by the anglophones in Montreal. Bourhis (1984a) also obtained results from field studies attesting to the high vitality of anglophones in Montreal. He found that pedestrians' actual response language choices to pleas, voiced either in French or in English, favoured English language usage by both anglophones and francophones in Montreal. This was in marked contrast to the results of self-reported language use and attitudinal surveys (e.g. Bourhis, 1983) favouring French usage in all domains.

In Quebec City, the overwhelming dominance of French makes communication more predictable, allowing interpersonal accommodation to play an important role earlier on in bilingual encounters. Indeed, the large and stable vitality advantage enjoyed by francophones in Quebec City may be expected to result in evaluations favouring French rather than English by both francophones and anglophones, *in spite of* normative and accommodative factors. In accordance, results from Genesee and Bourhis's (1988) study in Quebec City showed that all groups of listeners consensually evaluated the client's switches to French more positively than switches to English, and especially so when the client was depicted as an anglophone. The favourable evaluation of high-vitality languages by majority and minority groups has also been obtained in other multilingual situations characterized by large and stable vitality differentials (e.g. Bourhis and Sachdev, 1984; Sachdev et al., 1987).

Clearly, neither normative nor motivational factors are sufficient to account for the evaluation of multilingual and code-switching in the studies discussed above – an analysis of group vitality is necessary better to understand bilingual communication. Unfortunately, previous research on group vitality and bilingual and multilingual communication has generally been of a descriptive nature. Field investigations incorporating the construct of group vitality provide a realism that is almost impossible to capture in laboratory investigations of the relationship between sociostructural factors and intergroup behaviour. Due to their largely correlational nature, field approaches clearly need to be complemented by more predictive, experimental approaches to fill in the sociostructural lacunae of bilingual and multilingual communication. Since the vitality construct encompasses three fundamental features of intergroup relations, viz. group numbers, status and power, some interesting theoretical and empirical possibilities are raised by making links with recent experimental research in the social psychology of intergroup relations.

FILLING THE SOCIOSTRUCTURAL LACUNAE

Results of the classic 'minimal group' studies have consistently shown that anonymous and arbitrarily categorized ingroup subjects discriminate against outgroup members to achieve positive social identities (e.g. Sachdev and Bourhis, 1985;

Tajfel, 1978). Minimal group discrimination has been conceptualized as the outcome of the interplay between the processes of social categorization, social identity and social comparison, functioning to attain psychological distinctiveness (Tajfel and Turner, 1979). In multilingual contexts, languages (codes) often serve as powerful categorization cues, which trigger social categorization effects in much the same way that arbitrary categorization processes operate in the 'minimal group' paradigm. From an SAT perspective, language divergence and maintenance have been conceptualized as reflecting motivations for positive 'psycholinguistic' distinctiveness in multilingual contexts (Giles et al., 1977, 1987b).

Giles (1978) provided a taxonomy of ethnolinguistic group contact situations in terms of group members' language skills; this implied the importance of sociostructural factors such as power, status and group numbers in shaping the dynamics of relations between ethnolinguistic groups without making specific distinctions between the three sociostructural factors. Recent studies using the minimal group paradigm have shown that group numbers, status and power differentials have predictably independent and interactive effects on patterns of intergroup behaviour and perceptions (Sachdev and Bourhis, 1984, 1985, 1987, 1988).

In brief, results of these intergroup studies showed that increases in own group power and own group status led to increased discrimination. Dominant and high-status group members favoured members of their own groups, while subordinate and low-status group members were more egalitarian in their treatment of outgroup members. Results also showed that arbitrary numerical minority group members tended to be more discriminatory than their majority counterparts. Generally, membership in minority groups accentuated patterns of intergroup behaviour present in majority group conditions. For instance, dominant high-status group members were much more discriminatory when they were in a minority than in a majority. Similarly, subordinate low-status group members favoured *outgroup* members more when they were in a minority than in a majority. Other results from the intergroup studies showed that, relative to group numbers and group status, group power was more predictive of actual behaviour. However, group status accounted for most of the variance in intergroup evaluations and social identifications.

Conceptually, Sachdev and Bourhis (1988) argue that their results show that group status and group numbers factor variables are causally related to intergroup differentiation, in that they make direct contributions to the *a priori* positivity and security of members' group identities, which in turn motivate subsequent behaviour. In contrast, group power may be best conceptualized as affecting the range of behavioural options available to group members, regardless of their degree of identification with the ingroup. How are these conceptualizations likely to be useful in understanding the impact of the sociostructural context within which multilingual communication takes place?

The simplest expectations may be that the dynamics of language choice and language evaluation strategies are influenced by group numbers, status and power differentials in a manner that is similar to the intergroup studies. For instance, on the basis of the experimental findings that arbitrary numerical majorities – having 'security in numbers' – were less discriminatory than numerically equal groups,

Bourhis and Sachdev (1984) predictably found that English Canadians were more tolerant of Italian usage when they comprised a numerical majority rather than a numerically equal group relative to the Italian outgroups in their local school settings. In a similar vein, insecurities associated with being members of a dominant and high-status *minority* group in Montreal may have contributed to the ingroup favouritism in language evaluations displayed by anglophone listeners in the study by Genesee and Bourhis (1982). Such examples illustrate how some findings of the experimental intergroup studies on sociostructural variables may inform real-life issues in bilingual and multilingual communication, though systematic research has yet to be done to assess their generalizability, and their interaction with normative and motivational variables in multilingual contexts.

EPILOGUE AND FUTURE DIRECTIONS

Reviews of the literature on the social psychology of bilingual and multilingual communication show that normative and motivational approaches have yielded invaluable insights and provided useful frameworks for understanding code-switching phenomena. Both theoretically and empirically, the reviews of past research and recommendations for future work emphasize integrative approaches. Recent theoretical approaches (e.g. Bourhis, 1985; Giles *et al.*, 1987b) outline some of the multifactorial complexities underlying multilingual communication. Conceptually, as Hamers and Blanc (1989) have argued, the complexity of some of the recent propositional frameworks (e.g. Giles *et al.*, 1987b; Gudykunst, 1986) may provide the impetus for more integrative yet parsimonious meta-analyses of the determinants of bilingual and multilingual code-switching.

The sociostructural lacunae in these conceptualizations need to be filled. Empirically, field studies from different sociostructural contexts may be designed explicitly to assess systematically the findings of the intergroup studies in detail. Research in intergroup relations is also likely to benefit from this enterprise, particularly as bilingual and multilingual code-switching represent ideal naturally occurring intergroup phenomena, where language choices are inextricably linked to the expressive and symbolic salience of group identity. Theoretically, taxonomies of ethnolinguistic group contact situations such as the classification by Giles (1978) may be reformulated in terms of differences in power, status and group numbers as these variables have been shown to have independent and different effects on behaviour.

One point worthy of attention is that much of the previous research in the social psychology of language has focused on evaluations of code-switching and self-reports of code-switching. Interestingly, Bourhis (1983, 1984a) has obtained evidence showing that evaluations and self-reports of language choice were not always predictive of actual language behaviour. Future studies that include actual code-switching responses as dependent measures would improve the predictive utility of models.

Finally, as the findings of recent studies have emphasized (Bourhis, 1985), future research should focus on sequential analyses of bilingual and multilingual communication. The determinants of code-switching are not only multifactorial but also interact dynamically throughout the course of communication as was illustrated by an interesting instance of multilingual switching in India. Luthra (1986) reported that after accepting witness testimony in eight languages – Persian, Tamil, English, Hindi, Sinhala, Latin, Arabic and Sindhi – an Indian High-Court judge delivered his final, classically differentiating judgment in Sanskrit! In conclusion, the use of laboratory and field methodologies in future research will help us better understand the fundamental aspects of bilingual and multilingual communication.

REFERENCES

d'Anglejan, A. (1984). Language planning in Quebec: An historical overview and future trends. In R.Y. Bourhis (Ed.), *Conflict and language planning in Quebec*, pp. 29–52. Clevedon (England): Multilingual Matters.

Beardsley, R.B. and Eastman, C.M. (1971). Markers, pauses, and code-switching in bilingual Tanzanian speech. *General Linguistics*, **11**, 17–27.

Beebe, L. (1981). Social and situational factors affecting communicative strategies of communicative code-switching. *International Journal of the Sociology of Language*, **46**, 139–49.

Bentahila, A. (1983). *Language attitudes in Morocco*. Clevedon (England): Multilingual Matters.

Berger, C.R. and Bradac, J.J. (1982). *Language and social knowledge*. London: Arnold.

Bourhis, R.Y. (1979). Language in ethnic interaction: A social psychological approach. In H. Giles and B. Saint-Jacques (Eds), *Language and ethnic relations*, pp. 117–142. Oxford: Pergamon.

Bourhis, R.Y. (1983). Language attitudes and self-reports of French–English usage in Quebec. *Journal of Multilingual and Multicultural Development*, **4**, 163–179.

Bourhis, R.Y. (1984a). Cross-cultural communication in Montreal: Two field studies since Bill 101. *International Journal of the Sociology of Language*, **46**, 33–47.

Bourhis, R.Y. (Ed.) (1984b). *Conflict and language planning in Quebec*. Clevedon (England): Multilingual Matters.

Bourhis, R.Y. (1985). The sequential nature of language choices in cross-cultural communication. In R.L. Street, Jr and J.N. Cappella (Eds), *Sequence and pattern in communicative behaviour*, pp. 120–141. London: Arnold.

Bourhis, R.Y. and Giles, H. (1977). The language of intergroup distinctiveness. In H. Giles (Ed.), *Language, ethnicity and intergroup relations*, pp. 119–136. London: Academic Press.

Bourhis, R.Y., Giles, H., and Lambert, W.E. (1975). Social consequences of accommodating one's style of speech: A cross-national investigation. *International Journal of the Sociology of Language*, **6**, 55–72.

Bourhis, R.Y., Giles, H., Leyens, J.-P., and Tajfel, H. (1979), Psycholinguistic distinctiveness: Language divergence in Belgium. In H. Giles and R. St Clair (Eds), *Language and social psychology*, pp. 158–185. Oxford: Blackwell.

Bourhis, R.Y., Giles, H., and Rosenthal, D. (1981). Notes on the construction of a 'Subjective Vitality Questionnaire' for ethnolinguistic groups. *Journal of Multilingual and Multicultural Development*, **2**, 144–55.

Bourhis, R.Y. and Sachdev, I. (1984). Vitality perceptions and language attitudes: Some Canadian data. *Journal of Language and Social Psychology*, **3**, 97–126.

Brietborde, L.B. (1983). Levels of analysis in sociolinguistic explanation: Bilingual code-switching, social relations, and domain theory. *International Journal of the Sociology of Language*, **39**, 5–43.

Brown, P. and Fraser, C. (1979). Speech as a marker of situation. In K.R. Scherer and H. Giles (Eds), *Social markers in speech*, pp. 33–62. Cambridge: Cambridge University Press.

Brown, P. and Levinson, S. (1980). Universals in language usage: Politeness phenomena. In E.N. Goody (Ed.), *Questions and politeness: Strategies and social interaction*, pp. 256–289. Cambridge: Cambridge University Press.

Byrne, D. (1969). Attitudes and attraction. *Advances in Experimental Social Psychology*, **4**, 35–89.

Coleman, W. (1984). Social class and language policies in Quebec. In R.Y. Bourhis (Ed.), *Conflict and language planning in Quebec*, pp. 130–147. Clevedon (England): Multilingual Matters.

Davidson, D. (1974). Psychology as philosophy. Reprinted in Davidson, D. (1982). *Essays on actions and events*. Oxford: Clarendon.

Ervin-Tripp, S.M. (1968). An analysis of the interaction of language, topic and listener. In J.A. Fishman (Ed.), *Readings in the sociology of language*, pp. 192–211. The Hague: Mouton.

Fasold, R. (1984). *The sociolinguistics of society*. Oxford: Blackwell.

Ferguson, C.A. (1959). Diglossia. *Word*, **15**, 125–140.

Fishman, J.A. (1967). Bilingualism with and without diglossia; Diglossia with and without bilingualism. *Journal of Social Issues*, **32**, 29–38.

Fishman, J.A. (1972). *The sociology of language*. Rowley, MA: Newbury House.

Fishman, J. (1977). Language and ethnicity. In H. Giles (Ed.), *Language, ethnicity and intergroup relations*, pp. 15–57. London: Academic Press.

Gal, S. (1983). Comment. *International Journal of the Sociology of Language*, **39**, 63–72.

Genesee, F. and Bourhis, R.Y. (1982). The social psychological significance of code-switching in cross-cultural communication. *Journal of Language and Social Psychology*, **1**, 1–28.

Genesee, F. and Bourhis, R.Y. (1988). Evaluative reactions of language choice strategies: Francophones and anglophones in Quebec City. *Language Sciences*, **8**, 229–250.

Gibbons, J.P. (1986). *Code-mixing and code-choice: A Hong Kong case study*. Clevedon (England): Multilingual Matters.

Giles, H. (Ed.) (1977). *Language, ethnicity, and intergroup relations*. London: Academic Press.

Giles, H. (1978). Linguistic differentiation between ethnic groups. In H. Tajfel (Ed.), *Differentiation between social groups*, pp. 361–393. London: Academic Press.

Giles, H., Bourhis, R.Y., and Taylor, D. (1977). Towards a theory of language in ethnic group relations. In H. Giles (Ed.), *Language, ethnicity and intergroup relations*, pp. 307–348. London: Academic Press.

Giles, H. and Byrne, J. (1982). The intergroup model of second language acquisition. *Journal of Multilingual and Multicultural Development*, **3**, 17–40.

Giles, H., Garrett, P., and Coupland, N. (1987a). Language acquisition in the Basque Country: Invoking and extending the intergroup model. Paper presented at the 2nd World Basque Congress, San Sebastian, Spain.

Giles, H. and Hewstone, M. (1982). Cognitive structures, speech and social situations: Two integrative models. *Language Sciences*, **4**, 187–219.

Giles, H. and Johnson, P. (1981). The role of language in ethnic group relations. In J.C. Turner and H. Giles (Eds), *Intergroup behaviour*, pp. 199–243. Oxford: Blackwell.

Giles, H. and Johnson, P. (1986). Perceived threat, ethnic commitment, and interethnic language behaviour. In Y. Kim (Ed.), *Interethnic communication: Recent research*, pp. 91–116. Beverly Hills, CA: Sage.

Giles, H. and Johnson, P. (1987). Ethnolinguistic identity theory: A social psychological approach to language maintenance. *International Journal of the Sociology of Language*, **68**, 256–269.

Giles, H., Mulac, A., Bradac, J.J., and Johnson, P. (1987b). Speech accommodation theory: The first decade and beyond. In M.L. McLaughlin (Ed.), *Communication Yearbook*, No. 10, pp. 13–48. Beverly Hills, CA: Sage.

Giles, H. and Powesland, P.F. (1975). *Speech style and social evaluation*. London: Academic Press.

Giles, H., Rosenthal, D., and Young, L. (1985). Perceived ethnolinguistic vitality: The Anglo- and Greek-Australian setting. *Journal of Multilingual and Multicultural Development*, **3**, 253–269.

Giles, H., Taylor, D., and Bourhis, R.Y. (1973). Towards a theory of interpersonal accommodation through language: Some Canadian data. *Language in Society*, **2**, 177–192.

Grandy, R. (1973). Reference, meaning and belief. *Journal of Philosophy*, **70**, 439–52.

Grice, H.P. (1975). Logic and conversation. In P. Cole and J.L. Morgan (Eds), *Syntax and semantics*, Vol. 3, *Speech acts*, pp. 41–58. New York: Academic Press.

Grosjean, F. (1982). *Life with two languages: An introduction to bilingualism*. Cambridge, MA: Harvard University Press.

Gudykunst, W.B. (1986). Towards a theory of intergroup communication. In W.B. Gudykunst (Ed.), *Intergroup Communications*, pp. 152–167. London: Arnold.

Gumperz, J.J. (1982). *Discourse strategies*. Cambridge: Cambridge University Press.

Gumperz, J.J. and Hymes, D. (Eds). (1972). *Directions in sociolinguistics*. New York: Holt, Rinehart and Winston.

Hamers, J.H. and Blanc, M.H. (1982). Towards a social-psychological model of bilingual development. *Journal of Language and Social Psychology*, **1**, 29–49.

Hamers, J.H. and Blanc, M.H. (1989). *Bilinguality and bilingualism*. Cambridge: Cambridge University Press.

Heider, P. (1958). *The psychology of interpersonal relations*. New York: Wiley.

Herman, S. (1961). Explorations in the social psychology of language choice. *Human Relations*, **14**, 149–164.

Homans, G.C. (1961). *Social behaviour*. New York: Harcourt, Brace and World.

Husband, C. and Saifullah Khan, V. (1982). The viability of ethnolinguistic vitality: Some creative doubts. *Journal of Multilingual and Multicultural Development*, **3**, 193–205.

Hymes, D. (1972). Models of the interaction of language and social life. In J.J. Gumperz and D. Hymes (Eds), *Directions in sociolinguistics*, pp. 35–71. New York: Holt, Rinehart and Winston.

Johnson, P., Giles, H., and Bourhis, R.Y. (1983). The viability of ethnolinguistic vitality: A reply. *Journal of Multilingual and Multicultural Development*, **4**, 255–69.

Kelley, J.J. (1973). The process of causal attribution. *American Psychologist*, **28**, 107–128.

Kramarae, C. (1981). *Women and men speaking*. Rowley, MA: Newbury House.

Labrie, N. and Clément, R. (1986). Ethnolinguistic vitality, self-confidence and second language proficiency: An investigation. *Journal of Multilingual and Multicultural Development*, **7**, 269–282.

LaFrance, M. (1979). Nonverbal synchrony and rapport: Analysis by the cross-lag panel technique. *Social Psychology Quarterly*, **42**, 66–70.

Lambert, W.E. (1967). A social psychology of bilingualism. *Journal of Social Issues*, **23**, 91–109.

Luthra, H.R. (1986). A classic pronouncement. *New Language Planning Newsletter*, **1**, 7–8.

Moscovici, S. (1981). On social representations. In J. Forgas (Ed.), *Social cognition*, pp. 181–209. London: Academic Press.

Pandit, P.B. (1979). Perspectives on sociolinguistics in India. In W.C. McCormack and S.A. Wurm (Eds), *Language and society*, pp. 171–182. The Hague: Mouton.

Pierson, H.D., Giles, H., and Young, L. (1987). Intergroup vitality perceptions during a period of political uncertainty: The case of Hong Kong. *Journal of Multilingual and Multicultural Development*, **8**, 451–460.

Platt, J. (1977). A model for polyglossia and multilingualism with special reference to Singapore and Malaysia. *Language in Society*, **6**, 361–378.

Platt, J. (1980). The *lingua franca* of Singapore: An investigation into strategies of inter-ethnic communication. In H. Giles, W.P. Robinson, and P.M. Smith (Eds), *Language: Social psychological pespectives*, pp. 171–177. Oxford: Pergamon.

Rubin, J. (1962). Bilingualism in Paraguay. *Anthropological Linguistics*, **4**, 52–58.

Ryan, E.B., Giles, H., and Sebastian, R.J. (1982). An integrative perspective for the study of attitudes towards language variation. In E.B. Ryan and H. Giles (Eds), *Attitudes towards language variation: Social and applied contexts*, pp. 1–19. London: Arnold.

Sachdev, I. and Bourhis, R.Y. (1984). Minimal majorities and minorities. *European Journal of Social Psychology*, **14**, 35–52.

Sachdev, I. and Bourhis, R.Y. (1985). Social categorization and power differentials in group relations. *European Journal of Social Psychology*, **15**, 415–434.

Sachdev, I. and Bourhis, R.Y. (1987). Status differentials and intergroup behaviour. *European Journal of Social Psychology*, **17**, 277–293.

Sachdev, I. and Bourhis, R.Y. (1988). Power and status in minority–majority relations. Unpublished manuscript, Birkbeck College, University of London.

Sachdev, I., Bourhis, R.Y., Phang, S.-W., and D'Eye, J. (1987). Language attitudes and vitality perceptions: Intergenerational effects amongst Chinese Canadian communities. *Journal of Language and Social Psychology*, **6**, 287–307.

Saville-Troike, M. (1982). *The ethnography of communication*. Oxford: Blackwell.

Scotton, C.M. (1980). Explaining linguistic choices as identity negotiations. In H. Giles, W.P. Robinson, and P.M. Smith (Eds), *Language: Social psychological perspectives*, pp. 359–366. Oxford: Pergamon.

Scotton, C.M. (1983a). Comment. *International Journal of the Sociology of Language*, **39**, 119–128.

Scotton, C.M. (1983b). The negotiation of identities in conversation: A theory of markedness and code-choice. *International Journal of the Sociology of Language*, **44**, 115–136.

Scotton, C.M. (1986). Diglossia and code-switching. In J.A. Fishman, A. Tabouret-Keller, M. Clyne, B. Krishnamurti, and M. Abdulaziz (Eds), *The Fergusonian impact*, Vol. 2, pp. 403–415. Berlin: Mouton.

Sechrest, L., Flores, L., and Arellano, L. (1968). Language and social interaction in a bilingual culture. *Journal of Social Psychology*, **76**, 155–161.

Simard, L., Taylor, D., and Giles, H. (1976). Attribution processes and interpersonal accommodation in a bilingual setting. *Language and Speech*, **19**, 374–387.

Singh, R., Lele, J., and Martohardjono, G. (1988). Communication in a multilingual society: Some missed opportunities. *Language in Society*, **17**, 43–59.

Street, R.L. (1982). Evaluation of non-content speech accommodation. *Language and Communication*, **2**, 13–31.

Tajfel, H. (Ed.) (1978). *Differentiation between social groups: Studies in the social psychology of intergroup relations*. London: Academic Press.

Tajfel, H. (1982). Social psychology of intergroup relations. *Annual Review of Psychology*, **33**, 1–39.

Tajfel, H. and Turner, J.C. (1979). An integrative theory of intergroup conflict. In W.G. Austin and S. Worchel (Eds), *The social psychology of intergroup relations*, pp. 33–47. Monterey, CA: Brookes/Cole.

Taylor, D. and Royer, L. (1980). Group processes affecting anticipated language choice in intergroup relations. In H. Giles, W.P. Robinson, and P. Smith (Eds), *Language: Social psychological perspectives*, pp. 185–192. Oxford: Pergamon.

Triandis, H.C. (1960). Cognitive similarity and communication in a dyad. *Human Relations*, **13**, 175–183.

Trudgill, P. (1974). *Sociolinguistics*. Harmondsworth (England): Penguin.

van den Berg, M.E. (1986). Language planning and language use in Taiwan: Social identity, language accommodation and language choice behaviour. *International Journal of the Sociology of Language*, **59**, 97–115.

Young, L., Giles, H., and Pierson, H. (1986). Sociopolitical change and perceived vitality. *International Journal of Intercultural Relations*, **10**, 459–469.

15

Ethnic Identity, Language and Communication Breakdowns

WILLIAM B. GUDYKUNST AND STELLA TING-TOOMEY

Department of Speech Communication, California State University, Fullerton, USA

Ethnic identity, for the most part, is activated and regulated through the dynamics of language and communication. Extensive research on various aspects of language and ethnicity (e.g. language attitudes, second-language learning, code-switching, speech norms, communication accommodation, ethnolinguistic identity) has been conducted in recent years using a variety of theoretical and methodological perspectives. It is impossible to examine all of the research here (for other recent reviews, see Chapter 14, by Sachdev and Bourhis; Giles and Franklyn-Stokes, 1989; Gudykunst, Ting-Toomey, Hall, and Schmidt, 1989; Hogg and Abrams, 1988). Our purpose, therefore, is to overview the interrelationships among ethnicity, language, and communication, with a focus on how language and ethnicity can affect communication breakdowns. We develop the chapter in four sections. We begin by assessing the overall relationship between ethnicity and language. Next we look at the relationship between language and ethnolinguistic identity. In the third section, we examine the relationship between ethnolinguistic identity and communication breakdowns. We try to integrate several different frameworks in this section in order to explain the conditions under which intergroup communication breakdowns are likely. To conclude, we offer suggestions for future theorizing and research.

Handbook of Language and Social Psychology
Edited by H. Giles and W.P. Robinson. © 1990 John Wiley & Sons Ltd

ETHNICITY AND LANGUAGE

Ethnicity is a slippery concept. There is little consensus among scholars across or within disciplines on how to define ethnicity (Ross, 1979). Conceptualizations of ethnicity tend to involve 'objective criteria', 'subjective' criteria, or some combination (Cohen, 1978). Objective definitions are based upon categorization by non-members. While the objective position predominated in early anthropological work (e.g. naming of 'tribes'), the objective approach to defining ethnicity has not been used widely since Barth's (1969) analysis. Barth pointed out that ethnic labels often are imposed inaccurately. He went on to suggest that ethnicity should be viewed as a subjective process whereby individuals use labels to define themselves and their communication with others.

DeVos (1975) argued that the 'ethnic identity of a group of people consists of their subjective symbolic or emblematic use of any aspect of culture, in order to differentiate themselves from other groups' (p. 16). Giles and Johnson (1981), in contrast, suggested that an ethnic group includes 'those individuals who identify themselves as belonging to the same ethnic category' (p. 202). The focus of their conceptualization is on drawing and maintaining ethnic group boundaries, which are necessary for a self-conscious ethnic identity (Paulston and Paulston, 1980). While these definitions avoid the pitfalls of the objective view of ethnicity, they do not take into consideration that others do categorize individuals and impose an identity on them. Despres (1975) incorporates both self-categorization and other-categorization when he claims that 'ethnic groups are formed to the extent that actors use ethnic identities to categorize themselves and others for purposes of interaction' (pp. 190–191). Fishman (1977) takes a similar position, arguing that 'ethnicity is rightly understood as an aspect of a collectivity's self-recognition as well as an aspect of its recognition in the eyes of outsiders' (p. 16).

For purposes of our analysis, we treat ethnicity as a function of self-categorization and/or other-categorization. Our position is consistent with social identity theory. Turner (1987), for example, points out that any self-categorization – 'cognitive groupings of oneself and some class of stimuli as the same' (p. 44) – is made by contrasting the stimuli being used to some other. Self-categorization involves the recognition of intraclass similarities and interclass differences. Self-categorizations involve at least three levels of abstraction: self as a human being, self as a member of ingroup or outgroup, and self as similar or different to other members of the ingroup. These correspond to the individual's 'human', 'social', and 'personal' identities, respectively (Turner, 1987). All self-categorizations inherently impose a categorization on others (another person either is or is not a member of the ingroup). The relevant ingroup may be based on ethnicity, nationality, sex, social class, etc.

There are four possible intergroup impression presentation options (Ting-Toomey, 1989):

(1) member categorizes or identifies self as a typical group member, and behaves typically;
(2) member categorizes or identifies self as an atypical group member, and behaves atypically;

(3) member categorizes or identifies self as a typical group member, but acts atypically;
(4) member categorizes or identifies self as an atypical group member, but acts typically.

The four options probably are influenced more by the individual's perceptions and interpretations than by the member's projected sense of self in the encounter. The individual's knowledge of an outgroup, the degree of favorableness towards the outgroup, the levels of expectations of the role enactment from outgroup members, and the degree of tolerance of ambiguity will create either a positive or negative climate for the initial intergroup contact. Hewstone and Brown (1986) argue that positive feelings towards outgroup members as a whole are more likely to be generated from intergroup interaction involving an outgroup member who is perceived as typical of his/her group rather than from interaction involving an outgroup member who is perceived as atypical. It may be necessary to qualify this finding, however, by adding on the variables of degree of favorable outgroup attitude and the valence of typical/atypical outgroup members' behavior. A favorable outgroup attitude, in conjunction with desirable typical/atypical outgroup members' behavior, will promote the development of an interpersonal relationship, while an unfavorable outgroup attitude, with undesirable typical/atypical outgroup members' behavior, will impede further relationship progress. Language salience plays a critical role in this process.

Before moving on to examine the relationship between ethnicity and language, a distinction should be drawn between the 'old' and 'new' ethnicity. The 'old' view of ethnicity can be traced to the writing of Park (1950), who argued that the 'race' relations cycle 'of contact, competition, accommodation and eventual assimilation, is apparently progressive and unreversible' (p. 150). According to Patterson (1977), the assimilationist view of ethnicity was based on individualism, where societal forces 'push us toward the creation of ourselves as separate and distinct individual beings' (p. 13). The 'new' view of ethnicity, in contrast, is based on a pluralistic model, where individuals carry their ethnicity with them in their interactions with others. The 'new' ethnicity' views ethnicity as a psychological state, not a property of groups (see e.g. Gans, 1979). Alba and Chaplin's (1983) research, which indicates that people from mixed ethnic ancestry still tend to identify with one group, supports this view. Hraba and Hoiberg (1983) succinctly summarize the new view when they point out that 'this "new ethnicity" is an internal attitude which predisposes, but does not make compulsory, the display of ethnic identification in interaction. When it facilitates self-interest, ethnic identity will be made evident; it is left latent when it would hinder' (p. 385). The display of ethnic identity, then, is part of a broader self-management and self-presentation process (see Chapter 9, by Holtgraves, and Chapter 10, by Tracy).

The positions regarding the relationship between ethnicity and language or ethnic identity are as numerous as the scholars writing on the subject. Gumperz and Cook-Gumperz (1982), for example, see language as relatively critical to ethnicity when they argue that 'social identity and ethnicity are in large part established and maintained through language' (p. 7). Haarmann (1986) supports this view in part, arguing that the relationship between language and ethnicity can be viewed only as one way: language affects ethnicity, not the other way around. It is through language that ethnic boundary is marked. According to Haarmann, while the statement 'ethnicity is definitely related to language' (p. 260) is false, the claim that 'whenever language is involved in boundary making of ethnic groups, it is definitely related to ethnicity' (p. 261) is true. He suggests that language can be a basic aspect of ethnicity but it is not a 'crucial' feature. Haarmann concludes that ethnic identity, not language, is the major generative mechanism for intergroup behavior; the effect of language on intergroup behavior is indirect through ethnicity. Edwards (1985), however, argues that, 'while language is commonly held to be a highly important or, indeed, essential component of group identity, it is not *necessary* to retain an original variety in order to maintain the continuity of a sense of groupness . . . identities can and do survive the loss of the original group language' (p. 159).

Overall, it is not language *per se*, but language salience issues that should constitute the focus of study on the relationship between ethnicity and language usage. For some ethnic groups, language serves as a critical dimension to the formation and the preservation of group membership. For other ethnic groups, the subscription to group values and norms and/or other means of communication patterns is enough to qualify members into different ingroup roles and positions. The issue of whether language comes before ethnicity, or ethnicity comes before language, is probably a chicken-and-egg question.

LANGUAGE AND ETHNOLINGUISTIC IDENTITY

Giles and Johnson (1981) argue that language performs at least four psychological functions with respect to ethnicity. They contend that 'a certain speech style or language is often a necessary attribute for membership of a particular ethnic group, a salient cue for interethnic categorization, an important aspect of ethnic identity, and the ideal medium for facilitating intragroup cohesion' (p. 241). Giles and Johnson go on to argue that there are at least three major approaches to the study of ethnicity and language: sociolinguistic, sociological, and communication breakdown. Sociolinguists focus on developing linguistic taxonomies of ethnic markers, while sociologists studying language examine 'language erosion' as a function of sociostructural factors in a society. Scholars studying breakdowns look at how and why interethnic communication is perceived to 'break down' or involve miscommunication.

While each of these approaches has made important contributions to the study of ethnicity and language, none of them 'take into account between-group and within-group diversity in language and ethnic attitudes, speech repertoires and strategies . . . [nor] structural features of, and influences on, groups in contact' (p. 216). In order to address these issues, Giles and Johnson adapted Tajfel's (1978) social identity theory and proposed a social psychological theory of language and ethnicity which has become known as 'ethnolinguistic identity theory' (a label first used by Beebe and Giles, 1984).

Drawing upon research on ethnolinguistic vitality ('individuals' cognitive representations of the sociostructural forms operating in interethnic contexts'; Giles and

Johnson, 1981, p. 229; see also Chapter 14, by Sachdev and Bourhis), group boundaries, interethnic comparisons, status, and social/ethnic identity, Giles and Johnson (1981) concluded that people tend to adopt positive linguistic distinctiveness strategies with members of outgroups when they:

(1) identify with an ingroup which considers its language important;
(2) make insecure comparisons with other ethnic groups;
(3) perceive their group's ethnolinguistic vitality to be high;
(4) perceive boundaries between their group and other groups to be closed and hard;
(5) do not identify strongly with other social categories;
(6) perceive little category-membership overlaps with the person with whom they are interacting;
(7) do not derive a strong social identity from other social category memberships;
(8) perceive their status to be higher in their ethnic group than in other social category memberships.

More recently, Giles and Johnson (1987) elaborated the theory, linking it to the attitudes/motivations of members of dominant and subordinate groups (this theory is discussed in the section on communication breakdowns), and Gallois, Franklyn-Stokes, Giles, and Coupland (1988) articulated the theory with communication-accommodation theory (e.g. Giles, Mulac, Bradac, and Johnson, 1987).

Several recent studies support the application of Tajfel's (1978) social identity theory to the study of ethnicity and language, and/or support Giles and Johnson's (1981, 1987) ethnolinguistic identity theory. McNamara (1987), for example, found that changes in social identity are accompanied by changes in language attitudes favoring English over Hebrew and a shift to the use of English among Jewish immigrants' children in Australia. Ros, Cano, and Huici's (1987) study revealed that social identity and perceived ethnolinguistic vitality affect intergroup relations and attitudes toward the major languages (Castilian, Catalan, Basque, Valencian, and Galician) in Spain. Specifically, they found that subtractive identity (i.e. the difference between identification with a specific linguistic ingroup and identification with Spain) is a better predictor of specific intergroup relations than identification with ingroup alone. Louw-Potgieter and Giles (1987) examined the linguistic strategies used to deal with imposed identities. Their research revealed that, when there is an incongruity between self-definition by members of one group and the identity imposed on them by members of another group, individuals attempt to escape the imposed identity by changing the criteria for group membership and by differentiating themselves from the group with which they are associated. Both of these processes involve specific language-usage strategies, but the specific strategies vary depending upon the groups and the relations between them.

Recent research also has linked code-switching to ethnolinguistic identity. Banks (1987), for example, extended traditional discourse-analytical work to examine the influence of language-in-use on changing ethnolinguistic identities. He argues that the boundary between marked and unmarked discourse (cf. Scherer and Giles, 1979) is soft and permeable, while the boundary between low- and high-power positions is hard and less permeable. Banks presents evidence to support four general propositions:

(1) members of ethnolinguistic minority groups must cross the soft boundary from marked ethnic discourse before crossing the boundary from a low- to high-power position;
(2) crossing the boundary from marked to unmarked ethnic discourse is a function of the individual's strategies for maximizing rewards, as well as of the norms, values, and discourse routines in the organization;
(3) there is an implicit promise from the organization that, if members of ethno-linguistic minorities cross the boundary from marked to unmarked ethnic discourse, they will have the opportunity to cross the low to high boundary;
(4) individuals who cross the boundary from marked to unmarked ethnic discourse 'subtract from' their ethnolinguistic identity (cf. Giles, 1979).

San Antonio (1987) also examined language-in-use as an ethnolinguistic identity marker in her study of intergroup communication in a US corporation in Japan. Her observations revealed that the use of English by Japanese employees was a marker for the claimed identity of being a Japanese with whom the North Americans could work, and it increased their status within the organization. The employees who were fluent in English 'protected' employees who did not speak English well in meetings by speaking up and answering North Americans' questions. Employees who did not speak English well were grateful for the help of those who spoke it better. The use of English in this particular setting, therefore, did not 'subtract' from the Japanese's ethnolinguistic identity.

Ethnolinguistic identity also is related to language attitudes. Consistent with ethnolinguistic identity theory, Giles and Ryan (1982) explained language attitudes of group members as a function of the situation in which the language is used. Two specific dimensions (status-stressing/solidarity-stressing and person-centered/group-centered) are used to evaluate the situation and language choice. In those situations where the solidarity-stressing or group-centered dimensions are dominant, individuals are likely to diverge linguistically from members of the outgroup. When the status-stressing and person-centered dimensions are most salient, individuals tend to converge linguistically with the members of the outgroup.

Ryan, Hewstone, and Giles (1984) extended Giles and Ryan's (1982) analysis to take into account intergroup dynamics, social attributional processes, and cognitive representatives of forces operating in the general society. They argue that evaluations of speakers is a function of the sociostructural context (i.e. the standardization and vitality of the languages), the immediate social situation (e.g. its domain and degree of formality), the language speakers themselves (i.e. the linguistic/para-linguistic features of the language, the individual/group attitudes, and the content of messages), the judges (especially their individual and group attributes), and cognitive processes (both individual and collective). Their intergroup model of language attitudes further distinguishes four patterns or 'language-preference profits':

(1) *Profile A* involves a preference within both groups for the dominant group (this

profile is subdivided into (A1), where the subordinate group's preference for the dominant group is due to 'self-hate', and (A2), where the subordinate group attributes its status to its 'negatively valued' group membership);

(2) *Profile B* involves a preference for the dominant group in terms of status, but a preference for the ingroup in terms of solidarity;

(3) *Profile C* involves situations where there is equal status between the groups, with an ingroup preference;

(4) *Profile D* involves a preference for the dominant group in terms of status, but a solidarity preference for the subordinate group.

Each of these patterns leads to different language attitudes and occurs under different conditions (e.g. vitality, standardization, and cognitive processes vary across profiles).

Ethnolinguistic identity also affects the nature of accommodation that occurs in interethnic encounters. There is a tendency for members of ingroups to react favorably to outgroup members who linguistically converge toward them (Bourhis and Giles, 1976; Giles and Smith, 1979). This, however, is not always the case. Giles and Byrne (1982) point out that, as an outgroup's members begin to learn the speech style of the ingroup, ingroup members will diverge in some way so as to maintain linguistic distinctiveness. Outgroup members' reaction to speech convergence depends upon the intent attributed to the speaker (Bourhis, 1984; Genesee and Bourhis, 1982; Simard, Taylor, and Giles, 1976). Speech divergence and/or speech maintenance can be used to assert a positive group identity (Bourhis, 1984; Bourhis and Giles, 1977; Giles, Bourhis, and Taylor, 1977). Further, cultural/ethnic values influence the nature of the accommodation that occurs. Bond and Yang's (1982) research, for example, revealed that the more important Chinese in Hong Kong place on Chinese values, the more they display ethnic affirmation and the less they display interethnic accommodation.

Giles *et al.* (1987) argue that communication convergence is a function of a speaker's desire for social approval, for high communication efficiency, for a shared self- or group-presentation, and for an appropriate identity definition. The preconditions for communication convergence also require a match between the speaker's view of the recipient's speech style and the actual speech being used, that speech is valued in the situation, and the specific speech style being used is appropriate for both the speaker and the recipient. Divergence, in contrast, is a function of the speaker's desire for a 'contrastive' self-image, to dissociate from the recipient, to change the recipient's speech behavior, and to define the encounter in intergroup terms. Divergence further occurs when recipients use a speech style which deviates from a norm which is valued that is consistent with the speaker's expectations regarding the recipient's performance.

Recently, Gallois *et al.* (1988) integrated Giles and Johnson's (1987) ethnolinguistic identity theory and Giles *et al.*'s (1987) theory of communication-accommodation processes. Gallois *et al.*'s (1988) theory differentiates the nature of communication accommodation, which occurs in encounters where the participants have either high or low dependence on their ingroup and either high or low identification with their ingroup. Differences between how members of subordinate and dominant groups react are specified and situational constraints on accommodation are isolated. Specific behaviors of 'speakers' and 'receivers' in intercultural encounters also are identified in the theory.

In summary, language-in-use in an interethnic communication context is a strategic choice (which can be either conscious or unconscious) that individuals make to maximize situational rewards to self and/or for other group members while not incurring the costs of the outcome. Further, the underlying motivations to use one language (or language variety) over another, the situation at hand, and the nature of the conversational task (instrumental as versus socio-emotional purposes) influence the use of a particular language or language variety.

ETHNOLINGUISTIC IDENTITY AND COMMUNICATION BREAKDOWN

Ethnolinguistic identity theory (Giles and Johnson, 1981, 1987) focuses on the influence of ethnic identity on individuals' intentions to maintain their distinctive language features. Gallois *et al.* (1988) integrated the theory with communication-accommodation theory (Giles *et al.*, 1987). Our purpose in this section is to extend the theory by linking it to intergroup communication breakdowns (e.g. instances of misunderstanding or miscommunication between members of different groups).

Language often is used synonymously with 'speech' and 'communication'. There are, however, important differences in these three concepts. Language is an abstract system of rules (phonological, syntactic, semantic, and pragmatic). As such, it is a medium of communication. The abstract rules are translated into a channel (spoken, written, or sign language) in order to create messages. When the channel is the spoken word, speech occurs. 'Communication is a more general concept involving the exchange of messages which may or may not be spoken and linguistic in form' (Berger and Bradac, 1982, p. 52). The primary function served by the exchange of messages is the reduction of uncertainty (Berger and Calabrese, 1975). Uncertainty in this context refers to individuals' inability to understand or predict their own and others' beliefs, attitudes, and behavior in a given situation. Linking language and the interpersonal/intergroup salience of encounters to uncertainty-reduction processes will help to clarify the relationship between ethnolinguistic identity and communication breakdowns.

Language affects uncertainty reduction in interethnic encounters. Berger and Bradac (1982) suggest four alternative models (see Figure 15.1) regarding the relationship between language and uncertainty reduction:

Model 1 specifies that people use others' language to develop hypotheses about their group affiliations, and, on the basis of these hypotheses, judgments of similarity are made. The greater the similarity, the more uncertainty is reduced.

Model 2 is similar except that a 'judgment of psychological trait or state' replaces the judgment of group membership as the mediator for judging similarity.

Model 3 posits that language leads to a judgment of group membership, which in turn

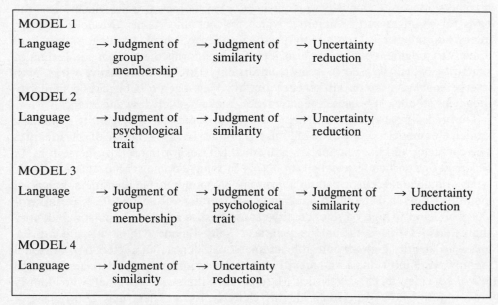

FIGURE 15.1 Models of the relationship between language and uncertainty reduction (Berger and Bradac, 1982).

leads to a judgment of psychological trait or state, which then forms the basis of a judgment of similarity. Similarity then leads to uncertainty reduction.

Model 4 posits that only a judgment of similarity intervenes between language and uncertainty reduction.

Each of the four models 'is probably valid in particular circumstances' (Berger and Bradac, 1982, p. 55); however, Berger and Bradac do not specify under which circumstances each model might be valid. Recognizing that the interpersonal and intergroup salience of encounters are orthogonal dimensions (Gudykunst and Lim, 1986) provides a way to define the circumstances under which each of Berger and Bradac's models should be valid.

Following Stephenson (1981), Gudykunst and Lim (1986) argued that encounters can be classified into one of four categories:

(1) high intergroup and low interpersonal salience;
(2) high intergroup and high interpersonal salience;
(3) low intergroup and high interpersonal salience;
(4) low interpersonal and low intergroup salience.

We contend that when intergroup salience is high and interpersonal salience low, individuals use language to make judgments of group affiliation on which judgments of similarity are made and uncertainty is reduced (Model 1). When intergroup salience is high and interpersonal salience also is high, a judgment of group membership is used to make a judgment of a psychological trait, which forms the basis for a judgment of similarity, which reduces uncertainty (Model 3). When intergroup salience is low and interpersonal salience is high, language should lead directly to judgment of a psychological trait, which forms the basis of a judgment of similarity, which is used to reduce uncertainty (Model 2). Finally, when both interpersonal and intergroup salience are low, language probably cues a similarity judgment (Model 4) because the interaction is of relatively low importance.

The preceding analysis is consistent with Ting-Toomey's (1986) identity-validation model. Her model is based upon McCall and Simmons' (1978) notion of role identity, 'the character and the role that an individual devises for himself [or herself] as an occupant of a particular social position' (p. 65). Ting-Toomey argues that four basic types of individuals participate in intergroup encounters: role identifiers, balanced identifiers, personal identifiers, and marginal identifiers. Role identifiers are individuals who identify high on role identity characteristics and low on personal identity characteristics (that is, the unique qualities of self). Balanced identifiers are individuals who identify high on both role and personal identity characteristics. Personal identifiers are individuals who identify high on personal identity characteristics and low on role identity characteristics. Marginal identifiers are individuals who identify low on both role and personal identity characteristics. There may also be a fifth identifier category in the validation model: the ambivalent identifiers. Ambivalent identifiers define themselves as being moderate with respect to either role or personal identity characteristics, or a combination of both. They are located in the crux of the identity-validation model – the ambivalent identifiers probably are characterized by perpetual dialectical tensions between their role identities and their idiosyncratic, personal identities.

Role identifiers tend to make evaluations of others on the basis of role traits and role attributes, and the language strategies that they use focus more on eliciting role-membership information, especially in the initial interactions with members of other groups. The balanced identifiers, on the other hand, tend to make an inferential linkage between group-membership information and psychological-trait information, and with the combined information, make a judgment about strangers. The personal identifiers use language strategies to elicit information concerning the psychological or the motivational states of the stranger, and, finally, the marginal identifiers may be at a loss as to how to use language strategically to gain information on a role identity level or a personal identity level.

The balanced identifiers probably are the most likely group to risk relational uncertainties and initiate interpersonal ties with members of the other groups because of their secure sense of self on both group (e.g. culture/ethnicity) and personal grounds. It seems likely that since balanced identifiers define themselves high on both identity salience and personal identity salience dimensions, they have more role identity and personal identity options to cultivate similarity of interests and attitudes with dissimilar others. The personal identifiers probably are the next likely group to risk establishing affective, interpersonal ties with an outgroup member because their idiosyncratic, unique personal characteristics propel them to test out different identity performance behaviors in different idiosyncratic relational situations, and, hence, the likelihood of their initiating interpersonal ties with dissimilar others is increased. In comparison, the role identifiers, who identify high on role characteristics and low on personal identity characteristics, probably are less likely to initiate interpersonal ties with an outgroup member because of the normative cultural constraints that are placed on their role enactments as compared to either the balanced identifier group or the personal identifier group. Finally, the marginal identifiers, who have a meager sense of both role identity and personal identity, probably are the least likely group to actively invest time and energy on the formation of interpersonal ties across group boundaries. Because of their perceived lack of self-worth and low self-value, they perceive any relational context as threatening and disconfirming.

Berger and Bradac's (1982) four language models also can be linked directly to Giles and Johnson's (1987) reformulation of ethnolinguistic identity theory, which is summarized in six sets of propositions. The first three sets of propositions relate to the predispositional conditions that influence the degree to which individuals define interethnic encounters in terms of ethnicity and the likelihood they will use language maintenance strategies. The first set of propositions posits that members of subordinate groups who consider language to be an important dimension of their identity, identify strongly with their ethnic group, and make insecure comparisons with other groups are predisposed to act in terms of ethnic solidarity, define intergroup encounters in terms of ethnicity, and try to maintain their distinctive language features.

The conditions outlined in the first set of propositions appear to apply in those situations where the intergroup salience of encounters is high and interpersonal salience is low (i.e. the role–identifier group). As indicated above, Berger and Bradac's (1982) Model 1 of the relationship between language and uncertainty reduction applies in this situation (see Figure 15.1). Ethnolinguistic identity is the major generative mechanism for intergroup attitudes (including language attitudes) and motivation to study, and competence in, outgroup languages, and these in turn influence uncertainty reduction in these situations (Gudykunst, 1985). When ethnic solidarity increases in importance, negative language attitudes increase, and motivation to study, and competence in, outgroup languages decreases. The effect of second-language competence on uncertainty reduction depends on the vitality of the outgroup language. If the outgroup language has high vitality, uncertainty will not be reduced *vis-à-vis* behavior of members of the outgroup, because competence is low; in fact, uncertainty may increase. If the outgroup languages has low vitality, then competence in the language should have little effect on uncertainty reduction with respect to the outgroup.

'Interpersonal' variables such as interpersonal attraction, frequency of communication, intimacy of communication and attitude similarity should not be positively related to uncertainty reduction in intergroup encounters when ethnic solidarity is stressed. Rather, uncertainty reduction should be a function of 'intergroup' variables such as group similarity, shared networks, knowledge of other group, and intergroup attitudes/stereotypes. Language is one of the major cues that activates stereotypes. Bond (1983), for example, found that language has a significant effect on activating different autostereotypes (Chinese) and heterostereotypes (Westerners) of Chinese bilinguals in Hong Kong. This research is consistent with studies which demonstrate that the language of questionnaires used in research can affect the responses to items dealing with ethnicity (Bond and Yang, 1982; Marin, Triandis, Betancourt, and Kashima, 1983; Punetha, Giles, and Young, 1987). Other research demonstrates that the effect of language on stereotypes is different from that of ethnicity. Specifically, Bond (1985) found that language influences Chinese bilinguals' judgments of the likability, Westernization, and benevolence of Chinese and British speakers, while ethnicity influences the speakers' ethnic-group preference.

Stereotypes also influence language choice. Beebe (1981), for example, found that when Chinese-Thai bilingual children are interviewed by a person who looks Chinese, but speaks standard Thai, they use Chinese phonological variants. Similarly, Bell (1982) discovered that stereotypes of listeners influence how New Zealand broadcasters read scripts. More recently, Mgbo-Elue (1987) examined the stereotypes Yorubas and Ibos in Nigeria hold regarding the other group and the effect these stereotypes have on individuals' desire to learn the outgroup language. She found a positive association between attitudes toward the outgroup and its language and desire to learn the outgroup language. Her research also revealed that positive stereotypes of the outgroup increase the likelihood that individuals will learn the outgroup language.

While any stereotype can reduce uncertainty, only accurate stereotypes allow accurate predictions to be made. Since intergroup contact is a novel form of interaction for most people (Rose, 1981) and contact is necessary to develop accurate stereotypes (Rothbart, Dawes, and Park, 1984), it is unlikely that accurate predictions are made when extreme ethnic solidarity is stresssed. A breakdown in interethnic communication, therefore, is likely.

Hewstone and Giles' (1986) stereotype-based model of intergroup communication breakdown focuses upon sociolinguistic stereotypes and language production/reception strategies. They argue that in intergroup situations sociolinguistic stereotypes are activated. The stereotypes activated and the speech pattern used are a function of the individuals' ethnolinguistic identities that are relevant in the particular context, as well as of the relations between the groups involved in the context (cf. Taylor and McKirnan, 1984). The relations between the groups influence the communicative distance established between the groups (e.g. Lukens' (1979) distances of 'indifference', 'avoidance', and 'disparagement', or Gudykunst and Kim's (1984) distances of cultural relativism, 'sensitivity', and 'equality'). The ethnolinguistic stereotypes are used to explain difficulties in intergroup communication and make accurate attributions about members of the outgroup (see Hewstone and Jaspars, 1982). Language production and reception strategies feed back and reinforce ethnolinguistic stereotypes and, in combination with the context, can lead to breakdowns in, or dissolutions of, intergroup encounters. The breakdowns or dissolutions, in turn, can increase uncertainty in intergroup relationships (cf. Sodetani and Gudykunst, 1987).

Giles and Johnson's (1987) second set of propositions in the reformulated ethnolinguistic identity theory posits that members of subordinate groups who consider language an important part of their identity, moderately identify with their ethnic group, and make insecure comparisons with other ethnic groups are predisposed to conform with ingroup norms, but display only weak or moderate ethnic solidarity, do not define all ethnic encounters in terms of ethnicity, and are not likely to maintain distinctive language features. These conditions exist when intergroup salience is high and interpersonal salience is high (i.e. the balanced-identifier group). Berger and Bradac's (1982) Model 3 (see Figure 15.1), therefore, applies to the relationship between language and uncertainty reduction. In this situation, ethnolinguistic identity is only one generative mechanism for the communication that occurs. Since individuals are less likely to maintain language distinctiveness, increases in the competence of the outgroup language should occur. Language cues associated with ethnolinguistic identity provide the basis for judgments of group membership, but these judgments are used to make judgments of psychological traits. The judgments of psychological traits include interpersonal factors (e.g. attitude similarity) which reduce uncertainty. Since there is moderate identification with the ethnic group and a few overlapping group memberships, the interpersonal factors are activated by judgments of psychological traits and are more central than ethnolinguistic identity in the reduction of uncertainty. The activation of interpersonal factors should decrease the effect of sociolinguistic stereotyping on language production and reception strategies and, thereby, decrease the likelihood of a breakdown in interethnic communication.

Giles and Johnson's (1987) third set of propositions posits that members of subordinate groups who do not see language as an important part of their identity, identify moderately or weakly with their ethnic group, and make secure comparisons with other ethnic groups are predisposed to conform to societal norms, show weak ethnic solidarity, define few intergroup encounters in terms of ethnicity, and are not likely to maintain their distinctive language features. These conditions occur when intergroup salience is low and interpersonal salience is high (i.e. the personal-identifier group). Berger and Bradac's (1982) Model 2 (see Figure 15.1), therefore, should explain the relationship between language and uncertainty reduction. In this situation, ethnolinguistic identity is not a major generative mechanism for communication. Since language is not an important aspect of group identity and intergroup salience is low, ethnolinguistic identity does not cue group membership. Language, therefore, leads directly to a judgment of psychological trait, which activates interpersonal factors (e.g. attitude similarity, attraction, frequency and intimacy of communication), which serve the major generative mechanisms for the reduction of uncertainty. Since ethnolinguistic identity is not a major factor influencing behavior, sociolinguistic stereotypes have only a minor effect on language production and reception strategies. The likelihood of a breakdown in interethnic communication, therefore, is low.

The first three sets of propositions deal with predispositional conditions. While Giles and Johnson (1987) did not link these propositions to differing levels of intergroup and interpersonal salience, each set of propositions appears to be applicable to a different combination of intergroup and interpersonal salience. The only combination not included is low intergroup and low interpersonal salience (i.e. the marginal-identifier group). Encounters under these conditions do not involve individuals who can provide rewards, who will be encountered in the future, or who act in a deviant fashion (the conditions under which people try to reduce uncertainty; Berger, 1979). If any of these were relevant, the encounter would involve high intergroup or high interpersonal salience. Since none of these conditions are met, uncertainty reduction is not a high priority. The only question relevant to these encounters is whether or not the other person will follow situational norms. Language, therefore, is used as a cue for a similarity judgment (e.g. this person is from the same culture and understands the norms), which reduces uncertainty in a sufficient amount so that interaction can take place (Berger and Bradac, 1982, Model 4).

Giles and Johnson (1987) argue that situational factors can override predispositional conditions. The fourth and fifth sets of propositions focus on specific ways situational factors moderate ethnic solidarity. When situational factors override the desire for ethnic solidarity, there is an increase in the use of outgroup (e.g. the dominant group) language or dialect, an increase in shared networks, interpersonal factors are attuned to, and, therefore, ethnolinguistic identity plays a less important role in uncertainty reduction. Since societal norms, rather than ingroup norms, are followed under these conditions, the situation itself serves as a mechanism for uncertainty reduction. The chances for communication breakdowns due to ethnicity and/or language, therefore, are minimized.

To summarize, when Giles and Johnson's (1987) first set of propositions is applicable, social categorization (a judgment of perceived group membership based on language cues) leads to a judgment of similarity, which influences uncertainty levels (i.e. if similarity is perceived, uncertainty is reduced; if dissimilarity is perceived, uncertainty is increased). The likelihood for interethnic communication breakdowns is high under these conditions. When the second set of propositions applies, language cues social categorization, but trait attributions (perceived traits) intervene between the initial judgment of group membership and the judgment of similarity, which in turn influences uncertainty. The likelihood of interethnic communication breakdowns is moderate under these conditions. When the third set of propositions applies, language serves as a cue that activates trait attribution, and, in turn, trait attribution is used as a basis for a judgment of perceived similarity, which affects uncertainty. The likelihood of interethnic communication breakdowns is low under these conditions. As the fourth and fifth sets of propositions indicate, situational factors may override those conditions where the first set of propositions is applicable. The situational factors also can influence use of, and competence in, the outgroup language/dialect.

Extending this line of argument to communication breakdowns, accurate attributions are critical in interethnic encounters that involve either intergroup salience and/or interpersonal salience. Accurate attributions based on salient group-membership characteristics will reduce uncertainty in interethnic interaction. Inaccurate attributions or typifications based on salient or non-salient group-membership characteristics will result in an increase of uncertainty, and ultimately, communication breakdowns. Accurate attributions based on salient interpersonal identity characterisics also will reduce uncertainty in interethnic interaction. Inaccurate attributions or mistypifications based on salient or non-salient interpersonal-typed characteristics will result in an increase of uncertainty. If such episodes repeat over time, communication breakdown is the most likely end-result. Of course, both interperceptual factors and situational factors across time will act as critical mediating variables that affect interethnic communication breakdowns.

Before concluding, one potential criticism of our formulation needs to be addressed. Our analysis is based upon the assumption that individuals attempt to reduce uncertainty in their interactions with strangers (cf. Berger and Calabrese, 1975). Sunnafrank (1986) disagrees with this assumption, arguing that individuals do not necessarily try to reduce uncertainty, but rather try to access the predicted outcome value of the relationship. He contends that individuals will pursue relationships with positive predicted outcomes and try to curtail or terminate relationships with negative predicted outcomes. We reject his criticism of uncertainty-reduction theory for several reasons. First, Sunnafrank's predictions regarding relationships with potential predicted outcomes are consistent with uncertainty-reduction theory predictions and Berger's (1979) assumption that individuals try to reduce uncertainty when others provide rewards. Second, we contend that individuals often cannot curtail and/or terminate relationships with negative predicted outcomes, especially in an interethnic context. Rather, situational demands often require individuals to continue intergroup relationships that have negative predicted outcomes. As Berger argues, however, individuals who find themselves in the situation will still try to reduce uncertainty because the outgroup member will be encountered in the future.

CONCLUSION

To conclude, our purpose in this chapter was to overview the interrelationships among ethnic identity, language, and communication breakdowns. We have attempted to integrate recent theoretical formulations in the social psychology of language (e.g. ethnolinguistic identity theory, communication-accommodation theory) with uncertainty-reduction theory to proffer a plausible explanation of how language and ethnicity contribute to interethnic communication breakdowns. The explanations suggested, however, must be considered tentative until they are tested empirically.

Several issues remain to be resolved theoretically and methodologically. Theoretically, most perspectives and frameworks that focus on the relationships among ethnicity, language, and communication do not account for the interperceptual processes that affect communication breakdowns. Since a communication breakdown episode minimally involves two participants in an interactive situation, future theoretical effort should emphasize the importance of studying the congruence versus incongruence of perceptions, attributions, and categorizations in the analysis of interethnic communication breakdowns. Further, the situational and contextual variables that mediate the effect of language and ethnicity on communication breakdowns (see for example Forgas's (1988) work on social episodes) should be isolated in future theoretical work. The focus on social episodes is necessary because effective interethnic communication is, to a large extent, based on the 'shared episode representations between the interactants [that] are present' (Forgas, 1988, p. 188), and ineffective interethnic communication is, to a large extent, based on misaligned episode representations, which, ultimately, may lead to communication

breakdowns. Finally, we believe that future research should use uncertainty-reduction theory in conjunction with an expectations states perspective (e.g. Berger and
Zelditch, 1985) in the theorizing about ethnic identity, language, and communication breakdowns. Uncertainty increases when someone's expectations regarding
situational episodes have been violated and this, in turn, should feed back to create
more uncertainty in an interethnic miscommunication situation.

Methodologically, a process orientation to the study of interethnic uncertainty-
reduction episodes is needed. Attributions, categorizations, and interethnic typifications are all based on the dynamic interplay of language exchange. If language plays
such a critical role in the marking or unmarking of ethnic identity, and language itself
is also a prime contributor to communication breakdowns, it is vital for researchers
to study the verbal and non-verbal moves and counter-moves that lead to communication, miscommunication, and, eventually, to interethnic communication
breakdowns.

REFERENCES

Alba, R.D. and Chaplin, M.B. (1983). A preliminary examination of ethnic identification
among whites. *American Sociological Review*, **48**, 240–247.
Alert, E. (1979). *Implications of ethnic renewal in modern industrialized society*. Helsinki:
Commendations Scientiarum Socialism.
Banks, S.P. (1987). Achieving 'unmarkedness' in organizational discourse: A praxis perspec-
tive on ethnolinguistic identity. *Journal of Language and Social Psychology*, **6**, 171–190.
Barth, F. (1969). *Ethnic groups and boundaries*. London: Allen and Unwin.
Beebe, L.M. (1981). Social and situational factors affecting the strategy of dialect code-
switching. *International Journal of the Sociology of Language*, **32**, 139–149.
Beebe, L.M. and Giles, H. (1984). Speech accommodation theories: A discussion in terms of
second-language acquisition. *International Journal of the Sociology of Language*, **46**, 5–32.
Bell, A. (1982). Radio: The style of news language. *Journal of Communication*, **32**, 150–164.
Berger, C.R. (1979). Beyond initial interactions. In H. Giles and R. St Clair (Eds), *Language
and social psychology*. Oxford: Blackwell.
Berger, C.R. and Bradac, J. (1982). *Language and social knowledge: Uncertainty in interper-
sonal relations*. London: Arnold.
Berger, C.R. and Calabrese, R. (1975). Some explorations in initial interactions and beyond.
Human Communication Research, **1**, 99–112.
Berger, C.R. and Zelditch, M. (Eds) (1985). *Status, rewards and influences*. San Francisco,
CA: Jossey-Bass.
Bond, M.H. (1983). How language variation affects inter-cultural differentiation of values by
Hong Kong bilinguals. *Journal of Language and Social Psychology*, **2**, 57–66.
Bond, M.H. (1985). Language as a carrier of ethnic stereotypes in Hong Kong. *Journal of
Social Psychology*, **125**, 53–62.
Bond, M.H. and Yang, K.S. (1982). Ethnic affirmation versus cross-cultural adaptation: The
variable impact of questionnaire language on Chinese bilinguals in Hong Kong. *Journal of
Cross-Cultural Psychology*, **13**, 169–185.
Bourhis, R.Y. (1984). Cross-cultural communication in Montreal: Two field studies since the
Charter of the French Language. *International Journal of the Sociology of Language*, **46**,
33–47.
Bourhis, R.Y. and Giles, H. (1976). The language of co-operation in Wales. *Language
Sciences*, **42**, 13–16.

Bourhis, R.Y. and Giles, H. (1977). The language of intergroup distinctiveness. In H. Giles (Ed.), *Language, ethnicity and intergroup relations*. London: Academic Press.

Cohen, R. (1978). Ethnicity: Problem and focus in anthropology. *Annual Review of Anthropology*, **7**, 379–403.

Despres, L.A. (1975). Toward a theory of ethnic phenomena. In L. Despres (Ed.), *Ethnicity and resource competition in plural societies*. The Hague: Mouton.

DeVos, G. (1975). Ethnic pluralism. In G. DeVos and L. Romanucci-Ross (Eds), *Ethnic identity*. Palo Alto, CA: Mayfield.

Edwards, J. (1985). *Language, society and identity*. London: Blackwell.

Fishman, J.A. (1977). Language and ethnicity. In H. Giles (Ed.), *Language, ethnicity and intergroup relations*. New York: Academic Press.

Forgas, J. (1988). Episode representations in intercultural communication. In Y.Y. Kim and W.B. Gudykunst (Eds), *Theories in intercultural communication*. Newbury Park, CA: Sage.

Gallois, C., Franklyn-Stokes, A., Giles, H., and Coupland, N. (1988). Communication accommodation theory and intercultural encounters: Intergroup and interpersonal considerations. In Y.Y. Kim and W.B. Gundykunst (Eds), *Theories in intercultural communication*. Newbury Park, CA: Sage.

Gans, H.M. (1979). Symbolic ethnicity: The future of ethnic groups and cultures in America. *Ethnic and Racial Studies*, **2**, 1–20.

Genesee, F. and Bourhis, R.Y. (1982). The social psychological significance of code-switching in cross-cultural communication. *Journal of Language and Social Psychology*, **1**, 1–27.

Giles, H. (1979). Ethnicity markers in speech. In K. Scherer and H. Giles (Eds), *Social markers in speech*. Cambridge: Cambridge University Press.

Giles, H., Bourhis, R., and Taylor, D.M. (1977). Towards a theory of language in ethnic group relations. In H. Giles (Ed.), *Language, ethnicity and intergroup relations*. London: Academic Press.

Giles, H. and Byrne, J.L. (1982). An intergroup approach to second language acquisition. *Journal of Multilingual and Multicultural Development*, **3**, 17–40.

Giles, H. and Franklyn-Stokes, A. (1989). Communicator characteristics. In M.K. Asante and W.B. Gudykunst (Eds), *Handbook of international and intercultural communication*. Newbury Park, CA: Sage.

Giles, H. and Johnson, P. (1981). The role of language in ethnic group relations. In J. Turner and H. Giles (Eds), *Intergroup behavior*. Chicago, IL: University of Chicago Press.

Giles, H. and Johnson, P. (1987). Ethnolinguistic identity theory: A social psychological approach to language maintenance. *International Journal of the Sociology of Language*, **68**, 69–91.

Giles, H., Mulac, A., Bradac, J.J., and Johnson, P. (1987). Speech accommodation theory: The next decade and beyond. In M. McLaughlin (Ed.), *Communication yearbook*, No. 10. Beverly Hills, CA: Sage.

Giles, H. and Ryan, E. (1982). Prolegomena for developing a social psychological theory of language attitudes. In E. Ryan and H. Giles (Eds), *Attitudes toward language variation*. London: Arnold.

Giles, H. and Smith, P.M. (1979). Accommodation theory: Optimal levels of convergence. In H. Giles and R. St Clair (Eds), *Language and social psychology*. Oxford: Blackwell.

Gudykunst, W.B. (1985). A model of uncertainty reduction in intercultural encounters. *Journal of Language and Social Psychology*, **4**, 79–98.

Gudykunst, W.B. and Kim, Y.Y. (1984). *Communicating with strangers*. Reading, MA: Addison-Wesley.

Gudykunst, W.B. and Lim, T.S. (1986). A perspective for the study of intergroup communication. In W. Gudykunst (Ed.), *Intergroup communication*. London: Arnold.

Gudykunst, W.B., Ting-Toomey, S., Hall, B.J., and Schmidt, K. (1989). Language and intergroup communication. In M.K. Asante and W.B. Gudykunst (Eds), *Handbook of international and intercultural communication*. Newbury Park, CA: Sage.

Gumperz, J.J. and Cook-Gumperz, J. (1982). Introduction. In J. Gumperz (Ed.), *Language and social identity*. Cambridge: Cambridge University Press.

Haarmann, H. (1986). *Language in ethnicity*. Berlin: Monton de Gruyter.

Hewstone, M. and Brown, R. (1986). Contact is not enough. In M. Hewstone and R. Brown (Eds), *Contact and conflict in intergroup encounters*. Oxford: Blackwell.

Hewstone, M. and Giles, H. (1986). Stereotypes and intergroup communications. In W. Gudykunst (Ed.), *Intergroup communication*. London: Arnold.

Hewstone, M. and Jaspars, J. (1982). Intergroup relations and attribution processes. In H. Tajfel (Ed.), *Social identity and intergroup relations*. Cambridge: Cambridge University Press.

Hogg, M.A. and Abrams, D. (1988). *Social identification*. London: Routledge.

Hraba, J. and Hoiberg, E. (1983). Identical origins of modern theories of ethnicity. *Sociological Quarterly*, **24**, 381–391.

Louw-Potgieter, J. and Giles, H. (1987). Imposed identity and linguistic strategies. *Journal of Language and Social Psychology*, **6**, 258–284.

Lukens, J. (1979). Interethnic conflict and communicative distance. In H. Giles and R. Saint-Jacques (Eds), *Language and ethnic relations*. Elmsford, NY: Pergamon.

Marin, G., Triandis, H.C., Betancourt, H., and Kashima, Y. (1983). Ethnic affirmation versus social desirability: Explaining discrepancies in bilinguals' responses to a questionnaire. *Journal of Cross-Cultural Psychology*, **14**, 173–186.

McCall, G. and Simmons, J. (1978). *Identities and interactions*. New York: Free Press.

McNamara, T.F. (1987). Language and social identity: Israelis abroad. *Journal of Language and Social Psychology*, **6**, 202–226.

Mgbo-Elue, C.N. (1987). Social psychological and linguistic impediments to the acquisition of a second Nigerian language among Yoriba and Ibo. *Journal of Language and Social Psychology*, **6**, 309–319.

Park, R.E. (1950). Our racial frontier on the Pacific. In R.E. Park (Ed.), *Race and culture*. New York: Free Press.

Patterson, O. (1977). *Ethnic chauvinism*. New York: Stein and Day.

Paulston, C.B. and Paulston, R.G. (1980). Language and ethnic boundaries. *Language Sciences*, **2**, 69–101.

Punetha, D., Giles, H., and Young, L. (1987). Ethnicity and immigrant values: Religion and language choice. *Journal of Language and Social Psychology*, **6**, 229–242.

Ros, M., Cano, J.I., and Huici, C. (1987). Language and intergroups perception in Spain. *Journal of Language and Social Psychology*, **6**, 240–258.

Rose, T.L. (1981). Cognitive and dyadic processes in intergroup contact. In D. Hamilton (Ed.), *Cognitive processes in stereotyping and intergroup behaviour*. Hillsdale, NJ: Erlbaum.

Ross, J.A. (1979). Language and the mobilization of ethnic identity. In H. Giles and B. Saint-Jacques (Eds), *Language and ethnic relations*. Oxford: Pergamon.

Rothbart, M., Dawes, R., and Park, B. (1984). Stereotyping and sampling biases in intergroup perception. In J. Eiser (Ed.), *Attitudinal judgment*. New York: Springer-Verlag.

Ryan, E., Hewstone, M., and Giles, H. (1984). Language and intergroup attitudes. In J. Eiser (Ed.), *Attitudinal judgment*. New York: Springer-Verlag.

San Antonio, P.M. (1987). Social mobility and language usage in an American company in Japan. *Journal of Language and Social Psychology*, **6**, 191–200.

Scherer, K. and Giles, H. (Eds) (1979). *Social markers in speech*. Cambridge: Cambridge University Press.

Simard, L., Taylor, D., and Giles, H. (1976). Attributional processes and interpersonal accommodation in a bilingual setting. *Language and Speech*, **19**, 374–387.

Sodetani, L.L. and Gudykunst, W.B. (1987). The effects of surprising events on intercultural relationships. *Communication Research Reports*, **4**(2), 1–6.

Stephenson, G. (1981). Intergroup bargaining and negotiation. In J. Turner and H. Giles (Eds), *Intergroup behavior*. Chicago, IL: University of Chicago Press.

Sunnafrank, M. (1986). Predicted outcome value during initial interactions: A reformulation of uncertainty reduction theory. *Human Communication Research*, **13**, 3–33.

Tajfel, H. (1978). Social categorization, social identity, and social comparison. In H. Tajfel (Ed.), *Differentiation between social groups*. London: Academic Press.

Taylor, D.M. and McKirnan, D. (1984). A five-stage model of intergroup relations. *British Journal of Social Psychology*, **23**, 291–300.

Ting-Toomey, S. (1986). Interpersonal ties in intergroup communication. In W. Gudykunst (Ed.), *Intergroup communication*. London: Arnold.

Ting-Toomey, S. (1989). Identity and interpersonal bonding. In M.K. Asante and W.B. Gundykunst (Eds), *Handbook of international and intercultural communication*. Newbury Park, CA: Sage.

Turner, J. (1987). *Rediscovering the social group*. Oxford: Blackwell.

16

Social Class, Social Status and Communicative Behavior

BETH HASLETT

Department of Communication, University of Delaware, USA

Any social group, whether it be a culture, subculture or family, develops communicative patterns that enable group members to cooperate and co-exist with one another. These communication practices reflect the social power of particular group members or subgroups in a larger society, and provide a distinct social identity for social groups.

Social power or influence may derive from many factors, such as age, wealth, education, religion or race. Mazur (1985) argues that social status ranks are allocated in all face-to-face groups. Across primate species (including humans), social rank may be signalled through a vocal or physical display (e.g. erect posture, glares, eye contact, assertive speech among humans, etc.). For human beings, one of the most important historic factors contributing to a group's or individual's social power has been social class. The main focus of this chapter will be to examine social class influences on communicative processes.

Social class ranks as one of the classic demographic variables in social science research. It is typically measured by income, education and occupation, although some studies rely only on economic indicators like income. In some countries, castes or religious systems may define who has the highest social class ranking. While all societies discriminate among subgroups and individuals on the basis of social class

Handbook of Language and Social Psychology
Edited by H. Giles and W.P. Robinson. © 1990 John Wiley & Sons Ltd

(most broadly, social status or rank), it must be clearly kept in mind that each society may utilize different criteria for making these social judgments. In the USA, for example, the culture generally tends to be highly individualistic and egalitarian, whereas Middle Eastern countries tend to mark social status and position more (Yousef, 1974). Tieri (1973) suggests that different social class and ethnic groups develop language variety which incorporates sociocultural factors as well as cognitive factors.

Thus, while we can talk generally about the communicative effects of social class, these effects may stem from very diverse cultural practices. Because of such differences, the concept of social class itself has become more diffuse and a more general term, social status, is often used. For the purposes of this overview, I shall be using the more generic term, social status.

Social status may be broadly viewed, then, as social prestige. Those possessing high social status will be more respected, more rewarded and will exercise more power than those having lesser social status. As noted, social groups will differ on the criteria for status: status markers will include such factors as age, sex, religion, social class and occupation. Generally, status, class and power are related as follows:

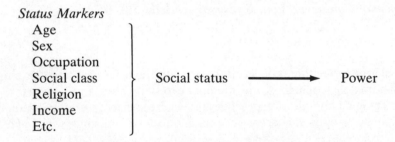

The status markers used by a particular group will result in a perceived or accorded social status ranking. In turn, the higher the social status ranking, the more power the individual possesses, both in material goods and social influence.

Three major lines of research will be covered. First, a body of research that explores the social evaluation of speech will be reviewed, focusing particularly on social class differences in speech. Second, the work of Bernstein (1973, 1975, 1977), which theoretically and empirically explores the linkages between social class and communication, will be discussed. A final major line of research is found in the work of Tajfel and his associates (Tajfel, 1978; Tajfel and Turner, 1979), which explores the speech patterns by which groups mark and maintain their social identity. Although Tajfel and his associates focus on language and social identity, I believe the work has implications for social status and language use generally. It should be noted, however, that this extension of their work is my own, and the original scholars may or may not agree with it. Generally, we shall look at a variety of studies which have explored a range of communicative practices, such as forms of address, that differ as a function of social status. Although the bulk of research covered here is based on the study of Western nations, these status differences are believed to be applicable to societies and social groups generally.

SOCIAL EVALUATION OF SPEECH: SOCIAL STATUS DIFFERENCES

A substantial literature supports the idea that an individual's speech characteristics influence how he or she is perceived and evaluated by others. Norms concerning appropriate speech and language behavior emerge within social groups, and determine the speech style used by that group. These norms may be context-related standards, which set speech standards in particular situations (Giles and Powesland, 1975). Norms are also set with respect to class-related standards, in which the most preferred (or prestigious) form for speaking is established. Giles and Powesland note that there is no simple, straightforward correlation between social class and social status because of social mobility within groups. Nor is the distinction between a standard and non-standard language usage clear-cut. They suggest that there is a continuum of judgment, such that greater deviation from the preferred speaking norm (the received pronunciation; RP) results in judgments of lesser social status. In some cases, languages themselves can be ranked in order of preferred usage and higher social status. Herman (1961) found a .84 correlation between the prestige of a language and the relative social prestige of a particular subgroup in a country.

The bulk of research has been conducted in Great Britain, the USA and French-speaking Canada. Speech characteristics studied include dialect, accent, pronunciation, vocal quality and listener characteristics. In Great Britain, Giles (1970, 1971) found accents and regional dialects were ranked in terms of their relative social prestige. Giles (1972) found that broadness of accent influenced judgments of social prestige, with older respondents being more sensitive to accent variation and more tolerant of differences. Generally, research indicates that RP has the most prestige and status; that speakers discriminate clearly between various accents and dialects and rank them differentially in terms of prestige; that accents of industrial towns are accorded least prestige; and that age and personality of listeners influenced their judgments of language usage (Giles and Powesland, 1975).

In the USA, similar results have been found. Ellis (1967), using audiotapes, found high correlations between judged social status and actual social status. Labov (1964) investigated judgments of varying speech characteristics. He found that listener's social status and language usage influenced his or her judgments of others' speech. Individuals who had the highest frequency of non-standard usage in their own speech were most sensitive to use of those features by others. Shuy, Baratz, and Wolfram (1969) found that middle-class speakers were more accurate judges of actual social status in speech than their lower-class counterparts. Williams and his colleagues (1969) investigated ethnicity and status in speech. They found that sounding 'white' was judged as high status, and that ethnicity/non-standardness appeared to be an important judgmental dimension in assessing speech. There does not appear to be a ranking of various regional US accents or dialects like that in Great Britain. However, there may be certain regional variations that may generally be accorded lower status (Giles and Powesland, 1975). Further work is needed to explore the complexities of regional variation, ethnicity and social status in speech.

Generally, these studies (and we have reviewed only a small portion of the voluminous literature in this area) confirm that individuals have the ability accurately to assess social class differences in speech, and to accord regional and accent variation with differing prestige. In addition, such judgments tend to be relatively uniform within a given social group. Across these studies, standard speakers are more positively perceived and judged than non-standard speakers. Prestigious speech is associated with higher social status and higher social class. Higher social class speakers are also regarded as more personable and well-liked (Giles and Powesland, 1975).

Why have various accents and dialects been accorded different social status? Two alternative explanations have been proposed. One view suggests that certain language forms possess an inherent value such that they are more aesthetically or structurally acceptable. The alternative explanation suggests that certain language forms are imposed norms and thus have become preferred forms as a result of social or political factors that have nothing to do with the language forms themselves. Current views tend to incorporate both explanations and cite both inherent value and imposed norms as explaining different usage standards (Giles and Powesland, 1975).

Several general criticisms of this research can be made. First, the matched-guise technique, which has been used in many of these studies, is limited in its reliance on neutral messages and voice qualities alone. As Edwards (1985) notes, this gives listeners very artificial conditions under which to evaluate someone's speech. Second, studies have focused on very specific features and specific judgments. Further research is needed to assess how these features and judgments may influence one another. Edwards (1985) also notes that there is the standard problem of the relationship between attitude and behavior: most measures report attitudinal judgment, but it is not clear whether such judgments may affect behavior directed toward particular speakers in a given situation.

In contrast to the work previously reviewed, Bernstein's (1973, 1975, 1977) work reflects an attempt to explain how communicative differences across social classes are developed, maintained and transmitted across generations. As such, Bernstein's work addresses different social functions of language as used by lower-class and middle-class speakers.

CLASS, CODES AND SOCIAL CONTROL

Bernstein (1973, 1975) hypothesizes that communication passes along the 'genes' of social class from generation to generation (see Table 16.1). A complex network of social relationships, including work, community and family relationships, determines people's communicative behaviors (codes). These codes subsequently influence future social interactions and relationships. Thus any social group, through its social relationships and unique communicative codes, passes along its dominant values to future generations.

Social roles are learned through the family, peer group, school and work. Families

TABLE 16.1   Bernstein's Sociolinguistic Approach to Socialization

I.   Social Influences on Communication and Social Development
    A. Work relationships, community relationships, and family role systems influence and determine communication code(s)
    B. This communication code(s) is taught to children and they too are influenced by (A)
    C. Therefore communication code(s) transmits 'genes' or characteristics of the social class.

II.   Roles Learned Four Ways
    A. Family
    B. Age or peer group
    C. School
    D. Work

III. Role Systems
    A. Open
        1. Meaning in one's own terms (individualistic meanings)
        2. Motivation to explore
        3. Has to cope with ambiguity

    B. Closed
        1. More communal and collective meanings (group-oriented meanings)
        2. Strictly defined in social context
        3. Little ambiguity in roles

IV.   Communication Codes
    A. Elaborated
        1. Relies on verbal 'explicitness'
        2. Has wide range of syntactic alternatives
        3. Flexibly organized
        4. Complex planning involved
        5. Doesn't rely on shared objects, events or meanings
        6. Verbal communication is important
        7. Intent of other person is not taken for granted
        8. Oriented toward individual persons
        9. Verbally 'elaborate'

    B. Restricted
        1. Relies on gesture, intonation and metaphor
        2. Has a narrow range of syntactic alternatives
        3. Rigidly organized
        4. Little planning involved
        5. Relies on shared identifications and common assumptions
        6. Extra-verbal means important (non-verbal dimension stressed)
        7. Intent is taken for granted
        8. Oriented toward common group or status membership

V.   Role Systems of Families
    A. Personal
        1. Decisions are a function of the psychological qualities of the individual
        2. Roles not clearly defined
        3. Children's peer group associations subject to family discussion
        4. *Achieved* status
        5. Role discretion (range of alternatives) wide
        6. Verbal elaboration of individual differences

(*continued overleaf*)

Table 16.1 (*cont.*)

        B. Positional
           1. Decision-making is invested in the member's formal status
           2. Clear separation of roles
           3. Children's peer group associations subject to legislation by adults
           4. *Ascribed* status important
           5. Little role alternatives
           6. Verbal elaboration of judgment (its consequences)

VI.   Modes of Social Control
        A. Imperative Mode
           1. Demands, e.g. 'shut up'
           2. Learns hierarchy of social control prescribed by the role structures

        B. Appeals
           1. Positional
              a. Process of learning the rules
              b. Child reminded of what he or she shares with others
              c. Required to follow norm defined by status, e.g. 'Little girls don't do that'
              d. Rules *assigned* to individuals
              e. Learns role obligation and differentiation

           2. Personal
              a. Learning social relationships
              b. Deals with motivation and individual attention
              c. Explanation given, e.g. 'I know you don't want to but she will feel bad if you don't'
              d. Rule *achieved* by individuals

VII. Code-switching occurs and some of the possible contributing actors are:
        A. Greater affluence
        B. Greater geographical mobility
        C. Wife enters workforce
        D. Change in solidarity of workers
        E. Shift in the division of labor

        (All of the above could influence a switch from restricted to elaborated codes.)

---

vary between two role systems: open and closed. Individuals raised in open role systems have personal, individualized meanings; an ability to cope with social ambiguity; and a motivation to explore the environment. At the other end of the continuum, individuals raised in closed role systems have communal, collective meanings and values, and strictly defined social contexts with little social ambiguity. While open role systems encourage individual development, closed role systems encourage a person to fulfill socially prescribed roles.

These role systems are supported by elaborated and restricted communicative codes. Restricted codes support closed role systems, while elaborated codes facilitate open roles. Disciplinary activities which are carried out through the use of positional appeals (e.g. 'We don't do things that way', etc.) support communal values and restricted role systems. In contrast, personal appeals, which rely on individual motivation and intent, are disciplinary activities fostering an open role system.

As can readily be seen, elaborated codes encourage individuals to develop their own meanings and to verbalize their ideas. Such codes require complex planning and flexible organization. In contrast, restricted codes require little planning, and rely on shared values and social identities. As Bernstein (1977) notes, a communicative code is a 'socially constituted regulative principle, tacitly acquired, which integrates 1. the relevant meanings; 2. the form of their realization; [and] 3. their evoking contexts' (p. ix). He further notes that:

> What we observe are the *productions* of text. What we infer is the performance or ground rule which regulates the *production* of specific texts. What we infer at a structural level is the regulation on the relationships *between* performance rules and specific contexts. It is this level which refers to codes. Codes are no more directly observable than are grammatical rules. This does not mean that there are any more heuristic devices than the rules of grammar. As codes change, so do what count as relevant meanings, what count as appropriate realisations and what count as evoking contexts. Codes are constituted by social relationships which regulate the selection and structure of meanings and the mode of their *contextual* realisations. (Bernstein, 1977, p. ix)

The point that communicative codes are not directly observable is a very important one since many educators and linguists have attempted to test directly for restricted or elaborated code characteristics. Most of these empirical studies have found mixed results. Bernstein's (1975) research on middle-class and working-class messengers found that working-class messengers used shorter words, longer phrases, shorter pauses and more personal pronouns than their middle-class counterparts. Middle-class messengers used more uncommon adjectives and adverbs, and more subordinate clauses and passive verbs.

What are the implications of these code differences across social classes? In a nutshell, Bernstein (1975) argues that the educational system (in Great Britain) transmits a middle-class elaborated code which systematically disenfranchises lower-class children. Adlam (1977) found that lower-working-class children, in instructional contexts, relied primarily on narrative speech. This use of narrative speech, especially among girls, was strongly correlated with mothers who reported favoring positional control strategies and less 'educationally' focused communication. Lineker (1977) found class differences in the mode of instruction used by children when explaining a game to other children. Middle-class children tended to use a context-independent mode, whereas lower-working-class children used a more context-dependent mode of instruction.

In summarizing class differences across children's responses to open-ended questions in a variety of settings, Bernstein (1977) notes that:

> These very different situations have one feature in common. The eliciting instruction does not specify the form the response should take. Yet the middle-class children translate this open request into a request for a particular type of response. We know that this translation is independent of the 'measured intelligence' of the children, and that

> the translation is made in very different situations within a structured context. . . . The interview context (adult-task, child-response, adult-evaluation) appears to be seen by the middle-class child as calling for a specialised response irrespective of a question which appears to offer the child a variety of ways of responding. Indeed, the child translates or rather re-codes an open question into a closed question. . . . The child learns to distinguish between open questions, according to their context; the child learns which open questions are in fact *testing* rather than eliciting questions . . . (Bernstein, 1977, p. xii)

As Bernstein goes on to point out, middle-class children's code usage is similar to code usage in the educational system and thus the educational system legitimates that code usage, whereas this is not the case for lower-class children.

Several important criticisms have been made of Bernstein's work. As Trudgill (1975) points out, it may be most appropriate (as Bernstein himself notes) to regard codes as distinct language styles rather than as linguistic units. Second, differences in code usage appear to be differences in the *frequency* of usage since it has been demonstrated that lower-working-class children can use an elaborated code (Robinson, 1965). Finally, there is the issue of the educational implications of restricted and elaborated codes. Are these merely differences, or is there a deficit for the restricted code speakers?

Despite these criticisms, others have valued Bernstein's work for its emphasis on the interrelationship between society and language (Hymes, 1974). Halliday (1973) suggests that Bernstein's research contributes to our understanding of functional differences in language use. Edwards (1985) concludes that Bernstein's research can be placed in the language-difference perspective, although it has been used to support language-deficit theorists.

Social Class Differences in Maternal and Child Language

Considerable research has been stimulated by Bernstein's (1973, 1975, 1977) work, both in the USA and England. Although the research reported here is primarily from those two countries, it seems reasonable to assume that class or status differences will be present elsewhere, although taking a different communicative form and function.

In assessing children's language, Pap and Pleh (1972) found differences in language across Hungarian children of differing social class that paralleled those found by Bernstein. Although Piche, Rubin, and Michlin (1978) did not find any significant social class differences across children's communicative appeals, this may have been confounded by an interaction between age and appeal in which older children tended to use significantly more positional appeals (i.e. appeals to role-oriented behaviors) than did younger children. Edwards (1976) also failed to find any persistent restricted or elaborated codes in the speech of 11-year-old British school-children of differing social classes.

In contrasting class differences in the speech of 10- to 13-year-old children, Williams and Naremore (1969) looked for functional, rather than structural, differences in the use of language. Lower-class children had a higher proportion of incomplete sentences; made more use of minimal responses like 'yeah'; made more use of the general 'you' in responding to questions; and were less organized than middle-class children. The results seem to indicate a limited set of situations in which lower-class children function effectively.

These mixed results suggest that restricted and elaborated codes may only influence certain aspects of linguistic or cognitive functioning. Gianotti (1979) found significant differences in causal reasoning and classification between upper- and lower-class children, with upper-class children having superior performances on these tasks. Bruck and Tucker (1974) found that lower-class children understood the grammar of language just as well as middle-class children; however, they had less understanding of the communicative demands of situations (e.g. the need for relevant information, etc.). Johnston (1977) found that working-class children used more pronouns than did middle-class children, who used more numbers of cases. She suggests that these differences may come from social class differences in functional language used by young children. Stipek and Nelson (1980) suggest that the ability of lower-class children to communicate efficiently is very dependent on the task itself. Jewson, Sachs, and Rohner (1981), using descriptive tasks with three different stimuli, found significant class differences as a function of stimulus type and of communication strategies used in each situation.

Some of these differences appear to be related to maternal styles of interaction with their children. As Wells (1985) points out, different communicative environments are offered by different parenting styles, and thus children may learn some skills, while others are not developed. Cook-Gumperz (1973) found social class differences across mothers' style of interaction and control, and a moderate relationship between the mothers' reported strategies and their children's responses several years later. Robinson and Rackstraw (1967), analyzing class differences in mothers' responses about how to answer their children's questions, found that middle-class mothers were more likely to answer questions; gave more factual information; gave more explanations to 'why' questions; and had more accurate information. Robinson (1972) found that middle-class mothers used more different kinds of explanation when answering children's questions, and integrated their responses with one another.

Similar studies completed in the USA also found social class differences in maternal communicative styles. Hess and Shipman (1965) explored social class differences in mothers' control strategies and teaching styles. Middle-class mothers tried to motivate their children, gave specific instructions and positively reinforced their children. Hess, Shipman, Bear, and Brophy (1968) explored family control strategies and their impact on communication. Three types of control strategies were investigated:

(1) appeals to status through ascribed role norms;
(2) appeals to the subjective state of the individual;
(3) appeals in terms of an action's logical consequences.

Lower-class families are prdominantly status-oriented, using appeals to 'what the child should do in terms of shared social expectations' and using a restricted code based on communal meanings and values. Mothers who use personal appeals or logical consequences as control strategies are predominantly middle class, and use an elaborated code to support the reasoning required by those control strategies. Olim, Hess, and Shipman (1964) also note that the use of appeals to his or her ascribed status gives the child no opportunity to develop abstract concepts or complex problem-solving strategies. (For a more thorough review of social class differences in socialization and communicative behaviors, see Robinson (1972). Williams (1971) offers an excellent overview of poverty, class and communication issues.)

Social Class Differences in Adult Communicative Behavior

Thus far, we have examined some of the social class differences in the communicative behavior of young children. Class differences appear to carry over to adult communicative patterns, and build upon the early socialization differences in maternal and child speech.

A study by Schatzman and Strauss (1955) is particularly interesting since it relies on naturalistic data: the authors assessed differences in how people reported their own experiences in a tornado. Working-class individuals related events from their own perspective, often failing to set the scene for the listener or to give necessary qualifications. Their experiences were given using narratives that often went off on a tangent. In contrast, middle-class respondents supplied the context for events and referred to other people and organizations in discussing the tornado. Their narratives were well-organized, and provided an overall framework for understanding the effect of the tornado, rather than focusing only on their own direct experiences.

More recent studies examine the effect of class differences on communication in varied contexts. Gudykunst and Lim (1985) found that ethnicity and class interact to predict people's perceptions of their own communication style. Ward, Seccombe, Bendel, and Carter (1985) suggest that social status inequities in societies interact with sex differences in explaining why women seem more easily persuaded than men. Pearlin (1975) investigated status inequities in marriage and found that inequities negatively influenced everyday marital interactions. Hawkins, Weisberg, and Ray (1977) explored social class and marital communication style (the manner in which messages are sent). After analyzing taped discussions between spouses, they found that higher-status couples used a contactful style and perceived themselves as being less controlling. McMullen and Murray (1986) explored the effect of status and solidarity on verbal familiarity with others. They found that higher-status members of a dyad were more familiar than their lower-status partners, and friends were more familiar than strangers.

Other studies have focused on politeness and status. Ferguson (1976) found that politeness strategies varied as a function of the relative social status of the communicators. In an ethnographic study of a Fijian village, Hickson (1986) found that apologies in resolving disputes were determined by the interdependence and hierarchical status differences among the disputees. Cross-cultural evidence from 56 countries tends to support this. Brown and Gilman (1960) found status differences in forms of address and expressions of solidarity and power.

Research has also emphasized the effects of status differences on communicative processes in medical settings. Wilkinson (1975) suggests that, when patients' social class rating differs from that of their psychiatrist, communicative differences lead to the patients being diagnosed as more severely ill. Daly and Hulka (1975), reviewing the literature on physician–patient communication, found that such communication is often hampered by educational and social class distinctions, the use of jargon, and characteristics of the physician and patient. Pendleton and Bochner (1980) found that social class differences across patients significantly influenced physicians' explanations. Srivastava (1983) found that differences in caste (social class) among Indian health professionals influenced their interaction with other colleagues and patients. Waitzkin (1985) found that physicians' transmission of information was significantly influenced by patients' social class. It was suggested that linguistic differences based on social class hamper patient–physician communication.

In summary, Bernstein's (1973, 1975, 1977) work on the linkages between control, class and communication codes established a basis for exploring relationships between social class and communication. Bernstein and his colleagues focused primarily on the family and early socialization as an explanation for persistent class differences, and investigated its educational and social impact. Although the empirical studies based on Bernstein's model show mixed results, this may partly be due to the generality of Bernstein's predications about code characteristics and the varying ways scholars have applied these code characteristics. More recently, scholars have explored the effects of social class in more specific settings, like marital communication and doctor–patient communication. These studies show consistent class effects on communication, with superior performance by, or an advantage to, those of higher social status.

A significant line of research has focused on communication as a powerful source of social identity. This has been especially important in looking at the assimilation of new ethnic groups into the cultural mainstream: communication has been used to keep new groups isolated as well as to provide social identity for different groups. Social class or status becomes a relevant concern here because new groups are usually perceived as having lower status than mainstream groups. Thus communication and status are linked in groups' efforts to assimilate as well as to maintain their unique cultural heritage. It is to this area we now turn.

COMMUNICATION, SOCIAL STATUS AND SOCIAL IDENTITY

Significant research in this area has been done by Tajfel, Scherer, Giles and their colleagues. Taken as a whole, their work suggests that interactants can emphasize their ingroup status (e.g. by using jargon, special terms of address, etc.), or their differentiation from others (e.g. by using a formal mode of address; different codes, languages or dialects). Although this research was not intended to reflect on status differences, I believe it can be viewed usefully from that perspective and can illuminate the subtle ways in which status differentiation can be expressed in language behavior.

Giles and Hewstone (1982) outline a number of ways in which communication signals social and situational identity:

(1) Communication helps define ambiguous situations, or situations in which several different norms might apply.
(2) Communication is most salient as a situation-defining cue when other obstacles may limit the defining and redefining of the situation.
(3) Situational definitions are more likely to be accepted when given by a high-status individual.
(4) Situations may be redefined when a high-status person is threatened; when goals are not being met; when people are more predictable; or when a low-status person believes that status has been distributed unfairly and that a change is necessary.

Thus communication appears to play a central role in how participants define situations and their roles within those situations.

Furnham (1986), reviewing situational influences on intergroup communication, suggests that language choice itself helps define situations and social identities. He suggests that language choice may be governed by:

(1) the activity itself (e.g. using one's native language at home and a 'national' language at school, etc.);
(2) a desire to express and emphasize social identity through language choice;
(3) language tolerance or flexibility;
(4) formality of the social setting;
(5) the public/private nature of the situation.

Situations may be clearly defined by communication, but social identity is also defined, in part, by communication. Tajfel (1978) suggests that, whenever groups interact, participants socially identify themselves as well as construct their own view of the social setting. When participants define the interaction as an *intergroup* interaction, the participants tend to separate or distance themselves from a perceived outgroup (Tajfel and Turner, 1979). Some factors influencing intergroup interaction are: the perceived status of the groups as contrasted with one another (Tajfel, 1978); beliefs as to which group may be favored (Bourhis, Giles, and Rosenthal, 1981); and the person's own status in the group (Giles and Johnson, 1981). DeGreve (1983) proposed a model of bilingualism in which an individual's competence is a function of personal competence and the sociocultural situation. Colfer (1983) found that, in situations involving development personnel and the populations they are working with, status, communication and social identity are all powerful forces at work.

Generally, as can be readily seen, status and social identity influence communicative behavior; communicative behavior, in turn, helps define social settings and expresses social identity. Status, social identity, social settings and communicative behavior mutually interact and influence one another. Any individual, at any given point in time, may choose to emphasize or de-emphasize a particular social identity, depending on its desirability in the current situation. For example, a person's bilingualism may be dispreferred at home, but be a very desirable attribute at school. Individuals may code-switch, and thus signal what is the relevant social identity for them at any given point. A person's choice of code, in turn, signals to listeners his or her interpretation of the setting and the norms being applied.

CONCLUDING REMARKS

Social class, more broadly viewed as social status, clearly influences communicative behavior. Communicative behaviors that may be influenced range from interpersonal effects, like forms of address and topics of discourse, to group differences in how language functions for lower-class as opposed to middle-class speakers/ listeners.

Earlier research primarily viewed class or status as a function of education, occupation and income. More recently, concepts of social status have become more diffuse, in that they include or reflect a wider range of measures. However, status has become more specific as well, in that only one of several factors which influence status, for example ethnicity, may be measured in a particular study. These trends can be seen as reflecting the fact that, while social status is an influential variable in virtually all social groups, the ways in which social groups measure that status are very diverse, judgments may be based, for example, on wealth, aristocratic lineage, occupation, race or religion.

Given the aforementioned diversity, it is very difficult to make generalizations about the way in which a communicator's status may influence his or her communicative behaviors. Researchers are moving in the right direction, however, when measures of social status are appropriately linked to cultural values and when they are specific, rather than diffuse. Such precision enables researchers to link status with its communicative effects more specifically.

Perhaps the most profound question to be raised here concerns the implications – both social and educational – of status differences in language behavior. As previously noted, higher status results in more prestige, more liking, more power and so forth. With respect to educational implications, there are two views concerning the implications of code differences. One view argues that these differences are merely differences; the other view suggests that these differences are deficits – that lower-class children are at a serious disadvantage in schooling. In judging this issue, the strong middle-class bias in society must be clearly kept in mind (Cole and Bruner, 1972). Finally, as Edwards (1985) notes, consideration of class as a variable masks the fact that a number of important differences exist within the same social class. More research is needed to assess such variation. These issues are discussed more thoroughly elsewhere in this handbook; they are mentioned here to underscore the importance of research in this area and its profound social and educational significance.

Finally, I want to call attention to the research linking social status with mass communication systems and the new information technology. It is suggested that those possessing high status in a society also control communication processes (including both interpersonal and mass media resources), and, through communication, exercise control economically and politically (Kirkpatrick, 1979). Smith (1984) suggests that gender and class oppression exists in capitalistic societies, and that this oppression is supported by most social institutions. Steeves and Smith (1987) analyzed the portrayal of women in ten top television programs, and found that the portrayal of gender and social class reflected distorted views of gender and class differences.

Other scholars suggest that a new information gap is being created; that is, those having highest social status (commanding most educational and economic resources) can afford products of the new information technology, like personal computers, video cassette recorders and related services. Such information resources permit their owners to exert more power and influence, and perpetuate existing social status differences.

REFERENCES

Adlam, D. (1977). *Code in context*. London: Routledge and Kegan Paul.

Bernstein, B. (1973). *Class, codes and control*, Vol. 1. London: Routledge and Kegan Paul.

Bernstein, B. (1975). *Class, codes and control*, Vol. 3. London: Routledge and Kegan Paul.

Bernstein, B. (1977). Foreword. In D. Adlam (Ed.), *Code in context*. London: Routledge and Kegan Paul.

Bourhis, R., Giles, H., and Rosenthal, D. (1981). Notes on the construction of a 'subjective vitality' questionnaire for ethnolinguistic groups. *Journal of Multicultural and Multilingual Development*, **2**, 145–155.

Brown, R. and Gilman, A. (1960). The pronouns of power and solidarity. In T. Sebeok (Ed.), *Style in language*, pp. 253–276. New York: Wiley.

Bruck, M., and Tucker, G.R. (1974). Social class differences in the acquisition of school language. *Merrill-Palmer Quarterly*, **20**, 205–220.

Cole, M. and Bruner, J.S. (1972). Preliminaries to a theory of cultural differences. In I. Gordon (Ed.), *Early childhood education*. Chicago: University of Chicago Press.

Colfer, C. (1983). On communication among 'unequals'. *International Journal of Intercultural Relations*, **7**, 263–288.

Cook-Gumperz, J. (1973). *Social control and socialization*. London: Routledge & Kegan Paul.

Daly, M. and Hulka, B. (1975). Talking with the doctor. *Journal of Communication*, **25**, 148–152.

DeGreve, M. (1983). Receptive competence: An eventual solution? *Recherches-Sociologiques*, **14**, 59–73.

Edwards, A. (1976). Speech codes and speech variants. *Journal of Child Language*, **3**, 247–265.

Edwards, J. (1985). *Language and disadvantage*. New York: Elsevier.

Ellis, D. (1967). Speech and social status in America. *Social Forces*, **45**, 431–437.

Ferguson, C. (1976). The structure and use of politeness formulas. *Language in Society*, **5**, 137–151.

Furnham, A. (1986). Social situations. In W. Gudykunst (Ed.), *Intergroup communication*. London: Arnold.

Gianotti, M. (1979). Conceptions of the world and concrete operations: A comparative study of children from different social classes. *Italian Journal of Psychology*, **6**, 43–52.

Giles, H. (1970). Evaluative reactions to accents. *Educational Review*. **22**, 211–227.

Giles, H. (1971). Ethnocentrism and the evaluation of accented speech. *British Journal of Social and Clinical Psychology*, **10**, 187–188.

Giles, H. (1972). The effects of stimulus mildness–broadness in the evaluation of accents. *Language and Speech*, **15**, 262–269.

Giles, H. and Hewstone, M. (1982). Cognitive structures, speech and social situations: Two integrative models. *Language Sciences*, **4**, 188–219.

Giles, H. and Johnson, P. (1981). The role of language in inter-ethnic behavior. In J. Turner and H. Giles (Eds), *Intergroup behavior*. Oxford: Blackwell.

Giles, H. and Powesland, P. (1975). *Speech style and social evaluation*. New York: Academic Press.

Gudykunst, W. and Lim, T. (1985). Ethnicity, sex and self perceptions of communicator style. *Communication Research Report*, **2**, 68–75.

Halliday, N.A.K. (1973). Foreword. In B. Bernstein (Ed.), *Class, codes and control*, Vol. 2, *Applied studies towards a sociology of language*. London: Routledge and Kegan Paul.

Hawkins, J., Weisberg, C., and Ray, D. (1977). Marital communication style and social class. *Journal of Marriage and the Family*, **39**, 479–490.

Herman, S. (1961). Explorations in the social psychology of language choice. *Human Relations*, **14**, 149–164.

Hess, R. and Shipman, V. (1965). Early experience and the socialization of cognitive modes in children. *Child Development*, **36**, 869–886.

Hess, R., Shipman, V., Bear, R., and Brophy, J. (1968). *The cognitive environments of urban preschool children*. Chicago, IL: University of Chicago Press.

Hickson, L. (1986). The social contexts of apology in dispute settlement: A cross-cultural study. *Ethnology*, **25**, 283–294.

Hymes, D. (1974). *Foundations in sociolinguistics; An ethnographic approach*. Philadelphia, PA: University of Pennsylvania Press.

Jewson, J., Sachs, J., and Rohner, R. (1981). The effect of a narrative context on the verbal style of middle-class and lower-class children. *Language in Society*, **10**, 201–215.

Johnston, R. (1977). Social class and grammatical development: A comparison of the speech of five year olds from middle and working class backgrounds. *Language and Speech*, **20**, 317–324.

Kirkpatrick, J. (1979). Politics and the new class. *Society*, **10**, 42–48.

Labov, W. (1964). Phonological correlates of social stratification. *American Anthropologist*, **66**, 164–176.

Lineker, L. (1977). The instructional context. In D. Adlam (Ed.), *Code in context*. London: Routledge and Kegan Paul.

Mazur, A. (1985). A biosocial model of status in face to face primate groups. *Social Forces*, **64**, 377–402.

McMullen, L. and Murray, W. (1986). Effects of status and solidarity on familiarity in verbal behavior. *Journal of Language and Social Psychology*, **5**, 49–52.

Olim, E., Hess, R., and Shipman, V. (1964). Role of mothers' language styles in mediating their preschool children's cognitive development. *School Review*, **75**, 414–424.

Pap, M. and Pleh, C. (1972). Language and social class. *Szociologia*, **2**, 211–234.

Pearlin, L. (1975). Status inequality and stress in marriage. *American Sociological Review*, **40**, 344–357.

Pendleton, D. and Bochner, S. (1980). The communication of medical information in general practice consultations as a function of patients' social class. *Social Science and Medicine*, **14**, 669–673.

Piche, G., Rubin, D., and Michlin, M. (1978). Age and social class in children's use of persuasive communicative appeals. *Child Development*, **49**, 773–780.

Robinson, W.P. (1965). The elaborated code in working class language. *Language and Speech*, **8**, 243–252.

Robinson, W.P. (1972). *Language and social behaviour*. Harmondsworth: Penguin.

Robinson, W.P. and Rackstraw, S. (1967). Variations in mothers' answers to children's questions. *Sociology*, **1**, 259–279.

Schatzman, L. and Strauss, A. (1955). Social class and modes of communication. *American Journal of Sociology*, **60**, 329–338.

Shuy, R., Baratz, J., and Wolfram, W. (1969). Sociolinguistic factors in speech identification. NIMH Research Project No. MH–15048–01. Center for Applied Linguistics, Washington, DC.

Smith, D. (1984). The deep structure of gender antitheses: Another view of capitalism and patriarchy. *Humanity and Society*, **8**, 395–402.

Srivastava, A. (1983). Job satisfaction and conflict in the task performance of allied health professionals in a North Indian hospital. *Journal of Social and Economic Studies*, **11**, 118–131.

Steeves, L. and Smith, M. (1987). Class and gender in prime-time television entertainment: Observations from a socialist-feminist perspective. *Journal of Communication Inquiry*, **11**, 43–63.

Stipek, D. and Nelson, K. (1980). Communication efficiency in middle- and lower-SES dyads. *Human Communication Research*, **6**, 168–177.

Tajfel, H. (1978). *Differentiation between social groups*. London: Academic Press.

Tajfel, H. and Turner, J. (1979). An integrative theory of intergroup conflict. In W. Austin and S. Worchel (Ed.), *The social psychology of intergroup relations*. Monterey, CA: Brooks/Cole.

Tieri, P. (1973). Sociolinguistics and Whorf's hypothesis. *Critica Sociologica*, **26**, 57–76.

Trudgill, P. (1975). *Accent, dialect and the school*. London: Arnold.

Waitzkin, H. (1985). Information giving in medical care. *Journal of Health and Social Behavior*, **26**, 81–101.

Ward, D., Seccombe, K., Bendel, R., and Carter, L. (1985). Cross-sex context as a factor in persuasibility sex differences. *Social Psychology Quarterly*, **48**, 269–276.

Wells, G. (1985). *Language development in the preschool years*. Cambridge: Cambridge University Press.

Wilkinson, G. (1975). Patient–audience social status and the social construction of psychiatric disorders: Toward a differential frame of reference hypothesis. *Journal of Health and Social Behavior*, **16**, 28–38.

Williams, F. (1970). *Language and poverty*. Chicago, IL: Markham.

Williams, F. and Naremore, R. (1969). On the functional analysis of social class differences in modes of speech. *Speech Monographs*, **36**, 77–102.

Yousef, F. (1974). Cross-cultural communication: Aspects of contrastive social values between North Americans and Middle Easterners. *Human Organization*, **33**, 383–387.

17

Changing the Complexion of Gender in Language Research

CHERIS KRAMARAE

Department of Speech Communication, University of Illinois, USA

Western men say they have to watch their language when a lady is around. This 'watching' can take many forms, and might include using curse words followed by an 'apology'; interrupting the lady's talk; ignoring the words, topics, and presence of the lady; using a specialized category of address terms; and giving her order to a waitress in a restaurant.

If she is no lady – for example a woman walking by herself on 'public' streets – then she can be treated in a wide variety of ways, from no remark, to comments on her appearance or morals, to threats to her safety. Her response options to any of the above events are the topics not only of her own internal dialogues but also of articles, workshops, and home talks, as children and adults talk about and talk out *gender*. This talk will be influenced by the confluence of forces including racism, economics, ageism, and homophobia. As this introduction indicates, gender is a complex relationship, with everyday seriousness. As this review will illustrate, gender is not looking the same as it did in textbooks a decade ago.

In this chapter I review several basic framing explanations used in some recent language and gender studies, and I then discuss the work on interaction practices in several kinds of female–male relationships. The review focuses on studies and concerns expressed in English, and thus on Western research. Because of such pressing influences as US and UK colonizing actions (including military activities, and sales of Western TV programming to Eastern countries), and because of the importing into Europe and North America of products produced by low-paid 'Third

Handbook of Language and Social Psychology
Edited by H. Giles and W.P. Robinson.   © 1990 John Wiley & Sons Ltd

World' workers, there are many, often unexplored, relationships between women and men in English-speaking countries and those in other countries. The complexion of gender will continue to change as we pay more attention to the ways that our knowledge and theorizing have been influenced by the assumption that West and East are *separate* parts of the world rather than hierarchical divisions created by political actions.

If there were space enough, this review could usefully begin with information about language and gender discussions in previous centuries or with mention of current research about that earlier theoretical work. For example, in the nineteenth century 'strong-minded women' wrote at length about men's use of 'chivalrous' behaviour as a weapon, administered by men only to women who did not need it, to remind them that men were not their protectors as much as their controllers. (The kind words of respect, the helping hand, and other forms of chivalrous behaviour were not offered, these critics pointed out, to the women advocating voting rights for women, to working-class women on their knees scrubbing other people's floors, or to homeless women.) The 'strong-minded women' (later the self-label became 'feminist') also wrote about the everyday behaviours which supported the legal and social acceptance of men's sexual violence and exploitation (Jeffreys, 1985). The history of the nineteenth-century sex-reform movement and of the development of the 'science' of sexology (in response to feminist ideas about the sexual and other behaviours of men) affects (some would say infects) current research, whether we wish it or not. For example, influential sexologist Havelock Ellis, who began writing about 'sexual inversion' and 'real sexuality' at the turn of the century, thought males naturally aggressive and sadistic, and women passive and masochistic (see Jeffreys, 1987). His prescriptions, which entered literature and art as well as psychological and social analysis, were central to the development of 'sexual liberation' and are still a part of contemporary ideology.

Many people today do not know about the massive debates in which feminists and their critics engaged during the nineteenth and early twentieth century – debates which included support, justification, and denial of binary and hierarchical sex differences such as male/female, mind/body, and reason/emotion, with many feminists insisting that masculist ideas about sexuality contributed to the massive use of women in prostitution, to wife battering and sexual abuse of children, and to the undermining of women's attempts at economic and psychological independence. For their critiques these earlier feminists have been labelled Victorian prudes. The history of labels stuck on women has received attention by a few scholars (such as linguist Julia Penelope, 1975), but needs much more attention as we attempt to explain the language practices, expected and actual, of women and other marginalized social groups (see Chapter 22, by Coupland and Coupland).

The labels and terminology change, of course, as our ideas about the relationship of women and men change. In the 1970s this field of study was called 'language and sex'. Then, with increasing attention to the social construction of 'female' and 'male', we shifted to the use of 'gender' to avoid connotations of biological, bipolar opposites. 'Gender differences' have come to mean distinctions resulting from the differing socialization of boys and girls. However, the current use of this term is also the subject of controversy. Some researchers seem to use 'sex' and 'gender' as interchangeable, or talk about 'gender differences' as if they come only from previous biological or environmental conditions; others stress the ongoing, everyday process of gender-making (see MacKinnon, 1987). In this chapter, gender is used in the latter sense. An important point is that the terminology and category systems of research are challenged and changed not primarily because of academicians' questions and critiques but because of activists' questions, critiques, and demands. Because the thousands of language and gender studies (hundreds of which are mentioned by Thorne, Kramarae, and Henley, 1983) are all influenced by the often-conflicting language and ideas about race, gender, class, and age, I first review some of the more frequently discussed theoretical approaches.

THEORETICAL APPROACHES

Sex Differences

From the first days after birth, boys and girls in Western cultures are treated as somewhat different species. Division of the sexes is a pervasive structural aspect of our institutions – including religion, education, family, politics, and mass media. So it is not surprising that the increased academic interest in language and gender studies in the early 1970s also stressed sex differences. Researchers searched for different ways language deals with women and men, different ways females and males use words, and differences in verbal and non-verbal interaction. As Thorne and Henley pointed out in their introduction to a 1975 volume of articles on language, gender, and society, 'the cataloguing of sex *difference* in language has seemed the primary task to most investigators' in this research area. In their introduction, these editors discussed the limitations of this approach and the importance of studying any themes of differences through a recognition of structures of male dominance and the division of labour by sex. Most of the essays in their volume, however, focused on difference (in actual speech or in stereotypes of female and male speech), with little analysis of power. In contrast, 8 years later, Thorne *et al.* (1983) wrote of the research move from isolated variables and differences to: social context; larger units of speech and writing; speech strategies; closer attention to women's use of language, especially with each other; power structures; issues of age and race; and *similarities* as well as differences. During the intervening years there was also a shift from considering sex as a dichotomous 'natural fact' to considering sex or gender as historically changing social relationships which are socially regulated with the assignment of women and men to hierarchical positions and privileges (see Chapter 13, by Ng).

One line in the sex-differences research has followed the theories of speech accommodation (Giles and Powesland, 1975; Giles and Smith, 1979) and speech reciprocity, with studies testing, for example, whether 'low-power speakers' will reciprocate the style of speakers who are higher in power. Not surprisingly, it appears that speech accommodation processes (matching of speech styles) are less likely in situations where shared linguistic norms exist (as in client/counseller or patient/doctor interaction) than in less formalized situations.

Work in the sex-differences tradition also continues along another line in many investigations of evaluative reactions to 'powerless' and 'powerful' speech styles. O'Barr (1982) and colleagues conducted studies to determine if such linguistic features as tag questions (e.g. 'This example is silly, isn't it'), qualifiers, hedges, and superpolite forms are tied more closely to social status than to sex. While in the early 1980s, stimulus messages used in some of the studies were scripted by researchers (who payed too little attention to the customary location of these linguistic features in actual speech), Mulac and colleagues in a series of studies developed written stimulus messages from transcriptions of actual monologues by men and women performing such tasks as oral descriptions of photographs (see descriptions and citations in the articles by Mulac and Lundell, 1982; Mulac, Lundell, and Bradac, 1986). In several of these studies the linguistic productions of males were, for example, rated by listeners as higher in dynamism but lower in aesthetic quality than female productions, a pattern of evaluation called 'gender-linked language effect' by Mulac and associates.

In general, this research line of sex-related speech differences uses rating categories and methodology from traditional social psychology research rather than from feminist theory and methodology.

Androgyny

With the renewed questioning in the 1970s and 1980s concerning gender-related divisions of labour, some theoreticians have proposed the possibility and desirability of a society of androgynous persons living without gender-role distinctions or prescriptions (see Heilbrun (1973) for a general discussion of this). Researchers working with similar assumptions about the flexibility of women's and men's 'natures' developed and used a variety of models of psychological androgyny, masculinity–femininity constructs, and sex-role identification or gender schema. The assumptions were that women and men differ in the degree to which they identify and associate with traditional masculine and feminine attitudes and behaviours, that those people who claimed or exhibited both 'feminine' and 'masculine' characteristics had better mental health, and that we could all develop more androgynous, desirable attitudes and behaviours. The focus was on *individual* orientations to stereotypes of 'female' and 'male' characteristics, and what effect these orientations had on interaction.

This approach and the use of masculinity–femininity measurements (e.g. Bem, 1974; Spence and Helmreich, 1978) supplied a critique of the concept of *sex* as a single, categorical variable, and promoted many communication studies in which (whatever the focus of study, be it the use of adjectives or reports of heterosexual courtship habits) participants first filled out questionnaires (used to determine 'sex-role' orientation) before being observed or asked to write reports on their behaviours. For example, Smith (1985) examined the correspondence between speakers' self-assessed 'masculinity' and 'femininity' and listeners' impressions of speakers' 'masculinity' and 'femininity'. He concluded that people do form reliable impressions of others' 'femininity' and 'masculinity' on the basis of speech alone, and that listeners' impressions resemble speakers' own self-characterizations. (Also see several studies in the volumes by Berryman and Eman (1980) and Mayo and Henley (1981); Smith (1985) reviews many of the studies as well as some of the criticisms of the masculinity/femininity measures.) In many of the studies, hypotheses of specific behaviours (observed or reported) of individuals were predicted on the basis of the subjects' 'masculinity' and 'femininity' scores. In some studies a person with approximately equal masculine and feminine scores was said to be 'androgynous'.

Although the questioning of the meaning and measurement of 'masculinity' and 'femininity' was valuable, there has been continual theoretical and methodological confusion about how the measures were constructed and what they measured (Bem, 1981; Spence and Sawin, 1985). The concept of androgyny has been criticized by many. For example, some critics point out that the organizing constructs 'masculine' and 'feminine' are from patriarchal ideology. 'Merger does not correct the distortion', writes Knight (1981, p. 30); that is, combining some of the traits of, say, John Wayne with those of another creation, Marilyn Monroe, does not lead to a unified, balanced wholeness (see also Rich, 1977). Further, while introduced by feminists concerned by the prevalence of notions about biological sex as determining behaviour, the psychological scales were also being used by some researchers, it seems, to avoid mention of *social* influences and restrictions on people. Putting a stress on behavioural flexibility and adaptiveness in interaction deflected or delayed analysis of the constraints and status hierarchies present in institutional structures (including family, education, religion, law).

Two Cultures

The basic argument for this theoretical approach is set forth by Maltz and Borker (1982) in an article which is based largely on research dealing with difficulties in cross-ethnic communication (see Chapter 15, by Gudykunst and Ting-Toomey). On the basis of their own experience and studies of children's play, Maltz and Borker suggest that the amount of time girls and boys spend in single-sex groups means that they learn and practise different types of communication strategies. Girls use interaction forms that stress cooperation and equality of power, and learn to deal sensitively with relationships and situations. In contrast, boys' interaction is more likely to be based on establishing and maintaining hierarchical relations, on gaining and keeping an audience, and on asserting their identity. These gender differences are extended into adult interaction, with women more concerned with cooperatively building on each other's contributions and men more likely to include story-telling, arguing, and verbal posturing in their interactions. In some cases, the same syntactic form will mean different things to women and men. Maltz and Borker suggest, for example, that women are more likely to use questions as efforts to encourage conversation; men, to hear questions as requests for information.

In contrast to the still pervasive misogynist critiques of women's talk as trivial and irrational, this approach presents women's interaction (with women or with men) as meaningful, connected to children's interaction and socialization, and as a system, rather than a jumble of strange, inexplicable habits. There are two cultures, men's and women's, with definable speech patterns. (See Johnson (1989) for a presentation of the value of this approach for communication research.) Many of the problems between men and women, these theorists suggest, results from 'miscommunication' between speakers of these different cultures (see Chapter 15, by Gudykunst and Ting-Toomey). However, as Henley and Kramarae (in press) have noted, missing in this approach is explicit attention to patterns of dominance in conversation. Men's and women's speech patterns are not merely *different* interactive styles. The traits associated in the research with boys' and men's speech (e.g. treating questions as requests for information rather than as conversation-maintenance devices, and using delayed minimal ('uh huh') responses) can be viewed as not just different but as dominance strategies.

The Androgyny approach stresses the possibilities of *similarities* in the interaction styles of women and men. The Two-Cultures approach stresses the existence of *differences*. Both downplay the gender *hierarchy* and the links between the specifics of female–male interactions and the inequities women experience through family policies, property laws, salary scales, and the many other repressive practices. Both approaches ignore the interaction of race, class, age, and sexual orientation.

Hierarchy

A focus on difference as a result of inequalities (MacKinnon, 1987) encourages us to deal with the ways that race, age, class, and gender are all related divisions which are used to maintain hierarchies within hierarchies. These divisions have become standard categories in language research because of social movements.[1] While at any one time researchers usually treat these categories as separate, standard, and unproblematic, they are, of course, social constructs which undergo change because of continued social movements and other political events.

Gender, far from being a separate 'variable', is a part of all interactions as a hierarchical ordering – even if, for example, girls and women are not present. Since gender-ranking locates everyone within a hierarchy, it is an important shaping factor even in single-sex interactions. Men are *men* because of their insistence upon the subordinate category *women*; much of their understanding of their behaviours and power (whether they are together in the corporate boardroom or on the street corner) comes from their constantly reiterated *otherness* from women.

Further, gender as an oppositional, hierarchical division is used by dominant people via sexist and opportunistic terminology and interactions to *augment* hierarchical comparisons among people also identified, for example, as black, Hispanic, old, lesbian, or poor. Consider, for example, the attention of US researchers to 'The Dozens', verbal 'games' in which players, usually young black males, compete with each other in trying to make the most outrageously demeaning comments about the other's mother: often comments about her sexual organs and sexual activity. These researchers do not point out that hierarchical standing within the male community is based on hierarchical concepts of gender; neither do they consider the terminology that is often used by younger people to express a lack of respect for old people. Much of the terminology of old separates old women and old men, with many of the terms for old men being associated with being old-fashioned, uncouth, or stingy, and those for old women being associated with witchery, bossiness, and bad temper (see Chapter 22, by Coupland and Coupland). Women receive old-age labels much earlier in life than do men (Benjamin, 1986; Covey, 1988). There is thus a gender hierarchy within the hierarchy based on age. This is just one illustration of how age and gender are interrelated. Listening critically to this terminology we can better understand the relationships among race, class, age, gender, sexual orientation, and other categories often treated in social sciences as independent variables; the gender hierarchy is also used to organize other social categories (Kramarae, 1988b).

Moral Development

As in other fields, researchers in communication have tested and extended Gilligan's (1982) theory and empirical findings which suggest that traditional descriptions of the stages of moral development describe men's but not women's experiences and talk. Gilligan argues that, in this research on moral development, as in other psychological research, too often a single scale of measurement, derived from men's interpretations of data from studies of males, is used, ignoring girls' and women's divergent development and interpretations. According to research done with male participants, their fundamental development is directed to separation from others and independent actions, and to a morality based on principles of equality, objectivity, individual rights, and rule-governed justice. For girls and women, the Gilligan work posits, development is based on relatedness, cooperation, relationships, care equity, flexibility, and responsibility.

This theory has obvious explanatory and methodological interest for people doing communicative/gender studies. For example, Wood (1986) used Gilligan's (1982) theory of gender-differentiated moral reasoning as a guide while coding men's and women's accounts of a crisis in a serious romantic relationship (see Chapter 20, by Wilmot and Shellen). She found that, in evaluating their participation, women reported concern with the adequacy of their attention to self, other, and the processes that connected them, awarding about equal importance to all three. Men were more likely to report following more abstract principles to resolve crises and to depict themselves as separate from relationships.

This study underscores the importance of building communication theory and studies from both women's and men's experiences. (Obvious, it would seem, but still rare.) However, to consider gender as a variable separate from age, class, and race still means creation of an illegitimate segregation. Theories which do not deal with power relations of *race*, for example, are not just partial, they are inaccurate.

Hayles (1986) suggests other problems with the initial uncritical acceptance of Gilligan's (1982) *In a different voice*: first, the theory is based on *stories* people tell about themselves, and, second, in selecting and shaping those stories for her illustrations, Gilligan has suppressed women's anger, present in the original texts. One implication of this suppression is that the ethics of the males and females are made to appear to be just different and complementary – rather than conflicting. Her conciliatory voice, describing the men's and women's development as having separate but equally valid characteristics, is likely one of the reasons so many male researchers have found her framework congenial for their explanations of the gender differences they find. She has revealed important problems in male-dominated theorizing, but what is concealed may be as important.

Ecofeminism and Language

Ecofeminism is a growing movement and theory that raises questions about fundamental assumptions of most socialist and liberal feminist approaches to communication. It draws on, but differs from, feminist social theory, ecology, philosophy, deep
ecology, ethics, and spirituality. Ecofeminist theorists and activists criticize the
widespread focus, present in communication studies as elsewhere, on individual
autonomy – which describes and encourages attention to personal empowerment as
an agent of social transformation – and on the dualism of mind/nature and reason/
emotion. As a part of this focus, discussions about 'equal rights to communicate' are
heard increasingly as women extend the traditional listing of 'human rights' to
include and stress communication 'rights'. (This language of 'rights' is used, for
example, by Finlay (1987) and in the 1980 UNESCO publication.)

People working with an ecofeminist approach suggest that this language of 'rights',
so basic to communication studies in capitalistic countries (as well as to popular
courses on assertiveness training for women), is very problematic because it is based
on a concept of *individual* human rights, obscuring the webs of connection necessary
for continual survival on this earth and contributing to current forms of domination
(Diamond and Quinby, 1988). Ecofeminists suggest that this language of individual
'rights' comes from a masculinist ideology and vision of *control*, objectification, and
domination (King, 1988; see also Chapter 13, by Ng).

Theories and Politics

All theories are built on the theorists' ideas about psychological and social interests
and forces – what they are and should be. Because they are explicitly linked to
debates about social consciousness and change in the broader women's movement,
the political positions of feminists (who are doing most of the language/gender
research) are more obvious than others. There is no one feminist theory or
theoretical approach, nor much attempt to create a totalizing set of rules and claims
to truth for studying and explaining people's language and human interaction. What
feminist theories do offer are critiques, questions, and propositions which are much
more inclusive than most other analyses of communicative actions, and which show
possibilities for changes in personal and institutional practices. This review of
theoretical approaches in language and gender research can help explain the types of
research and theorizing of several kinds of female–male relationships.

FEMALE–MALE RELATIONSHIPS

'Love' Relationships

In most textbooks on interpersonal relationships, *love relationships* are assumed to
be intimate (emotionally and sexually) heterosexual relationships.[2] (Wolfe (1988)
has documented some of the ideological structures which maintain heterosexuality as
the norm, as well as the legal and social structures which have made 'homosexual' a

male-specific noun, increasing lesbian invisibility.) The introduction to a recent book on 'couples' begins: 'The couple is the basic unit of society. It is the unit of reproduction, the wellspring of the family, and most often the precinct of love, romance, and sexuality' (Blumstein and Schwartz, 1983, p. 11).

Most of the book deals with the roles played by money, paid work, and sex in the lives of the 'couples' (i.e. heterosexual women and men), but a final section has reports of interviews with 'lesbian couples' and 'gay male couples'. It is assumed that the words 'money', 'work', and 'sex' mean much the same thing to these different kinds of couples. However, Frye (1988) writes that 'sex' is a phallocentric term which has little to do with lesbian passion. 'Love', 'passion', and 'lust' are also seductive, deceiving words which conceal the social construction of 'love' relationships. As Lakoff (1987) spells out, the ways passion or lust are usually talked about reflect very particular, restrictive approaches to intimate relationships. (Frequently used metaphors for sexual desire include: hunger (piece of meat, a dish, sex-starved); animal (wolf, chickadee); heat (the hots, on heat); insanity (crazy for her, sex maniac); machine (you turn me on); war (conquest, surrender); physical force (bombshell, knockout).) The way we talk about passion, Lakoff points out, is related to the way we talk about anger.

This work advises us to look at the language and related ideology which constrains the ways we have to describe our experiences. Most studies of messages exchanged and negotiated in close relationships do not delineate the basic assumptions embedded in the words available to couples and researchers; most of the time, the vision and blinkers of conventional terminology lie outside our awareness, exposed only during times, and in areas of, conflict and social movements (see Chapter 13, by Ng). Current discussions about how we talk about relationships and whose meanings are validated bring new questions to some of the coding schemes used in relational communication studies (see Chapter 20, by Wilmot and Shellen, and Chapter 21, by Fitzpatrick). (Also see Elgin's (1984, 1986) novels, *Native tongue* and *Native tongue II* for what might be involved in the construction and use of a woman-made language.)

Abusive Relationships: Home-Grown and On the Streets

A Montgomery County woman accused her estranged husband yesterday of assaulting and raping her, then dangling her nude body over a bridge early last Sunday as he professed his love for her . . . 'I'd drop you if I didn't love you,' Mrs. Ludwig said he told her. (Quoted by Russell, 1982, p. 373)

Men's violence toward women comes in many forms in many places. By the mid-nineteenth century, feminists in several Western nations were documenting and discussing violence in the home and on the streets. More than 130 years later, the topic is again receiving attention because of the work of those involved in setting up and maintaining rape crisis centres and homes for battered women.

There has been very little attention to the relationship between physical and verbal abuse of children and women in the home. Most of the academic and popular articles which do make reference to the talk are based on interviews and surveys with women, not with the abusers. Sociologists claim that the abusers are difficult to contact. But Baughman (1988) suggests that, if they can find abused women, then they simply need to look at the women's spouses. And, if they can manage to find ways of getting the women to talk about the difficult topics of marital rape and other abuse, the researchers can also discover a way to get abusive men to talk. Baughman believes the most important reason for the paucity of research with the men can be found in the *researcher's* rhetorical strategies. She found that they used gender-neutral language to discuss the clearly gendered problem of wife abuse: terms such as 'spouse abuse', 'conjugal abuse', 'family violence', 'marital violence', and 'domestic violence', although they were describing situations of men hitting women.

In related work, and blowing the whistle on men who make street remarks to women, Gardner (1980) has written an explanation of street harassment, an analysis which utilizes theories about the relationship of women and men in 'public' places and about symbolic communication. In urban streets, she writes, women (all races, classes and ages, but especially young women) who walk alone face the possibility of a continual series of announcements of their physical status as evaluated (verbally and by gaze, hand gesture, posture) by men of all races, classes, and ages.

Men appear to be using these remarks to serve several functions. Often the remarks or noises draw the attention of the women to the man or men; they remind women that men control the 'public' streets and could and may control the women; they make women unwilling participants in often ambiguous interactions. (For example, if a woman responds in kind to a 'Good morning, miss!', she may then hear the man reply with 'Good boobs!' If she does not respond, she may receive a contemptuous, 'Miss Snot!') Gardner points out that street remarks are exploitation of the rules of civil inattention that supposedly operate among unacquainted people in public. As she points out, men in general find men's street remarks unobjectionable.

In addition to giving us information about abusive talk in particular settings, study of street remarks can also give information about who can talk where and with what sanctions (Kissling and Kramarae, 1985). Public places are inaccurately described as areas open to the community or the people as a whole. In many countries, public places and most public streets are actually places governed primarily by males, as even the police caution women that for their own safety they should not be in 'public' places when it is dark.

Business Relationships

The research in organizational communication is still overwhelmingly involved with the concerns and analyses of men – particularly management men (whose money and/or problems fund much of the research). Research which does include analysis of women in business also usually focuses on the relatively few women at corporate-management level. These days any research on the talk of the majority of women working in business – secretaries and VDT (VDU) operators – usually deals with sexual harassment,[3] which is treated as separate from other organizational communication problems and research.

The current focus on sexual harassment, while valuable in highlighting issues which have far-reaching implications for women in many organizations, may shift attention away from the professional achievements and advancement of women (Balsamo, 1985a,b), especially if the analyses do not deal with the entire gender systems of organizations, including the status and expectations of women and men in the organization, and the kind of talk and interaction that is prized. For example, Chase (1988) and Kanter (1977) note that maintaining a masculine ethic (incorporating tough-mindedness, unemotionality, abstract reasoning) has been an important accomplishment for people who want to be 'successful' in business. Discussion of individual sexual harassment episodes without discussion of how the masculine ethic (and other politics of the organization) is played out in everyday experiences in the business encourages people to see sexual harassment, and other problematic interactions, as events particular to the participants rather than as events endemic to the structure of the organization. The research on sexual harassment seems more concerned with documenting the presence or absence of it than with understanding the communicative implications of sexual messages in the workplace (Putnam and Fairhurst 1985).

Professional Relationships

One area of study that has received systematic attention has been the treatment of women patients by male doctors (see Chapter 25, by Hinkley, Craig, and Anderson). During the past 20 years, analyses of doctors' treatment of women's bodies and reproductive functions have been written by researchers in history, sociology, nursing, and anthropology, providing several ways of listening to and understanding patient–doctor consultations.

Using a conversation-analysis method which includes close reading of carefully transcribed tapes, West (1984) found extensive use of interruptions by male doctors (used, West argues, to communicate control); dictation of conversation structure through the doctors' questions, asymmetrical joking, salutations and naming; and a great deal of mishearings and misunderstandings. However, she did not find that physicians always had control of interaction; patients interrupted women doctors more than the reverse. Further, she points out that the organization of the interviews was *jointly* produced by the participants, who were using their understandings of options and status privileges in patient–doctor encounters.

In another study, Davis (1988) describes ways that paternalism pervades the consultation, as an asymmetrical relationship (modelled on that of parent and child) is established through the doctor's pleasant jokes and platitudes and devaluation of the women's experience. The patient–doctor analyses of Fisher (1983) and Fisher and Todd (1986) also document the specific conversational devices that doctors often use to structure an interaction and to withhold medical information.

Friendship Relationships

Many communication researchers tend to see friendship groups as pleasant but unimportant adjuncts to more important relationships within business, military and family structures (see Chapter 20, by Wilmot and Shellen). Women's friendships have been especially trivialized, in part by millions of jokes about chatting women playing bridge or women talking for hours on the phone. With increased studies of informal communication networks, friendship has been given a more social historical context. Working with women's diaries, novels, and letters, historians have documented the immense importance nineteenth-century women put on their friendships outside marriage and family. Studies of contemporary friendships explore the extent and the reasons for the differences – in topics, frequency of encounters, satisfaction level, evaluation – in men's and women's friendships. For example, Borker (1980) reviews studies of gossip (a word associated with women's information and analysis exchange) in seven countries, and suggests that women and men in these cultures have quite different concerns, with women's talk being primarily about people and taking place primarily in homes. (See Smith (1983) for a discussion of the contrasts in meanings 'home' has for white and black women in the USA.) Goodwin (1980), through her studies of girls' and boys' single-sex play on urban streets, demonstrates that girls and boys in similar locations and activities may talk in quite different ways. The boys in her study often organized their activities hierarchically, with some boys issuing directions to others by direct commands. The girls she studied were skilful in their use of commands when, for example, they were playing the part of a teacher or arguing with the boys, but they did not use the same forms when they were organizing task activities among themselves. Then they often proposed joint actions with phrases such as 'Let's . . .' and 'We could . . .'.

In her interviews with black and white friends, McCullough (1987) heard a lot of discussion about communication style, with both self and other descriptions of black friends including words such as 'confrontive', 'quick-tempered', and 'sceptical'. Contrasting descriptions of self and other for white friends included 'non-confrontive', 'withdrawn', and 'tactful'. As the friends and the researcher point out, these styles have been developed and used historically by black and white women to survive under different kinds of pressures. How friendship is talked about differs not only according to gender, but also (as above) according to age, location, race, class, and ethnic background and acceptance.

The reasons for the differences need to be found in the culture, traditions, conflicting pressures, and resistance of the speakers (see essays in Kramarae, 1988a). For example, Marshall, author of *Brown girl, brownstones*, has written about the New York kitchen-table talk of her mother and her friends – talk which was formed and connected by skin colour, African origin, and colonized status to the oral traditions of their ancestors, family, and friends in the West Indies (see Washington, 1981). Set-recipe surveys are not going to get at the home truths of women's friendships. There is often a lot of movement, especially for women of colour, between social groups with quite different communicative norms. Stanback (1985) points out that black middle-class women often live or socialize in black social contexts, and work in a primarily white social context where they may also have friends. She notes that the movement of influences upon speech works both ways, although whites often do not recognize the influences of 'West African cultures and languages, slave heritage, racism, [and] the traditional black church' on their talk.

General Relational Communication Issues

Women and men are involved in many types of relationships, only a few of which are mentioned above. In most research on two-person relationships, the stress is put on such communicative functions as expression of feelings, confirmation, and stages of relationships – especially in heterosexual romantic relationships. There is very little attention to unequal relations of power existing between women and men prior to any specific interaction; and, although people may 'belong' to different social groups, they are assumed to have equal economic, social, and political resources. The entire field of the social psychology of language would undergo a transformation if these basic notions of gender neutrality and equality were challenged, and if the joined systems of social structure, social movements, social interaction, and self-concept made clearer.

Then, traditional, individualistic interpersonal communication terminology (such as 'the true meaning of life', 'relational intricacies', 'relational enhancement', 'relational control', 'openness' and 'disorder') would take on new meanings incorporating issues of strategy, power, authority, establishment of respectability, control, subversion of control, and alternatives to the heavy reliance on the language of control (see Chapter 13, by Ng).

Probably the most dramatic and deserving changes in the theoretical frameworks and specific language/gender studies are likely to result from increased attention to speech communities and interactions other than of white, middle-class speakers. For example, new research perspectives and directions are suggested by revisionary ethnography of native American culture. In Powers' (1986) book based on 25 years of study, Oglala women (living in Pine Ridge reservation, South Dakota) are seen as receiving status from their cooking and child-care work and are generally accepted as good judges of disputes because they are accustomed to making and sticking with unpopular decisions with their children; men are believed to change their minds if they come to think that many of their fellows have another point of view. In Oglala culture, there is an emphasis on complementary and cooperative relationships among women and men in comparison with the more competitive relationships between the sexes in the surrounding white culture. Medicine (1987) writes of the many social functions which American Indian women fulfil through their language. These observations from contemporary cultures show whites their culture in a new light. They also show us that, when studies are contextualized in a particular social and economic context, there is value in treating gender not just as a difference or individual characteristic, but as social relations and power (Torres, in press), with power and dominance taking very diverse forms depending upon such factors as speaker characteristics and behaviour, specific situation, the levels of prejudice, and the economic or any other threat the speaker is thought to pose (Gallois, Callan, and Johnstone, 1984). The more attention is given to the words and realities of minority groups in Western countries and to those of speakers in other cultures, the more challenges are raised to the research questions, methodology, and interpretations of language and gender research.

NOTES

1 Increasingly, *ageism* is being discussed, particularly in the women's movement, as a serious social problem. Attention to power relations of age will alter our communication theory as, for example, old people are considered as more than extensions of 'women and men', which usually means people aged 18 to 50 years. See Thorne (1987) for a discussion of the inaccurate and inadequate ways social sciences theorize about children. See Giles and Ryan (1986) for communication research which attends to communication of old people. And see Macdonald, with Rich (1983), for information on the controversies of the terminology of age and ageism.

2 One of the reasons Hite's (1987) book *Women and love* so surprised and outraged male reviewers is likely that most interpersonal communication research and mass-media treatment of heterosexual relationships stress the ways the *individual* can and should deal with conflicts and problems – which are in many cases actually created by power hierarchies supported by institutions including the mass media. The disclosures of the 4500 women (most of whom were very dissatisfied with their conversations with husbands and male lovers) led to a lot of criticism of her methodology and low survey-return rate, but to relatively little discussion of the need to change our assumptions about heterosexual 'love' being the central and most satisfying emotion in most married women's lives. Hite argues that what women say in her survey shows that personality theory in general and Freud's ideas in particular (based on case studies of a few women) can neither 'predict what we do, nor seriously explain what we have done' (Hite, 1987, p. xli).

3 The use of different terminology – 'sexual harassment' and 'street remarks' – obscures the links in men's harassment of women in these different settings (Kramarae, 1985; Stanko, 1985; Wise and Stanley, 1987).

REFERENCES

Balsamo, A. (1985a). Beyond female as variable: Constructing feminist perspective on organizational analysis. Paper presented at Conference on Critical Perspectives in Organizational Analysis, Baruch College, New York.

Balsamo, A. (1985b). Women and organizational communication: An annotated bibliography. *Women and Language*, 9, 1/2, 6–32.

Baughman, L. (1988). A critique of sociologists' study of wife abuse within a patriarchal society. Unpublished paper, Institute of Communication Research, University of Illinois, IL.

Bem, S. (1974). The measurement of psychological androgyny. *Journal of Consulting and Clinical Psychology*, 42, 155–162.

Bem, S. (1981). The BSRI and gender schema: A reply to Spence and Helmreich. *Psychological Review*, 88, 369–371.

Benjamin, B.J. (1986). Dimensions of the older female voice. *Language and Communication*, 6, 1/2, 34–45.

Berryman, C.L. and Eman, V.A. (Eds) (1980). *Communication, language and sex*. Rowley, MA: Newbury House.

Blumstein, P. and Schwartz, P. (1983). *American couples*. New York: Morrow.

Borker, R. (1980). Anthropology: Social and cultural perspectives. In S. McConnell-Ginet, R. Borker, and N. Furman (Eds), *Women and language in literature in society*, pp. 26–44. New York: Praeger.

Bradac, J.J. and Mulac, A. (1984). Attributional consequences of powerful and powerless speech styles in a crisis-intervention context. *Journal of Language and Social Psychology*, 3, 1–19.

Chase, S.E. (1988). Making sense of 'The woman who becomes a man'. In A.D. Todd and S. Fisher (Eds), *Gender and discourse: The power of talk*, pp. 275–295. Norwood, NJ: Ablex.

Covey, H.C. (1988). Historical terminology used to represent older people. *The Gerontologist*, **28**, 291–298.

Davis, K. (1988). Paternalism under the microscope. In A.D. Todd and S. Fisher (Eds), *Gender and discourse: The power of talk*, pp. 19–54. Norwood, NJ: Ablex.

Diamond, I. and Quinby, L. (1988). American feminism and the language of control. In I. Diamond and L. Quinby (Eds), *Feminism and Foucault: Reflections on resistance*, pp. 193–206. Boston, MA: Northeastern University Press.

Elgin, S.H. (1984). *Native tongue*. New York: DAW.

Elgin, S.H. (1986). *Native tongue II: The Judas rose*. New York: DAW.

Finlay, M. (1987). *Powermatics: A discursive critique of new communications technology*. New York: Routledge and Kegan Paul.

Fisher, S. (1983). Doctor talk/patient talk: How treatment decisions are negotiated in doctor–patient communication. In S. Fisher and A.D. Todd (Eds), *The social organization of doctor–patient communication*, pp. 135–157. Washington, DC: Center for Applied Linguistics.

Fisher, S. and Todd, A.D. (1986). Friendly persuasion: The negotiation of decisions to use oral contraceptives. In S. Fisher and A.D. Todd (Eds), *Discourse and institutional authority: Medicine, education, and law*. Norwood, NJ: Ablex.

Frye, M. (1988). Lesbian 'Sex'. *Sinister Wisdom*, **35**, (Summer/Fall), 46–64.

Gallois, C., Callan, V.J., and Johnstone, M. (1984). Personality judgements of Australian aborigine and white speakers: Ethnicity, sex and context. *Journal of Language and Social Psychology*, **3**, 39–57.

Gardner, C.B. (1980). Passing by: Street remarks, address rights, and the urban female. *Sociological Inquiry*, **50**, 328–356.

Giles, H. and Ryan, E. (Eds) (1986). Language, communication and the elderly. *Language and Communication*, **6** (Nos 1 and 2).

Giles, H. and Smith, P. (1979). Accommodation theory: Optimal levels of convergence. In H. Giles and R.N. St Clair (Eds), *Language and social psychology*, pp. 46–65. Baltimore: University Park Press.

Gilligan, C. (1982). *In a different voice: Psychological theory and women's development*. Cambridge: Harvard University Press.

Goodwin, M.H. (1980). Directive-response speech sequences in girls' and boys' task activities. In S. McConnell-Ginet, R.A. Borker, and N. Furman (Eds), *Women and language in literature and society*, pp. 157–173. New York: Praeger.

Hayles, N.K. (1986). Anger in different voices: Carol Gilligan and The Mill on The Floss. *Signs: Journal of Women in Culture and Society*, **12**, 23–39.

Heilbrun, C. (1973). *Toward a recognition of androgyny*. New York: Harper and Row.

Henley, N. and Kramarae, C. (in press). Miscommunication and sex/gender. In N. Coupland et al. (Eds), *The handbook of miscommunication and problematic talk*. Clevedon (England): Multilingual Matters.

Hite, S. (1987). *Women and love: A cultural revolution in progress*. New York: Knopf.

Jeffreys, S. (1985). *The spinster and her enemies, feminism and sexuality 1880–1930*. London: Pandora.

Jeffreys, S. (1987). *The sexuality debates*. New York: Routledge and Kegan Paul.

Johnson, F. (1989). Women's culture and communication: An analytical perspective. In C.M. Lont and S. Friedley (Eds), *Beyond boundaries: Sex and gender diversity in communication*, pp. 301–316. Fairfax, VA: George Mason University.

Kanter, R.M. (1977). *Men and women of the corporation*. New York: Basic.

King, Y. (1988). Ecofeminism: On the necessity of history and mystery. *Signs: Journal of Women in Culture and Society*, **9**, 42–44.

Kissling, E. and Kramarae, C. (1985). Stranger compliments: The interpretation of street remarks. Paper presented at the Language, Gender, and Communication Conference, October 1985, University of Nebraska.

Knight, I. (1981). The feminist scholar and the future of gender. *Alternative Futures*, **4**, (2/3), 17–35.

Kramarae, C. (1985). Linguistic crimes which the law cannot reach. In Berkeley Women and Language Group (Eds), *Proceedings of the First Berkeley Women and Language Conference*, pp. 84–95. Berkeley, CA: Linguistics Department, University of California.

Kramarae, C. (1988a). Gotta go Myrtle, technology's at the door. In C. Kramarae (Ed.), *Technology and women's voices: Keeping in touch*, pp. 1–14. New York: Routledge and Kegan Paul.

Kramarae, C. (1988b). Redefining gender, class and race. In C.M. Lont and S. Friedley (Eds), *Beyond boundaries: Sex and gender diversity in communication*, pp. 321–333. Fairfax, VA: George Mason University Press.

Kramarae, C., Schultz, M., and O'Barr, W.M. (1984). *Language and power*. Beverly Hills, CA: Sage.

Lakoff, G. (1987). *Women, fire, and dangerous things: What categories reveal about the mind*. Chicago, IL: University of Chicago Press.

Lapata, H.Z. and Thorne, B. (1978). On the term 'sex roles'. *Signs: Journal of Women in Culture and Society*, **3**, 718–721.

Macdonald, B., with Rich, C. (1983). *Look me in the eye: Old women, aging and ageism*. San Francisco, CA: Spinsters/Aunt Lute.

MacKinnon, C.A. (1987). *Feminism unmodified: Discourses on life and law*. Cambridge, MA: Harvard University Press.

Maltz, D.N. and Borker, R.A. (1983). A cultural approach to male–female miscommunication. In J.J. Gumperz (Ed.), *Language and social identity*, pp. 196–216. New York: Cambridge University Press.

Mayo, C. and Henley, N.M. (1981). *Gender and nonverbal behavior*. New York: Springer-Verlag.

McCullough, M. (1987). Women's friendships across cultures: Black and white friends speaking. Paper presented at the Speech Communication Association Meeting, November 1987, Boston, MA.

Medicine, B. (1987). The role of American Indian women in cultural continuity and transition. In J. Penfield (Ed.), *Women and language in transition*, pp. 159–166. Albany, NY: State University of New York Press.

Mulac, A. and Lundell, T.L. (1982). An empirical test of the gender-linked language effect in a public speaking setting. *Language and Speech*, **25**, 243–256.

Mulac, A., Lundell, T.L. and Bradac, J.J. (1986). Male/female language differences and attributional consequences in a public speaking setting: Toward an explanation of the gender-linked language effect. *Communication Monographs*, **53**, 115–129.

O'Barr, W.M. (1982). *Linguistic evidence: Language, power, and strategy in the courtroom*. Academic Press: New York.

Penelope, J.S. (1975). Prescribed passivity: The language of sexism. In R. Ordoubadian and W. von Raffler-Engel (Eds), *Views on language*, pp. 96–108. Urbana, IL: National Council of Teachers of English.

Powers, M. (1986). *Oglala women: Myth, ritual, and reality*. Chicago, IL: University of Chicago Press.

Putnam, L.L., and Fairhurst, G. (1985). Women and organizational communication: Research directions and new perspectives. *Women and Language*, **9**, 2–4.

Rich, A. (1977). *The dream of a common language (Poems 1974–1977)*. New York: Norton.

Russell, D. (1982). *Rape in marriage*. New York: Macmillan.

Smith, B. (1983). Introduction. In B. Smith (Ed.), *Home girls: A black feminist anthology*, pp. xix–lvi. New York: Women of Color Press.

Smith, P.M. (1985). *Language, the sexes and society*. Oxford: Blackwell.

Spence, J.T. and Helmreich, R.L. (1978). *Masculinity and femininity: Their psychological dimensions, correlates, and antecedents*. Austin, TX: University of Texas Press.

Spence, J. and Sawin, L.L. (1985). Images of masculinity and femininity: A reconceptualization. In V.E. O'Leary, R.K. Unger, and B.S. Wallston (Eds), *Women, gender, and social psychology*, pp. 35–66. Hillsdale, NJ: Erlbaum.

Stanback, M.H. (1985). Language and black woman's place: Evidence from the black middle class. In P.A. Treichler, C. Kramarae, and B. Stafford (Eds), *For alma mater: Theory and practice in feminist scholarship*, pp. 177–193. Urbana, IL: University of Chicago.

Stanko, E. (1985). *Intimate intrusions: Women's experience of male violence*. London: Routledge and Kegan Paul.

Thorne, B. (1987). Re-visioning women and social change: Where are the children? *Gender and Society*, **1**, 85–109.

Thorne, B. and Henley, N. (1975). *Language and sex: Difference and dominance*. Rowley, MA: Newbury House.

Thorne, B., Kramarae, C., and Henley, N. (Eds) (1983). *Language, gender and society*. Rowley, MA: Newbury House.

Torres, L. (in press). Women and language. In D. Spender and C. Kramarae (Eds), *Knowledge explosion: Disciplines and debates*. Oxford: Pergamon.

UNESCO (1980). *Many voices, one world: Towards a more just and more efficient world information and communication order*. London: Kegan Page.

Washington, M.H. (1981). Afterword. In the reprint of Marshall, P. (1959). *Brown girl, brownstones*, pp. 311–324. Old Westbury, NY: Feminist Press.

West, C. (1984). *Routine complications: Troubles with talk between doctors and patients*. Bloomington, IN: Indiana University Press.

Wise, S. and Stanley, L. (1987). *Georgie Porgie: Sexual harassment in everyday life*. London: Pandora.

Wolfe, S.J. (1988). The rhetoric of heterosexism. In A.D. Todd and S. Fisher (Eds), *Gender and discourse: The power of talk*, pp. 199–224. Norwood, NJ: Ablex.

Wood, J.T. (1986). Different voices in relationship crises: An extension of Gilligan's theory. *American Behavioral Scientist*, **29**, 273–301.

18

Language and Communication in Mental Handicap

IVANA MARKOVA

Department of Psychology, University of Stirling, UK

The terms 'mental retardation' and 'mental handicap' have traditionally been associated with a variety of disabilities, including subnormal intellectual and cognitive functioning; social, linguistic and communicative incompetence; and educational failure (e.g. Clarke and Clarke, 1985; Heber, 1961). Unfortunately, these general terms do not specify the types and levels of severity of the disabilities in question. At one end of the continuum, they cover very mild and hardly noticeable impairments; at the other, very severe states of mental subnormality. Since the labels 'mental retardation' and 'mental handicap' carry a social stigma (Goffman, 1968), those so labelled, and in particular those with a mild handicap, suffer not only a *mental* but also a *social* handicap.

It is generally acknowledged that most people with a mental handicap have language and communication deficiencies of some kind (Mittler, 1974), ranging from difficulty with articulation and pronunciation to problems with grammatical construction, vocabulary, and the memory demands of speech production. In the 1960s and 1970s, most of the research in mental handicap was based on the *model of language deficiency*, focusing on three main issues:

(1) specific linguistic deficiencies, for example syntax, speech production and phonetics; and inadequacies in various social skills (for reviews see Bloom, 1972; Blount 1968; Cromer, 1974; Rondal, 1975, 1978a; Yoder and Miller, 1972);
(2) the relationships between such deficiencies and other psychological

Handbook of Language and Social Psychology
Edited by H. Giles and W.P. Robinson. © 1990 John Wiley & Sons Ltd

characteristics, for example cognition and intelligence (e.g. McLean, Yoder, and Schiefelbusch, 1972; O'Connor and Hermelin, 1963; Schiefelbusch, 1972; Schiefelbusch, Copeland, and Smith, 1967; Schiefelbusch and Lloyd, 1974);
(3) the assessment of language; training in language and communicative skills; and therapeutic processes (Berry, 1976; McLean *et al.*, 1972; Schiefelbusch and Bricker, 1981).

Speech therapy and intervention programmes were designed with the aim of rectifying deficiencies in the individual by exposing him or her to correct or normative performances in teaching situations. The role of the psychologist or therapist was similar to that of a mechanic attempting to find the faulty parts of a machine and to restore it to normal functioning. A general assumption of researchers and therapists was that language and communication problems were to be located solely in the mentally handicapped person; his or her handicap was due to his or her lack of competence and skill (Leudar, 1981). The focus on deficiencies in the individual with a mental handicap rather than on social and communicative aspects of language in interpersonal communication thus followed the dominant individualistic paradigm in linguistics and psycholinguistics (Markova, 1982).

The study of specific features of the individual's speech and the exploration of his or her linguistic deficiencies are, of course, important issues. However, it is too narrow to limit the study of language and communication solely to such problems because it means ignoring the fact that language is primarily, and above all, a means of social interaction. Moreover, as we shall see in this chapter, deficiencies in articulation, speech production and grammar may be the consequence of the individual's social and communicative problems.

The main research methods for the investigation of language and communication in people with a mental handicap in the 1960s and 1970s were experiments and observations based on the principles of either Skinnerian behaviourism or Chomskyan psycholinguistics (for reviews see Blount, 1968; Clarke and Clarke, 1985; O'Connor and Hermelin, 1963). In the 1970s, the general shift from an individualistic to a social psychological approach took place in mainstream research on language and communication (e.g. Giles and Powesland, 1975; Markova, 1978; Rommetveit, 1974; Ryan and Giles, 1982; St Clair and Giles, 1980). In the field of mental handicap, too, some researchers started to evaluate critically the narrowness of the laboratory experiment and, instead, to emphasize the important role of the social context of speech and communication (Rondal, 1980). However, although individual researchers did argue for a social and interactive approach, the general trend in the study of language and communication in mental handicap lagged behind mainstream social psychology of language. A more fundamental shift in the focus of research and intervention occurred only in the 1980s. The 1980s, therefore, can be seen as a transition period towards more interactive and social approaches in the study of language and communication in mental handicap. This period is characterized by a search for new ideas, concepts and research methods and for new techniques of language intervention. This chapter is concerned with these significant changes. It is divided into three main sections. First, it focuses on the *quality of communicative contexts* of people with a mental handicap. Second, it explores the problem of identifying their *linguistic and communicative problems*. Third, it draws attention to the *communicative strategies* of people with a mental handicap.

COMMUNICATIVE CONTEXTS OF THE MENTALLY HANDICAPPED

A communicative context is not only a physically, historically or culturally defined environment in which communication takes place, be it a family, a peer group, a speech-therapy room or a hospital. A communicative context is defined, above all, by the participants' roles in the interpersonal interaction, by the ways power is distributed between them, and by the implicit and explicit expectations they have with respect to each other. The communicative context affords participants certain options with respect to language and communication, and excludes others (Gumperz, 1982; Sabsay and Kernan, 1984). It determines, therefore, the kind and quality of what is said, how it is said, with what purpose, and with what consequences. In this section, three kinds of communicative context of the mentally handicapped will be discussed: parent–child communication, communication with the non-handicapped layperson, and communication with the professional.

Parent–Child Communication in Mental Handicap

An important issue that has preoccupied researchers for some time is whether children with a mental handicap experience an inferior linguistic environment compared to non-handicapped children (for a review see Rondal, 1980). Earlier findings that mothers' speech to their non-handicapped children includes longer utterances, and more advanced types of sentences and linguistic structures (Buium, Rynders, and Turnure, 1974; Marshall, Hegranes, and Goldstein, 1973; Mitchell, 1976) led some researchers to argue that mentally handicapped children are deprived of the richness of language spoken to non-handicapped children and, consequently, that their communicative environment is inferior. However, as Rondal (1980) pointed out, such arguments were not always well justified for the following reasons. First, the authors did not take into consideration the truly interactive nature of language, and, second, they matched handicapped and non-handicapped children on the basis of their chronological age rather than according to their language level. With respect to the first point, Rondal argued that, just as parents of non-handicapped children actively respond to the level of speech of their children when, for example, using 'motherese', so do parents of children with mental handicap. They use the kind of language they find suitable for their children and this does not mean that such communicative contexts are inappropriate (Leifer and Lewis, 1983; Rondal, 1978b). Concerning the second issue, Leifer and Lewis (1984) found that, when matched for linguistic competence at the one-word level, handicapped children produced more advanced conversational responses than non-handicapped children. The authors concluded that the development of language in children with mental handicap is not only delayed but also different with respect to the synchrony of syntactic development and communicative competence. It appears that social experience dependent on a child's chronological age has a vital influence on his or her language and communicative ability. These findings suggest that, until there has been further investigation, the claim that theories of parent–child communication applicable to normal development also apply to parent–child communication in mental handicap (Mahoney, 1988) must be treated with some caution.

Recently, research has focused on *reciprocity* rather than on the level of linguistic and communicative complexity of parent–child communication. It has been found that the mothers of handicapped children are more directive and dominant when talking to their children than are the mothers of non-handicapped children (Cunningham, Reuler, Blackwell, and Deck, 1981; Eheart, 1982; Mahoney and Robenalt, 1986; Maurer and Sherrod, 1987; Petersen and Sherrod, 1982; Stoneman, Brody, and Abbott, 1983). Mentally handicapped children, for their part, have been found to be more passive than the non-handicapped in interacting with their parents, initiating fewer interactions and often failing to respond to their parents (Cunningham *et al.*, 1981; Davis and Oliver, 1980; Eheart, 1982; Jones, 1977, 1980; Stoneman *et al.*, 1983).

Jones (1980) found that all the Down's syndrome children in her sample, even those very severely handicapped, could participate in prelinguistic communication with their mothers, and provide them with sufficient feedback for interaction to take place. Although, in her study, an overall count of frequencies did not show any general differences in interaction between mothers and their handicapped and non-handicapped children, there were differences with respect to immediately preceding and subsequent intercommunicative activities. Down's syndrome children produced less referential eye contact, i.e. eye contact with respect to the focus of a dialogue such as a toy or an activity in which both mother and child were engaged. They thus deprived themselves of feedback on their activities which the mothers could have provided. They did not show adequate timing pauses and thus did not give their mothers enough time to respond, and clashed with them more often in turn-taking in interactions than did non-handicapped children. They were unable to anticipate the responses from their mothers and thus could not establish the general turn-taking pattern that is essential for the development of language.

Mahoney (1988) found that mentally handicapped children are more likely to communicate verbally when their mothers are highly responsive to their initiations. In addition, the author points out that there are considerable individual differences among mothers in the manner in which they communicate with their children. These differences, Mahoney says, should be carefully explored, rather than glossed over as has happened so much in the past, when researchers tended to emphasize uniformities in communicative styles rather than differences. Moreover, it is important to explore how styles vary across communicative contexts and how assessments of style at a certain period relate to children's communicative development when they are older.

Rogers-Warren, Warren, and Baer (1984) maintain that in order to learn language through dyadic interactions it is essential that the child be an active participant in the process. He or she must participate in two kinds of interaction. First, there must be an interaction between the child and his or her ecological environment so that a proper communicative context is established for talking and teaching. If the child has an opportunity to explore his or her environment, he or she will have a great deal of material to talk about. Consequently, the child's interaction with his or her environment will provide the caregiver with information of the child's focus of attention at a particular moment and with a proper communicative context. Second, the child must actively interact with the caregiver, signalling his or her availability as speaker and listener, and as a participant in joint activities.

Communication of the Mentally Handicapped with the Non-Handicapped

People with a mental handicap start with a considerable disadvantage when communicating with the non-handicapped. They are *perceived* as socially unskilled and linguistically incompetent (Brewer and Yearley, 1989). The non-handicapped have preconceptions about the ability of the handicapped to organize and present information, observe, make inferences and remember things (Kernan, Sabsay, and Rein, 1986). Moreover, they think they are experts on the handicapped persons' needs, feelings and wishes (Jahoda, Markova, and Cattermole, 1988). The process of social segregation of people with mental handicap starts in their childhood. It has been well documented that children with a mental handicap are rarely sought as interactional partners by their peers (Guralnick, 1986; Guralnick and Groom, 1987; Guralnick and Weinhouse, 1984) and are often rejected by them (Taylor, Asher, and Williams, 1987). Moreover, they are perceived by teachers as shy, avoidant and less cooperative than non-handicapped children (Taylor *et al.*, 1987). Discourse analysis of the communicative interactions of preschool children has shown that, when communicating with mentally handicapped children, non-handicapped children simplify their speech (Guralnick and Paul-Brown, 1980). While on the one hand such simplified speech may well suit the level of speech and cognitive abilities of handicapped children, it also has the consequence that such children become socially segregated.

People recognize someone as mentally handicapped primarily because of the way that person talks (Kernan and Sabsay, 1988). If an interlocutor becomes aware that his or her partner in conversation is mentally handicapped, he or she will undergo a change in behaviour towards that person. For example, he or she may withdraw from the conversation, use highly simplified speech, or indicate by some other means his or her reduced expectations of that person (Aloia and MacMillan, 1983; Edgerton, 1967; Kernan *et al.*, 1986; Sabsay and Platt, 1985). These changes, in turn, have negative consequences for the handicapped person's performance. Thus it was found (Raber and Weisz, 1981; Weisz, 1981, 1982) that consistently negative feedback provided to a mentally handicapped child by his or her teacher leads to a striking deterioration of the child's performance. Children who receive negative feedback eventually get into a state of learned helplessness, believing that their activities, however hard they may try, will always be a failure.

Malgady, Barcher, Towner, and Davis (1979) carried out a study exploring whether verbal and communicative ability is a criterion on the basis of which a person is judged to be employable. Vocational teachers were asked to rate 28 kinds of maladaptive linguistic and communicative behaviours. It was found that irritating communicative manners, such as using abusive language, yelling, calling others names and arguing, were judged as much more likely causes of termination of employment than poor verbal ability. A series of studies evaluating the job-seeking interview skills of people with a mental handicap showed that positive impressions made by applicants were determined by their language and communicative skills (Elias, Sigelman, and Danker-Brown, 1980; Elias-Burger, Sigelman, Danley, and Burger, 1981; Sigelman, Elias, and Danker-Brown, 1980).

A number of researchers have set themselves the task of trying to discover the aspects of language and communication that a non-handicapped person identifies as characteristic of mental handicap, so that intervention programmes could be developed to modify those behaviours. Several studies have confirmed that laypersons are able to judge whether a person is mentally handicapped, solely on the basis of his or her speech (Kernan and Sabsay, 1982, 1984; Kernan et al., 1986; Sabsay and Kernan, 1984). Kernan et al. (1986) have found that, the lower the IQ of the speaker, the more likely lay judges are to identify such a speaker as mentally handicapped. Moreover, the lay judges reported that the quality of the speaker's voice tended to be the most important factor in making their judgment. Such qualities as articulation, pronunciation, and prosodic features including fluency, rate of speech, intonation, rhythm and hesitancy seem to be the first characteristics of which the listener takes notice. Disfluency, erratic tempo, childlike (singsong) intonation, and speech which is unusually fast or slow often indicate lack of confidence, uncertainty about the task or nervousness, suggesting that the speaker has a handicap. Kernan, Sabsay, and Shinn (1988) found that particular characteristics of discourse were highly indicative of the speaker's perceived intellectual level. Amongst these, ability to provide the listener with *detail*, to give a *coherent narrative*, and *to construct a good story* counted as most important in judges' decisions. In particular, omission of relevant detail, inclusion of trivial or irrelevant detail, and concentration on detail rather than general movement of the story led laypersons to believe that the speaker was mentally handicapped (Kernan et al., 1986). A similar effect was produced by provision of information in a piecemeal manner, voicing incomplete thoughts, and running unconnected thoughts together in the same utterance (Kernan and Sabsay, 1988). In contrast, grammar and vocabulary were seen as far less indicative of the level of intellectual development than the above features of discourse. If vocabulary *was* given as a reason for handicap, it was because the person could not find a word or used a wrong word, rather than because of a lack of a varied vocabulary (Kernan et al., 1986).

These findings are important for several reasons. First, tests of intelligence usually involve items relying on competence in grammar and vocabulary rather than on performance in a discourse. Second, assessment of language is mostly based on linguistic and grammatical competence and so are most language intervention programmes. The finding reported above that non-handicapped interlocutors focus their attention primarily on discourse characteristics should, therefore, have some effect on the ways language and communication are assessed and intervention programmes devised. Training people with a mental handicap in discourse characteristics and changing the qualities of their communicative contexts would make them more efficient participants in conversation and would, in turn, have a positive influence on their feelings of participation in the community.

Communicating with the Professional in Therapeutic Contexts

The deficiency model has always been implicit in training programmes of language and communicative skills. Most training programmes in the 1960s and 1970s assumed that the individual's language deficiencies could be rectified, so long as he or she had sufficient prelinguistic competencies. Such competencies include, for example, the ability to follow a simple instruction, or to generalize from training stimuli to other situations, or to remember instructions. Thus the training programmes were orientated towards teaching grammar, vocabulary and specific communicative functions such as requesting or questioning (Rogers-Warren et al., 1984).

More recently, a number of researchers have criticized the assessment of communicative skills carried out in clinical settings. Leudar (1981) suggested that, in a clinical setting, people with a mental handicap are always placed in a non-reversible communicative role. In such settings, Leudar argued, people with a mental handicap are not given equal opportunities to initiate and perpetuate discourse, to put forward their own point of view, to question the statements, explanations or justifications of others, to express their feelings and attitudes openly, or to regulate interaction by giving commands or permissions, or by opposing commands that have been given. Moreover, communications of people with a mental handicap in institutional settings do not seem to be taken seriously by professionals. Cullen, Burton, Watts, and Thomas (1983), in a study of staff reactions to 'appropriate' and 'inappropriate' communications of residents in a mental handicap hospital, found that there were few or no staff responses to any kind of communications by residents, whether 'appropriate' or 'inappropriate'. On similar lines, a study by Prior et al. (1979) showed that, in a mental handicap hospital, communications between staff and young mentally handicapped adults were based most on staff instructions and least on conversations with the residents. Goode (1984) was critical of the fact that assessment and training in communicative skills was usually carried out in clinics, that is in the home territory of the professional, rather than in that of the person with the mental handicap. Quite often, the trainer or assessor had had little or no previous contact with the assessed person, which contributed to the unfamiliar and threatening nature of the situation for the latter. Goode suggested that the only important criterion of competence is the person's ability to communicate in the situations that actually occur in his or her real life, and that clinical situations are not relevant to these. In a clinical assessment in which the behaviour of the person is viewed in isolation from his or her environment, such behaviour is likely to be interpreted, incorrectly, as evidence of lack of skills or even as deviance on the part of the individual.

Recently, the relationship between person and environment necessary for training in language and communicative skills has received more attention in research and intervention (Bailey and Wolery, 1984; Beveridge and Brinker, 1980; Campbell and Stremel-Campbell, 1986; Martin, McConkey, and Martin, 1984; Robertson, Richardson, and Youngson, 1984; Rogers-Warren and Warren, 1980; Warren and Rogers-Warren, 1980, 1984; Warren et al., 1980).

Recent models of language learning in a family (Rogers-Warren et al., 1984), and in institutional settings (Warren and Rogers-Warren, 1984), focus on critical components of environments related to language. The authors of these models emphasize the importance of generalization from training to real-life situations. They point out that training in grammatical or semantic structures does not necessarily result in improved communicative competence or in substantial increases in students' actual language use because such training does not easily generalize across settings and persons. Their *functional model* of training in language and communication requires that a student be actively involved with his or her environment. Such involvement can be achieved even in institutional settings by appropriate environmental modifications. Thus institutional living-unit and dining-hall settings are not very functional environments in terms of demand and support for language usage. Such settings are designed to operate efficiently, safely and economically, while little verbal or non-verbal exchange other than compliance is required from residents. Therefore, to increase demands on language usage, it is important to ensure that staff frequently talk to residents in ways that require verbal responses from them. Residents' communication with staff in situations that are functional and in which the resident is actively involved has a greater chance of also being applied by the resident in other situations (Halle, Marshall, and Spradlin, 1979). Functional staff–resident interactions can be increased by restructuring the environment in ways that change basic interaction patterns, or by requiring staff to utilize interaction techniques such as incidental teaching strategies.

Methodological Issues

The discussion in previous sections, concerned with the importance of proper communicative contexts, brings into focus methodological issues in research into the language and communication of people with mental handicap. About 15 years ago, Mittler (1974) pointed to the importance of collecting samples of language in everyday situations. However, only recently have observation and the collection of data in real-life situations become the main research method. The ethnographic approach has been pioneered by Edgerton (1967) and his students and followers (e.g. Kernan, Begab, and Edgerton, 1984; Platt and Sabsay, 1985). In using the ethnographic approach, the researcher fully and naturally engages in the life events of the participants he or she studies, observes what they do, asks questions when appropriate, and investigates the management of their communicative interactions (Kernan and Sabsay, 1988). The underlying philosophy of such research is one of establishing a relationship of trust with the participant. The researcher must actively seek to break down the barriers created by the traditional asymmetrical relationship based on the power of the professional. Establishing rapport with participants is an important and time-consuming aspect of research (Markova, Jahoda, and Cattermole, 1988; Platt, 1985).

Data obtained through the ethnographic method and through observations in family and institution most often take the form of field notes, and video- and audio-transcripts of recorded conversations, and are analysed by statistical and qualitative methods.

IDENTIFICATION OF PROBLEMS IN LANGUAGE AND COMMUNICATION OF PEOPLE WITH A MENTAL HANDICAP

There are two main areas of research focusing on problematic aspects in the speech of the mentally handicapped. The first is concerned with psycholinguistic issues, such as cognitive prerequisites of language acquisition, the relationship between cognition and language development, the production and comprehension of language, and the like. The second area of research takes as starting points interpersonal communication and units of discourse. It focuses on problematic aspects in the handicapped person's performance in conversation, for example on his or her giving of information, his or her social sensitivity, and the like. This section discusses solely the latter area of research.

Not surprisingly, problems in speech and communication are related to the level of severity of mental handicap. It appears, however, that even individuals whose speech is very limited can, to a considerable degree, communicate effectively with one another. Price-Williams and Sabsay (1979) found that severely mentally handicapped persons satisfy the basic requirements of discourse, such as securing the attention of the hearer, and establishing referents, i.e. directing the hearer's attention to a person, object or event in the immediate environment. This study has shown that the participants took turns in conversation, responded to one another's questions, and used repair devices if the hearer did not understand what the speaker had said.

One of the most difficult tasks for the researcher in the study of the communication of mildly mentally handicapped people is to identify what exactly it is in their speech that gives the hearer the impression that something is wrong (Kernan and Sabsay, 1982). Kernan and Sabsay have found 13 different kinds of error in the narratives of mentally handicapped people that commonly are also present in the conversations of non-handicapped people. These are, for example, grammatically ill-formed sentences, semantic blends, incorrect lexical selection, saying one thing while intending another, logical errors, inadequately presented background information and inadequately identified referents. However, what is different between the conversations of handicapped and non-handicapped people, the authors pointed out, is the frequency and multiplicity of such problems in a particular stretch of discourse. The frequency and multiplicity of the problems have a cumulative effect on the listener. The findings by Kernan and Sabsay were confirmed by Brewer and Yearley (1989), who carried out conversation analysis of the speech of a group of hospital residents. In addition, these authors found that, when talking amongst themselves, residents conformed to the basic structural conversational regularities better than when talking to visitors and strangers. However, because of the residents' linguistic difficulties and memory failings, their conversations did not exhibit all of the higher-level organizational features present in conversations of non-handicapped people. The authors argued that conversational incompetence often resulted from attempts of the handicapped to manage their spoilt identity as stigmatized persons (see next section).

It appears that one of the most important problems in speech of the mentally handicapped is that of *referential* defect. There have been studies of the speech of children and adolescents (Beveridge, Newton, and Grantley, 1982; Biasini and Bray,

1986; Bray, Biasini, and Thrasher 1982; Halle, Baes, and Spradlin, 1981; Rueda and Chan, 1980) as well as of adults (Kernan and Sabsay, 1987; Sabsay and Kernan, 1984). It was found that even participants with low intellectual abilities provided some definite referents in their speech, although referential competence was clearly related to the severity of the individual's handicap (Rueda and Chan, 1980). Kernan and Sabsay (1987) studied definitive referents in narratives of mildly handicapped adults. They found that the participants introduced less than half as many referents into their narratives as did the non-handicapped and often introduced information about which their interlocutors could not have had prior knowledge. They used indefinite forms of referents with respect to non-shared knowledge for about 85% of the time. Their ability to cope with referents clearly was dependent on the complexity of the task.

As Kernan and Sabsay (1987) say, linguistic theory can provide a framework for the analysis of units of discourse but it cannot offer an explanation for deficiencies in the construction of discourse units. Such explanations must be based on the study of social-interactional and cognitive abilities. Thus it is interesting that mildly handicapped speakers on some occasions produce discourse that is perfectly formed. For example, at these times they provide necessary background information and their narratives are coherent and to the point. However, speech situation or context does not seem to be predictive of the particular quality of a discourse (Kernan and Sabsay, 1987; Kernan, Sabsay, and Shinn, 1989). It is likely that the individual's self- and other-awareness and his or her motivation and emotions interplay with the quality of his or her performance in communication.

Conversational analysis, however, involves more than description of basic dialogical structures. Equally important is speakers' sensitivity to their conversational partners and the way they construct their utterances to fit in with the communicative situation. Speakers' sensitivity with respect to each other is essential for the maintenance of conversation, and it has been found that it is present in the talk of the mentally handicapped (Kernan and Sabsay, 1984; Sabsay and Kernan, 1984; Turner, Kernan, and Gelphman, 1984). However, while these studies provide numerous examples showing sensitivity of handicapped participants towards their interlocutors, lack of communicative sensitivity is, nevertheless, an important factor in many of the misunderstandings. Sabsay and Platt (1985) point out that lack of communicative sensitivity is particularly pronounced in conversations with the mildly mentally handicapped, and is more significant than are grammatical, phonological and lexical deficiencies, which, in consequence, may pass unnoticed.

It has been well documented that many of the negative social consequences for a person with a mental handicap are related to his or her lack of sensitivity in interpersonal communication (Edgerton, 1967; Greenspan, 1979, 1981). Sensitivity of mentally handicapped children to emotional states of others has been explored by Marcell and Jett (1985). The authors presented non-handicapped and handicapped children with audio-tapes in which speakers expressed happiness, sadness, anger or fear. It was found that handicapped children were accurate in their identifications of emotions although those more severely handicapped were less competent. Abbeduto (1984) explored the effect of communicative situations on the type of directive requests produced by handicapped and non-handicapped kindergarten children. Directive requests were elicited in role-playing situations which differed with respect to the addressee's age, and the cause and purpose of directive request. Both groups of children were sensitive to different communicative contexts, although the child's preferred form of directive appeared to overrule any different response that he or she might reasonably have been expected to make to a changed situation. The differences between the handicapped and non-handicapped children were not statistically significant, due to considerable individual differences in both groups. Owings, McManus, and Scherer (1981) studied sensitivity to different communicative contexts in a case study of one moderately handicapped person. The authors found considerable variability in the person's use of communicative functions, such as giving information, imitation, repetition, praise and criticism, across different contexts. Thus, in spite of severe limits in his production of language, the individual was well aware of existing communicative conventions. Turner *et al.* (1984) studied speech etiquette in a workshop involving mildly handicapped people. It was found that the members of the speech community were highly sensitive with respect to what was and was not to be said publicly about matters of personal concern to them. For example, they would never discuss severe speech impediments of individuals in their presence unless they intended to insult them.

COMMUNICATIVE STRATEGIES OF PEOPLE WITH A MENTAL HANDICAP

People with a mental handicap, just like everybody else, want to be recognized as effective communicative partners and to be acknowledged as fully human (Markova, 1987). Many mildly mentally handicapped individuals are deeply aware of the stigma attached to mental handicap that discredits them in the eyes of others (Edgerton, 1967; Jahoda *et al.*, 1988; Platt and Sabsay, 1985; Zetlin and Turner, 1984). Their efforts, mostly unsuccessful, to achieve recogition by others often lead the handicapped into adopting one or more communicative strategies to avoid stigma and to protect their fragile self-concepts. In this section we shall discuss three main communicative strategies of handicapped people used in their conversations with the non-handicapped.

Withdrawal

Leudar and Fraser (1985) claim that withdrawal from communication is an active, complex and inherently paradoxical process. The authors distinguished three types of withdrawal in psychiatric assessments, taking into consideration the manner and extent to which a withdrawn individual with a mental handicap manages to regulate the communicative context. First, the person may give the impression that he or she is cooperative while refusing to provide information in chosen areas. In this case, informativeness in some areas masks uninformativeness in others. The second type of withdrawal reveals itself as the individual's attempt to distance himself or herself from communicative partners. The third type of withdrawal is inertia resulting from an intellectual handicap.

Another withdrawal strategy is the individual's attempt to conceal his or her incompetencies as a conversational partner by giving as minimum as possible a response or by repeating the other interlocutor's turn (Brewer and Yearley, in press). Brewer and Yearley (1989) argue that minimal responses are attempts to 'pass' (Edgerton, 1967) as non-stigmatized. By using this strategy, however, the individual achieves, paradoxically, quite the opposite effect. Incompetence is not a feature of everyday conversational interaction, and withdrawal from conversation further contributes to the individual's stigmatization. In a similar vein, Leudar, Fraser, and Jeeves (1981) suggest that individuals with Down's syndrome may actively avoid speech when interacting with the non-handicapped. Instead, they reflect their familiarity with speakers by body posture such as the orientation of head and arm, by leaning either forward or backward, and by changes in body posture.

Self-Aggrandisement

In contrast to withdrawal, self-aggrandisement strategy is based on an attempt by the individual to weave for himself or herself a 'cloak of competence' (Sabsay and Platt, 1985) and to project a favourable image. Kernan and Sabsay (1988) point out that individuals may do this by using any of a variety of strategies in their interactions with others. They may attempt to present themselves as bright and aggressive by blustering, being funny, and pretending understanding. They may try to demonstrate competence (Graffam, 1985), or display their knowledge of the discussed subject (Platt, 1985) and their personal accomplishments (Turner *et al.*, 1984). Platt (1985) discusses a variety of verbal strategies for displaying competence, which include announcements of facts about daily life and challenging the accuracy of others' statements, by pervasive use of 'I know' and the like. An aspect of self-aggrandisement strategy is 'normalcy fabrication' (Anderson-Levitt, 1985; Platt, 1985; Turner, 1984; Turner *et al.*, 1984): the preoccupation of the mildly mentally handicapped with appearing normal and avoiding topics in discussion that might touch on the question of mental handicap.

Gap-Filling

Kernan and Sabsay (1988) maintain that one of the greatest problems for mildly handicapped people is their limited repertoire of conversational topics. Some of them compensate for this problem by using idiosyncratic techniques which allow them to participate actively in a conversation, though inappropriately. They do this by using a gap-filling strategy. Gap-filling, in contrast to self-aggrandisement, is a desemanticized strategy. This means that it is not the subject of the conversation that is at issue. Rather, the individual is aware of the rules and conventions in conversation such as turn-taking and question–answer pairs, and he or she uses gap-filling devices to maintain the flow of the conversation. Kernan and Sabsay (1988) present a number of examples of this strategy: repetition of key words of another speaker's utterance; turning questions around and asking the same question of the interlocutor even if the question could not possibly pertain to him or her; asking questions to which he or she obviously knows the answers.

Impression-management strategies may create difficulties for the non-handicapped interlocutor who can either ignore them or challenge them, depending on the communicative context in which they appear (Sabsay and Platt, 1985). An effective response on the part of the non-handicapped to impression-management strategies by the handicapped requires sensitivity and a deep insight into this problem of stigma. One must bear in mind, though, that the communicative strategies discussed in this section are not specific to people with mental handicap. All human beings, because they are self- and other-aware, do their best to cope with their social situations using strategies of self-presentation designed to put them in the best possible light with others.

CONCLUSION

Studies of language and communication in people with a mental handicap in the 1980s have directed attention to several important areas. First, there has been a genuine effort to investigate language and communication in ecologically valid situations. Knowledge and understanding of the environment in which the individual lives are now considered more often than in the past in the evaluation of the need for intervention and of programmes in the training of communicative skills. Second, studies in parent–child communication, communication between the handicapped and non-handicapped, and between the handicapped and the professional have brought into focus the importance of managing a truly interactive relationship in which a person with a handicap can participate as a valued human being. It is essential that systematic studies in different environmental contexts be carried out to explore the role of active engagement in practical activities for language acquisition and for communication. Third, studies in impression management have focused attention on the handicapped person's persistent struggle to avoid stigma and be accepted as a normal member of society. These advances in theory and practice have been facilitated by methodological changes. In contrast to laboratory experiments and clinical testing, the main method of collecting information about language and communciation in people with a mental handicap has become participant observation and video- and audio-recording of naturally occurring conversations.

Finally, one can expect that research in language and communication of people with mental handicap in the 1990s will continue in the direction started in the 1980s. In particular, it is to be hoped that most studies will be carried out in ecologically valid situations and that mutuality and reciprocity between speaker and listener will form the basis for all research in language and communication.

REFERENCES

Abbeduto, L. (1984). Situational influences on mentally retarded and non-retarded children's production of directives. *Applied Psycholinguistics*, **5**, 147–166.
Aloia, G.F. and MacMillan, D.L. (1983). Influence of the EMR label on initial expectations of regular-classroom teachers. *American Journal of Mental Deficiency*, **88**, 255–262.

Anderson-Levitt, K.M. (1985). Taking sides: Resolution of a peer conflict in a workshop for retarded adults. In M. Platt and S. Sabsay (Eds), *Social setting, stigma, and communicative competence: Explorations of the conversational interactions of retarded adults*. Amsterdam and Philadelphia: Benjamin.

Bailey, D.B. and Wolery, M. (1984). *Teaching infants and preschoolers with handicaps*. Columbus, OH: Merrill.

Berry, P. (Ed.) (1976). *Language and communication in the mentally handicapped*. London: Arnold.

Beveridge, M. and Brinker, R. (1980). An ecological developmental approach to communication in retarded children. In M. Jones (Ed.), *Language disability in children*. Lancaster: MTP.

Beveridge, M., Newton, S., and Grantley, J. (1982). Referential communication as a technique in the teaching of work skills to severely subnormal adolescents. *British Journal of Disorders of Communication*, **17**, 15–21.

Biasini, F.J. and Bray, N.W. (1986). Comparison and message-formulation skills in the referential communication of severely mentally retarded children. *American Journal of Mental Deficiency*, **90**, 686–693.

Bloom, L. (1972). Semantic features in language development. In R.L. Schiefelbusch (Ed.), *Language of the mentally retarded*. Baltimore, MD: University Park Press.

Blount, W.R. (1968). Language and the more severely retarded: A review. *American Journal of Mental Deficiency*, **1**, 21–29.

Bray, N.W., Biasini, F.J., and Thrasher, K.A. (1982). The effect of communication demand on request-making in the moderately and severely retarded. *Applied Research in Mental Retardation*, **4**, 13–27.

Brewer, J.D. and Yearley, S. (1989). Stigma and conversational competence A conversational analytic study of the mentally handicapped. *Human Studies*, **12**, 97–115.

Buium, N., Rynders, J., and Turnure, J. (1974). Early maternal linguistic environment of normal and Down's syndrome language-learning children. *American Journal of Mental Deficiency*, **89**, 451–458.

Campbell, R.C. and Stremel-Campbell, K. (1986). Programming 'Loose training' as a strategy to facilitate language generalization. *Journal of Applied Behavioral Analysis*, **15**, 295–301.

Clarke, A.M. and Clarke, A.B.D. (1985). Experimental studies: An overview. In A.M. Clarke, A.B.D. Clarke, and J. Berg (Eds), *Mental deficiency: The changing outlook*, 4th edn. London: Methuen.

Cromer, R.F. (1974). Receptive language in the mentally retarded: Processes and diagnostic distinctions. In R.L. Schiefelbusch and L.L. Lloyd (Eds), *Language perspectives: Acquisition, retardation and intervention*. Baltimore, MD: University Park Press.

Cullen, C., Burton, M., Watts, S., and Thomas, M. (1983). A preliminary report on the nature of interactions in a mental-handicap institution. *Behaviour Research and Therapy*, **21**, 579–583.

Cunningham, C.E., Reuler, E., Blackwell, J., and Deck, J. (1981). Behavioral and linguistic development in the interactions of normal and retarded children with their mothers. *Child Development*, **52**, 62–70.

Davis, H. and Oliver, B. (1980). A comparison of aspects of the maternal speech environment of retarded and non-retarded children. *Child: Care, Health and Development*, **6**, 135–145.

Edgerton, R.B. (1967). *The cloak of competence: Stigma in the lives of the mentally retarded*. Berkeley, CA: University of California Press.

Eheart, B.K. (1982). Mother–child interactions with non-retarded and retarded preschoolers. *American Journal of Mental Deficiency*, **87**, 20–25.

Elias, S.F., Sigelman, C.K., and Danker-Brown (1980). Interview behaviour of and impressions made by mentally retarded adults. *American Journal of Mental Deficiency*, **85**, 53–60.

Elias-Burger, S.F., Sigelman, G.K., Danley, W.E., and Burger, D.L. (1981). *American Journal of Mental Deficiency*, **85**, 655–657.

Giles, H. and Powesland, P.F. (1975). *Speech style and social evaluation*. London: Academic Press.

Goffman, E. (1968). *Stigma*. Harmondsworth: Penguin.

Goode, D.A. (1984). Socially-produced identities, intimacy and the problem of competence among the retarded. In L. Barton and S. Tomlinson (Eds), *Special education and social interest*. New York: Croom Helm.

Graffam, J. (1985). About ostriches coming out of communist China: Meanings, functions, and frequencies of typical interactions in group meetings for retarded adults. In M. Platt and S. Sabsay (Eds), *Social setting, stigma, and communicative competence: Explorations of the conversational interactions of retarded adults*. Amsterdam and Philadelphia: Benjamin.

Greenspan, S. (1979). Social intelligence in the retarded. In N.R. Ellis (Ed.), *Handbook of mental deficiency: Psychological theory and research*, 2nd edn. Hillsdale, NJ: Erlbaum.

Greenspan, S. (1981). Social competence and handicapped individuals. *Advances in Special Education*, **3**, 41–82.

Gumperz, J.J. (1982). *Discourse strategies*. Cambridge: Cambridge University Press.

Guralnick, M.J. (1986). The peer relations of young handicapped and non-handicapped children. In P.S. Strain, M.J. Guralnick, and H.M. Walker (Eds), *Children's social behavior: Development, assessment, and modification*. New York: Academic Press.

Guralnick, M.J. and Groom, J.M. (1987). The peer relations of mildly delayed and non-handicapped preschool children in mainstreamed playgroups. *Child Development*, **58**, 1556–1572.

Guralnick, M.J. and Paul-Brown, D. (1980). Functional and discourse analysis of non-handicapped preschool children's speech to handicapped children. *American Journal of Mental Deficiency*, **84**, 444–454.

Guralnick, M.J. and Weinhouse, E. (1984). Peer-related social interactions of developmentally delayed young children: Development and characteristics. *Developmental Psychology*, **20**, 815–827.

Halle, J., Baes, D., and Spradlin, J. (1981). Teachers' generalised use of delay as a stimulus control procedure to increase language use in handicapped children. *Journal of Applied Behavior Analysis*, **14**, 389–409.

Halle, J., Marshall, A., and Spradlin, J. (1979). Time delay: A technique to increase language use and facilitate generalization in retarded children. *Journal of Applied Behavioral Analysis*, **12**, 431–439.

Heber, R. (1961). Modifications in the manual on terminology and classification in mental retardation. *American Journal of Mental Deficiency*, **66**, 499–500.

Jahoda, A., Markova, I., and Cattermole, M. (1988). Stigma and the self-concept of people with a mild mental handicap. *Journal of Mental Deficiency Research*, **32**, 103–115.

Jones, O.H.M. (1977). Mother–child communication with prelinguistic Down's syndrome and normal infants. In H.R. Schaffer (Ed.), *Studies in mother–infant interaction*. London: Academic Press.

Jones, O.H.M. (1980). Prelinguistic communication skills in Down syndrome and normal infants. In T.M. Fields, S. Goldberg, D. Stern, and A.M. Sostek (Eds), *High risk infants and children*, pp. 205–225. New York: Academic Press.

Kernan, K.T., Begab, M.J., and Edgerton, R.B. (Eds) (1984). *Environments and behavior: The adaptation of mildly retarded persons*. Baltimore, MD: University Park Press.

Kernan, K.T. and Sabsay, S. (1982). Semantic deficiencies in the narratives of mildly retarded speakers. *Semiotica*, **42**, 169–193.

Kernan, K.T. and Sabsay, S. (1984). Getting there: Directions given by mildly retarded and non-retarded adults. In R.B. Edgerton (Ed.), *Lives in process: Mildly retarded adults in a large city*. Monograph No. 6. Washington, DC: American Association on Mental Deficiency.

Kernan, K.T. and Sabsay, S.L. (1987). Referential first mention in narratives by mildly mentally retarded adults. *Research in Developmental Disabilities*, **8**, 361–369.

Kernan, K.T. and Sabsay, S. (1988). Communication in social interactions: Aspects of an ethnography of communication of mildly retarded adults. In M. Beveridge, G. Conti-

Ramsden, and I. Leudar (Eds), *Language and communication in mentally handicapped persons*. London: Chapman and Hall.

Kernan, K.T., Sabsay, S., and Rein, R.P. (1986). Aspects of verbal behaviour cited by listeners in judging speakers as retarded or not retarded. *Mental Retardation and Learning Disabilities Bulletin*, **14**, 24–43.

Kernan, K.T., Sabsay, S., and Shinn, N. (1988). Discourse features as criteria in judging the intellectual ability of speakers. *Discourse Processes*, **11**, 203–220.

Kernan, K.T., Sabsay, S., and Shinn, N. (1989). Lay people's judgements of storytellers as mentally retarded or not retarded. *Journal of Mental Deficiency Research*, **33**, 149–157.

Leifer, J. and Lewis, M. (1983). Maternal speech to normal and handicapped children: A look at question-asking behavior. *Infant Behavior and Development*, **6**, 175–187.

Leifer, J.S. and Lewis, M. (1984). Acquisition of conversational response skills by young Down syndrome and non-retarded young children. *American Association on Mental Deficiency*, **88**, 610–618.

Leudar, I. (1981). Strategic communication in mental retardation. In W.I. Fraser and R. Grieve (Eds), *Communication with normal and retarded children*. Bristol: Wright.

Leudar, I. and Fraser, W.I. (1985). How to keep quiet: Some withdrawal strategies in mentally handicapped adults. *Journal of Mental Deficiency Research*, **29**, 315–330.

Leudar, I., Fraser, W.I., and Jeeves, M.A. (1981). Social familiarity and communication in Down syndrome. *Journal of Mental Deficiency Research*, **25**, 133–142.

Mahoney, G. (1988). Maternal communication style with mentally retarded children. *American Journal of Mental Retardation*, **92**, 352–359.

Mahoney, G.J. and Robenalt, K. (1986). A comparison of conversational patterns between mothers and their Down syndrome and normal infants. *Journal of the Division of Early Childhood*, **10**, 172–180.

Malgady, R.G., Barcher, P.R., Towner, G., and Davis, J. (1979). Language factors in vocational evaluation of mentally retarded workers. *American Journal of Mental Deficiency*, **83**, 432–438.

Marcell, M.M. and Jett, D.A. (1985). Identification of vocally expressed emotions by mentally retarded and non-retarded individuals. *American Journal of Mental Deficiency*, **89**, 537–545.

Markova, I. (Ed.) (1978). *The social context of language*. Chichester and New York: Wiley.

Markova, I. (1982). *Paradigms, thought and language*. Chichester and New York: Wiley.

Markova, I. (1987). *Human awareness: Its social development*, London: Century Hutchinson.

Markova, I., Jahoda, A., and Cattermole, M. (1988). The meaning of independent living for people with a mental handicap. *Health Bulletin*, **46**, 246–253.

Marshall, N.R., Hegranes, J.R., and Goldstein, S. (1973). Verbal interactions: Mothers and their retarded children vs. mothers and their non-retarded children. *American Journal of Mental Deficiency*, **77**, 415–419.

Martin, H., McConkey, R., and Martin, S. (1984). From acquisition theories to intervention strategies. *British Journal of Communication Disorders*, **19**, 3–14.

Maurer, H. and Sherrod, K. (1987). Context of directives given to young children with Down syndrome and non-retarded children: Development over two years. *American Journal of Mental Deficiency*, **91**, 579–590.

McLean, J.E., Yoder, D.E., and Schiefelbusch, R.L. (Eds) (1972). *Language intervention with the retarded developing strategies*. Baltimore, MD: University Park Press.

Mitchell, D. (1976). Patterns of interactions in the mentally handicapped. In P. Berry (Ed.), *Language and communication in the mentally handicapped*. London: Arnold.

Mittler, P.J. (1974). Language and communication. In A.M. Clarke and A.B.D. Clarke (Eds), *Readings from mental deficiency: The changing outlook*, 3rd edn. London: Methuen.

O'Connor, N. and Hermelin, B. (1963). *Speech and thought in severe subnormality*. Oxford: Pergamon.

Owings, N.A., McManus, M.D., and Scherer, N. (1981). An analysis of communication functions in the speech of a deinstitutionalised adult mentally retarded client. *Mental Retardation*, **18**, 309–314.

Petersen, G.A. and Sherrod, K.B. (1982). Relationship of maternal language to language development and language delay of children. *American Journal of Mental Deficiency*, **86**, 391–398.

Platt, M. (1985). Displaying competence: Peer interaction in a group home for retarded adults. In M. Platt and S. Sabsay (Eds), *Social setting, stigma and communicative competence: Explorations of the conversational interaction of retarded adults*. Amsterdam and Philadelphia: Benjamin.

Platt, M. and Sabsay, S. (Eds) (1985). *Social setting, stigma and communicative competence*. Amsterdam and Philadelphia: Benjamin.

Price-Williams, D. and Sabsay, S. (1979). Communicative competence among severely retarded persons. *Semiotica*, **26**, 35–63.

Prior, M., Minnes, P., Coyne, T., Golding, B., Hendy, J., and McGillivary, J. (1979). Verbal interactions between staff and residents in an institution for the young mentally retarded. *Mental Retardation*, **17**, 65–69.

Raber, S.M. and Weisz, J.R. (1981). Teacher feedback to mentally retarded and non-retarded children. *American Journal of Mental Deficiency*, **83**, 432–438.

Robertson, I., Richardson, A.M., and Youngson, S.C. (1984). Social skills training with mentally handicapped people: A review. *British Journal of Clinical Psychology*, **23**, 241–264.

Rogers-Warren, A. and Warren, S. (1980). Mands for verbalization: Facilitating the display of newly-taught language. *Behavior Modification*, **4**, 361–382.

Rogers-Warren, A.K., Warren, S.F., and Baer, D.M. (1984). Interactional basis of language learning. In K.T. Kernan, M.J. Begab, and R.B. Edgerton (Eds), *Environments and behavior: The adaptation of mildly retarded persons*. Baltimore, MD: University Park Press.

Rommetveit, R. (1974). *On message structure*. Chichester and New York: Wiley.

Rondal, J.A. (1975). Développement du langage et retard mental: Une revue critique de la littérature en langue anglaise. *L'Année Psychologique*, **75**, 513–547.

Rondal, J.A. (1980). The interactive point of view in language development, disorders and intervention. *Psychologia Belgica*, **20**, 185–204.

Rondal, J.A. (1978a). Le développement linguistique des handicapes mentaux: Est-il simplement retardé ou proprement déficitaire! Une revue de la littérature avec référence particulière à la littérature de langue anglaise. *Journal de Psychologie Normale et Pathologique*, **3**, 347–368.

Rondal, J.A. (1978b). Maternal speech to normal and Down's syndrome children matched for mean length of utterance. In C.E. Meyers (Ed.), *Quality of life in severely and profoundly mentally retarded people: Research foundations for improvement*. Monograph No. 3. Washington, DC: American Association on Mental Deficiency.

Rueda, R. and Chan, K.S. (1980). Referential communication skill levels of moderately mentally retarded adolescents. *American Journal of Mental Deficiency*, **85**, 45–52.

Ryan, E.B. and Giles, H. (Eds) (1982). *Attitudes towards language variation*. London: Arnold.

Sabsay, S.L. and Kernan, K.T. (1984). Communicative design in the speech of mildly retarded adults. In K.T. Kernan, M.J. Begab, and R.B. Edgerton (Eds), *Environments and behavior: The adaptation of mildly retarded persons*. Baltimore, MD: University Park Press.

Sabsay, S. and Platt, M. (1985). Weaving the cloak of competence: A paradox in the management of trouble in conversation between retarded and non-retarded interlocutors. In M. Platt and S. Sabsay (Eds), *Social setting, stigma, and communicative competence: Explorations of the conversational interactions of retarded adults*. Amsterdam and Philadelphia: Benjamin.

Schiefelbusch, R.L. (Ed.) (1972). *Language of the mentally retarded*. Baltimore, MD: University Park Press.

Schiefelbusch, R.L. and Bricker, D. (1981). *Early language: Acquisition and intervention*. Baltimore, MD: University Park Press.

Schiefelbusch, R.L., Copeland, R., and Smith, J. (Eds) (1967). *Language and mental retardation: Empirical and conceptual considerations*. New York: Holt, Rinehart and Winston.

Schiefelbusch, R. and Lloyd, L. (Eds) (1974). *Language perspectives: Acquisition, retardation and intervention*. Baltimore, MD: University Park Press.

Sigelman, C.K., Elias, S.F., and Danker-Brown, F. (1980). Interview behaviours of mentally retarded adults as predictors of employability. *Journal of Applied Psychology*, **65**, 67–73.

St Clair, R.N. and Giles, H. (Eds) (1980). *The social and psychological contexts of language*. Hillsdale, NJ: Erlbaum.

Stoneman, C., Brody, G.H., and Abbott, D. (1983). In-home observations of young Down syndrome children with their mothers and fathers. *American Journal of Mental Deficiency*, **87**, 591–600.

Taylor, A.R., Asher, S.R., and Williams, G.A. (1987). The social adaptation of main-streamed mildly retarded children. *Child Development*, **58**, 1321–1334.

Turner, J.L. (1984). Workshop society: Ethnographic observations in a work setting. In K.T. Kernan, M.J. Begab, and R.B. Edgerton (Eds), *Environments and behavior: The adaptation of mildly retarded persons*. Baltimore, MD: University Park Press.

Turner, J.L., Kernan, K.T., and Gelphman, S. (1984). Speech etiquette in a sheltered workshop. In R.B. Edgerton (Ed.), *Lives in process: Mildly retarded adults in a large city*. Monograph No. 6. Washington DC: American Association on Mental Deficiency.

Warren, S.F. and Rogers-Warren, A. (1980). Current perspectives in language remediation. *Education and Treatment of Children*, **3**, 133–152.

Warren, S.F., Rogers-Warren, A., Baer, D.M. and Guess, D. (1980). Assessment and facilitation of language generalization. In W. Sailor, B. Wilcox and L. Brown (Eds), *Methods of instruction of severely handicapped students*. Baltimore, MD: Paul H. Brookes.

Warren, S.F. and Rogers-Warren, A.K. (1984). Because no one asked. . . Setting variables affecting the generalisation of trained vocabulary within a residential institution. In K.T. Kernan, M.J. Begab, and R.B. Edgerton (Eds), *Environments and behavior: The adaptation of mildly retarded persons*. Baltimore, MD: University Park Press.

Weisz, J.R. (1981). Learned helplessness in black and white children identified by their schools as retarded and non-retarded: Performance deterioration in response to failure. *Developmental Psychology*, **17**, 499–508.

Weisz, J.R. (1982). Learned helplessness and the retarded child. In E. Zigler and D. Balla (Eds), *Development and difference theories of mental retardation*. Hillsdale, NJ: Erlbaum.

Yoder, D.E. and Miller, J.G. (1972). What we may know and what we can do: Input towards a system. In J.E. McLean, D.E. Yoder and R.L. Schiefelbusch (Eds), *In language intervention with the retarded: Developing strategies*. Baltimore, MD: University Park Press.

Zetlin, A.G. and Turner, J.L. (1984). Self-perspectives on being handicapped: Stigma and adjustment. In R.B. Edgerton (Ed.), *Lives in process: Mildly retarded adults in a large city*. Washington DC: American Association on Mental Deficiency.

Section 5

Language in Social Relations

Introduction to Section 5

Many of the previous sections have highlighted the importance of understanding the *sequential* patterning of language forms and their social implications during a conversation. In this section, we elaborate on the developmental perspective by examining the ways in which adult language is contextualized in relational and personal histories.

Bradac's chapter starts us on this road by critiquing the voluminous literature showing how we use language, variably adhering or non-adhering as it does to valued norms, in forming impressions of strangers in *initial* encounters. A plethora of language features (e.g. accent/dialect, lexical diversity/intensity) induces listeners to make inferences about users' sociopsychological make-ups, as well as decisions about their likely past and future actions. Such social judgments are multidimensional and derived on the basis of speakers' known role characteristics, and the social and applied contexts in which a complex combination of these language features are purportedly produced. Bradac provides six very useful generalizations and an implicit model of the kinds of dynamic sociolinguistic factors which may be linked to various attitude patterns. He claims, however, that language cues (and doubtless distinct combinations of them) are utilized differentially in more established social relationships (in which the interactants have high levels of mutual knowledge) and where the process is one of inferring the other's emotional state as well as his or her relational status.

Wilmot and Shellen extend the discussion to take into account this and other functions of language in friendship formation *and* decline within and between the sexes. The language and communication correlates of increasing relational closeness are discussed – including non-verbal intimacies, immediacies, forms of address, self-disclosures, discourse strategies (e.g. topic-shifting), and gossip – yet the ways in which language also determines the nature and trajectories of friendships are underscored throughout. In addition to the various influence tactics friends adopt in

---

Handbook of Language and Social Psychology
Edited by H. Giles and W.P. Robinson. © 1990 John Wiley & Sons Ltd

an attempt to influence each other or account for themselves, what is *not* said is just as important, and is explored through the complex exchange of 'taken-for-granteds' on the one hand, and the adherence to various (sometimes strategic) conversational taboos on the other. By means of their 'relational schemata model', which illuminates how people decide whether they are which kinds of friends or not, Wilmot and Shellen provide some cognitive and promisory substance to the complexity and ambiguity which underlies the bidirectional, causative links between friendship and language.

Fitzpatrick's chapter investigates the role of language in one of the next stages in bonding between certain kinds of friends, namely marriage. Language and communication are integral to this institution and non-verbal sequences and the ways in which these are linked to measured arousal on the one hand and expressed attributions on the other are predictive of satisfied and dissatisfied marital states. Research and theories (both 'individual' and 'interpersonal') in this large and increasingly sophisticated area are discussed critically, and in their wake are unfolded male and female spouses' differential interpretations of each others' non-verbal and discoursal cues, thereby providing insights into the different views the genders can have of the same marriages. After an introduction to her own typology of marriages and the extensive communicative research attending it, Fitzpatrick shows (and in a manner which complements well the previous chapter) how her process model of marital schemata can synthesize previous models of marital interaction as well as, and perhaps more importantly, elucidate the *transactive* nature of marriage and language.

The final chapter in this section can be seen to make the case, amongst many other points, that different social relationships need to be considered from a *lifespan* perspective. In other words, friendships and marriage, and the roles of language within them, may be quite different at different stages of adulthood, maturity, and accomplishment. The Couplands point out that the elderly in general – as with many other social groups encountered in the previous section – can suffer from pernicious stigmas, evident, for example, in the manner in which negative stereotypes of elderly competence mediate some younger people 'talking down' or 'over-accommodating' to them. In reviewing the extant literature on sociolinguistics and communication in the elderly, the Couplands make the case that much of this may be ageist to the extent that it has examined intergenerational differences from a *decremental* stance only; that is, from the perspective that older people's language becomes progressively deficient, even regresses, as age increases yet further. However, they review another, so-called 'anti-ageist', approach (to which they have contributed substantively), which makes the case that communicative practices of elderly people – even those which involve, seemingly excessive, disclosures of age, health, and painful events – have considerable functional significance for them. Such an emancipating analysis takes on even more theoretical (as well as pragmatic) significance from both an appreciation of the collective subjectivity of 'elderliness' as well as from a thorough grasp of the particular contextual (and sometimes institutional) mores in which the interaction is localized.

In this section, then, we shall see how relational and lifespan developments find their reflections in, and give meaning to, differential language use in communication, but also that the very meaning itself of these personal and interpersonal histories is often grounded in language processes.

19

Language Attitudes and Impression Formation

JAMES J. BRADAC

Department of Communication, University of California, Santa Barbara, USA

The title of this chapter suggests a hypothesis: persons have attitudes toward language which are especially salient and influential in initial interactions. This means that various linguistic features trigger in message recipients beliefs ('Her way of talking leads me to think she is a professor') and evaluations ('She is intelligent') regarding message senders, and that these beliefs and evaluations are most likely to affect recipients' behaviours toward senders in contexts of low mutual familiarity. (It should be noted at the outset that even in the briefest initial interactions both parties are alternately or even simultaneously functioning in the role of sender and recipient; this distinction is primarily an expository convenience which nevertheless is frequently honoured in the literature (e.g. Krauss, 1987).)

The idea that language is an especially important trigger of evaluations and beliefs in initial-impression contexts is consistent with the findings of much research in this area, in large part because this research has overwhelmingly employed message senders who are unknown to message recipients. In other words, there has been very little examination of the influence of language upon beliefs and evaluations of persons who are well known to each other, for example intimates. In the last section of this chapter, a few suggestions will be offered regarding belief-generative and evaluative consequences of language in contexts of mutual familiarity.

Initially, it will be useful to examine (albeit briefly) the historical underpinnings of the language-attitudes area. The earliest studies established themes and procedures which are still with us today (this is either a testament to their excellence or a sign of

Handbook of Language and Social Psychology
Edited by H. Giles and W.P. Robinson. © 1990 John Wiley & Sons Ltd

some stagnation in the field). This examination will be followed by a discussion of some important, more recent studies which participate directly in the historical tradition: studies of consequences of accent and dialect. It will be useful then to discuss other language variables which have been investigated recently. Following this, the important general variable of 'context' will be examined, and specific examples of the role of context in mediating evaluations and beliefs produced by language will be gleaned from research. It will be useful next to discuss the *kinds* of message-recipient judgments which can be affected by language in context; this should be a good place for broaching measurement possibilities and issues. Finally, a few tentative conclusions will be offered and pertinent limitations will be noted; this will suggest possibilities for future work in the field.

EARLY RESEARCH ON LANGUAGE ATTITUDES

As with many other types of research, one can find precursors which go back hundreds of years. For example, Aristotle (trans. Cooper, 1932) believed that the type of language which speakers used had an effect upon their credibility or *ethos*, and a similar idea is apparent in Renaissance rhetoricians' preoccupation with the details of verbal expression, for example schemes and tropes (Sherry, 1961). More pertinently, although essentially and primarily descriptive, the research of dialect geographers in the early twentieth century called attention to language varieties which were stigmatized or, on the other hand, accorded prestige (Bloomfield, 1933). Equally pertinently, a number of studies conducted in the 1930s and 1940s in Britain and the USA attempted to demonstrate that persons can make reliable and accurate judgments of speaker physical characteristics and personality attributes on the basis of speech (Cantril and Allport, 1935; Pear, 1931; Taylor, 1934).

But if one construes the concept of 'language-attitudes research' rather narrowly to refer to the explicit, scientific study of attitudinal consequences of dissimilar language varieties, one can usefully cite as the first contemporary study the investigation of Lambert, Hodgson, Gardner, and Fillenbaum in 1960. The purpose of this study was to examine listeners' evaluative reactions to English and French. To achieve this purpose the researchers used a French prose passage and an English translation of it; four bilingual speakers audio-recorded both passages, and these recordings served as experimental stimuli. French- and English-speaking respondents listened to the English and French versions of the passage and, after each exposure to a reading, rated the speaker on 14 six-point scales pertaining to intelligence, likability, and sociability, for example. The ratings of the eight speaker–text combinations were subsequently compared statistically. Lambert *et al.* (1960) found that both English- and French-speaking respondents rated the speakers of the English versions more favourably on several traits, including perceived kindness and intelligence. Thus, even the French-speaking respondents found the English speakers relatively attractive.

Several features of this study are worth noting. First, this was an early (perhaps the earliest) attempt to exert experimental control over potentially confounding speaker idiosyncracies through the use of the 'matched-guise' technique (cf. Lambert, 1967).

The basic idea here is that each speaker used in a given study of language attitudes should cross all conditions; thus, for example, a speaker with a very high-pitched voice should not appear in a French-speaking condition only but in conditions of both French and English. Obtained differences between French and English guises would not be attributable in this case to a confounding of high pitch with French. Another point worth noting is that respondents reacted to the various guises via standard rating scales. The use of semantic-differential-type or Likert-type paper-and-pencil instruments has predominated in the measurement of language attitudes for more than 25 years, and this heavy reliance upon a single mode of measurement has been criticized in recent years (more about this below). Finally, the researchers' use of a formal passage of French prose as a 'kernel' message represented an attempt to minimize the effect of message content upon respondent reactions. This now seems misguided, and indeed more recent studies have used more naturalistic messages as vehicles for comparing the effects of language or dialect differences (Giles, Wilson, and Conway, 1981; Ryan and Bulik, 1982). But throughout the 1960s the purposeful use of standard message content with little real-world import was a methodological mainstay; perhaps the ultimate example of this is the use by Buck (1968) of passages from *Alice in wonderland* to compare the attitudinal effects of white versus black English.

Another important early study, somewhat more complex in design, was conducted by Lambert, Anisfeld, and Yeni-Komshian (1965). In this case a standard philosophical passage was recorded in Hebrew and Arabic by bilingual speakers, and in the case of Hebrew two dialectal variants were used (Ashkenazic and Yemenite). Jewish and Arab high-school students were the respondents, and they listened to the various versions and, following each, reacted to the speaker on six-point rating scales. Additionally, the Jewish respondents completed standard measures designed to assess directly general attitudes toward Ashkenazic Jews, Arabs, and Yemenite Jews.

Among other things, the results indicated that the Jewish respondents were relatively negative toward the Arabic guises on the traits of humour, friendliness, and honesty. For their part, the Arab respondents downgraded the Hebrew guises on intelligence, self-confidence, good-heartedness, friendliness, and honesty. In current parlance, these data provide evidence of devaluation of outgroup speakers among both the Arab and the Jewish respondents (Giles and Ryan, 1982). The fact that there were low to zero correlations between the generalized attitude measures and the matched-guise ratings for the Jewish respondents suggested to the investigators that the two types of assessment procedures tapped at least somewhat dissimilar attitudinal domains and that the matched-guise procedure potentially elicits responses which are relatively low in stereotypy and which are less subject to demand features of the measurement process.

This study by Lambert *et al.* (1965), like that of Lambert *et al.* (1960), is a prototypical example of traditional language-attitudes research in its use of the matched-guise procedure and its comparison of the effects of between-group language differences. The early language-attitudes research, conducted between 1960 and 1970, to give rough chronological markers, was primarily concerned with evaluative consequences of linguistic differences produced by speakers representing groups which were culturally dissimilar, typically as a function of geographical differences. (Of course, such geographical differences were, and are, in many cases highly correlated with ethnic, political, and socio-economic differences.) In this respect, one can relate this work to the earlier research of dialectologists referred to above. More recent work in the language-attitudes area continues to explore between-group differences, but in some cases interest has shifted away from geographically based differences toward differences rooted in social roles as in the case of research on attitudinal consequences of male/female language (Hogg, 1985; Mulac and Lundell, 1986).

Two other studies, characterized by Giles and Powesland (1975) as 'the early research in [British] culture' (p. 66), merit brief discussion here. Strongman and Woolsey (1967) used the matched-guise technique to compare northern and southern English listeners' evaluative reactions to Yorkshire and London accents. Across both groups of listeners, the London accent produced relatively high ratings of speaker self-confidence, whereas the Yorkshire accent enhanced ratings of speaker honesty, reliability, and generosity. The northern judges also gave high ratings to the Yorkshire guises on good-naturedness, kind-heartedness, and industriousness, and a low rating on irritability, which may be an example of accent loyalty (cf. Giles and Powesland, 1975). Cheyne (1970) compared the evaluative reactions of Scottish and English listeners to Scottish and English accent differences. Both groups of listeners gave relatively high ratings to the English accent for prestige, status, intelligence, etc. On the other hand, the Scottish accent was rated more highly on friendliness, likability, etc., especially by the Scottish listeners. This is a clear, early example of the distinction between status and solidarity judgments which pervades language-attitudes research (more about this below; cf. Giles and Powesland, 1975).

A study by Giles (1970) greatly elaborated the strategy employed in the Strongman and Woolsey (1967) and Cheyne (1970) studies. This investigator compared status ratings of 13 accents apparent in the United Kingdom. Highest ratings were given to Received Pronunciation (RP) English, while the lowest ratings were given to urban varieties (e.g. Cockney and Birmingham); ratings of particular foreign (e.g. Italian) and regional (e.g. South Welsh) accents fell between these extremes. Several early studies in the USA similarly examined evaluative reactions to accent variations. For example, Tucker and Lambert (1969) had northern and southern college students evaluate several types of white and black accents. Houck and Bowers (1969) had northern college students respond to a speaker who delivered a persuasive speech using northern- and southern-accented guises. Buck (1968) compared evaluative reactions to standard and non-standard accents when these were used by black and white speakers.

In discussing the results of some of this research, Giles and Powesland (1975) suggest:

> Whereas in Britain the mere possession of a regional accent tends to be regarded as a mark of low status [compared to RP], there appears to be no such discrimination against regional accents *per se* in the United States of America . . . it seems that the user of any regional variety of speech is capable of exhibiting 'standard' or 'nonstandard' features of that particular regional speech form. (Giles and Powesland, 1975, p. 45)

It would seem that this logic of cross-region × standardness orthogonality may not hold – or at least may not have held when the early research was conducted – for US ethnic (as opposed to regional) sources of accent (or dialect) variation. The early research suggests that there may be a tendency for untutored persons in everyday life to link ethnicity with language non-standardness perceptually and cognitively (Williams, Whitehead, and Miller, 1972) and conversely to link standardness with the dominant Anglo-American culture (Buck, 1968).

Many other studies of historical interest could be discussed here were there room enough, but this small sample is sufficient to reveal some important tendencies, for example the development and heavy use of the matched-guise technique and the strong reliance upon reactive paper-and-pencil forms of measurement. Additionally, it should be noted that the great majority of early language-attitudes studies were essentially concerned with *describing* attitudinal differences attached to different forms of accent and dialect; there was relatively little concern with *explaining* results, with postulating mechanisms, and with developing theories. This kind of descriptive work can be very useful (and even interesting) but it is limited in a particular way: as the culture within which an attitudinal pattern is isolated changes, the pattern may change also – some results may become outdated rather quickly. On the other hand, some patterns – perhaps, for example, the prestige structure for accents uncovered by Giles (1970) – may endure for many years. It may be important, both theoretically and practically, to discriminate between patterns which are very fragile and others which are quite robust.

RECENT RESEARCH IN THE HISTORICAL TRADITION

Since 1970, researchers have continued to study attitudinal consequences of ethnically and regionally determined language variation. Indeed, research in this area has proliferated greatly, so in this section an extremely selective sample of studies will be discussed in order to illustrate some recent trends.

Whereas the early studies of accent (and dialect) compared attitudinal consequences of one accent with those of another, several more recent studies have recognized that there is variation *within* a given accent type and that this variation may have consequences for speakers. For example, Giles (1972) compared the effects of mild and broad regional accents on the evaluations of adults and pre-adolescents. He found that both groups could discriminate along the mildness–broadness dimension and that the broader accent versions produced relatively negative evaluations. Brennan, Ryan, and Dawson (1975) demonstrated that linguistically non-sophisticated listeners can reliably distinguish among several degrees of Spanish-accented English, and the results of a later study by Ryan, Carranza, and Moffie (1977) indicated that degree of Spanish accent affects listeners' evaluations – the more highly accented the speech, the more negative the evaluation.

Researchers have also recognized that accent, dialect, and particular language spoken potentially interact with a variety of other linguistic features in producing evaluative consequences. For example, Giles *et al.* (1981) examined the evaluative effects of RP and Welsh accent when these were encoded in lexically diverse or lexically redundant language. Giles and Sassoon (1983) investigated the combined effects of accent and lexical diversity also, in this case comparing RP and Cockney guises. Perhaps because there was a rather small difference between the high- and low-diversity message versions used in this study, there were few effects for diversity. Still, a social distance measure indicated that RP speakers were rated especially favourably when they exhibited high lexical diversity and especially unfavourably when their diversity level was low; ratings for the Cockney speakers were between these extremes for both the high- and the low-diversity message versions, which did not differ from each other on the social distance measure.

Bradac and Wisegarver (1984) compared the effects of standard American versus Mexican-American accents when these were encoded in high- or low-diversity language. For measures of perceived intellectual competence and perceived control of communication behaviour, the high-diversity/standard American combination was rated most favourably; the high-diversity/Mexican-American combination was rated somewhat less favourably; and least favourably rated were the low-diversity/ standard American and the low-diversity/Mexican American combinations, which did not differ from each other. For ratings of solidarity, Mexican-American accent produced higher ratings than did standard American, an outcome which parallels the finding of Giles *et al.* (1981).

Thus, recent research has attended to relatively subtle effects of gradations in between-group speech and language differences and to effects produced by one linguistic variable in conjunction with another. There has also been a move away from the use of artificial prose monologues as experimental stimuli, replacing such stimuli with more realistic messages representing familiar interpersonal exchanges. For example, the Bradac and Wisegarver (1984) study cited above used responses which were ostensibly produced by an interviewee in a simulated employment interview. Another example is a series of studies by Genessee and Bourhis (1982) which examined the evaluative consequences of code-switching, in this case from English to French or vice versa. For these studies, actors recorded interchanges between a salesman and a customer; each interchange represented three or four speaking turns, for example salesman (French) – customer (English) – salesman (French); or salesman (French) – customer (English) – salesman (English). Not only were these stimuli relatively realistic, they were also dynamic. The researchers viewed language *change* as a variable of interest, recognizing that such change is a feature of many real-world communication contexts. A great deal of attention has been paid in recent years to evaluative consequences of code-switching or style-shifting and the major impetus of this attention has been speech-accommodation theory (Giles, 1973; more about this below).

Perhaps related to the use of realistic and dynamic stimulus materials is the concern with particular *applications* of the general concept of language attitudes which is apparent in a number of recent studies. For example, de la Zerda and Hopper (1979) found that potential employers were more likely to assign speakers exhibiting a Mexican-American accent to low-status positions than to positions of high status; the converse was true for speakers exhibiting a standard American accent. A similar result was obtained by Bradac and Wisegarver (1984): speakers exhibiting a Mexican-American accent received high suitability ratings on a Low-

Status Jobs factor. Using Canadian university students as respondents, Kalin and Rayko (1980) found that speakers exhibiting a variety of foreign accents were perceived to be well suited for relatively low-status positions, whereas speakers exhibiting an English Canadian accent were viewed as better suited for high-status positions. Giles *et al.* (1981) obtained a parallel result for Welsh versus RP accents. Kalin (1982) suggests that these outcomes fit a 'matching' hypothesis: on the basis of status-related speech and language cues, speakers will be matched to positions representing their status level.

Other types of applications have been investigated also. For example, Fielding and Evered (1980) provide some evidence that accent can affect the diagnoses of physicians; specifically, a speaker exhibiting an RP accent was relatively likely to be diagnosed as having a psychosomatic problem, whereas a speaker exhibiting a rural regional accent was more likely to be seen as having a physical problem. A large number of studies have examined the extent to which teachers' judgments of students' abilities and performance are affected by accent and dialect. Some of these studies indicate that non-standard forms can bias teachers' judgments in a negative direction (Williams *et al.*, 1976). As Edwards (1982) notes, 'Since teachers are people first, we should not be surprised that they too have . . . language attitudes . . . In particular, we should expect them to hold less than completely favourable views of varieties other than their own in many cases' (pp. 27–28).

Since applications involve practical considerations and since there is nothing as practical as a good theory (as Lewin suggested), this may be the place to note that recent studies in the historical tradition have invoked increasingly, and in some cases have directly tested, theories. A desire to *explain* attitudinal consequences of language variation is now evident in the literature; such a desire was not at all apparent prior to 1970. Without a doubt, the most influential of the explanatory structures has been speech-accommodation theory (SAT), originally articulated and primarily developed by Giles (1973) and discussed at length by Giles and Powesland (1975).

Briefly, in an interpersonal encounter a given speaker can move toward (convergence) or away from (divergence) the accent or dialect of another. Such movement can be perceived by the target of convergence or divergence (or by third-party observers of the exchange) as voluntary or as externally coerced by circumstances, for example by social pressure. Movement which is perceived to be voluntary will result in relatively extreme evaluations, extremely favourable for convergence and extremely unfavourable for divergence. Perceptions that speaker changes are externally coerced will attenuate these favourable and unfavourable reactions.

In some cases, perceptions of speaker convergence or divergence will compete with perceptions of adherence or non-adherence to norms regarding appropriate speech and language forms ('valued norms') in the production of evaluative consequences. For example, one speaker may voluntarily converge to a second speaker's broad accent, moving away from his or her initial use of a mild accent. Use of a broad accent may represent non-adherence to a valued norm and accordingly may be evaluated negatively, but such use also represents an act of convergence which should result in positive evaluations – will normative non-adherence or convergence be more consequential? A study by Ball, Giles, Byrne, and Berechree (1984) indicates that adherence or non-adherence to a valued norm will override perceptions of convergence in affecting evaluations. Recent revisions of SAT incorporate the notion of valued norms (as well as other notions) in an attempt to achieve a richer sense of explanation which accords with available data (Giles, Mulac, Bradac, and Johnson, 1987; Street and Giles, 1982). It is worth noting in passing that much of the language-attitudes research prior to 1970 examined consequences of accents and dialects which exhibited adherence or non-adherence to valued norms; in a sense this research was designed to discover through respondents' evaluative reactions which forms were valued and which forms were not.

Other theories are also apparent in the recent literature. For example, Heider's (1958) attribution theory has been invoked to explain results of research (e.g. Bradac, Courtright, Schmidt, and Davies, 1976a); indeed, this theory was an important influence upon the early statements of SAT. Uncertainty-reduction theory has had a considerable impact in this area (Berger and Calabrese, 1975). The key idea here is that a speaker's speech style is used by message recipients for the primary purpose of reducing their uncertainty about him or her; uncertainty reduction occurs through a process of social categorization (Berger and Bradac, 1982). The concept of 'ethnolinguistic vitality' merits discussion here also (Bourhis and Sachdev, 1984; Giles and Johnson, 1981). Ryan, Giles, and Sebastian (1982) suggest that 'the more numerous and more important the functions served by the [language] variety for the greater number of individuals the greater is its vitality' (p. 4). A general model has been offered which indicates that the two underlying sociostructural factors which affect language attitudes are standardness versus non-standardness (adherence or non-adherence to valued norms, as discussed above) and decreasing versus increasing vitality (Ryan *et al.*, 1982). Thus, maximally favourable evaluations will be made when a speaker uses standard forms which are also high in perceived vitality; maximally unfavourable evaluations will be made when both standardness and vitality are low. When standardness is high but vitality is low, one might expect status ratings to be high but ratings of dynamism and sociability to be low; when standardness is low but vitality is high, ratings of status should be low but ratings of dynamism and sociability should be high.

Thus, recent studies of language attitudes incorporate theories for the purpose of explanation, and explore applications of these theories in various domains. It was suggested in this section also that recent studies have attended to subtle gradations in between-group linguistic phenomena, that joint influences of two (or more) language variables have been investigated, and that language samples presented to respondents now typically are relatively high in realism. Two other characteristics of the post-1970 language-attitudes research remain to be discussed: the investigation of an increasing number and variety of language variables, and the inclusion of 'communication context' in studies of language effects. These are large-scale topics, which accordingly will be discussed at some length now.

MORE AND MORE VARIETIES OF LANGUAGE

As suggested above, the major focus of traditional language-attitudes research has been upon language variation which is rooted in between-group differences reflecting geographical dispersion. Recent studies have broadened the focus to include language variation based upon between-group differences reflecting social roles. Also, forms of language varying *within* groups as a function of changes in speaker states have been examined.

Gender-linked Language

Although speculation (Jesperson, 1922) and empirical research (Wood, 1966) pertaining to male/female language differences can be found in the literature prior to 1970, the idea that gender-differentiated speech styles have attitudinal consequences received its strongest initial statement in 1975 in Lakoff's *Language and woman's place*. The general implication of her discussion in this work is that use of the 'female register' weakens the force of a speaker's claims – it is a 'powerless' style. Research by Kramerae (1974, 1977) indicates that students (at least) have stereotypical beliefs which are consistent with the 'female-register' hypothesis: males are dominant, loud, concise, blunt, etc.; females are gentle, emotional, verbose, polite, etc. Newcombe and Arnkoff (1979) found that specific linguistic indicators of the 'female register', for example hedges and tag questions, produced judgments of low speaker assertiveness. On the other hand, it is not clear that men's and women's actual verbal behaviours differ in the way that the 'female-register' hypothesis suggests (Smith, 1979).

But, apart from Lakoff's notion, Mulac and associates have consistently found that samples of male and female language collected in a variety of contexts are differentiated attitudinally (e.g. Mulac and Lundell, 1980, 1986; Mulac, Lundell, and Bradac, 1986). Specifically, male language is rated higher in Dynamism, represented by the semantic differential scales strong–weak, active–passive, aggressive–unaggressive, and loud–soft, whereas female language is rated higher in Aesthetic Quality, represented by the scales pleasing–displeasing, sweet–sour, nice–awful, and beautiful–ugly. This attitudinal difference has been obtained even with respondents unable to guess beyond chance levels the gender of speakers whose language is presented in transcript form, and, where information regarding speaker gender is provided, the 'gender-linked language effect' is enhanced (Mulac, Incontro and James, 1985). Thus far it has proven difficult to isolate specific language features which are implicated in the consistently obtained effect; it may be that there are clusters of features that differentiate male–female language and that any sample of these manifest on a given occasion is capable of producing the attitudinal difference for Aesthetic Quality and Dynamism (Mulac and Lundell, 1986; Mulac *et al.*, 1986).

Finally, gender-linked language differences are obviously between-group differences (males versus females), but interestingly a recent study indicates that some situations may make gender psychologically salient, thereby affecting the production of gender-linked language; specifically, Hogg (1985) found that women speaking in mixed-sex groups were more likely to exhibit particular language features associated with maleness than were women speaking in same-sex dyads. The implication is that women tended to converge to the male style in the mixed groups because gender emerged as a salient social identity issue. Thus, gender-linked language may have a within-group component: in one situation male language will be used by a particular group of speakers, whereas in another situation these same speakers will use female language.

Powerful and Powerless Styles

Male/female language differences represent a particular type of between-group difference reflecting socialization into dissimilar social roles. Another language variable labelled 'powerful/powerless styles' by O'Barr (1982) and associates may reflect social role differences as well. In the original work on this variable, O'Barr uncovered a cluster of linguistic features exhibited by persons ostensibly low in social power in courtroom trials (e.g. inexpert witnesses with little education): hesitation forms, tag questions, deictic phrases, polite forms, intensifiers, and hedges. This was accordingly labelled the 'powerless style' and its unmarked counterpart characterized by the absence of these features was labelled the 'powerful' style. There is a clear similarity between the 'powerless' features and the features representing Lakoff's (1975) 'female register'.

It has been suggested that 'powerful/powerless styles' may in fact be a within-speaker variable: that, as persons for whatever reasons experience increases in subjective uncertainty, their speech may become increasingly hesitant, hedging, etc. (Berger and Bradac, 1982). Regardless of the possible objective association with social power on the one hand or subjective uncertainty on the other, there is evidence that the 'powerless' style is *perceived* by naive respondents to indicate low communicator power (Bradac, Hemphill, and Tardy, 1981; Bradac and Mulac, 1984a). And, in predicting evaluative reactions to speakers, it is precisely these sorts of perceptions which are important (Robinson, 1979; Street and Hopper, 1982). Regarding such reactions, there is evidence that communicators' use of 'powerless' language reduces respondent ratings of attractiveness and competence, and that this attitudinal effect is independent of both communicator and respondent gender (Bradac *et al.*, 1981; Bradac and Mulac, 1984b; Erickson, Johnson, Lind, and O'Barr, 1978). One study indicates that the features which reduce attractiveness and competence ratings are hedges, tag questions, and hesitations, not polite forms or intensifiers (Bradac and Mulac, 1984a; cf. Hosman and Wright, 1987).

Lexical Diversity

Another language variable which has a somewhat ambiguous status with regard to its between-group or within-group characterization is 'vocabulary richness', 'verbal redundancy', or 'lexical diversity', as it is variously labelled in the literature. One can construe the Bernstein (1971) hypothesis of elaborated and restricted codes as indicating that speakers from lower socio-economic groups will exhibit relatively low lexical diversity in their verbal productions, whereas their upper socio-economic group counterparts will exhibit relatively high lexical diversity. And there is evidence that naive respondents perceive speaker socio-economic status to vary with diversity level (Bradac, Konsky, and Davies, 1976b; cf. Robinson, 1979). But the evidence regarding objective connections between socio-economic status and lexical diversity level is not consistently supportive, to put it mildly (cf. especially Sankoff and

Lessard, 1975). On the other hand, there is sound evidence pointing to a within-group source of variation for this variable: as speaker anxiety increases, lexical diversity tends to decrease (e.g. Howeler, 1972).

Research on the attitudinal consequences of this variable has indicated rather consistently that a communicator's level of lexical diversity is directly related to evaluations of competence and message effectiveness (along with socio-economic status) and inversely related to judgments of communicator anxiety (Bradac, Bowers, and Courtright, 1980). This basic effect can be enhanced or diminished by various features of the communication context as this is perceived by respondents. (More about contextual qualifiers of language effects below.) There is some evidence that low lexical diversity may lead to judgments that a speaker is well suited for relatively low-status employment: positions requiring friendliness and good humour as opposed to technical expertise (Giles *et al.*, 1981).

In the light of data indicating that an average lexical diversity level for college-student speakers is .82 (for 25-word segments) with a standard deviation of .05 (Bradac, Konsky, and Elliott, 1976c), one study found that messages exhibiting a lexical diversity level of .72 were evaluated very negatively, while messages at a .92 level were evaluated no more positively than messages at a level of .82. Apparently, listeners are more sensitive to negative departures from an average level of diversity than to positive departures. Another study found that *reductions* in diversity level may be evaluated especially favourably if (a) they result in the speaker moving closer to the diversity level of the person he or she is conversing with (convergence) and (b) they are within the .92 to .82 range; conversely, reductions may be evaluated especially unfavourably if (a) they result in the speaker moving away from his or her conversational partner (divergence) and (b) they are in the range of .82 to .72 (Bradac, Mulac, and House, 1988).

Rate

Speakers vary in the number of words or syllables they utter per unit of time (per minute is the standard unit), primarily as a function of situational and personality factors. For example, persons who are high in trait anxiety and persons who are high in state anxiety as a result of situational stress may speak especially rapidly (Siegman and Pope, 1972). Rate is primarily a within-group language variable, the attitudinal effects of which have been explored extensively since 1970. However, there is some evidence that there is an inverse relationship between rate and age (Helfrich, 1979), so there is a between-group aspect to this variable too: elderly persons versus non-elderly. Apart from objective evidence, there are data which indicate that a perceptual bias exists such that slower elderly speakers are judged to be older than their counterparts who speak relatively rapidly (Stewart and Ryan, 1982).

Regarding the effects of speaker rate on evaluative reactions, the research has produced a rather consistent pattern: as speech rate increases, evaluations of speaker competence increase linearly (e.g. Brown, 1980; Street and Brady, 1982; Street, Brady, and Putman, 1983). Increases in speech rate also produce increases in ratings of speaker social attractiveness (trustworthiness, benevolence) up to a point at which ratings plateau or decrease; in other words, the relationship between speech rate and

ratings of social attractiveness likely assumes a quadratic form. There is some
evidence that these relationships are mediated by the similarity of the speaker's rate
to that of the evaluator: there is a preference for faster rates especially when the
listener typically speaks at a rapid rate also; positive reactions to rapid speech rate
may be attenuated when the listener typically speaks very slowly (Giles and Smith,
1979; Street *et al.*, 1983). This outcome is consistent with predictions of SAT
discussed above (Giles *et al.*, 1987).

Language Intensity

Research on this variable began in the 1960s with the work of Bowers (1964), who
defined intensity as 'that quality of language which indicates the degree to which the
speaker's attitude toward a concept deviates from neutrality' (p. 416). A speaker's
use of terms such as 'extremely', 'definitely', 'horrible', etc. and his or her use of sex
and death metaphors will lead listeners to rate a message's language as highly intense
(Bowers, 1964; Bradac, Hosman, and Tardy, 1978). Language intensity will increase
as a speaker's commitment to a position increases. Thus, this is rather clearly a
within-groups variable; high or low intensity is not attached to particular groups of
speakers across contexts.

There is evidence that language intensity is directly related to perceived communicator 'internality' (Bradac *et al.*, 1978), that is, the extent to which he or she is
perceived to be in control of daily circumstances (Rotter, 1966), and there is
evidence that internality is a positively evaluated trait (Stern and Manifold, 1977).
The use of obscenity, a particular form of intensity, has been shown to reduce postcommunication ratings of communicator competence (Mulac, 1976). Other research
results pertaining to the effects of intensity are highly dependent upon features of the
communication context; for example, the use of high-intensity language may lead to
positive reactions when the message source is a male and when the source is high in
precommunication credibility (Burgoon, Jones, and Stewart, 1975). Indeed, it is
difficult to offer 'main-effect' claims regarding the effects of language intensity (cf.
Bradac *et al.*, 1980).

Accordingly, this is a useful point to move to the next major topic: the role of
perceived communication context in language-attitudes research. Before doing this,
it should be suggested by way of summary that, in the 1970s and 1980s, researchers
increasingly investigated attitudes toward forms of language variation linked to
diverse social and psychological sources. For example, attitudes toward sources
exhibiting language reflecting states of high anxiety have been investigated, as have
attitudes toward persons using language reflecting gender socialization. The recent
language-attitudes research has moved beyond the almost exclusive concern with
geographically based language varieties which characterized the early research in
this area, but it must be noted that important work on attitudes toward dialect,
accent, and minority–majority languages continues. It is probably most accurate to
say that there has been a broadening of scope in recent years in terms of language
varieties investigated.

THE ROLE OF COMMUNICATION CONTEXT

Sociolinguists investigating the bases of language performance or message encoding have long attended to contextual influences. If one observes that speakers shift back and forth between styles, one must attend to factors which precipitate these shifts, and one's attention is rather quickly drawn to contextual features such as status relationships, formality–informality, etc. On the other hand, persons investigating language *de*coding, for example evaluative reactions to speech styles, have tended to ignore contextual variables until rather recently. Indeed, as recently as 1983, commenting upon Ryan and Sebastian's (1980) study of relationships between the contextual variable initial perceptions of speaker status and standard/non-standard accent, Giles and Sassoon note that the Ryan–Sebastian data 'suggest that the mechanisms mediating between accent perception and personality inferences are far more complex than hitherto acknowledged' (p. 305). Giles and Sassoon's suggestion is that much of the previous work on language and status had ignored aspects of context and had therefore produced an overly simplified picture of connections between standard/non-standard language and evaluations of speakers.

One can only speculate about causes of the 'decontextualizing' of much of the early (and even some of the recent) research on language attitudes. For one thing, it may be that a particular conception of attitude was apparent in this work: the idea that attitudes are rather stable predispositions to respond across a variety of contexts – if language type *A* is valued, it will be valued in situation types *B* and *C*. Notions of personality–situation interaction had an impact upon this view (Mischel, 1973) and may have been a factor in the increasing incorporation of contextual variables apparent in the 1980s. Also, much of the early language-attitudes research was experimental, and practice may have been influenced by a particular conception of the experiment: the behaviouristic idea that the neatest experiments were those that stripped stimuli to their barest essentials while keeping irrelevant non-stimulus influences (i.e. contextual factors) to a minimum by maintaining environmental constancy across trials for purposes of control. This view of experimentation now seems misguided (Cook and Campbell, 1979), and it may have been the demise of this view that led to the increasing incorporation of contextual variables in studies of language attitudes.

Whatever the explanation, during the last decade, studies of language attitudes have increasingly provided respondents with information regarding the context in which language performance occurred. In some cases, this contextual information is held constant across all conditions (in experimental studies) (e.g. Bradac *et al.*, 1976b, study 2), while, in other cases, levels or types of context are included as variables in the research design (e.g. Ryan and Bulik, 1982). Providing contextual information that is held constant is an attempt to increase the naturalness of the response to one or another variety of language and thereby potentially to increase the generalizability of results. Probably more interestingly, varying levels or types of context through manipulation in conjunction with manipulation of one or more language variables can represent an attempt to construct or test theories regarding the influence of communication context on reactions to language variation. For example, Burgoon and Miller (1985) have outlined an expectancy theory which

Nature

Communicator Role

indicates that message recipients enter situations with expectations regarding appropriate language performance and that these expectations may be fulfilled or violated by message senders. Positive violations may enhance credibility and persuasiveness, while negative violations may have the opposite effect.

The major contextual variables that have been studied can be grouped under the rubrics 'communicator role' and 'communication situation'. Regarding the former, several investigators have studied the effect of precommunication perceptions of communicator status in conjunction with status-related language variations. For example, Ryan and Bulik (1982) compared the effects of standard American English with German-accented English when these were attributed to both middle- and lower-class speakers. For ratings of status, main effects were obtained for both standard versus German accent and for middle versus lower class; an interactive effect was not obtained. Thus, status-related contextual information and status-related accent cues combined additively to affect postcommunication ratings of speaker status. This pattern has been obtained in several other studies also (e.g. Giles and Sassoon, 1983; Stewart, Ryan, and Giles, 1985).

Commenting on these results in the light of the results of their study of initial perceptions of status in conjunction with Mexican-American versus standard American accent and high versus low lexical diversity, Bradac and Wisegarver (1984) write:

> A clear picture of connections between [initial perceptions of speaker status] and language is beginning to emerge. Persons process descriptive information regarding speaker status and status-related linguistic information additively, not multiplicatively . . . This is something of an overstatement . . . but the data from our study and *all* of the other studies indicate that persons *combine* linguistic and descriptive information in constructing their judgments of speaker status. This combinatorial model differs from a plausible, alternative model which would picture one sort of information *or* the other being used in forming status judgments. (Bradac and Wisegarver, 1984, p. 252)

gender

Another communicator role variable which has been studied in conjunction with language variation is communicator gender. For example, Erickson *et al.* (1978) examined evaluative consequences of powerful and powerless styles when these were exhibited by male and female speakers. The powerful style produced higher credibility and attractiveness ratings, regardless of gender. Similarly, Bradac and Mulac (1984b) found that both males and females playing both counsellor and client roles were judged to be higher in socio-intellectual status in a hypothetical crisis-intervention situation when they used a powerful style. Here the relationship between the counsellor–client role and power of style was again additive: the counsellor/high-power condition received the highest ratings for status, while the lowest ratings were given to the client/low-power condition; the other conditions fell between these extremes. The relationship between speaker gender and power of style was also additive: male/high power received the highest rating, while female/low power received the lowest. It may be that a wide variety of status-related communicator characteristics and language forms yield this additive pattern. On the other hand, non-status related language variation, for example variations in language intensity, may *interact* with communicator gender, as suggested above: males using high-intensity language and females using low intensity may be evaluated relatively favourably, whereas relatively unfavourable judgments may be made of males using low-intensity language and females using high-intensity (Burgoon *et al.*, 1975). A similar interactive pattern has been obtained for language intensity and initial perceptions of source credibility: high-credibility sources are evaluated favourably when they use high-intensity language, while low-credibility sources are evaluated favourably when they use low-intensity language (Burgoon *et al.*, 1975).

It will be useful in future theoretical endeavours to explain just why it is that certain communicator role/language feature combinations yield additive attitudinal patterns, whereas others yield interactive patterns, in some cases of the dramatic cross-over type. It may be that some forms of language gain meaning *only* in context: high-intensity language used by a male means something completely different than does high-intensity language used by a female. On the other hand, other forms of language may have some meaning *apart* from context, which serves primarily to diminish or intensify that meaning – to diminish or intensify judgmental certainty: a non-standard accent denotes low-status and the certainty of this inference is strengthened by corroborating information that the speaker is from a lower socio-economic group.

Communication situation is the other variable which has been examined extensively in recent language-attitudes research. For example, Brown, Giles, and Thackerar (1985) created a situation where respondents were led to believe that a communicator was delivering a technical talk to an audience unfamiliar with the topic; in another condition no contextual information was given to respondents. Slow, moderate, and fast speech rates constituted a variable manipulated orthogonally with the context/no context variable, as did accent (RP versus Welsh). The most interesting result was that for both RP and Welsh accents, for ratings of intelligence and ambition, a slow rate was *not* downgraded in the technical talk/unfamiliar audience condition, whereas it was downgraded compared to moderate and fast rates in the no-context (monologue) condition; that is, results for the monologue condition adhered to the familiar linear relationship between rate and competence judgments described above, whereas the provision of situational information upset this relationship. Presumably, the speaker's slow rate was justified in the minds of respondents by the difficult communication situation.

Another situational variable examined in recent studies is 'formality/informality'. For example, Bradac *et al.* (1976b) found that low lexical diversity was evaluated especially negatively in formal situations, while high lexical diversity was evaluated especially positively in informal situations; this was an additive effect for situational formality and diversity. A similar additive effect was obtained by Street and Brady (1982) for rate and formality: high rate in an informal situation and low rate in a formal situation produced maximally different evaluations, positive in the former case and negative in the latter. Ryan and Carranza (1975) compared the evaluative effects of standard and non-standard accents when these were exhibited in a school context (formal) on the one hand and a home context (informal) on the other. Generally, the difference between standard and non-standard accents was greater for ratings of status in the school context than in the home context.

It should be noted that the results of Bradac *et al.* (1976b) and Street and Brady (1982) are somewhat disparate from those of Ryan and Carranza (1975): the former workers found that valued forms (high diversity and rapid rate) were evaluated especially favourably in informal contexts, whereas the latter investigators found that a valued form (standard accent) was evaluated especially favourably in a formal context. On the other hand, all of these researchers found that non-valued or stigmatized forms were reacted to especially negatively in contexts that were formal.

Another situational variable, suggested by attribution theory (Heider, 1958), is attributed communicator intention – what do respondents perceive the communicator's intention to be in this situation? Does perceived intention affect reactions to speech or language style? From one perspective, the Brown *et al.* (1985) study described above can be viewed as examining evaluative consequences of an implicit connection between perceived communicator intention and speech style – respondents may have inferred that the communicator intended to inform his audience about a difficult topic while recognizing the communicative difficulty (especially in the case of slow speech rate; hence the elevated evaluations in this condition). More directly, Bradac and Mulac (1984a) manipulated respondent perceptions of communicator 'intention to appear authoritative' and 'intention to appear sociable', believing that these dissimilar intentions would interact with power of style in affecting evaluations. And indeed there was an interaction which indicated that ostensibly powerless forms were judged somewhat more effective in the case of the sociability intention. There is ample room for further research on this variable (and on the other situational variables as well).

More generally, a large number of studies show that a person's perception of various features of communication context can affect his or her attitude toward between-group and within-group language variation. In some cases, the context–language variation relationship assumes an additive form, while in other cases the form is interactive. Regardless of form, the many positive results for context suggest that persons attempting to explain or predict attitudinal reactions to language must take context into account in a way that many of the early studies did not.

In concluding this section, it is worth noting that most of the studies of context and language attitudes have adopted contextual distinctions which are salient to researchers, for whatever theoretical or practical reasons: formal–informal situation, male–female communicator, etc. In many cases, researchers have attempted to check contextual manipulations against respondent perceptions in order to certify that contextual distinctions are perceived in the expected way. But an alternative approach to understanding the role of context is to *start* with distinctions that are important or especially meaningful to respondents, discovering what these are through one or another type of subjective assessment procedure and then incorporating the distinctions in the next phase of research, for example a language style × context experiment. In the terminology of Giles and Hewstone (1982), researchers have relied almost exclusively upon 'objective taxonomies of situation' in their studies of language attitudes, whereas they could rely upon 'subjective' situational taxonomies. This move from 'objective' to 'subjective' context is likely to assume importance for special groups whose members may define their social universes in ways which are idiosyncratic from the standpoint of the dominant culture, for example drug users, hypochondriacs, sports enthusiasts, and the elderly. A similar move is possible at the level of *measuring* responses to language in context by discovering unique evaluative dimensions which may be especially salient to particular groups of respondents, a point which leads us to the next (and penultimate) section.

MEASURING LANGUAGE ATTITUDES

At the heart of language-attitudes research is the idea that language can trigger an evaluative reaction. Indeed, one view of the human social animal is that he or she is constantly evaluating self and other for purposes of social comparison (Giles and Wiemann, 1987). Language is both a cause of social evaluation and a primary vehicle for its expression – one says: 'He has an unfriendly style' or 'He doesn't sound very smart'. And, with very few exceptions, language-attitude researchers have recognized the last-mentioned fact: reactions to language variation have been assessed with verbal measures.

There are three primary verbal measurement strategies apparent in the extant research: use of diverse evaluative items of interest to the researcher; use of general personality measures; and use of items representing empirically derived or theoretically motivated factors. The first 'scatter-gun' strategy is less and less apparent in the literature, which may be a sign of the increasing role being played by theories. Nevertheless, in this case, individual items are used, for example single scales measuring perceptions of the communicator's socio-economic status, anxiety level, intelligence, or leadership abilities (Bradac *et al.*, 1976b; Brown, 1980; Lambert *et al.*, 1965). The second strategy, which exploits existing personality instruments, has been used only infrequently. In this case, the usual approach is to ask respondents to complete a given personality instrument (or items from such an instrument) as they believe the communicator would. Thus, respondents may assess a communicator's degree of internality–externality (Bradac *et al.*, 1978; Miller, 1970; Rotter, 1966).

The third 'factor analytic' strategy is now widely apparent in the language-attitudes literature. For example, Mulac (1975, 1976) devised the Speech Dialect Attitudinal Scale (SDAS) as a general instrument for measuring reactions to speech and language variations. Three primary dimensions or factors have emerged repeatedly in a number of studies using the SDAS: Socio-Intellectual Status, Aesthetic Quality, and Dynamism (e.g. Mulac *et al.*, 1985, 1986). Zahn and Hopper (1985) have proposed a variant of the SDAS, a measure they label the Speech Evaluation Instrument (SEI). Three factors comprise the SEI also: Superiority (a generalized version of Socio-Intellectual Status), Attractiveness (a generalized version of Aesthetic Quality), and Dynamism.

The factor structures described above reflect a basic distinction that several theorists have posited in discussions of speech evaluation and, more generally, interpersonal behaviour. For example, Brown (1965) has suggested that the two primary dimensions of interpersonal relations are status and solidarity, which are conceptualized as orthogonal factors having poles representing high and low values.

Giles and Ryan (1982) have suggested that a third dimension intersects with status and solidarity, namely person–group orientation. Thus, in some circumstances one focuses upon a speaker's individual characteristics, while in others one focuses upon the speaker's group affiliations. In person-centred situations stressing status, message recipients will attend to speaker competence, expertise, and confidence, whereas in group-centred situations they will attend to hierarchical variables such as social class and power. Along the solidarity dimension, in person-centred situations message recipients will attend to speaker likableness and attractiveness, whereas in group-centred situations they will attend to ingroup versus outgroup membership, ethnic identification, etc. The person–group dimension might be labelled 'individualism', which can assume high or low values (paralleling status and solidarity).

Thus, a three-dimensional model can be invoked when conceptualizing speech and language evaluation: status × solidarity × individualism. Dynamism can probably be added as a fourth independent dimension, since in several studies it has emerged as a separate factor and in one programme of research it has served consistently to distinguish speaker types (males from females; Mulac *et al.*, 1985). This four-dimensional structure will undoubtedly generate particular measures in future language-attitudes research. Influences upon judgments of individualism seem especially worth examining at this point, since this is an under-explored area.

Although the heavy – almost exclusive – reliance upon paper-and-pencil evaluative instruments is criticizable from the now-familiar standpoints of reactivity, low potential correspondence to overt behaviour, etc., this same heavy reliance has allowed investigators of language attitudes to specify in some detail at least some of the dimensions that are important to persons as they perceive and think about communicators exhibiting one or another form of language; that is, had a rigidly behaviouristic paradigm dominated this area, with the focus upon overt (usually nonverbal) behaviour, it is difficult to imagine that the four-dimensional structure described above could have been articulated. The use of verbal measures reflects the social-cognitive paradigm which has guided activity in this area since its inception.

What may be a more severe limitation than the use of verbal measures *per se* is the use of such instruments in situations where respondents are aware of their respondent status. More precisely, the evaluations of respondents in virtually all of the language-attitude studies have been made in situations carrying few consequences for respondents and few responsibilities as well: the respondent behaves appropriately and thereby succeeds in language-attitude studies by merely reacting via an evaluative instrument (regardless of the nature of the reaction) as long as the reaction is apparently seriously intended. But in many actual communication situations, the reactions of message recipients have serious consequences. Attached to a given judgment of incompetence is the decision not to vote for the communicator who produces it or the decision not to continue seeing this doctor, etc. Potentially, the serious consequences attached to evaluative reactions in real-world situations may influence the nature or the intensity of these reactions. In some contexts, language variation may interact with decisional importance in producing evaluative reactions. Such an interactive effect would qualify previously obtained results and would also suggest avenues for theory construction. What is needed is language-attitudes research which systematically manipulates the context of evaluation, for example high versus low personal decisional consequence. In some respects, this research would be analogous to the work of Street, Mulac, and Wiemann (1988) which has manipulated the context of message processing in order to compare the effects of participant versus observer roles in the production of evaluative reactions.

A brief discussion of two additional issues will conclude this section. First, in many of the language-attitude experiments reported in the literature, respondent perceptions have not been assessed; that is, although evaluative reactions have been measured, the perceptual basis for these reactions is unclear. (There are notable exceptions, e.g. Ball *et al.*, 1984.) It is possible that in some cases the manipulated variable, for example non-standard accent, was not perceived by respondents or was misperceived, for example as 'poor grammar'. Where respondent perceptions do not correspond to researcher intentions, there exists the possibility of explanatory error. More interestingly, systematic misperceptions may represent cognitive processing biases which are theoretically interesting in their own right. The second issue is also related to respondent (as opposed to researcher) cognitions: as suggested above, measures of language attitudes have generally reflected distinctions which are of interest to researchers, for example status and solidarity. And the reliable results of many empirical investigations indicate that these distinctions have been meaningful to many respondents. But there may be evaluative distinctions which have not been examined which are important to *some* groups of respondents or which are important to many groups of respondents in *some* situations. For example, Bradac and Wisegarver (1984) suggest that 'perceived control of communicative behaviour' is an evaluative dimension which is independent of perceived status, solidarity, and dynamism, and which is potentially important to many message recipients in a variety of contexts. It would be useful to see if respondents would generate evaluative terms pertaining to communicator control on a free-response task when exposed to communicators who are 'out of control' on the one hand and rigidly self-possessed on the other.

CONCLUDING COMMENTS

Over the last 30 years, language-attitudes research has matured considerably: studies of the attitudinal consequences of accent and dialect variation have become increasingly theoretical and complex; researchers have gone beyond accent and dialect in order to investigate a broad range of language variables; communication context increasingly has been incorporated as a feature of research; and measurement procedures have become increasingly sophisticated. Indeed, the field has matured to the point where there are sets of stable results capable of yielding generalizations. For example, and perhaps most basically:

G1: All of the levels of language (i.e. phonology, syntax, semantics, and pragmatics) affect message recipients' beliefs about and evaluations of message sources.

An implication of G1 is that there is no level of language which does not carry social psychological information, at least potentially. On this view, language is something more than an abstract system designed for the formulation of propositions (although it is this too).

Other generalizations suggested by studies cited above (and by others) are:

G2: Message recipients distinguish between valued and non-valued (or even counter-valued) linguistic forms.

G3: Valued linguistic forms are positively associated with message recipients' judgments of a message sender's status or competence.

G4: Message recipients distinguish between convergent and divergent linguistic acts.

G5: A message sender's convergence to message recipients' language is positively associated with message recipients' judgments of the message sender's sociability or solidarity (assuming perceptions of non-malevolent sender intent).

Generalizations 2 to 5 imply that message-sender convergence–divergence and normative adherence–non-adherence are independent dimensions of performance, and that message-sender status/competence and solidarity/sociability are independent dimensions of message-recipient evaluation. The cell representing convergent normative adherence in the four-cell performance matrix should collect the most favourable evaluations of message senders, while the cell representing divergent normative non-adherence should collect the least favourable evaluations. The cell representing divergent normative adherence should collect favourable evaluations for status/competence but unfavourable evaluations for solidarity/sociability, while the cell representing convergent normative non-adherence should reverse this pattern.

A final generalization to be offered is:

G6: Perceptions of communication context affect reactions to valued/non-valued and convergent/divergent language performance.

Obviously, and also very importantly, this generalization qualifies G2 to G5. It suggests that in particular contexts the use of valued language may *reduce* status judgments. It suggests that in particular contexts convergent linguistic acts may be judged as *low* in sociability. Generalization 6 reminds us that, although G2 to G5 have some validity and force, their main-effect logic will be inappropriate in particular cases.

With the exception of G1, the generalizations have as their implicit scope first-impression situations, where message recipients are exposed to message senders for the first time. As suggested at the beginning of this chapter, virtually all of the language-attitudes studies have employed stimulus persons and respondents who are unknown to each other at the time of contact. In situations of initial contact, inferences generated about message senders are likely to pertain to stable personality attributes, for example intelligence, and to enduring characteristics, for example ethnic-group affiliation. This is the realm of 'from acts to dispositions' (Jones and Davis, 1965).

But of course in many important communication contexts persons are well acquainted with each other. The question becomes: does speech and language variation have attitudinal consequences among intimates? This is a virtually unresearched area, but some speculations are possible. Since persons who are well acquainted have high levels of mutual knowledge regarding dispositions, it seems likely that language cues (or non-verbal cues for that matter) will not stimulate dispositional inferences. Instead, language may be used as an indicator of emotional states and moods. It also seems likely that the language features which are taken to indicate moods and feelings will be somewhat idiosyncratically connected to particular relationships. Such indicators will evolve as the relationship develops. For example, a person may have learned that her partner tends to use especially powerful and intense language when he is feeling insecure and vulnerable; the stereotypical inference would be misleading in such a case (cf. Bradac and Street, 1986).

Along this line are two studies of the use of 'personal idioms' in developing relationships. In an initial study, Hopper, Knapp, and Scott (1981) found that a high percentage of couples in a heterosexual relationship invented special terms unique to the relationship which had meaning primarily to the two partners; such terms were interpreted by the researchers as serving a bonding function. In a recent extension of the 1981 study, Bell, Buerkel-Rothfuss, and Gore (1987) obtained evidence of a type of personal idiom used by couples in public contexts for self-presentational purposes. Specifically, these personal–public idioms were apparently designed to generate attributions of couple intimacy or solidarity in third parties. Evidence of personal–private idioms was also obtained by Bell et al. (1987), as in the Hopper et al. (1981) study. It seems likely that one partner's use of personal–private idioms generates self-attributions of solidarity and attributions of solidarity in the other partner as well.

The attitudinal effects of speech and language variation in established relationships is an important topic for future research. A related topic also deserving intensive study is the long-term attitudinal consequences of repeated exposure to messages exhibiting particular forms of language. In a sense, one can think of most consumers of the mass media as persons establishing ongoing relationships with particular newscasters, commercial spokespersons, etc. A newscaster, for example, may exhibit a particular accent (RP in Britain, general American in the USA), and a particular group of adolescent viewers of this person may exhibit a different accent (Welsh or Mexican-American). What will be the adolescent viewers' attitudes toward the newscaster upon initial exposure? What will be their attitudes after 20 exposures? Will initial attitudes intensify or decay? The exploration of these and other questions pertaining to long-term relational consequences will probably necessitate the use of descriptive research designs and the collection of qualitative data, as well as continued use of the experimental approaches which have always dominated this field.

REFERENCES

Aristotle (1932). *The rhetoric* (trans. L. Cooper). New York: Appleton.
Ball, P., Giles, H., Byrne, J., and Berechree, P. (1984). Situational constraints on the

evaluative significance of speech accommodation: Some Australian data. *International Journal of the Sociology of Language,* **46**, 115–129.

Bell, R.A., Buerkel-Rothuss, N.L., and Gore, K.E. (1987). 'Did you bring the yarmulka for the Cabbage Patch Kid?' The idiomatic communication of young lovers. *Human Communication Research,* **14**, 47–67.

Berger, C.R. and Bradac, J.J. (1982). *Language and social knowledge: Uncertainty in interpersonal relations.* London: Arnold.

Berger, C.R. and Calabrese, R.J. (1975). Some explorations in initial interaction and beyond: Toward a developmental theory of interpersonal communication. *Human Communication Research,* **1**, 99–112.

Bernstein, B. (1971). *Class, codes, and control,* Vols 1 and 2. London: Routledge and Kegan Paul.

Bloomfield, L. (1933). *Language.* New York: Holt, Rinehart and Winston.

Bourhis, R.Y. and Sachdev, I. (1984). Vitality perceptions and language attitudes: Some Canadian data. *Journal of Language and Social Psychology,* **3**, 97–126.

Bowers, J.W. (1964). Some correlates of language intensity. *Quarterly Journal of Speech,* **50**, 415–420.

Bradac, J.J., Bowers, J.W., and Courtright, J.A. (1980). Lexical variations in intensity, immediacy, and diversity: An axiomatic theory and causal model. In R.N. St Clair and H. Giles (Eds), *The social and psychological contexts of language,* pp. 193–223. Hillsdale, NJ: Erlbaum.

Bradac, J.J., Courtright, J.A., Schmidt, G., and Davies, R.A. (1976a). The effects of perceived status and linguistic diversity upon judgments of speaker attributes and message effectiveness. *Journal of Psychology,* **93**, 213–220.

Bradac, J.J., Hemphill, M.R., and Tardy, C.H. (1981). Language style on trial: Effects of 'powerful' and 'powerless' speech upon judgments of victims and villains. *Western Journal of Speech Communication,* **45**, 327–341.

Bradac, J.J., Hosman, L.A., and Tardy, C.H. (1978). Reciprocal disclosures and language intensity: Attributional consequences. *Communication Monographs,* **45**, 1–17.

Bradac, J.J., Konsky, C.W., and Davies, R.A. (1976b). Two studies of the effects of lexical diversity upon judgments of communicator attributes and message effectiveness. *Communication Monographs,* **43**, 70–79.

Bradac, J.J., Konsky, C.W., and Elliott, N.D. (1976c). Verbal behavior of interviewees: The effects of several situational variables on verbal productivity, disfluency, and lexical diversity. *Journal of Communication Disorders,* **9**, 211–225.

Bradac, J.J. and Mulac, A. (1984a). A molecular view of powerful and powerless speech styles: Attributional consequences of specific language features and communicator intentions. *Communication Monographs,* **51**, 307–319.

Bradac, J.J. and Mulac, A. (1984b). Attributional consequences of powerful and powerless speech styles in a crisis-intervention context. *Journal of Language and Social Psychology,* **3**, 1–19.

Bradac, J.J., Mulac, A., and House, A. (1988). Lexical diversity level and magnitude of convergent versus divergent style shifting: Perceptual and evaluative consequences. *Language and Communication,* **8**, 213–228.

Bradac, J.J. and Street, R.L., Jr (1986). Powerful and powerless speech styles re-visited: A theoretical analysis of language and impression formation. Paper presented at the meeting of the Speech Communication Association, November 1986, Chicago.

Bradac, J.J. and Wisegarver, R. (1984). Ascribed status lexical diversity, and accent: Determinants of perceived status, solidarity, and control of speech style. *Journal of Language and Social Psychology,* **3**, 239–255.

Brennan, E.M., Ryan, E.B., and Dawson, W.E. (1975). Scaling of apparent accentedness by magnitude estimation and sensory modality matching. *Journal of Psycholinguistic Research,* **4**, 27–36.

Brown, B.L. (1980). Effects of speech rate on personality attributions and competency evaluations. In H. Giles, W.P. Robinson, and P. Smith (Eds), *Language: Social psychological perspectives*, pp. 294–300. Oxford: Pergamon.

Brown, B.L., Giles, H., and Thackerar, J.N. (1985). Speaker evaluations as a function of speech rate, accent, and context. *Language and Communication*, **5**, 207–220.

Brown, R. (1965). *Social psychology*. New York: Free Press.

Buck, J. (1968). The effects of Negro and white dialectal variations upon attitudes of college students. *Speech Monographs*, **35**, 181–186.

Burgoon, M., Jones, S.B., and Stewart, D. (1975). Toward a message-centered theory of persuasion: Three empirical investigations of language intensity. *Human Communication Research*, **1**, 240–256.

Burgoon, M. and Miller, G.R. (1985). An expectancy interpretation of language and persuasion. In H. Giles and R.N. St Clair (Eds), *Recent advances in language, communication, and social psychology*, pp. 199–229. London: Erlbaum.

Cantril, H. and Allport, G.W. (1935). *The psychology of radio*. New York: Harper.

Cheyne, W. (1970). Stereotyped reactions to speakers with Scottish and English regional accents. *British Journal of Social and Clinical Psychology*, **9**, 77–79.

Cook, T.D. and Campbell, D.T. (1979). *Quasi-experimentation: Design and analysis issues for field settings*. Chicago, IL: Rand McNally.

de la Zerda, N. and Hopper, R. (1979). Employment interviewers' reactions to Mexican American speech. *Communication Monographs*, **46**, 126–134.

Edwards, J.R. (1982). Language attitudes and their implications among English speakers. In E.B. Ryan and H. Giles (Eds), *Attitudes toward language variation: Social and applied contexts*, pp. 20–33. London: Arnold.

Erickson, B., Johnson, B.C., Lind, E.A., and O'Barr, W. (1978). Speech style and impression formation in a court setting: The effects of 'powerful' and 'powerless' speech. *Journal of Experimental Social Psychology*, **14**, 266–279.

Fielding, G. and Evered, C. (1980). The influence of patients' speech upon doctors: The diagnostic interview. In R.N. St Clair and H. Giles (Eds), *The social and psychological contexts of language*, pp. 51–72. Hillsdale, NJ: Erlbaum.

Genessee, F. and Bourhis, R.Y. (1982). The social psychological significance of code switching in cross-cultural communication. *Journal of Language and Social Psychology*, **1**, 1–27.

Giles, H. (1970). Evaluative reactions to accents. *Educational Review*, **22**, 211–227.

Giles, H. (1972). The effects of stimulus mildness–broadness in the evaluation of accents. *Language and Speech*, **15**, 262–269.

Giles, H. (1973). Accent mobility: A model and some data. *Anthropological Linguistics*, **15**, 87–105.

Giles, H. and Hewstone, M. (1982). Cognitive structures, speech, and social situations: Two integrative models. *Language Sciences*, **4**, 187–219.

Giles, H. and Johnson, P. (1981). The role of language in ethnic group relations. In J. Turner and H. Giles (Eds), *Intergroup behaviour*, pp. 199–243. Oxford: Blackwell.

Giles, H., Mulac, A., Bradac, J.J., and Johnson, P. (1987). Speech accommodation theory: The first decade and beyond. In M. McLaughlin (Ed.), *Communication yearbook*, No. 10, pp. 13–48. Newbury Park, CA: Sage.

Giles, H. and Powesland, P. (1975). *Speech style and social evaluation*. London: Academic Press.

Giles, H. and Ryan, E.B. (1982). Prolegomena for developing a social psychological theory of language attitudes. In E.B. Ryan and H. Giles (Eds), *Attitudes toward language variation: Social and applied contexts*, pp. 208–223. London: Arnold.

Giles, H. and Sassoon, C. (1983). The effect of speaker's accent, social class background and message style on British listeners' social judgements. *Language and Communication*, **3**, 305–313.

Giles, H. and Smith, P. (1979). Accommodation theory: Optimal levels of convergence. In H. Giles and R.N. St Clair (Eds), *Language and social psychology*, pp. 45–65. Baltimore, MD: University Park Press.

Giles, H. and Wiemann, J.M. (1987). Language, social comparison, and power. In C.R. Berger and S.H. Chaffee (Eds), *Handbook of communication science*, pp. 350–384. Newbury Park, CA: Sage.

Giles, H., Wilson, P., and Conway, T. (1981). Accent and lexical diversity as determinants of impression formation and employment selection. *Language Sciences*, **3**, 92–103.

Heider, F. (1958). *The psychology of interpersonal relations*. New York: Wiley.

Helfrich, H. (1979). Age markers in speech. In K.R. Scherer and H. Giles (Eds), *Social markers in speech*, pp. 63–107. Cambridge: Cambridge University Press.

Hogg, M.A. (1985). Masculine and feminine speech in dyads and groups: A study of speech style and gender salience. *Journal of Language and Social Psychology*, **4**, 99–112.

Hopper, R., Knapp, M.L., and Scott, L. (1981). Couples' personal idioms: Exploring intimate talk. *Journal of Communication*, **31**, 23–33.

Hosman, L.A. and Wright, II, J.W. (1987). The effects of hedges and hesitations on impression formation in a simulated courtroom context. *Western Journal of Speech Communication*, **51**, 173–188.

Houck, C.L. and Bowers, J.W. (1969). Dialect and identification in persuasive messages. *Language and Speech*, **12**, 180–186.

Howeler, M. (1972). Diversity of word usage as a stress indicator in an interview situation. *Journal of Psycholinguistic Research*, **1**, 243–248.

Jesperson, J.O.H. (1922). *Language: Its nature, development, and origin*. London: Allen and Unwin.

Jones, E.E. and Davis, K.E. (1965). From acts to dispositions: The attribution process in person perception. In L. Berkowitz (Ed.), *Advances in experimental social psychology*, pp. 219–266. New York: Academic Press.

Kalin, R. (1982). The social significance of speech in medical, legal, and occupational settings. In E.B. Ryan and H. Giles (Eds), *Attitudes toward language variation: Social and applied contexts*, pp. 148–163. London: Arnold.

Kalin, R. and Rayko, D. (1980). The social significance of speech in the job interview. In R.N. St Clair and H. Giles (Eds), *The social and psychological contexts of language*, pp. 39–50. Hillsdale, NJ: Erlbaum.

Kramerae, C. (1974). Stereotypes of women's speech: The word from cartoons. *Journal of Popular Culture*, **8**, 622–638.

Kramerae, C. (1977). Perceptions of male and female speech. *Language and Speech*, **20**, 151–161.

Krauss, R.M. (1987). The role of the listener: Addressee influences on message formulation. *Journal of Language and Social Psychology*, **6**, 81–98.

Lakoff, R. (1975). *Language and woman's place*. New York: Harper and Row.

Lambert, W.E. (1967). A social psychology of bilingualism. *Journal of Social Issues*, **23**, 91–109.

Lambert, W.E., Anisfeld, M., and Yeni-Komshian, G. (1965). Evaluational reactions of Jewish and Arab adolescents to dialect and language variations. *Journal of Personality and Social Psychology*, **2**, 84–90.

Lambert, W.E., Hodgson, R., Gardner, R.C., and Fillenbaum, S. (1960). Evaluational reactions to spoken languages. *Journal of Abnormal and Social Psychology*, **60**, 44–51.

Miller, A.G. (1970). Social perception of internal–external control. *Perceptual and Motor Skills*, **30**, 103–109.

Mischel, W. (1973). Toward a cognitive social learning reconceptualization of personality. *Psychological Review*, **80**, 252–283.

Mulac, A. (1975). Evaluation of the Speech Dialect Attitudinal Scale. *Speech Monographs*, **42**, 182–189.

Mulac, A. (1976). Assessment and application of the Revised Dialect Attitudinal Scale. *Communication Monographs*, **43**, 238–245.

Mulac, A., Incontro, C.R., and James, M.R. (1985). A comparison of the gender-linked language effect and sex-role stereotypes. *Journal of Personality and Social Psychology*, **49**, 1099–1110.

Mulac, A. and Lundell, T.L. (1980). Differences in perceptions created by semantic–syntactic productions of male and female speakers. *Communication Monographs*, **47**, 111–118.

Mulac, A. and Lundell, T.L. (1986). Linguistic contributors to the gender-linked language effect. *Journal of Language and Social Psychology*, **5**, 81–101.

Mulac, A., Lundell, T.L., and Bradac, J.J. (1986). Male/female language differences and attributional consequences in a public speaking situation: Toward an explanation of the gender-linked language effect. *Communication Monographs*, **53**, 115–129.

Newcombe, N. and Arnkoff, D.B. (1979). Effects of speech style and sex of speaker on person perception. *Journal of Personality and Social Psychology*, **37**, 1293–1303.

O'Barr, W.M. (1982). *Linguistic evidence: Language power, and strategy in the courtroom*. New York: Academic Press.

Pear, T.H. (1931). *Voice and personality*. London: Wiley.

Robinson, W.P. (1979). Speech markers and social class. In K.R. Scherer and H. Giles (Eds), *Social markers in speech*, pp. 211–249. Cambridge: Cambridge University Press.

Rotter, J.B. (1966). Generalized expectancies for internal versus external control. *Psychological Monographs*, **80**, No. 609, 1–28.

Ryan, E.B. and Bulik, C.M. (1982). Evaluations of middle class speakers of standard American and German-accented English. *Journal of Language and Social Psychology*, **1**, 51–62.

Ryan, E.B. and Carranza, M. (1975). Evaluative reactions of adolescents toward speakers of standard English and Mexican American accented English. *Journal of Personality and Social Psychology*, **31**, 855–863.

Ryan, E.B., Carranza, M., and Moffie, R.W. (1977). Reactions toward varying degrees of accentedness in the speech of Spanish–English bilinguals. *Language and Speech*, **20**, 267–273.

Ryan, E.B., Giles, H., and Sebastian, R.J. (1982). An integrative perspective for the study of attitudes toward language. In E.B. Ryan and H. Giles (Eds), *Attitudes toward language: Social and applied contexts*, pp. 1–19. London: Arnold.

Ryan, E.B. and Sebastian, R. (1980). The effects of speech style and social class background on social judgements of speakers. *British Journal of Social and Clinical Psychology*, **19**, 229–233.

Sankoff, D. and Lessard, R. (1975). Vocabulary richness: A sociolinguistic analysis. *Science*, **190**, 689–690.

Sherry, R. (1961). *A treatise of schemes and tropes* (1550), introduction and index by H.H. Hildebrandt. Gainesville, FL: Scholars' Facsimiles and Reprints.

Siegman, A.W. and Pope, B. (1972). *Studies in dyadic communication*. New York: Pergamon.

Smith, P.M. (1979). Sex markers in speech. In K.R. Scherer and H. Giles (Eds), *Social markers in speech*, pp. 109–146. Cambridge: Cambridge University Press.

Stern, G.S. and Manifold, B. (1977). Internal locus of control as a value. *Journal of Research in Personality*, **11**, 237–242.

Stewart, M.A. and Ryan, E.B. (1982). Attitudes toward younger and older adult speakers: Effects of varying speech rates. *Journal of Language and Social Psychology*, **1**, 91–109.

Stewart, M.A., Ryan, E.B., and Giles, H. (1985). Accent and social class effects on status and solidarity evaluations. *Personality and Social Psychology Bulletin*, **11**, 98–105.

Street, R.L., Jr, and Brady, R.M. (1982). Speech rate acceptance ranges as a function of evaluative domain, listener speech rate, and communication context. *Communication Monographs*, **49**, 290–308.

Street, R.L., Jr, Brady, R.M., and Putman, W.B. (1983). The influence of speech rate stereotypes and rate similarity on listeners' evaluations of speakers. *Journal of Language and Social Psychology*, **2**, 37–56.

Street, R.L., Jr, and Giles, H. (1982). Speech accommodation theory: A social cognitive approach to language and speech behaviour. In M.E. Roloff and C.R. Berger (Eds), *Social cognition and communication*, pp. 193–226. Beverly Hills, CA: Sage.

Street, R.L., Jr, and Hopper, R. (1982). A model of speech style evaluation. In E.B. Ryan and H. Giles (Eds), *Attitudes toward language variation: Social and applied contexts*, pp. 175–188. London: Arnold.

Street, R.L., Jr, Mulac, A., and Wiemann, J.M. (1988). Speech evaluation differences as a function of perspective (participant versus observer) and presentational medium. *Human Communication Research*, **14**, 333–363.

Strongman, K. and Woolsey, J. (1967). Stereotyped reactions to regional accents. *British Journal of Social and Clinical Psychology*, **6**, 164–167.

Taylor, A.C. (1934). Social agreement on personality traits as judged from speech. *Journal of Social Psychology*, **5**, 244–248.

Tucker, G.R. and Lambert, W.E. (1969). White and Negro listeners' reactions to various American-English dialects. *Social Forces*, **47**, 463–468.

Williams, F. *et al.* (1976). *Explorations of the linguistic attitudes of teachers*. Rowley, MA: Newbury House.

Williams, F., Whitehead, J.L., and Miller, L.A. (1972). Relations between attitudes and teacher expectancy. *American Educational Research Journal*, **9**, 263–277.

Wood, M.M. (1966). The influence of sex and knowledge of communication effectiveness on spontaneous speech. *Word*, **22**, 112–137.

Zahn, C.J. and Hopper, R. (1985). Measuring language attitudes: The speech evaluation instrument. *Journal of Language and Social Psychology*, **4**, 113–123.

20

Language in Friendships

WILLIAM W. WILMOT AND WESLEY N. SHELLEN
Department of Interpersonal Communication, University of Montana, USA

You can probably remember times in your life when you were a stranger to everyone around you; perhaps as a 'new kid' in school, your first meeting when you joined a club, or your first day on a new job. Remember what it was like to be introduced, how talking with others at first may have seemed a little stiff and formal, mostly an exchange of names and impersonal generalities about one another's backgrounds? Then, as you watched the others in boisterous play during recess, or closing off into conversational cliques at the meeting, or breaking from work and going to lunch together, you were reminded of your newness and longed to get over the stranger stage so you could be included in the apparently effortless and friendly interaction going on around you. And gradually it happened, the newness wore off, you became more familiar with the others and felt included in their activities and conversations. By some unspoken mutual agreement, you grew particularly close to a few of them, and you became friends.

As your reminiscence of similar experiences tells you, the ways we talk with friends are greatly different from the ways we talk with strangers. What is not so apparent is that the development and maintenance of friendships depends in part on the language processes used by the participants. Duck and Pond (1989) claim that language has three important functions in personal relationships:

(1) an *indexical* function indicating the emotional status of a relationship;
(2) an *instrumental* function used to negotiate the relationship's development, roles, and climate through initiation, maintenance, repair, or dissolution;

Handbook of Language and Social Psychology
Edited by H. Giles and W.P. Robinson.   © 1990 John Wiley & Sons Ltd

(3) an *essential* function, which means that the talk itself embodies or frames the essence of the relationship for the participants.

Obviously, friendships are influenced by a host of other factors besides language. Variables such as cognitive development (Sants, 1984), returning to college (Suitor, 1987), and getting involved in a heterosexual romantic relationship (Rose, 1984) can also affect the development of friendship. Similarly, friendships which develop at various points in the participants' life-cycle present some interesting features. Adolescents, for example, adopt their own language – a 'unique argot' (McCandless and Evans, 1973) – as part of creating a 'world of their own' (Proefrock, 1983). While most studies show a decline in friendships in the elderly, they nevertheless are important because of the social support and sense of intimacy they bring (Bell, 1981; Dickens and Perlman, 1981). One recent study suggests that 'across various age groups, relationships may not be very different, at least in relation to self-disclosure' (Dickson-Markman, 1986, p. 262). Clearly, one could cast a large net over the topic of friendship, scooping up numerous communication, psychological, gender, and age issues related to friendships. Our net, however, will bring to the surface issues related to:

(1) language features of friendships;
(2) language about relationships;
(3) an examination of the limits of using language to understand friendships.

FRIENDLY LANGUAGE

Becoming Friends

As Brenton (1974) put it, 'we are limited in our choice of friends by the boundaries of the worlds we live in. After all, we can only be friends with people as we encounter them; it follows that the more curtailed our environments are, the smaller is our pool of potential friends' (p. 113). Many factors influence the likelihood that acquaintanceships will become transformed into friendships. Bell and Daly (1984) describe affinity-seeking as a multiple-act phenomenon which occurs over time. Sykes (1983) found that previous acquaintance and proximity were the best predictors of preference for interaction partners in his study, but added that similarity and other variables related to interpersonal attraction did not, even when taken together, completely predict how people chose one another for interaction. Even factors of dissimilarity have been shown to relate to attraction (Broome, 1983). Whatever it is that causes two people to come into contact – a shared workplace, a common hobby, other friends held in common, etc. – a relationship does not become a friendship until the two share commitment to interdependence. According to Wright (1978), 'it is the beginning of friendship *per se* in the sense that the commitment of the persons to one another is just as important, if not more so, than the commitment of either to the specific context providing the rationale for their interaction' (p. 203).

Some key communication markers are evident as a friendship develops. As Altman and Taylor (1973) and Knapp (1984) propose, there is a systematic unfolding of increasing intimacy (Hays, 1984). While Altman and Taylor (1973) first set forth the model for development of personal relationships, Knapp's work added some critical communication elements to the original notions. Basically, as a friendship develops toward intimacy there are attendant increases in broadness and uniqueness of interaction (breadth and depth of self-disclosure), more efficiency, flexibility, smoothness in interaction, and an increase in personalness and spontaneous exchanges. Finally, it is also suggested that overt judgment is given in interaction (Knapp, 1984). Basically, as a relationship develops there is an increase in both the frequency and quality of interaction (Hays, 1984).

Closeness: The Solidarity and Immediacy Metaphors

Friendships evolve and grow at different rates and stabilize at different levels depending on the extent of voluntary interdependence and mutual rewards sought by the participants (Baxter and Wilmot, 1983b; Wright, 1978). The terms 'casual', 'close', or 'best' friend describe three potential levels of stability in the achievement of friendship. Unlike romantic relationships, friendships do not demand exclusivity and in several surveys respondents reported having an average of about 20 friends each and from two to five close friends (Bell, 1981; Shellen and Cole, 1982). Also, the amount of involvement and commitment required to maintain these levels of friendship varies depending upon the nature and closeness of each relationship. However, some tending of the friendship garden appears to be necessary even if it is merely the yearly Christmas card sent to 'milestone' friends with whom we no longer share much in common except memories (Block, 1980). The notion that social relationships require energy for their maintenance is not new (Cattell, 1948). Bell (1985) showed, for example, that chronically lonely people with few or no friends differed from non-lonely people in the amount of *involvement*, that is, talkativeness, interruptions, vocal back-channels, and attention, they showed to others in conversation.

Language serves many simultaneous purposes in established relationships:

(1) as an indicator of the level and closeness of the relationship;
(2) as a medium for maintaining the relationship;
(3) as a consequence or outcome of the relationship.

We see the connection between language and friendship development not as dependent and independent variables, but as inseparably mutual reflections of one another. Just as Heider (1958) was forced to conclude that cause and effect worked in both directions in his propositions about the linkages between similarity, liking, and contact, we believe that the relationship between language and friendship is reciprocal, inseparable, and symmetrical.

An excellent example of the mutual interplay of language and relational development was presented in Roger Brown's (1965) pioneer work on the semantics of power and solidarity. *Solidarity*, a sense of closeness, kinship, and liking for another, is reflected, according to Brown, in the choices people make in their forms of address for one another. To speak most European languages, for example, one must acquire the relational distinction between familiar and formal pronouns such as *tu* and *vous* in French, or similar distinctions in Spanish, German, Dutch, Russian, Hungarian, and others. The Germans even have a word for the evolution of relationships into friendship, the *Brüderschaft*, in which two people ceremonially agree that they have come to know one another well enough to call each other *du* instead of *Sie*. Such pronoun distinctions have disappeared from the English language (except among groups such as the Society of Friends, who appropriately use the familiar 'thee' to other Friends and 'you' to outsiders), and explicit *Brüderschaften* to show friendship and solidarity are rarely performed by English-speaking adults. English shares with other languages some of the forms of address which signify solidarity, including mutual first-name usage, and multiple naming such as nicknames or name shortening (Brown and Ford, 1961; Harré, Morgan, and O'Neill, 1979; Knapp, 1984), but is otherwise more subtle in its solidarity semantics than other European languages.

   Embedded within the language of friendship are implicit spatiotemporal metaphors of closeness versus distance which symbolize the amount of positive affect and levels of interdependency friends feel for one another. Wiener and Mehrabian (1968) used the term *immediacy* to describe the subtle ways in which we use language to show inclusion or exclusion. 'We', for instance, is more immediate and shows less separation than 'you and I' although the denotative referents are the same. Denotative specificity is one of several ways that friends indicate their positive identification with one another. For example, as co-authors of this chapter we could refer to one another as 'we', 'my friend', 'my colleague', 'my co-worker', 'my assistant', 'the other guy', or simply 'him', which provides a roughly descending semantic scale of association or disassociation in the immediacy of our relationship. Factor analytic studies have confirmed that friendships are perceived to vary on dimensions related to immediacy and solidarity, including closeness, intimacy, affect, character, supportiveness, predictability, and degree of spatiotemporal constraints on the relationship (Berger and Bradac, 1982). Tannen (1984) reported four language indices of interpersonal involvement used by friends to show rapport in conversations:

(1) topic management;
(2) pacing;
(3) narrative strategies;
(4) expressive paralinguistics.

Topic management in highly involved relationships included preference for personal topics, more abrupt topic shifts, ability to introduce topics without hesitation, and persistence or freedom to reintroduce new topics if not picked up immediately. Pacing in highly involved relationships included faster rate of speech, faster turn-taking, pause avoidance, cooperative overlap, and participatory listenership. High-involvement narrative strategies included telling more stories, telling stories in rounds, and dramatizing the point of stories. Expressive paralinguistics included more expressive phonology, marked pitch and amplitude shifts, marked voice quality, and strategic within-turn pauses.

Gender appears to be quite salient in predicting the degree of closeness friends feel towards one another. Block (1980) surveyed over 2000 men and women about their friendships and found that people tended to form their closest friendships with members of their own gender. Further, women were found to have a greater number of friends and felt closer to their friends than did men. Shellen and Cole (1982) found no difference between men and women in the number of friends reported but agreed with Block that women reported closer relationships with friends of both sexes than did men. For both men and women, same-sex friendships were perceived to be closer and longer in duration than opposite-sex friendships. Wright (1982) found that women's friendships emphasized personalism and supportiveness, were holistic and undifferentiated, and were concerned about maintenance of the affective quality of the relationship. Men's friendships emphasized external interests and activities, were more delimited or differentiated in terms of needs served by each friendship, and tended to overlook or work around sources of affective strain. Although gender difference is a salient variable in friendship research, Wright (1988) cautions against dichotomous thinking and reminds us that most gender differences represent widely overlapping distributions: 'Concerning within-group variability, for any gender difference in central tendency, regardless of the level of statistical significance, there will almost always be a sizable number of women and men who do not fit the overall pattern' (p. 369).

Talking with Friends

Attempting to construct theories that uniquely describe the language used in conversations between friends is a bit like the mathematicians' problem of trying to find models to predict random events – it is possible to do both, but neither is easy and exceptions abound for every normative pattern described. The literature on relational development does not (or, perhaps it is fairer to say, cannot) always clearly separate communication behaviors associated with friendships, loveships, or kinships, because such relationships have overlapping attributes (Bradac, 1983). Therefore, some statements about friendships may also be true of other intimate relationships, not to mention the fact that some friends are also lovers or kin. Also, some statements in the literature which have the high-sounding connotation of scientific veracity, such as 'close friendship dyads develop their own idiolect' or 'intimate relationships develop idiosyncratic rules', are actually the social science equivalents of the random-event models referred to earlier; that is, they are at such high levels of abstraction that they say very little about friendships in general and nothing about friendships in particular. Even for any particular individual the experience of conversations with friends will differ from episode to episode and from friend to friend. But all this is not to say that people tolerate chaos in their relationships with others. Strong evidence exists that people strive for reduction of uncertainty in their relationships and develop cognitive prototypes to create normative explanations about people and events (see Berger and Bradac, 1982; Hewes and Planalp, 1982; Pavitt and Haight, 1986). Thus, conversations with friends can be

described in terms of their normative regularities but with the added qualifier that
our friends have the effect of turning us into adaptive social chameleons. Prather
(1977) illustrated this in musing about a magical day when he visited three friends,
one at a time. The first made him wise, the second made him gentle, and the third
turned him into a clown, as he was transformed by each conversation. 'It's nothing to
them: they do it so often. I expect I must also cause a change in them. And so we . . .
each a separate we . . . exist only in each other's presence' (p. 42).

What friends talk about

As mentioned earlier, communication in stable friendships is generally described as
unique, efficient, flexible, smooth, personal, spontaneous, judgmental, and broadly
based (Altman and Taylor, 1973; Ayres, 1982; Knapp, 1984). Studies of the topics
friends talk about show agreement with this description but differ for male and
female friendships. Self-reports among college students indicate that the most
common topic that both males and females discuss with their same-sex friends is the
other sex (Haas and Sherman, 1982). The same study showed, however, that the
frequency rankings for discussions of other topics differed by gender. Women friends
reported food, relationship problems, family, and clothing as their next most
frequent topics. Men ranked news, music and art, spectator sports, and participant
sports as the next highest categories of topics discussed with their friends. Rankings
of topics among friends differed from those discussed with co-workers, siblings,
parents, and children.

A similar study (Aries and Johnson, 1983) surveyed middle-aged parents of
college students to generate lists of the frequency and depth of conversational topics
they discussed with their close same-sex friends. Since 83% of the sample were
currently married, discussions about the opposite sex did not dominate the list of
topics as it did in the study among college students. Seventeen topics were generated
from the survey and the analysis showed that the women reported greater frequencies and depth of conversations about personal and family matters with their friends
than did the men. Only one topic, sports, was reported to be discussed significantly
more often and in greater depth by men than women.

Davidson and Duberman (1982) found that men's conversations with their friends
tended to be dominated by non-intimate topics (politics, current events, etc.). The
content of women's conversations with their friends also included non-intimate
topics, but emphasized relational and personal topics to a significantly greater degree
than did the content of men's conversations. The men in this study perceived
themselves to be conversing more spontaneously and with more trust than did the
women. The authors argued that this did not show greater intimacy in men's
friendships 'because men interact less than women on personal and relational levels,
and are therefore less vulnerable' (Davidson and Duberman, 1982, p. 820). Studies
showing that females are more expressive than males dominate the literature (Baxter
and Wilmot, 1983b; Knapp, Ellis, and Williams, 1980), but contradictory findings
exist as well (Shimanoff, 1983).

For both sexes, conversations of a highly personal nature are relatively rare within
the overall amount of time spent interacting with friends. Duck and Miell (1986)

analyzed reports from 74 college students who kept a log of their interactions with friends and acquaintances for 18 weeks. Superficial conversation or 'chat' was the most often-used category for reported conversations with friends. McCarthy (1986), who studied adult friendship dyads in a small coastal community in England, also found a low incidence of discussion of private or intimate matters reported among friends. Nearly all of the friendship dyads, however, reported engaging in gossip 'often' or 'very often'. Even though chats or gossip are not very intimate descriptions of talk among friends, they should not be considered unimportant. One study among adolescent friends, for example, showed that gossip functions as a means of vicarious learning and transmission of culural norms and rules for acceptable social behavior among the participants (Poulsen, 1988).

Not only do friends develop their relationships through talk, they sometimes actively *avoid* talk as a route to relationship development. Baxter and Wilmot (1985) in a survey of 'taboo topics' in close relationships found that certain topics were off-limits to opposite-sex friends. Friends chose to bypass discussion of the state of the relationship itself, extra-relationship activity, relationship norms, prior relation-ships, conflict-inducing topics, and negative self-disclosure. Of these topic cate-gories, discussing the 'state of the relationship' was the most pervasive taboo. Such explicit relational metacommunication, communication about the relationship itself (Wilmot, 1980), was seen by the participants as destructive, inefficient, futile, risky, and only appropriate for the very closest relationships.

The participants saw placing the relationship 'on the table' for discussion as destructive because it could bring unequal commitment levels into focus and therefore destroy the relationship. Metacommunication was also viewed as ineffec-tive – an inadequate means to express relationship feelings and perceptions. Rather, the participants felt the relationship should be magically 'understood' without the need for words. Those who mentioned that relationship talk was futile saw it as an exercise for naught. The dominant view was that external forces determined the success or failure of a relationship, not talk about the relationship. Finally, relationship-level metacommunication was seen as something that should occur only in the closest relationships. Overwhelmingly, the accounts portrayed relationship talk negatively. Explicit relationship talk was 'taboo', which meant that it was actively avoided.

The avoidance of explicit relationship metacommunication may serve a 'boundary-setting' function in relationships and inform us about why friends *do* talk about some topics and not others. Friends may limit their topics to the lowest common denominator – finding topics that will be 'safe' for the relationship to advance without conflict. Hocker and Wilmot (1985), for example, note the perva-sive nature of avoidance as a tactic to keep from precipitating a conflict. It could well be that female discussions of food, relationship problems, family, and clothing are exact parallels to male discussions of news, music, art, spectator sports, and participant sports. Both sets of topics function as 'guaranteed facilitators' for the building of the relationship. Stated another way, the relationship is built implicitly by restricting the topics to prescribed arenas. Additional indirect evidence for the implicit nature of relationship-building comes from the work by Baxter and Wilmot (1984). They noted that friends (as well as romantic partners) employed 'secret tests' to ascertain the status of the relationship. Clearly, further exploration of *why* certain topics are utilized and avoided in friendship development is warranted.

Self-disclosure among friends

One of the most active and perhaps the friendliest communication strategy for reducing uncertainty in relationships is self-disclosure (Berger and Bradac, 1982). Altman and Taylor's (1973) original conception of social penetration theory generally viewed relationship growth as an increasing progression of the depth and breadth of disclosure. Wheeless (1976, 1978) and Wheeless and Grotz (1976, 1977) identified five dimensions of disclosure (amount, honesty, valence, intent, and depth) and found a linear relationship between these factors and measures of social solidarity and trust in individual relationships. While some early conceptions of disclosure suggested a U-curve in disclosure frequency, with highest levels occurring with intimates and with absolute strangers with whom the discloser would have no further contact (Pearce and Sharp, 1973), the dominant theme of research suggests that disclosures between friends are sequenced from low to high intimacy in cyclical stages as relationships grow (Baxter and Wilmot, 1983a; Berger, Garner, Clatterbuck, and Schulman, 1976; VanLear, 1987). Deep disclosures of private and personal information can be used by others not only for confirmation and support but also for control and power, which explains why such disclosures are reserved for trusted best friends (Rawlins, Leibowitz and Bochner, 1986). Studies of gender differences in disclosure have resulted in inconsistent findings. A majority of the findings tend to show that women disclose to greater depth and breadth in same-sex friendships than men. However, Cline (1986) showed that these differences account for only a small percentage of variance in behavioral studies, and that men tend to overestimate their actual disclosures more than women in self-report studies. Hacker (1981) showed that in cross-sex friendships men disclose more than women and that the valence of disclosures also differs in male–female friendships. Men tend to conceal their weaknesses and women conceal their strengths.

The restricted code of solidarity

The unique and efficient qualities of conversation between friends are largely explainable by speech-accommodation theory and the extent of their shared personal history. Speech-accommodation theory posits that individuals in conversations shift their speech styles to become similar (convergent) or different (divergent) as a function of their social evaluations of one another (see Street and Giles (1982) for a review of theoretical approaches to speech accommodation). Convergence or synchrony occurs when the individuals seek attraction or social approval from one another (Simard, Taylor, and Giles, 1976). Convergence has been observed on a wide array of speech variables, including switches in language, dialects and accents, conversational structures, content, speech rates, pausing, and utterance length. Sociolinguistic evidence exists which links these convergent switches in speech style to conform to vernacular norms as one of the ways people show solidarity within their social networks (Cheshire, 1982; Milroy, 1982). This effect occurs at the level of the dyad as well, for it has also been demonstrated that people adjust the familiarity and informativeness of their language when speaking and writing to friends (McMullen and Krahn, 1985; McMullen and Murray, 1986). Thus, as friendships become established, conversations between friends take on a form of uniqueness characterized not only by convergent speech styles but also other features of personalized communication including personal idioms and what Hopper has referred to as 'taken-for-grantedness' (Hopper, 1981; Hopper, Knapp, and Scott, 1981; Knapp *et al.*, 1980). All conversation, not just that of friends and other intimates, relies on 'bridging inferences' (Clark, 1977) to make sense out of the taken-for-granted linkages between utterances or propositions in discourse. But the shared history of friends enables them to take *more* for granted in inferring what will be mutually understood by one another. This is especially well illustrated by Clark and Haviland's (1977) *given/new strategy*, which explains how people bridge and connect new information in discourse to concepts they already know or take for granted. For example, the statement, 'Hopper's "Doctor" example is a great case of TFG', might be understandable to people who have read Hopper's (1981) article, but would be meaningless to those for whom the referents for ' "Doctor" example', 'TFG', or even 'Hopper' were not 'given' as part of their prior knowledge. Similarly, personalized communication between friends is replete with assumed or unstated 'givens' so that the 'new' or informative portion of content shared among friends appears incomplete, sometimes even uninterpretable, to outsiders. Such language is a 'restricted code' in the full sense of the restatement by Ball, Giles, and Hewstone (1985) of Bernstein's (1972) general theory of sociolinguistic codes. Had Bernstein applied his theory to the study of social solidarity instead of social class, a great deal of criticism and controversy might have been avoided.

Friendly persuasion and relational maintenance

As Wright (1978) pointed out, friendships on all levels encounter strain and tension which require the partners to negotiate, work around, or tolerate the strain. As friends get to know one another, the chances increase that some undesired behaviors or attitudes will be discovered that create conflict. Rawlins (1983) identified another source of potential difficulty, the mutually contingent choice between interdependence versus freedom which must be negotiated even within the best of friendships. Therefore, compliance-gaining efforts between friends, such as attempts to influence behavior or requests for favors, operate within the presupposition of the right to ask for compliance but also may entail the obligation to grant the same rights to the friend in return. Research on conversational influence strategies has resulted in conflicting findings, with some studies showing that friends use politeness and 'friendly persuasion' with one another (Baxter, 1984a; Miller, Boster, Roloff, and Seibold, 1977; Tracy, Craig, Smith, and Spisak, 1984) and others showing that the obligation to use politeness is not as necessary with friends as with acquaintances and strangers (Brown and Levinson, 1978; Cody, McLaughlin, and Schneider, 1981; Fitzpatrick and Winke, 1979). It is likely that the contradictory findings are reflective of the highly situational nature of conflict and persuasion among friends and that both sets of findings may be true in different instances. Tracy *et al.* (1984) found that the frequencies with which people used various strategies involving reward or punishment appeals, altruism, and argument all varied, depending upon the status and familiarity of the requestee and the size of the request. Baxter (1984b) demonstrated that when the target of conflict was identified as 'someone you regard as a good friend' the strategies chosen reflected politeness and positive face-saving acts in attempts to persuade the friend. The choice of strategies also differed by gender and perceived closeness of the friendship. Face-threatening strategies were less likely to be employed by females than males and less likely to be used with close friends than with more distant friends.

Cushman and Cahn (1985) suggest that when norms are violated by friends and the relationship is threatened, alignment strategies, disclaimers, and accounts are used to attempt to rebuild and maintain the relationship. Such strategies, according to Stokes and Hewitt (1976), excuse, justify, offer concessions, or deny blame for the misdeed in an attempt to bring the relationship back into line and account for the violation of what was expected. McLaughlin, Cody, and O'Hair (1983) found that excuses were most often used in managing failure events unless they were quite severe, in which case concessions to repair the situation were most common. The choices of strategies in their study were not affected by relational intimacy, dominance, or orientation toward relational maintenance, and this suggests that these strategies may be used in a wide array of relationships, not just findings. However, some forms of alignment talk have been shown to invoke relational inferences of perceived friendliness and concern for cooperation (Jordan, 1987). Male/female differences have also been noted in the use of account strategies (Petronio, 1984), with women tending to use excuses and denials of responsibility as repair strategies. Males tended to use justifications as their maintenance and repair strategies and thus accepted more responsibility for their actions.

Exiting the Friendship

There are, of course, many reasons for the decline of a relationship for which the verbal interaction becomes a marker. Rose (1984) examined the decline in same-sex college-student friendships and found it was due to physical separation, new friends replacing old, a friend revealing or doing something that one disliked, and interference due to dating or marriage. At this juncture, however, we can say that the dissolution of friendships is marked by (a) a decrease in verbal interaction and (b) probably a reversal in some of the interaction qualities.

Dissolution processes, however, are not a complete reversal of communication elements associated with more intimacy. Baxter (1983) demonstrated that the 'reversal hypothesis' was particularized and not global across all the dimensions of interaction specified by Knapp (1984). Basically, Baxter (1983) found that those aspects of communication most linked to knowing the other were least susceptible to reversal during the waning of a friendship. Others have found that the attenuation of a friendship is not marked by a shift in mode of interaction; rather, people simply reduce their frequency of interaction (Glueck and Ayres, 1988). Duck (1982) adds his voice to those cautioning against an uncritical adoption of the 'reversal hypothesis'. Clearly, even with the limited data available, the 'reversal hypothesis' needs careful examination. The communicative features of friendship dissolution may be more characterized by a 'reduction hypothesis' (Glueck and Ayres, 1988), or a partial reversal in some interaction spheres, as noted by Baxter.

A close examination of extant studies of friendship dissolution reveals startlingly large gaps in our knowledge about 'talk' in the dissolution process. Even the best research suffers from a second-level perspective on language usage. Typically, research subjects are asked to respond to lists of disengagement strategies. For example, in the Baxter (1982) study, respondents reacted to a list of 35 disengagement strategies. Some sample items were: 'openly express to the pe..son my desire to disengage'; 'keep our conversation brief whenever we talk'; 'drop subtle "hints" that things had changed between us'; 'try to convince the other person that disengagement was in both our interests'; and 'verbally blame the other person for causing the disengagement, even if I thought s/he wasn't totally to blame'. While it is possible to factor-analyze such responses into dimensions of disengagement, they do not fully inform us of the actual language processes involved. Without conversational data, conclusions about the 'talk' during dissolution will be indirect at best and erroneous at worst.

FRIENDSHIP SCHEMATA

Often, language processes are seen as reflective of static relationship types. For example, as summarized above, researchers study 'friendship' and note the content themes and other interactive elements such as frequency and quality of verbal interaction. One attempt to extend the usual view that communication is simply a dependent variable within a relationship is that by Wilmot and Baxter (1989). They offer the Relationship Schemata Model (RSM) as a clarification of:

(1) the interconnection of communication and relationships:
(2) the process of relationship defining;
(3) the mechanisms of relationship change via communication.

Put another way, they treat the 'language about the relationship' as a central concern, specifying the processes individuals use to decide when they are 'friends'.

The RSM argues that relationships are defined, renegotiated, and reinforced by language choices of the participants. Basically, Wilmot and Baxter (1989) posit that individuals have templates, or schemata, for understanding the social world. These schemata are 'internal to the perceiver, modifiable by experience and specific to what is being perceived' (Neisser, 1976, p. 54). In perceiving their personal relationships, individuals use a *prototype* – an ideal representation for a pure type against which to pigeon-hole their judgments. Two people, for example, who are acting in a 'friendly' way, have yet to develop a 'friendship'. Wilmot and Baxter point out that relationship schemata such as 'friendship' are characterized by three elements:

(1) a natural language label;
(2) a set of criterial attributes which typify the prototype;
(3) communicative indicators of criterial attributes.

The natural language labels for 'friends' demonstrate some divergence from what one might expect. In their study, people in same-sex friendships completed extensive ethnographic interviews. They were asked to describe the kinds of relationships people have. Respondents used from two to five labels to distinguish types of friends. For example, one male respondent distinguished two types of friends: 'face–name relationship' and 'friend'. A female drew sharp lines between 'casual', 'good', and 'best' friends, and yet another between 'acquaintance', 'friend', 'close friend', and 'very best friend'. All the respondents put types of friends on a continuum ranging from least to most intimate. Across the respondents, there was an average of 2.6 natural language labels for 'friends'. Clearly, there is a culturally supported domain of 'friendship' reflected in the language for typifying friends; yet, there is considerable variation in the number and specific natural language labels people use for friends.

The RSM also specifies that the natural language labels are applied only when criterial attributes match the friendship prototype. The criterial attributes that must be met before one can be called a 'friend' were found to be: trust, respect, caring, ease in communicating, general comfort and security in the other's presence, and openness (Wilmot and Baxter, 1989). Of course, many of these criteria for 'friendship' also apply to other personal relationships. In their data comparing friendship to romantic prototypes, Wilmot and Baxter found the above criteria (trust, etc.) to be conjunctive – descriptive of both friendship and love relationships. However, disjunctive attributes also arose. Romantic relationships are characterized by 'mysticism' or inexplicableness, are seen as more intimate, especially in a sexual sense, involve more direct talk about the relationship *per se*, require more effort than do friendships, and are more fragile and exclusive.

Clearly, the language choices used to explicate the essential nature of friendships involve some ambiguity. For example, to say a friend is one who can be 'trusted' carries potentially different meaning than to say a date can be 'trusted'. Wilmot and Baxter's third level of specification in their model, therefore, was that participants utilize 'communicative indicators' of the criterial attributes (Forgas, 1978). Interestingly, when participants talked about their friendships in open-ended interviews, it was easier for them to generate language choices about natural language labels and criterial attributes which typify the prototype than it was to generate the communicative indicators. In a second study, participants were asked to specify the communicative indicators for the conjunctive attributes of friendship and romantic relationships. The indicators were wide ranging and diverse. For example, to communicate 'trust' in a friendship, one could:

- be able to be open
- be willing to be open
- let go of the other
- not do any 'put ons'
- keep a secret
- defend the other if he or she needed it
- put one's life in the other's hands

– express anger with the other
– listen to the other's problems

Some of the findings about the communicative indicators were that:

(1) people have difficulty capturing communicative indicators without being specifically queried about them;
(2) communicative indicators vary in their density – some are rich and some are lean without any symbolic importance;
(3) there can be a wide diversity of communicative indicators for the same criterial attribute (like 'trust' above);
(4) the same communicative indicators may be connected to different relationship attributes: for one respondent 'no phoniness' is a sign of 'feeling comfortable', while for another it is a sign of 'trust'.

A simplified example of the three levels of the RSM appears in Figure 20.1. Note that in this example, the natural language labels ('romantic relationship' and 'friendship') are just two of the many possible relationship types. For example, whereas one person might use the category 'lover', another might prefer 'dating partner'. Similarly, 'friend' might not be the label of choice, but 'buddy' or 'mate' might be. Whatever the chosen label, there are criterial attributes associated with each. And, as presented in the figure, the same criterial attribute might serve for both types of relationships. Since the subjects used the notions of 'sex, mysticism, and relationship talk' in the interviews, these are placed in the model. Finally, at the last level the communicative indicators 'touch', 'keep a secret', 'be willing to be open', and 'listen to other's problems' all were derived from the interviews. Note that

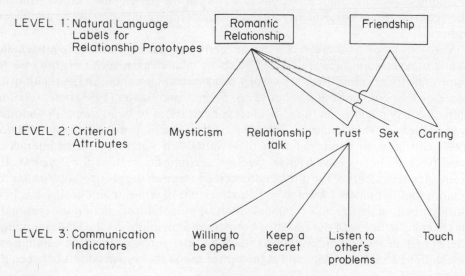

FIGURE 20.1

'touch' might signify 'caring' in a friendship while serving to connote 'sex' in a romantic relationship. The communicative indicators may be connected to different relationship criteria.

Basically, the three levels of this model indicate just how complex language about relationships can be. Language choices in friendship both reflect and create the nature of the prototype. The use of words, while meant to be communicative, is a 'fuzzy set' – with many attendant meanings. While the 'language about friendship' seems to be straightforward, upon closer inspection it contains much ambiguity across the three hierarchical levels of natural language labels, criterial attributes, and communicative indicators.

CAUTIONS AND CAVEATS

The principal issues regarding language and relationships center on (a) language as a consequence of relationships, and (b) language as a causative force in constructing relationships. As a consequence of relationships, language clearly serves as an intimacy marker. As a relationship develops and wanes, there are concomitant alterations in the forms of address, frequency, and breadth and depth of disclosure. While there is some dispute regarding the specific language features associated with the decline in a friendship, there is, at the least, a decline in the frequency of interaction. Language processes are one of the most obvious markers of the state of a relationship – one has only to overhear conversations to make estimates of the status of a given friendship. Basically, information about whether participants in a relationship are 'getting closer' or 'getting farther apart' is provided by the obvious verbalizations shared by the participants. If you are interested in the status of a given relationship, you need not do extensive testing of the participants; rather, tracking their conversations for frequency, breadth, and depth would normally be a sufficient indicator.

Verbal processes, however, can also be seen as a cause of relationship movement. While some relationships are altered by changing activities, such as is the case for some male friendships, there are usually concomitant alterations in the relationship based on the communication behavior. As Wilmot and Baxter (1983) note, relationships are dependent upon the individual conversations to build them. Put another way, the relationship definitions emerge from the recurring episodic events (Wilmot, 1987). Similarly, when one definition of a relationship is at odds with the interaction base (such as being 'best friends', yet not seeing one another for 2 years), the frequency and quality of the interaction exert pressure on the participants to alter the relationship definition (Wilmot and Baxter, 1983). While relationships are built through both activities and communication, the relationship definition eventually has to come in line with the expected normative interaction. As the RSM pinpoints, there are three levels of information and cognition occurring during the building and dissolution of a relationship, and at the center reside the conversations between the participants.

The exploration of the reciprocal influence of relationships and conversations – as both cause and consequence – needs additional work. In addition, the data often used to generate knowledge about language in friendships have some limitations. Most studies do not follow the ebb and flow of relationships over time, and the 'snapshot' view of relationships fails to capture the essential inherent dynamics. Further, most of the data is dependent on participant self-reports of disclosure and other communication elements of their interactions. Basically, we are trusting our participants to be 'conversational historians', without any guarantee that they can accurately report on micro-communication events. It may be that the link between intimacy and communication behavior resides in the schemata of an individual rather than in actual events that would be classified as 'close'. In one experiment, subjects were given a manipulation of a relationship 'getting closer' while others were told it was 'getting farther apart', and all were presented with identical conversations to assess. Their perceptions of the conversations were altered on the basis of the general global assessment of 'getting closer or farther apart' (Wilmot and Baxter, 1983). In free-flowing interactions, participants may be making conversational judgments based on general intuitive feeling about the progress or decline of the relationship. In any event, the interconnection of language and friendship offers intriguing challenges for insight into the function of language in all personal relationships.

REFERENCES

Altman, I. and Taylor, D.A. (1973). *Social penetration: The development of interpersonal relationships*. New York: Holt, Rinehart, and Winston.

Aries, E.J. and Johnson, F.L. (1983). Close friendship in adulthood: Conversational content between same-sex friends. *Sex Roles, 9*, 1183–1196.

Ayres, J. (1982). Perceived use of evaluative statements in developing, stable, and deteriorating relationships with a person of the same or opposite sex. *Western Journal of Speech Communication, 46*, 20–31.

Ball, P., Giles, H., and Hewstone, M. (1985). Interpersonal accommodation and situational construals: An integrative formalisation. In H. Giles and R.N. St Clair (Eds), *Recent advances in language, communication, and social psychology*, pp. 263–286. London: Erlbaum.

Baxter, L.A. (1982). Strategies for ending relationships: Two studies. *Western Journal of Speech Communication, 46*, 223–241.

Baxter, L.A. (1983). Relationship disengagement: An examination of the reversal hypothesis. *Western Journal of Speech Communication, 47*, 85–98.

Baxter, L.A. (1984a). An investigation of compliance-gaining as politeness. *Human Communication Research, 10*, 427–456.

Baxter, L.A. (1984b). Trajectories of relationship disengagement. *Journal of Social and Personal Relationships, 1*, 29–48.

Baxter, L.A. and Wilmot, W.W. (1983a). An investigation of openness–closedness cycling in ongoing relationship interaction. Paper presented at the Annual Meeting of the Western Speech Communication Association, Albuquerque, NM.

Baxter, L.A. and Wilmot, W.W. (1983b). Communication characteristics of relationships with differential growth rates. *Communication Monographs, 50*, 264–272.

Baxter, L.A. and Wilmot, W.W. (1984). 'Secret tests': Social strategies for acquiring information about the state of the relationship. *Human Communication Research, 11*, 171–201.

Baxter, L.A. and Wilmot, W.W. (1985). Taboo topics in close relationships. *Journal of Social and Personal Relationships, 2*, 253–269.

Bell, R.A. (1985). Conversational involvement and loneliness. *Communication Monographs,* **52**, 218–235.

Bell, R.A. and Daly, J.A. (1984). The affinity-seeking function of communication. *Communication Monographs,* **51**, 91–115.

Bell, R.R. (1981). *Worlds of friendship.* Beverly Hills: Sage.

Berger, C.R. and Bradac, J.J. (1982). *Language and social knowledge.* London: Arnold.

Berger, C.R., Garner, R.R., Clatterbuck, G.W., and Schulman, L.S. (1976). Perceptions of information sequencing in relationship development. *Human Communication Research,* **3**, 29–46.

Bernstein, B. (1972). Social class, language and socialisation. In P.P. Giglioli (Ed.), *Language and social context: Selected readings.* Harmondsworth (England): Penguin.

Block, J.D. (1980). *Friendship.* New York: Macmillan.

Bradac, J.J. (1983). The language of lovers, flovers, and friends: Communicating in social and personal relationships. *Journal of Language and Social Psychology,* **2**, 141–162.

Brenton, M. (1974). *Friendship.* New York: Stein and Day.

Broome, B.J. (1983). The attraction paradigm revisited: Responses to dissimilar others. *Human Communication Research,* **10**, 137–152.

Brown, P. and Levinson, S. (1978). Universals in language use: Politeness phenomena. In E. Goody (Ed.), *Questions and politeness: Strategies in social interaction,* pp. 56–289. New York: Cambridge University Press.

Brown, R. (1965). *Social psychology.* New York: Free Press.

Brown, R. and Ford, M. (1961). Address in American English. *Journal of Abnormal and Social Psychology,* **62**, 375–385.

Cattell, R.B. (1948). Concepts and methods in the measurement of group syntality. *Psychological Review,* **55**, 48–63.

Cheshire, J. (1982). Linguistic variation and social function. In S. Romaine (Ed.), *Sociolinguistic variation in speech communities,* pp. 153–166. London: Arnold.

Clark, H.H. (1977). Bridging. In P. Johnson-Laird and P.C. Wason (Eds), *Thinking: Readings in cognitive science,* pp. 411–420. Cambridge: Cambridge University Press.

Clark, H.H. and Haviland, S.E. (1977). Comprehension and the given–new contract. In R.O. Freedle (Ed.), *Discourse production and comprehension,* pp. 1–40. Norwood, NJ: Ablex.

Cline, R.J. (1986). The effects of biological sex and psychological gender on reported and behavioral intimacy and control of self-disclosure. *Communication Quarterly,* **34**, 41–54.

Cody, M., McLaughlin, M., and Schneider, M. (1981). The impact of relational consequences and intimacy on the selection of interpersonal tactics: A Reanalysis. *Communication Quarterly,* **29**, 91–106.

Cushman, D.P. and Cahn, D.D. (1985). *Communication in interpersonal relationships.* Albany, NY: State University of New York Press.

Davidson, L.R. and Duberman, L. (1982). Friendship: Communication and interactional patterns in same-sex dyads. *Sex Roles,* **8**, 809–822.

Dickens, W.J. and Perlman, D. (1981). Friendship over the life-cycle. In S. Duck and R. Gilmour (Eds), *Personal relationships,* Vol. 2, *Developing personal relationships,* pp. 91–122. New York: Academic Press.

Dickson-Markman, F. (1986). Self-disclosure with friends across the life cycle. *Journal of Social and Personal Relationships,* **3**, 259–264.

Duck, S.W. (Ed.) (1982). *Personal relationships,* Vol. 4, *Dissolving personal relationships.* New York: Academic Press.

Duck, S. and Miell, D. (1986). Charting the development of personal relationships. In R. Gilmour and S. Duck (Eds), *The emerging field of personal relations,* pp. 133–144. Hillsdale, NJ: Erlbaum.

Duck, S. and Pond, K. (1989). Friends Romans countrymen, lend me your retrospections: Rhetoric and reality in personal relationships. In C. Hendrick (Ed.), *Review of social behavior and personality,* Vol. 10, *Close relationships,* pp. 17–38. Newbury Park, CA: Sage.

Fitzpatrick, M.A. and Winke, J. (1979). You always hurt the one you love: Strategies and tactics in interpersonal conflict. *Communication Quarterly,* **29**, 3–11.

Forgas, J.P. (1978). Social episodes and social structure in an academic setting: The social environment of an intact group. *Journal of Experimental Social Psychology,* **14**, 434–448.

Glueck, L. and Ayres, J. (1988). Personalization patterns in developing, stable, and deteriorating relationships. *Journal of the Northwest Communication Association,* **16**, 61–81.

Haas, A. and Sherman, M.A. (1982). Reported topics of conversation among same-sex adults. *Communication Quarterly,* **30**, 332–342.

Hacker, H.M. (1981). Blabbermouths and clams: Sex differences in self-disclosure. *Psychology of Women Quarterly,* **5**, 385–401.

Harré, R., Morgan, J., and O'Neill, C. (1979). *Nicknames: Their origins and social consequences.* London: Routledge and Kegan Paul.

Hays, R.B. (1984). The development and maintenance of friendship. *Journal of Social and Personal Relationships,* **1**, 75–98.

Heider, F. (1958). *The psychology of interpersonal relations.* New York: Wiley.

Hewes, D.E. and Planalp, S. (1982). There is nothing as useful as a good theory . . .: The influence of social knowledge on interpersonal communication. In M.E. Roloff and C.R. Berger (Eds), *Social cognition and communication,* pp. 107–150. Beverly Hills, CA: Sage.

Hocker, J.L. and Wilmot, W.W. (1985). *Interpersonal conflict.* Dubuque: Brown.

Hopper, R. (1981). The taken-for-granted. *Human Communication Research,* **7**, 195–211.

Hopper, R., Knapp, M.L., and Scott, L. (1981). Couples' personal idioms: Exploring intimate talk. *Journal of Communication,* **31**, 23–33.

Jordan, J.M. (1987). Relational inferences and the use of alignment talk. Unpublished thesis, University of Montana.

Knapp, M.L. (1984). *Interpersonal communication and human relationships.* Boston: Allyn and Bacon.

Knapp, M., Ellis, D., and Williams, B. (1980). Perceptions of communication behavior associated with relationship terms. *Comunication Monographs,* **47**, 262–278.

McCandless, B.R. and Evans, E.E. (1973). *Children and youth: Psychosocial development.* Hinsdale: Dryden.

McCarthy, B. (1986). Dyads, cliques and conspiracies: Friendship behaviors and perceptions within long-established social groups. In R. Gilmour and S. Duck (Eds), *The emerging field of personal relations,* pp. 77–90. Hillsdale, NJ: Erlbaum.

McMullen, L.M. and Krahn, E.E. (1985). Effects of status and solidarity on familiarity in written communication. *Language and Speech,* **28**, 391–402.

McMullen, L.M. and Murray, W.A. (1986). Effects of status and solidarity on familiarity in verbal behavior. *Journal of Language and Social Psychology,* **5**(12), 49–52.

McLaughlin, M.L., Cody, M.J., and O'Hair, H.D. (1983). The management of failure events: Some contextual determinants of accounting behavior. *Human Communication Research,* **9**, 208–224.

Miller, G., Boster, F., Roloff, M., and Seibold, D. (1977). Compliance-gaining message strategies: A typology and some findings concerning effects of situational differences. *Communication Monographs,* **44**, 37–51.

Milroy, L. (1982). Social network and linguistic focusing. In S. Romaine (Ed.), *Sociolinguistic variation in speech communities,* pp. 141–152. London: Arnold.

Neisser, V. (1976). *Cognition and reality.* San Francisco: Freeman.

Pavitt, C. and Haight, L. (1986). Implicit theories of communicative competence: The semantics of social behavior. *Central States Speech Journal,* **37**, 204–219.

Pearce, W.B. and Sharp, S.M. (1973). Self-disclosing communication. *Journal of Communication,* **23**, 409–425.

Petronio, S. (1984). Communication strategies to reduce embarrassment: Differences between men and women. *Western Journal of Speech Communication,* **48**, 28–38.

Poulsen, S. (1988). Gossip as a prominent speech form in young female adolescents' talk. Paper presented to the Western Speech Communication Association Convention, San Diego, CA.

Prather, H. (1977). *Notes on love and courage.* New York: Doubleday.

Proefrock, D.W. (1983). The uncertainty principle in adolescent research. *Adolescence,* **18,** 339–343.

Rawlins, W.K. (1983). Negotiating close friendship: The dialectic of conjunctive freedoms. *Human Communication Research,* **9,** 255–266.

Rawlins, W.K., Leibowitz, K., and Bochner, A.P. (1986). Affective and instrumental dimensions of best, equal, and unequal friendships. *Central States Speech Journal,* **37,** 90–101.

Rose, S.M. (1984). How friendships end: Patterns among young adults. *Journal of Social and Personal Relationships,* **1,** 267–277.

Sants, H. (1984). Conceptions of friendship, social behavior and school achievement in six-year-old children. *Journal of Social and Personal Relationships,* **1,** 293–309.

Shellen, W.N. and Cole, C.M. (1982). Friendly relations: Same and opposite sex friendships among the married and unmarried. Paper presented to the Western Speech Communication Association Convention, Denver, CO.

Shimanoff, S.B. (1983). The role of gender in linguistic references to emotive states. *Communication Quarterly,* **31,** 174–179.

Simard, L., Taylor, D.M., and Giles, H. (1976). Attribution processes and interpersonal accommodation in a bilingual setting. *Language and Speech,* **19,** 374–387.

Stokes, R. and Hewitt, J.P. (1976). Aligning actions. *American Sociological Review,* **41,** 838–849.

Street, R.L. and Giles, H. (1982). Speech accommodation theory: A social cognitive approach to language and speech behavior. In M.E. Roloff and C.R. Berger (Eds), *Social cognition and communication,* pp. 193–226. Beverly Hills, CA: Sage.

Suitor, J.J. (1987). Friendship networks in transitions: Married mothers return to school. *Journal of Social and Personal Relationships,* **4,** 445–461.

Sykes, R.E. (1983). Initial interaction between strangers and acquaintances: A multivariate analysis of factors affecting choice of communication partners. *Human Communication Research,* **10,** 27–54.

Tannen, D. (1984). *Conversational style: Analyzing talk among friends.* Norwood, NJ: Ablex.

Tracy, K., Craig, R.T., Smith, M., and Spisak, F. (1984). The discourse of requests: Assessment of a compliance-gaining approach. *Human Communication Research,* **10,** 513–538.

VanLear, C.A. (1987). The formation of social relationships: A longitudinal study of social penetration. *Human Communication Research,* **13,** 299–322.

Wheeless, L.R. (1976). Self-disclosure and interpersonal solidarity: Measurement, validation, and relationships. *Human Communication Research,* **3,** 47–61.

Wheeless, L.R. (1978). A follow-up study of the relationships among trust, disclosure, and interpersonal solidarity. *Human Communication Research,* **4,** 143–157.

Wheeless, L.R. and Grotz, J. (1976). Conceptualization and measurement of reported self-disclosure. *Human Communication Research,* **2,** 338–346.

Wheeless, L.R. and Grotz, J. (1977). The measurement of trust and its relationship of self-disclosure. *Human Communication Research,* **3,** 250–257.

Wiener, M. and Mehrabian, A. (1968). *Language within language: Immediacy, a channel in verbal communication.* New York: Appleton–Century–Crofts.

Wilmot, W.W. (1980). Metacommunication: A re-examination and extension. In D. Nimmo (Ed.), *Communication Yearbook,* No. 4, pp. 61–69. New Brunswick: Transaction.

Wilmot, W.W. (1987). *Dyadic communication.* New York: Random House.

Wilmot, W.W. and Baxter, L.A. (1983). Reciprocal framing of relationship definitions and episodic interaction. *Western Journal of Speech Communication,* **47,** 205–217.

Wilmot, W.W. and Baxter, L.A. (1989). The relationship schemata model: On linking relationships with communication. Paper presented to Western Speech Communication Association Convention, Spokane, WA.

Wright, P.H. (1978). Toward a theory of friendship based on a conception of self. *Human Communication Research,* **4**, 196–207.

Wright, P.H. (1982). Men's friendships, women's friendships and the alleged inferiority of the latter. *Sex Roles*, **8**, 1–20.

Wright, P.H. (1988). Interpreting research on gender differences in friendship: A case for moderation and a plea for caution. *Journal of Social and Personal Relationships*, **5**, 367–373.

21

Models of Marital Interaction

MARY ANNE FITZPATRICK

Center for Communication Research, University of Wisconsin, USA

It may strike the reader as curious that a book on language and social psychology should include a chapter on marriage, for what possible connections can be drawn between language, social psychology and marriage? To appreciate the interconnections among the three areas, it is important to understand the functions of modern family life. Since the traditional functions of marriage and the family (e.g. its economic function, care for the aged, education of the children and so forth) have gradually been delegated to other social agencies, the only function remaining to the family is the nurturance of its members (Lasch, 1977). In contrast to previous decades, a 'good spouse' must be more than a good housekeeper, breadwinner and sexual partner. Today's values require that spouses listen to the worries and anxieties of their partners and are leisure-time companions and friends. Because both of these new marital requirements place demands in each spouse's ability to communicate, the study of language and social psychology becomes important in understanding modern relationships.

Thus, communication difficulties are the major cause of marital unhappiness and hence marital failure; that is, the quality of a marriage or the subjective evaluation of a marriage as good, happy or satisfying (Lewis and Spanier, 1979) depends upon good communication between husbands and wives. The meaning of 'good' marital communication, however, varies by couple. What constitutes functional marital communication (i.e. that which leads to satisfaction in the relationship) differs according to the underlying beliefs husbands and wives hold about the nature of marriage (Fitzpatrick, 1984). For some couples, 'communication' means close,

Handbook of Language and Social Psychology
Edited by H. Giles and W.P. Robinson. © 1990 John Wiley & Sons Ltd

supportive and flexible speech. Their marriage and the communication between them is analyzed, taken apart and put back together in an improved form, for this is how these couples 'work' on their relationships (Katriel and Philipsen, 1981). For other couples, good marital communication is the clear specification and discussion of mutual rights and obligations (Sillars, Weisberg, Burgraff, and Wilson, 1987). In deciphering a couple's definition of 'good' marital communication, linguistic and social psychological work is necessary. Only our theoretical work can help us to answer the question basic to this area: how do husbands and wives actively perceive, interpret, create and negotiate their relationship?

The study of social psychology and language thus helps us to understand marriage; however, the converse is also true: an examination of marital processes informs the study of social psychology and language in a number of significant ways. Marriage constitutes a rich, important and neglected domain for studying dyadic interaction in everyday life – from household chores and childcare, to aspects of self and sexual behavior. Virtually every area of social psychology comes together in marriage. Studies of group dynamics, causal attribution, equity and justice processes, person perception, personality traits and so forth all consider phenomena and processes that are basic to marriage (Anderson and Armstrong, 1989). Language between intimates, each person sharing extensive common history, illuminates the workings of private codes. The study of marriage and the family must, then, take into account an important dimension of depth: long-term marital interactions depend on underlying knowledge systems. Such knowledge systems are undoubtedly complex and related to affect. And, these systems push current theories beyond simple scope conditions. Marriage thus constitutes a central arena for the study of social psychology and language and one with the potential for unifying social psychological theory and language.

To help in this unification process, the review that follows selects and emphasizes the micro-societal theories related to marital communication. Such theories include analyses of both *individual* and *interactional* processes. Those of the former type use the individual as the unit of analysis and attempt to interpret and explain marital behavior (e.g. attitudes, values, motives and experiences) in those terms. Theories of the latter type use the marital system as the unit of analysis and attempt to interpret and explain how the influence each spouse exerts on the other, relative to his or her typical or baseline patterns (Cappella, 1987), affects the emergence of, as well as the stability or change in, the marital dyad. After surveying both individual and interactional models, I demonstrate that such models are neither contradictory nor mutually exclusive. Finally, I propose a theory of marital interaction which incorporates insights from both linguistic and social psychological theories.

THE INDIVIDUAL AND THE MARRIAGE

This section focuses on the individual and his or her underlying disposition, level of social competence, and cognitions about a spouse and marriage.

Trait Models

These approaches to communication in marriage place the locus of action in the predispositions of husbands and wives to initiate or react to communication from their spouses. The areas studied today include:

(1) psychological variables in mate selection (e.g. Buss and Barnes, 1986);
(2) the relationship between such variables and marital satisfaction (e.g. Baucom and Aiken, 1984);
(3) the relationship between the accuracy of interspousal perceptions of personality or role behavior and marital satisfaction (Sillars, Pike, Jones, and Murphy, 1984).

Major longitudinal investigations link low neuroticism in both partners, and high impulse control on the part of the husband, to the long-term maintenance of a marriage (Kelly and Conley, 1987). The highly valued traits for a mate are to be: kind, exciting, intelligent, physically attractive and healthy (Buss and Barnes, 1986). These traits may be clues to marital survival and satisfaction (e.g. the kind person is understanding and easy to get along with) or signal that the other is a good reproductive investment (e.g. the physically attractive person is usually young and healthy).

Psychological differences between males and females may also influence marital interaction (see Chapter 17, by Kramarae). Men are likely to prefer their spouses to be physically attractive, whereas women are likely to prefer mates who are college-educated with good earning potential (Buss and Barnes, 1986). Such consensually valued characteristics probably enter into the equity and exchange processes in the marital marketplace. In addition to these gender differences, females, in contrast to males, may place greater relative values on satisfying and close relationships (Gilligan, 1982; but see Kerber et al., 1986). The level of marital satisfaction experienced by husbands and wives often interacts with the gender of the communicator (e.g. Noller, 1984). A number of husband and wife communication differences are documented by Noller and Fitzpatrick (1988): particular interaction patterns appear to be initiated more by wives than by husbands (Christensen, 1988; Schaap, Buunk, and Kerkstra, 1988); communication channels used effectively by husbands and wives differ (Noller and Gallois, 1988); and the physiological responses of husbands and wives differ to marital messages (Gottman and Levenson, 1988).

Many of these differences between husbands and wives, however, can be better explained by the ideological orientations of the spouses than by their gender. Burgraff and Sillars (1987), comparing sex differences in marital communication during conflict, found that the ideological values, and levels of companionship in the marriage, were significantly more predictive of the conflict tactics used in conversation than was the sex of the speaker. In other words, the sex of a communicator is less likely to predict how a husband and wife talk to one another than are the values held by individuals about appropriate behavior for husbands and wives as well as the type of relationship the two people have evolved with one another.

Recently, the personality variables relevant to the explanation of individual

behavior have been reconstructed in terms of flexible mental structures and processes, rather than the stable and consistent behavioral dispositions envisaged by
conventional psychometric approaches. Aspects of Bem's (1984) work on gender-
schemata and Markus's (1977) work on self-schemata could be profitably applied to
the understanding of individual differences in marital communication. Although
extremely promising, very little of this new look in personality has been applied to
marital interaction.

Social Competence Models

These models examine the quality of a spouse's communication performance overall
in the marriage. Competent marital communication includes the ability to self-
disclose or reveal private thoughts and feelings about the self to the spouse (Burke,
Weir, and Harrison, 1976; Hendrick, 1981). Discrepancies in affective self-disclosure between married partners (Davidson, Balswick, and Halverson, 1983) and
the disclosure of negative rather than positive feelings to the spouse (Chelune,
Waring, Vosk, Sultan, and Ogden, 1984; Levinger and Senn, 1967; see also Chapter
9, by Holtgraves), are related to dissatisfaction with the marriage.

A problematic assumption undergirding the self-disclosure research is that relationships progress in a linear and unidirectional fashion with increasing openness
between partners (Altman, Vinsel, and Brown, 1981). Marital communication
functions dialectically, rather than linearly, in at least two senses. First, relationships
are dialectical in that they continually cycle through superficial and deeper contact
with repeated ebbs and flows of self-disclosure. Second, marital communication
performs at least five functions around which spouses must continually balance
opposite ends of a continuum. The need to open and disclose to one's spouse, for
example, must be balanced against the need to protect the spouse from the
consequences of such openness (Bochner, 1983).

The self-disclosure model implies that marital communicators have expressive
rather than rhetorical ideologies. In other words, spouses express whatever they
happen to be thinking rather than seeing communication as a strategic medium
through which social selves are created, negotiated and constituted (Fitzpatrick,
1977, 1987c). A rhetorical model leads theorists to pose questions like: what implicit
theories do spouses hold about the ways in which communication can be shaped to
serve as a means to an end? When researchers view communication as a vehicle for
structuring and evoking contexts, they examine marital communication in terms of:
compliance-gaining (Witteman and Fitzpatrick, 1986); generating positive affect in
an interaction (Bell, 1986); or tactics for maintaining one's marriage (Dindia and
Baxter, 1986).

Non-verbal communication is central to many competence models (see Chapter
7, by Cappella and Palmer, and Chapter 12, by Friedman and Tucker). Harmonious marital relationships are marked by closer physical distances, direct body
orientation, and more immediate and relaxed posture than are less harmonious
ones (Beier and Sternberg, 1977). Newly-wed couples are better able to read the
non-verbal messages of their spouse than are dating couples. The wife's skill
seems to be particularly important here (Sabatelli, Buck, and Dreyer, 1982).

Wives who are good encoders (easy for judges to read) have husbands with few marital complaints and are relatively satisfied themelves. Wives who are especially skilled at decoding their husband's poorly sent non-verbal messages are also in happier marriages. Contrary to this finding is that of Gottman and Porterfield (1981), who suggest that the husband's ability to read his wife's non-verbal communication is more predictive of the degree of marital happiness than the wife's ability to read the husband.

Noller (1984), who has extensively studied this issue, argues that husbands in distressed marriages seem to suffer a 'communication-skills deficit'. Husbands in unhappy marriages appear unable to receive the messages of their spouses correctly and have problems in sending clear messages, especially positive ones. In comparing spouses and strangers, however, what appears to be a 'communication-skills deficit' is actually a 'performance deficit'. Husbands and wives in distressed marriages do less well in reading the marital communication of their spouses than they do in reading the communication of strangers. Individuals in unhappy marriages appear capable of reading non-verbal communication but they fail to do so when interacting with one another.

Are the happily married more socially or communicatively competent than the unhappily married? As we have seen, a good deal of research emphasizes the cataloging of self-report and behavioral communication differences between the happily and the unhappily married (see Fitzpatrick and Badzinski, 1985). *Because* individuals are happily married, their communication practices must be the competent ones. The working assumption of this research is that the set of communication practices adopted by the happily married causes that marital happiness. Equally valid is its opposite: a happy marriage causes the use of certain interactional practices. Thus, the catalog studies are problematic because of the 'correlation and causality' question. Even more importantly, cataloging communication differences between the happily and the unhappily married passes for an *explanation* for communication in marriage, and so deflects deeper and more serious considerations of the issues. Social competence cannot be identified with any absolute standard of behavior but rather needs to be viewed as the spouse's ability to adapt to a given situation.

Before pursuing any study of social competence in marriage, the researcher must have a clear theory explicating the relationships among the observed variables. For example, a symbolic interactionist framework on marital competence hypothesizes that, the greater the ability to function effectively in a long-term and fairly complex relationship such as marriage, the greater the marital satisfaction. Effective functioning is defined as demonstrating role-taking ability, role skills and the capacity for negotiation. The question for communication researchers within this theoretical framework is: how do couples communicatively demonstrate their role-taking ability, their role skills and so forth.

Research which indicates that husbands and wives may have the skills to communicate accurately and effectively, yet choose not to use these skills in communicating with each other, suggests that theory must consider the cognitive or motivational processes underlying these decisions.

Cognitive Models

These models emphasize a spouse's complex abilities to produce and interpret marital messages (see Chapter 1, by McCann and Higgins). Husbands and wives represent external reality internally, often in a language-like form. Spouses can manipulate this internal representation in a variety of ways. Individuals have implicit theories of relationships that guide their information processing: they can hold dysfunctional beliefs about relationships (Eidelson and Epstein, 1982). The strong correlations between marital satisfaction and self-reports of communication behavior may reflect strongly held beliefs in our culture about the role of communication in marriage (Fitzpatrick and Badzinski, 1985). The happily married believe that they have remarkably 'good' marital communications: openness (Chelune, 1979); self-disclosure of thoughts and feelings (Levinger and Senn, 1967); perceived accuracy of non-verbal communication (Navran, 1967); and frequent successful communicative exchanges (Bienvenu, 1970).

Attribution theories consider how couples arrive at estimates of the causes of their own as well as their spouses' behavior (e.g. Bernal and Golann, 1980; Doherty, 1981; Newman, 1981). In order to study content themes in marital interaction, Sillars *et al.* (1987) have developed a coding scheme which has a strong attributional flavor (see Holtzworth-Munroe and Jacobson, 1985). Dissatisfied spouses often dwell on the attributed personality deficits of the partner, at the same time overlooking situational and interactional causes of behavior (Orvis, Kelley, and Butler, 1976). Distressed spouses tend to form rigid attributions about the partner's motives and personality (Fincham, 1985). Attribution theory cannot, however, be directly important from laboratory tests with strangers into the study of marital interaction. Traditional attribution theories tend to describe quasi-scientific judgments about causal influence as formulated by a reasonably disinterested observer. Statements about the cause of the individual's own marital behavior or that of the spouse tend to have strong evaluative implications (Fincham, Beach, and Nelson, 1987).

Husbands and wives may act less like scientists with one another and more like lawyers (Fincham and Jaspars, 1980). In other words, models of responsibility attribution that focus on the spouses' concerns with establishing accountability may be more important in understanding marital dynamics (Fincham, 1985). Accountability or responsibility attributions are concerned with the acceptability of the outcome (behavior) according to a set of standards. A spouse may cause an outcome but not be blamed for it because his or her actions met expected standards. In support of this contention, empirical attempts to focus on happily and unhappily married couples' distinctions between internal and external causes for spouse behavior have produced mixed results (Fincham and O'Leary, 1983; Jacobson, McDonald, Follette, and Berley, 1985). More consistent results have been obtained when other properties of causes have been examined (e.g. global versus specific: Fincham, 1985; Holtzworth-Munroe and Jacobson, 1985; positive versus negative attribution biases for self versus spouse: Fincham, Beach, and Baucom, 1987). Responsibility attributions predict both affective impact and the individual's intended response to the behavior of the spouse (Fincham *et al.*, 1987). In sum, relative to non-distressed spouses, distressed spouses view the causes of their partners' negative behavior as reflecting enduring, global characteristics of their partners and consider the behavior more negative in intent, selfishly motivated and blameworthy, whereas they tend to view their partners' positive behaviors as reflecting temporary, situation-specific causes. The inverse pattern holds for the non-distressed.

Two areas within the attribution framework could benefit from a communication perspective. First, how and when do attributions occur in conversation? Holtzworth-Munroe and Jacobson (1985) and Bradbury and Fincham (in press) offer methodological and conceptual considerations in assessing spontaneous attributions in marital conversations. Second, a variety of other attributions that couples can make (e.g. self-presentational, interpersonal, descriptive and so forth) could profitably be examined.

Despite their merits, attribution theories present static models of cognition. Such perspectives argue that individuals assign causes to the behaviors of themselves and of others but ignore how such processes operate. Furthermore, most experimental tests of attribution theory focus exclusively on how perceivers make sense of the situations that are already defined, not on how they rate information in attempting to define social situations. One move toward a more dynamic model of cognitive processes in husband and wife interaction is the recent work of Anderson and Armstrong (1989). These researchers have applied principles of cognitive algebra to marital interaction and decision-making. More work like this, exploring the dynamic nature of the cognitive processes underlying marital interaction, is needed.

Summary

In this section, I have reviewed the major individual-level approaches to the study of marriage: the trait, social competence, and cognitive models. Three trends are apparent in this literature. The first is the renewed interest in gender and sex differences in marital communication. The second is the concern for more dynamic models of cognitive processes that can account for how spouses perceive and interpret one another's messages. The third trend is the integration of affect and cognition into one model by linking the cognitive processes that underlie affect and the affective processes that may underlie cognition. In the next section, I argue that husbands and wives are *social* as well as cognitive creatures. Born into established and continuing social contacts, generally dependent on others, spouses are seldom, if ever, completely alone. And, spousal interaction forms the core of the marital relationship.

THE INTERACTION AND THE MARRIAGE

The assessment of marital interaction, which by definition reflects an interpersonal focus, entails conceptual and methodological considerations distinct from the consideration of the individual. How can the intricate system connecting two intimate partners be described, analyzed and explained?

Transactional Models

The study of transaction processes, defined as the sequential analysis of verbal and non-verbal messages involving chains of interpersonal exchanges, represents a revolution in thinking and research about interpersonal relationships (Gottman, 1982; Penman, 1980). Over 25 years ago, Haley (1962) argued that such a perspective required a new language to include dyadic constructs. More recently, new research technologies have been called for (Gottman, 1982; Lamb, Suomi, and Stephenson, 1979). This approach advocates the observation of patterns of communication, directly assessed and systematically coded. Theoretical arguments in the interactional framework (Watzlawick, Beavin, and Jackson, 1967) and in the family literature (Kantor and Lehr, 1975) are replete with statements about the primacy of transactional sequences. Therapeutic programs are built on such concepts as *quid pro quo* (Lederer and Jackson, 1968).

A number of theories and models have been proposed as explanations of interaction in marriage. Many of the early models are based on principles of behavioral exchange (Jacobson, Follette, and McDonald, 1982; Weiss, 1981). Newer models, however, have found it necessary to include as important predictors of marital satisfaction the cognitions that couples hold about the relationship, the spouse and the nature of the rewards and costs (Jacobson, 1984).

A model which extends the behavioral exchange principles is the Structural Model of Marital Interaction. Four major hypotheses have been tested and supported in this model of marital communication (Gottman, 1979). Researchers in the USA (Fitzpatrick, 1988; Ting-Toomey, 1983) and Europe (Schaap, 1982; Schaap *et al.*, 1988) have replicated the interaction patterns advanced by Gottman (1979). The first hypothesis, which posits that communication is structure and pattern, argues that unhappily married couples are significantly more rigid and inflexible in their communication patterns than are happy couples. The second hypothesis argues that the unhappily married express significantly more negativity in verbal and non-verbal communication than do the happily married. Whereas there are no significant differences between the happily and unhappily married in the reciprocity of positive messages, unhappy couples are significantly more likely to reciprocate negative messages than are the happy couples. In all couples, a compliment begets a compliment, yet a sarcastic comment begets a sarcastic comment only in the unhappily married. The final hypothesis suggests that unhappy marriages are marked by asymmetry in predictability: in other words, one spouse dominates the other. For example, when one spouse calls for compliance, compliance is more likely than when the other spouse calls for it. The asymmetry comes in being much more able to predict how one spouse acts, given the behavior of the other, than vice versa.

There are a growing number of important and notable research programs that emphasize the interactional level (Fitzpatrick, 1984; Gottman, 1979; Hahlweg and Jacobson, 1984; Margolin and Wampold, 1981; Raush, Barry, Hertel, and Swain, 1974; Schaap, 1982; Sillars, Pike, Jones, and Redmon, 1983; Ting-Toomey, 1983). Despite the elegance of these interactional models and their concern for sequence and pattern, many investigators do not go beyond examining separate frequency measures of behaviors that husbands and wives emit in one another's presence.

Many excellent studies stop short of analyzing the patterning in the communication between spouses over time. The exclusive use of rate or frequency data may promote inferential errors. Interactional researchers refer to one major error as the pseudo-unilaterality problem (Duncan, Kanki, Mokros, and Fiske, 1984). For example, suppose the researcher finds that dissatisfied husbands make more justifications for their behavior than do dissatisfied wives. The conclusion might be that justifications are related to male marital dissatisfaction (an individual-level explanation). Because the coded behaviors (in this case, justifications) emerged during marital interaction, an equally plausible interpretation of these rates is that the wives of the dissatisfied husbands act in some way that makes their spouses feel compelled to justify their behavior. The link between marital discord could then be made at the *interactional* rather than at the individual level. The only way to test an interactional model of marital communication is to examine messages in sequence with a statistical technique that can demonstrate a systematic relationship between the messages of husbands and those of wives. The use of frequency or rate measures obscures the level of analysis at which the theorist is working.

Typological Models

Within any sample of couples, there are a limited number of marital types which can be isolated. Couples within different types are assumed to communicate similarly to couples in the same type and differently from couples in other types. In my work over the past decade (Fitzpatrick, 1984, 1988), I have developed an empirical, polythetic classification scheme of marriage which categorizes couples according to three basic dimensions of married life: ideology, interdependence and expressivity. These dimensions combine systematically to isolate, in any population of married couples, three basic definitions of marriage. When individuals are asked to respond to the Relational Dimensions Instrument (RDI; Fitzpatrick, 1977), three definitions emerge: Traditional, Independent or Separate. Traditionals hold conventional values about marriage and the family, are very interdependent in the marriage, and willingly argue over serious issues. Independents are more liberal in their orientation toward marital and family values, are moderately interdependent in their marriages, and are habituated to conflict. Separates are ambivalent about their family values, not very interdependent in their marriages, and tend to avoid marital conflict. The typology moves beyond the assignment of an individual to a couple type and uses the couple as the unit of analysis: husbands and wives are compared on the three basic definitions and categorized in a pure type if they agree and a mixed type if they disagree. Importantly, in our reseach we have found that it is the couple type and not the individual assignment that appears to regulate marital interaction.

Many other researchers and clinicians have developed a variety of conceptually interesting typologies of marriage and the family (see Fitzpatrick, 1988, for a review). A typology alone, however, scarcely deserves notice. Such systems are elegant yet useless without linking the couple types to a network of other constructs. Using a variety of empirical methods, my colleagues and I have extensively explored the ramifications of my system. We have assessed gender concepts and marital satisfaction within each couple type; made direct behavioral observations of control, power and compliance-gaining between couples; examined the modes by which emotions are conveyed; and so forth. Thus, the reliable assignment of a couple to a marital type predicts a number of self-report assessments of the marriage, and a variety of communication rates, frequencies and patterns (for a summary, see Fitzpatrick, 1988).

Summary

Transactional models emphasize the structure and patterning in marital dialogs. Capturing the complexity of human communication, these models ignore the complexity of relationships. Typological models attempt to deal with that relationship complexity. Unfortunately, both interactional and typological models, although powerful descriptions of marital processes, do not answer important causal questions about marriage. To demonstrate that Independents confront disagreements in their relationship rather than avoid them is descriptive and predictive, yet it does not answer the question 'why' or offer any theoretical explanation or understanding of the process.

MERGING INDIVIDUAL AND INTERACTIONAL APPROACHES

One major point can be derived from this review of micro-societal theories of marital communication. To understand the causal mechanisms driving marital communication, consideration must be given to explanations of individual speaker (encoding) and listener (decoding) processes as well as to an explanation for observed interaction patterns. The process of linking constructs across levels of analysis, although not a simple one, is not impossible. Take the recent work of Gottman and Levenson (1988; Levenson and Gottman, 1983, 1985). These authors have demonstrated a high degree of physiological linkage between unhappily married husbands and wives, with arousal rising in both during marital discussions. Such physiological linkage at one point in the relationship can predict subsequent unhappiness in the marriage as well. This linkage concept is clearly an interactional one. Does anything at the individual level of analysis of marital happiness and unhappiness correspond to this construct? Indeed, longitudinal investigations of the personality characteristics that are correlated to marital distress show that high levels of neuroticism and low impulse control (see Chapter 4, by Furnham) predict marital dissatisfaction and divorce. The unhappily married person with low impulse control is less likely to be able to control his or her physiological arousal. This, in turn, may lead the partner to become more aroused during marital talk. If the marital pair comprises two neurotics, the dyad may demonstrate greater physiological linkage during tense interactions. Both neuroticism and low impulse control are related to an indiviudal's ability (or lack thereof) to control his or her physiological arousal (cf. Kelly and Conley, 1987). This reasoning is purely speculative. But, what seem at first glance remarkably different explanations for marital satisfaction are actually explanations for different, related pieces of the puzzle.

The difficulty with a model that explains marital talk by referencing the participants' arousal and their underlying ability (or inability) to control that arousal is that 'talk' becomes the error variance in the model (see Chapter 12, by Friedman and Tucker); that is, a symbolic process like human communication, with its richness and power, is considered important only to the degree to which the autonomic nervous systems of the speaker and the listener respond to the message. Take two different husbands. During conflicts with their wives, each may experience precipitously accelerating arousal. At the same point, both arousal curves level off. In one case, the wife has made a joke or smiled or changed the topic; in the other, the wife has yelled. When debriefed, both husbands explain the deceleration by saying that the wife's communication signalled that the 'fight was over'. Such symbolically different messages must be taken into account.

An alternative approach of linking individual and interactional processes is to integrate the cognitions of spouses into the interactional stream. As the review indicates, cognitive models in general are being applied to dynamic processes, and researchers applying behavioral models to marital interaction have felt the need to incorporate the cognitions of spouses. An alternative explanation to one based on personality processes and the ability to regulate physiological arousal during talk is a social-cognitive marital interaction theory (Fitzpatrick, 1987a,b,d). Such a perspective incorporates the knowledge that spouses bring to interaction.

In general, communication between people requires an amazing array of world knowledge (that private schools cost money, that mothers love their children, that dogs bite, and so forth). To communicate, people have three different knowledge bases: knowledge about how discourse operates (including the rules for decoding context and coherence); knowledge about other people (including their personalities and goals); and knowledge about relationships between people. All three types of world knowledge are called *schemata*.

A schema is a cognitive structure that represents organized knowledge about a given concept or type of stimulus. A schema contains both the attributes of a concept and the relationship among the attributes (Hastie, 1981). Schemata are simplified representations in memory of our perceptions of people, objects and events. If the word 'doctor', for example, brings to mind a middle-aged male who is knowledgeable, efficient and somewhat aloof, this is your schema for 'doctor'. Whatever knowledge structure is primed in an interaction is the structure that affects stages in social information processing: attention, memory and inference. Schemata allow us to observe and interpret, to remember and forget, and to infer and judge, in ways that fit our expectations (Fiske and Taylor, 1984). Communication proceeds because many of us develop – not exactly the same, but highly similar – schemata about a variety of concepts and stimuli.

Specifically, individuals are hypothesized to have *marital schemata* (cf. Chapter 11, by Cody and McLaughlin). Marital schemata are knowledge structures that represent the external world of marriage and provide guidelines about how to interpret incoming data. Marital schemata operate to specify the nature and organization of information relevant to the partner and the marriage, and to plan and direct activity relevant to the schemata (Neisser, 1967). The social-cognitive marital interaction theory proposes that individuals encode and process messages from the spouse and about the marriage in terms of Traditional, Independent or Separate schemata. Traditionals, Independents and Separates differentially encode, retrieve and process information about the spouse and the marriage. This differentiated individual-level process explains the different interaction rates, frequencies and patterns in the couple types. The RDI, used to categorize individuals into marital types, does not contain all of the major dimensions of marital interaction nor does it isolate the content of an individual's schema. The instrument can tap subgroups of individuals who hold similar marital schemata.

This theory specifies three major scope conditions. First, the marital schema must be primed in order for it to be the knowledge structure guiding interaction. As a memory structure, the marital schema is a cross-cultural and transhistorical construct. The processing of marital messages is the same in all cultures. What differs dramatically from culture to culture is the content of the marital schema. Second, once the scheme is primed, marital messages are evaluated as to their relevancy–irrelevancy to the schema. Only relevant messages are processed for consistency and inconsistency. Third, relevant and consistent marital messages are processed in a mindless or scripted manner and probably trigger similar scripted responses from the spouse.

My colleagues and I have completed three studies to demonstrate that the marital types are marital schemata. In general, schemata direct spouses' attention, message creation and interpretation. A reaction-time study demonstrated that the RDI tapped marital schemata. An interaction study demonstrated that these schemata influenced the choice of either a pragmatic or a syntactic code in communicating with a spouse. A standard content study demonstrated that these schemata affected the accuracy of the interpretation of messages from the spouse.

In the reaction-time study, spouses are exposed to segments of marital interaction, designed to represent one of the three basic marital types. Couples in the various marital types can be clearly differentiated in their reaction times to viewing schematic marriages (Fitzpatrick, 1987d). Spouses in one of the three marital types are differentially attentive to schema-consistent versus schema-inconsistent information. This process is measured by the individual's reaction time to a series of tones, placed at random on the tapes. Reaction time in milliseconds to the audible tone is recorded.

The hypothesis that the marital typology represents different schemata of marriage is strongly confirmed for the females within each relationship. For females, there was a significant interaction between their own relationship definition and the relationship portrayed. Specifically, females exhibited faster reaction times to examples of marital interaction from their own marital type than to examples of marital interaction from other types. Schema-consistent portrayals of marriage evoked faster reaction times for females than schema-inconsistent ones. Although Independent males were more sensitive than other males to relationship issues in general, these males did not recognize their own marital type. All females, however, recognized their own marriage when similar processes were displayed to them.

For males, those who defined their marriage as Independent exhibited longer reaction times, and those who defined it as Separate, shorter reaction times, to Traditional, Independent and Separate portrayals of marriage. Males who defined their marriage as Independent were more attentive to all these portrayals than were males who defined their marriage as separate. The Independent males have a more differentiated and complex view of marriage than do either Separate or Traditional males. Traditional and Separate males, in other words, have relatively less differentiated schemata on the nature of marriage.

The second study measured the differential code usage of couples reflecting dissimilar cognitive organizations among the couple types (Fitzpatrick, Bauman, and Lindaas, 1987). Four minutes of casual marital interaction were transcribed. Separates use less linguistic complexity and more implicit roles and rules in their communication with their spouses. For Separates, everything they say to their spouses (and they say as little as possible) does more work. Meaning resides in the situation and is very dependent on the stable expectancies of the communicators. The closeness and interdependence of the Traditional relationship is represented by their consistent reference to themselves as a couple (e.g. 'We do this . . .') and the relative absence of references to the self. The Independents have an elaborated linguistic style in marital interaction. Less is assumed in their conversations with their spouses and Independents attend to linking and elaborating conversational topics. The Independent code involves more precise symbolization because the Independent schema supports flexible roles, change and novelty. Husbands and wives in the mixed couple types, with conflicting schemata on the marriage, exhibit significantly more disfluencies and more disruptive interaction signifying their conflicting schemata.

The third study measured the accuracy and confidence of husbands and wives in decoding the emotional messages of their spouses (Noller and Fitzpatrick, 1987), employing a standard content paradigm. This paradigm uses neutral or ambiguous words to express a number of different intentions. Spouses may say 'What are you doing?' using different non-verbal cues to communicate anger, pleasure, depression or sexual interest in one of 30 different situations. The spouses' (listeners') job was to decide what emotion had been communicated. The Separates are the least accurate in decoding the emotional communications of their spouses because close emotional connections are not part of the Separate schema of marriage. Further, these couples have particular difficulty in recognizing the positive emotions of pleasure and sexual interest. Independent couples, who include strong emotional states in their construction of marriage, recognized these emotions significantly more frequently than couples in the other types of marriages.

The effectiveness of communication systems is measured not only by the accuracy of a listener's perception but also how clearly communicators think they have communicated and how confident the listener is in his or her assessment. Separates misconstrue anger as some other emotion, usually neutrality. The schematic commitment to emotional distance and conflict avoidance affects the interpretation of anger and hostility in this marriage. The misperception occurs, yet both are confident in the clarity of their communication and the accuracy of their interpretation. Independents clearly communicate both positive (i.e. sexual interest) and negative (i.e. depression) emotions, and the Independent listener is confident that he or she understands the message. Independent couples have clear, open emotional communication systems and are confident in their ability to understand the non-verbal messages of their spouses. The emotional communication system in the Traditional marriage suggests some clearly sex-differentiated understanding of non-verbal communication. The wife understands her husband's communication of sexual interest yet not his pleasure; whereas he understands her pleasant moods but not her sexual interest.

Summary

The predominant trend of this research confirms the theoretically derived hypotheses. The RDI taps different subgroups of individuals who have similar schema of marriage and these schema affect both the encoding and decoding of messages by the spouse.

CONCLUSION

This chapter has reviewed some of the major theoretical and methodological issues in the study of marital interaction. I organized the chapter around the individual in marriage as well as the interactional system. Subsequent to the review, I turned to a model of marital interaction that can link both the individual and the interactional levels of analysis. The model was a social-cognitive one which used my typological frame as the building block.

To see the couple types as representing marital schemata not only allows the generation of specific theoretical predictions about communication in various types of relationships but also implies a reconsideration of the definition of marital and family communication. Much of the research on marital and family communication is based on the assumption that all talk in the presence of the relationship partner is 'marital' or 'family' communication. Within a social-cognitive model, such talk could be considered 'marital' only when the marital schema was primed. Potentially, a profound difference among couple types may be the number of times a marital schema is instantiated at all. Being married to an individual is neither a necessary nor a sufficient condition for that talk to be defined as marital. Thus, any given conversation between married people may not be marital talk and, furthermore, it is possible to have marital talk with those other than the spouse. Luckily for most marital interaction researchers, the fact of bringing couples into a laboratory for a study of marital communication is undoubtedly (albeit unwittingly) a major priming mechanism for a marital schema.

The social-cognitive model offers the most potential for merging individual and interactional explanations in order to develop our understanding of the communication that occurs between husbands and wives.

REFERENCES

Altman, I., Vinsel, A., and Brown, B.B. (1981). Dialectical conceptions in social psychology. In L. Berkowitz (Ed.), *Advances in experimental social psychology*, pp. 107–160. New York: Academic Press.

Anderson, N. and Armstrong, M.A. (1989). Cognitive theory and methodology for studying marital interaction. In D. Brinberg and J. Jaccard (Eds), *Dyadic decision-making*, pp. 3–50. New York: Springer-Verlag.

Baucom, D.H. and Aiken, P.A. (1984). Sex role identity, marital satisfaction, and response to behavioral marital therapy. *Journal of Consulting and Clinical Psychology*, **52**, 438–444.

Beier, E.G. and Sternberg, D.P. (1977). Subtle cues between newlyweds. *Journal of Communication*, **27**, 92–103.

Bell, R. (1986). Affinity seeking among married couples. Paper presented at Meeting of the Speech Communication Association, Denver, CO.

Bem, S. (1984). Androgeny and gender schema theory: A conceptual and methodological integration. In T.B. Sonderegger (Ed.), *Psychology and gender: Nebraska symposium on motivation*, pp. 179–226. Lincoln, NE: University of Nebraska Press.

Bernal, G. and Golann, S. (1980). Couple interaction: A study of the punctuation process. *International Journal of Family Process*, **2**, 47–56.

Bienvenu, M.J. (1970). Measurement of marital communication. *Family Coordinator*, **19**, 26–31.

Bochner, A.P. (1983). The functions of human communication in interpersonal bonding. In C.C. Arnold and J.W. Bowers (Eds), *Handbook of rhetorical and communication theory*, pp. 544–621. Boston, MA: Allyn and Bacon.

Bradbury, T.N. and Fincham, F.D. (in press). Assessing spontaneous attributions in marriage. *Journal of Social and Clinical Psychology*.

Burgraff, C. and Sillars, A. (1987). A critical examination of sex differences in marital communication. *Communication Monographs*, **54**, 276–294.

Burke, R.J., Weir, T., and Harrison, D. (1976). Disclosure of problems and tensions experienced by marital partners. *Psychological Reports*, **38**, 531–542.

Buss, D.M. and Barnes, M. (1986). Preferences in human mate selection. *Journal of Personality and Social Psychology*, **50**, 559–570.

Cappella, J.N. (1987). Interpersonal communication. In C.R. Berger and S.H. Chaffee (Eds), *Handbook of interpersonal communication*, pp. 184–238. Newbury Park, CA: Sage.

Chelune, G.J. (1979). Measuring openness in interpersonal communication. In G.J. Chelune (Ed.), *Self-disclosure*, pp. 1–27. San Francisco, CA: Jossey-Bass.

Chelune, G.J., Waring, E.M., Vosk, B.N., Sultan, F.E., and Ogden, J.K. (1984). Self-disclosure and its relationship to marital intimacy. *Journal of Clinical Psychology*, **40**, 216–219.

Christensen, A. (1988). Dysfunctional interaction patterns in couples. In P. Noller and M.A. Fitzpatrick (Eds), *Perspectives on marital interaction*, pp. 31–52. Clevedon (England): Multilingual Matters.

Davidson, B., Balswick, J., and Halverson, C. (1983). Affective self-disclosure and marital satisfaction. *Journal of Marriage and the Family*, **45**, 93–102.

Dindia, K. and Baxter, L. (1986). Strategies used by marital partners to maintain their relationships. Paper presented at Meeting of the International Communication Association, May 1986, Chicago, IL.

Doherty, W.J. (1981). Cognitive processes in intimate conflict. *American Journal of Family Therapy*, **9**, 1–13.

Duncan, S., Kanki, B.G., Mokros, H., and Fiske, D.W. (1984). Pseudounilaterality, simple-rate variables, and other ills to which interaction research is heir. *Journal of Personality and Social Psychology*, **46**, 1335–1348.

Eidelson, R.J. and Epstein, N. (1982). Cognition and relationship maladjustment. *Journal of Consulting and Clinical Psychology*, **50**, 715–720.

Fincham, F. (1985). Attributions in close relationships. In J.H. Harvey and G. Weary (Eds), *Attribution: Basic issues and applications*, pp. 203–234. New York: Academic Press.

Fincham, F., Beach, S., and Baucom, D.H. (1987). Attribution processes in distressed and nondistressed couples: 4. Self-partner attribution differences. *Journal of Personality and Social Psychology*, **52**, 739–748.

Fincham, F., Beach, S., and Nelson, G. (1987). Attribution processes in distressed and nondistressed couples: 3. Causal and responsibility attributions for spouse behavior. *Cognitive Therapy and Research*, **11**, 71–86.

Fincham, F. and Jaspars, J.M.F. (1980). From man the scientist to man as lawyer, In L. Berkowitz (Ed.), *Advances in experimental social psychology*, Vol. 13, pp. 43–85. New York: Academic Press.

Fincham, F. and O'Leary, K.D. (1983). Causal inferences for spouse behavior in maritally distressed and nondistressed couples. *Journal of Social and Clinical Psychology*, **1**, 42–57.

Fiske, S.T. and Taylor, S. (1984). *Social cognition*. Reading, MA: Addison.

Fitzpatrick, M.A. (1977). A typological approach to communication in relationships. In B. Rubin (Ed.), *Communication yearbook*, No. 1, pp. 263–275. Rutgers: Transaction Press.

Fitzpatrick, M.A. (1984). A typological approach to marital interaction: Recent theory and research. In L. Berkowitz (Ed.), *Advances in experimental social psychology*, Vol. 18, pp. 1–47. Orlando, FL: Academic Press.

Fitzpatrick, M.A. (1987a). The effect of marital schemata on marital communication. Paper presented at Meeting of the International Communication Association, Montreal, Canada.

Fitzpatrick, M.A. (1987b). Marital interaction. In C.R. Berger and S.H. Chaffee (Eds), *Handbook of communication science*, pp. 564–618. Newbury Park, CA: Sage.

Fitzpatrick, M.A. (1987c). Marriage and verbal intimacy. In V. Derlega and J. Berg (Eds), *Self-disclosure: Theory, research, and therapy*, pp. 133–154. New York: Plenum.

Fitzpatrick, M.A. (1987d). Final report on the effect of marital schemata on marital communication. Submitted to NIMH (RO1–MH–40813–01).

Fitzpatrick, M.A. (1988). *Between husbands and wives: Communication in marriage*. Newbury Park, CA: Sage.

Fitzpatrick, M.A. and Bradzinski, D. (1985). All in the family: Communication in kin relationships. In M.L. Knapp and G.R. Miller (Eds), *Handbook of interpersonal communication*, pp. 687–736. Beverly Hills, CA: Sage.

Fitzpatrick, M.A., Bauman, I., and Lindaas, M. (1987). A schematic approach to marital interaction. Paper presented at Meeting of the International Communication Association, Montreal, Canada.

Gilligan, C. (1982). *In a different voice*. Cambridge, MA: Harvard University Press.

Gottman, J.M. (1979). *Marital interaction: Experimental investigations*. New York: Academic Press.

Gottman, J.M. (1982). Temporal form. *Journal of Marriage and the Family*, **44**, 943–962

Gottman, J.M. and Levenson, R.W. (1988). The social psychophysiology of marriage. In P. Noller and M.A. Fitzpatrick (Eds), *Perspectives on marital interaction*, pp. 183–201. Clevedon (England): Multilingual Matters.

Gottman, J.M. and Porterfield, A.L. (1981). Communicative competence in the nonverbal behavior of married couples. *Journal of Marriage and the Family*, **43**, 817–824.

Hahlweg, K. and Jacobson, N.S. (1984). *Marital interaction: Analysis and modification*. New York: Guilford Press.

Haley, J. (1962). Family experiments. *Family Process*, **1**, 265–293.

Hastie, R. (1981). Schematic principles in human memory. In E. Higgins, C. Herman, and M. Zanna (Eds), *Social cognition*, pp. 155–177. Hillsdale, NJ: Erlbaum.

Hendrick, S.S. (1981). Self disclosure and marital satisfaction. *Journal of Personality and Social Psychology*, **40**, 1150–1159.

Holtzworth-Munroe, A. and Jacobson, N.S. (1985). Causal attributions of married couples: When do they search for causes? What do they conclude when they do? *Journal of Personality and Social Psychology*, **48**, 1398–1412.

Jacobson, N.S. (1984). A component analysis of behavioral marital therapy: The relative effectiveness of behavior exchange and communication/problem-solving training. *Journal of Consulting and Clinical Psychology*, **52**, 295–305.

Jacobson, N.S., Follette, W.L., and McDonald, D.W. (1982). Reactivity to positive and negative behavior in distressed and nondistressed married couples. *Journal of Consulting and Clinical Psychology*, **50**, 706–714.

Jacobson, N.S., McDonald, D.W., Follette, W.C., and Berley, R.A. (1985). Attribution processes in distressed and nondistressed married couples. *Cognitive Therapy and Research*, **9**, 35–50.

Kantor, D. and Lehr, W. (1975). *Inside the family*. New York: Harper and Row.

Katriel, T. and Philipsen, G. (1981). 'What we need is communication': 'Communication' as a cultural category in some American speech. *Communication Monographs*, **48**, 301–318.

Kelly, E.L. and Conley, J.J. (1987). Personality and compatibility: A prospective analysis of marital stability and marital satisfaction. *Journal of Personality and Social Psychology*, **52**, 27–40.

Kerber, L.K., Greeno, C.G., Maccoby, E.E., Luria, Z., Stack, C.B., and Gilligan, C. (1986). 'In a different voice': An interdisciplinary forum. *Signs*, **11**, 304–333.

Lamb, M., Suomi, S., and Stephenson, G. (1979). *Social interaction analysis*. Madison, WI: University of Wisconsin Press.

Lasch, C. (1977). *Haven in a heartless world*. New York: Basic.

Lederer, W.J. and Jackson, D.D. (1968). *The mirages of marriage*. New York: Norton.

Levenson, R.W. and Gottman, J.M. (1983). Marital interaction: Physiological linkage and affective exchange. *Journal of Personality and Social Psychology*, **45**, 587–597.

Levenson, R.W. and Gottman, J.M. (1985). Physiological and affective predictors of changes in marital satisfaction. *Journal of Personality and Social Psychology*, **49**, 85–94.

Levinger, G. and Senn, D.J. (1967). Disclosure of feelings in marriage. *Merrill-Palmer Quarterly*, **13**, 237–249.

Lewis, R.A. and Spanier, G. (1979). Theorizing about the quality and the stability of marriage. In W.R. Burr, R. Hill, F.I. Nye, and I.L. Reiss (Eds), *Contemporary theories about the family*, Vol. 1, pp. 268–294. New York: Free Press.

Margolin, G. and Wampold, B.E. (1981). Sequential analysis of conflict and accord in distressed and nondistressed marital partners. *Journal of Consulting and Clinical Psychology*, **49**, 554–567.

Markus, H. (1977). Self schemata and processing information about the self. *Journal of Personality and Social Psychology*, **35**, 63–78.

Navran, L. (1967). Communication and adjustment in marriage. *Family Process*, **6**, 173–184.

Neisser, U. (1967). *Cognitive psychology*. New York: Appleton Press.

Newman, H. (1981). Communication within ongoing intimate relationships: An attributional perspective. *Personality and Social Psychology Bulletin*, **7**, 59–70.

Noller, P. (1984). *Nonverbal communication and marital interaction*. New York: Pergamon.

Noller, P. and Fitzpatrick, M.A. (1987). Nonverbal communication accuracy in couple types. Paper presented at the Third International Conference on Social Psychology and Language, July 1987, Bristol, England.

Noller, P. and Fitzpatrick, M.A. (1988). *Perspectives on marital interaction*. Clevedon (England): Multilingual Matters.

Noller, P. and Gallois, C. (1988). Understanding and misunderstanding in marriage: Sex and marital adjustment differences in structures and free interaction. In P. Noller and M.A. Fitzpatrick (Eds), *Perspectives on marital interaction*, pp. 53–76. Clevedon (England): Multilingual Matters.

Orvis, B.B., Kelley, H.H., and Butler, D. (1976). Attributional conflict in young couples. In J.H. Harvey, W.J. Ickes, and R.E. Kidd (Eds), *New directions in attribution research*, Vol. 1, pp. 353–386. Hillsdale, NJ: Erlbaum.

Penman, R. (1980). *Communication processes and relationships*. New York: Academic Press.

Raush, H.L., Barry, W.A., Hertel, R.K., and Swain, M.A. (1974). *Communication, conflict, and marriage*. San Francisco, CA: Jossey-Bass.

Sabatelli, R.M., Buck, R., and Dreyer, A. (1982). Nonverbal communication accuracy in married couples: Relationship to marital complaints. *Journal of Personality and Social Psychology*, **43**, 1088–1097.

Schaap, C. (1982). *Communication and adjustment*. Lisse (Neth.): Swets and Zeitlinger.

Schaap, C., Buunk, B., and Kerkstra, A. (1988). Marital conflict resolution. In P. Noller and M.A. Fitzpatrick (Eds), *Perspectives on marital interaction*, pp. 203–244. Clevedon (England): Multilingual Matters.

Sillars, A., Pike, G.R., Jones, T.S., and Murphy, M.A. (1984). Communication and understanding in marriage. *Human Communication Research*, **10**, 317–350.

Sillars, A., Pike, G.R., Jones, T.S., and Redmon, K. (1983). Communication and conflict in marriage: One style is not satisfying to all. In R. Bostrom (Ed.), *Communication yearbook*, No. 7, pp. 414–431. Beverly Hills, CA: Sage.

Sillars, A.L., Weisberg, J., Burgraff, C.S., and Wilson, E.A. (1987). Content themes in marital conversations. *Human Communication Research*, **13**, 495–528.

Ting-Toomey, S. (1983). An analysis of verbal communication patterns in high and low marital adjustment groups. *Human Communication Research*, **9**, 306–319.

Watzlawick, P., Beavin, J.H., and Jackson, D.D. (1967). *Pragmatics of human communication*. New York: Norton.

Weiss, R.L. (1981). The new kid on the block: Behavioral systems approach. In E.E. Filsinger and R.A. Lewis (Eds), *Assessing marriage: New behavioral approaches*, pp. 22–37. Beverly Hills, CA: Sage.

Witteman, H. and Fitzpatrick, M.A. (1986). Compliance-gaining in marital interaction: Power bases, power processes, and outcomes. *Communication Monographs*, **53**, 130–143.

22

Language and Later Life

NIKOLAS COUPLAND AND JUSTINE COUPLAND

Centre for Applied English Language Studies, University of Wales College of Cardiff, UK

The language sciences have generally been slow to contribute to our understanding of social ageing. There is a dawning recognition (which has come later to the UK than to the USA) that academic research, like the broader community, must revise its assumptions and upgrade its knowledge about a rapidly ageing population (Tinker, 1984). But, as yet, the elderly do not feature at all consistently as a visible social group within the paradigms of the social psychology of language or sociolinguistics as a whole. When language research has considered age and human development, this has almost uniquely been taken to mean *child* language development. Several important overviews of communication and ageing have appeared, in many cases from clinical psychological and psycholinguistic traditions (e.g. Bayles and Kaszniak, 1987; Maxim and Thompson, forthcoming; Obler and Albert, 1980; Wilder and Weinstein, 1984; for more interdisciplinary perspectives, see also Giles and Ryan, 1986; Oyer and Oyer, 1976). But despite these efforts, the research we review in this chapter is incipient and partial in several respects. At the same time, it should be seen as raising issues that *no other* sociolinguistic domain can afford to ignore, since a lifespan perspective will inevitably both inform and challenge established findings in the study of virtually any context of language use. It will probably prove to be the case that generalizations made in other research areas are skewed by under-representing elderly populations' behaviours, beliefs, orientations and assessments.

In our review, we shall mainly be concerned to identify general orientations to language and later life that have emerged or are emerging. In doing this, we hope to

Handbook of Language and Social Psychology
Edited by H. Giles and W.P. Robinson. © 1990 John Wiley & Sons Ltd

contribute to a debate about what are the appropriate priorities for a 'gerontological sociolinguistics' which has yet to develop as a coherent subdiscipline. Although there is a very valuable fund of existing empirical work to draw upon, we believe there is a need to consider theoretical and ideological foundations before significant, concerted progress can be made. In particular, we shall overview existing work in relation to two key concepts – *diachrony* (the perspective on change-over-time) and *decrement* (progressive decline in health or competence). These are concepts which, we claim, inevitably bear upon gerontological sociolinguistic concerns, but which can be invoked in several, crucially different, particular ways.

We argue that a whole tradition of existing work, the 'deficit tradition', is in danger of adopting a stereotypically based set of assumptions about how diachrony and decrement 'naturally' relate to ageing as a process, and so to what is researchable and knowable about elderly populations. A second and converse orientation, which we discuss under the heading for the 'anti-ageist tradition', finds its place articulating a more liberal ideology, and *resistance* to societal assumptions about 'natural' decline-with-years – assumptions that are seen as pernicious and ill-founded. Reviews of particular studies of language and later life in these two traditions make up the body of our chapter, though a third and final section introduces a more integrated and better-contextualized approach, which can resolve much of the theoretical tension between the other two. In the preliminary section that follows, we give a more detailed account of orientations to diachrony and decrement in research on language and ageing.

INVOKING DIACHRONY AND DECREMENT

The study of linguistic and communicative impairment is in some ways a clear candidate for inclusion under the rubric 'language and later life'. Specific pathologies and syndromes of impairment are probabilistically associated with later life (Beasley and Davis, 1981), such as Alzheimer's (Emery and Emery, 1983), and Parkinson's disease, Huntington's chorea, and stroke-related aphasias (see Cummings, Benson, Hill, and Read, 1985). However, from another perspective, which is our own in this chapter, it is at least as important to establish 'the normal elderly' as a population open to language/communication research, and to resist the assumption that the normal linguistic condition of late ageing is predictably and progressively decremental; it clearly is not. Boone, Bayles, and Koopmann (1982) are adamant that 'the typical person over age 65 communicates very well. Age *per se* is not a deterrent to good communication' (p. 313). It can reasonably be argued that studies of impairment are necessary to establish the boundaries of some specific dimensions of normal language and communication in ageing, though this has been virtually the only goal underlying existing research into normal ageing. Yet, as we have argued elsewhere (see N. Coupland, Coupland, Giles, and Henwood, 1988a), there is an obligation upon *socially* grounded research to redress the balance away from the cognitive and psycholinguistic concerns that have come to dominate the literature. It is ultimately inadequate to characterize the linguistic dimension of normal social ageing as the avoidance of decremental pathologies.

Diachrony

Concern with change-over-time also appears to surface 'naturally', though we believe problematically, in the gerontological context, if only because the elderly's most obvious defining characteristic is their occupation of a certain band of the lifespan. In fact, the static concern with the elderly as a social group is a clear theoretical alternative to the dynamic concern with age*ing* as process. The issue is not merely terminological. There are important implications of old age being researched *in relation to* earlier and later time periods, not least that such treatments impose an essentially transitional character upon the condition of old age. Even where the focus of interest is apparently a more stable phenomenon – a social group, 'the elderly' – some diachronic focus can be implicit. Research questions are often generated relating to the group's language or communication behaviour, but framed by past or projectable changes in those behaviours. And since change, for the old, is represented in stereotyped formulations as ineluctable progress towards incapacity and eventually death, the key word is not generally development but in fact decrement.

Therefore, our own starting point is that diachrony and the associated expectation of decremental change are intrinsic to the mythology of ageing *and* to the ideologies and common practices of linguistic research into normal ageing. Left unchallenged, these assumptions systematically misrepresent later life conditions and experiences. A persistent perspective on decrement unnaturally constrains the questions that linguists and psychologists will ask about elderly language and communication, predisposing a deficit formulation. On the other hand, it seems to us, there is also a naivety in the converse position which explicitly or implicitly *denies* the salience of diachrony and decrement as elements of the experience of ageing. Some recent research that we shall review at the end of the chapter suggests that the social identities of many elderly people are bound up with precisely these parameters, influencing their conversational goals and styles. By these means, perhaps ironically, diachrony and decrement come to be crucial factors in the interpretation of elderly and intergenerational talk; but as themes in its constitution, and not as premises for its interpretation.

THE DEFICIT PARADIGM

Language and communication in normal ageing are most often characterized through an appraisal of *residual competence*, with research focusing on precisely those dimensions of language use which are known potentially to show or are suspected of showing decrement at some stage. *Normal* ageing may as a result be represented through evidence of a group's non-impaired competence in some respect or their achieving a higher score on some index than that obtained by a group diagnosed to be impaired. Sometimes, the normal elderly will themselves be shown to have declined on some psycholinguistic measure in relation to a younger group. Very many facets of speech production, linguistic knowledge and processing have been investigated from these perspectives over more than three decades, producing complex and sometimes inconsistent results. Only a small number of representative studies will be cited here.

A broad paradigm of research has characterized the acoustic and articulatory characteristics of the ageing voice. Studies have shown that elderly voices are regularly discriminable from younger voices. Ptacek and Sander (1966), for instance, showed that people over 65 and under 35 could be identified even on the basis of single prolonged vowels. Ramig (1983) found that physiological ageing is associated with increased vowel spectral noise, stemming from degenerative changes in the larynx. Clearly, then, voice quality, just like pitch perturbation and pitch itself (see below), has the potential to act as a social marker of elderly speech (see Helfrich, 1979, for a general review). On the issue of receptive processing of language, Obler, Nicholas, Albert, and Woodward (1985) report a linear decline by age (across decades from 30s to 70s) in scores on a sentence comprehension/completion task. In Feier and Gerstman's (1980) study, declining scores were again found among people in their 60s and 70s (and not in younger groups) on a task requiring comprehension and enactment of complex sentences. Goodglass and Kaplan (1972) found an age effect on sentence- and paragraph-reading tasks, but none on an auditory comprehension subtest. In an influential series of studies of discourse comprehension and recall, Ulatowska and colleagues (Ulatowska, Cannito, Hayashi, and Fleming, 1985; Ulatowska, Hayashi, Cannito, and Fleming, 1986) found significant differences between young-old (64 to 76) and old-old (77+) subjects on test items requiring inferencing from the original text. Gordon and Clark (1974) similarly found lower levels of information recall among older subjects.

In terms of sentence production, Obler (1980) found older speakers (50 to 80) to use more elaborate and indefinite terms than younger speakers. A recent study by Gold, Andres, Arbuckle, and Schwartzman (1988) considers 'off-target verbosity' among elderly speakers, a phenomenon they recognize when speech 'quickly becomes a prolonged series of loosely associated recollections increasingly remote from, relatively unconstrained by, and irrelevant to the present external contextual stimuli' (p. 27). The authors find no direct association between such talk and age itself, but suggest that it 'becomes manifest in older people who are extroverted, socially active, not concerned with others' impressions of them, undergoing more stress and experiencing declining performance in nonverbal cognitive functioning' (p. 32). While Gold et al. are not able to commit themselves to a single interpretation of their findings, they consider cognitive impairment once again as a candidate explanation for behavioural characteristics of elderly talk. From a series of formal tests of comprehension and manipulation of items (including many varying in syntactic complexity), Emery (1986) reports no significant age differences, either at phonological or at lexical levels, except in speed of response. But, in morphological respects and on every measure of syntactic function, she finds repeated, significantly lower levels of performance among the normal elderly (aged 75 to 93) than among the pre-middle-aged (30 to 42). Kynette and Kemper (1986) likewise report that subjects in their 70s and 80s produced more syntactic errors and used less complex syntactic structures (which impose lower memory demands) in interview responses than people in their 50s and 60s. Kemper (1986) also reports that elderly adults (70 to 89) were less able to imitate complex syntactic constructions than young adults (30 to 49). Nebes and Andrews-Kulis (1976), on the other hand, report no decremental age effects in subjects' construction of grammatical strings.

Bayles and Kaszniak's (1987) balanced conclusion, after a thorough review of a good deal of the available experimental psycholinguistic research on ageing, is that:

> The study of possible age effects on the ability to communicate is extremely demanding because effects, when present, are generally subtle, and most tasks are influenced by the subject's intelligence, education, life history, motivation, sensory integrity, mental status, and vigor. Few researchers have been able to control all of these variables in a convincing way. (Bayles and Kaszniak, 1987, p. 152)

The authors single out comprehension and inferencing as the areas of most clearly documented differential performance between young and old: 'Age effects are most obvious when information to be comprehended is new, complex, and implied and the time allowed for processing is short' (p. 153). But they suggest that in terms of linguistic production evidence is more difficult to interpret, but again suggestive of decline with age, though not necessarily through deterioration of the lexicon. Contra the findings of Emery (1986), Bayles and Kaszniak (1987) conclude that 'An individual's knowledge of grammar is well preserved across the life span' (p. 153).

As a whole, the deficit paradigm of later-life research sustains a confused concept of 'normality'. In most studies, the 'normal' elderly (so labelled according to criteria of general health, and particularly absence of specific sensory problems) are demonstrated to be performing 'abnormally' in some linguistic/communicative respect if the norm is defined by young adult performance. Emery (1986) thus concludes from her study that 'diminished linguistic processing appears to be a concomitant of normal aging' (p. 60). Reminiscent of early and problematic studies in the language and social class domain (see Chapter 16, by Haslett), the paradigm throws up results that are highly difficult to interpret in any socially sensitive frame. There is generally no consideration of attitudinal or motivational factors which might mediate differential performances (why do elderly people respond more slowly in some experimental conditions?); or of contextual factors (in what range of circumstances do elderly people use less complex syntax or underachieve on tests of receptive ability?); or of real-life implications (do measured differences have any contrastive or 'emic' significance (see Robinson, 1979) outside of the test situation?); or of semiotic impact (which elderly characteristics in fact connote elderliness, to whom, and with what evaluative weighting?).

The studies in question invoke a decrement continuum as their implicit rationale. Differential linguistic performance does demonstrably exist, selectively, and there is no suggestion that the investigation of linguistic (under)performance during normal ageing is without interest. Our point is that research, in all of these instances, aligns to the expectation of decrement. The research is seen to fit the decrement model, and therefore legitimizes it. According to Levin and Levin (1980), this ideological slant pervades gerontological research as a whole. They argue that 'The literature in gerontology is shot through both with the assumption of decline with age and, perhaps partly as a result of this assumption, with the findings of physical, psychological and sociological deterioration in ageing individuals' (p. 2). The deficit paradigm of ageing research needs, we suggest, to contextualize its findings more thoroughly, and, as part of this process, to look reflexively at the ideological climate in which it operates.

A more elaborate conceptualization of deficit in later life is the 'inverted-U' model of elderly decrement, implying that elderly behaviours (linguistic or other) are in some specific respects not only moving towards lower levels of competence but moving *back* to the levels and types of behaviour associated with the *early* years of life. The model feeds off the more general mythological association of the old with children in our society – the view of old age as a 'second childhood'. Realizations of this myth include visual images of the old as physically smaller and stooping (for example, as portrayed on UK road-signs near residential homes for the old); and the conventional grouping of the elderly with children as recipients of low-cost coach and rail fares, and cheaper admission to cinemas, theatres, etc. Myths of the 'success' and 'naturalness' of interaction between the elderly and children perhaps enter the same category.

In the language domain, explicit claims about regression in later life are sometimes made. Emery (1986) concludes that there is:

> a direct relationship between language deficits and age, a direct relationship between language deficits and linguistic complexity, and what appears to be the concomitant inverse relationship between sequence in language deterioration and sequence in [child] language development, i.e. the more complex the linguistic form, the later the development of that form . . . , the quicker the deterioration of that form. (Emery, 1986, p. 57)

Even though this same claim has been discredited in aphasia research and has in any case been shown to have no practical value for therapists (Lesser, 1978), we can speculate that the elderly-as-child myth recurs in other dimensions of ageing research. Several characteristics of elderly speech production beyond syntactic complexity can, sometimes with more creativity than theoretical justification, be taken to fit the inverted-U. The higher vocal pitch and lower speech rate reported for elderly males in some studies (e.g. Hollien and Shipp, 1972; Mysak, 1959) might be viewable as regressive and stereotypically associated with young children's speech. Egocentricity (one interpretation of Gold *et al*'s (1988) verbosity data) is again stereotyped as both an elderly and child characteristic, and so on.

As researchers, we are not immune from societal stereotypes and myths. Miller (1987) voices a concern about 'the degree to which our society imputes social and moral meanings [e.g. of rolelessness] even to unconditionally legitimate behaviors in the aging role [e.g. retirement]' (p. 146). Rolelessness (see Bengston, 1973; Rosnow, 1973) and disengagement (Cumming and Henry, 1961) have in fact, controversially, been elevated to the level of explanatory theories of social ageing (see also, for a review, J. Coupland, Coupland, Giles, and Henwood, in press), and it is easy to see the communicative deficit tradition deriving general support from these models of the ageing experience. Deficit research seems to have served to substantiate cultural prejudices against the elderly through its selective designs and pervasive concern with linguistic decrement. The fact that only modest and sporadic evidence of suppressed performance levels has been produced does not seem to have challenged the work's ideological assumptions and its concern with elderly linguistic deficit. Yet, where more positively construed elderly communicative characteristics have been looked for via experimental hypotheses, elderly subjects have on occasions been shown to 'outperform' young communicators. Smith, Reinheimer, and Gabbard-Alley (1981) found that elderly women (mean age 70.8) coped better with the demands of crowded and close communication environments than young women (mean age 20.4). Overall, it seems appropriate to remind ourselves of 'the pitfalls of the health/wholeness archetype' (Guggenbuhl-Craig, 1980, p. 21), the blinkered concern with perfect competence and with individuals' deviations from it to which Western society is arguably prone. If we can escape the dominance of these concerns, then we can begin to explore the diverse processes through which language and communication impinge upon the experience of old age and on society's orientation to the old.

THE ANTI-AGEISM PARADIGM

In social gerontology, as in many approaches to sex/gender, class and race across the social sciences, a coherent orientation has developed, spanning very different specific issues and methodologies, which assumes its research populations are generally disenfranchised and undervalued. There is no shortage of general statements to this effect in relation to the elderly. Tyler (1986), for example, argues that ageism is structurally integrated into contemporary British society. Levin and Levin (1980) consider diverse forms and origins of societal ageism. Among general factors in the construction of an ageist climate, they document hostility by groups concerned with their own status and self-esteem towards minorities they perceive as weak, powerless or inferior, and economic forces (competition between young and old over scarce resources and jobs). Levin and Levin also recognize a specific condition they term 'gerontophobia': fear of one's own ageing, of the elderly and of association with death (see also Bunzel, 1972). Butler (1969) similarly defines ageism as 'a deep-seated uneasiness on the part of the young and middle-aged – a personal revulsion to and distaste for growing older' (p. 243). A critical manifestation of gerontophobia is to be found in the caring professions, where, according to Norman (1987), 'The poor image of old age inevitably rubs off on those who are working in this field. Work with old people is not a prestigious occupation and there is a vicious circle in that jobs with low prestige tend to attract unambitious or less-skilled workers' (p. 9). For Levin and Levin, ageism is manifest in a propensity to 'blame the [elderly] victim', to blame 'biology or the ravages of time' for the states and conditions of old age, rather than focus on 'the *social* forces that make old age a difficult, even dreaded, stage of life' (p. 35).

Some recent research has sought to demonstrate the ways in which language functions in the reproduction of ageist attitudes. Covey (1988) traces the changing meanings of terms relating to old age. The etymology of the word 'old' itself, for example, associates it with the meaning 'to nourish', and it has long carried connotations of experience, skill and wisdom. More recently, it has variably been associated with meanings of endearment ('old friend', 'Old Bright'), but also conservatism ('old guard'); it has been used in references to the Devil ('Old Harry',

'Old Nick') and very often in derogative terms ('old hag', 'old fogey', 'dirty old man'). Covey claims that 'contemporary older people do not like to use the word *old* in describing themselves or their membership groups' (p. 293), and concludes generally that terminology in this area reflects 'a decline in the status of the elderly and the increased focus on the debilitative effects of aging' (p. 297). Nuessel (1984) likewise argues that there is a vast lexicon of ageist language in everyday usage, within which most terms are used to describe or refer to the elderly in a pejorative way, or at least carry negative overtones. Instances relating to females (often prefixed by 'old') include: 'biddy', 'crone', 'bag' and 'battleaxe'; and referring to males: 'gaffer' and 'geezer'. Attributives often used to describe the elderly show the same process of pejoration: 'cantankerous', 'crotchety', 'fussy', 'garrulous', 'grumpy', 'rambling' and 'wrinkly'. Studying elderly labels within an experimental paradigm, Barbato and Feezel (1987) asked groups of people in three different age categories for their evaluations of the connotative meanings of ten words referring to an older person. Some terms (including 'mature American', 'senior citizen' and 'retired person') were positively rated on the scales 'active', 'strong', 'good', 'progressive' and 'happy'. On the other hand, 'aged', 'elderly' and nouns using 'old' were more negatively evaluated. Interestingly, few between-generation evaluative differences were found.

There is much scope for further research, both observational and controlled/ evaluative, on the connotative content of age-related vocabulary. Key requirements will be to distinguish terms of reference (ingroup and outgroup) from terms of address, and to delimit the contextual scope of studies, geared to producing better-founded and more particular statements of the distribution both of terms in everyday usage and of the evaluative currency of particular expressions. Crucially, too, the *discursive contexts* of the use of these terms will be a major factor in interpreting their sociopsychological significance (see below). Oyer and Oyer's (1976) expressed hope of making vocabulary relating to the elderly 'more accurate and complete' and so of reducing or eliminating ageism from language seems to underestimate the durability of established usage.

Talk to the elderly has been the subject of some of the most sustained research to date, mostly driven by concern for what is, in context, the proper treatment of elderly people as conversational recipients (see Anderson and Hinckley (unpublished) for a recent overview of research on speech-style modifications with the elderly). Ashburn and Gordon (1981) compared specific formal and functional characteristics of caregivers' and volunteers' speech among themselves and to elderly residents in a nursing home. They found that more questions and repetitions were used by staff and volunteers in speaking to elderly residents than were used among their peers, and that staff used more questions to non-alert than to alert residents. Rubin and Brown (1975) found that students used significantly shorter utterances, and hence arguably simpler syntax, to explain the rules of a game to older adults (whom they assessed to have lower intellectual abilities) than they did to young adults. Anderson and Hinckley (unpublished) rightly point out the need for more contextual sensitivity in work of this sort, too, though it is also true that contrastive quantitative designs will obscure the dynamics of specific contexts. For instance, Greene, Adelman, Charon, and Hoffman (1986) found no differences in the frequencies of questions, compliments or negative remarks made by physicians to older (over 65) and younger (under 45) patients in medical interviews. *But* the authors' more qualitative assessments led them to conclude that 'it was more difficult for elderly patients than for young patients to get their agendas addressed'; and also that 'physicians were less respectful, less patient, less engaged and less egalitarian with their old than with their young patients' (p. 121). The authors take these differences of approach by physicians as evidence of ageist professional practices in medical encounters (see Chapter 25, by Hinkley, Craig, and Anderson).

The focus of research by Caporael and colleagues (Caporael, 1981; Caporael and Culbertson, 1986; Caporael, Lucaszewski, and Culbertson, 1983; Culbertson and Caporael, 1983) has been the use of 'secondary baby-talk' (BT) by caregivers in speaking to the institutionalized elderly. In the 1981 study, BT (defined as a specific set of prosodic configurations including high and variable pitch) was found to be frequent in caregivers' talk to residents (in up to 20% of such talk), and to be indistinguishable when content-filtered from primary BT (i.e. talk actually addressed to children). As Caporael's term shows, the research aligns itself at a general level with other sociolinguistic traditions investigating simplified addressee-registers – not only BT (or 'motherese'; see Snow and Ferguson, 1977), but also 'foreigner talk' (Ferguson, 1981). While overlaps in manifest language and communication styles to these diverse groups are of course interesting, and while there might be implications in these similarities for a universal theory of linguistic complexity/simplification, each demographic context subsumes its own unique clusters of considerations of social motivation, evaluation and consequence. For example, Brown (1977) considers a possible pedagogic intent behind using simplified registers to children; descriptively similar styles to non-native speakers may conceivably be intended to *suppress* linguistic and cultural integration (Valdman, 1981); simplified talk to the visually handicapped may be demeaning because it overgeneralizes from a particular sensory handicap (N. Coupland, Giles, and Benn, 1986). An approach that glosses 'talk to the elderly' as one of a family of speech registers will inevitably obscure key sociopsychological processes. Indeed, Caporael and colleagues' research (to which we return below) clearly demonstrates the value of probing the interdependence of linguistic and sociopsychological factors in a very *precisely* contextualized, multilevel analysis.

Research in the quantitative social evaluative paradigm has also considered age-discriminatory responses to vocal stimuli. Stewart and Ryan (1982), for example, found that younger adults can be rated more positively than older adults in competence-stressing situations (see also Rubin and Brown, 1975). Research findings have not been entirely consistent. Crockett, Press, and Osterkamp (1979) found relatively favourable reactions to older speakers, and attributed the finding to the effects of judges' negative stereotypical expectations of elderly speakers being disconfirmed. In Ryan and Johnston's (1987) study, the variable 'effective message' versus 'ineffective message' was the only significant factor for competence ratings across younger and older speakers, with no main effects emerging for age itself. Giles, Coupland, Henwood, and Coupland (in press) again found that, in a matched-guise design, varying speech rate was a more potent variable than either accent (standard versus non-standard) or age (older versus younger speaking guise). There was also some evidence, though, that an elderly voice combined with a non-standard accent and a low speaking rate produced very high ratings of perceived 'vulnerability' (see also Chapter 19, by Bradac). In an open-ended phase of the investigation, respondents invoked consolidated age- and class-stereotypes to rationalize the evaluative decisions they had made. While the non-standard speaking guises called up images of a homely, provincial speaker, the elderly vocal guises were associated with incompetence, forgetfulness and disaffection.

Stereotypes have been shown to intervene not only in abstract evaluative processes but also in behavioural choices, to the detriment of the elderly. Carver and de la Garza (1984) demonstrated that, following a supposed road accident, further information was requested from younger and older drivers in stereotype-consistent ways. Drivers labelled 'elderly' were asked to supply information to do with their physical, mental and sensory adequacies; 'young' drivers tended to be asked whether they had been speeding or had drunk alcohol. In an extension study, Franklyn-Stokes, Harriman, Giles, and Coupland (1988) found similar patterns of differential questioning, though distributed incrementally across ages 22, 54, 64, 74 and 84 years (the ages presented for the addressee). Health and physical condition were increasingly considered relevant to subsequent questioning as presented age increased. To this extent, information-seeking can be seen to be ageist across the adult lifespan.

Research as a whole in what we have been considering the anti-ageism paradigm has demonstrated highly diverse associations between language and generalized negative societal beliefs about elderly people. Cues to the elderly identity of speakers have been shown to result in downgraded evaluations of individuals' attributed competence and in discriminatory consequent behaviours. We have considered sporadic claims that even the language system itself might have come to reify society's ageist assumptions in its lexicon. There is growing evidence of elderly groups being spoken to in characteristic styles, and some suggestion that these styles can be unwarranted and demeaning. In medical encounters, age-differentiated patterns of patient management could have the most profound implications for the success of health-care delivery (Kreps, 1986). It is not surprising that a major current growth area in social gerontology (beyond the immediate linguistic scope of this chapter) is the impact of close relationships (Rook and Pietromonaco, 1987) and social support processes (see Krause, 1986) as buffers against stress in the promotion of elderly health and wellbeing. There is an urgent need for specifically linguistic research to contribute to our understanding of the communication/health/ageing complex (see Giles, Coupland, and Wiemann, 1990).

ELDERLY DISCOURSE: TOWARDS AN INTEGRATIVE PERSPECTIVE

Gerontological sociolinguistics can find a useful basis in the wide-ranging studies we have reviewed in previous sections. On the other hand, many of these studies have worked within laboratory confines and most have addressed the fundamental theme of language and social ageing in a fragmented and piecemeal fashion. Much existing work is arguably reminiscent of the early eras in other sociolinguistic domains where a variety of contrastive, decontextualized, non-interactional designs were dominant. There has been little evidence as yet of integrated theoretical models of communication in ageing which might draw together attitudinal, evaluative and behavioural observations and relate them to relational processes that are operative in specific contexts.

But Caporael and colleagues have shown the complexity of issues surrounding the use of secondary BT styles of speech with institutionalized elderly people. Even within one physical setting, goals, attributions and evaluations of sociolinguistic styles can be highly differentiated. The Caporael *et al.* (1983) study found that caregivers predicted that residents with low functional ability would like to be spoken to with BT, and felt that non-BT speech would be ineffective for interacting with them. Also, it emerges that BT is indeed variously evaluated as demeaning and nurturing by different categories of institutionalized elderly people. Dependent elderly people were more likely to hear BT as nurturing, and prosodically-defined BT was also found to be associated with a high frequency of 'encouraging comments'. Other dimensions of 'elderspeak' also may be facilitative in some instances. Cohen and Faulkner (1986), for example, report positive effects for speech styles with exaggerated primary word stress on elderly recipients' comprehension and recall. A recent study of our own (N. Coupland, Grainger, and Coupland, 1988c) suggests that nurses' use of politeness strategies (see Chapter 10, by Tracy) to elderly residents in a long-stay home needs to be interpreted in terms of institutional roles as much as interpersonal relations. Findings such as these mean that a central case of the anti-ageist paradigm, where negative stereotypes of ageing are taken to constrain communicative choices to the detriment of elderly recipients, needs to be invoked with caution in particular settings.

As contextual concerns come to the fore, it is to be hoped that research methods will increasingly embrace discourse analytic methods. Discourse analysis can and should trigger far more than a methodological shift in gerontological studies, however, for example in stressing the need for a fully interactive perspective. Elsewhere (N. Coupland *et al.*, 1988a), we have attempted to draw up an initial taxonomy of intergenerational strategies of talk that can be elaborated upon in future empirical work. Working within the theoretical compass of speech-accommodation theory (see Giles, Mulac, Bradac, and Johnson, 1987), we list particular constellations of 'over-accommodative' and 'under-accommodative' talk which may lie at the heart of intergenerational conflicts and problems. Patterns of demeaning, deindividuating talk to the elderly are represented as categories of over-accommodation, talk which transcends perceptually ideal levels of interpersonal adaptation. Under-accommodation to the elderly may on the other hand take the form of excessively regulative talk. Elderly styles can of course in themselves be problematical for younger conversationalists, possibly through diverse forms of elderly under-accommodating to the young's conversational and other needs. Strategies here would include over-assertiveness, or highly self-disclosive or self-deprecatory talk.

The detailed analysis of these and related discourse processes in intergenerational talk is in its infancy, though there have been some significant recent advances. In a series of studies, Boden and Bielby (1983, 1986) have shown that talk about the past frequently functions among peer-elderly pairs as a topic resource which informs talk about current states and circumstances. The essence of their case is that 'among old people there is a broad recalling of the past in the context of the present which achieves for them a shared sense of meaning: this feature of talk is far less salient amongst young adults' (1983, p. 308). Kemper's (in press) longitudinal analysis of written diaries again shows the importance that personal historical narratives have for elderly diary-writers. In fact, prevalence of personal narratives and references to death emerges as an important diagnostic feature of the older writers' diaries. Likewise, Taylor (1987) charts a dimension of elderly identity portrayal in talk through alignment to ill-health and death – the 'production of frailty' in discourse.

Previous work of our own (see J. Coupland, Coupland, Giles, and Wiemann, 1988; N. Coupland, Coupland, Giles, Henwood, and Wiemann, 1988b) has addressed overlapping themes. In analyses of videotaped interactions between women aged 70 to 87 and women in their 30s, we have found high frequencies of 'painful' self-disclosure (PSD) by elderly speakers, both among their peers and intergenerationally, accounting for approximately 16% of talk-time in each context (see Chapter 9, by Holtgraves). Painful self-disclosure designates the revelation of a cluster of categories of personal and often intimate information on ill-health, bereavement, immobility, loneliness and so on. Since it is in fact the ill-health category that dominates distributionally, discussion of health-related problems offers a major resource for the encoding of age-identity in the data, in line with the independent findings of Kemper (in press) and Taylor (1987) above. Very significantly, though, our own data show that the younger women in the study also play a significant part in the production and sustaining of PSD talk from older interlocutors. They occasionally elicit 'personal' painful information quite directly, and very often support the development of PSD sequences through further questioning and back-channel responses. Our conclusion from this series of studies is thus that PSD represents an interactional ritual available to elderly–young interaction with anticipated contents, roles and management practices which draws upon and perpetuates generational stereotypes (see N. Coupland, Henwood, Coupland, and Giles, in press).

At this point in our general argument, then, there is an irony. We have argued that theory-driven explorations of elderly language are often unduly narrow in being limited to considerations of diachrony and decrement. Now, in several data-driven, discourse analytic investigations into elderly and intergenerational communication, diachrony and decrement have been shown to underpin some of the most distinctive observable characteristics of talk, and to serve as important *resources* for speakers and hearers. When research has focused on the contents and processes of elderly talk, elderly speakers have been shown to manage temporal frames in characteristic ways and to topicalize their own ill-health and decrement. Of course, there is no contradiction in this. The discourse analytic approach, perhaps above all, invites an analysis of how social actors make sense of their social circumstances, and not least of *themselves*, through communicative practices. It is for these reasons that discourse theorists over a considerable period (see Berger and Luckmann, 1967; Potter, 1988) have resisted deterministic assumptions about the constitution of social categories and their 'effects' upon linguistic performance. In the gerontological sphere, as West and Zimmerman (1985) have recently suggested for gender research (see Chapter

17, by Kramarae), a shift of attention from a demographic category treated as an isolated sociolingistic variable to speech as a mode of action between humans of varying situational identities allows us to develop a much richer understanding of how discourse helps to construct the fabric of social life.

In conclusion, then, perhaps the greatest challenge for studies of language and later life is to explore how themes of ageing, ageism and anti-ageism arise in social discourse where the elderly are participating or in question. For those of us who find it appropriate to see 'elderliness' as a collective subjectivity as much as a physiological endpoint, a primary agenda is to explore the social construction and reproduction of old age through talk. An interactional focus is essential if we assume, as independent research suggests, that elderly people are prone to assimilate society's devalued appraisals of their own elderly group, and so lower their self-esteem (Bengston, Reedy, and Gordon, 1985). A rough template for future work in this tradition may be provided in the informal taxonomy of age-identity marking processes in Table 22.1 (J. Coupland et al., in press).

The processes listed (and perhaps others) together offer elderly speakers, and sometimes their interlocutors, scope to define the age-identity of the older person in more or less direct ways. To take one set of particular instances, we are finding (see N. Coupland, Coupland, and Giles, 1989) that elderly communicators regularly disclose their own age in first-encounter conversations with younger people, and employ age disclosures as a pivot for building positive face or avoiding face-threatening alternatives (see Chapter 10, by Tracy). Reported chronological age (or a variety of surrogate forms such as 'I'm a widow, I've lived here for more than 50 years') also gives rise to a predictable routine of praise- or admiration-giving or highly conventionalized expressions of surprise from interlocutors. Age, moreover, turns out to have a systematic relation to reports of health status, where own health can serve as a relevant precontext for age reporting, and vice versa. Elderly speakers will often offer some variant on the relativist self-appraisal: 'I'm good for my age' (returning us to the ageist decrement perspective). Chronological age thus becomes a token available to be manipulated in the presentation, denial or redefinition of a person's elderliness.

There is growing evidence in these studies of intergenerational discourse to suggest that, for at least some elderly people, locating oneself in relation to past

TABLE 22.1 Age-Identity Marking Processes in Intergenerational Talk

---

Age-categorization processes

The disclosure of chronological age
Own (age-related) category/role reference
Age-identity in relation to health, decrement and death

Temporal framing processes

Adding time-past perspective to current/recent past states/topics
Self-association with the past
Recognizing historical/cultural/social change

From J. Coupland et al. (in press).

experiences, to one's own state of health, to chronological age, and perhaps to projectable future decrement and death, is functional at a profound level. Discourse can enact a negotiative process centring on life position and life prospects, with immediate consequences for morale and psychological wellbeing. Since this perspective credits language with power to influence (see Chapter 13, by Ng) the most profound experiences of ageing, for better or for worse, the discourse tradition has an independent contribution to make to applied gerontological concerns. And there is no shortage of applied settings where the fruits of a better-developed, integrated sociolinguistic account could bear fruit. Social skills training with the elderly is an established practice (e.g. Lopez, 1980) which has tried to remedy some of the reported difficulty that withdrawn elderly residents have with interpersonal relationships (Kuypers and Bengston, 1973). Correspondingly, there have been repeated attempts to develop communication skills of professionals and carers routinely involved with the elderly (see Dreher, 1987; Gravell, 1988; Portnoy, 1985; Wooliscroft, Calhoun, Maxim, and Wolf, 1984; see also J. Coupland, 1989, for a review of two of these treatments). Interchange between these practically grounded, interventionist efforts and sociopsychological and other sociolinguistic work in the future should advance not only our understanding of language-related processes but also our social practices in the gerontological sphere.

ACKNOWLEDGMENT

The research on which this paper is based has been supported by the Economic and Social Research Council, reference number G0022220022.

REFERENCES

Anderson, L.A. and Hinkley, J.J. (unpublished). Speech style modifications with the elderly: A review of findings and implications for practice. University of Michigan.

Ashburn, G. and Gordon, A. (1981). Features of a simplified register in speech to elderly conversationalists. *International Journal of Psycholinguistics*, **8**, 7–31.

Barbato, C.A. and Feezel, J.D. (1987). The language of aging in different age-groups. *Gerontological Society of America*, **27**, 527–531.

Bayles, K.A. and Kaszniak, A.W. (1987). *Communication and cognition in normal aging and dementia*. London: Taylor and Francis.

Beasley, D.S. and Davis, G.A. (Eds) (1981). *Aging: Communication processes and disorders*. New York: Grune and Stratton.

Bengston, V.L. (1973). *The social psychology of aging*. New York: Bobbs-Merrill.

Bengston, V.L., Reedy, M.N., and Gordon, C. (1985). Aging and self-conceptions, personality processes and social contexts. In J.E. Birren and K. Warner Schaie (Eds), *Handbook of psychology and aging*, pp. 544–593. New York: Van Nostrand Reinhold.

Berger, P. and Luckmann, T. (1967). *The social construction of reality*. Harmondsworth (England): Penguin.

Boden, D. and Bielby, D. (1983). The past as resource: A conversational analysis of elderly talk. *Human Development*, **26**, 308–319.

Boden, D. and Bielby, D. (1986). The way it was: Topical organisation in elderly conversation. *Language and Communication*, **6**, 73–89.

Boone, D.R., Bayles, K.A., and Koopmann, C.F., Jr, (1982). Communicative aspects of aging. *Otolaryngologic Clinics of North America*, **15**, 313–327.

Brown, R. (1977). Introduction. In C.E. Snow and C.A. Ferguson (Eds), *Talking to children: Language input and acquisition*. Cambridge: Cambridge University Press.

Bunzel, J.H. (1972). Note on the history of a concept: Gerontophobia. *Gerontologist*, **12**, 116–203.

Butler, R.N. (1969). Age-ism: another form of bigotry. *Gerontologist*, **9**, 243–246.

Caporael, L. (1981). The paralanguage of caregiving: Baby talk to the institutionalized aged. *Journal of Personality and Social Psychology*, **40**, 876–884.

Caporael, L. and Culbertson, G.H. (1986). Verbal response modes of baby talk and other speech at institutions for the aged. *Language and Communication*, **6**, 99–112.

Caporael, L., Lucaszewski, M.P., and Culbertson, G.H. (1983). Secondary babytalk: Judgements by institutionalized elderly and their caregivers. *Journal of Personality and Social Psychology*, **44**, 746–754.

Carver, C.S. and de la Garza, N.H. (1984). Schema-guided information search in stereotyping of the elderly. *Journal of Applied Social Psychology*, **14**, 69–81.

Cohen, G. and Faulkner, D. (1986). Does 'elderspeak' work? The effect of intonation and stress on comprehension and recall of spoken discourse in old age. *Language and Communication*, **6**, 91–98.

Coupland, J. (1989). Review of B.B. Dreher *Communication Skills For Working with Elders*, New York: Springer, 1987; and R. Gravell *Communication Problems in Elderly People: Practical Approaches To Management*, London: Croom Helm, 1988. *Journal of Language and Social Psychology*.

Coupland, J., Coupland, N., Giles, H., and Henwood, K. (in press). Formulating age: The management of age identity in intergenerational talk. *Discourse Processes*.

Coupland, J., Coupland, N., Giles, H., and Wiemann, J. (1988). My life in your hands: Processes of self-disclosure in intergenerational talk. In N. Coupland (Ed.), *Styles of discourse*, pp. 201–253. London: Croom Helm.

Coupland, N., Coupland, J., and Giles, H. (1989). Telling age in later life: Identity and face implications. *Text*.

Coupland, N., Coupland, J., Giles, H., and Henwood, K. (1988a). Accommodating the elderly: Invoking and extending a theory. *Language in Society*, **17**, 1–42.

Coupland, N., Coupland, J., Giles, H., Henwood, K., and Wiemann, J. (1988b). Elderly self-disclosure: Interactional and intergroup issues. *Language and Communication*, **8**, 109–133.

Coupland, N., Giles, H., and Benn, W. (1986). Language, communications and the blind: Research agenda. *Journal of Language and Social Psychology*, **5**, 52–63.

Coupland, N., Grainger, K., and Coupland, J. (1988c). Politeness in context: Intergenerational issues. Review of P. Brown and S.C. Levinson (1987) *Politeness: Some Universals in language usage*. Cambridge: Cambridge University Press. *Language in Society*, **17**, 253–262.

Coupland, N., Henwood, K., Coupland, J., and Giles, H. (in press). Accommodating troubles-talk: The young's management of elderly self-disclosure. In G. McGregor and R. White (Eds), *Reception and response: Hearer creativity and the analysis of spoken and written texts*. London: Croom Helm.

Covey, H.C. (1988). Historical terminology used to represent older people. *Gerontologist*, **28**, 291–297.

Crockett, W.H., Press, A.N., and Osterkamp, M. (1979). The effects of deviations from stereotyped expectations upon attitudes toward older persons. *Journal of Gerontology*, **34**, 368–374.

Culbertson, G.H. and Caporael, L. (1983). Baby talk speech to the elderly: Complexity and content of messages. *Personality and Social Psychology Bulletin*, **9**, 305–312.

Cumming, E. and Henry, W.E. (1961). *Growing old: The process of disengagement*. New York: Basic.

Cummings, J.L., Benson, D.F., Hill, M., and Read, S. (1985). Aphasia in dementia of the Alzheimer type. *Neurology*, **34**, 394–397.

Dreher, B.B. (1987). *Communication skills for working with elders*. New York: Springer.

Emery, O. (1986). Linguistic decrement in normal ageing. *Language and Communication*, **6**, 47–64.

Emery, O. and Emery, P. (1983). Language in senile dementia of the Alzheimer type. *Psychiatric Journal of University of Ottawa*, **8**, 169–178.

Feier, C. and Gerstman, L. (1980). Sentence comprehension abilities throughout the adult life span. *Journal of Gerontology*, **35**, 722–728.

Ferguson, C.A. (1981). 'Foreigner talk' as the name of a simplifed register. *International Journal of the Sociology of Language*, **28**, 9–18.

Franklyn-Stokes, A., Harriman, J., Giles, H., and Coupland, N. (1988). Information seeking across the life span. *Journal of Social Psychology*, **128**, 419–421.

Giles, H., Coupland, N., Henwood, K., and Coupland, J. (in press). The social meaning of RP: an intergenerational perspective. In S. Ramsaran (Ed.), *Studies in the pronunciation of English: A commemorative volume in honour of A.C. Gimson*. London: Croom Helm.

Giles, H., Coupland, N., and Wiemann, J. (Eds) (1990). *Communication, health and the elderly*. Proceedings of Fulbright Colloquium 1988. Manchester: University of Manchester Press.

Giles, H., Mulac, A., Bradac, J., and Johnson, P. (1987). Speech accommodation theory: The first decade and beyond. In M.L. McLaughlin (Ed.), *Communication yearbook*, No. 10, pp. 13–48. Beverly Hills, CA: Sage.

Giles, H. and Ryan, E.B. (Eds) (1986). *Language, communication and the elderly*. Oxford: Pergamon. *Language and communication*, **6**, Nos 1/2.

Gold, D., Andres, D., Arbuckle, T., and Schwartzman, A. (1988). Measurements and correlates of verbosity in elderly people. *Journal of Gerontology: Psychological Sciences*, **43**, 27–33.

Goodglass, H. and Kaplan, E. (1972). *The assessment of aphasia and related disorders*. Philadelphia: Lea and Febiger.

Gordon, S.K. and Clark, W.C. (1974). Application of signal detection theory to prose recall and recognition in elderly and young adults. *Journal of Gerontology*, **29**, 64–72.

Gravell, R. (1988). *Communication problems in elderly people: Practical approaches to management*. London: Croom Helm.

Greene, M.G., Adelman, R., Charon, R., and Hoffman, S. (1986). Ageism in the medical encounter: An exploratory study of the doctor–elderly patient relationship. *Language and Communication*, **6**, 113–124.

Guggenbuhl-Craig, A. (1980). *Eros on crutches: On the nature of the psychopath*. Dallas, TX: Spring.

Helfrich, H. (1979). Age markers in speech. In K.R. Scherer and H. Giles (Eds), *Social markers in speech*. Cambridge: Cambridge University Press.

Hollien, H. and Shipp, T. (1972). Speaking fundamental frequency and chronologic age in males. *Journal of Speech and Hearing Research*, **15**, 155–159.

Kemper, S. (1986). Imitation of complex syntactic constructions by elderly adults. *Applied Psycholinguistics*, **7**, 277–288.

Kemper, S. (in press). Adults' diaries: Changes to written narratives across the life-span. *Discourse Processes*.

Krause, N. (1986). Social support, stress and wellbeing among older adults. *Journal of Gerontology*, **41**, 512–519.

Kreps, G.L. (1986). Health communication and the elderly. *World Communication*, **15**, 55–70.

Kuypers, J.A. and Bengston, V.L. (1973). Social breakdown and competence: A model of normal ageing. *Human Development*, **16**, 181–201.

Kynette, D. and Kemper, S. (1986). Aging and the loss of grammatical forms: A cross-sectional study of language performance. *Language and Communication*, **6**, 65–72.

Lesser, R. (1978). *Linguistic investigations of aphasia*. London: Arnold.

Levin, J. and Levin, W.C. (1980). *Ageism: Prejudice and discrimination against the elderly*. Belmont, CA: Wadsworth.

Lopez, M.A. (1980). Social skills training with institutionalized elderly: Effects of precounseling structuring and overlearning on skills acquisition and transfer. *Journal of Counseling Psychology*, **27**, 286–293.

Maxim, J. and Thompson, I. (forthcoming). *Language and the elderly: A clinical perspective.* London: Arnold.

Miller, L. (1987). The professional construction of aging. *Journal of Gerontological Social Work*, **10**, 141–153.

Mysak, E.D. (1959). Pitch and duration characteristics of older males. *Journal of Speech and Hearing Research*, **2**, 46–54.

Nebes, R.D. and Andrews-Kulis, M.S. (1976). The effect of age on the speed of sentence formation and incidental learning. *Experimental Aging Research*, **2**, 315–331.

Norman, A. (1987). Aspects of ageism: A discussion paper. London: Centre for Policy on Ageing.

Nuessel, F. (1984). Ageist language. *Maledicta*, **8**, 17–28.

Obler, L.K. (1980). Narrative discourse style in the elderly. In L.K. Obler and M.L. Albert (Eds), *Language and communication in the elderly*, pp. 75–90. Lexington, MA: Heath.

Obler, L.K. and Albert, M.L. (1980). *Language and communication in the elderly: Clinical, therapeutic and experimental issues.* Lexington, MA: Lexington.

Obler, L.K., Nicholas, M., Albert, M.L., and Woodward, S. (1985). On comprehension across the adult life span. *Cortex*, **21**, 273–280.

Oyer, H.J. and Oyer, E. (1976). *Aging and communication.* Baltimore, MD: University Park Press.

Portnoy, E. (1985). Enhancing communication with elderly patients. *American Pharmacy*, **25**, 50–55.

Potter, J. (1988). Cutting cakes: A study of psychologists' social categorisations. *Philosophical Psychology*, **1**, 17–33.

Ptacek, P.H. and Sander, E.K. (1966). Age recognition from voice. *Journal of Speech and Hearing Research*, **9**, 273–277.

Ramig, L.A. (1983). Effects of physiological aging on vowel spectral noise. *Journal of Gerontology*, **38**, 223–225.

Robinson, P. (1979). Speech markers and social class. In K.R. Scherer and H. Giles (Eds), *Social markers in speech*, pp. 211–249. Cambridge: Cambridge University Press.

Rook, K.S. and Pietromonaco, P. (1987). Close relationships: Ties that heal or ties that bind? *Advances in Personal Relationships*, **1**, 1–35.

Rosnow, I. (1973). The social context of the ageing self. *Gerontologist*, **13**, 82–87.

Rubin, K.H. and Brown, J. (1975). A life-span look at person perception and its relationship to communicative interaction. *Journal of Gerontology*, **30**, 461–468.

Ryan, E.B. and Johnston, D.G. (1987). The influence of communication effectiveness on evaluations of younger and older adult speakers. *Journal of Gerontology*, **42**, 163–164.

Smith, M.J., Reinheimer, R.E., and Gabbard-Alley, A. (1981). Crowding, task performance, and communicative interaction in youth and old age. *Human Communication Research*, **7**, 259–272.

Snow, C.E. and Ferguson, C.A. (Eds) (1977). *Talking to children: Language input and acquisition.* Cambridge: Cambridge University Press.

Stewart, M.A. and Ryan, E.B. (1982). Attitudes toward younger and older adult speakers: Effects of varying speech rates. *Journal of Language and Social Psychology*, **1**, 91–109.

Taylor, B. (1987). Elderly identity in conversation: Producing frailty. Paper presented at Meeting of the Speech Communication Association, November 1987, Boston, MA.

Tinker, A. (1984). *The elderly in modern society.* London: Longman.

Tyler, W. (1986). Structural ageism as a phenomenon in British society. *Journal of Educational Gerontology*, **1**, 38–46.

Ulatowska, H.K., Cannito, M.P., Hayashi, M.M., and Fleming, S.G. (1985). Language abilities in the elderly. In H.K. Ulatowska (Ed.), *The aging brain: Communication in the elderly*, pp. 125–139. San Diego, CA: College-Hill Press.

Ulatowska, H.K., Hayashi, M.M., Cannito, M.P., and Fleming, S.G. (1986). Disruption of reference. *Brain and Language*, **28**, 24–41.

Valdman, A. (1981). Sociolinguistic aspects of foreigner talk. *International Journal of the Sociology of Language*, **28**, 41–52.

West, C. and Zimmerman, D. (1985). Gender, language and discourse. In T. van Dijk (Ed.), *Handbook of discourse analysis*, Vol. 4, pp. 103–124. London: Academic Press.

Wilder, C.N. and Weinstein, B.E. (1984). *Aging and communication: Problems in management*. New York: Haworth.

Woolliscroft, J.O., Calhoun, J.G., Maxim, B.R., and Wolf, F.M. (1984). Medical education in facilities for the elderly. *Journal of the American Medical Association*, **252**, 3382–3385.

Section 6

Language Used in Applied Contexts

Introduction to Section 6

In the good old days sociologists offered taxonomies of complex societies that divided their subsystems into orders: the judiciary, the military, religion, the polity, the economy, and kinship. There was also a superordinate national citizenship for each member of society. Such a classification enables us to note vast areas of life as yet unexplored by social psychologists of language. How many studies have been made for the military, religious, political, and economic orders? Although it may be difficult to observe some of the conversations of the power-élites, much of the speech and writing is public. Here we have chosen one order, the judicial, because that is the one for which research has received the most sponsorship. Likewise, at the higher level of society, education of the young has attracted funding. Within health care, the physician–patient dyad has been the major focus for research. The massive amounts of research of the media for the media by the media have not invariably been conducted from a social psychological perspective, but Wober selects a number of issues which have been examined with or without such funding.

The selection of five topics on the grounds that enough research has been conducted to warrant reviews is not the best basis for choice, but each serves to highlight the crucial importance of social psychology of language to the social lives of ordinary people. The inefficiencies, biases, and discriminations already exposed begin to show just how much has to be done if we are to create more rational, humane, and equitable societies.

Much of the language work in education was underwritten by a *Zeitgeist* which judged some form of equality of opportunity principle an ideal towards which Western societies should move. Unfortunately, the educational problems of children quickly took second place to the difference versus deficit arguments among academics. Edwards addresses the relevance of social psychology to the superordinate general problems of language development, both as an end and as a means for other development; he selects reading and conversational competence as topics for review. In a middle section the state of the deficit versus difference debate is brought up to

Handbook of Language and Social Psychology
Edited by H. Giles and W.P. Robinson. © 1990 John Wiley & Sons Ltd

date, and this is expanded to the issues of pluralism versus uniformity and the role that language plays in this apparently useful but ultimately misleading binary opposition.

Gardner and Clément take us into greater depth with this issue as it is manifested in the special case of second language acquisition. Much of the work is the result of social psychologists taking up the challenge of Canada's historical problem of two powerful cultures and languages. The continued concern and empirical work has led directly into the construction of theory informative both to social psychology and to language learning. The review offers an excellent example of basic theory being advanced in the pursuit of practical problems in applied settings.

In contrast, studies of physician–patient interaction are as yet still essentially pragmatic, in both senses of the word. The linguistic stance is pragmatic, with a preference for derivations from interaction-process analysis of speech-act theory. The psychological concerns are also predominantly pragmatic. How might communication become more efficient? What would decrease the probability of physicians misunderstanding patients? How could patient compliance with prescriptions be further enhanced? How could patient satisfaction be increased? (Perhaps strangely, accuracy of diagnosis and curing have not figured as concerns.) As Hinkley, Craig, and Anderson illustrate, we now have a range of studies linking inferences about patients to physicians' reactions to them, and linking physicians' behaviour to patient outcomes. We have gained some knowledge of the mediating mechanisms. To date the field has been successfully parasitic on social psychology and linguistics to the practical advantage of patients and physicians.

Whereas one ideal for physician–patient communication would be an efficient exposure of facts and a consensual commitment to solving the health problems diagnosed, legal systems have had years to develop a vast symbolic apparatus for the confusion of the citizenry, the maintenance of the wealth and power of the legal profession, for the preservation of the status quo of the distribution of power, and for the execution of 'justice'. Danet begins by documenting some of the work of the Plain Language movement in various countries, although in the discussion she correctly warns that this movement may be more symbolic that real in its consequences. There is something strange and sinister about agreements which are understood by only one party to the contract, and both psychologists and linguists have contributed to simplifications of the legal jargon, particularly in written forms.

Likewise, the cause of justice is being advanced by social psychologists drawing attention to the influences at work in courtrooms. Of course, the forensic context was the one about which the Ancient Greeks became locked in dispute. Recent social psychological work in adversarial courts has essentially been warning juries and judges about the extent to which they are victims of Gorgias and his heirs. However, as Danet illustrates, adversarial systems are only one of a whole variety awaiting study by whatever combination of linguistic and psychological methods will best serve to describe and explain their modes of functioning.

Wober has to be selective, even within the confines of television. He omits educational uses of television but reviews studies of the effects of watching ordinary TV on attainments in reading and vocabulary. A brief section asks whether conversation in soap operas mirrors real life. Wisely avoiding the sparse evidence relevant to choice of language *per se*, Wober notes three salient issues about choices within language. The reader is spared from seeing in print any of the taboo words whose use has prompted surveys and helped to provoke official action. How and why British television came to generate and sustain the use of at least three variants of temperature descriptions is left unresolved, inevitably perhaps. Are Imperial units a symbol of social identity? Equally incomprehensible and therefore appropriate for investigation are the issues of Received Pronunciation (RP) and Standard English, again a review limited to British problems. Accents other than RP have been a reliable stimulus for evoking the response of apoplectic letters from that mystical character, Yours, Disgusted, Tunbridge Wells. If social psychology serves in part, to render the apparently irrational understandable, then Wober gives some good illustrations for us. In a final more general section the Sapir–Whorf questions of wordings as signposts, containers and channels of and for thinking are examined in relation to social scientists interested in the mass media and to the generators and managers of the messages.

As each of the chapters shows, we have massive amounts of work yet to do within each field. As the opening paragraphs of this introduction mentioned, the five fields are but a small sample of the institutions and organizations of society.

It is extraordinary that so little research is being funded in the social psychology of communication. Our societies continue to invest vast sums in technology, when if we did not insist on competitive edges, we have in fact solved our species' problems of generating more than enough goods for us all to live comfortably. We have not however managed to arrange for such goods to be equitably distributed. Neither have we realized the extent to which our current and future problems turn around problems of communication in applied contexts. At least we are now beginning to embark upon this last.

23

Language in Education

JOHN EDWARDS

Department of Psychology, St Francis Xavier University, Canada

Of all the applied settings relevant to the social psychology of language (SPL), education is among the most important. In fact, the general framework I wish to adopt here sees school as the arena in which many issues central to SPL are played out. The educational context obviously possesses a great deal of intrinsic interest, much of it reflecting language matters, and also has the potential to reveal theory-building elements for SPL. There are two major language-relevant strands in the fabric of education, particularly early education, which suggest themselves here. First, there is a *general developmental* strand; by this I mean the unfolding and progress of language development, which affect all children during the school years. Second, there is what might be termed a *group-contact* strand. Again this theoretically affects all children, to the extent to which all will perceive some discontinuity between home language and that reflected and encouraged at school. However, it can be argued that for so-called 'mainstream' children, this discontinuity is slight and presents relatively little in the way of obstacles to further language development, and school success generally. For some other children, however, there is a more serious home–school discontinuity in language (among other things), one which may well affect home life, school life and post-educational experience. One thinks here especially of children whose language or dialect is not that of the school. This second, group-contact strand is important because:

(1) it often proves to evoke contentious issues extending beyond school itself, to matters of public policy and values;

Handbook of Language and Social Psychology
Edited by H. Giles and W.P. Robinson. © 1990 John Wiley & Sons Ltd

(2) it provides a great source of purely in-school problems;
(3) it is of major immediate interest to SPL.

If one takes social psychology to be the discipline in which the 'thoughts, feelings and behaviours of individuals are influenced by the actual, imagined or implied presence of others' (Allport, 1935, cited by Alcock, Carment, and Sadava, 1988, p. 3), then *contact* of some variety is paramount.

EDUCATION: THE GENERAL DEVELOPMENTAL STRAND

Before they arrive at school, children are already in control of a well-formed grammatical system (though not of the 'fully-formed' one noted by Gumperz and Hernandez-Chavez, 1972). According to McNeill (1966), they are able at age four to 'produce sentences of every conceivable syntactic type' (p. 99). These observations apply generally, whatever the class, language, dialect or ethnic background; that is, any 'normal' child (i.e. one not handicapped by some variety of speech pathology) learns the language of its own speech community in a way which, while complex, is natural to the species. This developmental process has provided grist for the mills of linguists and psychologists and has in fact contributed to a theoretical position which postulates evolutionary brain readiness ('prewiring').

At the same time (*pace* McNeill and others), much of interest in language terms occurs during the school years. Not only does oral language development continue, but the more formal processes of reading and writing assume importance. In fact, grammar, vocabulary, semantics and pragmatics all develop substantially beyond the age of school entrance. In and through these developments, the child becomes sociolinguistically aware of variation, of repertoire expansion and appropriateness, of paralinguistic features, of language pragmatics, of all sorts of communicative conventions (above all, of course, conversation). In short, school is a powerful language context, both in its overt practices and curriculum and in its more subtle 'hidden agendas'. Yet some have observed that the study of child language, in all its elements, has traditionally focused more on the very young, in the preschool period. As implied above, it is entirely natural that such a hothouse time should be stressed, a time when children go from babbling to firm grasp of language but, as Durkin (1986) points out in his book on language development in the school years, there is an unevenness of approach, which could be corrected by giving more attention to events occurring after the very earliest, at-home years. Central, of course, to the educational context of language development are the interactions among children themselves and those between children and teachers. It is not, I think, fully appreciated how important here is the opportunity for children, in a social psychological sense, to compare, contrast and learn from *peers* at the same time as interactions, many of them more formal, occur with *adult* models and instructors. In this section, I wish to mention two language areas of particular interest to social psychology: reading and conversation/discourse. Not only are these illustrative of general development, but each has an importance which has only recently begun to be systematically investigated within SPL. This is interesting given the centrality of reading and oral communication to education; in fact, one could argue that they are the twin lynchpins of language-in-education and, as focal points of the teacher's attention, they figure largely in school success (or the lack of it).

Reading

As Gibson and Levin (1975) pointed out, a great deal of the emphasis in the psychology of reading has traditionally been upon comparisons of teaching methods. Some passing mention was typically made in the standard psychological works, but it is only relatively recently that attention has been paid to the social environment within which reading occurs (see, e.g., Downing and Thackray, 1978; Entwisle, 1979; Schonell and Goodacre, 1975). Among the more important features discussed are socio-economic background of pupils, cultural differences, motivational levels, classroom organization and dynamics, teacher expectations, and dialect differences. All of these are clearly areas inviting social psychological attention.

A recent treatment of the social psychology of reading (J. Edwards, 1981a) covers these and other features. Sex differences in reading ability and disability are examined cross-culturally by Downing (1981). While, in North America, girls are often found to be superior to boys in reading at the primary-school level, this is not a global phenomenon; we are not dealing here with a universal but rather with something affected by culture. For example, Downing notes that countries in which boys prove better than girls include Nigeria, India, Germany and Finland. Elsewhere, boy–girl differences may be insignificant. Some studies have shown this in Britain in fact. Downing also considers such relevant matters as the content of reading books, the sex of the teacher, and the power of sex-role expectations and standards as they apply differentially to males and females. Den Heyer (1981) discusses the large area of motivation, dealing particularly with the development of interest in reading. In so doing, he treats teacher-expectation effects, child self-concept and classroom experience. He also adverts to theoretical positions of relevance, for example locus-of-control, achievement motivation, and attribution theory. Motivation for reading is also dealt with by Carr and Evans (1981). They are particularly concerned to chart the effects of classroom organization and structure upon motivation and ability. Should we concentrate upon the development of formal reading skills in the classroom, or should we aim to encourage a more informal pupil self-motivation? Carr and Evans conclude that a compromise is called for between programmes of basic skill development and those which give considerable freedom to pupils to use these skills quickly and enjoyably. Hale and Edwards (1981) employ an ethnomethodological approach in their study of how teachers hear children read, and the teacher–pupil interactions which follow. These interactions, and the stress on ethnomethodology, is also the subject discussed by Pace and Powers (1981). In considering classroom dynamics and atmosphere, these authors look at teachers' effects upon pupils, but also pupils' impact on teachers; the point is that classroom climate is constructed by *all* participants and is not only a teacher-driven phenomenon.

These represent a sample of studies of reading at school which involve social psychological investigation. As well, they illustrate some of the more important directions recently taken; all of them, in their own way, view reading as a process in which cognitive skills interact with socially determined contextual definition. This interactionist approach involves, implicitly in some cases, explicitly in others, ethnographic and ethnomethodological frameworks. It may be useful to say a word or two about these here, not only because they figure in what has just been discussed, but also because they are central to the area I shall next be looking at – conversation and discourse in the classroom. Indeed, they are also of relevance in the following, *group-contact* section (see Gumperz, 1981).

Ethnomethodology is a term coined by the sociologist Garfinkel (1967), and refers generally to the study of how people construct a stable social world through their ordinary activities. Garfinkel himself states that it means 'the investigation of the rational properties of indexical expressions and other practical actions as contingent ongoing accomplishments of organized artful practices of everyday life' (1967, p. 11). This is quite a mouthful. Sevigny (1981) notes, more simply, that ethnomethodology concerns itself with the 'doings' which constitute the social order, 'the regularities and changes in selected features of behavior that are meaningful to the individual members of a social setting' (p. 71). It is a phenomenological approach which builds upon individuals' intentions, subsequent social action, and interpretations of social events; that is, implicit in it is a sense of the *meaning* events possess, rather than a more simplistic description or classification of them. Thus, Pace and Powers (1981) were particularly concerned with how classroom climates occur and what they mean for all participants, rather than with the more reductionist approach often associated with psychological study. Some of the essential assumptions of ethnomethodology, according to Sevigny, are that reality is a social phenomenon to be interpreted rather than discovered, that human behaviour is rule-governed, and that rule expectations inform social action, and form the basis of values and morality.

Ethnography refers to research involving 'participation in and observation of the daily lives [*sic*] of a particular social group. . . [in order to] understand the patterns and meanings of group members' lives' (Genishi and Dyson, 1984, p. 6). In a sense, ethnographic practice reminds one of classic anthropological fieldwork, although the duration of ethnographic participation found in the literature is sometimes so slight as to weaken that comparison. More detail is provided by Green and Wallat (1981a), who note that the thrust of ethnography is the study of a 'whole' culture (with accompanying participant observation, interview, field study and case study approaches) in order to properly understand and describe it, and to define what membership in it means. Since their own book involves school, however, it is apparent that an ethnographic focus is *not* strictly being applied, since school is but one aspect of a culture. Nevertheless, the holistic approach can be used, albeit in a scaled-down form, thus producing 'micro-ethnographies' (for further notes on educational ethnography, see D. Edwards and Mercer, 1986; Lutz, 1981).

In very general terms, ethnomethodology and ethnography overlap, inasmuch as both involve a holistic emphasis, and ethnomethodological inquiry would seem to be necessary for ethnography. Furthermore, the general approach is not necessarily inconsistent with social psychology; indeed, some might argue that, perhaps through the medium of discourse analysis (see below), social psychology will grow to embrace the ethnographic thrust. This coming together would mean a more holistic, less reductionist social psychology and would not be without difficulties, at least in the eyes of those who are firmly wedded to an empirically orientated social psychology with an emphasis upon quantification. However, recent theorists have stated that statistical procedures are not necessarily outlawed in ethnography, and stress the useful complementarity of qualitative and quantitative methods (Erickson, 1981; Green and Wallat, 1981a). There are, of course, problems with ethnographic approaches. One difficulty is that, like the study of applied settings generally, ethnographies and ethnomethodologies could lead to an endless proliferation of studies. Relatedly, the general phenomenological thrust can give rise to some bizarre offspring. Consider, for example, 'ethno-inquiry' – 'the world is seen as consisting of both people and things and it is the task of the ethno-inquirer to try to sort them out. . . the range is immense, spanning studies of backpacking to that [*sic*] of the hemispheres of the brain' (Kaplan, 1982, p. 15; for an outline of 'ethno-inquiry' see also Rose, 1982, and, for a critique, J. Edwards, 1983c).

Conversation and Discourse

The application of ethnomethodology to conversation and discourse analysis is central; indeed, 'conversational analysis' implies, to many, an ethnomethodological exercise which studies the ways in which people engage in verbal interaction. Given that conversational analysis interests itself in such phenomena as when to initiate and terminate conversation, when to interrupt or interject, what are appropriate topics (and styles for discussing them), and rules governing turn-taking, it is clear that classroom dynamics have a lot to offer our understanding of how conversational ability is developed and refined. As A. Edwards (1976) put it, traditional classrooms are 'places contrived for the controlled transmission of knowledge. This is what gives them their peculiar identity as settings for talk' (p. 180). (It should be noted here that some discourse analysts, insisting on study of 'natural' conversations, have seen classrooms as 'unnatural'. This raises questions, of course, about just what we are to construe as natural.)

Discourse analysis is sometimes differentiated from conversational analysis; while the latter aims to assess how conversation 'works', the former may involve more structural analysis. It may also be applied to written samples – although for this some might wish to use the term 'text analysis'. In short, there is a good deal of overlap, not to say imprecision, in these terms (see Stubbs, 1983; consider, by way of comparison, the common ground often trodden by SPL, sociolinguistics and the sociology of language). In any event, it is not difficult to see that a thoroughgoing analysis of conversation necessitates delving beyond the words to the context, and in this sense an ethnomethodological approach (or, a micro-ethnography) seems sound.

A good recent example of discourse analysis in the context of this *general developmental* strand is given by D. Edwards and Mercer (1986). Their investigation centres upon the creation of shared knowledge in the classroom, as this is revealed through the context and continuity of discourse. In outlining their work they present a useful overview of the relevant literature; of particular relevance here is the work of A. Edwards and Furlong (1978), Griffin and Mehan (1981), Mehan (1979), Sinclair and Coulthard (1975), Stubbs and Delamont (1976) and Willes (1983). Sinclair and Coulthard, for example, use classroom discourse as a convenient corpus for their more abstract concerns, an example of the applied context contributing to more general knowledge; Mehan and Griffin are also concerned to use classrooms as an arena. Willes provides an illustration of the ethnographic study of classroom life and discourse in an attempt to illuminate the very earliest days and weeks of school. Stubbs has argued for discourse analysis as *the* avenue for studying classroom interaction, and has cited an increasing dissatisfaction with traditional psychological work based upon experimental manipulation; in a later publication (Stubbs, 1986), he gives an up-to-date discussion of language and education in which discourse analysis figures prominently (perhaps too prominently; see V. Edwards, 1987). Further very useful studies in classroom ethnography and discourse analysis may be found in the collection edited by Green and Wallat (1981b; for treatments of discourse more generally, see Stubbs, 1983, and Van Dijk, 1985).

Finally here, we should note the recent appearance of a book which aims to place discourse analysis at the very centre of the social psychological enterprise. Social existence, according to Potter and Wetherell (1987), is largely a matter of discourse. But part of their argument is also to dismiss some of the traditional emphases in the area (e.g. attitudes, particularly as elicited via questionnaires). Antaki (1988) feels that their work could 'rescue' social psychology from its current laboratory-orientated 'sterility', Billig (1988) considers it something which cannot be ignored, and Smith (1988) sees it as of great heuristic value. In a review essay, Giles and Coupland (1989) offer some more detailed assessment. They note that:

(1) the book indeed has significance for social psychology;
(2) it tends to downplay an already potent emphasis existing in SPL;
(3) it elevates discourse analysis too highly over other worthwhile, complementary approaches.

The Potter and Wetherell (1987) book is undoubtedly an indicator of change in SPL, change which may centrally affect educational studies. Still, as Giles and Coupland (1989) imply, we should on principle be chary about 'new waves', and not be overly quick to jettison existing methods and insights. There are certainly difficulties with discourse and conversational analysis. One of the basic ones has to do with the underlying phenomenological perspective of much of the work; the history of phenomonological psychology is chequered, particularly in the British and North American mainstream social psychological context. Second, discourse analysis may lend itself to an endless series of fact-gathering exercises. Judicious selection of texts for analysis would seem vital, but some of the literature does not justify very well the particular choices made. Indeed, observers have noted the difficulties in a field in which the explanations can be so much more detailed (and take up much greater space) than the phenomena under study (see also Hymes, 1986, on 'Discourse: Scope without depth').

EDUCATION: THE GROUP-CONTACT STRAND

Although some have disputed it (see Feagans and Farran, 1982, countered by J. Edwards, 1983a, 1986), the school is basically a middle-class institution in terms of what it values and encourages. Since it is a setting which the middle class are more prepared for, as it were, and better able to use, and given that some of its pupils are *not* of middle-class background, the school is a place of contact and, perhaps, conflict. In this sense it is an arena involving minority–majority (and minority–minority) relations, a microcosm of larger social interaction. Matters concerning the validity and acceptance of dialect and language variation, the position accorded to standard language production, and social policy of the broadest kind (e.g. dealing with cultural pluralism and assimilation) are important here (see J. Edwards, 1989; J. Edwards and Giles, 1984). In this section, as in the last, I will focus upon two main areas. First, dialect contact at school suggests itself. How different dialects arise and what they are seen to imply in terms of ability are questions of great importance, particularly as they reflect the larger 'difference–deficit' debate (see below). Second, the perception of school as an agent of social language and cultural policy is important, particularly at a time of increased attention to the place of ethnic minority groups in society, to the debate over and around an enduring pluralism and linguistic diversity.

Dialects in Contact

This first issue is centrally concerned with group, educational and linguistic disadvantage, a phenomenon in which certain home backgrounds and lifestyles (e.g. of the working class, of immigrant and of ethnic minority groups) are seen to contribute to lowered academic achievement and extra-school success. There have been three main theoretical explanations of the aetiology of disadvantage – the *genetic deficiency*, *environmental deficit* and *group-difference* viewpoints. They have been discussed extensively elsewhere (J. Edwards, 1989), and so can be treated very briefly here.

The genetic deficiency argument holds that some groups of children are inherently less able than others; this was a popular view historically, but one which has latterly fallen into disrepute. However, the work of Jensen (1969, 1973) and others concluded that genetic influences accounted for a large percentage of black–white differences in IQ, giving new life to the perspective. Problems with the definition and measurement of intelligence, and methodological difficulties involved in separating environmental from hereditary forces have called this interpretation into question (an excellent review of intelligence, IQ, heredity–environment and race is that of Colman, 1987; see also Sutherland, 1988).

The second, environmental deficit argument is that deficiencies in early physical, social and psychological life lead to intellectual deficit. This is the perspective giving rise to programmes of compensatory education and 'resocialization'. It is also the perspective which has produced long lists of disadvantaging characteristics of homes and children. Difficulties with this viewpoint include the accuracy of data gathered about disadvantaged homes, inadequately made links between environment and characteristics, and then between characteristics and achievement, and, above all, the imposition of a middle-class bias which implicitly assumes the correctness of some types of behaviour or, at least, which sees that behaviour as the social standard which must be attained by all who are concerned with social mobility and success (in some 'mainstream' sense).

The final, group-difference position is that imputations of 'better' and 'worse' are inappropriate when comparing groups' attitudes, behaviour and values. Rather, disadvantage is seen as representing *difference* and not genetic or environmental deficit. However, it is acknowledged that differences become social deficits when groups are unequal in power and the standards of one consequently dominate while those of another are denigrated; this is one of two important points of great social psychological salience. The other is that disadvantage, as conceived here, is a product of social comparison among groups of differing status; without this comparison of non-equals, disadvantage would be an empty concept.

Careful analysis and assessment have shown that the difference viewpoint on disadvantage is the most likely of the three (J. Edwards, 1989). This does not mean, of course, that there are not further complexities. For example, many 'different' groups come to school, but they do not all experience the same success or failure. Ogbu (1978, 1982) has maintained that over and above simple difference there exists for some groups a 'caste-like' status from which members cannot escape, however well they do at school. Ogbu thus contrasts the school performance of American ghetto blacks with Chinese, Japanese and others (for a comment, see D'Amato, 1987). McDermott and Gospodinoff (1981) have also offered a more detailed insight into classroom failure, noting that it is not simply that language difference *per se* contributes to this, but rather that 'schools function to maintain ethnic borders, and. . . the continuing divergence of communicative codes has its roots in social and political forces which extend beyond the school' (J. Edwards, 1982a, p. 198). Ogbu would no doubt point out that only *some* groups fail in this way, not all. To give McDermott and Gospodinoff the last word: 'If we wanted a mechanism for sorting each new generation of citizens into the advantaged and the disadvantaged, into the achieving and the underachieving, we could have done no better than to have invented the school system we have' (1981, p. 229).

Rejecting genetic deficiency and environmental deficit arguments clearly does not eradicate the problem in societies in which differences are socially construed as deficits. This has particular relevance for disadvantaged *language*. In the educational setting it is obvious that schools have traditionally thought that some dialects were wrong, substandard and the products of deficient lifestyle and cognitive capabilities. Programmes were thus set in motion on the faulty assumption of the 'verbal deprivation' of some groups of children. Thus, Bereiter and Engelmann (1966) claimed that the disadvantaged were retarded in language ability, that language was 'dispensable' for them, and that it was 'an aspect of social behaviour which is not of vital importance' (p. 42). Similarly, Hess and Shipman (1968) noted, in an elegant but vacuous phrase, that 'the meaning of deprivation would thus seem to be a deprivation of meaning' (p. 103) and went on to recommend the 'resocialization' of the disadvantaged child. Other studies, particularly those of Bernstein, a British sociologist, fuelled the linguistic deficit argument (see, e.g., Bernstein, 1971, 1973, 1975) by suggesting that disadvantaged children did not have access to the range of language possessed by the middle class; that is, their speech varieties were 'restricted'; those of the middle class, 'elaborated' (see J. Edwards, 1987, 1989; the latter reference also discusses the difficulties with Bernstein's work which, while certainly *taken* as support for the deficit hypothesis, perhaps does not itself belong in the deficit camp). Trudgill (1975) pointed out how unfortunate this all was, reinforcing older prejudices about dialect at a time when a degree of tolerance was perhaps emerging.

This might all be taken as of historical interest, since the relevant evidence from academic quarters supports the difference viewpoint on disadvantage generally, and on language in particular. However, a number of points should be made:

(1) academic opinion does not always filter effectively to the public at large or, indeed, to the educational constituency;
(2) applied areas, by their nature, have potential interaction with social policy and standards, and this may mean that factual information is ignored or manipulated for specific political ends;
(3) even in academic circles differences of opinion may exist, and evidence can be reinterpreted in what remains a volatile area.

The price of accuracy is continuing, disinterested social psychological and socio-linguistic attention.

By way of illustration, and to conclude this section, I will briefly outline evidence of the continuation of the language-deficit argument in the literature (it goes without saying that it has continued unabated in general society, a fact which in itself argues for more dissemination of psychological and other insights in suitable and intelligible ways). For example, the work of Tough (1977) in the UK and of Ramey and his associates in the USA (e.g. Adams and Ramey, 1980; Ramey and Campbell, 1977) discusses developmental (including linguistic) retardation among poor children supposedly deprived of early stimulation and learning experiences. Rodick and Henggeler (1980) mention a programme to help parents 'restructure' the home environment of black inner-city children (shades of Hess and Shipman, 1968, see above). Jay, Routh, and Brantley (1980) and Gullo (1981) deal with social class language differences from a Bernsteinian (should we say 'unreconstructed' Bern-steinian; see below) position, and Gullo in particular seems to accept the view that the language of children of low socio-economic status is more linked to the concrete here-and-now, and less used for abstract reasoning. Feagans and Farran (1982) edit a book devoted to poor children's language, in which several contributors continue to give at least partial support to a deficit viewpoint (see J. Edwards, 1983a). More recently, Honey (1983) attacks recent linguistic theory supporting the view that all language varieties are valid systems, claims that non-standard English is an inferior variant, and recommends upgrading currently poor standards of written and spoken language at school (see Davies, 1985; J. Edwards, 1983b, 1986).

Much of this recent work which continues the deficit tradition has an allegiance to Bernstein's studies which, interpreted or misinterpreted (see J. Edwards, 1989), have greatly influenced this direction (see Atkinson, 1985, for a new 'introduction' to Bernstein; see also A. Edwards, 1987a,b). A very recent study by Mason (1986) on the deficit hypothesis deals explicitly with Bernstein. She claims that the hypothesis has 'remained alive in the minds of many practising school-teachers' (p. 279; see below), and wants to underline the distinction between concrete and abstract language, 'Bernstein's fundamental insight' (p. 287; see also the reply to Mason's article by Carrington and Williamson, 1987).

The issue of interest here is not the continuing debate about where best to place Bernstein along some difference–deficit continuum, but rather the impact of what has been *taken* to be Bernstein's position, an impact which 'continues to reinforce long-established views about the incorrectness of certain language styles . . . a continuing allegiance to a language-deficit philosophy . . . prejudices and attitudes about speech and speakers which are traditional, comfortable and . . . difficult to dislodge' (J. Edwards, 1987, p. 377). Certainly the work of Gordon (1978, 1981) with British teachers reveals this impact; he quotes the words of one teacher as follows: 'Bernstein . . . is saying something which most teachers "take in through their fingers", as you might say it, every day of their lives' (1978, p. 104). Similarly, a study of teachers by J. Edwards and McKinnon (1987) shows a continuing adherence to a language-deficit view, and suggests again at least an indirect influence of a Bernsteinian type. The work of writers like Atkinson (1985), A. Edwards (1987a,b), and Halliday (1973) would indicate that Bernstein has been badly used in support of linguistic deficit hypotheses, and Atkinson in particular is concerned to place Bernstein in the correct light. Yet in society at large, and among teachers in particular, the evidence suggests that the 'old' view of Bernstein, and of linguistic deficit, continues its baleful influence.

Education, Language and Pluralism

One of the most interesting features of education for SPL is its use as a support for a social policy of pluralism, for the protection of minority languages and group identities seen to be at risk of assimilation by a mainstream society. In some sense, schools have always been used to promote social policy, have always been a political instrument. In most cases, however, this has taken the form of an arm of the dominant social mainstream – that is, it has presented an assimilative, sink-or-swim face to minority groups – and has aimed to reinforce existing social currents. In some cases, however, schools have been seen as agents of widespread social change, again operating with a centralist perspective; the case of the attempted revival of Irish through the educational system is an apposite example. As well, some contemporary contexts have seen social change through education in the service of decentralization, of linguistic and cultural diversity, and of ethnic pluralism; in some instances this has been a result of movements by or on behalf of *minority* groups. In part, this has proved possible because of a greater tolerance of diversity in heterogeneous societies, but it should be made clear that tolerance cannot necessarily be equated with a more active promotion, nor is tolerance – often a product of relative social security and affluence – a quantity which, once in place, always remains.

This is a very broad area indeed, and I have treated it in detail elsewhere (see, e.g., J. Edwards, 1981c, 1982b, 1984a,b,c). Here I shall simply outline some of the more important matters which require further SPL input:

(1) What is the nature of the relationship between language and identity?
(2) Is cultural pluralism good, and assimilation bad?
(3) Is it realistic to ask schools to effect social change?

Further to (3) are four other points:

(a) Can schools support group identities at risk of change and contribute to pluralism and diversity?
(b) Can they do this by attending principally to language?
(c) What is the place of multicultural education?
(d) Can schools promote diversity *and* provide a strong core curriculum?

I have obviously stated these questions baldly and simplistically; perhaps in the following brief discussion (which draws heavily upon J. Edwards, 1985) something of their complexity, interrelatedness and relevance for SPL will emerge.

First, the relationship between language and identity is a complex one, but my reading of the literature and analysis of current and historical situations leads to the conclusion that continuity of the original group language need not be a necessary condition for identity continuation. Here I draw upon the work of Barth (1969) on the maintenance of boundaries coexisting with cultural change within them. Consider the Irish as an example here: language shift from Irish to English can hardly be said to have resulted, today, in an identity which is not strong or unique. Consider also the 'hyphenated' Americans who remain proudly linked to their forebears with whom they share, however, virtually no cultural manifestations.

Second, the simple dichotomy often assumed between pluralism (good) and assimilation (bad) is unrealistic; there are types and degrees of both. Some variety of modified pluralism (see, e.g., Higham's 1975 notion of *pluralistic integration*), in which degrees of diversity can coexist with minority penetration of the mainstream, would seem to appeal to many groups and individuals if the historical record is considered (see also Glazer, 1983, for a recent treatment of assimilation and pluralism).

Third, we should note that it is very difficult to use schools alone as agents of change, since by their nature they tend to reflect the society of which they are a part. Where schools *are* to be used for change, it is helpful, to say the least, if the direction they are asked to take is one being adopted outside the school as well; that is, given an existing social current, there is no doubt that the school's role can be complementary. However, the attempted revival of Irish, in a society committed in practice to English, exemplifies the difficulty when this complementarity is absent. Furthermore, not only is the school policy likely to fail, but the failure itself allows a scapegoat to be created, this resulting from an unfair burden being put on school in the first place. Is education in multicultural, 'receiving' societies like the USA going to be successful in promoting a permanent social, ethnolinguistic diversity? Examination of the modern centralist thrust of American bilingual education, the historical attempts at bilingual education on the part of minorities themselves, and the tenor of mainstream American life should lead to a certain caution here. In all situations of language contact (a) which appear to be leading towards linguistic assimilation, and (b) which some at least wish to transform into a stable linguistic diversity, we should remember that:

(1) linguistic change rather than stasis is the historical fact;
(2) diversity tends to reduce itself over time;
(3) language shift is a *symptom* of group contact – to attempt, therefore, to change aspects of language alone may well be fruitless without a much wider reworking of the social fabric which may itself be impractical, undesirable (even to those desiring language change) or impossible (short of revolution);
(4) populations typically do not maintain two (or more) languages indefinitely, once one has come to suffice across all domains.

Situations in which identities are at risk of alteration usually result from large-scale social dynamics and group contact, yet it is in precisely these situations that schools are typically asked to intervene on behalf of pluralism and diversity; that is, they are appealed to at points at which social currents make their task incredibly difficult. It follows that we should not ask too much of schools alone. Supposing, however, that schools *were* to intervene on behalf of group identity, should their efforts be directed mainly at language? This has been the rationale behind some programmes of bilingual education, for example. However, as a marker of groupness, communicative language is very susceptible to change; this is because it is a highly visible feature which may be perceived as stigmatizing, or because of pragmatic pressures to shift, or both (in the *process* of shift, incidentally, bilingualism is often but a stage on the road to monolingualism in the new variety). Thus, school efforts directed at identity maintenance through language preservation may indeed be battling against very strong counter-trends. It may be noted here that after *communicative* language shift has occurred, the original language may retain *symbolic* value (J. Edwards, 1977) and, in this way, continue to contribute to identity. For example, the report of the Committee on Irish Language Attitudes Research (1975) showed that most people valued the language as a national or ethnic symbol, while, at the same time, they expressed lack of interest in restoration of the Irish language and general pessimism about the future of Irish as a communicative medium. Relatedly, Eastman (1984) has pointed to what she terms an 'associated' language, one connected with group identity but no longer regularly used nor, perhaps, known at all.

Symbolic language is not particularly susceptible to educational treatment except, perhaps, as part of a multicultural curriculum, which, while not necessarily aiming to transmit given cultures in their entirety, is surely right to reflect a heterogeneous society in the classroom. As I have suggested elsewhere: 'all education worthy of the name is multicultural. It should be part and parcel of education generally to show an awareness of diverse cultures and to develop an appreciation of human difference' (J. Edwards, 1985, p. 131). Finally here, we should recall that one of the tensions in modern education is between what Bullivant (1981) has called 'civism' and 'pluralism', between a curriculum which transmits general knowledge and core elements necessary for all pupils (and perhaps *especially* so for minority children wishing to succeed in the wider society: see Stone, 1981; Tomlinson, 1984) and one which conveys a variety of cultural values. Of course, these two elements can and should coexist – indeed, in some cases it may be difficult (and unprofitable as well) to distinguish between them – but the distinction according to critics like Stone is roughly between curricula which heavily emphasize 'traditional' offerings like science, history and geography and those which consider rather more vague 'affective' goals (self-awareness, self-esteem and so on) to be central to the educational enterprise, particularly for disadvantaged minority-group pupils.

CONCLUSIONS

Although I have been able to focus only on a few specifics, I hope this chapter has shown that language issues in education are interesting, varied and complex. Furthermore, I believe it is clear that studies of an SPL nature have contributed much to our understanding – here I interpret SPL very broadly and include useful overlaps with the sociology of language and sociolinguistics. It is equally clear, however, that much more remains to be done and, in this final section, I shall indicate some possible directions of interest.

(1) Generally, SPL should continue to provide theoretical frameworks for our forays into applied contexts. One useful example is the accommodation model outlined by Giles and his colleagues (e.g. Giles, Bourhis, and Taylor, 1977; Giles and Powesland, 1975; Giles and Smith, 1979), incorporating Tajfel's ideas of social comparison and categorization (e.g. Tajfel, 1982). Education, with its interactions among pupils, teachers and parents, particularly where these cross lines of class, group, age and sex, is an obvious arena for studies of language accommodation, of convergence/divergence, and of social movement. Such studies will help to contribute both to our understanding of the educational context itself, in which linguistic interaction is so central, indeed providing the *raison d'être* of the traditional educational exercise, and to our emerging grasp of SPL *per se*.

An interesting theoretical analysis is provided by Giles and Johnson (1981) in which four elements are prominent:

(1) Tajfel's theory of social identity, comparison and group relations;
(2) *perceived* ethnolinguistic vitality (see Bourhis, Giles, and Rosenthal, 1981);
(3) the distinctiveness, strength and value of group boundaries, and the subsequent perceptions of boundary permeability;
(4) the importance of multiple group membership.

The impact of this model in an educational setting is outlined by J. Edwards and Giles (1984), who also extend the model in a discussion of the acquisition of standard dialects by non-standard-speaking children (see below).

(2) With regard to reading, we have seen that important elements include teacher expectations, cultural differences, pupil motivation and classroom organization, all areas benefiting from SPL input. There is, as well, another important social psychological perspective on reading which has not as yet been touched on here, and which has not been dealt with much in the literature. While our studies of expectations and motivation are important in reading development and proficiency, 'a social

psychology of reading should include not only a consideration of factors important in what one might term the *basics* of reading but also of those things related to the *uses* to which these basics are applied' (J. Edwards, 1981b, p. 217). After all, the intent is not only to produce reading skills but also to promote reading itself, for that happy combination of pleasure and learning. This takes us into areas like the encouragement of reading, guidance as to what is read, and the whole notion and influence of 'mass culture'. Not only is this a neglected area for social psychology, it is also one which yet again illustrates the necessary interconnections always to be made between school and the larger society.

Finally here, my remarks on reading led me to look briefly at ethnomethodology and ethnography. They represent an emphasis attractive to many who are somewhat disillusioned with more traditional approaches. Yet, as noted, common ground can be established here and it should be part of the social psychological agenda to investigate this.

(3) I can reiterate the point just made, making it more specific by mentioning conversation and discourse. Given that conversational analysis often comprises a central ethnomethodological emphasis, and given that conversation is a highly relevant part of SPL, it follows that some coming together of ethnomethodology and social psychology is to be looked for and encouraged. More generally, there is the recent proposal by Potter and Wetherell (1987) that discourse analysis should be placed firmly within social psychology (see also Robinson, 1985); this has already attracted critical notice, and more may be expected. It is my hope and belief that, while discourse analysis will come to occupy a greater position within SPL, it will not displace earlier approaches still of value, for example the study of attitudes towards languages, dialects, accents and their speakers (see J. Edwards, 1982c, 1983d).

(4) The attention given here to dialects in contact at school shows above all the continuing need for close psychological monitoring of teacher attitudes, expectations and stereotypes. The difference–deficit debate, and the perspectives on standard versus non-standard varieties are not settled matters by any means. Children's views of such language issues are also open to SPL study, and J. Edwards and Giles (1984) outline some basic questions to be asked or re-asked.

One feature emerging in this section was the influence of Bernstein upon teachers and others. This suggests, at the least, further and more pointed dissemination of SPL information. It also, however, points to possibilities for looking at Bernstein's work in new lights. One example involves the original assertion that schools promote and use the so-called 'elaborated' code, transmitting 'universalistic orders of meaning' (Atkinson, 1985, p. 78). It is clear that this is too simplistic a view and that, in fact, classroom language is often more 'restricted' to the particularistic and the concrete. Atkinson discusses some relevant studies here, and concludes that the 'relationship between language codes and classroom discourse needs to be revised' (p. 80). D. Edwards and Mercer (1986) make the same sort of point. What is required here is further study of classroom language through the detail of discourse (see point 3).

(5) My final section deals with education, language and pluralism. The SPL agenda here relates most clearly to the points I outlined at the beginning of the section. However, I wish to make two other observations. The first is that Giles's

model of ethnolinguistic vitality (Giles *et al.*, 1977) is of considerable relevance in understanding the perceptions which animate the whole notion of education as a servant to the cause of pluralism and enduring diversity. This takes on a particularly SPL aspect when one considers not so much the *actual* features of vitality (outlined by Giles and colleagues as status, demography and institutional support) as the *perceived* group vitality (see Bourhis *et al.*, 1981, on the Subjective Vitality Questionnaire). The approach is not without its difficulties (J. Edwards, 1985) but it aims at something important (further consideration of ethnolinguistic vitality and other similar approaches is given by J. Edwards, 1988a,b).

Second, this area highlights how important an interdisciplinary approach is. To understand the educational dynamics relating to language and diversity, we need to go beyond education itself, and beyond social psychology too – to sociology, sociolinguistics, anthropology, etc. However, perhaps the most important complement to psychological study here is a historical one. I have argued elsewhere (J. Edwards, 1985) that intelligent deduction from the historical record is revealing and necessary, and that history can provide the needed ballast for more fine-grained, contemporary excursions. A major example here is the language–identity relationship. Only a thorough knowledge of the course of Irish cultural history, for instance, will reveal the subtle interplay between Irish and English in the educational system (and elsewhere). Only an understanding of the early, group-initiated efforts in mother-tongue instruction in the USA will illuminate fully more contemporary, federally funded educational interventions whose success or failure ultimately depends upon the desires and circumstances of the potential beneficiaries themselves. At the same time, while historical analysis indicates much of importance for a grasp of the language–identity linkage, current and detailed studies in the SPL tradition need to be done to assess (for example) ordinary people's view of ethnicity, ethnic salience, symbolic aspects of identity, language and government policy. Work has been done here (e.g. Driedger, 1975, 1976; J. Edwards and Chisholm, 1987; J. Edwards and Doucette, 1987; J. Edwards and Shearn, 1987; Mackie, 1978; Mackie and Brinkerhoff, 1984) suggesting, among other things, an awareness that symbolic features of ethnicity are central to many well-settled immigrant minority-group members, and a realization that communicative language shift need not destroy identity continuity. More is required, for too much of our information still comes from spokesmen who may be atypical of ordinary group members, or from apologists for diversity in general.

(6) In conclusion, I would pick up on the point already noted about the mutually supportive relationship between educational studies and SPL in general. Consider, for example, conversation and discourse analysis. On the one hand, we have not only a strong theoretical argument for the centrality of this within social psychology (Potter and Wetherell, 1987), but also an increasing number of empirical studies. On the other hand, we see that a prime area for such analysis is the school. For example, ethnographically inspired investigations of classroom discourse hold the promise of a fine-grained and contextually rich method of better understanding, and perhaps reducing, educational/linguistic disadvantage. This could lead to practical suggestions of useful adaptations and repertoire expansions on the part of both teachers and pupils. The point, I think, is clear: discourse analysis may provide useful insights in

education, while further studies of discourse at school will inevitably feed back into the growing corpus of information and expertise characterizing such analysis as a subdisciplinary feature of an expanding social psychology.

In education, three elements of the greatest concern to SPL occur – communication, contact and comparison – and each of the topic areas I have so briefly dealt with here illustrate this. It is clear enough, then, that both SPL in general and the educational context in particular will continue to receive close attention from students of language and society. Part of this, an important part, will devote itself to theory construction. This is, in fact, a natural reaction to the perceived danger of that endless proliferation of potential studies already referred to. As Robinson (1985) has observed, we are in an area in which the possibilities for future work are infinite: 'spatially and temporally there can be no end to studies that would be of practical use to individuals in their daily lives' (p. 136). (One wonders, of course, about points of diminishing return, about bounds of practical utility beyond which further detail will be of interest only to a handful of specialists.) In any event, I am suggesting that the very breadth of our concern is perhaps the major reason for a desire to seek generalization in the form of theory. In pursuing this, we should bear in mind that meaningful returns from applied domains like education may be harder to achieve than the great (and increasing) quantity of empirical findings in the literature would first suggest. The twin dangers to be avoided are, on the one hand, premature and simplistic efforts at theory-building which demean the very idea of theory, and whose only conceivable application is within highly artificially constrained settings, and, on the other hand, efforts in which theory is so closely a restatement of observation that it would seem the ultimate (if unattainable) goal is a theoretical mapping of social reality on a scale of 1 : 1. What is the advantage in such a map? Where, indeed, could we unfold it?

REFERENCES

Adams, J. and Ramey, C. (1980). Structural aspects of maternal speech to infants reared in poverty. *Child Development*, **51**, 1280–1284.

Alcock, J., Carment, D., and Sadava, S. (1988). *A textbook of social psychology*. Scarborough (Ontario): Prentice-Hall.

Allport, G.W. (1935). Attitudes. In C. Murchison (Ed.), *Handbook of social psychology*, pp. 798–844. Worcester, MA: Clark University Press.

Antaki, C. (1988). Sounding board. *Times Higher Education Supplement*, 8 January.

Atkinson, P. (1985). *Language, structure and reproduction*. London: Methuen.

Barth, F. (Ed.) (1969). *Ethnic groups and boundaries*. Boston, MA: Little, Brown.

Bereiter, C. and Engelmann, S. (1966). *Teaching disadvantaged children in the preschool*. Englewood Cliffs, NJ: Prentice-Hall.

Bernstein, B. (1971). *Class, codes and control*. Vol. 1, *Theoretical studies towards a sociology of language*. London: Routledge and Kegan Paul.

Bernstein, B. (1973). *Class, codes and control*, Vol. 2, *Applied studies towards a sociology of language*. London: Routledge and Kegan Paul.

Bernstein, B. (1975). *Class, codes and control*, Vol. 3, *Towards a theory of educational transmissions*. London: Routledge and Kegan Paul.

Billig, M. (1988). Review of *Discourse and social psychology* (Potter & Wetherell). *Psychologist*, **1**, 23.

Bourhis, R., Giles, H., and Rosenthal, D. (1981). Notes on the construction of a 'Subjective Vitality Questionnaire' for ethnolinguistic groups. *Journal of Multilingual and Multicultural Development*, **2**, 145–155.

Bullivant, B. (1981). *The pluralist dilemma in education*. Sydney: Allen and Unwin.

Carr, T. and Evans, M. (1981). Classroom organization and reading ability: Are motivation and skill antagonistic goals? In J. Edwards (Ed.), *The social psychology of reading*, pp. 67–98. Silver Spring: Institute of Modern Languages.

Carrington, B. and Williamson, J. (1987). The deficit hypothesis revisited. *Educational Studies*, **13**, 239–245.

Colman, A. (1987). *Facts, fallacies and frauds in psychology*. London: Hutchinson.

Committee on Irish Language Attitudes Research (1975). *Report*. Dublin: Government Stationery Office.

D'Amato, J. (1987). The belly of the beast: On cultural differences, castelike status, and the politics of school. *Anthropology and Education Quarterly*, **18**, 357–360.

Davies, A. (1985). Standard and dialect English: The unacknowledged idealisation of sociolinguistics. *Journal of Multilingual and Multicultural Development*, **6**, 183–192.

Den Heyer, K. (1981). Reading and motivation. In J. Edwards (Ed.), *The social psychology of reading*, pp. 51–65. Silver Spring: Institute of Modern Languages.

Downing, J. (1981). Cultural expectations and sex differences in reading. In J. Edwards (Ed.), *The social psychology of reading*, pp. 1–27. Silver Spring: Institute of Modern Languages.

Downing, J. and Thackray, D. (1978). *Reading readiness*. London: Hodder and Stoughton.

Driedger, L. (1975). In search of cultural identity factors. *Canadian Review of Sociology and Anthropology*, **12**, 150–162.

Driedger, L. (1976). Ethnic self-identity. *Sociometry*, **39**, 131–141.

Durkin, K. (1986). Introduction. In K. Durkin (Ed.), *Language development in the school years*, pp. 1–16. London: Croom Helm.

Eastman, C. (1984). Language, ethnic identity and change. In J. Edwards (Ed.), *Linguistic minorities, policies and pluralism*, pp. 259–276. London: Academic Press.

Edwards, A. (1976). *Language in culture and class*. London: Heinemann.

Edwards, A. (1987a). Review of *Language, structure and reproduction* (Atkinson). *Journal of Language and Social Psychology*, **6**, 67–70.

Edwards, A. (1987b). Language codes and classroom practice. *Oxford Review of Education*, **13**, 237–247.

Edwards, A. and Furlong, V. (1978). *The language of teaching*. London: Heinemann.

Edwards, D. and Mercer, N. (1986). Context and continuity: Classroom discourse and the development of shared knowledge. In K. Durkin (Ed.), *Language development in the school years*, pp. 172–202. London: Croom Helm.

Edwards, J. (1977). Ethnic identity and bilingual education. In H. Giles (Ed.), *Language, ethnicity and intergroup relations*, pp. 253–282. London: Academic Press.

Edwards, J. (Ed.) (1981a). *The social psychology of reading*. Silver Spring: Institute of Modern Languages.

Edwards, J. (1981b). The reading public and the school. In J. Edwards (Ed.), *The social psychology of reading*, pp. 217–229. Silver Spring: Institute of Modern Languages.

Edwards, J. (1981c). The context of bilingual education. *Journal of Multilingual and Multicultural Development*, **2**, 25–44.

Edwards, J. (1982a). Review of *Culture and the bilingual classroom* (Trueba, Guthrie, and Au). *Modern Language Journal*, **66**, 197–198.

Edwards, J. (1982b). Bilingual education revisited: A reply to Donahue. *Journal of Multilingual and Multicultural Development*, **3**, 89–101.

Edwards, J. (1982c). Language attitudes and their implications among English speakers. In E. Ryan and H. Giles (Eds), *Attitudes towards language variation*, pp. 20–33. London: Arnold.

Edwards, J. (1983a). Review of *The language of children reared in poverty* (Feagans and Farran). *Journal of Language and Social Psychology*, **2**, 80–83.

Edwards, J. (1983b). Review of *The language trap* (Honey). *Journal of Language and Social Psychology*, **2**, 67–76.

Edwards, J. (1983c). Ethno-inquiry: Renaissance or illusion? Unpublished manuscript.

Edwards, J. (1983d). Language attitudes in multilingual settings: A general assessment. *Journal of Multilingual and Multicultural Development*, **4**, 225–236.

Edwards, J. (1984a). The social and political context of bilingual education. In R. Samuda, J. Berry, and M. Laferrière (Eds), *Multiculturalism in Canada*, pp. 184–200. Toronto: Allyn and Bacon.

Edwards, J. (1984b). Irish and English in Ireland. In P. Trudgill (Ed.), *Language in the British Isles*, pp. 480–498. Cambridge: Cambridge University Press.

Edwards, J. (Ed.) (1984c). *Linguistic minorities, policies and pluralism*. London: Academic Press.

Edwards, J. (1985). *Language, society and identity*. Oxford: Blackwell.

Edwards, J. (1986). Language and educational disadvantage: The persistence of linguistic 'Deficit' theory. In K. Durkin (Ed.), *Language development in the school years*, pp. 139–154. London: Croom Helm.

Edwards, J. (1987). Elaborated and restricted codes. In U. Ammon, N. Dittmar, and K. Mattheier (Eds), *Soziolinguistik: Ein internationales Handbuch zur Wissenschaft von Sprache und Gesellschaft*, pp. 374–378. Berlin: De Gruyter.

Edwards, J. (1988a). Socio-educational issues concerning indigenous minority languages: Terminology, geography and status. Paper presented to the Colloquy on Lesser Used Languages in Primary Education, April 1988, Riis.

Edwards, J. (1988b). Sociopolitical aspects of language maintenance and loss. Paper presented to the International Conference on Maintenance and Loss of Ethnic Minority Languages, August 1988, Noordwijkerhout.

Edwards, J. (1989). *Language and disadvantage*, 2nd edn. London: Cole and Whurr.

Edwards, J. and Chisholm, J. (1987). Language, multiculturalism and identity: A Canadian study. *Journal of Multilingual and Multicultural Development*, **8**, 391–408.

Edwards, J. and Doucette, L. (1987). Ethnic salience, identity and symbolic ethnicity. *Canadian Ethnic Studies*, **19**, 52–62.

Edwards, J. and Giles, H. (1984). Applications of the social psychology of language: Sociolinguistics and education. In P. Trudgill (Ed.), *Applied sociolinguistics*, pp. 119–158. London: Academic Press.

Edwards, J. and McKinnon, M. (1987). The continuing appeal of disadvantage as deficit: A Canadian study in a rural context. *Canadian Journal of Education*, **12**, 330–349.

Edwards, J. and Shearn, C. (1987). Language and identity in Belgium: Perceptions of French and Flemish students. *Ethnic and Racial Studies*, **10**, 135–148.

Edwards, V. (1987). Review of *Educational linguistics* (Stubbs). *Journal of Language and Social Psychology*, **6**, 141–144.

Entwisle, D. (1979). The child's social environment and learning to read. In T.Waller and G. MacKinnon (Eds), *Reading research*, pp. 45–70. New York: Academic Press.

Erickson, F. (1981). Some approaches to inquiry in school-community ethnography. In H. Trueba, G. Guthrie, and K. Au (Eds), *Culture and the bilingual classroom*, pp. 17–35. Rowley: Newbury.

Feagans, L. and Farran, D. (Eds) (1982). *The language of children reared in poverty*. New York: Academic Press.

Garfinkel, H. (1967). *Studies in ethnomethodology*. Englewood Cliffs, NJ: Prentice-Hall.

Genishi, C. and Dyson, A. (1984). *Language assessment in the early years*. Norwood, NJ: Ablex.

Gibson, E. and Levin, H. (1975). *The psychology of reading*. Cambridge, MA: MIT Press.

Giles, H., Bourhis, R., and Taylor, D. (1977). Towards a theory of language in ethnic group relations. In H. Giles (Ed.), *Language, ethnicity and intergroup relations*, pp. 307–348. London: Academic Press.

Giles, H. and Coupland, N. (1989). Discourse: Realignment or revolution? *Journal of Language and Social Psychology*, **8**, 63–68.

Giles, H. and Johnson, P. (1981). The role of language in ethnic group relations. In J. Turner and H. Giles (Eds), *Intergroup behaviour*, pp. 199–243. Oxford: Blackwell.

Giles, H. and Powesland, P. (1975). *Speech style and social evaluation*. London: Academic Press.

Giles, H. and Smith, P. (1979). Accommodation theory: Optimal levels of convergence. In H. Giles and R. St Clair (Eds), *Language and social psychology*, pp. 45–65. Oxford: Blackwell.

Glazer, N. (1983). *Ethnic dilemmas, 1964–1982*. Cambridge, MA: Harvard University Press.

Gordon, J. (1978). The reception of Bernstein's sociolinguistic theory among primary school teachers. University of East Anglia Papers in Linguistics, No. 1.

Gordon, J. (1981). *Verbal deficit: A critique*. London: Croom Helm.

Green, J. and Wallat, C. (1981a). Introduction. In J. Green and C. Wallat (Eds), *Ethnography and language in educational settings*, pp. xi–xviii. Norwood, NJ: Ablex.

Green, J. and Wallat, C. (Eds) (1981b). *Ethnography and language in educational settings*. Norwood, NJ: Ablex.

Griffin, P. and Mehan, H. (1981). Sense and ritual in classroom discourse. In F. Coulmas (Ed.), *Conversational routine*, pp. 82–97. The Hague: Mouton.

Gullo, D. (1981). Social class differences in preschool children's comprehension of Wh-questions. *Child Development*, **52**, 736–740.

Gumperz, J. (1981). Conversational inference and classroom learning. In J. Green and C. Wallat (Ed.), *Ethnography and language in educational settings*, pp. 3–23. Norwood, NJ: Ablex.

Gumperz, J. and Hernandez-Chavez, E. (1972). Bilingualism, bidialectalism, and classroom interaction. In C. Cazden, V. John, and D. Hymes (Eds), *Functions of language in the classroom*, pp. 84–108. New York: Teachers College Press.

Hale, A. and Edwards, A. (1981). Hearing children read. In J. Edwards (Ed.), *The social psychology of reading*, pp. 117–130. Silver Spring: Institute of Modern Languages.

Halliday, M. (1973). Foreword. In B. Bernstein (Ed.), *Class, codes and control*, Vol. 2, *Applied studies towards a sociology of language*, pp. ix–xvi. London: Routledge and Kegan Paul.

Hess, R. and Shipman, V. (1968). Maternal influences upon early learning: The cognitive environments of urban pre-school children. In R. Hess and R. Bear (Eds), *Early education*, pp. 91–103. Chicago, IL: Aldine.

Higham, J. (1975). *Send these to me*. New York: Atheneum.

Honey, J. (1983). *The language trap*. Kenton: National Council for Educational Standards.

Hymes, D. (1986). Discourse: Scope without depth. *International Journal of the Sociology of Language*, **57**, 49–89.

Jay, S., Routh, D., and Brantley, J. (1980). Social class differences in children's comprehension of adult language. *Journal of Psycholinguistic Research*, **9**, 205–217.

Jensen, A. (1969). How much can we boost IQ and scholastic achievement? *Harvard Educational Review*, **39**, 1–123.

Jensen, A. (1973). *Educability and group differences*. New York: Harper and Row.

Kaplan, C. (1982). Report on the Kassel University Conference. *Sociolinguistics Newsletter*, **13**(1), 15–18.

Lutz, F. (1981). Ethnography: The holistic approach to understanding schooling. In J. Green and C. Wallat (Ed), *Ethnography and language in educational settings*, pp. 51–63. Norwood, NJ: Ablex.

Mackie, M. (1978). Ethnicity and nationality. *Canadian Ethnic Studies*, **10**, 118–129.

Mackie, M. and Brinkerhoff, M. (1984). Measuring ethnic salience. *Canadian Ethnic Studies*, **16**, 114–131.

Mason, M. (1986). The deficit hypothesis revisited. *Educational Studies*, **12**, 279–289.

McDermott, R. and Gospodinoff, K. (1981). Social contexts for ethnic borders and school failure. In H. Trueba, G. Guthrie, and K. Au (Eds), *Culture and the bilingual classroom*, pp. 212–230. Rowley, MA: Newbury.

McNeill, D. (1966). The creation of language by children. In J. Lyons and R. Wales (Eds), *Psycholinguistic papers*, pp. 90–104. Edinburgh: Edinburgh University Press.

Mehan, H. (1979). *Learning lessons*. Cambridge, MA: Harvard University Press.

Ogbu, J. (1978). *Minority education and caste*. New York: Academic Press.

Ogbu, J. (1982). Societal forces as a context of ghetto children's school failure. In L. Feagans and D. Farran (Eds), *The language of children reared in poverty*, pp. 117–138. New York: Academic Press.

Pace, A. and Powers, W. (1981). The relationship between teachers' behaviors and beliefs and students' reading: In J. Edwards (Ed.), *The social psychology of reading*, pp. 99–115. Silver Spring: Institute of Modern Languages.

Potter, J. and Wetherell, M. (1987). *Discourse and social psychology*. London: Sage.

Ramey, C. and Campbell, F. (1977). Prevention of developmental retardation in high risk children. In P. Mittler (Ed.), *Research to practice in mental retardation*, pp. 157–164. Baltimore, MD: University Park Press.

Robinson, W.P. (1985). Social psychology and discourse. In T. Van Dijk (Ed.), *Handbook of discourse analysis*, Vol. 1, *Disciplines of discourse*, pp. 107–144. London: Academic Press.

Rodick, J. and Henggeler, S. (1980). The short-term and long-term amelioration of academic and motivational deficiencies among low-achieving inner-city adolescents. *Child Development*, **51**, 1126–1132.

Rose, E. (1982). Epistle to Kaplan: Remarks on the ethno-inquiries. *Sociolinguistics Newsletter*, **13**(1), 18–23.

Schonell, F. and Goodacre, E. (1975). *The psychology and teaching of reading*. Edinburgh: Oliver and Boyd.

Sevigny, M. (1981). Triangulated inquiry: A methodology for the analysis of classroom interaction. In J. Green and C. Wallat (Eds), *Ethnography and language in educational settings*, pp. 65–85. Norwood, NJ: Ablex.

Sinclair, J. and Coulthard, R. (1975). *Towards an analysis of discourse*. London: Oxford University Press.

Smith, J. (1988). Review of *Discourse and social psychology* (Potter and Wetherell). *Psychologist*, **1**, 109.

Stone, M. (1981). *The education of the black child in Britain: The myth of multiracial education*. London: Fontana.

Stubbs, M. (1983). *Discourse analysis*. Oxford: Blackwell.

Stubbs, M. (1986). *Educational linguistics*. Oxford: Blackwell.

Stubbs, M. and Delamont, S. (1976). *Explorations in classroom observation*. Chichester (England): Wiley.

Sutherland, S. (1988). Review of *Facts, fallacies and frauds in psychology* (Colman). *Times Higher Education Supplement*, 12 February.

Tajfel, H. (1982). *Social identity and intergroup relations*. Cambridge: Cambridge University Press.

Tomlinson, S. (1984). Home, school and community. In M. Craft (Ed.), *Education and cultural pluralism*, pp. 21–37. London: Falmer.

Tough, J. (1977). *Talking and learning*. London: Ward Lock.

Trudgill, P. (1975). *Accent, dialect and the school*. London: Arnold.

Van Dijk, T. (Ed.) (1985). *Handbook of discourse analysis* (4 Vols). London: Academic Press.

Willes, M. (1983). *Children into pupils*. London: Routledge and Kegan Paul.

24

Social Psychological Perspectives on Second Language Acquisition

ROBERT C. GARDNER AND RICHARD CLÉMENT

Department of Psychology, University of Western Ontario and School of Psychology, University of Ottawa, Canada

The term 'second language' is often used interchangeably with that of 'foreign language', and some readers may find it strange that there is a chapter dealing with second language acquisition (or foreign language learning) in a handbook on language and social psychology. To many, studying another language like French, or German, or English, is much like studying any other school subject like mathematics or history, so that the topic might seem more suited to a handbook on educational psychology. But, in fact, there is considerable literature on the topic of second language acquisition, and much of the research in this area is conducted by social psychologists, or at least has a very definite social psychological perspective. The purpose of this chapter is to provide an overview of this literature.

Why, you may ask, would social psychologists be interested in second language learning? The answer is, in fact, fairly straightforward. In discussing the history of social psychology, Allport (1954) pointed out that social psychologists are concerned with understanding the behaviour of individuals that results because of their membership in a cultural group. Social psychology is concerned with such things as the development of attitudes; relationships among members of the same and different ethnic, political, or social groups; individuals' feelings about various groups; and characteristics of individuals that influence interpersonal relationships. It thus is quite reasonable to expect social psychologists to be interested in a situation where individuals of one ethnic group are learning the language of another. The

Handbook of Language and Social Psychology
Edited by H. Giles and W.P. Robinson.   © 1990 John Wiley & Sons Ltd

situation leads to a number of very specific questions, many of them dealing with central issues in ethnic relations. For example, are there specific skills, attitudes and motivations, or personality traits that might facilitate or impede the acquisition of a second language? Are there particular tricks that students might use to help them overcome any reticence they feel or difficulties they experience in learning a language? Does the nature of the social environment have any bearing on students' relative degree of success in learning a second language? Is one's sense of identity modified in any way by learning a language, or, contrariwise, does one's sense of identity influence achievement in a second language? These are some of the questions we address in this chapter, but we anticipate that the material presented will help you to formulate a series of questions of your own.

The acquisition of language is complex and has both biological (Lenneberg, 1967) and social (Mowrer, 1950) foundations. Generally, the first language is learned in infancy and early childhood, and is an integral part of a developmental sequence. The acquisition of a second language, however, is somewhat more complex. It can take place in very many different settings and at different ages, and there are many reasons for learning second languages. They can be learned at home in infancy and early childhood, at school as part of the regular educational system, or later in life in educational contexts or interpersonal settings for occupational or personal reasons. Because of this diversity, it is often difficult adequately to summarize the relevant research literature.

Even if one limits oneself to reviewing studies focusing on individuals learning a second language in an educational context, there are a number of different pro-grammes in which this can take place. Tucker (1974) describes three different types of language courses: core second language programmes, where students receive instruction in 20- to 75-minute classes on anything from a daily to a weekly basis; partial immersion programmes, where students learn some but not all school subjects in a second language; and total immersion programmes, where students receive virtually all of their education in the second language. These programmes, moreover, can take place in communities where the second language is the dominant one, where both languages tend to co-exist, or where the second language is encountered infrequently. There are a number of reviews and summaries of these types of programmes which give an appreciation of the complexities involved (see, e.g., Genesee, 1987; Lambert and Tucker, 1972; Swain and Lapkin, 1982; Willig, 1985).

When one considers the many different measures of individual differences that might be involved in second language learning and the many possible definitions and measures of second language proficiency, any stability in results is remarkable. In the literature, the term 'proficiency' has many definitions. Often it is taken to mean primarily 'knowledge *about* the second language' which is assessed by means of objective (multiple-choice, true–false) measures of vocabulary, grammar, aural comprehension, reading comprehension, etc., or grades in the language class. It can also, however, refer to 'communicative competence in the language', assessed in terms of the ability to interact in the language (Canale and Swain, 1980). Then, too, it can refer to self-perceptions of competence defined either globally in terms of being able to 'speak' the language or in terms of specific language acts such as being able to order a meal in a restaurant (Clark, 1981). Each of the preceding can be viewed as possible linguistic outcomes of any language learning programme (see Gardner, 1985). There is, however, another aspect of proficiency, viz. the willingness and capacity to use the language in interpersonal contexts. This is equally important and can be considered as a non-linguistic outcome of second language programmes. Each aspect has been investigated to varying degrees in this area of research.

This review will focus on the social psychological aspects of second language learning, and will consider second language proficiency as comprising all of the above facets. In reviewing this topic, attention first will be directed toward three classes of individual difference variables that conceivably influence second language acquisition:

(1) cognitive characteristics;
(2) attitudes and motivation;
(3) personality attributes.

Following this, we will consider the role of context and its effects on both proficiency and individual difference correlates of such proficiency.

INDIVIDUAL DIFFERENCES

Cognitive Characteristics

Any discussion of the social psychological aspects of second language acquisition would be derelict if it did not include a consideration of cognitive factors associated with learning a second language, because this would ignore a very basic component of the learning process. Obviously, there are individual differences in language learning that reflect differences in abilities or approaches to the task at hand; and these are typically subsumed under the general category of cognitive variables. This section focuses attention on two major cognitive variables: language aptitude and language learning strategies. As discussed here, language aptitude is a general term referring to those abilities that facilitate language learning, whereas language learning strategies are those techniques and/or tricks that individuals use to help them acquire language material. Both classes of variables have been shown to have appreciable relations to measures of achievement.

The concept of language aptitude dates back to 1929 when it was proposed that one could develop special prognosis tests to predict success in second language learning (Henmon, 1929). The major measures used in North America today are the Modern Language Aptitude Test (Carroll and Sapon, 1959); the Elementary form of the Modern Language Aptitude Test, intended for young children (Carroll and Sapon, 1967); and the Pimsleur Language Aptitude Battery (Pimsleur, 1966). The Defense Language Aptitude Battery (Petersen and Al-Haik, 1976) has been developed largely for use with American military personnel. These tests are similar in that they assess verbal abilities and skill in English, and/or employ miniature artificial language learning tasks in order to differentiate between potential successful and unsuccessful language learners. The tests are presumed to measure such underlying variables as phonetic coding, grammatical sensitivity, rote memory, inductive language learning ability, verbal intelligence (including analytic reasoning), motivation, and auditory ability.

The primary validity data for these measures consist of their correlations with indices of second language proficiency, which generally tend to be significant (Carroll and Sapon, 1959, 1967; Petersen and Al-Haik, 1976; Pimsleur, 1966). Carroll (1962) demonstrated that correlations between aptitude and second language achievement tend to increase from high school to college to military language intensive programmes, and argued that this reflected the growing importance of aptitude in influencing achievement once factors such as motivation, opportunity to learn, and quality of language teaching improve and become more homogeneous. Lambert (1963a) considered the concept of language aptitude in the context of various theoretical approaches in psychology and proposed that it is quite probable that the underlying abilities develop at different rates and that different training programmes may be more suited to some patterns of abilities than to others. He argued that language educators should consider matching particular programmes to particular ages and ability groupings.

The concept of language learning strategies has a somewhat shorter history than that of language aptitude. This concept grew out of attempts to characterize the good language learner, through which it was found that many such learners often relied on particular techniques to assist them (Rubin, 1975; Stern, 1975). These strategies run the gamut of activities from those that facilitate memorization of material to those that make the task more meaningful, maintain motivation, encourage active participation, and/or reflect personality characteristics such as risk-taking. Studies in this area have used a number of different assessment devices to assess individual differences in the use of such strategies (e.g. Bialystok, 1984; Oxford, Nyikos, and Crookall, 1987; Politzer and McGroarty, 1985; Reiss, 1985). Oxford et al. (1987), for example, factor-analyzed responses to the Strategy Inventory for Language Learners (Oxford, 1986) and found clear evidence for five factors defined as General Study Habits, Functional Practice, Speaking and Communicating Meaning, Studying or Practising Independently, and Mnemonic Devices. Reiss (1985) reported that some strategies were much more commonly used than others, and Politzer (1983) and Politzer and McGroarty (1985) have demonstrated that individual differences in the use of certain strategies are related to differences in both proficiency and motivation.

As this section indicates, both the individual's ability and the strategies that he or she uses to help acquire the language are significant factors that must be recognized in any theoretical model or empirical study of language learning. As we shall see, however, this remains to be done in many cases.

Attitudes and Motivation

There is a large body of research concerned with the relation of attitudinal and motivational variables to second language proficiency. Two early studies, conducted in Great Britain, investigated the relation of proficiency defined by school grades to attitudes toward learning the language, and reported significant but low correlations (Jones, 1950; Jordan, 1941). Later studies in Great Britain, the USA, and Canada tended to confirm these relationships (Duckworth and Entwistle, 1974; Neidt and Hedlund, 1967; Randhawa and Korpan, 1973). Other research has focused instead on a complex of variables assessing a wide range of attitudes and motivation, and often including various measures of language learning abilities as well as measures of different aspects of proficiency. These studies have also tended to use factor analytic procedures to uncover the dimensionality underlying such measures.

The original study using this approach was conducted by Gardner and Lambert (1959), who reported that achievement in French (the second language) loaded on two independent factors: social motivation (defined primarily by indices of attitudes toward French Canadians, an integrative orientation toward French study, and motivation) and language aptitude (defined by measures of language learning abilities and verbal intelligence). They argued that such a configuration supported the notion that proficiency in a second language was dependent upon at least two independent factors: language aptitude and a socially based motivation that involved a 'willingness to be like valued members of the (second) language community' (p. 271).

This type of research has been replicated in a number of different cultural contexts with different ages of students and with different first and second languages. Many more attitudinal and motivational measures have been added since the original study, but by and large they tend to belong in one of three categories, viz. integrativeness, attitudes toward the learning situation, or motivation. Measures of integrativeness are those that refer to attitudes toward the other language group, outgroups in general, other languages, etc., while indices of attitudes toward the learning situation typically involve evaluations of the course or the teacher. Measures of motivation, on the other hand, refer to different characteristics of the motivated individual such as effort expended to learn the language, desire to learn the language, etc.

In these later studies, although the factor structures are sometimes more complex than in the original study, they generally lead to similar conclusions. Two books have been written that discuss this research in considerable detail (see Gardner, 1985; Gardner and Lambert, 1972). These studies have been conducted with English-speaking Canadian students learning French, French-speaking Canadian students learning English, English-speaking American students learning French or Spanish, Franco-Americans learning French, Filipinos learning English in the Philippines, children of Belize in Central America learning English, and students in Finland learning English.

Other researchers have sometimes used different measures and analytic procedures. Often, they have conducted factor analyses of the relationships among the predictors and used the resulting factor scores as predictors, so that the interpretation of the predictors themselves is not straightforward. These studies have tended to produce equivocal results. For example, measures of favourable attitudes toward the other community were found to relate both positively and negatively to proficiency among Chinese students learning English (Oller, Hudson, and Liu, 1977). In discussing these and other studies of this type, Gardner (1985) points out a number of reasons as to why these findings are less consistent than those described earlier, and why their interpretation is ambiguous.

Some studies have summarized correlations across a number of samples. Generally, they have shown that indices of motivation correlate more highly with proficiency than do the measures of attitudes involving other language groups or the language learning situation. Gardner, Smythe, Clément, and Gliksman (1976), for example, showed that motivation was among the top three predictors in all of 15 sets of correlations investigated, while language aptitude was among the top three in 14 sets, and French classroom anxiety in 11. Lalonde and Gardner (1985) contrasted correlations between proficiency and indices of each of motivation, integrativeness, and attitudes toward the learning situation in 39 samples. The correlations were generally highest for motivation. Gardner (1980) found, furthermore, that correlations of attitude/motivation indices with proficiency were comparable to those between language aptitude and proficiency. He reports that the median correlation between the Attitude/Motivation Index and Grades in French was .37 for 29 samples (range = .15 to .50), while that for language aptitude was .41 (range = .19 to .59).

Such results have often been interpreted as indicating that attitudes and motivation facilitate second language acquisition, though different processes are sometimes invoked to explain the relationships, and different concepts are often emphasized (see, e.g., Clément, 1980; Gardner, 1985; Gardner and Lambert, 1972; Giles and Byrne, 1982; Krashen, 1981; Lambert, 1963b, 1967, 1972; Schumann, 1978a; Smythe, Stennett, and Feenstra, 1972). There are, however, alternative perspectives. Burstall, Jamieson, Cohen, and Hargreaves (1974), for example, argued that it is more likely the case that success in learning a second language would foster favourable attitudes and high levels of motivation. Oller and Perkins (1978), on the other hand, proposed that factors such as intelligence could account for the relationships obtained, while Oller (1982) suggested that the relationships could be due to a confounding of verbal intelligence and social desirability with measures of both second language proficiency and attitudinal/motivational characteristics. In a somewhat different vein, Au (1988) has criticized the socio-educational model of second language acquisition proposed by Gardner (1985) to explain how attitudes and motivation can influence proficiency. Au (1988) argues that the results obtained in many of the studies linking attitudes and motivation to second language achievement are ambiguous. He argues further that the concept of the social milieu proposed in that model permits *post-hoc* explanations for these ambiguities and thus makes the model itself untestable. As indicated in a following section in this chapter dealing with contextual aspects, however, it is clear that the social milieu plays a significant role in language learning and that it isn't simply a convenient explanatory device.

In replying to the various criticisms, Gardner (1980, 1988) has demonstrated that many of the criticisms are based on misconceptions, and that the 'inconsistent' results reflect methodological, measurement, or analytic problems with some specific studies. One value that derives from the various criticisms and counter-criticisms, however, is that they serve to highlight important issues in this area of research and focus attention more directly on the processes involved in second language learning.

One issue that is particularly problematic is that of the cause/effect sequence. The basic data are correlational, and when dealing with individual differences one cannot make unequivocal generalizations as to which are cause and which are effect. In his seminal discussions of this area, Lambert (1963b, 1967) demonstrated how attitudes and motivation were both cause and effect of successful second language achievement, and a number of theoretical models developed since then are based in part on similar notions, though they emphasize different process variables (see, e.g., Clément's (1980) social context model, Gardner and Smythe's (1975) socio-educational model, and Giles and Byrne's (1982) intergroup model). In recent years, increased use has been made of causal modelling procedures to provide tests of specific causal links, and this new development has been extremely beneficial in clarifying concepts and refining our understanding of underlying process variables. Such tests have been made of the social context model (Clément and Kruidenier, 1985), the socio-educational model (Gardner, Lalonde, and Pierson, 1983), and the intergroup model (Hall and Gudykunst, 1986).

Other research has considered the relation of attitudes and motivation to other aspects of second language acquisition. Research has demonstrated that attitudes and motivation are related negatively to the intention and/or actual act of dropping out of second language study (Bartley, 1969, 1970; Clément, Smythe, and Gardner, 1978; Gardner *et al.*, 1976), and positively to the amount of participation in language class (Gliksman, Gardner, and Smythe, 1982; Naiman, Fröhlich, Stern, and Todesco, 1978). These studies direct attention to the more non-linguistic outcomes of language study referred to earlier. These results, as well as those demonstrating correlations between proficiency in the second language and attitudes and motivation, demonstrate the very important role they play in the language learning process.

Personality Variables

Viewed from a different perspective, it is reasonable to assume that an individual's personality could influence second language achievement, and a number of personality characteristics have been considered as possible determinants of second language proficiency. Among the most frequently studied are sociability and/or extraversion, field dependence/independence, empathy, and anxiety.

On the surface, it might appear that sociability is an obvious correlate of proficiency since it is reasonable to assume that sociable people would be more outgoing, would communicate more, and thus would learn more of a second language. Kawcyznski (1951) argued, however, that both extraverted (sociable) and introverted individuals would be successful, and that language programmes should be geared to both types of individuals, a belief that also is shared by many language teachers (Naiman, Fröhlich, and Stern, 1975). To a considerable extent, the research literature supports this position. Chastain (1975) found positive correlations between sociability and grades in both German and Spanish, but not French. Smart, Elton, and Burnett (1970), on the other hand, found negative relationships between sociability and proficiency, once differences in ability were controlled. Lalonde (1982) and Ely (1986) failed, however, to find any relationship between sociability and proficiency.

Field dependence/independence is another variable that seems potentially relevant. Witkin, Goodenough, and Oltman (1979) characterize field-dependent individuals as sensitive and interested in others, while field-independent individuals are self-sufficient and somewhat analytic. Krashen (1981) views someone with an analytic orientation as being a potentially better language learner; thus it seems reasonable to assume that field independence would relate to achievement. Naiman *et al.* (1978) found, in fact, that field independence related positively to both oral and aural second language skills, while Tucker, Hamayan, and Genesee (1976), Genesee and Hamayan (1980), and Hansen and Stansfield (1981) also found relations between field independence and second language achievement. This last study offers a note of caution in interpreting these results, however, since most of the relationships obtained were eliminated once the effects of scholastic ability were partialled out. Thus, although it seems clear that field-independent individuals may be more successful at learning a second language, this may reflect less on their personality characteristics and more on the relation of field independence to ability.

Another potential correlate is empathy, in that one might expect that individuals who are sensitive to cues in interpersonal situations would be more likely to acquire an authentic pronunciation in a second language. This type of hypothesis was supported by Guiora, Lane, and Bosworth (1967), who found a positive correlation between their measure of empathy, the Micro-Momentary Expression Test, and accuracy of pronunciation among French teachers. Unfortunately, subsequent studies (see, e.g., Guiora, Brannon, and Dull, 1972) yielded equivocal results, possibly because of measurement artifacts. Schumann (1975) has commented that the rationale underlying these studies is reasonable, but that the studies themselves have failed to provide an adequate test, probably because of difficulties involved with the measure of empathy used. In any event, the concept itself seems appropriate, and is one that would have obvious links with the attitudinal/motivational variables discussed earlier.

The concept of anxiety is another one that is meaningfully linked with the development of proficiency in a second language. Scovel (1978) proposed that there are possibly two forms of anxiety, facilitating and debilitating anxiety, which could have opposing relations with proficiency. This characterization, however, does not seem necessary to interpret the various results obtained. By and large, measures such as general anxiety, test anxiety, manifest anxiety, and the like that do not refer directly to second language anxiety usually fail to relate to indices of achievement (Clément, Gardner, and Smythe, 1977a, 1980; Tarampi, Lambert and Tucker, 1968). Chastain (1975) did find a negative correlation between test anxiety and grades in Spanish, but similar relationships were not obtained for German or French, or other measures of anxiety.

Studies concerned with measures of anxiety that deal directly with the second language (e.g. Language Class Anxiety, Language Use Anxiety, Language Test Anxiety) fairly consistently report negative relationships with achievement (see Clément *et al.*, 1977a, 1980; Horwitz, Horwitz, and Cope, 1986); that is, increased levels of anxiety are associated with lower levels of proficiency, suggesting that anxiety has a debilitating effect on second language learning.

In a series of studies, Clément and his colleagues (Clément, 1986; Clément *et al.*, 1977a, 1980; Clément and Kruidenier, 1985) have proposed that a major dimension underlying second language acquisition is Self-Confidence with the language. This self-confidence is viewed as a combination of low levels of language-specific anxiety, confidence in one's language skills, and self-perceptions of high levels of proficiency. Using causal modelling techniques, Clément and Kruidenier (1985) demonstrated that self-confidence can be viewed as one cause of motivation that in turn is one cause of second language achievement. In a subsequent study, Clément (1986) obtained high correlations between self-confidence, defined in terms of an aggregate of low anxiety, high linguistic confidence, and high self-ratings of proficiency, and both second language (i.e. English) oral production skills and acculturation, defined in terms of a tendency to use English in communication situations. This type of conceptualization, therefore, links the anxiety concept directly with attitudinal/ motivational attributes as well as second language proficiency. At the same time, it describes a process by which they might interrelate. Clément (1980) has argued previously that this process is itself influenced by the sociocultural milieu in which language training takes place.

As this section demonstrates, there is considerable research literature indicating that various individual difference variables such as language aptitude, language learning strategies, attitudes and motivation, and various personality traits are related to proficiency in a second language. In the discussion to now, other variables such as the ethnic background of the students, their sociocultural contexts, and the nature of the language learning environment have not been considered even though they are often factors involved in the studies themselves. The next section of this review considers the more general role played by such social context effects, and discusses processes by which such environmental factors could be implicated.

CONTEXTUAL ASPECTS

Whereas individual differences have had their place for some time within social psychology, interest in contextual effects is more recent (but see Lambert, Havelka, and Crosby, 1958, for an exception). It is even questionable whether or not social psychology has developed concepts that permit the scientific description of contextual effects in a manner that would be compatible with discussing individual differences in second language acquisition.

The description of the context of utterances can be seen to involve three inter-related levels:

(1) the context of a particular language characterized by a specific lexicon and rules governing its verbal and paraverbal communication systems;
(2) the context of a particular interpersonal encounter within a specific situation;
(3) the wider societal and intergroup context in which the utterance is made.

Categories (2) and (3) clearly refer to the social context within which the acquisition (or maintenance) and usage of a language take place, whereas category (1) refers to the linguistic, cognitive, developmental, and, to some extent, anthropological context. Although the last category shows much controversy and research (see, e.g., Hagège, 1985; Hamers and Blanc, 1988; Heller, 1984; McLaughlin, 1984), it will be considered here only insofar as it has implications for categories (2) and (3). Given this restriction, as well as current trends in second language pedagogy (e.g. Kramsch, 1983; Tardif and Weber, 1987), and anticipating the forthcoming discussion, the social psychological perspective on context is proposed here to encompass all interpersonal and intergroup phenomena, real or imagined, likely to influence or result from the acquisition of a second language.

This definition gives the social psychological study of context in second language acquisition a scope which is out of proportion with the evidence collected to date. Hopefully, the contrast will motivate future research. The structure of what follows is meant to reflect the attention given in the empirical literature to the various factors proposed to influence second language acquisition. Theoretical developments which are in themselves integrations and abstractions from empirical evidence (such as those of Hamers and Blanc, 1988) will, however, not be reviewed here. In terms of the present perspective, it seems that two clusters of empirical evidence can be identified: (a) a sociostructural perspective and (b) a socioperceptual perspective.

The Sociostructural Perspective

The sociostructural perspective is characterized by attempts at dealing with the influence on bilingualism of 'objective' community characteristics. Bilingualism is defined in terms either of the individual capacity to use two languages *or* of the collective acquisition and maintenance of two languages in a community. These two outcomes should not be confused because they entail different determinants and consequences. Collective bilingualism does not necessarily imply individual bilingualism. It may, however, promote interethnic contact, which may or may not have positive consequences, depending on other factors. Thus, the studies by McAllister and Mugham (1984) concerning the maintenance of Welsh in Wales, by Cartwright (1987) concerning the level of bilingualism of Quebec anglophones, and by Driedger (1984) concerning factors likely to affect heritage language maintenance in Canada attest to the positive influence of demographic aspects on language acquisition, maintenance, and use. It does seem that the relative proportion of a language group within a community is positively related to the extent to which that language is learned and/or maintained.

The positive effect of the presence of the second language-speaking group in the immediate environment does not imply, however, that a second language cannot be learned within a milieu from which the second language-speaking group is relatively absent. The results obtained by Gardner and Smythe (1975) with anglophones learning French as a second language show that, in an English monolingual setting, the attainment of a relatively high level of proficiency in a second language is possible and, furthermore, that such proficiency is positively correlated with attitudes and motivation (see also Gardner, 1979). Students participating in immersion programmes (e.g. Genesee, 1987; Swain and Lapkin, 1982) in settings where the second language group is not present also develop high levels of proficiency, at least with respect to the more contextualized aspects of communicative competence.

Without direct contact with the second language-speaking group, at least two contextual aspects may influence the student's achievement. The first aspect corresponds to the second language learning situation, including the course itself and the teacher (see Gardner, 1979, 1983). There is also evidence (e.g. Clément, 1978; Gardner and Smythe, 1975) that there is a relationship between attitude toward the second language teacher and attitude toward the second language group. This suggests that the teacher may be perceived as representing the second language-speaking group for students living in unilingual communities and, consequently, be an important agent of attitude formation and change.

The second contextual aspect pertaining to unicultural settings is related to the role of parents in supporting the language learning efforts of their children. Gardner (1968) suggested that parents may play an active role through their open support and monitoring of children's curricular activities. As well, parents may play a passive role by modelling and communicating attitudes and values related to the acquisition of the second language and the second language-speaking group. Empirical research has shown a positive relationship between the student's perception of parental encouragement and motivation to learn a second language (e.g. Clément, 1978; Gardner and Smythe, 1975). Furthermore, Colletta, Clément, and Edwards (1983), from a survey of parental attitudes, report results supporting the existence of separate constructs corresponding, respectively, to the passive and active roles hypothesized by Gardner (1968), though no direct relationship to the child's second language fluency was reported by the authors. The results of their application of causal modelling techniques would rather suggest that the dual influence of parents on proficiency is mediated through the student's motivational characteristics. These results corroborate those obtained previously in numerous studies (see Gardner, 1985, for review).

Apart from the influence of the learning situation and parental encouragement, students learning a second language in an environment where the second language group is not available may benefit from the indirect contact afforded through mass media as well as the sporadic contact permitted through travel (e.g. Clément, Gardner, and Smythe, 1977b; Desrochers and Gardner, 1981). The results obtained by Clément (1979) would, however, suggest that the format of the contact programme (i.e. length of residence, closeness to target language group) may affect differentially the motivational outcome of the programme.

When the second language group is available in the community, parental influence and the learning situation remain important, but in conjunction with structural characteristics, one of which is the relative political power of the first and second language-speaking groups. The importance of this factor is illustrated by Bourhis (1986) in his account of the history of language legislation in Quebec and by Olson and Burns (1983) in their analysis of the variable effects of immersion programmes in different provinces of Canada. It seems evident that increased political power and recognition have, by themselves and together with an important demographic representation, a positive effect on the maintenance of a language and the extent to which that language will be learned by other ethnolinguistic groups.

Both demographic and political aspects were included together with socio-economic status under the structural formulation of the construct of ethnolinguistic vitality proposed by Giles, Bourhis, and Taylor (1977). They proposed that ethnolinguistic vitality is that which causes a group to behave distinctively and act as a collectivity. They argued as well that minorities that have little vitality will ultimately cease to exist. Thus, embodied within their formulation is the expectation that structural factors would have a direct impact on the maintenance of a language within a community. The evidence provided by Giles *et al.* (1977; see also Mougeon and Heller, 1986) tends to support the hypothesized effect of ethnolinguistic vitality on first language maintenance.

Results pertaining to second language acquisition and use, however, originate for the most part from the education literature. A survey of various forms of bilingual education (Hamers and Blanc, 1988) shows that the outcomes of bilingual education are a function of status of the learners and of the extent of their control over the schooling system. Members of majority groups are more likely to be more successful in developing bilingual competence, and less likely to suffer social and cognitive deficits than are members of minority groups.

According to the interdependence and threshold hypotheses (see Cummins, 1984a; Cummins and Swain, 1986), a second language will be learned properly to the extent that an individual attains a minimal level of fluency in the first language. Such conditions also apply to the cognitive and social advantages of an additive form of bilingualism, while subtractive bilingualism (i.e. loss of the first language and culture) results from a failure to acquire an appropriate knowledge of the first language (see Lambert, 1978).

Cummins (1979, 1984a,b) and Cummins and Swain (1986) use the above argument as well as empirical evidence (but see Holobow, Genesee, Lambert, Gastright, and Met, 1987; McLaughlin, 1984) as support for monolingual mother-tongue education for minority children as well as for the general 'empowerment' (Cummins, 1986) of minority groups *vis-à-vis* their own schooling system. They argue that subtractive forms of bilingualism can be avoided to the extent that the family and school milieux are consistent in affording children social support and education in their first language and culture.

In contrast, a home–school language switch may be beneficial for majority students, whose first language is valued and widely used in the community. In such cases, the available evidence suggests that immersion students are comparable to regular school students in all subject matters and that while maintaining their command over the second language they will not lag behind in terms of their knowledge of the first language (Lambert and Tucker, 1972). The school environment is thus presented as a counterweight (see Landry and Allard, 1987a,b) to societal forces; it may be positioned in support or against the home environment, depending on the minority or majority status of the learner.

Most of the available evidence and theorizing on the influence of the structural context on second language acquisition, therefore, hinges on the distinction between the relative status of the learner group and target language group. This emphasis has obscured and confounded to some extent the effects of interethnic contact. Minority individuals would be expected to have greater contact with members of the second language group, whereas little such contact would be available to majority students learning a minority second language. Yet, the effect of interethnic contact on interethnic attitudes has been well documented (e.g. Desrochers and Clément, 1979). For example, d'Anglejean and Renaud (1985) report that the use of French in the community is a significant predictor of French proficiency among adult immigrants in Montreal. Clément (1986) reports that for both majority (from Quebec) and minority (from Ontario) French Canadians, a strong association is found between frequency and pleasantness of contact with anglophones and proficiency in English. In fact, social psychological models of second language acquisition (e.g. Clément, 1980; Gardner and Smythe, 1975; Schumann, 1978a) have all hypothesized that interethnic contact is an important determinant of second language achievement.

Such acknowledgment of the influence of 'real-life' contact in the target language can also be found in the education literature. For example, Wong Fillmore (1976, as quoted by McLaughlin, 1984) links the 'natural' acquisition of a second language to the acquisition of 'formulaic' speech enabling the individual to be accepted and supported by the target language group. Both Harley (1986) and Cummins and Swain (1986) conclude from their study of different types of second language programmes that exposure to, and use of, the second language in the environment has a positive effect on the student's achievement in the second language.

These results, taken in conjunction with other research dealing with interethnic contact (e.g. Clément and Kruidenier, 1985; Schumann, 1978b, 1986), raise the question of the relative importance and/or interactive role of status and contact in the second language. Although much has been attributed to the minority/majority distinction, few studies have controlled systematically for amount of contact. In one such study, Clément and Kruidenier (1983; see also Kruidenier and Clément, 1986) have varied systematically:

(1) the status of the learning group;
(2) the status of the target language group;
(3) the linguistic composition of the community.

The goal of the study was to assess the relationship between these factors and the endorsement of various reasons (i.e. orientations) for learning the target language. The results show that instrumental, knowledge, friendship, and travel orientations were common to all groups. The relative status of the learning group produced by factors (1) and (2) and the availability of the target language group in the community (factor 3), however, influenced the students' orientations. Control and prestige-seeking orientations emerged as a result of the relative dominance of the learning group, whereas integration and identification orientations emerged as a result of the relative familiarity of the target language group. Although the studies did not assess second language proficiency and use, these results link second language learning motivation to independent effects of status and contact.

The Socioperceptual Perspective

The sociostructural factors described in the preceding section as well as the relevant evidence demonstrate that the acquisition and use of a second language are intimately linked to the social context of interethnic contacts. The scientific understanding of the relationship, however, requires that we also specify the manner in which phenomena that are external to individuals come to influence the psychological mechanism of language acquisition and use.

A first step towards bridging the structural–psychological gap has usually been to recast structural factors as subjective perceptions of the individual. The concept of 'ethnolinguistic vitality', for example, was proposed initially (Giles *et al.*, 1977) to describe the objective features associated with the strength of ethnic group membership in a community. The initial statement, however, allowed for the possibility that subjective vitality might be more important than its 'objective' counterpart. The Subjective Vitality Questionnaire (SVQ) subsequently developed by Bourhis, Giles, and Rosenthal (1981) was meant to assess perceived ethnolinguistic vitality.

The format of the SVQ still retained, however, the elements of the 'structural' construct, assessing demographic representation, socio-economic status, and institutional support. Subsequent studies using this instrument showed that, in some situations, objective and subjective vitality tended to correlate positively (e.g. Bourhis and Sachdev, 1984; Clément, 1986), though sometimes the relationship was weak (and intriguingly so; see Pierson, Giles, and Young, 1987). Although subjective vitality was proposed by Clément (1984) to relate to measures of motivation to learn the second language as well as to proficiency in the language, subsequent research found no such relationship for motivation (Labrie and Clément, 1986) or for proficiency and use of the second language (Clément, 1986). Using a somewhat different measure, however, Gardner, Lalonde, Nero, and Young (1988) did find that perceived ethnolinguistic vitality was related to self-evaluations of proficiency in the second language.

These results, as well as criticisms (i.e. Husband and Saifullah Khan, 1982) levelled against the concept of ethnolinguistic vitality, led Landry and Allard (1985) to reconceptualize ethnolinguistic vitality as a belief system and to devise a measuring instrument patterned after Kreitler and Kreitler's (1982) theory rather than after the original structural concept. Using their scale, Landry and Allard (1985) were able to predict choice of language of schooling among minority francophones from New Brunswick. The contrast between these results and those obtained with the original scale is confirmed in a recent study by Bourhis and Bédard (1988) which shows the greater predictive power of the Landry and Allard scale relative to the SVQ. This illustrates the necessity of translating structural constructs into constructs that are congruent with hypothesized psychological mechanisms. More importantly, it illustrates the fact that a structurally adequate construct is not necessarily psychologically meaningful.

But even before this methodological issue came to the fore, the introduction of subjective ethnolinguistic vitality to the area of second language acquisition was meant to link the intergroup situation prevailing in the community to the affective process hypothesized to influence the individual's motivation to acquire a second language (Clément, 1980). Giles and Byrne (1982), Giles and Johnson (1987), and Garret, Giles, and Coupland (in press) subsequently introduced more elaborated versions of the individual's perception of the intergroup situation, in an attempt to reconcile 'ethnolinguistic identity theory' (see Giles and Johnson, 1981) with the evidence stemming from the research on second language proficiency and speech accommodation as they apply to a minority situation.

The model proposed by Giles and his colleagues predicts that strong identification with one's group, the perception of cognitive alternatives to a subordinate intergroup status, the perception of ingroup and outgroup boundaries which are hard and closed, identification with few categories other than ethnicity, and the perception of relatively high ingroup vitality would lead one to preserve the first language and culture and not to strive for proficiency in a second language (but see Giles and Johnson, 1987). The converse condition would promote second language acquisition.

The 'intergroup model' of second language acquisition, therefore, represents situations in which the second language would be learned, as well as situations in which such proficiency would not only *not* be sought, but would be systematically avoided. The more recent formulation of the model (i.e. Garrett *et al.*, in press) also describes possible differences between members of the ingroup and their influence on ingroup identification as well as the influence of outgroup reaction on ingroup status and identification.

Contrasting with this wide conceptual scope is the limited amount of empirical research generated by the model. To date, two attempts have been made to validate hypotheses derived from the 'intergroup model' (i.e. Giles and Johnson, 1987; Hall and Gudykunst, 1986) and results have been interpreted as providing moderate support for the original framework. The obtained results also lead Giles and Johnson (1987) to revise the model by adding new contingencies and alternatives which complicate further the predictions of the model (see also Garrett *et al.*, in press).

Other formulations seem to have generated clearer results, but again in very limited quantity when compared to the evidence pertaining to individual attitude and motivation research. The framework proposed by Gardner and Smythe (1975), for example, suggests that cultural expectations will influence an individual's motivation to learn a second language, and his or her eventual proficiency. Gardner *et al.* (1983), using causal modelling, report a positive association between the extent to which students perceived school officials to be favourably predisposed toward second language course objectives and integrativeness. In a similar vein, Genesee, Rogers, and Holobow (1983), working from Schumann's (1976) social distance model, showed that the student's expectation of support from the target language group was significantly related to various measures of second language use, proficiency, and willingness to affiliate with members of the target language group.

Both studies, therefore, underline the importance of the individual learner's perception of community support for the acquisition of a second language. The study of Genesee *et al.* (1983) also demonstrates the importance of outgroup support, where available. The perceived pleasantness and frequency of such contact have been shown to be the immediate determinant of self-confidence in the second language (see Clément and Kruidenier, 1985), which has, in turn, been associated most strongly with indices of communicative competence (cf. Clément, 1986). Taken together with Harley (1986) and Cummins and Swain's (1986) conclusions regarding the importance of second language usage, these results support the important role of perceived community values and interethnic attitudes in determining second language proficiency.

Viewed within the context of languages in contact, a particular language is the badge of belonging to a particular ethnic group, and language variations (including second language use) are symptoms of contact between groups. These variations are taken as a reflection of the type of contact taking place between groups, as well as means used by locutors to influence the process and outcome of such contact. The social psychology of language has, therefore, assumed a form of isomorphism between language phenomena and ethnic identity.

Yet, the association between language and identity is not a stable one. Much of the relevant research has been done in studies of *acculturation*. Thus, Clément (1986) and Lalleman (1987) report a positive association between fluency in the second language and level of acculturation to that group. Pak, Dion, and Dion (1985), on the other hand, find a positive association between self-confidence in the second language and level of linguistic acculturation but *not* cultural acculturation among Chinese students in Toronto. Studying Gaelic Scots descendants living in Nova Scotia, Edwards and Chisholm (1987) report that ethnic identity remains, in spite of the loss of the ethnic language.

In a similar vein, but from a different perspective, when considering code-switching and cross-language interference, Pedersen (1987) interprets the intrusion of German words in Danish utterances as a form of creativity on the part of German minority children. The same phenomenon is, however, interpreted as a sign of assimilation (i.e. loss of first language) by Danesi (1985) who studied the introduction of English loan words in the discourse of Italo-Canadians. These studies suggest that the process of identity change or maintenance may very well be multidimensional, linguistic aspects defining only one of the dimensions. Also, it seems more likely that ethnic identity would be negotiated and result from particular interactions (see Heller, 1987; Weinreich, 1986) than that it would remain a stable and pervasive individual characteristic. These considerations (see also Edwards, 1985) call into question the strong relationship between language and identity which appears to be the base of much research and theorizing in the social psychology of language.

CONCLUSION

The scope of the social psychology of second language acquisition has grown from initial attempts to explain second language competence on the basis of individual difference variables. This evolution is particularly evident with respect to four related aspects of the field. First, applications of the original framework generated by Gardner and Lambert (1959) have been made to languages other than French. Although some of the results quoted herein are at variance with the theory, most confirm the fundamental importance of motivation and affective predispositions toward the second language group.

Second, the initial focus on individual differences in language aptitude was expanded to include other individual differences such as personality characteristics and language learning strategies. The introduction of these supplementary determinants complicates to a degree our understanding of the individual mediation mechanism. To some extent, though, an empirical test of more complex models is now permitted through recent advances in causal modelling techniques.

A third area of evolution has to do with an increase in the number and kinds of outcomes associated with second language acquisition. Besides second language competence, researchers have tried to tackle the issues of persistence in second language study, second language use and retention, second language classroom behaviour, interethnic contact, and acculturation. The process once targeted at explaining second language competence appears to be relevant to a 'family' of phenomena resulting from the contact between language groups. In addition to those that have already been studied, future research may bring language replacement and shift, code-mixing and switching, and lexical borrowing under the umbrella of this paradigm.

The fourth and last evolution of the field is represented as a separate subsection in the structure of this text: it concerns contextual effects. Although the hypothesis of the influence of the milieu had been formulated relatively early, it is only recently that systematic conceptualizations have been proposed. These are varied in their focus and theoretical foundations, and emphasize aspects such as the relative status of the first and second language, interethnic contact, and ethnic group membership. As these formulations have grown in complexity to account for disparate results, so has the language used to cast them. Such complexity may, at times, result in abstract models able to account, *ex post facto*, for just about any pattern of results. Relatedly, the fact that some hypotheses are common to all models reduces the possibility of conducting comparative tests of the validity of different explanations. While speaking for the vitality of the field, these difficulties bolster, in our view, the argument for conceptual parsimony and precision.

Notwithstanding the 'growing pains', more than three decades of careful and systematic research have supported the relationship between second language fluency and socially bound individual differences. The social psychology of second language acquisition is now in a position to face the problems created by the expansion of paradigms to accommodate contextual effects, the increase in the number of phenomena falling within its scope, and the less than well understood relationship between identity and language. If the past speaks for the future, there is every reason to believe that a powerful explanatory system will eventually evolve that will have implications for our understanding of language phenomena and interethnic relations, as well as for our comprehension of cognitive processes and the relationship between the individual and society.

ACKNOWLEDGEMENTS

Preparation of this chapter was facilitated by Social Sciences and Humanities Research Council of Canada grants 410-85-0190 and 410-88-0087 to the first and second author, respectively. The authors would like to express their appreciation to V. Galbraith, P.D. MacIntyre, and A. Young, from the University of Western Ontario, and K. Noels and L.S. Laplante from the University of Ottawa for their invaluable assistance in the preparation of this chapter.

REFERENCES

Allport, G.W. (1954). The historical background of modern social psychology. In G. Lindzey (Ed.), *The handbook of social psychology*, pp. 3–56. Cambridge, MA: Addison Wesley.

Au, S. (1988). A critical appraisal of Gardner's social psychological theory of second language (L2) learning. *Language Learning*, **38**, 75–100.

Bartley, D.E. (1969). A pilot study of aptitude and attitude factors in language dropout. *California Journal of Educational Research*, **20**, 48–55.

Bartley, D.E. (1970). The importance of the attitude factor in language dropout: A preliminary investigation of group and sex differences. *Foreign Language Annals*, **3**, 383–393.

Bialystok, E. (1984). Strategies in interlanguage learning and performance. In A. Davies, C. Cuper, and A.P.R. Howett (Eds), *Interlanguage*, pp. 37–48. Edinburgh: Edinburgh University Press.

Bourhis, R.Y. (1986). Language planning and language use in Québec. Paper presented at the II International Catalan Language Congress, Lleida, Catalonia, Spain.

Bourhis, R.Y. and Bédard, M. (1988). Usage des langues et vitalité ethnolinguistique en milieu Franco-Ontarien. Paper presented at the Annual Meeting of the Canadian Psychological Association. Abstract in *Canadian Psychology*, **29**(2a), 84.

Bourhis, R.Y., Giles, H., and Rosenthal, D. (1981). Notes on the construction of a 'Subjective Vitality Questionnaire' for ethnolinguistic groups. *Journal of Multilingual and Multicultural Development*, **2**, 145–155.

Bourhis, R.Y. and Sachdev, I. (1984). Vitality perceptions and language 'attitudes': Some Canadian data. *Journal of Language and Social Psychology*, **3**, 97–126.

Burstall, C., Jamieson, M., Cohen, S., and Hargreaves, M. (1974). *Primary French in the balance*. Windsor (England): NFER.

Canale, M. and Swain, M. (1980). Theoretical basis of communicative approaches to second language teaching and testing. *Applied Linguistics*, **1**, 2–43.

Carroll, J.B. (1962). The prediction of success in intensive language training. In R. Glaser (Ed.), *Training research and education*. Pittsburgh: Pittsburgh Press.

Carroll, J.B. and Sapon, S.M. (1959). *Modern Language Aptitude Test (MLAT)*. New York: Psychological Corporation.

Carroll, J.B. and Sapon, S.M. (1967). *Modern Language Aptitude Test, Elementary form*. New York: Psychological Corporation.

Cartwright, D. (1987). Accommodation among the anglophone minority in Quebec to official language policy: A shift in traditional patterns of language contact. *Journal of Multilingual and Multicultural Development*, **8**, 187–212.

Chastain, K. (1975). Affective and ability factors in second language acquisition. *Language Learning*, **25**, 153–161.

Clark, J.L.D. (1981). Language. In T.S. Barrows (Ed.), *A survey of global understanding: Final report*. New Rochelle, NY: Change Magazine Press.

Clément, R. (1978). Motivational characteristics of francophones learning English. International Center for Research on Bilingualism, Laval University, Quebec City.

Clément, R. (1979). Immersion and residence programs: Their effects on attitude and anxiety. *Interchange*, **9**, 52–58.

Clément, R. (1980). Ethnicity, contact and communicative competence in a second language. In H. Giles, W.P. Robinson, and P.M. Smith (Eds), *Language: Social psychological perspectives*. Oxford: Pergamon.

Clément, R. (1984). Aspects socio-psychologiques de la communication inter-ethnique et de l'identité sociale. *Recherches Sociologiques*, **15**, 293–312.

Clément, R. (1986). Second language proficiency and acculturation: An investigation of the effects of language status and individual characteristics. *Journal of Language and Social Psychology*, **5**, 271–290.

Clément, R., Gardner, R.C., and Smythe, P.C. (1977a). Motivational variables in second language acquisition: A study of francophones learning English. *Canadian Journal of Behavioural Science,* **9**, 123–133.

Clément, R., Gardner, R.C., and Smythe, P.C. (1977b). Inter-ethnic contact: Attitudinal consequences. *Canadian Journal of Behavioural Science,* **12**, 205–215.

Clément, R., Gardner, R.C., and Smythe, P.C. (1980). Social and individual factors in second language acquisition. *Canadian Journal of Behavioural Science,* **12**, 293–302.

Clément, R. and Kruidenier, B.G. (1983). Orientations in second language acquisition: I. The effects of ethnicity, milieu, and target language on their emergence. *Language Learning,* **33**, 273–291.

Clément, R. and Kruidenier, B.G. (1985). Aptitude, attitude and motivation in second language proficiency: A test of Clément's model. *Journal of Language and Social Psychology,* **4**, 21–37.

Clément, R., Smythe, P.C., and Gardner, R.C. (1978). Persistence in second language study: Motivational considerations. *Canadian Modern Language Review,* **34**, 688–694.

Colletta, S., Clément, R., and Edwards, H.P. (1983). Community and parental influence: Effects on student motivation and French second language proficiency. International Center for Research on Bilingualism, Laval University, Quebec City.

Cummins, J. (1979). Bilingualism and educational development in anglophone and minority fracophone groups in Canada. *Interchange,* **9**, 40–51.

Cummins, J. (1984a). *Bilingualism and special education: Issues in assessment and pedagogy.* Clevedon (England): Multilingual Matters.

Cummins, J. (1984b). Educational linguistics and its sociological context in heritage language research. In J. Cummins (Ed.), *Heritage languages in Canada: Research perspectives.* Ottawa: Department of the Secretary of State of Canada.

Cummins, J. (1986). Empowering minority students: A framework for intervention. *Harvard Educational Review,* **56**, 18–36.

Cummins, J. and Swain, M. (1986). *Bilingualism in education.* New York: Longman.

Danesi, M. (1985). Ethnic languages and acculturation: The case of Italo-Canadians. *Canadian Ethnic Studies,* **17**, 98–103.

d'Anglejean, A. and Renaud, C. (1985). Learner characteristics and second language acquisition: A multivariate study of adult immigrants and some thoughts on methodology. *Language Learning,* **35**, 1–19.

Desrochers, A. and Clément, R. (1979). The social psychology of inter-ethnic contact and cross-cultural communication: An annotated bibliography. International Center for Research on Bilingualism, Laval University, Quebec City.

Desrochers, A. and Gardner, R.C. (1981). Second language acquisition: An investigation of a bicultural excursion experience. International Center for Research on Bilingualism, Laval University, Quebec City.

Driedger, L. (1984). Sociology of language and Canadian heritage language research. In J. Cummins (Ed.), *Heritage languages in Canada: Research perspectives.* Ottawa: Department of the Secretary of State of Canada.

Duckworth, D. and Entwistle, N.J. (1974). Attitudes to school subjects: A repertory grid technique. *British Journal of Educational Psychology,* **46**, 76–83.

Edwards, J. (1985). *Language, society and identity.* Oxford: Oxford University Press.

Edwards, J. and Chisholm, J. (1987). Language, multiculturalism and identity: A Canadian study. *Journal of Multilingual and Multicultural Development,* **8**, 391–408.

Ely, C.M. (1986). Language learning motivation: A descriptive and causal analysis. *Modern Language Journal,* **70**, 28–35.

Gardner, R.C. (1968). Attitudes and motivation: Their role in second language acquisition. *TESOL Quarterly,* **2**, 141–150.

Gardner, R.C. (1979). Social psychological aspects of second language acquisition. In H. Giles and R. St Clair (Eds), *Language and social psychology,* pp. 193–220. Oxford: Blackwell.

Gardner, R.C. (1980). On the validity of affective variables in second language acquisition: Conceptual, contextual and statistical considerations. *Language Learning*, **30**, 255–270.

Gardner, R.C. (1983). Learning another language: A true social psychological experiment. *Journal of Language and Social Psychology*, **2**, 219–239.

Gardner, R.C. (1985). *Social psychology and second language learning: The role off attitudes and motivation*. London: Arnold.

Gardner, R.C. (1988). The socio-educational model of second language learning: Assumptions, findings and issues. *Language Learning*, **38**, 101–126.

Gardner, R.C., Lalonde, R.N., Nero, A.M., and Young, M.Y. (1988). Ethnic stereotypes: Implications of measurement strategy. *Social Cognition*, **6**, 40–60.

Gardner, R.C., Lalonde, R.N., and Pierson, R. (1983). The socio-educational model of second language acquisition: An investigation using LISREL causal modeling. *Journal of Language and Social Psychology*, **2**, 1–15.

Gardner, R.C. and Lambert, W.E. (1959). Motivational variables in second language acquisition. *Canadian Journal of Psychology*, **13**, 266–272.

Gardner, R.C. and Lambert, W.E. (1972). *Attitudes and motivation in second language learning*. Rowley, MA: Newbury House.

Gardner, R.C. and Smythe, P.C. (1975). Second language acquisition: A social psychological approach. *Research Bulletin*, No. 332, Department of Psychology, University of Western Ontario, London, Canada.

Gardner, R.C., Smythe, P.C., Clément, R., and Gliksman, L. (1976). Second-language learning: A social psychological perspective. *Canadian Modern Language Review*, **32**, 198–213.

Garrett, P., Giles, H., and Coupland, N. (1989). The contexts of language learning: Extending the intergroup model of second language acquisition. In S. Tine-Toomey and P. Causeney (Eds), *Language communication and culture: Current directions*. Annual of International and Intercultural Communication, Vol. 13, pp. 201–221. Newbury Park, CA: Sage.

Genesee, F. (1987). *Learning through two languages*. Cambridge, MA: Newbury House.

Genesee, F. and Hamayan, E. (1980). Individual differences in second language learning. *Applied Psycholinguistics*, **1**, 95–110.

Genesee, F., Rogers, P., and Holobow, N. (1983). The social psychology of second language learning: Another point of view. *Language Learning*, **33**, 209–224.

Giles, H., Bourhis, R.Y., and Taylor, D.M. (1977). Towards a theory of language in ethnic group relations. In H. Giles (Ed.), *Language, ethnicity and intergroup relations*, pp. 307–348. New York: Academic Press.

Giles, H. and Byrne, J.L. (1982). An intergroup approach to second language acquisition. *Journal of Multilingual and Multicultural Development*, **1**, 17–40.

Giles, H. and Johnson, P. (1981). The role of language in ethnic group relations. In J.C. Turner and H. Giles (Eds), *Intergroup behaviour*, pp. 199–243. Oxford: Blackwell.

Giles, H. and Johnson, P. (1987). Ethnolinguistic identity theory: A social psychological approach to language maintenance. *International Journal of the Sociology of Language*, **68**, 69–99.

Gliksman, L., Gardner, R.C., and Smythe, P.C. (1982). The role of the integrative motive on students' participation in the French classroom. *Canadian Modern Language Review*, **38**, 625–647.

Guiora, A.Z., Brannon, R.C., and Dull, C.Y. (1972). Empathy and second language learning. *Language Learning*, **22**, 111–130.

Guiora, A.Z., Lane, H.L., and Bosworth, L.A. (1967). An exploration of some personality variables in authentic pronunciation of a second language. In H.L. Lane and E.M. Zale (Eds), *Studies in language and language behavior*, Progress Report, No. IV. Ann Arbor, MI: Center for Research on Language and Language Behavior.

Hagège, C. (1985). *L'Homme de paroles*. Paris: Fayard.

Hall, B.J. and Gudykunst, W.B. (1986). The intergroup theory of second language ability. *Journal of Language and Social Psychology*, **5**, 291–302.

Hamers, J.F. and Blanc, M. (1988). *Bilinguality et bilingualism*. Cambridge: Cambridge University Press.

Hansen, J. and Stansfield, C. (1981). The relationship of field dependent–independent cognitive styles to foreign language achievement. *Language Learning, 31*, 349–367.

Harley, B. (1986). *Age in second language acquisition*. Clevedon (England): Multilingual Matters.

Heller, M. (1984). Language and ethnic identity in a Toronto French-language school. *Canadian Ethnic Studies, 16*, 1–14.

Heller, M. (1987). Language and identity. In U. Ammon, N. Dittmar, and K.J. Mattheier (Eds), *Sociolinguistics*, pp. 780–784. Berlin: Walter de Gruyter.

Henmon, V.A.C. (1929). Prognosis tests in the modern foreign languages. In V.A.C. Henmon (Ed.), *Prognosis test in the modern foreign languages*. New York: Macmillan.

Holobow, N.E., Genesee, F., Lambert, W.E., Gastright, J., and Met, M. (1987). Effectiveness of partial French immersion for children from different social class and ethnic backgrounds. *Applied Psycholinguistics, 8*, 137–152.

Horwitz, E.K., Horwitz, M.B., and Cope, J. (1986). Foreign language classroom anxiety. *Modern Language Journal, 70*, 125–132.

Husband, C. and Saifullah Khan, V. (1982). The viability of ethnolinguistic vitality: Some creative doubts. *Journal of Multilingual and Multicultural Development, 3*, 193–205.

Jones, W.R. (1950). Attitude towards Welsh as a second language, a further investigation. *British Journal of Educational Psychology, 20*, 117–132.

Jordan, D. (1941). The attitudes of central school pupils to certain school subjects and the correlation between attitude and attainment. *British Journal of Educational Psychology, 11*, 28–44.

Kawcyznski, A.S. (1951). The two psychological types of language students. *Modern Language Journal, 35*, 113–118.

Kramsch, C.J. (1983). Culture and constructs: Communicating attitudes and values in the foreign language classroom. *Foreign Language Annals, 16*, 437–448.

Krashen, S.D. (1981). *Second language acquisition and second language learning*. New York: Pergamon.

Kreitler, H. and Kreitler, S. (1982). The theory of cognitive orientation: Widening the scope of behavior prediction. In B. Maher and W. Maher (Eds), *Progress in experimental personality research*. New York: Academic Press.

Kruidenier, B.G. and Clément, R. (1986). The effect of context on the composition and role of orientations in second language acquisition. International Center for Research on Bilingualism, Laval University, Quebec City.

Labrie, N. and Clément, R. (1986). Ethnolinguistic vitality, self-confidence and second language proficiency: An investigation. *Journal of Multilingual and Multicultural Development, 7*, 269–282.

Lalleman, J. (1987). A relation between acculturation and second-language acquisition in the classroom. *Journal of Multilingual and Multicultural Development, 8*, 409–431.

Lalonde, R.N. (1982). Second language acquisition: A causal analysis. Unpublished master's thesis, University of Western Ontario, London, Canada.

Lalonde, R.N. and Gardner, R.C. (1985). On the predictive validity of the Attitude/Motivation Test Battery. *Journal of Multilingual and Multicultural Development, 6*, 403–412.

Lambert, W.E. (1963a). Psychological approaches to the study of language. I: On learning, thinking and human abilities. *Modern Language Journal, 14*, 51–62.

Lambert, W.E. (1963b). Psychological approaches to the study of language. II: On second language learning and bilingualism. *Modern Language Journal, 14*, 114–121.

Lambert, W.E. (1967). A social psychology of bilingualism. *Journal of Social Issues, 23*, 91–109.

Lambert, W.E. (1972). *Language, psychology and culture: Essays by Wallace E. Lambert* (Selected by A.S. Dil). Stanford, CA: Stanford University Press.

Lambert, W.E. (1978). Cognitive and socio-cultural consequences of bilingualism. *Canadian Modern Language Review, 34*, 537–547.

Lambert, W.E., Havelka, J., and Crosby, C. (1958). The influence of language acquisition contexts on bilingualism. *Journal of Abnormal and Social Psychology, 60*, 44–51.

Lambert, W.E. and Tucker, G.R. (1972). *Bilingual education of children: The St Lambert experiment.* Rowley, MA: Newbury House.

Landry, R. and Allard, R. (1985). Choix de la langue d'enseignement: Une analyse chez des parents francophones en milieu bilingue soustractif. *Canadian Modern Language Review, 41*, 480–500.

Landry, R. and Allard, R. (1987a). Can schools promote additive bilingualism in minority group children? Faculté des sciences de l'éducation, Université de Moncton, Canada.

Landry, R. and Allard, R. (1987b). Contact des langues et développement bilingue: Un modèle macroscopique. Paper presented at the Colloque sur 'Contacts de langues: Quels modèles?', Nice, France.

Lenneberg, E. (1967). *Biological foundations of language.* New York: Wiley.

McAllister, I. and Mugham, A. (1984). The fate of the language: Determinants of bilingualism in Wales. *Ethnic and Racial Studies, 7*, 321–347.

McLaughlin, B. (1984). *Second-language acquisition in childhood: School-age children.* Hillsdale, NJ: Erlbaum.

Mougeon, R. and Heller, M. (1986). The social and historical context of minority French language education in Ontario. *Journal of Multilingual and Multicultural Development, 7*, 199–227.

Mowrer, O.H. (1950). On the psychology of 'talking birds' – A contribution to language and personality theory. In O.H. Mowrer (Ed.), *Learning theory and personality dynamics: Selected papers.* New York: Ronald Press.

Naiman, N., Fröhlich, M., and Stern, H.H. (1975). *The good language learner.* Toronto: Ontario Institute for Studies in Education.

Naiman, N., Fröhlich, M., Stern, H.H., and Todesco, A. (1978). The good language learner. *Research in Education Series*, No. 7. Toronto: Ontario Institute for Studies in Education.

Neidt, C.O. and Hedlund, D.E. (1967). The relationship between changes in attitude toward a course and final achievement. *Journal of Educational Research, 61*, 56–58.

Oller, J.W. (1982). Gardner on affect: A reply to Gardner. *Language Learning, 32*, 183–189.

Oller, J.W., Hudson, A., and Liu, P. (1977). Attitudes and attained proficiency in ESL: A sociolinguistic study of native speakers of Chinese in the United States. *Language Learning, 27*, 1–27.

Oller, J.W. and Perkins, K. (1978). Intelligence and language proficiency as sources of variance in self-reported affective variables. *Language Learning, 28*, 85–97.

Olson, P. and Burns, G. (1983). Politics, class and happenstance: French immersion in a Canadian context. *Interchange, 14*, 1–16.

Oxford, R.L. (1986). Development of a new survey and taxonomy for second language learning. Paper presented at the Learning Strategy Symposium, New York.

Oxford, R.L., Nyikos, M., and Crookall, D. (1987). Learning strategies of university foreign language students: A large scale factor-analytic study. Unpublished manuscript.

Pak, A.W., Dion, K.L., and Dion, K.K. (1985). Correlates of self-confidence with English among Chinese students in Toronto. *Canadian Journal of Behavioural Science, 17*, 369–378.

Pedersen, K.M. (1987). German minority children in the Danish border region: Code switching and interference. *Journal of Multilingual and Multicultural Development, 8*, 111–120.

Petersen, C.R. and Al-Haik, A.R. (1976). The development of the Defense Language Aptitude Battery (DLAB). *Educational and Psychological Measurement, 36*, 369–380.

Pierson, H.D., Giles, H., and Young, L. (1987). Intergroup vitality perceptions during a period of political uncertainty: The case of Hong Kong. *Journal of Multilingual and Multicultural Development, 8*, 451–460.

Pimsleur, P. (1966). *Pimsleur Language Aptitude Battery.* New York: Harcourt Brace Jovanovitch.

Politzer, R.L. (1983). An exploratory study of self reported language learning behaviors and their relation to achievement. *Studies in Second Language Acquisition, 6*, 54–68.

Politzer, R.L. and McGroarty, M. (1985). An exploratory study of learning behaviors and their relationship to gains in linguistic and communicative competence. *TESOL Quarterly, 19*, 103–123.

Randhawa, B.S. and Korpan, S.M. (1973). Assessment of some significant affective variables and the prediction of achievement in French. *Canadian Journal of Behavioural Science, 5*, 24–33.

Reiss, M.A. (1985). The good language learner: Another look. *Canadian Modern Language Review, 41*, 511–523.

Rubin, J. (1975). What the good language learner can teach us. *TESOL Quarterly, 9*, 41–51.

Schumann, J.H. (1975). Affective factors and the problem of age in second language acquisition. *Language Learning, 25*, 209–235.

Schumann, J.H. (1976). Social distance as a factor in second language acquisition. *Language Learning, 25*, 135–143.

Schumann, J.H. (1978a). Social and psychological factors in second language acquisition. In J.C. Richards (Ed.), *Understanding second and foreign language learning*. Rowley, MA: Newbury House.

Schumann, J.H. (1978b). The acculturation model for second-language acquisition. In R.C. Gingras (Ed.), *Second-language acquisition and foreign language teaching*. Arlington, VA: Center for Applied Linguistics.

Schumann, J.H. (1986). Research on the acculturation model for second language acquisition. *Journal of Multilingual and Multicultural Development, 1*, 379–392.

Scovel, T. (1978). The effect of affect on foreign language learning: A review of the anxiety research. *Language Learning, 28*, 129–142.

Smart, J.C., Elton, C.F., and Burnett, C.W. (1970). Underachievers and overachievers in intermediate French. *Modern Language Journal, 54*, 415–422.

Smythe, P.C., Stennett, R.G., and Feenstra, H.J. (1972). Attitude, aptitude and type of instructional programme in second language acquisition. *Canadian Journal of Behavioural Science, 4*, 307–321.

Stern, H.H. (1975). What can we learn from the good language learner? *Canadian Modern Language Review, 31*, 304–318.

Swain, M. and Lapkin, S. (1982). *Evaluating bilingual education: A Canadian case study*. Clevedon (England): Multilingual Matters.

Tarampi, A.S., Lambert, W.E., and Tucker, G.R. (1968). Audience sensitivity and oral skill in a second language. *Philippine Journal for Language Teaching, 6*, 27–33.

Tardif, C. and Weber, S. (1987). French immersion research: A call for new perspectives. *Canadian Modern Language Review, 84*, 67–77.

Tucker, G.R. (1974). Methods of second language teaching. *Canadian Modern Language Review, 31*, 102–107.

Tucker, G.R., Hamayan, E., and Genesee, F.H. (1976). Affective, cognitive and social factors in second language acquisition. *Canadian Modern Language Review, 32*, 214–226.

Weinreich, P. (1986). The operationalization of identity theory in racial and ethnic relations. In J. Rex and D. Mason (Eds), *Theories of race and ethnic relations*. Cambridge: Cambridge University Press.

Willig, A.C. (1985). A meta-analysis of selected studies on the effectiveness of bilingual education. *Review of Educational Research, 55*, 269–317.

Witkin, H., Goodenough, D., and Oltman, P. (1979). Psychological differentiation: Current status. *Journal of Personality and Social Psychology, 37*, 1127–1145.

Wong Fillmore, L. (1976). The second time around: Cognitive and social strategies in second language acquisition. Unpublished doctoral dissertation, Stanford University, Stanford, CA.

25

Communication Characteristics of Provider–Patient Information Exchanges

JACQUELINE J. HINCKLEY, HOLLY K. CRAIG AND LYNDA A. ANDERSON

*Medical Center, Communicative Disorders Clinic, and School of Public Health,
University of Michigan, USA*

Physician–patient interactions are complex social phenomena to which both parties contribute a variety of attitudes and expectations about each other. Examination of communication processes reveals highly relevant information about the roles, goals, and content of the interaction. Variations in communication processes have been shown to influence important patient outcomes such as patient satisfaction with the health encounter, patient compliance with treatment recommendations, and reductions in patient concerns.

To illustrate, imagine a video-recording of what may be considered a typical consultation between a doctor and patient. If one was to watch the video-tape without any sound, one might be able to identify the doctor and patient roles and general affective states. If the picture was blackened and one listened to the sound alone, information regarding topic, types of speech patterns, and emotional status would become available. These communication processes are affected by the characteristics of the doctor and patient and the specific circumstances of their interaction. The result of this interaction will be changes in the patient's knowledge, concerns, or behaviors.

Research has shown that the presentation and clarity of information given by health-care providers has important effects on patient comprehension and patient satisfaction (Buller and Buller, 1987; Ley, 1983; Ley, Bradshaw, Eaves, and Walker,

Handbook of Language and Social Psychology
Edited by H. Giles and W.P. Robinson.   © 1989 John Wiley & Sons Ltd

1973; Ley *et al.*, 1976), and that the amount of time the provider spends with the patient, giving information, is related to better recall (Bertakis, 1977) and higher levels of patient satisfaction (DiMatteo, Prince, and Taranta, 1979; Stiles, Putnam, James, and Wolf, 1979). Patients also display clear preferences for physicians' affective presentation, including friendliness (Pendleton, Schofield, Tate, and Havelock, 1984), seriousness (Hall, Roter, and Rand, 1981; Rost and Roter, 1987; Waitzkin, 1985), and concern (Street and Wiemann, 1987). It is clear that communication patterns have important effects on patient comprehension, recall of information, compliance to treatment regimen, and satisfaction with care.

The purpose of this chapter is to review the sociolinguistic characteristics of physician–patient information exchanges. First, a conceptual framework for the analysis of interactions between mediating variables and communication processes is described. Next, information regarding specific communication behaviors in physician–patient interactions is reviewed. The effects of various mediating variables with possible theoretical explanations are offered. Finally, future directions for research in provider–patient interactions are discussed.

CONCEPTUAL FRAMEWORK

Pragmatic language approaches offer a helpful framework for examining physician–patient information exchanges. Pragmatic language models propose that communication can be conceptualized as the use of linguistic content and form in conversational contexts (Austin, 1962; Halliday, 1978; Sacks, Schegloff, and Jefferson, 1974; Searle, 1969). Content can be considered to be the meaning of a communication, whereas form includes the word and grammar choices employed to convey the meaning. Successful communication exchanges typically entail an integration of linguistic structural knowledge with psychosocial knowledge of a range of interactive contexts. Indeed, the nature of the conversational context can determine the patterns of talk involved. This type of communication model permits the examination of linguistic variations as a function of specific contextual constraints, the identification of verbal and non-verbal forms of conversational rules, and the determination of psychosocial characteristics of speakers and listeners associated with linguistic differences.

Pragmatic language approaches have traditionally focused on examining the effects of certain mediating variables on patterns of discourse. Research that applies pragmatic language approaches to the study of doctor–patient communication has included the relationship between communication processes, mediating variables, and subsequent outcomes. Potentially, pragmatic language approaches can relate two major components important to provider–patient communication: psychosocial variables in their role as contextual mediators, and linguistic behaviors in their role as process variables. Patient-care outcomes are believed to be the result of the interaction between mediating variables and communication processes (see Figure 25.1).

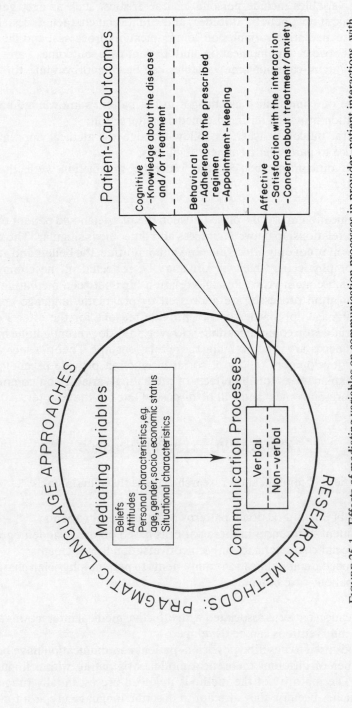

FIGURE 25.1 Effects of mediating variables on communication processes in provider–patient interactions, with subsequent effect on patient-care outcomes. Pragmatic language approaches are proposed as a system of investigating methods into the relationships between mediating variables and communication behaviors.

Mediating variables include personal characteristics, such as age, gender, and socio-economic status; beliefs; attitudes; and situational characteristics. The direct effects of these mediating variables on communication processes, and the proposed relationship between communication and patient-care outcomes, are shown in Figure 25.1. Patient-care outcome variables can be categorized into three groups:

(1)   cognitive outcomes, such as changes in the patient's knowledge base due to information provided during the medical interaction;
(2)   behavioral outcomes, such as follow-through on medical appointments or adherence to particular treatment regimens;
(3)   affective outcomes, such as the patient's satisfaction with the medical encounter.

As communication must take place between the physician and patient to effect an outcome, the relationship between process and outcome is singular. The communication process may not only affect outcome but may affect the beliefs and attitudes of the patient or physician, which in turn may be reflected in the communication processes of subsequent visits. Possible relationships between mediating variables and communication processes are addressed by pragmatic language approaches. Pragmatic language approaches do not provide reasons for the effects of certain mediating variables on communication; however, they do present unique methods of measurement necessary in determining those relationships. Theories such as attribution and the development theory of social interaction provide psychological and sociological explanations for the effects of mediating variables on communication and patient-care outcomes, and will be discussed later in the chapter.

COMMUNICATION PROCESSES

Physician–patient communication research reflects three main goals:

(1)   to describe the interactional patterns of doctors and patients;
(2)   to document differences in these patterns based on the sociodemographic and psychosocial characteristics of both conversational participants;
(3)   to link specific communication components to patient–physician characteristics and to patient-care outcomes.

As communication patterns associated with effective medical interactions are identified, specific interventions can be developed.

The methods used to describe physician–patient communication have been based upon a number of different theoretical models originating within linguistics and psychology. The majority of the methods involved are essentially pragmatic language approaches because they attempt to describe language use as a function of a particular context. Specific communication behaviors observed to change with particular role relationships and interactant characteristics are discussed below.

Communicative Intent

The intentions behind physicians' and patients' utterances in medical interactions have been examined in an effort to understand what interactants are attempting to accomplish through their choice of communication behaviors. Particular patterns of intent and communication behaviors were found to be associated with the history-taking, physical examination, and concluding segments of medical interactions. For example, patients' explanations and physicians' questions were typical of the history-gathering section, whereas information-giving generally characterized the conclusion segment (Putnam, Stiles, Jacob, and James, 1985; Stiles, Putnam, and Jacob, 1982). Some communicative intentions occurred throughout the interview, such as checking accuracy of communication. An example of this 'checking' function would be the doctor's sentence in the following example:

Doctor: 'So your pain started on Monday.'
Patient: 'Yeah.'

This illustrates the doctor's attempt to ensure that his comprehension of the patient's statement was correct. It has also been shown that when physicians' verbal responses indicated their intent to use the patient's frame of reference, patients were more satisfied with the interaction (Putnam *et al.*, 1985).

Affective content can also carry important information about intentionality, along with verbal content and form (Bales, 1968; Roter, 1977). Affect can be conveyed through choice of words and grammar as well as intonational patterns. For example, a concern regarding a medical issue may become an indirect question, or physicians may convey information about the seriousness of a disease or the importance of a treatment regimen through affective communication.

Communicative intentions are measured through analyses which have generally developed from speech-act theory (Austin, 1962; Searle, 1969). Speech-act theory has been a major influence on pragmatic language approaches. This theory proposes that communication can be understood as a series of speech acts that integrate speaker intentions, utterance productions, and listener effects. In brief, a speech act can be defined as the intent underlying production of an utterance, for example to request, to advise, to warn, or to give orders (Austin, 1962; Searle, 1969). Speech-act analysis relates utterance forms to underlying intentions and therefore can reveal patterns of language use for each speaker.

Three main analysis systems based on speech-act theory have been developed and used to investigate communicative intent in medical interactions. Bales' Interaction Process Analysis (Bales, 1968) was developed from small-group interactional analysis, and assigns communication segments from a written transcript to one of 12 intention categories, which broadly reflect affective and content categories. Roter (1977) modified Bales' system specifically for the analysis of doctor–patient communication, by developing eight specific categories for the physician and eight categories for the patient. Utterances are scored into categories directly from audio-tape, allowing for consideration of paralinguistic information in the coding process. Paralinguistic information carries important effective information in determining intentionality. Stiles' Verbal Response Mode taxonomy (Stiles, 1979) provides scoring procedures for intentions as well as specific grammatical forms. Coding of verbal forms is a unique contribution. Stiles' method allows for the development of profiles of verbal form and intentions.

Verbal Form

A single message can often be conveyed using many different words and grammars, all maintaining an equivalent meaning. For example, the two statements 'Where does it hurt?' and 'Please tell me where you have pain' are requests with the same meaning but different verbal forms. This section will examine vocabulary choice and questions as two important verbal forms in doctor–patient interaction.

Vocabulary choice in a medical setting necessarily involves using more or less complex terms and medical jargon. Technical jargon may be used to establish physicians' authority, affirm their knowledge, or determine their role in relation to the patient. It has been found that, when pediatric physicians used less medical jargon, the mothers of the children being treated indicated greater satisfaction with medical care, and more compliance with the treatment regimen (Davis, 1971; Korsch, Gozzi, and Frances, 1968). It is possible, but has not yet been shown, that patients with varying socio-economic levels may have differing preferences for amount of medical jargon.

Question-asking is a speech act that has attracted considerable investigation, due to its importance in the role relationships of doctor–patient interactions and its potential for intervention development. Physicians who utilize open-ended questions (i.e. allowing a large set of responses) rather than closed-ended questions (i.e. requiring yes/no or brief answers) allow the patient to provide information more freely (Byrne and Long, 1976). More frequent questions by doctors may also occur when they provide new information to patients, such as when new medications are being prescribed (Scherwitz, Hennrikus, Yusum, Lester, and Vallbona, 1985). Particular patient populations, such as those who have lower educational levels, are unskilled, or are older, tend to ask fewer questions of their doctors (Waitzkin, 1985). Though not all researchers agree, when patients are encouraged to ask more questions, they tend to be more satisfied with their medical care (Freemon, Negrete, Davis, and Korsch, 1971; Stiles et al., 1982). For these reasons, advocates of patient consumerism have encouraged more active participation by patients (Haug, 1976; Haug and Lavin, 1981, 1983; Reeder, 1972) and interventions focused on coaching question-asking have developed.

These interventions have emphasized the identification and rehearsal of patient questions prior to the consultation (Greenfield, Kaplan, and Ware, 1985; Roter, 1984). Booklets encouraging patients to ask more questions of their family-practice physicians have also been attempted (Tabak, 1988). However, these trials of interventions focused specifically on a particular communication act have not yet yielded consistent effects on the frequency of question-asking or on patient satisfaction.

Verbal forms sensitive to possible interventions have been the most extensively investigated. Frequency of medical jargon in the discourse of physicians and frequency of patient question-asking have been researched. Overall vocabulary choices, exclusive of medical terms, have not been investigated. This line of research may reveal patterns based on patients' presentations, physicians' perceptions, and/or physicians' stylistic differences. Likewise, complexity of grammar forms by patients and physicians and potential effects on the listener have yet to be demonstrated.

Verbal Content

Content refers to the underlying message or information being conveyed, regardless of the form being used to express it. Topic, although related to content, is a discourse unit involving sequences of utterances. One may identify the topic of a conversation and the content of one utterance.

Of particular interest is the work correlating initiation and response patterns of physicians and patients with types of topics in medical interviews. Physicians have been found to raise psychosocial topics less frequently with elderly patients than with younger patients (Greene, Hoffman, Charon, and Adelman, 1987; see Chapter 22, by Coupland and Coupland). Response patterns of types of topics constitute an important area, because they relate communicative behaviors to role relationships and perceptions regarding patient groups, such as in the above example.

Non-Verbal and Paralinguistic Communication

Non-verbal communication, such as gestures, facial expressions, and intonation, may significantly add to interactants' impressions and perceptions (see Chapter 6, by Street, and Chapter 7, by Cappella and Palmer). Pragmatic language approaches have emphasized the inclusion of non-verbal communication behaviors, as these may be important conversational regulators or alternatives to conventional verbal conversational forms.

Physicians' skill in decoding non-verbal messages, as portrayed in video-taped examples, has been shown to be related to patient satisfaction with physician listening behaviors (DiMatteo, Taranta, Friedman, and Prince, 1980). Further, the manner in which physicians' behaviors relate to medical procedures during the interaction has been shown to affect patient impressions and satisfaction in an analog study (Roter, Hall, and Katz, 1987). Roter et al. (1987) filtered speech samples so that the content of the utterances could not be identified. The highest satisfaction ratings from patients were obtained on samples containing intonational patterns judged as 'negative', in combination with positive, supportive verbal content. The authors suggest that negative intonation conveys seriousness to the patient whereas the positive verbal content demonstrates concern and respect. Differences in reported patient satisfaction with physician seriousness have been observed to be dependent on the acuity of the illness as well (Korsch et al., 1968; Street and Wiemann, 1987).

Descriptive research of the non-verbal communication behaviors within physician–patient interactions has revealed characteristic profiles associated with physician and patient role relationships. Patients tend to elicit physicians' attention and eye contact by using pauses and specific body movements before initiating utterances (Heath, 1984). Heath (1984) surmised that patients desired full attention of their physicians, particularly as physicians often were checking the medical chart during the sampled interactions. The coordination of eye gaze and body movements has been shown in one study to remain constant throughout interactions (Smith and Larsen, 1984) and this result raises the possibility that these non-verbal behaviors are characteristic of the role each participant plays within the interaction. These findings indicate that desires for control, role relationships, and affective information are conveyed through non-verbal communication behaviors.

Summary

Patterns in types and frequency of specific communication behaviors have been reviewed. These communication patterns are manifestations of the role relationships, perceptions, attitudes, and beliefs of the interactants. Pragmatic language approaches provide unique ways of investigating the relationships between communication variables, characteristics of interactants, and environmental effects.

MEDIATING VARIABLES

This section will examine specific mediating processes, potential psychological and sociological reasons for their effects on communication, and the resultant changes in patient-care outcomes. Patient-care outcomes are crucial, in that positive changes in outcome are the gauge used by the health-care system to consider the quality of health-care delivery and to modify procedures.

Patient Beliefs About, and Desires for, Control in Health-Care Interactions

There is considerable variability in specific patient populations in their desire for involvement in health-care processes, with the notable exception of systematic age differences. Consistent differences between older and younger adult patients have been found (Beisecker, 1988; Haug, 1981; Strull, Lo, and Charles, 1984), with older adults indicating less desire for involvement in health-care processes than younger adults. Additionally, older patients exhibit less desire to make or assist in medical decisions than do younger adult patients (Beisecker, 1988). Interestingly, patients' desire for self-control (versus shared control or clinician control) of clinical interactions was inversely related to patient satisfaction. In contrast, desire for clinician control was positively related to patient satisfaction with the clinical interaction (Anderson, DeVellis, Boyles, and Feussner, 1989). This would suggest, at least among the samples studied, that patients who desire more control over their clinical interactions with providers may be dissatisfied with what actually transpires. Future work should focus on how patients' beliefs influence communication processes.

It has been hypothesized that older patients have grown up during an era when more authority was given to physicians, and there was no emphasis on patient involvement and patient consumerism. This hypothesis is one potential explanation for the striking differences between older and younger adult patients. A second hypothesis suggests that physicians' communication modifications with elderly patients may in some way elicit different patient beliefs and expectations. This latter idea is expanded further in the next section.

Overall, patients tend to be more satisfied when their beliefs about clinical interactions are consistent with actual events in the interaction (Korsch *et al.*, 1968). Therefore, one might suspect that when physicians' and patients' beliefs about the interaction are congruent, increased patient satisfaction and treatment adherence would result. However, little agreement has been found, and patients' beliefs about their care generally go unrecognized by health-care providers (Freemon *et al.*, 1971). For example, physicians treating patients for hypertension indicated that patients who were young, white, and highly educated would be most likely to desire information and participate in the decision-making process. These physicians incorrectly assumed that patients who were older and with less education would desire less information. Physicians generally overestimated patients' desire for decision-making participation and underestimated their desire for information (Strull *et al.*, 1984).

Taken as a whole, these studies provide important evidence that patients do have specific beliefs about, and desire for, information and involvement in clinical interactions. Additionally, patients' desires for control are related to health-care outcomes, such as satisfaction. Finally, the studies indicate that there are mismatches between patients' and physicians' beliefs, and this may be an important area for potential intervention.

Attribution Theory and Social Interaction

Personal characteristics refer to those individual or group attributes that contribute to variability in interpersonal interactions (Patterson, 1983, and see Chapter 5). An individual's status, gender, and age are some of the more salient characteristics that have been shown to impact on patient–provider interactions. These characteristics have been shown to evoke inferences about the person as well as to influence subsequent behaviors towards him or her (Botwinick, 1984; Sebastian and Ryan, 1985; van Dijk, 1984).

There is considerable evidence, particularly in social psychology, that stereotypes about certain patient groups are salient and prevalent among health-care professionals (Blalock and DeVellis, 1986; Dryden and Giles, 1987). However, as researchers concerned with stereotyping suggest, biases held toward these groups may be more subtle than general attitude measures reflect (Patterson, 1983). As a result, they recommend that more attention should be given to studying how stereotyping influences communication processes and patient–care outcomes.

The effect of attributional processes on social interaction has been a topic of interest since the inception of attribution theory (Kelly and Michlea, 1980). Attribution theorists typically assume, either implicitly or explicitly, that attributions influence behavior or mediate the relationship between other factors and behaviors. Stereotyping is a particular type of attribution, and refers to a process in which a person imposes his or her general beliefs about a category of people on an individual, simply because that person is thought to be a member of that group (Blalock and DeVellis, 1986). For example, when health-care providers impose the stereotype of 'patient' on a hospitalized person, they may assume, solely on the basis of the observation that the individual is occupying a bed in the hospital, that the person is dependent and anxious (DeVellis, Wallston, and Wallston, 1980).

The effects of stereotyping by health-care providers are widely documented in the health-care literature. The way in which the attitudes of health-care providers affect communication is revealed in a number of investigations (Ervin-Tripp, 1968; Morimoto, 1955; Platt and Weber, 1984; Waitzkin, Stoeckle, Beller, and Mons, 1978). Morimoto (1955) found that, when nurses interacted with patients, 'preferred' patients were treated in a more personalized way, whereas 'non-preferred' patients were treated in a business-like manner. Similarly, Rosenthal, Blanck, and Vannicelli (1984) documented that the way psychotherapists spoke about their patients was predictive of the intonation they used during sessions with the patient.

Further direct evidence about the effects of attributional processes on patient evaluation and communicative behaviors is available. Wallston, Wallston, and DeVellis (1976) found that stereotypes about an 'alcoholic patient' exerted a powerful influence over nurses' perceptions of a specific patient. Nurses' ratings of a patient labeled 'alcoholic' were found to be similar to their relatively negative ratings of the concept of an alcoholic patient. It appeared that, once the patient was labeled an alcoholic, the nurses reacted to the label rather than to the individual characteristics of the patient. In another study in this area, information about responsibility for the decision to be childless (voluntary versus medically necessary sterilization) and intelligence of women making the decision (mildly retarded or not classified intellectually) was manipulated (DeVellis, Adams, and DeVellis, 1984). When the patient was thought to be mildly retarded or to be seeking sterilization because of medical necessity, nurses expressed more positive attitudes and more person-centered communicative behaviors than when the patient was thought to be seeking sterilization voluntarily or was not classified intellectually. These studies indicate how the strength of particular labels, and the attitudes of health-care providers, may be affected by labeling.

Specific patient characteristics and the possible categorical responses they elicit in physicians' and others' interaction patterns have been studied. Female patients have been found to receive more time from doctors and more explanations at the same technical level as their questions than have male patients (Waitzkin, 1985). However, the opposite findings also have been reported (Wallen, Waitzkin, and Stoeckle, 1979). Furthermore, West (1984) documented significant differences in the number of interruptions produced by male patients with female physicians than interruptions produced by female patients. Despite the fact that patients' personalities and diagnoses were varied, a subsequent study (DeVellis et al., 1980) found that female patients were liked less by nurses and seen as less mentally healthy compared to male patients. Although additional research on various gender combinations, communication processes, and patient-care outcomes is needed, the evidence thus far indicates the presence of communication differences based on gender in medical interactions (see Chapter 17, by Kramarae). These differences can potentially be explained by attribution theory.

The special importance of patients' age in influencing physicians' behaviors in clinical interactions is widely noted in the literature. Greene, Adelman, Charon, and Hoffman (1986) did not find any differences between older and younger adult patients in the frequency of questions, compliments, or negative remarks made to them by physicians in medical encounters. Other reports indicate that physicians are more courteous, empathic, and informative with older patients (Hooper, Comstock, Goodwin, and Goodwin, 1982) and tend to respond to questions raised by older patients at the same level of technicality as that at which they were asked (Waitzkin, 1985). However, age effects may be much more subtle than these findings suggest. For example, physicians occasionally attempted to diminish the significance of some illnesses by ascribing them to ageing (Waitzkin, *et al.*, 1978), and have been found to be less responsive to psychosocial issues raised by older patients than younger patients (Greene *et al.*, 1987). Moreover, significant decreases in the amount of time physicians spent with patients over the age of 65 have been reported (Keeler, Solomon, Beck, Mendenhall, and Kane, 1982).

The lack of consensus may be due, at least in part, to methodological variations across studies. Research documenting no differences between physician's communication to older patients and that to younger patients measured smaller, utterance-level analytical units, such as politeness or technicality. Differences in communication components between physicians and older patients compared with between physicians and younger patients were found when larger units of analysis were utilized, such as topics and time duration of visit. Determining sources of variation for disparate results will be important first steps in establishing the most revealing analysis systems by which sociolinguistic patterns can be documented.

Recent research also indicates that stereotypes can function as self-fulfilling prophecies (Snyder, Tanke, and Berscheid, 1977), and this has important implications for attributional processes in health-care encounters. For example, a clinician who believes that older adults are generally passive may treat an older patient as though he or she was helpless and dependent. This may lead to the patient becoming anxious and frightened, and elicit a more passive response from a normally self-assertive individual. Research reveals that, when a subject was led to believe that a person with whom he or she was interacting fell into a certain stereotypical category, the subject's behaviors led the person to behave in a manner consistent with the stereotype (Snyder *et al.*, 1977). This has negative connotations for medical encounters in which patients increasingly are requested to participate in decision-making processes and treatment regimens.

Attributional processes and stereotyping, then, have effects on communication behaviors within health-care encounters. Specific examples have been provided that document changes in clinicians' behaviors based on their beliefs about patients' socio-economic status, gender, and age. A potential negative implication, namely self-fulfilling prophecy, has been discussed.

Situational Characteristics

Situational characteristics are those environmental characteristics external to the physician and patient which may affect the perceptions of either one. Two primary examples will be discussed here: the effects of first-time interactions, and the presence of a companion.

As discussed in the preceding section, perceptions of individuals with particular sociodemographic characteristics may invoke certain social stereotypes. However, the role of social stereotypes may be magnified in first-time medical encounters (Strecher, 1981). Hypothetically, this occurs due to interactants' needs to evaluate an individual based on little information. As physicians and patients continue in an ongoing relationship, initial stereotypical responses may decrease. This observation is an outgrowth of the developmental theory of interaction communication (Berger and Calabrese, 1975), which purports that the saliency of sociodemographic characteristics decreases as an interpersonal relationship develops. Although this dynamic relationship has been anecdotally reported as occurring within ongoing physician–patient interactions, little empirical evidence on long-term doctor–patient communication patterns has been collected. Indeed, it must be emphasized that the majority of the work on physician–patient discourse has focused on first-time interactions.

It has been noted that young children and older adults, particularly those in very late life, are frequently accompanied to the doctor's office by a companion, generally a family member or a spouse (Rosow, 1981). Physicians in a rehabilitation clinic saw half of their patients in the presence of a companion (Beisecker, 1988). In this situation, doctors spent their time talking to both the companion and the patient, and provided a considerable amount of information to the companion during the interaction. Companions were also found to interact rarely with the patient during the medical encounter. This is an important first step in the investigation of the effects of the presence of a companion on the perceptions and communication patterns of doctors and patients.

Summary

Processes and characteristics that mediate communication patterns between physicians and patients include patients' beliefs about, and desires for, control and decision-making participation; personal characteristics of physicians and patients, such as socio-economic status (see Chapter 16, by Haslett), age, or gender; and situational characteristics. These processes affect communication patterns and patient-care outcomes (see Figure 25.1). Theoretical explanations for these processes and their effects on communication and outcomes include attribution and development theories.

DISCUSSION

Key questions should be posed, based upon what the present literature review demonstrates is known currently about provider–patient communication.

Do the findings warrant the investigative effort involved?

Research has shown that informational exchanges between health-care providers and patients are affected by sociodemographic variables, situational characteristics, beliefs, and attitudes. The utility of this information to the quality of health-care interactions is clear (Inui and Carter, 1985; Wasserman and Inui, 1983). Furthermore, conclusions can be drawn about the effects of communication characteristics on patient-care outcomes. This result has important implications for the quality, efficacy, and efficiency of health-care provision. The importance of these findings increases the urgency with which more information regarding the occurrence of communication modifications in health-care interactions, and potential remedies and interventions are pursued.

How can current analysis systems be ameliorated in order to further knowledge about provider–patient communication?

Investigations of provider–patient exchanges, although revealing, have generally examined only two of the following three components: mediating variables, communication processes, and/or patient-care outcomes. With few exceptions have all three components been examined in a single research study (e.g. Greenfield, Kaplan, and Ware, 1985). Studies have linked mediating variables with outcomes, or communication processes with outcomes, and pragmatic language approaches have focused on relating mediating variables with communication processes. More emphasis on inclusion of all three components is needed in order to track these crucial relationships more fully.

Mediating factors such as beliefs have generally been assessed after the interaction and communication-process variables. Unfortunately, it is unclear how measurement of beliefs subsequent to the interaction affects the reporting of beliefs. It is possible that patients bring their expectations in line with what actually occurred in the interaction.

Current methods of communication analysis have varied widely in origin and type. Two important considerations in the utilization of various methods are the size of the analysis unit and method reliability levels. Analysis units vary in size from single utterances, as in the speech-act approaches measuring communicative intentionality, to topics. These different unit sizes have the ability to reveal different types of communication information, as demonstrated by the conflicting results of research on communication modifications with elderly patients. Indeed, it should not be presumed that these methods are just different ways of obtaining similar information; rather, it should be noted that various units of analysis display different kinds of communication information, and may relate to mediating variables and health outcomes in unique ways.

Interestingly, the reliability of different interaction analysis systems varies with the size of analysis unit. For example, speech-act analysis systems have reported a high inter-rater reliability (i.e. agreement between different raters). The systems based on speech-act scoring categories, such as those of Bales (1968) and Roter (1977), range from 81% to 99% in inter-rater agreement. However, inter-rater reliability tends to decrease as analysis units increase in size. Reliability for the larger topic analysis segments within physician–patient information exchanges has been reported at a somewhat lower, but still acceptable, reliability level of 70% to 85% agreement. Studies utilizing larger segmentation units are fewer in number than those employing speech-act analyses, and so these observations are preliminary. The reliability of methods utilizing larger scoring units is an important area in which to continue investigation, since these analyses reveal more subtle language changes in relation to beliefs, attitudes, and personal and environmental characteristics.

In addition, the differences between contextual variables within physician–patient interaction and those within typical conversation should be considered (Fisher, 1984; Shuy, 1979). Inequalities in medical knowledge, and possible levels of anxiety on the part of the patient, affect the interaction and alter it from typical conversation. Therefore, the application of conversational analyses must be chosen with careful consideration of the special circumstances under which provider–patient communication occurs.

What new directions should research in doctor–patient communication pursue?

Future research in health-care communication will need to address the following questions, among others. Are disparities in current results due to different analysis methods? How does patient–provider communication change from the first encounter through to a well-established doctor–patient relationship? How many communication modifications can be attributed to stylistic differences? What are the communication preferences of particular groups of patients? Finally, given associations between patient preferences and patient-care outcomes with specific communication behaviors, what are the effective interventions that will improve physician–patient communication?

Some of these questions can be effectively addressed by adopting methodological principles frequently used in pragmatic language approaches. Primarily static measures have been utilized to analyze the dynamic communication processes in provider–patient exchanges. Research to date has relied extensively on the use of frequency measures; that is, how often a particular communication behavior or profile occurs. Duration, the length of time a behavior occurs, and latency, the length of time a behavior does not occur, have been utilized successfully in the description of communication behaviors in other pragmatic language analyses (Bloom, Rocissano, and Hood, 1976; Craig and Evans, 1989; Ervin-Tripp, 1979; Prutting and Kirchner, 1983). Preliminary evidence of the efficacy of these measures in doctor–patient communication research is offered by two analog studies (Anderson, De-Vellis, and DeVellis, 1987; Wallston, Wallston, and DeVellis, 1979). These measures have the potential to reveal dynamic communication relationships and should be explored further.

Doctor–patient communication research has adopted primarily *a priori* categories for the coding of data. This type of analysis can be described as an *etic* approach, in which a set of hypotheses or categories is developed initially, prior to collection of data (Bloom and Lahey, 1978; Blurton-Jones, 1972; Harris, 1964; Pike, 1967). Etic approaches can be distinguished from *emic* studies of behavior, in which, internal to the data collection, behaviors are re-evaluated and reclassified, and new hypotheses are established on the basis of the trends revealed.

Three possible combinations of the etic–emic distinction for research applications have been discussed (Bloom and Lahey, 1978). A strictly etic approach involves the establishment of categories and the coding of data into those categories. This describes the majority of research in doctor–patient communication to date. A second possibility is the etic to emic approach that begins with previously identified categories but reanalyzes data in such a way that more contextually relevant accounts are obtained. Third, and perhaps ideally, an etic to emic to etic approach could be utilized successfully in the study of doctor–patient communication, in which conclusions evolving from an emic level are utilized later to construct relevant categories for future examinations. These last two possibilities generally have not been employed in doctor–patient communication research, although they have been advocated (Pendleton and Hasler, 1983). Emic, and emic to etic, approaches have the potential to create opportunities for coding behavior patterns within physician–patient information exchanges in a way that will be maximally revealing.

REFERENCES

Anderson, L.A., DeVellis, B.M., and DeVellis, R.F. (1987). Effects of modeling on patient communication, satisfaction, and knowledge. *Medical Care*, **25**, 1044–1056.

Anderson, L.A., DeVellis, R.F., Boyles, B., and Feussner, J.R. (1989). Patients' perceptions of their clinical interactions: Development of the multidimensional desire for control scales. *Health Education Research*, **4**, 383–397.

Austin, J. (1962). *How to do things with words*. London: Oxford University Press.

Bales, R.F. (1968). Interaction Process Analysis. In D.L. Sills (Ed.), *International encyclopedia of the social sciences*, Vol. 7. New York: Macmillan.

Beisecker, A.L. (1988). Aging and the desire for information and input in medical decisions: Patient consumerism in medical encounters. *Gerontologist*, **28**, 330–335.

Berger, C.R. and Calabrese, R.J. (1975). Some explorations in initial interaction and beyond: Toward a developmental theory of interaction communication. *Human Communication Research*, **1**, 99–112.

Bertakis, K. (1977). The communication of information from physician to patient: A method for increasing patient retention and satisfaction. *Journal of Family Practice*, **5**, 217–222.

Blalock, S.J. and DeVellis, B.M. (1986). Stereotyping: The link between theory and practice. *Patient Education and Counseling*, **8**, 17–25.

Bloom, L. and Lahey, M. (1978). *Language development and language disorders*. New York: Wiley.

Bloom, L., Rocissano, L., and Hood, L. (1976). Adult–child discourse: Developmental interaction between information processing and linguistic knowledge. *Cognitive Psychology*, **8**, 521–552.

Blurton-Jones, N. (1972). Introduction: Characteristics of ethological studies of human behavior. In N. Blurton-Jones (Ed.), *Ethological studies of child behavior*. London: Cambridge University Press.

Botwinick, J. (1984). *Aging and behavior*. New York: Springer.

Buller, M.K. and Buller, D.B. (1987). Physicians' communication style and patient satisfaction. *Journal of Health and Social Behavior*, **28**, 375–388.

Byrne, P.S. and Long, B.E.L. (1976). *Doctors talking to patients*. London: HMSO.

Craig, H.K. and Evans, J. (1989). Turn exchange characteristics of SLI children's simultaneous and non-simultaneous speech. *Journal of Speech and Hearing Disorders*, **54**, 334–337.

Davis, M.S. (1971). Variation in patients' compliance with doctors' orders: Medical practice and doctor–patient interaction. *Psychiatry in Medicine*, **2**, 31–54.

DeVellis, B.M., Adams, J.L., and DeVellis, R.F. (1984). Effects of information on patient stereotyping. *Research in Nursing and Health*, **7**, 237–244.

DeVellis, B.M., Wallston, B.S., and Wallston, K.A. (1980). Stereotyping: A threat to individualized patient care. In M.H. Miller and B. Flynn (Eds), *Current perspectives in nursing: Social issues and trends*, Vol. 2. St Louis: Mosby.

DiMatteo, M.R., Prince, L.M., and Taranta, A. (1979). Patients' perceptions of physicians' behavior: Determinants of patient commitment to the therapeutic relationship. *Journal of Community Health*, **4**, 280–291.

DiMatteo, M.R., Taranta, S.A., Friedman, H.S., and Prince, L.M. (1980). Predicting patient satisfaction from physicians' nonverbal communication skills. *Medical Care*, **18**, 376–387.

Dryden, C. and Giles, H. (1987). Language, social identity and health. In H. Beloff and A. Coleman (Eds), *Psychology Survey*, No. 6. Leicester: British Psychological Society Press.

Ervin-Tripp, S. (1968). An analysis of the interaction of language topic and listener. In J.A. Fishman (Ed.), *Readings in the sociology of language*. The Hague: Mouton.

Ervin-Tripp, S. (1979). Children's verbal turn-taking. In E. Ochs and B. Schieffelin (Eds), *Developmental pragmatics*, pp. 391–414. New York: Academic Press.

Fisher, S. (1984). Institutional authority and the structure of discourse. *Discourse Processes*, **1**, 201–224.

Freemon, B., Negrete, V.F., Davis, M., and Korsch, B.M. (1971). Gaps in doctor–patient communication: Doctor–patient interaction analysis. *Pediatric research*, **5**, 298–311.

Greene, M.G., Adelman, R., Charon, R., and Hoffman, S. (1986). Ageism in the medical encounter: An exploratory study of the doctor–elderly patient relationship. *Language and Communication*, **6**, 113–124.

Greene, M.G., Hoffman, S., Charon, R., and Adelman, R. (1987). Psychosocial concerns in the medical encounter: A comparison of the interactions of doctors with their old and young patients. *Gerontologist*, **27**, 164–168.

Greenfield, S., Kaplan, S., and Ware, J.E. (1985). Expanding patient involvement in care: Effects on patient outcomes. *Annals of Internal Medicine*, **102**, 520–528.

Hall, J.A., Roter, D.L., and Rand, C.S. (1981). Communication of affect between patients and physicians. *Journal of Health and Social Behavior*, **22**, 18–30.

Halliday, M.A.K. (1978). *Language as social semiotic*. Baltimore, MD: University Park Press.

Harris, M. (1964). *The nature of cultural things*. New York: Random House.

Haug, M.R. (1976). The erosion of professional authority: A cross-cultural inquiry in the case of the physician. *MMFQ/Health and Society*, 83–106.

Haug, M. (1981). *Elderly patients and their doctors*. New York: Springer.

Haug, M.R. and Lavin, B. (1981). Practitioner or patient – Who's in charge? *Journal of Health and Social Behavior*, **22**, 212–229.

Haug, M.R. and Lavin, B. (1983). *Consumerism in medicine: Challenging physician authority*. Newbury Park, CA: Sage.

Heath, C. (1984). Participation in the medical consultation: The coordination of verbal and nonverbal behaviour between the doctor and patient. *Sociology of Health and Illness*, **6**, 311–338.

Hooper, E.M., Comstock, L.M., Goodwin, J.M., and Goodwin, J.S. (1982). Patient characteristics that influence physician behavior. *Medical Care*, **20**, **6**, 630–638.

Inui, T.S. and Carter, W.B. (1985). Problems and prospects for health services research on provider–patient communication. *Medical Care*, **23**, 521–538.

Keeler, E.B., Solomon, D.H., Beck, J.C., Mendenhall, R.C., and Kane, R.L. (1982). Effect of patient age on duration of medical encounters with physicians. *Medical Care*, **20**, 1101–1108.

Kelly, H.H. and Michlea, J.L. (1980). Attribution theory and research. *Annual Review of Psychology*, **31**, 457–501.

Korsch, B.M., Gozzi, E.K., and Frances, V. (1968). Gaps in doctor–patient communication: Doctor–patient interaction and patient satisfaction. *Pediatrics*, **42**, 855–871.

Ley, P. (1983). Patients' understanding and recall in clinical communication failure. In D. Pendleton and J. Hasler (Eds), *Doctor–patient communication*. London: Academic Press.

Ley, P., Bradshaw, P.W., Eaves, D., and Walker, C.W. (1973). A method for increasing patients' recall of information presented by doctors. *Psychology and Medicine*, **3**, 217–223.

Ley, P., Whitworth, M.A., Skilveck, C.E., Woodward, R., Pinsent, R.J.H.F., Pike, L.A., Clarkson, M.E., and Clark, P.B. (1976). Improving doctor–patient communication in general practice. *Journal of the Royal College of General Practitioners*, **26**, 720–724.

Morimoto, F.R. (1955). Favoritism in personnel–patient interactions. *Nursing Research*, **3**, 109–112.

Patterson, M.L. (1983). *Nonverbal behavior: A functional perspective*. New York: Springer-Verlag.

Pendleton, D. and Hasler, J.C. (1983). *Doctor–patient communication*. London: Academic Press.

Pendleton, D., Schofield, T., Tate, P., and Havelock, P. (1984). *The consultation: An approach to learning and teaching*. London: Oxford University Press.

Pike, K. (1967). *Language in relation to a unified theory of the structure of human behavior*. The Hague: Mouton.

Platt, J. and Weber, H. (1984). Speech convergence miscarried: An investigation into inappropriate accommodation strategies. *International Journal of Society and Language*, **46**, 131–146.

Prutting, C. and Kirchner, D. (1983). Applied Pragmatics. In T. Gallagher and C. Prutting (Eds), *Pragmatic assessment and intervention issues*, pp. 29–64. San Diego, CA: College Hill Press.

Putnam, S.M., Stiles, W.B., Jacob, M.C., and James, S.A. (1985). Patient exposition and physician explanation in initial medical interviews and outcomes of clinic visits. *Medical Care*, **23**, 74–83.

Reeder, L.G. (1972). The patient–client as a consumer: Some observations on the changing professional–client relationship. *Journal of Health and Social Behavior*, **134**, 406–412.

Rosenthal, R., Blanck, P.D., and Vannicelli, M. (1984). Speaking to and about patients: Predicting therapists' tone of voice. *Journal of Consulting and Clinical Psychology*, **52**, 679–686.

Rosow, I. (1981). Coalitions in geriatric medicine. In M.R. Haug (Ed.), *Elderly patients and their doctors*. New York: Springer.

Rost, K. and Roter, D. (1987). Predictives of recall of medical regimens and recommendations for life style changes in elderly patients. *Gerontologist*, **27**, 510–515.

Roter, D.L. (1977). Patient participation in the patient–provider interaction: The effects of patient question-asking on the quality of interaction, satisfaction, and compliance. *Health Education Quarterly*, **5**, 281–330.

Roter, D.L. (1984). Patient question asking in physician–patient interaction. *Health Psychology*, **3**, 395–409.

Roter, D.L., Hall, J.A., and Katz, N.R. (1987). Relations between physicians' behaviors and analogue patients' satisfaction, recall, and impressions. *Medical Care*, **25**, 437–451.

Sacks, H., Schegloff, E.A., and Jefferson, G. (1974). A simplest systematics for the organization of turn-taking for conversation. *Language*, **50**, 696–735.

Scherwitz, L., Hennrikus, D., Yusum, S., Lester, J., and Vallbona, C. (1985). Physician communication to patients regarding medications. *Patient Education and Counseling*, **7**, 121–136.

Searle, J. (1969). *Speech acts: An essay in the philosophy of language*. London: Cambridge University Press.

Sebastian, R.J. and Ryan, E.B. (1985). Speech cues and social evaluation: Markers of ethnicity, social class, and age. In H. Giles and R.N. St Clair (Eds), *Recent advances in language, communication and social psychology*, pp. 112–143. Hillsdale, NJ: Erlbaum.

Shuy, R.W. (1979). Three types of interference to an effective exchange of information in the medical interview. Paper presented at Meeting of the Society for Computer Medicine, Atlanta, GA.

Smith, C.K. and Larsen, K.M. (1984). Sequential nonverbal behavior in the patient–physician interview. *Journal of Family Practice*, **18**, 257–261.

Snyder, M., Tanke, E.D., and Berscheid, E. (1977). A social perception and interpersonal behavior: On the self-fulfilling nature of social stereotypes. *Journal of Personality-Psychology*, **35**, 656–666.

Stiles, W.B. (1979). Discourse analysis and the doctor–patient relationship. *International Journal of Psychiatry in Medicine*, **9**, 263–274.

Stiles, W.B., Putnam, S.M., and Jacob, M.C. (1982). Verbal exchange structure of initial medical interviews. *Health Psychology*, **1**, 315–336.

Stiles, W.B., Putnam, S.M., James, S.A., and Wolf, M.H. (1979). Dimensions of patient and physician roles in medical screening interviews. *Social Science and Medicine*, **13A**, 335–341.

Strecher, V.J. (1981). Improving physician–patient interactions: A review. *Patient Counselling and Health Education*, **4**, 129–136.

Street, R.L. and Wiemann, J.M. (1987). Patient satisfaction with physicians' interpersonal involvement, expressiveness, and dominance. In M.L. McLaughlin (Ed.), *Communication yearbook*, No. 10, pp. 591–610. Newbury Park, CA: Sage.

Strull, W.M., Lo, B., and Charles, G. (1984). Do patients want to participate in medical decision-making? *Journal of the American Medical Association*, **252**, 2990–2994.

Tabak, E.R. (1988). Encouraging patient question-asking: A clinical trial. *Patient Education and Counseling*, **12**, 37–49.

van Dijk, T.A. (1984). *Prejudice in discourse*. Philadelphia, PA: Benjamin.

Waitzkin, H. (1985). Information-giving in medical care. *Journal of Health and Social Behavior*, **26**, 81–101.

Waitzkin, H., Stoeckle, J.D., Beller, E., and Mons, C. (1978). The informative process in medical care: A preliminary report with implications for instructional communication. *Instructional Science*, **7**, 385–419.

Wallen, J., Waitzkin, H., and Stoeckle, J.D. (1979). Physician stereotypes about female health and illness: A study of patient's sex and the informative process during medical interviews. *Women and Health*, **4**, 135–146.

Wallston, B.S., Wallston, K.A., and DeVellis, B.M. (1979). Modification of question-asking behavior in high and low assertive women through modeling and specific instructions. *Social Behavior and Personality*, **6**, 195–204.

Wallston, K.A., Wallston, B.S., and DeVellis, B.M. (1976). Effect of a negative stereotype on nurses' attitudes toward an alcoholic patient. *Journal of Studies on Alcoholism*, **37**, 659–665.

Wasserman, R.C. and Inui, T.S. (1983). Systematic analyses of clinician–patient interactions: A critique of recent approaches with suggestions for future research. *Medical Care*, **21**, 279–293.

West, C. (1984). Medical misfires: mishearings, misgivings, and misunderstandings in physician–patient dialogues. *Discourse Processes*, **7**, 107–134.

26

Language and Law: An Overview of 15 Years of Research

BRENDA DANET

*Departments of Communication and Sociology/Social Anthropology,
Hebrew University of Jerusalem, Israel*

In the mid-1970s, the Law and Social Science Program of the National Science Foundation launched the empirical study of language in American legal settings by funding four interdisciplinary studies: two on questioning in American courtrooms, conducted by William M. O'Barr, John Conley, and E. Allen Lind, and by Kenneth Hoffman and myself, and two on the comprehensibility of pattern jury instructions, led by Bruce Sales, Amiram Elwork, and James Alfini, and by Veda and Robert Charrow. In the 15-year period since these studies were funded, research activity has continued to focus on the nature and consequences of communication processes in dispute-processing, and on the comprehensibility of legal language to laypersons. The latter work is, in turn, one expression of another development: the rise of the Plain Language movement, which calls for greater transparency and accessibility of language in institutional settings. Similar trends occurred in the United Kingdom: a major study of courtroom interaction was undertaken by J. Maxwell Atkinson and Paul Drew, and, in a quite separate development, a demand for plain language in public life also crystallized.

By the late 1980s, this new interdisciplinary field of law and language has expanded to such an extent that it is no longer possible to review all relevant work in one short article. Basic and applied research on linguistic aspects of communication in legal settings has also blossomed in Canada, Australia, and Israel, as well as in continental Europe, particularly in Sweden, West Germany, and Austria. As might be expected

Handbook of Language and Social Psychology
Edited by H. Giles and W.P. Robinson.   © 1990 John Wiley & Sons Ltd

in such a new and highly interdisciplinary area of research activity, there is enormous diversity in the range of issues investigated, the theoretical orientations advocated, the research methods used, and in the relevance of the various studies for applied social issues. The achievements of the field, and of specific researchers within it, are becoming evident in the publication of a number of increasingly specialized review articles and essays (e.g. Brenneis, 1988; Danet, 1980a, 1985; Drew, 1985; Goodrich, 1984; Maynard, 1985, in press; O'Barr, 1981, 1983; Philips, 1984c; Pomerantz and Atkinson, 1984; Shuy, 1986a; Wodak-Engel, 1985). A number of books, mono-graphs, and edited collections have also appeared (e.g. Atkinson and Drew, 1979; Bennett and Feldman, 1981; Berk-Seligson, in press, c; Danet, 1984a; Goldberg, 1988; Goldman, 1983, 1987; Kurzon, 1986; Levi and Walker, in press; Maynard, 1984a; O'Barr, 1982).

This chapter will focus on three topics:

(1) the Plain Language movement and the reform of legal language;
(2) language and disputing in modern Western legal systems;
(3) disputing in non-Western settings.

Of the three themes, the second will be treated in the greatest detail. For reviews of work on disputing among children, not discussed here, see Brenneis (1988) and Shantz (1987). Another topic deserving of attention but omitted from this chapter, for lack of space, is the issue of 'words as evidence'. Linguists have increasingly begun to appear in courts as expert witnesses, in relation to this issue, which includes both the problem of criminal liability for utterances, as in slander, and civil liability for what is said or implied, as in the language of an insurance policy or landlord–tenant contract (see Danet, Hoffman, and Kermish, 1980a; Green, in press; Johnson, in press; Philips, 1986; Prince, 1984; Shuy, 1981a,b, 1986a).

THE PLAIN LANGUAGE MOVEMENT AND THE REFORM OF LEGAL LANGUAGE

History of the Movement

In the 1970s, there was a call in many Western countries for greater accountability of both public and private institutions – government, the professions, bureaucracy, as well as private-sector business interests. Just as the consumer movement argued that consumers have a right to get fair value for money, so there was growing recognition of citizens' *right to understand*. Citizens should be able to understand critical written documents of all kinds, it was argued, including tax forms, social security benefits pamphlets, credit loan forms, and landlord–tenant leases. In addition, the claim was increasingly made that citizens have a right to understand what is *said to them or about them* in legal, bureaucratic, or professional settings. Attention focused on the well-known fact that jurors have difficulty understanding the complex instructions addressed to them by judges, just before they exit the courtroom to deliberate their verdict. About the same time, serious attention also began to be paid to the difficulties of defendants and witnesses who cannot speak the official language of the court.

There is much debate as to just what constitutes plain language, both in general, and in specific, contexts. A useful first approximation for the purposes of this chapter is a definition by Redish:

> Plain English means writing that is straightforward, that reads as if it were spoken. It means writing that is unadorned with archaic, multisyllabic words and majestic turns of phrase . . . Plain English is clear, direct, and simple. (Redish, 1985, p. 125)

In the USA, the insurance and banking industries were the first to institute reform of documents. The government soon followed. While interest in plain language was not really new (Danet, 1980a; Redish, 1985), the movement gained new momentum when President Carter issued two Executive Orders calling for plain English to be used in federal regulations, and for a serious attempt to reduce the amount of paperwork in government. Reform began to take hold at the state level too; while only seven American states now have plain English legislation, the movement has succeeded in spurring businesses to seek out the services of professional document designers (Redish, 1985).

In the United Kingdom, a grass-roots movement called the 'Plain English Campaign' was launched in 1979, with support from the National Consumer Council. A White Paper called *Administrative forms in government* served, in effect, as the declaration of a plain English policy for official publications by the British government (Eagleson, 1985, in press). Australia followed a similar pattern. An insurance company took the lead when in 1976 it issued its first policy in plain English. Other insurance companies, as well as the real-estate profession, soon followed suit. In 1984 an Australian Senate Committee recommended the establishment of a national Task Force to make recommendations for the reform of legal language (Law Reform Commission of Victoria, 1986). Sweden undertook language reform long before the USA and Britain; already in 1944 a language committee was formed, and since 1976 language consultants have advised government officials (Gunnarsson, in press).

Characteristics of Legal Language

Although no systematic description of legal English (LE), based on a wide variety of genres, has been carried out, many linguistic features of the legal register or dialect are by now quite well known. Since they have been reviewed elsewhere, they are summarized here only briefly. Psycholinguistic research has demonstrated that many of these features are associated with difficulties of comprehension (Charrow and Charrow, 1979; Danet, 1980a; Holland, 1981).

Lexical features

Legal English, especially in its written varieties, is full of technical terms; words of Latin or Old French origin, like *habeus corpus*; archaic expressions like 'hereafter'; polysyllabic words; unusual prepositional phrases (e.g. 'in the event of' instead of 'if'); binomial expressions like 'aid and abet' or 'cease and desist'; words belonging to a formal register; and expressions which seem either overly vague or overly precise.

Syntactic features

Legal English typically contains many nominalizations (e.g. 'payment' from the verb 'to pay'), passives, unusual anaphora (absence of pronouns), conditionals, whiz deletion (e.g. 'covenant contained' instead of 'covenant that is contained'), unusually placed prepositional phrases, and sentences of unusual length and syntactic complexity (see Hiltunen, 1984).

Discourse-level features

Recent research has demonstrated that the difficulties of comprehension of legal or bureaucratic language derive not so much from their surface-level lexical or syntactic features as from text-level features which are less easily identifiable by laypersons. Documents are often poorly organized, and their headings and tables of contents are frequently uninformative (Redish, 1983). More important, they do not make clear what actions citizens/readers are to take; they are overly abstract and implicit in communicating meaning (Gunnarsson, 1984, in press). For these reasons, the readability formulas still widely used are an inadequate basis on which to evaluate the comprehensibility of documents to lay readers (Redish, 1980, 1981).

Prosodic features

The formulaic varieties of LE show traces of poetization. Both LE and legal Hebrew show signs of alliteration, assonance, rhyme, rhythm, meter, and even phonemic contrast (Danet, 1980a, 1984b). In addition, there is evidence for the principle of end-weight, whereby there are more beats, or more phonetic material, in the second half of a two-part expression, as in 'cease and desist' (Danet, 1984b; Gustafsson, 1975). (For further discussion of the linguistic features of LE, see, e.g., Charrow and Charrow, 1979; Charrow, Crandall, and Charrow, 1982; Danet, 1980a, 1985; Gustafsson, 1975, 1984; Hiltunen, 1984; Kurzon, 1984; Mellinkoff, 1963.)

Progress in Reform

Redish (1985) summed up the accomplishments of the Plain English movement in the USA. Since the mid-1970s only a handful of government documents, but many insurance and banking documents, have been revised. Many new handbooks have been written, including some for law students and lawyers (e.g. Givens, 1981; MacDonald, 1979; Mellinkoff, 1982; Wydick, 1979), and are now widely used. Lawyers and consumers increasingly accept revised documents. In Sweden, the language of legislation was regularly critiqued for vocabulary and sentence structure in the 1960s and 1970s, but only in the last few years have legal drafters begun to pay attention to deeper, text-level features (Gunnarsson, in press). Public awareness of 'gobbledegook' has grown everywhere. In Australia, most insurance companies have adopted plain English, but implementation in government, for the most part, has yet to come (Eagleson, in press).

Evaluating the Impact of Reform

The business world has discovered that plain language is good business. Thus, an Australian insurance company that revised its policies found that the number of invalid claims dropped dramatically, and that litigation declined. Also, landlords forced to confront formerly hidden injustices in reformed tenant lease-forms agreed to remove them (Eagleson, in press). In Britain, government departments now have programs to monitor the language of forms systematically every 3 to 4 years (Eagleson, in press). As for the USA, by 1979, 30 states had passed or proposed laws or regulations requiring readable insurance policies (Pressman, 1979).

Research evidence is accumulating that reforming the language of pattern jury instructions can significantly improve comprehension, and, perhaps more important, the ability to apply them correctly, although there is still much room for improvement (Charrow and Charrow, 1979; Elwork, Sales, and Alfini, 1982; Jones and Myers, 1979; Kess, Hoppe, and Copeland, 1985; Severance and Loftus, 1982). What are called usability studies of reformed documents are becoming standard operating procedure among those engaged in document design; they regularly show that reformed documents improve the ability of readers to understand and use them (Redish, 1985). Language reformers busy simplifying forms no doubt throw out, along the way, the traces of poetization mentioned above; it remains to be seen whether such features just might sometimes be desirable, in order to preserve the authoritative nature of language.

Too much simplification can also erode the substance of legal documents significantly (Bhatia, 1983; Redish, 1985). Furthermore, Procaccia (1979) reminds us that linguistic reform can never be a substitute for substantive justice. To be effective, linguistic reformers must learn to pay attention to the organizational constraints affecting openness to linguistic reform (Keller-Cohen, 1987).

LANGUAGE AND DISPUTING: MODERN SETTINGS

The Range of Settings Studied

As we have seen, a second major theme of research undertaken in the mid-1970s was the nature of communication processes in trials. Although much of the more recent work continued to focus on the high drama of trials, researchers also began to study other types of proceedings, for example plea bargaining (Maynard, 1984a,b); insanity hearings (Holstein, 1987, 1988a,b); change-of-plea and initial appearance hearings (Phillips, 1984a,b, 1985, 1988); Congressional hearings (Danet, 1976; Molotch and Boden, 1985); small-claims courts (Conley and O'Barr, 1987; O'Barr and Conley, 1985; Pomerantz, 1987); depositions (Walker, 1982a,b, 1988); magistrates' interrogation of persons dilinquent in payment of fines or maintenance (Harris, 1984); and lawyer–client interaction (Bogoch and Danet, 1984; Hosticka,

1979; Sarat and Felstiner, 1986, in press). This development is to be applauded, since only a small proportion of either civil or criminal legal actions ever actually goes to trial, and most of the routine business of modern legal systems is conducted in these other types of settings.

Empirical work on disputing outside the formal judicial system appears to be less common. Francis (1986) analyzed disputing in industrial negotiation. Fraser (1988) critiqued the applicability of Grice's (1975) Cooperative Principle to disputatious discourse everywhere; his critique draws not only on his expertise as a linguist, but also on experience as a professional mediator and arbitrator (for another critique of the applicability of Grice's Cooperative Principle to disputing, see Penman, 1987). O'Donnell (in press) has analyzed labor–management conflict talk. Ethno-methodologically oriented studies like those of Pomerantz on blamings, provision of evidence, and strategies to legitimate claims, as they occur in everyday conversation, are all pertinent (see Pomerantz, 1978, 1984, 1986).

If the domain of language and law is understood broadly to mean 'the role of language in the negotiation of social order', other, older research traditions, such as those of symbolic interaction and the sociology of deviance, are also relevant (see, for example, the literature on accounts for untoward behavior, e.g. Austin, 1970; Marshall, 1981; Scott and Lyman, 1968, 1970; Sykes and Matza, 1957; Weinstein, 1980).

Approaches to the Study of Discourse in Disputing

Two main methodological approaches to the study of legal discourse have developed, those of ethnomethodology and conversational analysis on the one hand, and of sociolinguistics and the ethnography of communication, on the other. The two approaches share a commitment to the study of naturally occurring conversation, and typically tape-record and transcribe whole sequences of interaction.

Ethnomethodology and conversation analysis

Ethnomethodologists seek to elucidate the methods of practical reasoning by which individuals determine facts, produce decisions, and attribute responsibility (Pomerantz and Atkinson, 1984). They are interested in the social organization of conversation in legal settings, including such phenomena as turn-taking, adjacency pairs – question–answer sequences in the case of courtroom questioning – and the interactional work involved in blaming, accusing, justifying, excusing etc. (Drew, in press, a,b; Maynard, 1984a; Pollner, 1979). At first, the work in legal settings (e.g. Atkinson and Drew, 1979) stressed the similarities between procedures observed there and ordinary conversation. Although Atkinson and Drew (1979) were also interested in the techniques of control which were specific to courtroom interaction, their main goal was to illuminate the general nature of interaction, not the nature of the legal system.

More recent work has begun to address the issue of socio-legal relevance directly. Thus, Holstein's (1987, 1988a,b) studies of communication in insanity hearings elucidate how the communicative competence or incompetence of patients is interactionally produced, and how aspects of their biographies do not so much determine interaction patterns and outcomes as provide resources for their inter-rogators. Similarly, Maynard's (1984a, 1985, 1988) work on plea bargaining is a way of critiquing traditional, positivistically oriented sentencing research, which assumes that justice is done when characteristics of individuals' backgrounds do *not* influence decision-making. Maynard's research suggests, to the contrary, that decision-makers make decisions fit with known features of individuals' biography.

Sociolinguistics and the ethnography of communication

The second main approach to the study of communication processes in legal settings falls within the rubric of empirical sociolinguistics and the ethnography of communi-cation. This research focuses generally on one or more speech acts which occur during the elicitation of testimony. The central concern of this literature is the nature and consequences of patterns of questioning. Two studies have also investigated objections (Bogoch and Danet, 1980; Danet and Bogoch, 1980; Walker, 1982b). A number of these studies have developed typologies of question form, and have sought to tease out the complicated and elusive interrelations between question form and function (Adelsward, Aronsson, and Linell, 1988; Danet and Bogoch, 1980; Danet, Hoffman, Kermish, Rafn, and Stayman, 1980b; Harris, 1984, 1987a,b; Philips, 1984a, 1987, 1988; Walker, 1988; Woodbury, 1984). This type of research often aspires to examine the influence on linguistic choices of interrogators, defen-dants, and witnesses of factors such as type of examination (Bogoch and Danet, 1980; Danet, 1980b; Danet and Bogoch, 1980; Harris, 1984; Valdes, 1986; Wood-bury, 1984), seriousness of offense (Adelsward *et al.*, 1988; Danet and Bogoch, 1980), the institutional role of the questioner (Philips, 1984a, 1985, 1988), and the social class of defendants (Wodak-Engel, 1984, 1985). The comparison between direct examination and cross-examination is, of course, possible only in the Anglo-American adversary system. In the continental European system, the judge asks the questions, and there is no distinction between these two types of examination.

Critique of the Discourse Constraints on Witnesses

One of the most important themes to emerge from this literature is the criticism of constraints on witnesses' freedom to tell their version of events, particularly on cross-examination in adversary trials. Even when witnesses are eager to cooperate in helping courtroom participants to arrive at a constructed 'true' version of 'what happened', the discourse rules operating in legal situations may well prevent them from providing needed information. The work of Molotch and Boden (1985), Penman (1987), Valdes (1986), Walker (1982b), and a Swedish group based at the University of Linkoping (Adelsward *et al.*, 1988; Adelsward, Aronsson, Jonsson, and Linell, 1987; Aronsson, Jonsson, and Linell, 1987; Jonsson, 1988) has added grist for the mills of all those concerned with this issue.

Not surprisingly, then, many researchers, of both the ethnomethodological and the sociolinguistic persuasions, are seeking to further our understanding of how cross-examination, or any sequence of questioning which challenges the credibility of the witness or the validity of the testimony, is accomplished, and by what means witnesses can resist the view of reality being imposed on them by questioners. (In addition to the earlier work on courtroom questioning (e.g. Atkinson and Drew, 1979; Danet, 1980b; Danet and Bogoch, 1980), see Adelsward *et al.*, 1987, 1988; Drew, 1985, in press a,b; Harris, 1984, 1987a,b; Jonsson, 1988; Penman, 1987; Valdes, 1986; Walker, 1982b. On power and control in lawyer–client communication, see Bogoch, in preparation; Bogoch and Danet, 1984; Hosticka, 1979.)

The Search for Methods Which Capture Sequence

An important development of both theoretical and methodological significance is the effort by researchers in the tradition of sociolinguistics and discourse analysis to go beyond the question–answer sequence as the basic unit of analysis. Valdes (1986) developed a model which aspires to encompass both macro- and micro-level aspects of trials; her unit of analysis is the exchange, a unit consisting of an *initiate* and a *terminate*. An initiate is a request for display of information in direct examination, and a request for admission or defense in cross-examination. Such exchanges may be completed in one question–answer sequence, or they may take longer. The Linkoping group developed what they call Initiative–Response Analysis (Linell *et al.*, 1988). Turns are ranked on a scale from 1 to 6, as to the degree to which they are independent of preceding dialogue and govern the following turn, or are determined by the interlocutor's preceding turn. This technique provides an incisive empirical profile of the imbalance between interrogators and witnesses, and also enables the researchers to demonstrate that seriousness of offense makes a difference for the degree of imbalance (Adelsward *et al.*, 1987).

The differences between ethnomethodological and sociolinguistic approaches are becoming increasingly blurred. In earlier work, the sociolinguists and ethnographers of communication had tended to be more overtly concerned with implications of patterns of communication for justice, and, at least in some cases, to have an interest in the substance of what was talked about. Ethnomethodological work had declined to become involved in such issues. Today, at least some ethnomethodologists and others influenced by them are also addressing themselves to issues of justice and of power beyond the micro-situation of interaction. Methodological developments have also brought the two approaches increasingly together, as sociolinguists turn from quantitative to qualitative methods, in the search for better ways to take account of the complexities of context.

Narrative in Disputing

A relatively new development in the study of the language of disputing in modern legal settings is the focus on narrative. It should be evident that virtually all of the work on the language of disputing reviewed thus far has dealt in one way or another with highly structured sequences of questioning, in which a legal professional maintains relatively tight control over the flow of testimony, and witnesses are allowed to tell their 'story' only bit by bit, in relatively short segments. In 1980, I contrasted this mode of constructing 'facts', so characteristic of disputing in formal legal settings in modern societies, with the less structured narrative mode more typical of tribal disputing (Danet, 1980a).

It is now clear that this was too sharp a contrast; varieties of narrative continue to be important in at least some kinds of modern legal settings, for example in written genres such as lawyers' briefs (Kurzon, 1985), as well in such oral genres as plea-bargaining sessions (Maynard, 1984a, in press), attorneys' summations (Goldberg, 1986, 1988), and small-claims court proceedings (O'Barr and Conley, 1985). Bennett and Feldman (1981) argue that jurors reconstruct evidence to create a 'story'. However, they use the term 'story' in a broader sense than most of the others interested in narrative. (For a critique of Bennett and Feldman's (1981) work, see Philips, 1983.)

At the other end of the spectrum is the approach of O'Barr and Conley (1985), who define narrative as 'a telling [by one person, the witness] that occurs in a relatively uninterrupted manner, with the witness having an opportunity to determine both the form and the substance of the telling' (p. 665). They find that narratives by plaintiffs in small-claims courts resemble everyday talk about trouble, but fail to meet standards of legal adequacy. In contrast, Maynard (1988) analyzed plea-bargaining sessions as *jointly* constructed narratives, in which the prosecutor, defense attorney, and judge all take part.

Bilingualism in the Courtroom

One of the most important developments in the 1980s has been the focusing of research attention on the special problems of defendants who have an inadequate command of the official language of the court. A major step forward in the USA was the passing in 1978 of the federal Court Interpreters Act, which formalized the provision of court interpreters to non-English-speaking defendants, litigants, and witnesses, and created high professional standards of training and practice for this purpose. Similar developments at the state and municipal levels soon followed.

One type of research which has been stimulated, at least in part, by these developments looks closely at the communication problems encountered by non-native English speakers who testify in court. Exploratory research by Bresnehan (1979) and Naylor (1979) (summarized by Danet, 1980a), pointing to problems of linguistic interference, was followed by the more extensive studies of Gumperz (1982) and Underwood (1987). At issue in these analyses is the fact that interference from the native language can make a truthful speaker appear evasive.

An entirely different set of issues is raised by the presence of interpreters in court. In theory, at least, the interpreter is a neutral presence, a mere conduit for the flow of information. Berk-Seligson (1987, in press, a,b,c) and Morris (1989) have demonstrated that this is not the case. Interpreters often alter the flow of testimony, for example by prompting a witness to speak, and call attention to themselves by addressing other participants in a trial, albeit often for a good reason, for example to clarify the intent of a lawyer's question. Moreover, they tend to lengthen the witnesses' replies, to shift their wording to a higher, more formal register, and to make subtle changes in the degree of politeness, adding or deleting 'sir' or 'madam', or in 'Yes, sir, he did' versus 'Yes, he did'. Interpreters unwittingly even alter the degree of blame for wrongdoing implied by such choices as the active or passive voice (Berk-Seligson, 1987, in press, c).

The Consequences of Speech Patterns

One of the most intriguing questions for researchers and trial lawyers alike is that of the effect of speech patterns of trial participants on decision-makers. O'Barr and his colleagues have shown that testimony presented in a 'powerful' style is perceived as more credible than the same testimony presented in a 'powerless' style (see O'Barr, 1982). Troutzer (1982) adapted the design used by O'Barr to an Israeli courtroom setting, creating three degrees of powerlessness, instead of two. Her study confirmed the basic finding that speech style affects perceptions of credibility. While the male witness was evaluated the most favorably when he spoke in the most powerful style, the female witness was rated most favorably when she spoke in only a moderately powerful style (Danet and Troutzer, 1983; Troutzer, 1982).

Parkinson (1979; summarized by Danet, 1980a) found that polite witnesses were perceived more favorably than less polite ones. There is also some indication that matters of lexical choice can influence jurors. Bell and Loftus (1985) report that when witnesses offer testimony that is vivid, it may be more persuasive than the same testimony delivered in a pallid manner. Walker (1985b) found that witnesses' tendency to hesitate before answering influences lawyers' impressions of them. Her data suggested that witnesses who hesitate, and who also violate other rules of discourse in a situation of interrogation, are especially likely to be evaluated negatively by attorneys.

A series of experiments by Berk-Seligson (1988b, in press, b), using mock jurors, demonstrated that alterations in testimony by interpreters are likely to affect jurors' judgments of witnesses. Testimony with the polite 'sir' or 'madam', and in a relatively more formal register, was evaluated more favorably than less polite, and less formal versions of the same testimony. The work by both Berk-Seligson and by Morris (1989) strongly suggests that interpreting makes it difficult for the parties to a case to object when the opposing attorney is questioning a witness.

LANGUAGE IN NON-WESTERN DISPUTING

The Challenges of Studying Disputing in Non-Western Societies

Despite the large literature on non-Western disputing, few studies provide details on the nature of communication processes in these settings (Danet, 1980a). Typically, the materials studied are treated too globally to allow for examination of their linguistic aspects. Close linguistic analysis of disputing in non-Western contexts is also fraught with problems not faced by researchers who study the language of disputing in the West. It is not simply a matter of mastering an exotic language. On the theoretical level, anthropologists investigating these societies are committed to the holistic study of disputing as a general social phenomenon. The lack of formal institutions like courts makes it difficult to isolate sequences of interaction for analysis; the response to normative breaches and conflicts of interest is embedded in the flow of daily life.

One solution has been to study the repertoire of genres of disputing in a given society and the interrelations among them (Abrahams, 1983; Arno, 1985; Brenneis, 1984a, 1987; Duranti, 1984; Goldman, 1980, 1987; Hertzfeld, 1985). Others prefer to use the extended-case method, to follow particular cases from start to finish (Goldman, 1983, 1986a,b, 1987; Rumsey and Merlan, 1988). The advantage of the latter approach is that it enables the transformation of a dispute to be followed over time (Mather and Yngvesson, 1980–81). Even in the more structured context of Western legal systems, to follow a case from start to finish is a formidable, if not impossible, task.

Despite all the difficulties, in the last decade a number of legal and linguistic anthropologists have begun to pay closer attention to the details of communication processes in disputing (e.g. Arno, 1980, 1985; Besnier, in press; Boggs and Chun, in press; Brenneis, 1983, 1984a,b, 1987; Brenneis and Myers, 1984; Goldman, 1980, 1983, 1986a,b, 1987; Hayden, 1987; Hutchins, in press; Katriel, 1986; Lindstrom, in press; McKellin, in press; Watson-Gegeo and Gegeo, in press). I will devote the remainder of the discussion in this section to the work of two anthropologists who, in my opinion, raise issues of especially great interest for persons working on the language of disputing in modern societies, which has been the central focus of this chapter.

Disputing Among the Huli in New Guinea

Goldman (1983, 1986a,b, 1987) has carried out an extensive series of detailed studies of the language of disputing among the Huli, a New Guinea Highlands society of 80 000 persons. He studied both informal moots, or mediation sessions, and formal adjudication in local courts. Most pertinent here is his analysis of three aspects of questioning in Huli disputes: the syntactic form of questions, constraints on choice of question form, and the nature of questioning sequences and structures (Goldman, 1987). Moots are rather informal; there is no pre-allocation of turn order or prespecification of turn-type, as Atkinson and Drew (1979) had pointed out is the case for modern Western trials, and neither is there segmentation into sequences resembling direct examination and cross-examination, as known in Anglo-American adversary trials. Talk is primarily addressed to the group, not to a specific questioner. Question–answer sequences in which an interrogator directly addresses a witness are relatively rare; rhetorical questions are a common way of referring to group norms. The language of these discussions shows evidence of poetization, including assonance and alliteration, parallelism, play with rhythm, and so on. Comparing moots with court adjudication, Goldman found that structured interrogation sequences were more common in the courts; women were especially likely to be interrogated in this way. Moreover, in both the moots and the courts, question form was more coercive, in the sense developed in our research (Danet and Bogoch, 1980), when a woman was being questioned.

Turn-Taking in Indian and Fijian *Panchayats*

Hayden's (1987) analysis of turn-taking and overlap of speech in disputing in Fiji and India raises important issues about how legal systems and culture relate to turn-taking generally. Contesting the view that overlapping speech is dysfunctional, as is implied or claimed by researchers such as Walker (1982a) and O'Barr (1982), Hayden claims that a high degree of control over the flow of speech in disputing is correlated with an emphasis on the function of 'fact' finding. He compares his own data on *panchayats* in an area of northern India with a similar genre of disputing among Fijian Indians. *Panchayats* are gatherings to discuss a case of trouble, dispute, or misconduct.

The north Indian variety is a rowdy, disorderly affair, with many people speaking at once, and very little questioning in the sense known in the West. In contrast, in the Fijian version, carefully controlled questioning is well institutionalized. In the former, the focus is not on determining the 'facts' of a case, but on debate about how to evaluate them; in the latter, the goal is to arrive at a consensually created, authoritative version of the 'facts'. Hayden (1987) thus argues for a correlation between controlled questioning and a commitment to construction of evidence. He rejects an alternative explanation that it is simply culture that explains a preference for highly ordered speech.

DISCUSSION

This chapter has pointed to a number of important developments in the empirical study of law and language since its beginnings in the mid-1970s. To recapitulate, one major trend has been the rise of the Plain Language movement, and the enlistment of linguists in its cause. We have seen that linguists have become involved in the planning and reform of many kinds of documents. The movement is increasingly accepted, in the English-speaking world, and in some countries in continental Europe too. Both government and business now regularly seek out the services of experts on reform like the staff of the Document Design Center at the American Institutes of Research in Washington DC. At the same time, there is still room for debate and research on the long-term impact of the movement: whether it is, for example, primarily a symbolic gesture, or a genuine substantive improvement enabling citizens to obtain their due.

Research on disputing in modern societies has expanded greatly. Not only has it spread to countries other than Britain and the USA, but also, as we have seen, many types of legal settings besides trials are now being studied. Research on trials still constitutes a major focus of interest. The work of the Swedish group at the University of Linkoping (Adelsward *et al.*, 1987, 1988; Aronsson *et al.*, 1987; Jonsson, 1988) constitutes, to my knowledge, the first substantial research program outside of countries using the Anglo-American adversary model to tackle the kinds of issues which have interested researchers in the English-speaking world. However, their results are not entirely comparable to those of any study in an adversary system, both because they used largely different empirical criteria and methods, and because they studied a set of trials not comparable to any set studied by other researchers.

For the most part, even the various studies conducted within the Anglo-American adversary model, in the United Kingdom, Australia, and New Zealand, as well as in the United States and Israel, are not very comparable, because, once again, different researchers have investigated different phenomena, using different methods, and focusing on different types of trials. As we have seen, some studied low-level magistrates' courts, and others have investigated trials at higher levels in the court system. Thus, there is a great need for well-designed, systematic, comparative analyses of trials, both in different countries following the Anglo-Saxon adversarial model, and, even more important, comparing the handling of similar types of cases in adversary and inquisitorial systems.

Whatever its limitations to date, research on disputing, both in trials and in the many other legal settings reviewed earlier, has already made a strong case that communication processes are no mere conduit for the doing of justice, but in fact play a critical role in the social construction of 'facts' and in the application of rules to those 'facts'. Moreover, work on the consequences of features of testimony, notably that of O'Barr (1982) and Berk-Seligson (in press, a,b,c) has shown that such ostensibly unimportant matters as the speech styles of witnesses and the provision of interpretation in court may affect judgments of credibility of those witnesses.

As for research on disputing in non-Western settings, it is obvious that more studies of a detailed nature would be helpful, although few may have the stamina that Goldman (1983, 1987) had to pursue this challenge. There is still much work to be done to help us to understand why disputing is so highly controlled in some settings, and so spontaneous in others. Whether or not Hayden (1987) is right that cultural differences do not account for the different communication patterns in Indian and Fijian *panchayats*, there *is* evidence for cultural differences in disputing styles, not just in tribal or modernizing societies, but in modern societies as well.

Much of the evidence for the influence of culture comes from research on informal, rather than formal, disputing. To take just one example, which is close to 'home' for me as an American-Israeli Jew, there is by now a good deal of research on disputatiousness among American Jews (Schiffrin, 1984, 1985, in press; Tannen, 1981). In an American study of a group of elderly Jews in a day program, conducted by Myerhoff (1979), a psychologist was called in to urge them to live in harmony, rather than fighting all the time. Unmoved, one woman told Myerhoff, 'He doesn't understand us . . . we fight to keep warm!'

While middle-level trials in Israel are characterized by tight control of questioning on direct examination and cross-examination, as in the English-speaking world (Bogoch and Danet, 1980; Danet, 1980b), Grebler's (1981) research on lower-level magistrates' court hearings in Jerusalem found the proceedings to be extremely disorderly. A challenge for researchers interested in pursuing this issue of why some trials, or other modes of disputing, seem so controlled, while others are spontaneous and even rowdy, is to try to separate the notions of order and disorder, on the one hand, from those of formality and informality, on the other (Atkinson, 1982).

Other ethnic groups besides Jews also show a preference for disorderly conversation. Thus, not only in less modern societies, but even among some subgroups in modern ones, and perhaps in entire modern societies as well, the expressive aspects of disputing may continue to be important, along with the instrumental or 'fact'-oriented ones. Expressiveness in disputing survives in modern society for other, less colorful reasons too. As O'Barr and Conley (1985; Conley and O'Barr, 1987) showed in their research on American small-claims courts, the chance to be heard was central for plaintiffs, regardless of the outcome. In short, one direction future research might take is to search for more probing ways to analyze how the instrumental and expressive aspects of disputing interrelate, in both tribal and in modern societies, and why one or the other tends to predominate.

REFERENCES

Abrahams, R.D. (1983). *The man-of-words in the West Indies: Performance and the emergence of Creole culture*. Baltimore, MD: Johns Hopkins.

Adelsward, V., Aronsson, K., Jonsson, L., and Linell, P. (1987). The unequal distribution of interactional space: Dominance and control in courtroom interaction. *Text, 7*, 313–346.

Adelsward, V., Aronsson, K., and Linell, P. (1988). Discourse of blame: Courtroom construction of social identity from the perspective of the defendant. *Semiotica*.

Arno, A. (1980). Fijian gossip as adjudication: A communication model of informal social control. *Journal of Anthropological Research, 36*, 343–360.

Arno, A. (1985). Structural communication and control communication: An interactionist perspective on legal and customary procedures for conflict management. *American Anthropologist, 87*, 40–55.

Aronsson, K., Jonsson, L., and Linell, P. (1987). The courtroom hearing as a middle ground: Speech accommodation by lawyers and defendants. *Journal of Language and Social Psychology, 6*(2), 99–115.

Atkinson, J.M. (1982). Understanding formality: The categorization and production of 'formal' interaction. *British Journal of Sociology, 33*, 86–117.

Atkinson, J.M. and Drew, P. (1979). *Order in court: The organization of verbal interaction in judicial settings*. London: Macmillan.

Austin, J.L. (1970). *Philosophical papers*. Oxford: Oxford University Press.

Bell, B.E. and Loftus, E.F. (1985). Vivid persuasion in the courtroom. *Journal of Personality Assessment, 49*, 659–665.

Bennett, F.L. and Feldman, M.S. (1981). *Reconstructing reality in the courtroom: Justice and judgment in American culture*. New Brunswick, NJ: Rutgers.

Berk-Seligson, S. (1987). The intersection of testimony styles in interpreted judicial proceedings: Pragmatic alterations in Spanish testimony. *Linguistics, 25*, 1087–1125.

Berk-Seligson, S. (1988a). The need for quality interpreting services in the courtroom. *Court Manager, 3*(2), 10–17.

Berk-Seligson, S. (1988b). The impact of politeness in witness testimony: The influence of the court interpreter. *Multilingua, 7*, 411–439.

Berk-Seligson, S. (1988c). The role of linguistic pragmatics in court interpreting. *La Raza Law Journal*, fall.

Berk-Seligson, S. (in press, a). Bilingual court proceedings: The role of the court interpreter. In J.N. Levi and A.G. Walker (Eds), *Language in the judicial process*. New York: Plenum.

Berk-Seligson, S. (in press, b). The role of register in the bilingual courtroom: Evaluative reactions to interpreted testimony. In I. Wherritt and O. Garcia (Eds), *US Spanish: The language of Latinos*. Special issue of *International Journal of the Sociology of Language*.

Berk-Seligson, S. (in press, c). *The bilingual courtroom*. Chicago, IL: University of Chicago Press.

Besnier, N. (in press). Conflict management, gossip and affective meaning on Nukulaelae. In K.A. Watson-Gegeo and G.M. White (Eds), *The discourse of disentangling: Conflict, person and emotion in the Pacific*.

Bhatia, V.K. (1983). Simplification is falsification: The case of legal texts. *Applied Linguistics*, **4**, 42–54.

Bhatia, V.K. (1987). Textual mapping in British legislative writing. *World Englishes*, **6**(1), 1–10.

Boggs, S.T. and Chun, N.C. (in press). Ho'oponopono: An Hawaiian method for resolving interpersonal conflict. In K.A. Watson-Gegeo and G.M. White (Eds), *The discourse of disentangling: Conflict, person and emotion in the Pacific*.

Bogoch, B. (in preparation). Language and power in lawyer–client communication in a legal aid setting. PhD dissertation, Department of Communications, Hebrew University, Jerusalem.

Bogoch, B. and Danet, B. (1980). A sociolinguistic analysis of twelve Israeli and American criminal trials. Paper presented at the Annual Meeting of the Israel Sociological Society, February 1980.

Bogoch, B. and Danet, B. (1984). Challenge and control in lawyer–client interaction. In B. Danet (Ed.), *Studies of legal discourse*, pp. 249–275. Special issue of *Text*, **4**, Nos 1–3.

Brenneis, D. (1983). Official accounts: Performance and the public record. *Windsor Yearbook of Access to Justice*, **3**, 228–244.

Brenneis, D. (1984a). Straight talk and sweet talk: Political discourse in an occasionally egalitarian community. In D. Brenneis and F. Meyers (Eds), *Dangerous words: Language and Politics in the Pacific*, pp. 69–84. New York: New York University Press.

Brenneis, D. (1984b). Grog and gossip in Bhatgaon: Style and substance in Fijian Indian conversation. *American Ethnologist*, **11**, 487–506.

Brenneis, D. (1987). Performing passions: Aesthetics and politics in an occasionally egalitarian community. *American Ethnologist*, **14**, 236–250.

Brenneis, D. (1988). Language and disputing. *Annual Review of Anthropology*, **17**, 221–237.

Brenneis, D. and Myers, F.R. (1984). *Dangerous words: Language and politics in the Pacific*. New York: New York University Press.

Bresnehan, M.I. (1979). Linguistic limbo: The case of the non-native English-speaking defendant in the American courtroom. Paper presented at the Eighth Annual Colloquium on New Ways of Analyzing Variation in English (NWAVE-VIII), Montreal, Canada.

Charrow, R.P. and Charrow, V.R. (1979). Making legal language understandable: A psycholinguistic study of jury instructions. *Columbia Law Review*, **79**, 1306–1374.

Charrow, V.R. (1982). Linguistic theory and legal or bureaucratic language. In L. Obler and L. Menn (Eds), *Linguistic theory and exceptional languages*, pp. 81–102. New York: Academic Press.

Charrow, V., Crandall, J.A., and Charrow, R.P. (1982). Characteristics and functions of legal language. In R. Kittredge and J. Lehrberger (Eds), *Sublanguage: Studies of language in restricted domains*. Berlin: Walter de Gruyter.

Conley, J.M. and O'Barr, W.M. (1987). Fundamentals of jurisprudence: An ethnography of judicial decision making in informal courts. *North Carolina Law Review*, **66**, 467–507.

Cutts, M. and Maher, C. (1986). *The Plain English story*. Stockport (England): Plain English Campaign.

Danet, B. (1976). Speaking of Watergate: Language and moral accountability. Centrum: Working Papers of the Minnesota Center for Advanced Studies in Language, Style, and Literary Theory, No. 4.

Danet, B. (1980a). Language in the legal process. In R.L. Abel (Ed.), *Contemporary issues in law and social science*, pp. 445–565. Special issue of *Law and Society Review*, **14**.

Danet, B. (1980b). 'Baby' or 'fetus': Language and the construction of reality in a manslaughter trial. *Semiotica*, **32**, 187–219.

Danet, B. (1980c). Obstacles to the study of lawyer–client interaction. *Law and Society Review*, **14**, 905–922.

Danet, B. (1980d). Language in the courtroom. In H. Giles, P. Smith, and P. Robinson (Eds), *Language: Social psychological perspectives*, pp. 367–376. Oxford: Pergamon.

Danet, B. (1983). Law, bureaucracy and language. In A.D. Grimshaw (Ed.), *Language as a social problem*, pp. 49–55. Special issue of *Transaction-Society*, **4**, May–June.

Danet, B. (Ed.) (1984a). *Studies of legal discourse*. Special issue of *Text*, **4**, Nos 1–3.

Danet, B. (1984b). The Magic Flute: A prosodic analysis of binomial expressions in legal Hebrew. In B. Danet (Ed.), *Studies of legal discourse*, pp. 143–172. Special issue of *Text*, **4**, Nos 1–3.

Danet, B. (1985). Legal discourse. In T.A. van Dijk (Ed.), *Handbook of discourse analysis*, Vol. 1, pp. 273–291. New York: Academic Press.

Danet, B. and Bogoch, B. (1980). Fixed fight or free-for-all? An empirical study of combativeness in the adversary system of justice. *British Journal of Law and Society*, **7**, 36–60.

Danet, B., Hoffman, K.B., and Kermish, N.C. (1980a). Threats to the life of the President: An analysis of the linguistic issues. *Journal of Media: Law and Practice*, **1**, 180–190.

Danet, B., Hoffman, K.B., Kermish, N.C., Rafn, J., and Stayman, D. (1980b). An ethnography of questioning in the courtroom. In R. Shuy and A. Shnukal (Eds), *Language use and the uses of language*, pp. 222–234. Washington, DC: Georgetown University Press.

Danet, B. and Troutzer, I. (1983). Eve against Eve in the Promised Land: Sex of speaker, sex of listener, and speech style in an Israeli legal setting. Unpublished manuscript.

Drew, P. (1985). Analyzing the use of language in courtroom interaction. In T.A. van Dijk (Ed.), *Handbook of discourse analysis*, Vol. 3, *Discourse and dialogue*. London: Academic Press.

Drew, P. (in press a). Disputes in courtroom cross-examination: 'Contrasting versions' in a rape trial. In J. Heritage and P. Drew (Eds), *Talk at Work*. Cambridge: Cambridge University Press.

Drew, P. (in press b). Strategies in the contest between lawyer and witness in cross-examination. In J.N. Levi and A.G. Walker (Eds), *Language in the Judicial Process*. New York: Plenum.

Dunstan, R. (1980). Contexts for coercion: Analyzing properties of courtroom 'questions'. *British Journal of Law and Society*, **7**, 61–77.

Duranti, A. (1981). The Samoan Fono: A sociolinguistic study. *Pacific Linguistics, Series B*, **80**. (Canberra: Australian National University.)

Duranti, A. (1983). Samoan speechmaking across social events: One genre in and out of a Fono. *Language in Society*, **12**, 1–22.

Duranti, A. (1984). *Lauga* and *Talanoaga*: Two speech genres in a Samoan political event. In D. Brenneis and F.R. Myers (Eds), *Dangerous words: Language and Politics in the Pacific*, pp. 217–242. New York: New York University Press.

Eagleson, R.D. (1985). The Plain English debate in Australia. In *Festschrift in Honor of Arthur Delbridge*, pp. 143–150. Special issue of *Beitrage zur Phonetik und Linguistik*, **48**.

Eagleson, R.D. (in press). The Plain English movement in Australia and the United Kingdom. In E.T. Steinberg (Ed.), *Promoting Plain English*. Detroit: Wayne State University Press.

Elwork, A., Sales, B.D., and Alfini, J.J. (1982). *Making jury instructions understandable*. Charlottesville, VA: Mitchie.

Francis, D.W. (1986). Some structures of negotiation talk. *Language in Society*, **15**, 53–79.

Fraser, B. (1988). Disputing: The challenge of adversative discourse to the Cooperative Principle. In O. Tomic and R. Shuy (Eds), *The relation of theoretical and applied linguistics*. New York: Plenum.

Givens, R.A. (1981). *Drafting documents in plain language*. New York: Practicing Law Institute.

Goldberg, B.W. (1986). The jury summation as speech genre: An ethnographic study of what it means to those who use it. PhD dissertation, University of Pennsylvania. *Dissertation Abstracts International, A: The Humanities and Social Sciences, 46*, 3710–A.

Goldman, L. (1980). Speech categories and the study of disputes: A New Guinea example. *Oceania, 50*, 209–227.

Goldman, L. (1983). *Talk never dies: The language of Huli disputes*. London: Tavistock.

Goldman, L. (1986a). A case of 'questions' and a question of 'case'. *Text, 5*, 349–392.

Goldman, L. (1986b). The presentational styles of women in Huli disputes. *Papers in New Guinea Linguistics, 24*, 213–289.

Goldman, L. (1987). *Interrogative and evidential patterns in pre-marital sex cases among the Huli: A comparison between traditional and village court styles*. Sydney: Sydney Oceania Monographs.

Goodrich, P. (1984). Law and language: An historical and critical introduction. *Journal of Law and Society, 11*, 173–206.

Grebler, G. (1981). Negotiating priorities: Formality and informality in an Israeli court. Paper presented at Meeting of the Sociology of Law Research Committee, International Sociological Association, September 1981, Oxford.

Green, G.M. (in press). Linguistic analysis of conversation as evidence regarding the interpretation of speech events. In J.N. Levi and A.G. Walker (Eds), *Language and the judicial process*. New York: Plenum.

Grice, P. (1975). Logic and conversation. In P. Cole and M. Morgan (Eds), *Syntax and semantics*, Vol. 3, *Speech Acts*. New York: Academic Press.

Gumperz, J.J. (1982). Fact and inference in courtroom testimony. In J.J. Gumperz (Ed.), *Language and social identity*, pp. 161–194. Cambridge: Cambridge University Press.

Gunnarsson, B.L. (1984). Functional comprehensibility of a Swedish law: An experiment. In B. Danet (Ed.), *Studies of legal discourse*, pp. 71–106. Special issue of *Text, 4*, Nos 1–3.

Gunnarsson, B.L. (1987). The abstractness and implicitness of Swedish legal language. In A.-M. Cornu, J. Vanparijs, M. Delahaye, and L. Baten (Eds), *Bead or bracelet? How do we approach LSP?*, pp. 219–229. Oxford: Oxford University Press.

Gunnarsson, B.L. (in press). Text comprehensibility and the writing process: The case of laws and law making.

Gustafsson, M. (1975). *Some syntactic properties of English law language*. Publication No. 4, Department of English, University of Turku, Turku, Finland.

Gustafsson, M. (1984). The syntactic features of binomial expressions in legal English. In B. Danet (Ed.), *Studies of legal discourse*, pp. 123–142. Special issue of *Text, 4*, Nos 1–3.

Harris, S. (1984). Questions as a mode of control in magistrates courts. *International Journal of the Sociology of Language, 49*, 5–27.

Harris, S. (1987a). Courtroom discourse as genre: Some problems and issues. *Occasional Papers in Systemic Linguistics, 2*, 35–73.

Harris, S. (1987b). *Communication in court: The language of power and control*. London: Pinter.

Hayden, R. (1987). Turntaking, overlap and the task at hand: Ordering speaking turns in legal settings. *American Ethnologist, 14*, 251–170.

Hertzfeld, M. (1985). *The poetics of manhood: Contest and identity in a Cretan mountain village*. Princeton: Princeton University Press.

Hiltunen, R. (1984). The type and structure of clausal embedding in legal English. In B. Danet (Ed.), *Studies of legal discourse*, pp. 107–122. Special issue of *Text, 4*, Nos 1–3.

Holland, V.M. (1981). *Psycholinguistic alternatives to readability formulas*. Washington, DC: American Institutes for Research.

Holland, V.M. and Campbell, L.J. (1982). Understanding the language of public documents because readability formulas don't. In R. di Pietro (Ed.), *Linguistics and the professions*, pp. 157–171. Norwood, NJ: Ablex.

Holland, V.M. and Redish, J.C. (1981). Strategies for understanding forms – and other public documents. In D. Tannen (Ed.), *Analyzing discourse: Text and talk*, pp. 205–218. Washington, DC: Georgetown University Press.

Holstein, J.A. (1987). Producing gender effects on involuntary mental hospitalization. *Social Problems*, **34**, 141–155.

Holstein, J.A. (1988a). Studying 'family usage': Family image and discourse in mental hospitalization decisions. *Journal of Contemporary Ethnography*, **17**, 261–284.

Holstein, J.A. (1988b). Court ordered incompetence: Conversational organization in involuntary commitment hearings. *Social Problems*, **35**, 458–473.

Hosticka, C.J. (1979). We don't care what happened, we only care about what is going to happen: Lawyer–client negotiations of reality. *Social Problems*, **26**, 598–610.

Hutchins, E. (in press). Getting it straight in Trobriand land litigation. In K.A. Watson-Gegeo and G.M. White (Eds), *The discourse of disentangling: Conflict, emotion and person in the Pacific*.

Johnson, M.G. (in press). Language and cognition in products liability. In J.N. Levi and A.G. Walker (Eds), *Language in the judicial process*. New York: Plenum.

Jones, C.S. and Myers, E. (1979). Comprehension of jury instructions in a simulated court. In *Studies on the jury*, pp. 301–392. Law Reform Commission of Canada Report.

Jonsson, L. (1988). On being heard in court trials and police interrogations: A study of discourse in two institutional contexts. Linkoping Studies in Arts and Science, Linkoping, Sweden.

Katriel, T. (1986). *Talking straight: Dugri speech in Israeli Sabra culture*. Cambridge: Cambridge University Press.

Keller-Cohen, D. (1987). Organizational contexts and texts: The redesign of the Midwest Bell Telephone Bill. *Discourse Processes*, **10**, 417–428.

Kess, J.R., Hoppe, R.A., and Copeland, A.M. (1985). Formulating jury instructions: Applied linguistics and the law. *Rassegna Italiana di Linguistica Applicata*, **17**, 243–255.

Kurzon, D. (1984). Themes, hyperthemes, and the discourse structure of British legal texts. In B. Danet (Ed.), *Studies of legal discourse*, pp. 31–56. Special issue of *Text*, **4**, Nos 1–3.

Kurzon, D. (1985). How lawyers tell their tales: Narrative aspects of a lawyer's brief. *Poetics*, **14**, 467–481.

Kurzon, D. (1986). *It is hereby performed: Explorations in legal speech acts*. Amsterdam: Benjamins.

Kurzon, D. (1987). Latin for lawyers: Degrees of textual integration. *Applied Linguistics*, **8**, 223–240.

Lane, C. (1985). Mis-communication in cross-examinations. In J.B. Pride (Ed.), *Cross-cultural encounters: Communication and mis-communication*, pp. 196–211. Melbourne: River Seine.

Law Reform Commission of Victoria (1986). *Legislation, legal rights and Plain English*. Discussion Paper No. 1.

Levi, J.N. (1982). *Linguistics, language and law: A topical bibliography*. Bloomington, IN: Indiana University Linguistics Club.

Levi, J.N. (1983). Applications of linguistics to the language of legal interactions. In P.C. Bjarkman and V. Raskin (Eds), *Linguistic applications in the 1980's*.

Levi, J.N. and Walker, A.G. (Eds) (in press). *Language and the judicial process*. New York: Plenum.

Lindstrom, L. (in press). Straight talk on Tana. In K.A. Watson-Gegeo and G.M. White (Eds), *The discourse of disentangling: Conflict, person and emotion in the Pacific*.

Linell, P., Gustavsson, L., and Juvonen, P. (1988). Interactional dominance in dyadic communication: A presentation of the initiative–response analysis. *Linguistics*, **26**, 415–442.

Loftus, E.F. (1979). *Eyewitness testimony*. Cambridge, MA: Harvard.

Loftus, E.F. and Goodman, J. (1985). Questioning witnesses. In S.M. Kassin and L.S. Wrightsman (Eds), *The psychology of evidence and trial procedure*, pp. 253–279. Beverly Hills: Sage.

Lynch, M.E. (1982). Closure and disclosure in pre-trial argument. *Human Studies*, **5**, 285–318.

MacDonald, D.C. (Ed.) (1979). *Drafting documents in plain language*. New York: Practicing Law Institute.

Marshall, G. (1981). Accounting for deviance. *International Journal of Sociology and Social Policy*, **1** (1), 17–45.

Mather, L. and Yngvesson, B. (1980–81). Language, audience, and the transformation of disputes. *Law and Society Review*, **15**, 775–910.

Maynard, D. (1982a). Person-descriptions in plea bargaining. *Semiotica*, **42**, 195–213.

Maynard, D. (1982b). Aspects of sequential organization in plea bargaining discourse. *Human Studies*, **5**, 319–344.

Maynard, D. (1984a). *Inside plea bargaining: The language of negotiation*. New York: Plenum.

Maynard, D. (1984b). The structure of discourse in misdemeanor plea bargaining. *Law and Society Review*, **18**, 75–104.

Maynard, D. (1985). The problem of justice in the courts approached by the analysis of plea bargaining discourse. In T.A. van Dijk (Ed.), *Handbook of discourse analysis*, Vol. 4, pp. 153–179. New York: Academic Press.

Maynard, D. (1988). Narratives and narrative structure in plea bargaining. *Law and Society Review*, **22**(3), 449–482.

Maynard, D. (in press). On the ethnography and analysis of discourse in institutional settings. In J. Holstein and G. Miller (Eds). Greenwich, CT: JAI.

McGaughey, K. and Stiles, W. (1983). Courtroom interrogation of rape victims: Verbal response mode use by attorneys and witnesses during direct vs cross examination. *Journal of Applied Social Psychology*, **13**, 78–87.

McKellin, W.H. (in press). Self and inference: Intentional ambiguity in Managalase negotiations. In K.A. Watson-Gegeo and G.M. White (Eds), *The discourse of disentangling: Conflict, person and emotion in the Pacific*.

Medical Research Council Applied Psychology Unit (undated). *Improving the presentation of information to juries in fraud trials: A report of four research studies*. London: HMSO.

Mellinkoff, D. (1963). *The language of the law*. Boston, MA: Little, Brown.

Mellinkoff, D. (1982). *Legal writing: Sense and nonsense*. St Paul: West.

Milroy, J. (1984). Sociolinguistic methodology and the identification of speakers' voices in legal proceedings. In J. Milroy (Ed.), *Applied sociolinguistics*.

Molotch, H.L. and Boden, D. (1985). Talking social structure: Discourse, domination, and the Watergate hearings. *American Sociological Review*, **50**, 273–288.

Morris, R. (1989). An analysis of the role of interpreters in the Demjanjuk trial. Unpublished MA thesis, Department of Communications, Hebrew University, Jerusalem.

Myerhoff, B. (1979). *Number our days*. New York: Simon and Schuster.

Naylor, P.B. (1979). Linguistic and cultural interference in legal testimony. Paper presented at the International Conference on Language and Social Psychology, July 1979, University of Bristol.

O'Barr, W.M. (1981). The language of the law. In C.A. Ferguson and S.B. Heath (Eds), *Language in the U.S.A.*, pp. 386–406. New York: Cambridge University Press.

O'Barr, W.M. (1982). *Linguistic evidence: Language, power and strategy in the courtroom*. New York: Academic Press.

O'Barr, W.M. (1983). The study of language in institutional contexts. *Journal of Language and Social Psychology*, **2**, 241–251.

O'Barr, W.M. and Conley, J.M. (1985). Litigant satisfaction versus legal adequacy in small claims court narratives. *Law and Society Review,* **19**, 661–702.

O'Donnell, K. (in press). Difference and dominance: How labor and management talk conflict. In A.D. Grimshaw (Ed.), *Conflict talk: Sociolinguistic investigations of arguments in conversations.* Cambridge: Cambridge University Press.

Parkinson, M. (1979). Language behavior and courtroom success. Paper presented at the International Conference on Language and Social Psychology, July 1979, University of Bristol. Summarized in Danet, B. (1980). Language in the courtroom. In H. Giles, P. Smith, and P. Robinson (Eds), *Language: Social psychological perspectives,* pp. 367–376. Oxford: Pergamon.

Parkinson, M. (1981). Verbal behavior and courtroom success. *Communication Education,* **30**, 22–32.

Parks, W. (1986). Flyting, sounding, debate: Three verbal contest genres. *Poetics Today,* **7**, 439–458.

Penman, R. (1987). Discourse in courts: Cooperation, coercion and coherence. *Discourse Processes,* **10**, 201–218.

Philips, S.U. (1982). The language socialization of lawyers: acquiring the 'cant'. In G. Spindler (Ed.), *Doing ethnography in the classroom,* pp. 176–209. New York: Holt, Rinehart and Winston.

Philips, S.U. (1983). Review of *Reconstructing reality in the courtroom,* by W.L. Bennett and M.S. Feldman. *Language in Society,* **12**, 514.

Philips, S.U. (1984a). The social organization of questions and answers in courtroom discourse. In B. Danet (Ed.), *Studies of legal discourse,* pp. 225–248. Special issue of *Text,* **4**, Nos 1–3.

Philips, S.U. (1984b). Contextual variation in courtroom language use: Noun phrases referring to crimes. *International Journal of the Sociology of Language,* **49**, 29–50.

Philips, S.U. (1984c). Language, law and society: Report for the Center for Psychosocial Studies. Unpublished manuscript.

Philips, S.U. (1985). Strategies of clarification in judges' use of language: From the written to the spoken. *Discourse Processes,* **8**, 421–436.

Philips, S.U. (1986). Reported speech as evidence in an American trial. In D. Tannen and J. Alatis (Eds), *Language and linguistics: The interdependence of theory, data and application,* pp. 154–170. Washington, DC: Georgetown University Press.

Philips, S.U. (1988). Contextual variation in the use of Wh questions in American courtroom discourse. In L. Kedar (Ed.), *Power through discourse,* pp. 83–111. Norwood, NJ: Ablex.

Philips, S.U. (in press, a). The judge as third party in American trial court conflict talk. In A.D. Grimshaw (Ed.), *Conflict talk.* Cambridge: Cambridge University Press.

Philips, S.U. (in press, b). Evidentiary standards for American trials. In J. Hill and J. Irvine (Eds), *Responsibility and evidence in oral discourse.* Cambridge: Cambridge University Press.

Philips, S.U. (in press, c). The routinization of repair in courtroom discourse. In A. Duranti and C. Goodwin (Eds), *Rethinking language in context.*

Pollner, M. (1979). Explicative transactions: Making and managing meaning in traffic court. In G. Psathas (Ed.), *Everyday language: Studies in ethnomethodology.* New York: Irvington.

Pomerantz, A.M. (1978). Attributions of responsibility: Blamings. *Sociology,* **12**, 115–121.

Pomerantz, A.M. (1984). Giving a source or basis: The practice in conversation of telling 'how I know'. *Journal of Pragmatics,* **8**, 607–625.

Pomerantz, A.M. (1986). Extreme case formulations: A way of legitimizing claims. *Human Studies,* **9**, 219–229.

Pomerantz, A.M. (1987). Descriptions in legal settings. In G. Button and J. Lee (Eds), *Talk and social organization,* pp. 226–243. Clevedon (England): Multilingual Matters.

Pomerantz, A.M. and Atkinson, J.M. (1984). Ethnomethodology, conversation analysis, and the study of courtroom interaction. In D.J. Muller, D.E. Blackman, and A.J. Chapman (Eds), *Psychology and law*, pp. 283–297. London: Wiley.

Pressman, R. (1979). *Legislative and regulatory progress on the readability of insurance policies*. Washington, DC: American Institutes for Research.

Prince, E.F. (1984). Language and the law: Reference, stress and context. In D. Schiffrin (Ed.), *Meaning, form and use in context: Linguistic applications*, pp. 240–252. Washington, DC: Georgetown University Press.

Procaccia, U. (1979). Readable insurance policies: Judicial regulation and interpretation. *Israel Law Review*, **14**(1), 74–103.

Redish, J.C. (1979). How to draft more understandable legal documents. In D.C. MacDonald (Ed.), *Drafting documents in plain language*, pp. 121–156. New York: Practicing Law Institute.

Redish, J.C. (1980). Readability. In D. Felker (Ed.), *Document design: A review of the relevant literature*, pp. 69–94. Washington, DC: American Institutes for Research.

Redish, J.C. (1981). Understanding the limitations of readability formulas. *IEEE Transactions on Professional Communication*, March 1981, 46–48.

Redish, J.C. (1983). The language of the bureaucracy. In R.W. Bailey and R.M. Fosheim (Eds), *Literacy for life: The demand for reading and writing*, pp. 151–174. New York: Modern Language Association.

Redish, J.C. (1985). The Plain English movement. In S. Greenbaum (Ed.), *The English language today: Public attitudes toward the English language*, pp. 125–138. New York: Pergamon.

Redish, J.C., Battison, R.M., and Gold, E.S. (1985). Making information accessible to readers. In L. Odell and D. Goswami (Eds), *Writing in nonacademic settings*. New York: Guilford Press.

Rumsey, A. and Merlan, F. (1988). *The language of exchange: Social action in the Nebilyer Valley*. Cambridge: Cambridge University Press.

Sarat, A. and Felstiner, W.L.F. (1986). Law and strategy in the divorce lawyer's office. *Law and Society Review*, **20**, 93–134.

Sarat, A. and Felstiner, W.L.F. (in press). Legal realism in lawyer–client communications. In J.N. Levi and A.G. Walker (Eds), *Language in the judicial process*. New York: Plenum.

Schiffrin, D. (1984). Jewish argument as sociability. *Language in Society*, **13**, 311–316.

Schiffrin, D. (1985). Everyday argument: The organization of diversity in talk. In T.A. van Dijk (Ed.), *Handbook of discourse analysis*, Vol. 3. New York: Academic Press.

Schiffrin, D. (in press). The management of a cooperative self during argument: The role of opinions and stories. In A.D. Grimshaw (Ed.), *Conflict talk: Sociolinguistic investigations of arguments in conversations*. Cambridge: Cambridge University Press.

Scott, M.B. and Lyman, S.L. (1968). Accounts. *American Sociological Review*, **33**, 46–62.

Scott, M.B. and Lyman, S.L. (1970). Accounts, deviance and social order. In J.D. Douglas (Ed.), *Deviance and respectability*, pp. 89–119. New York: Basic.

Severance, L.J. and Loftus, E.F. (1982). Improving the ability of jurors to comprehend and apply criminal jury instructions. *Law and Society Review*, **17**, 153–197.

Shantz, C.U. (1987). Conflicts between children. *Child Development*, **58**, 283–305.

Shuy, R.W. (1981a). Topic as the unit of analysis in a criminal law case. In D. Tannen (Ed.), *Analyzing discourse: Text and talk*, p. 118. Georgetown University Round Table on Language and Linguistics. Washington, DC: Georgetown University Press.

Shuy, R.W. (1981b). Can linguistic evidence build a defense theory in a criminal case? *Studia Linguistica*, **35**(1–2), 33–49.

Shuy, R.W. (1986a). Some linguistic contributions to a criminal court case. In S. Fisher and A.D. Todd (Eds), *Discourse and institutional authority: Medicine, education, law*, pp. 234–249. Norwood, NJ: Ablex.

Shuy, R.W. (1986b). Language and the law. *Annual Review of Applied Linguistics,* **7**, 50–63.

Sykes, G.M. and Matza, D. (1957). Techniques of neutralization. *American Sociological Review,* **22**, 667–669.

Tannen, D. (1981). Jewish conversational style. *International Journal of the Sociology of Language,* **30**, 133–139.

Tannen, D. (1984). Relative focus on involvement in oral and written discourse. In D.L. Olson, W. Torrence, and A. Hildgard (Eds), *Literacy, language and learning*, pp. 124–147. Cambridge: Cambridge University Press.

Troutzer, I. (1982). Sex of speaker, sex of listener, and speech style and impression formation in a legal setting. Unpublished MA thesis, Department of Communications, Hebrew University Jerusalem. (Hebrew.)

Underwood, C.F. (1987). The Indian witness: Narrative style in courtroom testimony. PhD dissertation, University of California, Berkeley, CA. *Dissertation Abstracts International, A: The Humanities and Social Sciences,* **47**, 2640–A.

Valdes, G. (1986). Analyzing the demands that courtroom interaction makes upon the speakers of ordinary English: Toward the development of a coherent description framework. *Discourse Processes,* **9**, 269–303.

Walker, A.G. (1982a). Patterns and implications of cospeech in a legal setting. In R.N. di Pietro (Ed.), *Language in the professions*, pp. 101–112. Norwood, NJ: Ablex.

Walker, A.G. (1982b). Discourse rights of witnesses: Their circumscription in trial. Sociolinguistics Working Paper No. 95. SW Educational Development Laboratory, Austin, TX.

Walker, A.G. (1985a). From oral to written: The 'verbatim' transcription of legal proceedings. PhD dissertation, Georgetown University, Washington, DC.

Walker, A.G. (1985b). The two faces of silence: The effect of witness hesitancy on lawyers' impressions. In D. Tannen and M. Saville-Troike (Eds), *Perspectives on silence*, pp. 55–75. Norwood, NJ: Ablex.

Walker, A.G. (1986a). The verbatim record: The myth and the reality. In S. Fisher and A.D. Todd (Eds), *Discourse and institutional authority: Medicine, education and law*, pp. 205–222. Norwood, NJ: Ablex.

Walker, A.G. (1986b). Context, transcripts and appellate readers. *Justice Quarterly,* **3**, 409–427.

Walker, A.G. (1986c). Fallibility in the production of 'verbatim' transcripts: What and why. Paper presented at the Annual Meeting of the Law and Society Association, May–June 1986, Chicago, IL.

Walker, A.G. (1988). Linguistic manipulation, power, and the legal setting. In L. Kedar (Ed.), *Power through discourse*, pp. 57–79. Norwood, NJ: Ablex.

Walker, A.G. (in press). Transcription of legal proceedings: Theoretical issues and application to the appellate process. In A.G. Walker and J.N. Levi (Eds), *Language in the judicial process*. New York: Plenum.

Watson-Gegeo, K. and Gegeo, D. (1983). The structure of counselling in four speech events among the Kwarae. Paper presented at the Conference on 'Talk and Social Inference', October 1983, Claremont, NJ.

Watson-Gegeo, K. and Gegeo, D. (in press). Shaping the mind and straightening out conflicts: The discourse of Kwara'ae family counselling. In K.A. Watson-Gegeo and G.M. White (Eds), *The discourse of disentangling: Conflict, person and emotion in the Pacific.*

Weinstein, R.M. (1980). Vocabularies of motive for illicit drug use: An application of the accounts framework. *Sociological Quarterly,* **21**, 577–593.

Westman, M. (1984). On strategy in Swedish legal texts. In B. Danet (Ed.), *Studies of legal discourse*, pp. 57–70. Special issue of *Text,* **4**, 1–3.

Wodak-Engel, R. (1980). Discourse analysis and courtroom interaction. *Discourse Processes,* **3**, 369–380.

Wodak-Engel, R. (1984). Determination of guilt: Discourse in the courtroom. In C. Kramarae, M. Schulz, and W.M. O'Barr (Eds), *Language and power*, pp. 89–100. Beverly Hills: Sage.

Wodak-Engel, R. (1985). The interaction between judge and defendant. In T.A. van Dijk (Ed.), *Handbook of discourse analysis*, Vol. 4. New York: Academic Press.

Woodbury, H. (1984). The strategic use of questions in court. *Semiotica,* **48**, 197–228.

Wydick, R.C. (1979). *Plain English for lawyers*. Durham, NC: Carolina Academic Press.

27

Language and Television

J. MALLORY WOBER

Independent Broadcasting Authority, UK

In American homes television is reportedly switched on for an average of over 6 hours a day; in Britain for over 3. Apart from its cornucopia of entertainment, television is used as an extremely important way of taking political ideas and information to populations. Not only does each nation generate its own programming, but a great deal of imported material is shown in most nations, except the USA and USSR, raising questions of potential cross-cultural influence. Television may be said to be like the eye of a needle through which all of life is, at some time, drawn. Therefore, fully to examine the implications of television for the language experience of its audience would require not just one volume but several. A review chapter will therefore have to be selective.

In choosing which issues to discuss in some detail, certain socially important topics will have to be set aside. An example is that of the attempt to safeguard the languages of small nations such as Wales. The reason why this story, and others like it will not be treated more expansively is because there is, as yet, not enough research to evaluate the goals that have been tackled by television. The Welsh predicament is that, in a nation of some 2.7 million people (Howell, 1981), speakers of Welsh numbered fewer than one-fifth in 1980, and this proportion was falling. Welsh speakers were then watching 3 hours a day of television spoken in English, and it was feared that English would presently replace Welsh in all parts of the country.

Handbook of Language and Social Psychology
Edited by H. Giles and W.P. Robinson.   © 1990 John Wiley & Sons Ltd

After energetic political action the fourth television channel, provided in November 1982 in English for the rest of the United Kingdom, was started as a Welsh language channel in Wales. This provides original programming in Welsh, which is certainly viewed by that community, and it supplements the teaching of Welsh in schools. At the end of the decade it can be said that the channel provides a symbolic focus for, as well as a true fount of experience of, the Welsh language; but whether any decline has been halted or the language has begun to advance again with television's aid has not yet been definitively established.

The goal of the Welsh television channel is similar to those in Catalonia, Israel and elsewhere, where ancient national languages are conserved by use of the newest message system; and this use of television may eventually be fully enough evaluated to require a book on its own. Terrestrial television, by which language communicates and receives a particular service (though limited always by the high costs of producing appropriate programming), is, however, thought likely to be overtaken in the 1990s by satellite transmissions, by which major languages are likely to overwhelm minor ones.

A variant of the language conservational goals above has been described by Kuo (1984) in Singapore. Of the 2.4 million population of this country, 77% were Chinese, alongside Malay and Tamil minorities. Mandarin was spoken at home by only one in ten Chinese, but was selected over the Hokkien, Teochew and Cantonese dialects to be promoted as the official form of Chinese. An energetic campaign to promote Mandarin began in 1979, making full use of television, radio and the press; after 2 years Kuo reported some increased use of Mandarin, though dialects still predominated; further evaluation was intended at the end of the decade.

At the other end of the population scale India has used satellite transmission to beam entertainment and instructional television to its dispersed countryside communities. Mowlana and Wilson (1988) report that 'surveys showed significant gains in information about health and hygiene, politics, modernity and family planning . . . Children showed gains on four measures of language development (Shukla, 1979) and in learning to seek information from a variety of sources' (p. 38). Necessarily, in spite of a rotational scheme to use five or six main state languages, this system could not help to conserve dialects or minority languages; indeed, India's linguistic diversity makes a pan-Indian identity difficult to develop, which is one reason why English remains a common language among educated people.

Because the cultural dimension of language as served by television is not one which has yet been mastered by research, a more individual level of language competence will be selected for more detailed attention. Some indications are then given of studies which have documented the contents of television programmes and advertisements, mostly in terms of indicators of social relationships and forces. Following this, another detailed introduction is given to research on attitudes towards the ways in which language is used on television – with particular attention given to the socially important category of 'bad language'. Finally, some conceptual matters are explored, including the need to use a coherent and well-designed jargon with which to conduct social psychological research on language as a dimension of the television phenomenon.

TELEVISION AND LANGUAGE SKILLS

When television is first introduced, concern arises that it might swamp print not only in adults' lives, but especially for children. Two mechanisms for a possible effect of the arrival of this new phenomenon include that it might simply reduce the time available or used for reading, thus restricting the development of language skills of reading, writing and speaking; but also that, even if time was safeguarded for practising these skills, viewing television would nevertheless interfere with training in literacy because the mixture of pictures and music creates skills (motionacy, gesturacy, picturacy) which deflect interests in or interfere with the skills that are entailed in developing literacy.

Most research on this topic has used measures of reading comprehension or vocabulary and has set these alongside evidence on amount of television use. Becoming more sophisticated, researchers have measured these things at two, or three stages, years apart and have added measures of amounts of reading experience. The intention has been to explore evidence for two hypotheses: one, that television viewing in of itself, regardless of displacement of reading, might relate with language skills; and, two, that an effect may be discernible indirectly, through displacement of activities which do sustain language skills. The evidence for an effect by either process is becoming more and more slight, as researchers increase their sophistication. Little if any research has, however, taken place on any interaction between television and speech skills – of complexity, clarity or appeal – among 'ordinary' people; or on possible effects of television on skills or practice among politicians, clerics and other public speakers.

A substantial study by Morgan and Gross (1982) makes a good first mark in this area; they performed a 3-year analysis of over 200 children in the USA. Morgan (1985) himself says of the results that 'when IQ and other factors are controlled, the areas of achievement most related (negatively) to amount of viewing are reading comprehension and language usage and structure'. Of the same work, however, Ritchie, Price, and Roberts (1987) report that there had been:

> a negative correlation beween TV use and total reading in the first year, but positive correlations in the second and third years . . . the preponderance of empirical evidence to date, then, suggests that there is a negative relationship between television viewing and reading achievement, but does not suggest that the displacement of reading time by television viewing is an important factor in explaining this negative association. (Ritchie et al., 1987, pp. 293–294.)

In spite of their own mixed-outcome results, Morgan and Gross (1982) assessed them as similar to those of several other studies, with which contemporary reviews by Hornik (1981) and Comstock (1982) agree: the general finding is of an association between television viewing and reduced language skills. Hornik's review has particular merit as he had done his own research in El Salvador (Hornik, 1978), comparing students whose families had just acquired television, with others who either had sets over some years, or had no sets. Children in new-TV households did slightly worse on a reading test than did those who already had sets (though who were of higher socio-economic status), but also than did others who had no sets (who were of lower socio-economic status). However, these analyses were at the level of simple correlations between two measures, or of correlations partialling out a small number of interrelated measures. One of the early literature reviews (Williams, Haertel, Hachtel, and Walberg, 1982) made out that, for children who watch very little television, up to 10 hours a week, language achievement may be improved as a measure of this experience; from 10 to 35 hours' viewing a week, the effect is negative, but above that there is likely to be no further impact. A variant of this verdict is proposed by Potter (1987; see below), who reports that, at below 10 hours of viewing a week, students are not displacing much study time, so viewing has no detrimental effect on skills, or may be positive in some kinds of skill; at over 30 hours of viewing a week, more marked negative relationships with achievement measures, including language skills, are found.

This pattern was supported by the work of another group (Williams, 1986), whose study was based in three towns in Canada, one of which, Notel, acquired one channel after being without, and the others, Unitel and Multitel, already had one and four channels, respectively. As well as many other attitudes and abilities Williams and colleagues tested children's reading skills and vocabulary achievement. The reading test was 'automated' and consisted of showing words and phrases on a tachistoscope. The Canadian findings included that Notel children who had been in Grade 1 when television arrived were poorer readers than Unitel and Multitel children of the same grades. Williams diagnoses the first two grades as 'especially important for television's potential influence on the acquisition of fluent reading skills'. A further result was that non-verbal IQ was more strongly related to reading test scores in the presence than in the absence of television in the home. Children who have lower IQ but no television might spend more time practising reading then do brighter children, who reach fluency even with television; Williams agrees that this theory needs to be tested, and others have tackled the problem, as will be seen below.

The pointer to the importance of a second stage in the acquisition of reading skills, in which the rudiments of letter and number recognition are composed into fluent word recognition, matches with the findings of another group, at Yale (Singer and Singer, 1983), who studied children from the age of 4. The Singers employed measures of parents' own abilities and disciplinary styles and found that these interacted with simple amounts of viewing experience to produce different results. More imaginative parents who, moreover, kept more orderly household regimes were likely to produce better readers, especially if there had been less viewing in preschool years. Parents of lower socio-economic status on the other hand produced better reading children if there was a mixture of greater curiosity and imagination on the part of the parent, combined with heavier preschool television viewing. This is why Williams (1986) concludes that, to provide better reading skills, 'reducing the child's involvement with television may be necessary, but it is not likely to be sufficient' (p. 397).

Following Williams (1986), Gaddy (1986) used an extremely large high-school sample from which to draw very large subsamples of children, who were tested in two waves with various measures including ones of vocabulary and reading comprehension. Simple correlations showed the often-found negative relationship between (heavy) television viewing and (poor) achievement, not only on verbal measures but on all tests. Using a more sophisticated regression analysis examining second-wave achievement scores in the light of a variety of other measures, including amount of reading for pleasure, 'television' (it is not quite clear whether this was amount of viewing in 1980, or in 1982, or both) showed no significant negative links with language achievement scores, and there were some positive even if not quite significant beta weights among a 'medium educational resource' group. The drawback to this study is that it deals with much older children than are indicated by Williams' study as crucial for the diagnosis of any role of television viewing in affecting reading or vocabulary scores. Another study, by Potter (1987), tested over 500 eighth through twelfth grade adolescents using a reading and a language test, and obtained measures of viewing for nine separate programme types. Regression equations showed a small though significantly positive association between reading scores and news viewing, while language performance was negatively related with more viewing of Music TV, sports and cartoons.

Focusing on the more crucial early years, Ritchie et al. (1987) report the third-wave results of a panel study involving 270 children from first to fifth grades. Again, at the first level of analysis there were consistently negative correlations between television viewing time and reading achievement scores. Going on to the next stage, of partial correlation (controlling for first-year reading achievement), five out of nine correlations between viewing and reading achievement measures were non-significant and negative. Focusing, however, on the first cohort (grades 2 to 4), there was one negative and one significant positive correlation (depending on which measure and which pair of waves was involved). Rejecting the possibility of a curvilinear relationship, Ritchie et al. (1987) suggest instead that their young children had perhaps given inaccurate self-reports of their amounts of viewing.

The next stage of what Ritchie et al. (1987) did poses a genuine problem for assessment of the research in this field. On the one hand stand 'state of the art' statistical techniques; on the other hand stand 'dirty data'; dismissed to the wings are the arts of clinical style diagnosis combined with a sufficient level of statistical expertise. The analysis uses LISREL and shows that, out of six coefficients relating earlier viewing time to later reading achievement measures, only one is significant – and negative (their table 3); viewing time is significantly – and negatively – related to reading time in one out of six coefficients and reading time is likewise significantly – and negatively – related to viewing time in one out of six coefficients. All other coefficients are insignificant (their table 6).

Ritchie et al. (1987) sum up by saying, 'when the stability and unreliability of the measures are taken into account via structural equation models and the use of multiple indicators, the hypothesised relationships almost disappear' (p. 310); this becomes sharpened in the abstract to: 'what change there is in reading time or in reading skills does not seem to be related consistently to time spent viewing television'.

For all their sophistication most of the above reports (except that of Potter, 1987) treated television as a homogeneous experience; but a pilot study with 93 preschool children by Selnow and Bettinghaus (1982) used measures of viewing that distinguished between four types of programmes. There were negative correlations between a language-production measure, based on assessment of 50 sentences per child, collected in a guided interview, and amounts of viewing of family dramas and situation comedy; but there were positive links with amounts of viewing of cartoon and of educational material. When programmes were rated for language sophistication and viewing was weighted by these indices, a positive correlation was found between scores of language production and of sophistication of language in viewing experience.

It may be best to conclude from all this that each of these studies has some merit and some faults that are not shared with the other studies. The Singers (1983) included measures of parental behaviour and abilities – but only had a small group of children; Williams (1986) had a larger group, focusing on a crucial early stage in acquisition of reading skills – but lacked measures of reading time that might have been displaced; Gaddy (1986) had a very large study with many measures – but researched the 'wrong' developmental stage, well after basic reading skills had (or could not have) been established; Ritchie *et al*. (1987) dealt with early-grade children – but collected their own, and possibly inaccurate, estimates of viewing time, and no measures of parental behaviour.

A composite diagnosis is therefore required; and this may also take into account two more recent studies. In one of these Van Vuuren (1988) reviews studies of reading 'patterns' among large samples of South African children, following the introduction of television into that country in 1976; the data appear to focus on a wide range of reports of reading behaviour, rather than on tested abilities, but Van Vuuren concludes nevertheless that any 'changes were of a very small order . . . compared to overseas concern about a decline of reading skills in students, the South African situation seems to be different'. Morgan (1985), in the USA, turned to adults for whom a national survey had assembled data on verbal intelligence (choice of synonym for each of ten 'difficult' words), television viewing, and many other measures. Seventeen of these measures (age, sex, income, race, etc.) were used as controls and it was shown that amount of viewing was not related with ability to define the five less difficult words in the text; but with the five more difficult words 'heavier viewers did less well than did lighter viewers'.

In all, then, various studies suggest that television viewing may help less able people, or younger learners at an earlier stage, to progress in vocabulary, and not impede letter-recognition skills; however, it may then (and depending on how parents harness it) slightly impede further vocabulary acquisition and reading skills. There is little or no sign of studies on whether television viewing either promotes or detracts from the abilities to write or speak creatively, although Postman (1986) in a broadside attack on television has argued that it trivializes the presentation of thought. Whereas in the early nineteenth century the American public was highly literate and spent hours listening to sermons and political speeches, nowadays these messages have to be dramatically shorter, perhaps because the hasty style of (American) television accustoms people to be impatient. To test this kind of allegation it might serve to list the 20 most widely read novels for the years 1960 to 1980 (the television era), for 1920 to 1940 (radio), 1900–1920 (pre-radio) and for similar 'control' periods in the previous century and to apply tests of language complexity, controlling for overall length. On the basis of Postman's accusations, and reflecting some of the results on the measurements of abilities, one might expect to find similar levels of complexity across the eras, for shorter novels, but differences for the longer novels, with complexity reducing for the television era.

ANALYSES OF LANGUAGE CONTENTS OF TELEVISION

Some researchers have analysed measures of language, of what is heard rather than seen on television. Fine (1981) focused on soap operas, selecting episodes from five serials for analysis; in all, 232 conversations between characters were coded, of which 151 were male–female. Women-only conversations were more likely to be in family relationships, those between men and women in romantic relationships and men-only ones in professional relationships. The most frequent content, involving half the conversations, was 'small talk', defined as greetings and other conventional markers. Other frequent topics were occupation (26%), personality (23%), marriage and family (each 21%).

Fine (1981) cites various ethnographic studies of conversation to substantiate her verdict that soap-opera conversations mirror real-world conversations in style and content. However, in two ways this assertion may be unjustified. In one, Fine herself points out that 'the preponderance of male–female relationships, particularly intimate ones, is very unlike the world we live in'. In another dimension, unexamined in Fine's analysis, that of time, it is not known to what extent soap-opera conversations contain short- or long-term references to the past or the future, nor how such references might correspond with what happens in real life. Though the conclusion is that soap-opera talk serves to bind relationships, Fine presents no analysis, apart from a relatively low count for deviant behaviour, of hostile or fractious aspects of conversation such as taunts, insults, untrue or even true but harmful accusations, or other disruptive phenomena. Some of these may, if they are only at a mild level, have an eventual integrative function though it is likely to elude simple counts of content. In spite of these shortcomings, Fine's study does provide useful rudimentary information about actual conversational contents.

Arliss, Cassata, and Skill (1983) later analysed 316 soap-opera dyads according to whether each conversant was seeking to control the interaction or not. Intra-male and intra-female conversations were much more often one-sided then competitive or jointly submissive; but in male–female conversations the male partner was trying to dominate in 68% of instances and accepting submissive status in only 32% of the cases. The woman was trying to take control in 45% of the conversations but accepting the lesser role in 55% of the cases.

Male dominance may be linguistically signalled more markedly in advertisements than in programming. Knill, Pesch, Pursey, Gilpin, and Perloff (1981) analysed over 1600 commercials on American network television, finding 90% of the voice-overs to be male. In a smaller UK study Manstead and McCulloch (1981) found that males were typically portrayed as having reasons for buying products; while McArthur and Resko (1975) had shown that 30% of female figures used no argument in advocating a product, tending instead to display its use, Manstead and McCulloch found that 63% of central female figures used no argument. Livingstone and Greene (1986) replicated this result.

The direction of the studies which have examined language as it is used on television has been to look for signs of power relationships and status, and the general outcome has been to show that men dominate women. No similar analyses have examined features such as verbal complexity, age and social class of speakers or perceived likeability or merit of screen characters in relation to their spoken performance. It is not unlikely that language helps to sustain many, if not most, of the impressions formed by viewers of the characters whom they see.

ATTITUDES TOWARDS THE USE OF LANGUAGE ON TELEVISION

In the USA the right to free speech influences the extent to which there is any desire to curb indecent speech on television. Feldman and Tickton (1976) report that the Federal Communications Commission received 31 084 written complaints citing obscene, profane or indecent expression in broadcasts in 11 months of 1973. The Commission did not carry out any disciplinary action, in spite of this evidence of public concern; nor is it easy to find representative measures of such public concern. Feldman and Tickton cite some ripe scatological examples but say they prefer to see any proceedings on such matters resolved in the courts.

It is in Britain, and possibly mainly in Britain however, that the way in which language is used on television has been a matter for administrative regulation and, hence, for research. The Acts of Parliament governing Independent Television in the 1960s to 1980s specified that, so far as possible, nothing should be broadcast which offended against 'good taste and decency'. To some extent this applied to symbolic pictorial messages (since no tongue is involved, these should not be called language, as the analytic need is to relinquish such terms which would thus be metaphors, in favour of others which are explicit) so that women salaciously unpeeling bananas or other more directly sexual or excretory sights have been discouraged from being broadcast, other than on occasions where they are necessary to help convey the meaning of some drama or current-affairs theme being developed. However, regulation also applied to curb any unbridled use of spoken language.

Simple assessments of the proportions of the public who say they have been offended by what they have seen or heard on television have been carried out in Britain for two decades. Gunter and Svennevig (1988) have shown that every year from 1970 to 1987 inclusive approximately four in ten adults said they were at some time in the previous year offended by something seen or heard on television, and for these people 'the nature of the offensive material seen is also very consistent . . . "bad language" usually heads the list' (p. 51); one in five of the population cited bad language as a source of offence on the most widely watched channels.

This kind of offence is generally taken to mean utterance of words denoting sexual or excretory bodily parts and actions. The next question is why these labels and notions should and do excite offence, and remarkably few empirical researchers have offered or investigated any theories which might explain the case, though the psychoanalytic literature is, of course, a source of ideas on the matter. Drawing from this source, Wober (1980b, 1988) suggested that a core need for any individual is to protect the integrity of the self – the extent to which the boundary of the self is secure rather than invaded or torn – because the intact self provides physical and symbolic evidence of one's continued life, while any disruption of the boundary fractures this security of existence, putting one closer to the mysterious, threatening and feared realm of non-existence or death.

If these ideas or theories have any reality, then the propensity to take offence would be greater among those who have a higher need for keeping this symbolic boundary of the self intact; in day-to-day terms, people who express a greater need for bodily privacy and those who say that religion is more important to them are more likely to be sensitive about bad language. This is not merely a matter of 'Victorian morality' or a notion among middle-aged and younger adults that the culture of the 1930s or before was 'more repressive' in a number of ways, and is merely carried forward amongst the most aged sector of the population. To be sure, old people are more likely to report offence from bad language; but the old people in 1987 are two decades separate from those of 1970, and the 2 years produced very similar numbers of people saying they were offended by material encountered on television. Further, the importance of privacy was shown (Wober, 1980b) to be related to sensitivity to offence, when age was partialled out, as also was the importance of religion. In a subsequent national survey carried out in 1983, likeliness to be offended was measured by adding scores on a list of potentially sensitive items, such as advertisements for sanitary-protection devices, funeral parlours and homosexuals' advice services; for the present purpose, while this offensiveness measure did not focus on language, it can be accepted as being likely to identify those people who would also be offended by bad language. Measured alongside this sensitivity was extraversion–introversion, and need for privacy; analysis showed that the latter was correlated with sensitivity of offence, independently of introversion (Wober, 1988).

More recently another national survey measured expressed approval or disapproval for a list of 31 potentially sensitive scenes on television. Factor analysis revealed nine groups of items, one of which was verbal offence. Sensitivity to this was correlated with a measure of the personal importance of religion, not only at a simple level but also in a regression equation in which demographic measures were entered, as well as others of viewing religious television programmes, conversation about religion and other topics, and attitudes towards the possibility of a channel devoted to religious content (Wober, 1989). Disapproval of the five items (two about graffiti seen on public walls, two on newscasters either expressing political opinions – of their own – or letting slip 'a four-letter bad word', and one simply envisaging 'adult' shows broadcast before 9 p.m.) was also related in the regression equation to a smaller amount of viewing of action-thriller films and an attitude of unwelcome for a sex-films (satellite) channel.

Besides a theory as outlined above which relates sensitivity to verbal offence to some underlying dynamics of needs and personality structure, there is another which might be called a learning of social norms theory. This can be found implied in the writings of a number of dramatists and critics; they wish, in their words, to continue to press back the frontiers of what is acceptable. In practice, this has meant – in the early 1980s – showing scenes of explicit childbirth, more nakedness and sexual activity, and males urinating (defaecation has not been put forward by dramatists, or accepted, as yet) and a parallel increase in the utterance of sexual and excretory words. The social learning 'theorists' may expect the public to come to accept all this more readily; but their expectation has no deep grounding in observed fact or in theory. For, as has been indicated, 'recent years have . . . witnessed an upward trend in concern about bad language' (Gunter and Wober, 1988), while, as regards theory, there is no reason in this attempted explanation for what the public may come to find acceptable to say why scatological words are found offensive in the first place while others of similar length and sound, such as back, shot, pass and so on, which have quite different meanings, never were unacceptable.

It remains to be observed, as a footnote, that in the USA, where the First Amendment protecting the freedom of speech holds sway, it is reported by most observers that there is much less 'bad language' on domestic screens (and even in the cinema) than occurs in Britain. On the other hand it is commonly agreed, there is a great deal more violent behaviour on American than on British screens. It is tempting to theorize therefore that the utterance of 'bad language' is a symbolic projection of male aggression. The sexual and excretory referents (as well as the challenge, for example in the word 'bastard', to the social 'legitimacy' of an accused person) generally carry an existential threat; evidently this may be necessary for the display of what is usually male aggressive expression. The brandishing and use of guns and other weapons is merely a more real form of aggression, and may displace the need for bad language. On the basis of this hypothesis it would be expected that the screen cultures of Japan and overseas China, brimming with overt physical aggression, may have less symbolically aggressive verbal threat. This question remains to be investigated.

ATTITUDES TOWARDS NORMAL LANGUAGE USE ON SCREEN

In 1965 the Federation of British Industry told the government that its members favoured metrication, and the government set up a Metrication Board in 1969. Noticing that this centralized initiative existed in Britain to accomplish a major change in a minor sector of the language, from the use of what were called Imperial units of measurement towards the International System, a survey (Wober, 1980a) explored Londoners' attitudes towards these options. Amongst implications for broadcasting were that radio-station locations were now to be expressed in the hertz unit of frequency rather than the metre, previously used (even in Imperial Britain), and that weather temperatures were to be given in Centigrade (later termed Celsius) instead of (though often supplemented by) Fahrenheit. The survey showed majorities of disapproval for each of six items (replacement of miles, gallons, pounds, weight, feet, metres and Fahrenheit by their metric equivalents) from over 50% down to 11%, respectively. While sex and social class (hence educational level) bore no relation to degree of acceptance of the new metrics, younger people were better disposed to innovation, as were those who had (or had realized and reported that they had) radio sets calibrated in kilohertz.

On a much narrower question, broadcasters envisaging the use of the 24-hour-clock designation for programme times asked a large national sample in 1988: 'Do you personally feel you know the difference between the 12-hour and the 24-hour clock?' Over nine out of ten said yes. Asked which one out of three alternatives corresponded to '12 a.m.', one-quarter chose 00.00 and 10% 24.00; over six in ten were more conventionally correct with their choice of 12.00; likewise '12 p.m.' was given by one-third of respondents as equivalent to 12.00 and by 20% to 00.00. The ambiguity is not in the new but in the old designation, which should helpfully add 'noon' or 'midnight'. Nevertheless, the technical jargon lacks normative power over social custom since, when asked how they would find out what was being broadcast at 3 a.m. on Friday morning, 57% said they would turn in the programme journal to the Thursday page (25% felt it should appear in Friday's listing). Since this survey was taken, the Metrication Board has been dissolved, though the government and broadcasting bodies continue to support its purpose; however, popular use of Imperial units of size and weight remains entrenched, other than where institutional changes present the public with no alternative.

It may be doubted that opposition to imposed change in the jargon is motivated merely by inertia, as a British survey suggests (Gunter, 1984). In this survey, the situation in the North-East region – where sign-language inserts for severely deaf viewers (estimated as at least 8% of the population) had been experimentally used – was monitored. The result was a substantial majority (six in ten) in favour of the option that sign language should be used 'in general programmes for any topic' rather than for use to be restricted to 'programmes made specially for the deaf' or for the general public but on topics of special interest to the deaf. People who had not seen any programmes with sign-language inserts were not any less well disposed to the change in general than were those who had seen such examples; but people who had seen the provision were significantly more ready (than those who had not seen it) to support its use in news programmes.

In addition to their deeply rooted sensitivities to 'bad' language in the modes discussed above, and to deliberately introduced changes in jargon, many 'viewers' observe a range of other language features about which they have marked preferences or dislikes. One of these features, in Britain at least, is 'regional' accent. The history of accent is complex but it is said that in the last century there was not yet fully developed the 'Queen's English' or 'received pronunciation' as a standard of correct speech. The institutions which enabled this version to come forward included the boarding schools and universities which brought people from different parts of the country together who then shared an experience of being an élite in terms of education and social authority, and the home and overseas civil services; and, between the World Wars, radio, quickly established as a national instrument of public service broadcasting, expressed an ideal form of the language. After the Second World War, the arrival of a Labour government, and then television for the popular taste, structured in a system of regional franchises, created opportunities for the diverse forms of speech across the nation each to seek and assert the dignity of equals in a community of voices. While this became an ideal for many, Queen's English retained its perceived authority in several respects.

A survey carried out among a representative United Kingdom panel (i.e. including Northern Ireland) first asked: 'How much do you feel (each of the following accents) would be welcome in a TV news reader?' Over eight in ten endorsed Queen's English in this role, and the next most widely approved accent in this role was English West

Country, with fewer than three in ten approving this (Wober, 1987). Accents of foreign origin were not approved of for use by a television news reader: one in ten or fewer respondents approved of American, West Indian, Asian, French or German accents in this role. The last two were included in the question to explore the readiness amongst the British public to hear voices from the Community of Europe expressing the nation's affairs. By this index, shared European identity is still remote.

The same survey then showed that people had a much broader range of readiness to hear 'certain regional accents' in different genres of television; eight in ten found such variety welcome in drama programmes or comedies. Five in ten welcomed regional accents for reporters on national news and for weather forecasters, and even four in ten said they welcomed regional voices in national news – a figure which is not at odds with the smaller degrees of welcome for any particular named regional accent.

When asked whether they associated any sense of humour with particular accents, there was a very wide disparity in results. Over six in ten cited the working-class accents of the cities of Liverpool and London as indicating a strong sense of humour. Queen's English was associated with an excellent sense of humour by only three in ten, and the foreign accents again produce minority support.

It is noteworthy that differences of accent were perceived very similarly by people of all socio-economic statuses; this uniformity was less evident with the questions of whether people perceived what they considered to be mistakes by announcers and newsreaders in pronunciation, in grammar and in the use of words in their correct meanings. Examples were given in each case. The cited lapse – if such it is – in grammar was the omission of a verb from many sentences; thus 'Winds coming in from the west' omits a 'will be', 'are' or 'have been'. The reason is possibly because television and radio have taken over the newspaper headline form in which the sentence of discourse is replaced by a word string that is essentially an index, or the kind of utterance made by a town crier. The practice is marked by having one reader utter the (non-grammatical) headline before another reader continues in more complete sentences. The distinction is less clear between speakers of headlines and text on broadcast services than in print, and nearly seven in ten viewers say they notice errors of this kind – two out of these seven say they mind, and five say they do not mind such errors. Illustrated errors of meaning are problematic; an example given was that the word 'critical' is often said when the meaning would be better conveyed by 'crucial'; another example given was the use of 'anxious' when the meaning should be conveyed better by 'eager' (thus distinguishing positive from negative feeling in anticipation). However, there is no shortage of theorists of language who celebrate its evolution and who defend the process of change in meaning brought about by (mal)practice. Perhaps for this reason there were fewer – six in ten – who said they noticed errors in meaning than who had noticed errors in grammar.

As an overview, nearly two in ten considered the 'standards of speech on TV news and announcements' were getting worse: twice as many as those who said they were improving. Pessimism was equalled by optimism amongst those of lowest status, but was markedly in excess amongst those of highest socio-economic (and hence educational) status.

WORDS AS SIGNPOSTS, CONTAINERS AND CHANNELS FOR THOUGHT

One view of the use of terms in the field of 'mass communications' is essentially anarchic, holding that language is evolving so that meanings are never exactly shared, either within one person from one use of a term to the next, or between people, so in this view attempts to achieve precision in the process of communication are bound to fail. However, if two parties using the same words are found to understand them in effectively different ways, or if the words in use are ill-chosen (however well entrenched such misuses may be), then impediments exist to the development and use of knowledge, and such problems should be diagnosed and solutions put forward.

There are several kinds of ways of tackling the Whorfian challenge posed above. One is to hold that it is a false construction; another is to accept it passively; a third is to try to accept it dynamically, not trying to bring about an illusion of precision in the apparatus of communication but to be ever vigilant and striving in the attempt to sense what is being shared and what is being lost in verbal communication; and, fourth, the position to be adopted here, is to recognize that the attempt simply to be permanently vigilant is likely to fail and could benefit by considerable assistance in trying to stabilize and broaden acceptance of terms and their meanings, as far as the latter can be taken as shared across minds.

The first steps in what amounts to a campaign along these lines start from the position taken by Rosch (1986), which is that the bulk of work on linguistic relativity has involved language at the lexical level, and this is the plane on which examples will now be explored. Rosch has also stated that, in order to have a real test of Whorf's hypothesis, it is necessary to have at least two natural languages whose lexicons differ with respect to some domain of discourse; further, she asserts that effects of lexical linguistic categories are probably inseparable from the effects of the functions which led initially to the formation of just those categories.

Neither of these contentions is fully accepted in what follows; for language is taught, very largely without being created anew, to each generation whose thoughts are principally conditioned by, rather than have the opportunity to become, architects of that language. Second, if differences are found in between two languages as regards how their speakers think about two particular domains, then it could be argued that something else in the language and culture other than a narrow strip of lexicon has been responsible for how particular speech communities deal with this particular area (for example, perceptions of personal characters as labelled in English or Chinese; see Hoffman, Lau, and Johnson, 1986). In some respects it would be more convincing if one 'speech community' such as a professional group can be found whose jargon, within the same overall language, and whose practices are different from those of another professional group whose work deals largely with the same phenomena. Then, the words of the jargon will be found to express certain forms of thought which they serve to construct in acolytes and from whose subculture the new members will find it difficult to emerge.

In the world of broadcasting audience research two such professional subcultures go by the names of 'mass communication' and 'critical' studies (Jensen, 1988). The fact that both of these terms are themselves misnomers does not seem to occur to, let alone trouble, the adherents of each school. Mass communication it has been pointed out (Wober, 1988) should preferably be termed mass admunication; for it describes an overwhelmingly centrifugal flow of messages with very limited centripetal flow. The branch of critical studies (evolved from literary criticism to apply to the analysis of broadcast works) concerned with audience research takes care not to make judgments or criticisms, but strives dispassionately to discover the meanings developed in the minds of audience members from what they see and hear.

Within the overall field of broadcasting and audience research there are calls for a more multidisciplinary approach but, while mass-communications researchers generally know what flies under their own banner, there are signs that they are misled to some extent by the term critical research, and some of the jargon within that subculture. The following study has probably never been carried out, but it could be, at a convention of the International Communication Association, the International Association of Mass Communication Research, or of other related bodies. People would deal with a list of terms, rating each on its familiarity, usefulness to oneself or to other researchers, its appropriateness of definition, its openness to change its referent, pleasingness and other scales. The terms would be drawn from the mass-communications subculture and include normative, exposure, significant, information and ratings; and from the critical studies subculture and include appreciation, discourse, hegemony, readings, sign and syntax; for added interest dummy terms could be included which look to members of one camp as if they belong to the jargon of the other. The hypothesis is that 'members' of one research subculture would not understand the other's terms as well, or as favourably, as they understand their own. The point is, then, that investigators schooled in one tradition tend to be reinforced in accepting its ways, partly by using the words which carry forward its ideas.

A focal term which provides a deep channel containing 'mass-communication' thought is exposure. The verb 'to expose' requires an object which gets exposed; the subject who does the exposing does not become exposed unless the reflexive aspect is made explicit: I expose myself (to sunlight, to criticism, whatever). Whenever it is reported in a study that 'subjects were exposed' to some message or material it is strongly implied that initiative rests with the exposer, the experimenter, and not with 'the subject' – who is really functioning as an object. Even if 'the subject who is exposed' is then conceived of as able to contribute some element of processing in between specification of 'the stimulus' (some 'stimuli' should be recognized as boring, and hence lacking in stimulus attributes, so that all stimuli could more correctly be called messages) and 'emission of a response', this whole style of discourse has little or no place for the function of initiative on the part of the subject (which is an explicit interest of 'critical research'). This constraint of mass-communication thought appears to be rooted in the behaviourist 'psych'ology of the second quarter of this century in which experiments were generally done on rats or, if on humans, all too often purposely used nonsense syllables so as to make the 'subjects' of experiment as much like objects as was possible.

This is one reason why much of the work in the mass-communications tradition has continued to function without consideration of personality affecting subjects' behaviour. For, to open the door to personality required the experimenter to hand over or at least to share power with the subject, to acknowledge the reality of stimulus-seeking (or sensation-seeking, in the terms of one personality construct) instead of being exposed to messages by the experimenter. There is nevertheless a section of mass-communication audience research which sets out to consider the subject as a person, and this calls itself 'uses and gratifications' research; even this tradition, which acknowledges the postexperiential subjective reality of gratifications, focuses otherwise on the motivationally inert construct of uses – in other words behaviour. To make the subject autonomously real in this tradition requires it to be renamed and to be thought of, afresh, as a *needs* and gratifications perspective, where needs are a prior determinant of behaviour and mean that 'stimuli' can be either found by the subject, or even created internally (Wober, 1988).

The quite simple terms 'exposure' and 'uses and gratifications' are not just signs of a way of thinking which have nothing to do with constructing and sustaining that way of thought; these terms are dykes and ditches which determine the flow of ideas within this territory. Those who enter within and who use these terms constrain their thought accordingly.

A complementary restriction of action occurs amongst 'critical theorists'. In attempting to respect the experiences of broadcasting that viewers and listeners have, critical theorists deny themselves the ways of mass-communications empiricists who, in devising experiments or even using surveys in a quasi-experimental way, take control and initiative into their own hands. There are not many words written upon signposts; but, together with the initiative of the travellers they make a major difference to where people go. The words 'expose' and 'uses and gratifications' are such signposts to the territory of mass-communications empirical research and away from the realms of critical theory.

A solution recommended here is to abandon the terms used by the (unwitting) inheritors of stimulus–response 'psych'ology (in which the psyche or mind had actively been denied) but to retain an interest in and use of many of the methods used by such researchers. An example may help. One recent observational study (Morley, 1986) of (lower middle-class) families' viewing developed the point that the remote control switch had become within the family a symbol and instrument of power operated generally by the husbands. This point received considerable attention and credence in the press, where the idea (or myth?) of male domestic power was already current and was reinforced. The wives had been observed and their behaviour analysed, as 'subjects', but without enough attention to their opinions and justifications they were effectively treated as objects. Yet opinion surveys done at the same time yielded more equivocal evidence; it was by no means acknowledged by all women that all their menfolk controlled the remote switch or selected the majority of video-recordings made or seen. Empirical survey evidence gained within the mass-communications approach accorded autonomy of control to both male and female subjects, finding many families in which the women were reported to wield 'the power' of this electronic wand. Further, the question exists as to how interested in television the non-controllers are. If the empiricist mass-communications researchers remain aware of the subjectivity of their 'objects' of study, the values in their approach can be conserved. Note that asking people, in surveys or in observational studies, who operates the remote control is far removed from observing –

and speaking and writing in terms of who 'is exposed to' programmes brought up by a remote control device.

Besides the thought-formative terms 'mass communication', 'critical studies', 'subjects' and 'exposure', a whole new jargon has been advocated (Wober, 1988) based on principles put forward decades ago by Shannon and Weaver, and Colin Cherry, among others. In this scheme a focal term is 'medium', whose referent has to be clearly understood at the outset. Whereas colloquial and received 'scientific' practice applies the word generally to a social entity composed of institutions but also including the physical means of transmission, the advice now is to reduce ambiguity by clarifying the duties expected of each term in the jargon. This approach also points to a need for a number of new terms, because they should apply to phenomena which the existing 'smudgy' jargon have not allowed to emerge clearly.

The word 'medium' should refer to the physical continuum along which information passes from a sender to a perceiver. Thus air is not just one medium but two. It carries light and it carries sound. Light is perceived only through the eyes (discounting skin perception as insufficiently coded), and sound by the ears. While simple enough, these realities have been obscured by existing jargon and one of the important reasons why they should be marked in a better jargon is because the mental processing of codes in each of these two media is done in different ways. The phenomenon called television, it will be simply realized, is not one medium but two, and, instead of calling television a medium, it might be better termed a 'message system'.

If those who produced television never thought of it as 'a medium' but as a message system addressing individuals via two media, then the programme makers' task of composing an effective combination of what the French have called *son et lumière* would become clearer; the evidence that the composite use of two media has led to ineffective news (Gunter, 1987) and inefficient communication in other programme areas (Greenfield, 1984) is quite substantial, and it is proposed here that a root step towards realizing the difficulty and equipping programme makers to tackle it would be to clarify the processes involved with a more appropriate jargon.

The next focal term to tackle and clarify is 'literacy'. Qualified as visual literacy or audiovisual literacy, this skill is variously presumed to be the ability to encode, or decode, messages, or both; and the messages are variously presumed to be writing, pictures (still or moving) or combinations of sound (words or non-words) with writing, and still or moving pictures. It should be obvious, but even if not it is documented in research (Wober, 1976), that skills involved in decoding still and moving pictures are different, and have to be learned. A solution advocated by Wober (1988) is to reserve the term literacy for the two skills of being able to encode and to decode letters (writing and reading) and to use parallel terms to label other skills. Thus 'picturacy' (probably qualifying this also as moving or still) is the ability to make and to derive (close to the encoded) meanings from pictures; more arcane terms such as 'oracy' and 'auracy' (abilities to speak and to understand – by ear – spoken speech) immediately point to the physiologically different structures involved in encoding and decoding messages for and from different media. The face and body as 'sign agents' send messages by the visual medium which require the skills of 'expressionacy' and 'gesturacy' for comprehension. An important function that this specificity of jargon immediately evokes is the presence of imagery in the receiver which may assist or impede comprehension. Thus on seeing print some people may evoke auditory images of a voice reading the words, and on seeing gestures some people may feel internal proprioceptive imagery. The first phenomenon does not transform headlines into 'an auditory medium', because headlines are not a medium but signs, and they address the visual medium, and even in those who evoke auditory images the messages are still received in the first place by the eye and are dealt with through the corresponding cortical pathways.

The whole apparatus of a precise jargon in this field performs several functions. It helps to show how complex the neurophysiological phenomena are, in the enterprise of communicating meanings; it suggests that in different cultures there can be a different balance in the use of different media (involving message-system sociology, but also brain physiology and aesthetics); it helps in identifying what the basic processes in communication really are; and it suggests that the Whorfian idea is at work, so that those who possess and use a particular array of terms will think about the topic area in a different way than do others who do not use such terms.

The analysis above has dealt with jargon whose design has implications for the study of broadcasting both at a highly individual and also at an institutional level (by reference to message systems where others have applied the term media). Two final examples at the level of jargon concern the Dutch word *overheidsvoorlichting*, and the more universal word 'ratings'.

Nillesen and Stappers (1987) explained that *overheidsvoorlichting* is a unique Dutch concept referring to the precise way and context in which the Dutch government puts out information. The authors say there is no clear-cut translation into French, English or German. They explore the options of *oeffentlichkeitsarbeit, beratung, forderung, aufklarung, erziehung* and *auskunft*, education, guidance and extension; but evidently the Dutch concept is none of these. The English 'elucidation' is a close version but the Dutch concept evidently conveys more of a concern for the benefit of the receiver than a reflection of the motives of the elucidator. One example of the different practices of the Dutch from those elsewhere include a 'weekly television appearance of the Prime Minister . . . in which an account is given of what was discussed and decided upon in the Cabinet Council' (Nillesen and Stappers, 1987, pp. 498–499). The point being made is that Dutch society and culture make such ways of disclosing information possible, and make it necessary for the concept to be recognized and named. The name itself has no magic, but in order to understand it, it is necessary to find out something about the (Dutch) reality to which it refers, and it is not only insufficient but probably also misleading to try to represent it in translation. The word thus opens the way to its own concept and the use of the word enables its referent to be evaluated, which not only is useful in itself, but almost certainly also changes the evaluation of other entities named and labelled in other languages (propaganda, *glasnost*).

Another example of a concept that finds its apt expression in one language but that defies translation or full expression in another language is that *Lehrnschock* which the Germans say was brought about by knowledge of the Chernobyl disaster. It was not the loss of Ukrainian life, or the prediction of cancer increases in Germany, or the 'objective' radiation levels that *Lehrnschock* named; it was a new awareness brought about by confrontation by the broadcast news to which the word referred. It means something more sudden and alarming than insight and something more meaningful than mere shock. Germans who use this term will think more crisply about the topic than do English speakers who are still groping for a concept to coalesce into a word.

'Ratings' is now a term used not only in English to refer to a measurement of audience size. Because audience size is a direct indicator of economic potential value to vendors of advertising, the word ratings as applied to audience size has come to be regarded as a measure of programme merit, held up in public to indicate success. Thus newspapers publish lists of top ten (or 20, or whatever) programmes in order of audience size, given in 'the ratings' and these are called 'the most popular programmes'. This procedure, in which the word 'ratings' serves as a conceptual rut, blurs over the distinction between behaviour and attitude. It is well known in audience research that appreciation measurement shows that many programmes with large audience size have poor appreciation – that is, viewers when asked have given these items low ratings – while many programmes with low audience size have high appreciation. To understand what is meant by rating, one has to ask who has done the rating; and, if it is supposed to be the audience, then the rating is given by the appreciation score and not the audience size. If the rater is the vendor of advertising time, then the rating is understandably given by audience size. Yet these qualifications are rarely if ever explained or understood by those who 'use' (more correctly, misuse) the term; so the vernacular has enabled a misunderstanding to become widespread and entrenched.

The argument has been that one section of language, namely 'professional' jargon, has offered many examples of terms which acts as conduits of 'dirty' or sloppy thought, and eventually of inappropriate action. The notion of dirt, otherwise applied to 'matter out of place' is adapted here to refer metaphorically to ideas out of place. Since the topic at issue is that of communication, indicating a valid and equitable transfer of ideas and feelings, the situation is rife with irony. Mass communication is not communication, critical studies are not critical, so-called 'media' are really institution-level message systems each using one or more media, many conventional extensions of the term 'literacy' are to an extent illiterate, and there will be staunch resistance to having all these shortcomings pointed out or remedies proposed. Yet the physical sciences have arranged for internationally recognized jargon to be established, defining limits in an integrated metric system. Units of mass, extension, time, energy and power, and constants such as the gravitational force and refraction index, have been named. In many cases changes of name have taken place from terms quite familiar a generation ago.

All this has occurred in the world of physics, where it may be said that, at least at an everyday level, phenomena proceed according to reasonably exact laws and matters are thus quite predictable. It could be argued that, all the more so in a social science such as that of understanding the phenomenon of admunicating to the mass, there is a need for exact and appropriate design of jargon. Yet, perhaps because, unlike physics, broadcast admunication involves feelings as well as ideas, it will be difficult to alter existing jargon which offers a semblance of stability in an otherwise elusive field. Two ways in which jargon has been, or will be, changed include the elimination or reduction of sexist and racist terms. It has taken major changes in societies for these to be reflected in the language or jargon of social science and no such reinforcement is in sight to influence any review of the more technical features of mass-admunications science jargon. For the time being, therefore, those who are interested must remain content with taking stock of the matter and extending the number of those who contribute to this process of preliminary assessment.

SUMMARY AND DISCUSSION

Social science should always be reflexive in its awareness and take into account the behaviour of the observer who is simultaneously one of the observed. In a review of any study of language in broadcasting, this reflexivity means that the language of observation comes under scrutiny. The jargon (or specialist vocabulary) of the scientific language requires special attention, as this forms the conceptual armoury with which the science is to proceed. Engineers or surgeons trying to work with the wrong tools will not do good work. The same applies to communications scientists who seek to understand the ways in which the public encounter and use broadcast services, especially television. This review has therefore spent some time in examining the appropriateness of words such as 'rating' (which in the rest of social psychology implies the existence of one who performs the – subjective – act of rating, but which in audience research is applied to an objective assessment of audience size), 'communication', 'literacy', and many other terms. It may be that it will have to be accepted that there is no difference in practice between the 'use' and 'misuse' of these words; but it is less likely that science will advance unless there is a greater conceptual clarity behind this sloppy practice, and it is not impossible that communications scientists who are in earnest may even take the trouble to establish a more precisely defined and agreed jargon, or specialist vocabulary.

If there is demonstrable lack of clarity in expression among communications scientists, and a minority (though a large one) among the public who notice errors of practice in positions (such as the television news) where they hope to encounter high standards both of veracity of content and of practice in speech, then it is easier to understand the concerns of those who fear that increased experience of television may damage language skills among the population at large. For the most part, those who have tackled this question have used tests of verbal comprehension rather than of construction, and the outcome of the studies has seemingly changed. At first, television was seen as replacing time spent with (low-grade) comic-book 'reading', and hence not responsible for loss of skills; later, researchers reported an inverted-U relationship, with more hours of viewing associated with better reading skills among the least able performers, but detracting from comprehension and reading skills among average and above-average people.

A new wave of researchers has sought to pinpoint television experience as an independent feature of the environment which may, or may not, be responsible for affecting language skills. The more meticulous these studies, the less their authors implicate television viewing as an independent influence. Yet there is another perspective in which an acquittal of this kind can be seen as unsatisfactorily shallow.

For it can be hypothesized that television viewing does not function as an independent influence but, rather, precisely in conjunction with other features of a person's experience (indexed most easily by age, sex and class, but denoting differences in subculture and attitude) which, taken together, may entail that the use of television will have been detrimental more often than an asset to the development of language skills.

The problem with this 'state of the art' focus on statistical technique is that it aims to isolate 'atoms' of experience whose weights can then be separately evaluated, when it may be that in human experience these 'atoms' actually have different weights, depending on next to which other atoms they are placed. In particular, the role of radio (and music) listening has been ignored by most of the research on television's interaction with language skills, as have assessments of language production skills – of complexity and accuracy of written and spoken expression. The review therefore serves to indicate what a large field remains open for research.

Some will say that where the arts of precision in expression are sacrificed, the blunter weapons of emotive terms come to the fore. 'Bad' language, whose badness lies in its use of taboo to alarm the listener, is more often heard, though not, evidently more widely accepted. Some theory is needed to explain why and in what contexts certain terms are bad in this sense, and there are two contenders for this role. One theory holds that the designation of 'bad' is an arbitrary convention that could eventually be overcome by a tide of reassuring practice. This idea has either failed, or not really been put to the test; for the dramatists who press forward the use of bad language nearly always place the words where they will be experienced as bad, for their shock value; they rarely if ever introduce such terms as casual and innocent decorations or in order to convey their actual meanings but in non-emotive terms. The other theory links certain meanings – of words connected with procreation, life (cleanliness) and death (dirt) – to anxieties which may be aroused when listeners are made more aware of the boundaries of their security in existence. In this theory personality characteristics of need for privacy and depth of religious orientation may index sensitivities to bad language, and some evidence of such links has been reported.

Language is by no means a neutral conduit for sharing ideas and experience. Listeners (and speakers) have distinct attitudes to what kinds of language they want to hear – or to use – in various contexts. Features of language such as the jargons of measurement, regional and foreign accents, and standards of performance in vocabulary and grammar are all additional signs of currents of social change. Those who feel – and who might wish to shut out – the draught most keenly tend to be older people; but, again, a wide area of study of other personal characteristics that may relate to attitudes towards the 'normal' use of language in broadcasts remains enticingly open.

REFERENCES

Arliss, L.P., Cassata, M., and Skill, T. (1983). Dyadic interaction on the daytime serials: How men and women vie for power. In M. Cassata and T. Skill (Eds), *Life on daytime television: Tuning-in American serial drama*. Norwood, NJ: Ablex.

Comstock, G. (1982). Mass media. In H.E. Mitzel (Ed.), *Encyclopaedia of educational research*, 5th edn. New York: Free Press.

Feldman, C. and Tickton, S. (1976). Obscene/indecent programming: Regulation of ambiguity. *Journal of Broadcasting*, **20**, 273–282.

Fine, M.G. (1981). Soap opera conversations: The talk that binds. *Journal of Communication*, **31**, 97–107.

Gaddy, G.D. (1986). Television's impact on high school achievement. *Public Opinion Quarterly*, **50**, 340–359.

Greenfield, P.M. (1984). *Mind and media*. London: Fontana.

Gunter, B. (1984). *Attitudes towards sign-language inserts in TV news*. London: IBA Research Department.

Gunter, B. (1987). *Poor reception: Misunderstanding and forgetting broadcast news*. Hillsdale, NJ: Erlbaum.

Gunter, B. and Svennevig, M. (1988). *Attitudes to broadcasting over the years*. London: Libbey.

Gunter, B. and Wober, M. (1988). *Violence on television: What the viewers think*. London: Libbey.

Hoffman, C., Lau, I., and Johnson, D.R. (1986). The linguistic relativity of person cognition: An English–Chinese comparison. *Journal of Personality and Social Psychology*, **57**(6).

Hornik, R.C. (1978). Television access and the slowing of cognitive growth. *American Educational Research Journal*, **15**, 1–15.

Hornik, R.C. (1981). Out-of-school and schooling: Hypotheses and methods. *Review of Educational Research*, **51**, 199–204.

Howell, W.J. (1981). Britain's fourth television channel and the Welsh language controversy. *Journal of Broadcasting*, **25**, 123–137.

Jensen, K.B. (1988). Answering the question: What is reception analysis? *Nordicom Review*, **1**, 3–5.

Knill, B.J., Pesch, M., Pursey, G., Gilpin, P., and Perloff, R.M. (1981). Still typecast after all these years: Sex role portrayals in television advertising. *International Journal of Women's Studies*, **4**, 497–506.

Kuo, E.C.Y. (1984). Mass media and language planning: Singapore's 'Speak Mandarin' campaign. *Journal of Communication*, **34**, 24–35.

Livingstone, S. and Greene, G. (1986). Television advertisements and the portrayal of gender. *British Journal of Social Psychology*, **25**, 149–154.

Manstead, A.R.S. and McCullough, C. (1981). Sex role stereotyping in British television advertisements. *British Journal of Social Psychology*, **20**, 171–180.

McArthur, L.Z. and Resko, B.G. (1975). The portrayal of men and women in American television commercials. *Journal of Social Psychology*, **97**, 209–220.

Morgan, M. (1985). Television and adults' verbal; intelligence. Mimeographed paper, Department of Communication, University of Massachussets, Amherst, MA.

Morgan, M. and Gross, L. (1982). Television and educational achievement and aspiration. In D. Pearl, L. Bouthilet, and J. Lazar (Eds), *Television and behaviour: Ten years of scientific progress and implications for the eighties*, pp. 78–90. Washington, DC: US Government Printing Office.

Morley, D. (1986). *Family television: Cultural power and domestic leisure*. London: Comedia.

Mowlana, H. and Wilson, L.J. (1988). *Communication technology and development*. Reports and Papers on Mass Communication, No. 101. Paris: UNESCO.

Nillesen, A.B. and Stappers, J.G. (1987). The government as communicator: A Dutch dilemma. *European Journal of Communication*, **2**, 491–512.

Postman, N. (1986). *Amusing ourselves to death*. London: Heinemann.

Potter, W.J. (1987). Does television viewing hinder academic achievement among adolescents? *Human Communication Research*, **14**, 27–46.

Ritchie, O., Price, V., and Roberts, D.F. (1987). Television, reading and reading achievement. *Communication Research*, **14**, 292–315.

Rosch, E. (1986). Linguistic relativity, *ETC.: A Review of General Semantics*, **44**, 254–279.

Selnow, G.W. and Bettinghans, E.P. (1982). Television exposure and language development. *Journal of Broadcasting*, **26**, 469–479.

Shukla, S. (1979). The impact of SITE on primary school children. *Journal of Communication*, **29**, 99–103.

Singer, J.L. and Singer, D.G. (1983). Psychologists look at television: Cognitive, developmental, personality and social policy implications. *American Psychologist*, **38**, 826–834.

Van Vuuren, D. (1988). Television: Friend or foe? Some indications from research in South Africa. *Mentor*, Autumn, 99–102.

Williams, P.A., Haertel, E.H., Hachtel, G.D., and Walberg, H.J. (1982). The impact of leisure time television on school learning: A research synthesis. *American Educational Research Journal*, **19**, 19–50.

Williams, T.M. (Ed.) (1986). *The impact of television. A natural experiment in three communities*. Montreal: Academic Press.

Wober, M. (1976). *Psychology in Africa*. London: International African Institute.

Wober, M. (1980a). Attitudes towards metric and imperial systems of measurement. In H. Giles and W.P. Robinson (Eds), *Language: Social psychological perspectives*. Oxford: Pergamon.

Wober, M. (1980b). *Offence and defence in the home: Some reasons for viewers' reactions to bad language on television*. London: IBA Research Department.

Wober, M. (1987). *The quality of language on television. Listener–viewers' perceptions of and attitudes to what they hear*. London: IBA Research Department.

Wober, M. (1988). *The use and abuse of television: A social psychology of the changing screen*. Hillsdale, NJ: Erlbaum.

Wober, M. (1989). *Lines and liberties: Attitudes to religion, ethics and innovation in television*. London: IBA Research Department.

Epilogue

W. PETER ROBINSON AND HOWARD GILES

The Prologue promised diversity and variety. Some topics would be given comprehensive reviews. Others would offer an idiosyncratic perspective that might encourage a switch from traditional approaches. Some would focus on theory; others on evidence. Some would try to define difficulties for future research. Hopefully the promises have been kept. However, with most chapters taking a forward look for themselves, there is no point in repeating the prophesies at this stage. Neither is there any point in listing the fields or approaches that should have been included and were not or that still need pioneering development; we are only too aware of the long menu for both.

What might be more useful is to raise some methodological questions that have been relevant to the work reported so far and will be relevant in the future. By 'methodological' we do not mean simply 'methods'. We mean to pose questions about the propriety of methods, the relative places of explanation and data collection, and relationships to adjacent disciplines.

It is possible to generate binary oppositions that characterize preferences and prejudices of social psychologists concerned with language and its use. Some prefer surveys to experiments. Some reject both to examine naturally occurring activities. Some psychologists prefer theory – or hypothesis-driven research; others, empirically driven. The hypothetico-deductive versus inductive contrast appears to have been replaced by top-down versus bottom-up, or idea-led versus data-driven, but the contrasts intended are comparable. Should we be seeking abstract truths in real-world contexts or should we be demonstrating the essence of processes and structures in contrived situations?

None of these hoary old polarizations have been salient as controversial issues in the chapters, but they continue to constitute potential battlefields at conferences and seminars. Why? In part the preferences have historical precedents. Neither socio-

Handbook of Language and Social Psychology
Edited by H. Giles and W.P. Robinson. © 1990 John Wiley & Sons Ltd

logy nor linguistics traditionally included experimentation as a method of inquiry in their undergraduate courses. The Durkheim tradition included statistical analysis in the study of social facts but this strand seems to have weakened in recent years. Psychologists on the other hand are likely to have been led to believe that experiments are the ideal research technique. Very little psychology training yet involves encouraging students to observe and ask questions about people's everyday behaviour. We do not have field trips of the kind that bird-watchers or anthropologists engage in. Incredible as it may seem, the training is mainly within literature-guided questions about bits of behaviour to be studied in the Department.

Another factor affecting the arguments is the lack of an historical developmental perspective applied to areas of study. The more we learn about an area, the more we can consider the possibility of exercising control over relevant variables in experiments. The more we know, the better our techniques of measurement are likely to be. Conversely, the less we know, the more appropriate it is to use apt illustrations, or even fictional accounts, just to begin to define the phenomena. The fields covered show this variety. Non-verbal communication has been advanced very considerably in recent years. The utilization of video-recording with sophisticated associated instrumentation permits analysis that could not have been dreamed of 30 years ago. In contrast, the study of the language of emotions is still trapped by conceptual difficulties and the diversity of the usage of key words by ordinary people. Video and computer power have been two great technological boosts to research in language and social psychology but they cannot solve conceptual muddles. It may well be that speech synthesizers and decoders will be the next technological assets for systematic analysis of text and discourse. Certainly one of our difficulties with language is the sheer quantity of speech occurring in even brief encounters. Students who collect real conversations are prone to disappear into archives of transcripts and not to re-emerge. One of the objections to collecting real extended conversations is the avalanche of transcripts that buries the original questions. We may expect technological relief with some matters but by no means with all.

If we turn to some of the binary oppositions mentioned at the beginning, we can be happy in noting that none of the authors has actually engaged in cathartic diatribes against any particular *methods* of inquiry. Some have indeed risked those avalanches of naturally occurring speech. Others have relied more or solely on evidence arising from interrogation and experiment. We have already indicated the stereotypically presumed differences between the linguists, sociologists and anthropologists on the one hand and psychologists on the other. Here we would have to argue for eclectism in methods of observation, recognizing that ultimately explanations have to cope with behaviour wherever or however it occurs, whether deliberately or not. Oppositions can be improperly exaggerated. People can be constrained or encouraged in laboratories to say or do strange things, but they cannot, by definition, do what it is impossible for them to do. We might wonder why someone should bother to compare the incidence of certain linguistic features when 'subjects' are talking to stuffed versus real parrots, and we might wonder about the ecological validity of inferences drawn from the study, but those subjects can only have used their etic repertoire for their speech; the speech itself remains real. Conversely, what someone actually says or writes in a natural setting has no magical properties. It is but an example of what might have been said on such an occasion and it has no privileged status, just because its emic quality has been recorded.

Eventually data from all methods of observation should complement each other and form an integrated whole. It would be good to have the power to ban the dogmatic slogans that can be heard and seen around these problems. Typically, naturally occurring data reported in print are abused for being conveniently and especially selected (as are what are recorded as responses in experiments). They are abused for being samples from unknown universes (as are responses in experiments). They are abused for having a variety of possible interpretations (as do responses in experiments) and for being uncontrolled (as is the error variance and what is not thought about in experiments). On the other side, behaviour in experiments is condemned as 'artificial' (what does 'artificial' really mean and how is it a term of abuse?) and controlled (is natural behaviour not subject to control too?).

Certainly data obtained by certain methods are seen as more prone to some kinds of inferential errors than they are to others. That is a reason for needing a variety of methods, not a reason for rejecting all but one technique! In this handbook these issues have not reared their heads; they have been axes of dispute in the last 20 years, but perhaps our academic culture is becoming better informed and perhaps our training courses are now beginning to encourage a diversity of approaches to problems, thereby reducing the time wasted in sterile argumentation.

A nested variant of this contrast exists between the hard-line experimentalists and the interviewers (questionnaire-givers). Some of the latter apologize that their data are only correlational and cannot be used to infer direction of causation. Experimenters have no logical advantage. Their argument is: if A, then B should result; B observed; therefore A. As any teenage Aristotle can prove, this is not a valid syllogism. Yet experimenters are prone to claim *logical* and not just *psychological* advantages over their correlating colleagues. This old argument may take on a new guise with the technique used by Gardner and Clément in this volume. LISREL is sometimes presented as a causal analysis technique that can be used with correlational data. It is not. Causal interpretations are in the heads of investigators. Number crunching cannot of itself answer such questions. If we have theories and data distributed in time, LISREL can trace paths of associations whose numerical qualities may render it easier for us to prefer and justify one set of explanations to others. It cannot be those explanations. For Gardner and Clément LISREL is a good servant. In the future we may find it becoming an unwelcome master in the hands of weaker investigators.

In the field overall, there is a welcome move away from too heavy a reliance on college students as subjects, from what was a crazy triumph of convenience over concern to solve social psychological problems. Courtrooms are real and public. We cannot perform experiments, but we can record the data and relate these to theories of influence which are also testable in laboratories. Marriages are real and, in many respects, private. How are we to study the relationship and the talk associated with it? British undergraduate students are certainly suspicious of data in this area. How do investigators find couples? Who would permit being studied? Who would tell the truth? Their concerns are genuine, and we have very serious difficulties with such relationships. On the other hand experiments asking people to simulate being married or being imaginative in some relevant respect really cannot substitute for real spouses. Perhaps social psychologists need to face up to the fact that some behaviour is very difficult to observe. We have to find and seize rare opportunities as and when they become available.

The beginnings of some friendships can still usefully be studied among captive undergraduate populations; especially since these relationships are being created and dissolved at college and university. The issues of privacy remain problematic. Recent studies of the last two topics also register a profound change in focus away from the individuals in the relationship to the relationship itself. Why should social psychology focus only on individuals in their social context? Why not take dyadic or network relationships as units of analysis as we used to when studying small-group processes in the 1960s. Marriage provides a clear example in this handbook but other family relationships cry out for comparable approaches. As we knew long ago, the selection of terms of address and reference in those languages which permit such differentiation depends not only upon the context of situation and the absolute and relative status of the participants but upon the relationship between the participants.

Perhaps the importance of relationships *per se* will become more evident as our concerns lose their English-language dominance. Most social psychologists are primary speakers of English, and most work in environments where English is the dominant language. We can only look forward to studies extending beyond Standard Average European languages which will probe our ideas about the social psychology as well as about the interface with language.

These ideas have certainly developed strongly. Many concepts have moved from being ideas to being included in explanations. As Clément noted at the 1987 International Conference on Social Psychology and Language in Bristol, earlier preferences for the inductive are now being mixed with a higher proportion of theory-inspired investigations. Whilst these theoretical frameworks are likely to be overly restricted to Standard Average European communication in the first instance, they will be expanded. Some already are, but these are from other disciplines. Our linguistic and philosophical peers such as Grice, Leech and Levinson have already been generating frameworks of potentially universal generality. These frameworks might well be exploited soon by more social psychologists.

To date, the theoretical ideas have arisen mainly from what used to be called pure research. It is ironic but partly understandable that so little sponsored research has arisen out of applied contexts. The law counts as one semi-honourable exception. It is only semi-honourable because, in any applied context where winning is important, winners have vested interests in not having their techniques exposed. Not that the advocates today are using ideas which cannot be found in Plato. It is however one of the moral weaknesses of adversarial judicial systems that injustice can result from skilful applications of social psychological principles. Similarly, in the political arena, successful politicians have vested interests in not having the bases of their oratical competence made public. The *Journal of Language and Social Psychology* has been carrying a fascinating dialectic about Mrs Thatcher. One story is that she is more frequently interrupted by interviewers than are other senior politicians. The alternative story is that she is not actually treated differently from her political colleagues: she simply protests more about being interrupted. Likewise Atkinson's analyses of political speeches reiterate some Ancient Greek ideas which are not known or followed by many professional speakers. In industry and commerce too, inefficient and asymmetric communication systems can enable those with power to retain it. Applied contexts may appear to be problems looking for solutions but only naive social psychologists would accept the management's overt definition of these problems.

Such considerations, alas, are also relevant to the status of social psychological 'facts' as evidence to inform social policy. Social psychologists can analyse and expose the gender biases or ethnic biases in texts. We can show how history textbooks exalt our own national status and demean that of the barbarians. We can show how Plain English can substitute for legal jargon. When we offer such evidence we may not win the argument for at least two reasons. First, our kind of evidence may not be the sort of evidence that our hearers or readers appreciate as valid. Second, the policy makers may well already know and believe what we can demonstrate, but they will be taking a lot of no notice of our findings. As human beings and social psychologists we may well wish to see society taking note of our findings, but we are optimistic if we expect rationality rather than vested interests to guide and inform decisions. At least we can retain our optimism.

It is hoped that most readers will not merely have dipped into the topics with which they most identify. If this is the case, then much of the value of this handbook will be severely diluted. Put another way, we cannot fully understand marriage without recourse to the family, we cannot contain the family in a socio-economic vacuum, we cannot cope with the intricacies of the latter without considering the lifespan, and so on and so forth, virtually interminably. Indeed, cross-fertilization is evident in a number of fields as currently described. A few years ago, we would not have afforded much credence to the value of schemata in our analyses of accounting, relationships, and marriage. That said, their potency is just as valuable in the arenas of language and the elderly, multilingualism, and in the legal context. This handbook contains a vast repository of data and ideas with potential for imperializing areas not presently under their purview where we can all profitably feed off each other.

Let us provide just a flavour of the possibilities on creative offer. Accounting and deception, while interpersonally grounded in the literature, are also of course important elements at the intergroup level, for instance in certain intergenerational, between-gender, and cross-cultural communications. Similarly, sociostructural, de-politicization, and lifespan perspectives are not only pertinent to multilingual, gender, and gerontological concerns in the foregoing chapters, but function in important and under-researched ways in many topics from individual differences to relational communication. Finally here, the compensation strategies of coping with handicap may also feature in most situations where social stigma is at issue and thereby shed emancipatory light on the constructivist features of language use in context.

The next handbook therefore will likely attest to these cross-fertilizations as it doubtless will to constructs only invoked almost in passing, such as trust, morality, silence, and miscommunication. The field of language and social psychology is at an interesting stage of its development. A mere handful of years ago, we would not have been treated to the regularity of appearances of processual notions of variability, sequence, and negotiation and to the complementary idea that communication problems often arise from the frequency and multiplicity of certain language features as much if not more than they derive from something uniquely 'problematic' about any one of them. Furthermore, the appreciation that language is not dichotomously locked away from social constructs such as attitudes, relationships, attributions, health, and situations but rather is often an integral element of them is a minefield where language scholars are likely to have a significant impact on the development of social psychology as well. Indeed, the view that everyday language in social interaction sustains, perpetuates, and creates wider-scale social discriminations is a message that is well alluded to throughout. That said, we must be wary of elevating language to an untenable primary, explanatory force across situations. We need to spend time, as Markova would have us, in knowing more experientially about how individuals transact with their environments and how these are cognitively construed from a historical perspective as well as in the immediacy of the context studied.

In the future we shall need to confront the complexities of both the mediating role of self in generating and processing language, and the role of language in constructing our views of that self. But that is for the future.

Author Index

Subject Index